PURSUIT THROUGH DARKENED SKIES

PURSUIT THROUGH DARKENED SKIES

An ace night-fighter crew in World War II

MICHAEL ALLEN DFC**

An Airlife
CLASSIC

Copyright © 1999 Michael Seamer Allen

First published in the UK in 1999
by Airlife Publishing Ltd

This edition published 2001

British Library Cataloguing-in-Publication Data
      A catalogue record for this book
      is available from the British Library

ISBN 1 84037 355 5

Typeset by Phoenix Typesetting, Ilkley, West Yorkshire
Printed in England by Biddles Ltd, Guildford and King's Lynn

Airlife Publishing Ltd
101 Longden Road, Shrewsbury, SY3 9EB, England
E-mail: airlife@airlifebooks.com
Website: www.airlifebooks.com

For

HARRY WHITE

Air Commodore H. E. White CBE, DFC**, AFC

Acknowledgements

There are three people without whom there would have been no *Pursuit Through Darkened Skies*. In 1994, at the invitation of the Harrier pilots of No. 1 Squadron, I returned to RAF Wittering after a gap of fifty years – accompanied by my wife, Pam . . .

Although I must have looked to those young pilots – rather as a soldier from Lord Kitchener's Army of the Sudan would have appeared to us on No. 141 Squadron (had he come into the Mess in the Summer of 1943) they were kind enough to listen politely, when I got up on my feet and spoke:

> . . . of flak, intruders, beams,
> Of dummy runs and how to weave
> Sorties and strikes, and tales like dreams
> Which none but airmen would believe.

When I had finished speaking one of the pilots – a certain Squadron Leader Michael Harwood – and a Harrier addict (for some obscure reason he was known to his friends as 'The Prince of Darkness'), came rushing across to where Pam was sitting . . . burbling something to the effect 'Mike's got to write all this stuff down!' and again 'Mike's got to write a book!'

I had only been talking for a few minutes on how – after taking off from Wittering, half a century earlier, Harry White and I had gone wandering about in the vivid night skies above The Third Reich – hoping to have the chance of putting 'some round holes into square heads' before we came home . . . The young men had given the Dinosaur Navigator a polite hearing, so what more was there to fuss about . . . surely, now was the time to renew one's acquaintance with the bar in the Officers' Mess?

But it wasn't going to be like that! Once Mike Harwood had broached his preposterous idea to Pam, I did not stand a chance . . . Pam took up the challenge and from that moment – with a witches' brew comprised of a subtle mixture of 'sticks and carrots' – she relentlessly urged me to write 'my book'. Three years and 200,000 words later the great day came when I could place the completed manuscript in her hands. Subsequently she has gallantly undertaken the onerous task of 'proof-reading' for me. I am deeply grateful to her – but likewise I am aware that, if ever I were to contemplate writing another book, I would be sticking my neck out!

As for 'The Prince of Darkness' who started all the trouble – he is now a Wing Commander with an MBE, and the Commanding Officer of No. 20 Squadron based at RAF Wittering. I have been able to turn the tables on him, by making him an offer which he could not refuse . . . namely, to write the Foreword! Mike and I have (as he says) bridged 'the age gap' to become close friends – and I am grateful to him for accepting the task of writing the opening words for this story of a night-fighter crew, which he did so much to inspire . . . I, and my generation, are also grateful to him for the interest he has shown in linking the past with the

Royal Air Force of the present day – and hopefully of the years to come . . .

The third member of the trio, without whom there would have been no *Pursuit Through Darkened Skies*, is a remarkable man. He has served No. 141 Squadron devotedly – in war and in peace . . . in between whiles he managed to fit in a successful post-war career in business and commerce, spanning forty years. Don Aris served as an Armourer on 141 during the War. Like many others, he wanted to fly as aircrew but had to settle for a vital ground job. He joined the Squadron in May 1942 – servicing and maintaining the cannons, machine-guns, bombs and other weaponry on our Beaufighters and later . . . the Mosquitoes. He worked on Wing Commander Braham's aircraft *Betsy*, also that of another 141 C.O., W/Cdr Charles Winn, as well as others on 'A' Flight. Whenever the opportunity was there, he went up on the Air Tests which followed the servicing . . . Don was one of several of our ground crew members who was singled out for the award of a 'Mention in Dispatches'.

When he retired from business in the 'eighties Don looked back on his 2¼ years with 141 Squadron . . . and he proceeded to research and compile what is probably the finest Squadron History ever written by a single individual. It was an opus and ran to three Volumes and to over 900 pages. It is that History to which Don has generously allowed me unlimited access.

As related in the story, Harry and I first joined No. 141 Squadron in January 1943. With two breaks – one for ferrying to the Middle East, and the other when posted to the Bomber Support Development Unit – we remained on the Squadron until it was disbanded in September 1945. For the first 1½ years of my service in the Air Force (June '41 to Dec. '42) I had to rely on the details in my Flying Log-Books (and a handful of material I had doggedly retained over fifty years and numerous moves!) for accuracy, when piecing my story together. From January 1943 onwards – and through the whole course of the Bomber Support operations – I was able to refer to, and rely on, Don Aris' *History of the Squadron* . . . confident, that for painstaking research and meticulous compilation, it could not be faulted. There are no words with which I can thank him. This incomparable Squadron History was not Don's first 'labour of love'. Like many of us, he felt that our former Commanding Officer, Wing Commander J.R.D. 'Bob' Braham DSO & 2 Bars, DFC & 2 Bars, AFC, had not been given adequate recognition in the post-war years. Don – soon after his retirement from the business world – set himself to research and compile a biography of W/Cdr Braham. He did not do it for publication, or for any form of 'gain'. He eventually presented it to Bob's widow, Mrs Joan Braham, for her and for her family. He also sent a copy to some of the former members of the Squadron – of whom I was one of the lucky ones. Additionally, he presented copies to selected Military Museums and to the RAF Staff College.

With his single-minded and unselfish labours Don Aris has earned the undying gratitude of Mrs Braham and her family and the unstinted regard and affection of a small nucleus of former members of 141 Squadron – for whom he has become 'our Anchor Man'. For me, he is one of the greatest friends that the Air Force has ever given me.

The 'Hi-Tech' back-up was provided by my younger son, Simon, (assisted by Donna) who 'scanned' my 550 pages of A4, and turned them – by some miracle – into two small plastic discs. I am very grateful to them, because they had a number of other pressing commitments at the time I wanted to submit the finished work to Airlife.

It was the late 'Laddie' Lucas who suggested that I should send my manuscript to Airlife. In the early days I thought only of my story as being a record for the family and for Harry White's family. I had little hope that it would ever attract the attention of a publisher. Laddie had been at RAF Wittering when I had spoken to the Harrier pilots. He had also included some small contributions from Harry and myself in some of his own publications. After the Wittering visit he gave me just the support and encouragement which I needed to keep me going, and which today has resulted in the publication of *Pursuit Through Darkened Skies*. For someone attempting to write their first book at 75 years of age I could have had no better friend.

I am particularly indebted to Helena Engelbach. It was as the fiancée – and then wife – of 'Angels' (better known as 'Paddy' Engelbach) that I shall always think of her. Helena, who staunchly waited for 'Angels' to come back from the Prison Camp, gave me permission to use the Sonnet which opens: 'I have been near that state which men call death, . . .' It was one of several poems that Paddy wrote whilst he was a Prisoner-of-War. I am grateful to Helena and I hope that, in the future, some of his other poems may see the light of day.

I have known Norman Franks for many years and have been able to make one or two contributions towards his many publications in the field of military aviation. At one time he said that he would like to write my story; indeed, had it not been for that certain weekend I spent at RAF Wittering, he might well have done so. As things have worked out, Norman has compiled the Index for me – a task completely beyond my capabilities. I am extremely grateful to him for providing this vital component for the better understanding of my story.

Overseas, my cousin Neil Garlick in Cape Town and my old school friend, Hugh Franks now living in France, have given me their constant support. Both had distinguished Army careers in WWII. Neil offered to try and find a publisher in South Africa if I was unsuccessful in the UK. Hugh and I used to play in the Colts XV at Hurst more than sixty years ago – subsequently he became a successful author in his own right and has passed on to me the benefit of his own wide experience.

I am grateful to Martin Middlebrook for allowing me to quote freely from his book *The Peenemunde Raid*, published by Allen Lane in 1982.

I have endeavoured to make contact with the other authors, or publishers from whose work I have quoted and am grateful to: Mrs Joan Braham for permission to quote from *Scramble*; Martin Bowman in respect of *Confounding the Reich* and Chaz Bowyer in respect of *Bomber Barons* (NOTE: For further details please refer to the Bibliography).

Foreword

'I'd like to have flown with you.' I remember saying these words in 1994, not long after meeting Mike Allen for the first time. I was researching the tactics and psychology of Royal Air Force night operations, taking every opportunity to meet people who had operated 'through darkened skies'. Could the wit and wisdom that had once guided his pilot, Harry White, in the 1940s, now be working its charm on an impassioned single-seat pilot of the 1990s? Who knows, but I meant it. Mike and I 'clicked'. The age gap was – and is – meaningless, and I am over the moon that he has finally put down on paper some of the memories of his particular war. His generation needs to record, mine needs to take note. He has managed to put his story across with that wicked sense of humour I have found so endearing; his manuscript lies across my office floor, with pencil marks against the many paragraphs which strike a deep chord. I have found myself reading out loud, transported to his side as he recounts each absorbing episode.

There is a moving honesty within these pages, no brash attempt to say 'look how good we were' but the whole story, warts and all, with a few heartfelt 'home truths' thrown in for good measure. Witness the role of Lady Luck, the failures, the disasters, the tragedies and desolation, but also those elusive moments of success, all the sweeter because of their rarity. Allow men like Guy Gibson, Leonard Cheshire, 'Bob' Braham, 'Laddie' Lucas, Don Bennett and Rory Chisholm to come alive once more, with the power and charisma to influence still . . . And how good to meet so many new characters, such as Paddy Engelbach (nicknamed, inevitably, 'Angels'), whose stunning sonnet – describing his sensations as he faced what seemed to be certain death – is a masterpiece to savour. Then there's the raw courage of men like Herbert Farrow, Walter Ward and Jimmy Andrews, Norfolk farmers who braved a blazing aircraft to extricate the trapped Mike Allen and Harry White . . . only seconds before their crashed Mosquito blew up!

In 1945, after it was all over, Harry White wrote to Mike Allen 'Not only have I learned to fly an aeroplane better under your helpful, critical eye but have grown up a better and more wise man than I should have done without your companionship – something I shall always prize greatly'. I could not sum it up any better in 1999. We cannot all be fortunate enough to meet the likes of Mike Allen in person but his hard-won experiences can live on forever. By no means least, he has introduced me to some poetry that I shall always treasure, made all the more poignant in the context of the people and happenings of this book, with the following example a fitting anthem for those charged with delivering today's Royal Air Force night capability:

The heights by great men reached and kept
Were not attained by sudden flight,
But they, while their companions slept,
Were toiling upward in the night.

Longfellow

Mike Harwood

Wing Commander M. J. Harwood, MBE, MA, RAF
Office Commanding Number 20 Squadron (the Harrier Operational
   Conversion Unit)
Royal Air Force Wittering

Fifty years on. I returned to RAF Wittering to share the cockpit of a Harrier with W/Cdr 'Mike' Harwood, OC of No. 20 Squadron and author of the Foreword.

Contents

1 **'We Don't Want To Lose You Too'**
   – and how it all started   1
2 **The School for Secrets**
   – and how I came to 'crew-up' with Harry White   35
3 **Learning Our Trade with the Aid of an Airborne Searchlight**
   – and how we then became a Ferry Crew   55
4 **Operation 'Serrate'**
   – night-fighter versus night-fighter   91
5 **The Development of the Bomber Support Operations**
   – and the price paid for equipping the Serrate Squadrons
   with 'worn out' Mosquitoes   144
6 **One Party in Ashford – and Another Over Frankfurt**
   – and how Harry White received a kiss . . .   179
7 **Life With The Boffins and Death at Home**
   – and how we nearly lost our lives on Mosquito MM797   219
8 **Our Return to 141 Squadron – and the Napalm Attacks**
   – and how the German night-fighter force remained
   to the end – undefeated   272
9 **The Anti-climax and the Parting of the Ways**
   – 'Farewell! Othello's occupation's gone'   300

Epilogue   326

Appendices
1A   AI Mk IV   335
1B   AI Mk IV and the Serrate Homer   338
2   Citation for Awards to James Andrews,
     Herbert George Farrow and Walter William Ward   340
3   141 Squadron Order of Battle for 2 May 1945   341

Bibliography   342
Index   343

1 'We Don't Want To Lose You Too'

– and how it all started

In September 1941, amongst the new crews posted to No. 29 Squadron based at West Malling in Kent, were Sergeants H.E. White and M.S. Allen. Pilot and Navigator respectively, they were both of tender age, not mustering 37 years between them. But they did not let that factor, or their lack of training as a night-fighter crew, worry them. They were pleased, although somewhat bewildered, to find themselves on an operational squadron so quickly but were determined to make a name for themselves. In this, they were soon successful but not quite in the manner they had intended!

On reporting to the squadron orderly room they learnt that they were assigned to 'A' Flight and duly checked in at the Flight office. Here they found that their Flight Commander was a certain Squadron Leader Guy Penrose Gibson DFC & Bar . . .

'Two Nine' (as it was widely known) was a night-fighter squadron. Its reputation went back to November 1915, when it was formed in the early years of the First World War. It was now one of the crack night-fighter Squadrons in No. 11 Group of Fighter Command, equipped with the formidable Bristol Beaufighter. The aircraft were fitted with an airborne radar system known as Airborne Interceptor (AI), which had a maximum range of nearly four miles when the aircraft was flying at a height of 20,000 ft. At the time, it was 'leading edge' technology.

After the heavy night raids on England in the winter of 1940/41 – which became known as 'the Blitz' – there was a temporary respite from the German onslaught thanks to the short spring and summer nights. During these months the bombers of the *Luftwaffe* could not reach their targets and return to their new bases – just inside the French, Belgian and Dutch coastline – under cover of darkness.

No. 29 Squadron had, whenever possible, given chase to the few Heinkels, Dorniers and Junkers that had ventured out as they hurried to complete their missions in the five to six hours of darkness. For the Germans wanted to have their noses down for home, and their bomb bays empty, before dawn brought the Hurricanes and Spitfires of the day-fighter squadrons up after them.

The pilots and AI operators of 29 Squadron also trained hard when there were no 'bandits' in their Sector. They practised day and night with the co-operation of their Ground Controllers at the GCI station at Willesborough, to get in as many mock interceptions as possible, with first one Beau acting as 'target' whilst another was the defending 'fighter', and then the two changing places. With their aircraft, armament, airborne radar and radio equipment much improved during the first eight months of 1941, the squadron stood ready to give a good account

of itself when the night Blitz was resumed under cover of the long winter nights
– as surely it must be.

This was the cover of darkness to which the *Luftwaffe* had fled after their heavy
daylight losses in August and September 1940 during the Battle of Britain.
No. 29's base, near Maidstone in Kent, was in the direct line between the airfields
where the Heinkels and Dorniers were being made ready, and London which
seemed likely to continue as one of their main targets. Patrolling in the Channel
they might also get a chase after German bombers setting out, or returning home,
from raids on towns and cities in the Midlands or North of England. One way
and another, they were pretty well placed.

The Blitz, which had lasted effectively from 7/8 September 1940 throughout
the winter until 10/11 May 1941 was, in strict economic terms, a profitable
venture for the enemy. Their losses were slight and they inflicted a considerable
amount of damage to our cities and casualties amongst the civilian population.
The German bomber crews must have been quite looking forward to resuming
their night attacks in the winter of 1941/42 and, judging by the previous year,
they did not have much to fear.

On the other hand, 29 Squadron (not forgetting Sgts White and Allen!) during
the second year of Home Defence night-fighter operations, were hoping to take
some of the enemy's profit away from him by intercepting and destroying many
more of his bombers than in the previous year. The stage was set!

The squadron was to be successful, even though the German night raids during
the winter of 1941/42 were, thankfully, far less severe than expected. The two
young sergeants, on the other hand, were soon to build up a 'debit' balance, and,
within six weeks, were owing His Majesty a sum running well into five figures.
They were, in fact, of more use to the Germans than to their own side!

Sergeant Pilot Harold Edward White and his AI operator, more sophisti-
catedly called an Observer (Radio), Michael Seamer Allen, arrived on No. 29
Squadron at the beginning of September 1941, having crewed up at No. 54
Operational Training Unit at Church Fenton in Yorkshire, on 4 August. The
crewing up in those days was splendidly haphazard, and the story of how Harry
and I came to meet and fly together will be told in a later chapter. Suffice to say
that at the time I was in blissful ignorance of Harry's mid-air collision with
another aircraft the previous week whereby he already owed HM King
George VI money for his 50 per cent share in the destruction of an Airspeed
Oxford (his) and a Bristol Blenheim (under the temporary care of a Czech flight
sergeant).

Harry and the Czech pilot both finished up in much better shape than their
aircraft but there were some mutterings heard in 'D' Squadron crew room to the
effect that, had the results been the other way around, it might have been better
for the war effort!

It is only fair to add that I was ignorant about almost everything! Having
joined the Air Force on 14 June 1941, I had been in for less than three months
when I was posted with Harry to No. 29 Squadron.

We did our first flight together in a Beau on 13 September: a 'X-country'
(cross-country) in daylight lasting 1 hour 45 minutes. During the next two weeks
we carried out a number of practice flights using the AI and learning to work
with the Ground Controllers of the GCI station at Willesborough. But on 15
September I did my first 'op'.

I went up on a standing patrol – somewhere over Kent and the English Channel

– taking off at 23.10 hrs in Beaufighter 2144 and landing back at West Malling two hours later, but I was not flying with Harry! There is no other comment in my log-book, so it doesn't look as if I and my pilot (for the night!) had any chases or got to grips with any enemy bombers.

At some time during that afternoon, Flight Lieutenant Hugh Verity had come into the crew room and announced that his AI operator – one Sergeant Lawrence – was sick and as he was 'on' that night he was looking for an operator that was 'mad keen'. I said I'd go with him! So without doing a night flying test in the aircraft we were going to fly, and above all, without ever having carried out an AI interception at night, we took off in defence of King and Country against the potential hordes of Heinkels and Dorniers.

What a good thing it was – looking back – that none came that night, or if they did we certainly knew nothing about it! Still, I can remember that Harry was a bit cheesed off when I pushed off on ops without him!

Hugh Verity did not stay on night-fighters. He went on to make a name for himself on No. 161 (Special Duties) Squadron, based at Tempsford, ferrying agents in and out of France and elsewhere in Occupied Europe. Flying a Lysander, from the squadron's advanced base at Tangmere, Hugh carried out a large number of hazardous trips, earning himself a great reputation and great respect from the infinitely brave men and women of the Special Forces. He richly deserved his two DSOs and his DFC. Forty-five years later we met up again at the Royal Air Force church of St Clement Danes.

No. 29 Squadron, West Malling: NCO aircrew billeted at Malling Abbey in September 1941. Harry White and myself are at the back, on the right. Flight Sergeant James DFM – Guy Gibson's AI Operator – is in the middle row on the left. Flight Sergeant 'Sticks' Gregory (who flew with 'Bob' Braham and was, by the end of the war, Squadron Leader Gregory DSO, DFC, DFM) is kneeling on the left of the front row.*

The NCO aircrew of '29' were billeted in Malling Abbey and, in our early days on the squadron, I sent my younger brother a postcard of the Abbey. Rodney had left Hurstpierpoint College and was working for a year in a factory before himself joining the Air Force. He had obtained an exceptional School Certificate with five Distinctions, three Credits and a Pass in the nine subjects which he had taken. Normally this sort of result would have led on to a Higher School Certificate and an almost certain place at Oxford or Cambridge, but things weren't normal and Rodney, too, was influenced by our upbringing in the world of civil aviation and our father's exciting life as a pilot – or so it seemed to us.

But, as in my case, my father was keen that Rodney learned what it was to 'do a day's work' before he joined up. With the benefit of hindsight, it all now seems to be a bit of a waste. Rodney – with his exceptional natural talent for figures and these brilliant results at School Certificate level – should surely have gone on to university and the chance of high academic or business achievements. He would have been a natural for computers in their pioneering era of the fifties and sixties. Still, it was his choice to become aircrew – as it was for other exceptionally talented men, many of whom were lost during the war years: as he himself was to be lost in the post-war years.

Rodney, like many boys of his age (he had just turned 17) joined the Air Training Corps (formerly called the Air Defence Cadet Corps) and had already been promoted to corporal. On my postcard of our billet (with its 2d stamp!) I have addressed him as 'Cpl Allen R. Westwick, 60 Clarendon Road, Ashford, Middlesex' and I wrote on the card as follows, using his nickname of 'Tich', which really should have been spelt 'Titch':

> Dear Tich,
> Thanks for putting in your subscription book for the A.T.C. There seem to be a large number of cadets here, and some have been lucky to be taken up by our pilots. Harry did his solo trip yesterday so we shall soon be cracking. Look after Mumsie. Chin chin. Mick.

'Mumsie' was an affectionate term for my mother which we both used, and the language shows how fashions have changed in fifty years. I have some letters written by my uncle in the 1914–18 War when fashions in writing were different again; his read just like a P.G. Wodehouse novel and you can almost hear Bertie Wooster talking!

The card also shows how keen Harry and I were to get cracking i.e. to get 'on ops', and how I was now more conscious of the dangers for civilians during the night hours and the blackout, because of the job that Harry and I were about to undertake.

From those early squadron days, I have a vivid memory of Guy Gibson. Much has been written about him, as for other great figures of the war years, since 1945 and not all of it complimentary. But when Harry and I walked into a pub (I think it might have been The Strangled Saint) as two young 'sprog' sergeants, he saw us walk in, looking a bit strange and out of our depth. After all, we had hardly ever walked into a pub before! On the far side of the bar was this squadron leader (already twice decorated) with his wife and a crowd of other officers. But we were in his flight and he saw us standing there, not knowing quite what to do. In a moment he was across the floor, greeted us and took us over to meet his wife, buy us a drink and make sure that we were part of the crowd that was gathered around him. Some of those who presume to write about men like Guy Gibson lack the privilege of having known them, as they lack any real knowledge of the business on which we were engaged.

Our off-duty hours at West Malling were also enlivened by Harry's driving lessons! I had my car with me and some petrol in the tank. Those were still the days when I could drive my Ford 8 under the wing of our Beau, as it was being re-fuelled, and get my tank filled up by an obliging 'erk' on the petrol bowser, with 100 octane fuel!

Rumour had it that 100 octane was supposed to enhance the performance of one's car at the risk of sooting up the plugs. On balance, we were happy to take the risk! Another attraction was that it was free, by courtesy of His Majesty. Later in the war things were to be different! In 1942, dire penalties were threatened if anyone was found with 100 octane in their tanks. Still, it was good while it lasted. But I've allowed myself to be diverted from the hair-raising episode of Harry's driving lessons.

Although, by then, Harry must have had well over 150 hours' flying time, he had never driven a car. So I attempted to put matters right by giving him some driving lessons around the barrack blocks and aerodrome buildings. I don't think we ever ventured onto the roads outside West Malling. There is no doubt that he was a better pilot than he was a driver, and that's not saying much at that stage in his career as an aviator! He went too fast into his corners, too fast on the straight, and ignored anyone else on the road! I can still remember him trying to turn left and careering onto the grass and up a bank on the far side. I don't remember how we got the car back on the road but I do recall saying to him that he had better stick to his flying and I would look after our transportation when we were on the ground!

Our somewhat youthful appearance caught up with us soon after our arrival on the squadron. We had to take a Beaufighter into Gravesend to have the guns harmonised and, as we climbed out of the aircraft wearing our new Irvin jackets, we were greeted by the senior NCO in charge of the butts. A pre-war Regular, he did not mince his words. He took one look at us and said abruptly, 'Where are the crew?' He thought we were a couple of Air Training Corps cadets (like those mentioned in my postcard to Rodney, who had managed to scrounge a flight in the Beau). Harry had to take off his Irvin jacket for the irate warrant officer to see his pilot's wings before he would believe us!

Our determination to make a name for ourselves received a bit of a setback when Harry was carrying out his 'dusk landings'. One of the requirements before Guy Gibson would let us loose at night was that all pilots had to take off just before dusk and do 'circuits and bumps' round West Malling as the light faded and darkness fell. On the roads, driving at dusk is said to be one of the most dangerous times, as one's eyes adapt to night-time conditions. It is no different in flying as pilots have to change from flying on a visual horizon to flying on their instrument panel as night closes around them.

Dusk landings were an important stepping stone for us and I readily said that I would go with Harry. I was starting to get my kit together when I heard the voice of the flight commander behind me, 'Where do you think you're going?' I told him. 'Oh no you're not! He's going up on his own to do his Duskies', said Gibson. 'We don't want to lose you too,' he added cheerfully! In the light of what happened he was proved to be quite right!

Harry did two landings without any trouble, taking off each time and going round again. I was outside the old club house watching the proceedings and several others joined me. Dusk landings sometimes provided a bit of entertainment as the new pilots lurched down through the 'funnels' on the approach, touched down briefly and then immediately opened up to take off again, disappearing into the gathering gloom.

So it was that night, and as Harry came round for the third time we could all see that he was too high on the approach and, as he came over the boundary fence, he was still much too high. I heard 'Sticks' Gregory (Bob Braham's AI Operator and one of the finest night-fighter navigators ever produced by the Royal Air Force) starting to say, '*Go round again!*' By then Harry was almost halfway over the airfield and still 100 ft up. Then I heard Sticks shouting, '*For Christ's sake, go round again!*' About that time Harry, who was fast running out of airfield, decided that he might just get the Beau in – and 'pulled everything back'.

Before our agonised gaze, and from a height of about 60 ft, the Beau dropped like a brick out of the darkening sky and fell with an awful crunching sound into the very middle of West Malling airfield. There were a few seconds of silence but – thank God! – no pillar of fire and no explosion. I leapt into my car, which was standing close by, and with several others piling in drove straight out across the aerodrome towards the wreckage of the Beau lying on its belly at the intersection of the grass runways.

I had already seen a Blenheim 'go in' at Church Fenton and was terrified that, within the next few seconds, there would be a muffled *whumph* and the Beau would 'go up'. It didn't. I arrived in front of the wreckage to see that the pilot's cockpit was intact and just as Harry was climbing out. He saw me and blurted out 'Christ, Boy – what a bloody fool I was!' The aircraft was a write-off. Harry was unharmed.

The following day the station was due to receive a VIP in the shape of the Secretary of State for Air, Sir Archibald Sinclair. The Station Engineer Officer was unable to move the debris before the great man's arrival and so his aircraft had to land off the runway, and his first sight of West Malling was of the wreckage of Sergeant White's Beaufighter spread across the airfield! We heard later that the Station Commander was not at all pleased.

At the end of September we did fly at night together on a 'Searchlight Co-Op' and again on 3 October when my log-book tells me that we had to divert to Tangmere owing to bad weather and an obstruction on the flarepath at West Malling. On the afternoon of 4 October we flew back to Malling with a cloud ceiling of 600 feet and landed with the aid of 'Mother' (the AI radar beacon at our home base).

Things were coming on but little did we realise that Tangmere was soon to become our home base instead of Malling! Also, our own success in getting ourselves back in quite bad weather was soon tempered by the news that F/O Miles and Sgt Hall had crashed into the hills north of West Malling and both were killed.

We had carried out our first operational patrol together on 30 September, and three more followed in quick succession. In fact, on that first night we flew two details and a total of 6 hours and 5 minutes. We were given a number of chases by the Controllers but my log reports that three or four times we were told to break off the interception as we were in danger of crossing the enemy coast. At that time it was strictly forbidden to take aircraft fitted with AI over 'the other side' as the Germans were behind the British scientists in the race for radar superiority. If the Beau was shot down there was a serious risk that – from the wreckage – the Germans would glean vital information, which could be turned against us.

On 15 October we flew a Miles Magister to St Athan in Wales for it to be fitted out with BA (Blind Approach) equipment, but on landing we taxied over some metal stakes and damaged the flaps. Sergeant Webb came over in a Beau to pick us up and we were safely back at Malling in an hour, landing at dusk. We heard later that the Magister was used by some of our superiors for going off on the odd dirty weekend and that they were not pleased with White and Allen – who didn't even know what a dirty weekend was! We were indeed starting to make a name for ourselves!

On 16 October we flew twice during the day (including a successful interception with a target Beau under control of the GCI station to which we had recently paid a visit with another new crew) and carried out an operational patrol at night, during which we completed another successful interception and Harry got a visual on our target Beau; and, for the first time, was able to manoeuvre us into an attacking position, lining up the target in his gunsight, before breaking away. Little did we know that it was to be twenty-one months before he was to do it for real with a German aircraft in his sights. Also, we did not know that our days on 29 were numbered and that this was to be our last op with the squadron. Just when we thought we were getting the hang of things.

There is no record in my log-book of when the blow fell and we were 'sacked' from 29 Squadron, but by 23 October we were flying an American-built Douglas Havoc from Tangmere, where we had been posted at very short notice! The final straw – after the incidents of the wrecked Beau and the damaged Magister – came about on one of our six operational patrols. It could have been our second trip.

Taking off at 01.50 hrs we were up for 2 hours and 40 minutes and the 'Remarks' column of my log-book reads as follows:

> '. . . four chases but although gateing I had no joy and we were called off when we reached the bandit's coastline.'

Somewhere over the Channel, where we were patrolling between Dover and Beachy Head at a height of 12–15,000 ft, Harry and I discussed the secret code signals for the period. These were the Letters and the Colours of the night, which were used for messages sent by Aldis lamp and Very pistol respectively and changed every few hours. One of their prime uses was for identification between friend and foe. So they were fairly important to all concerned, i.e. the Navy and the Army, as well as the Air Force.

We discussed the Letters and the Colours of the night over the intercom system. This linked Harry – sitting up in front of the Beau, monarch of all he surveyed – with me sitting crouched over my cathode-ray tubes under the Perspex cupola, halfway back along the fuselage and, like the 'Wim Wam' bird, facing the way we had come.

This was a necessary discussion and there was nothing inherently wrong with it. We needed to be clear in our minds about the correct colours to be identified if fired off by another aircraft, or to use ourselves if one of our own patrolling Beaufighters were to attack us by mistake, which was a not unknown occurrence in daytime, let alone at night. As we shall see later on!

The only snag was that (unknown to us) Harry had left the VHF radio transmitter switch in the ON position. Every word of our interesting and revealing discussion was being heard by the German radio operators on the other side of the Channel, whose job it was to monitor all transmissions sent out by British aircraft. This serious and dangerous breach of security was also, of course, heard by the horrified Ground Controllers on our side who were powerless to stop it! Once a pilot left his radio transmitter on in those days there was no way that anybody else could get through to him. So, in blissful ignorance, Harry and I proceeded to compromise the secret code signals for the period, thereby rendering them useless. All the codes would have to be changed immediately before friend started firing on friend and lives were lost.

When we landed back at West Malling at 04.30 hrs on the Sunday morning and walked into the old club house which 29 used as a crewroom, it was already known that we had provided the Germans with some gratuitous information of a highly confidential nature. On the official level, so we learned later, the Officer i/c Night Flying had considered ringing up the guard room, sending for the Service Police and having us put under close arrest the moment our feet touched the ground.

Unofficially, amongst the other crews it was rumoured that we were being put up – by the Germans – for the Iron Cross (2nd Class)! A few days later, when the Flight Commander of 'A' Flight, S/Ldr Guy Gibson, was asked to find a crew for a rather 'down-market' job, on a night-fighter unit of little significance, he had no difficulty in deciding whose names should be on the top of his Transfer List. It was that crew which had made such a name for itself since it arrived on the squadron at the beginning of September 1941 – White and Allen.

I have often thought since that, if he had been the manager of a football team, he would not have asked for a transfer fee for us. As it was, Guy Gibson went on to win a Victoria Cross over the Möhne and Eder Dams on 16/17 May 1943 and, with it, immortal fame.

We were summarily posted off the squadron, and by Tuesday 21 October we had got our marching orders, although I seem to recall Harry saying, initially, that the posting was for him only and suggesting that it was up to me if I wanted to stay.

There was never any question of that. In my mind the almost immediate loyalties formed when people crewed up (irrational though they may have been) held strong and we left 29 together.

I remember heaving all our kit into the back of my car and we set off through the Kent and Sussex countryside to join No. 1455 Flight based at Tangmere – a famous fighter aerodrome dating back to the First World War and where my father had been stationed before leaving for France. This time Harry was occupying the passenger's seat.

When we drove into Tangmere, which lies three miles to the east of Chichester between the South Downs and the sea, and reported to the guard room, we got a surprise. Everywhere we looked, airmen were walking about in gas masks and those awful voluminous gas capes! Half the station personnel seemed to be in the air raid shelters. There was no hot food in the sergeants' mess – just emergency rations. And nobody seemed willing to take their gas masks off for long enough to tell us the location of our billets!

Arriving in the middle of a practice gas alert was not a propitious start at the station which was to be our home for the next fifteen months and where we were to serve our apprenticeship to the night-fighter trade.

To learn how Harry White and I came to share four years of war, and to clarify the relatively obscure world of night-fighter operations, we must go back to September 1940; long before Harry and I knew anything about such erudite matters, or each other. We must try to lay the ghost that, to achieve success as a night-fighter pilot and shoot down lots of invading German bombers, one either had to possess a pair of 'cat's eyes' or else consume vast platefuls of carrots.

As everyone knows – who has read the story of what came to be called the Battle of Britain – it was No. 11 Group of Fighter Command which was charged with the 'Home Defence' of the south-east corner of England. Air Vice-Marshal Park's squadrons had successfully ranged by day across the Home Counties south of a line drawn roughly from Yarmouth on the Norfolk coast to Bournemouth, just to the west of the Isle of Wight (including, of course, the North Sea, the Thames Estuary and the English Channel). They hunted down the enemy bombers until the German losses became prohibitive, and then, like the RAF in the early months of the war, the *Luftwaffe* were forced to seek the cover of darkness if they wished to maintain the aerial bombardment of England.

When the Heinkels and Dorniers came over in the dark they would not be able to fly in formation, although the Germans had developed, and were using, a radio beam and blind-bombing device system known as *Knickebein*. So they would have to take off one after the other – set course on their own – climb up singly – and cross the English coast, *en route* for their targets, spread out in a long loose gaggle – unseen by each other. They would have to return in the same manner to their bases in Occupied Europe after dropping their bombs.

Similarly, in the night sky, there could be no fighter escort. There was no way in which formations of Me 109s could have shepherded the embryo bomber stream, spread out along their track for many miles – or have protected the individual bombers from attack by British fighters – in the dark. Each bomber crew would have to fend for itself, as did their opposite numbers in the Wellingtons, Whitleys and Hampdens of Bomber Command.

But would there be any British fighters for the Heinkel and Dornier crews to defend themselves from as they flew towards London, Birmingham, Liverpool, Manchester and Coventry? Certainly it would not be the formations of Hurricanes and Spitfires, which had plagued them by day from July to September. The day-fighter squadrons could no more operate by night than the German *Jagdgeschwadern*. So would there be any opposition to the night attacks other than the ack-ack guns supported by searchlights to (hopefully from the British point of view!) illuminate the enemy aircraft long enough for them to receive a decisive hit and be brought down?

In fact, when the first of the big raids came at the beginning of September, on London, our defences against night attack were entirely inadequate. One or two individual day-fighter pilots took off on their own and flew a few sorties, mostly in Hurricanes; and there were a handful of squadrons equipped with Bristol Blenheims or the Boulton & Paul Defiant who were designated as night-fighter squadrons (amongst them 29 Squadron, then at Digby/Wellingore). Only the Blenheims had airborne radar, and that, the Mk III AI, was primitive and unreliable. The Boulton & Paul Defiant had, incidentally, been relegated to a night-fighting role after one terrible day during the Battle of Britain when the

Defiants of 141 Squadron were massacred by a group of Me 109s over the Channel.

There were a few successes, notably by Flight Lieutenant Richard Playne Stevens DSO DFC*. But with aircraft not designed for the job – undeveloped radar sets (or no radar at all!); inadequate radio-telephones; and poor fire power – most of those who ventured aloft spent their time milling aimlessly about for an hour or so looking for some indication of the presence of 'bandits', by peering out of their cockpits at the waving beams of the searchlights, the flash of the anti-aircraft guns as they fired and the bomb bursts far below. Even if they did catch a glimpse of the silhouette of a Heinkel 111 or a Dornier 217 they were most unlikely to be able to get into a firing position before they lost it again in the dark.

As few of the pilots had many hours' experience at night, for much of the time they would be concentrating on their instrument panels, in order to stay the right way up! For many of the day-fighter pilots in particular, experience of instrument flying was minimal.

Lastly, within a few minutes of having taken off into the unaccustomed blackness (plus the complete wartime 'blackout' on the ground), the major concern of these early night-fighter pilots and their crews was, quite understandably, how they were to find their way back to their base with the primitive radio homing devices and, sometimes, the aid of a friendly searchlight. Secondly, having found base could they get themselves down in one piece without overshooting or under-shooting the airfield in the dark (and always there was the added hazard of low cloud or fog).

The detailed story of the 'Blitz' of the winter of 1940/41 has been fully docu-mented in numerous accounts published since the war. Suffice for our purposes to record that throughout the long nights of the winter months the attacks continued causing widespread damage and loss of life, until the second week of May 1941. By the time the shorter nights of the summer months brought some relief, the Germans could claim a successful night campaign (their losses were only 1.5 per cent of sorties) after their failure to sustain their daylight attacks. They would surely return to renew this campaign with the advent of the longer nights in the autumn.

By September 1941, a year after the first heavy night raids, it was a different kettle of fish. Many of the lessons of the previous winter had been learned and the means to deal with the problems of defending England during the night hours had been miraculously provided. It was a case of 10/10 for effort on the part of the Air Ministry, the aircraft industry, the RAF itself and above all the British scientists (who became known by the endearing name of 'the boffins') who succeeded in keeping this country ahead of Germany in the technical and complex fields of radio countermeasures, electronic intelligence and radar throughout the Second World War.

Number 11 Group, under its new AOC, Air Vice-Marshal Trafford Leigh-Mallory, now had a formidable force of night-fighter squadrons. They were equipped with new aircraft, manned by newly trained crews and supported on the ground by the recently introduced GCI (Ground Control of Interceptions) stations which would put the defenders close enough to the enemy raider for the radar operator to pick up its echo (or 'blip') on his airborne radar set, thus enabling the crew to complete the interception on their own and without any further instructions from the ground.

The aircraft was the Bristol Beaufighter 1F. It was superbly designed – and speedily produced – for the night-fighter role. The 'Beau', as it instantly became known, with two Bristol Hercules 16-cylinder radial engines, had a maximum speed of 324 mph at 11,750 ft, a service ceiling of 27,000 ft and could climb to 15,000 ft in 9.4 minutes. The armament of four 20 mm cannon and six .303-in machine-guns (all firing forward) appealed to all who flew, or flew in, this robust and effective aeroplane. The more advanced radiotelephone (VHF) receivers and transmitters made communications with the GCI Controller and aerodrome Flying Control much easier with clarity of speech and less interference.

Above all, the Beaus were fitted with the newly developed Mk IV AI set. Designed and developed in the previous year by the incomparable boffins the equipment was compressed into half a dozen 'black boxes', including a viewing unit into which the radar (or AI) operator (RO) peered at two small cathode-ray tubes as if on Brighton Pier, hoping to have a glimpse at 'what the butler saw'.

On the nose of the aircraft was an arrow-shaped aerial from which the radar pulses were transmitted, and on the wings, a neat set of receiver aerials to pick up the vital echoes as the pulses bounced back off any other aircraft within the coverage of the set. This coverage, which was mainly forward-looking, had one important limitation: the range of the Mk IV AI set was limited to the height at which the Beaufighter was flying above the ground, i.e. at 10,000 ft the range of the set was two miles, whilst at 15,000 ft it was three miles. (*See* Appendix 1A.)

It is worth remembering, in this age of 'high tech', when many youngsters possess their own personal computers (and are adept in their use!), that many of the potential users of the Mk IV AI sets – the AI operators – who were first intro-duced to the concept of airborne radar, in the spring and summer of 1941, had seen nothing more complicated than the family wireless set made by courtesy of Messrs Phillips or Pye! So it did seem like a miracle to us.

Above all else – aircraft, armament and communications – AI bridged the gap which had to be closed before night interception could cease to be a hit or miss affair and became a practical proposition under operational conditions.

The AI sets were also the means of solving that other problem of the early night-fighter crews: how to get back to base after wandering about in the dark for two or three hours. Homing beacons transmitting on the same frequency as used for the Mk IV AI were set up at all the night-fighter stations like West Malling in Kent and Middle Wallop, north-east of Salisbury. When required, the AI operator could tune into a visual signal on his tubes, giving azimuth readings, distance and identification of his own airfield and guide his pilot back home. It was an extremely reliable system and easy to use: it was called appropriately enough 'Mother' and, like its namesake, its value was priceless!

Our home defences were therefore much improved when comparing the autumn of 1941 with that of 1940. The development of the Beaufighter and its new equipment had been taking place during this period, and some had started to reach the squadrons in late September 1940, although many of the crews were still having to use the older Bristol Blenheim. It was in November 1940 that a certain John Cunningham, with Aircraftman J.R. Phillipson as his AI operator, had opened his account with the destruction of a Junkers 88, which fell near Bridge Norton. By the end of the winter of 1940/41 things had improved in our favour; but – as I have already made clear – there was still every reason to fear the onset of winter in 1941.

For the sake of clarity we must now enlarge on the vital gap between day and night interception mentioned in an earlier paragraph. In the Battle of Britain the Ground Controllers – with the aid of the new radio-location stations – aimed to put the day-fighter squadrons within 5–10 miles of the incoming enemy formations. At that range, in reasonable weather conditions, the pilots in the cockpits of their Hurricanes and Spitfires were hopefully near enough to be able to spot the German aircraft, warn their colleagues, plan their attack and put it into effect.

To be within 5–10 miles of an enemy at night is patently not good enough, because you can't see him at that range. In fact, he could be within two–three hundred feet of you and it would still be useless in the darkness because, without airborne radar, the night-fighter pilot would not know where to look. Also, as we have already seen, because of the natural hazards of flying in formation in the dark, the defending fighters would be operating individually and seeking to find not a large formation spread out across miles of sky, but a single target, some-where amongst a loose gaggle over one hundred miles in length; the night business was very much a one-to-one confrontation.

The task of the Ground Controller – at his GCI station – was to watch a large cathode-ray tube (called a Plan Position Indicator) and look for the blips (radar echoes) of the incoming bombers on his screen. He would then identify one of the blips thrown up on the screen by a defending night-fighter, which he con-sidered to be in the most suitable position relevant to the track and height of the 'bandit', and by instructions over the VHF radiotelephone attempt to direct the fighter to within 2–3 miles of its quarry. Ideally the Controller would try to bring the fighter in on a 'cut-off' vector somewhere close behind the enemy bomber, so the pilot and his AI operator would not be faced with a prolonged stern chase.

Initially, the Controller might also pick the fighter which had some height in hand (on the bomber), in case some extra speed was needed to catch up on it. This was particularly the case if the bomber had dropped its load of bombs and had its nose down for home. Once the echo from the target appeared on the cathode-ray tubes of the airborne radar, the AI operator could gleefully shout '*Contact!*' to his pilot and take over, whilst the former passed on the good news to the GCI Controller. From that moment it was up to the crew of the Beaufighter to bring the interception to a satisfactory conclusion.

Either by direct instructions, i.e. '*Turn port . . . Throttle-back . . . Lose 500 ft . . . Turn 5 degrees starboard*', or by giving a running commentary to his pilot of the relevant position of the target (or a mixture of both!), the AI operator could, after a swift but vital scrutiny of the signals on his cathode-ray tubes, aim to bring his pilot to within 500–600 ft astern of the target and 5–10 degrees below it. The shimmering green lines of the time-traces and the indistinct shape of the blips on the two small tubes were not always easy to decipher when one was being bumped along in the back of a Beau. Additionally, the amount of working space on the tubes, unencumbered by the menacing 'Christmas tree' of the ground returns was woefully small (*c.*2 cm at 10,000 ft). If the two aircraft were converging fast – or even head on – the AI operator had only a second or two in which to act before the precious blip disappeared off his tubes as quickly as it had arrived.

Many an operator, in his early days, can recall (if he is honest with himself) his commentary to his astonished pilot going something like this over the intercom: '*Contact! It's coming . . . It's coming!! . . . It's coming!!! . . . . It's going!! . . . It's going! . . . It's gone!*' I sometimes think that the poet Longfellow would have made a good patron for the bewildered AI operators of those days. Amongst his splendid verse is to be found, '. . . only a look and a voice; then darkness again and silence.'

If all went well and the operator was able to bring them in as described above, i.e. to within 600 ft and 5–10 degrees below, the pilot, as they closed the range slowly from 600 ft, would start to see a shape which was different from the rest of the night sky. On all but the darkest of nights he would be able to pick up the outline of the other aircraft and, coming in below, he would see the silhouette as it became larger and larger and spread out above him. On the way in he might have caught a glimpse of twin exhaust flames (flame dampers on the exhaust manifolds quickly put an end to those helpful yellow bursts of flame), and if, on the final approach, he chanced to pull up onto the same level as his prey, he would feel – on his controls – the turbulence caused by its slipstream.

As soon as the pilot was able to pick out the silhouette (i.e. in night-fighter terms, had got a 'visual') the gap between day and night had been successfully bridged. However, he still had to identify his target before making his attack and opening fire, even though the GCI Controller might have already told him that it was a bandit. The problem of identification is as old as warfare itself, and even aided by certain new radar devices (Identification Friend or Foe, or IFF for short), accidents could and did happen, as we shall see! Once the pilot of the Beau had identified the shape in front of him as a Heinkel 111, Dornier 217 or Junkers 88 (or whatever type of German aircraft it might be) he could drop back, pull the nose up, line up the target in his sights and open fire. Sometimes in order to be quite sure he might ask his operator to have a look and confirm that it was a Heinkel 111, or whatever, before opening fire. But sometimes the harassed AI operator, pulled away from the brightness of his cathode-ray tubes to stare into the blackness of the night would come up with the wrong answer! I certainly know one who did and he can still recall Harry White's unprintable reply over the intercom!

There was great haste and effort made throughout the spring and summer of 1941 to rush the new night-fighter crews through to the squadrons. They would then be ready together with the first generation of AI operators and pilots for the resumption of the night Blitzes. They were all confident that the Heinkels, Dorniers, Junkers and Messerschmitts would not be able to traverse the night skies over England quite so freely as had been the case during the previous winter.

Swept up in the rush and carried along with the tide were Harry White and myself. But, before finding out how we fared after our short-lived career on No. 29 Squadron, it is necessary to go back in time once more. This time to the years immediately following the First World War . . .

*　　　*　　　*

Family legend has it that my father and mother met in 1920 whilst riding their motor-cycles in opposite directions! They 'met' twice a day: on their way to work in the morning, and on the return journey home in the evening, my father giving a merry wave of his hand, and my mother studiously ignoring it! Encumbered by those heavy leather coats favoured by the early motor-cyclists (and wearing helmets and goggles), they could not have seen very much of each other anyway!

My mother had come down from the Midlands during the First World War, with her sister, to work in London; and they were the proud owners of a

My uncle, Lieutenant Geoffrey Charles Allen, killed in France in 1918 whilst serving with the Buffs.

My father, 2nd Lieutenant Brian Seamer Allen RFC in 1918.

motor-cycle combination. My father, newly demobilised from the Royal Air Force, was already involved in the motor-cycle business and shortly to become a partner in the Allen Bennett Motor Cycle Company Ltd. His parents lived in south-east London, where my grandfather managed a branch of the Westminster Bank. My mother's family lived in the Burton-on-Trent area; she had two elder brothers and one sister; she had been born on St Swithin's Day in 1898 and christened Kathleen Margaret Jessie Gray, so she was aged 23 when she and my father were married in 1921.

Christened Brian Seamer Allen, after he was born on May Day 1899, my father was the youngest of three children. Joyce, his elder sister (of whom more will be heard later), was married during the First World War and went to live in South Africa. His elder brother, Geoffrey Charles, was killed in 1918 whilst serving as a Lieutenant in the Buffs. He lies in Doullens Communal Cemetery in northern France.

My father, who was crazy about anything mechanical (and that went fast!), joined the Royal Flying Corps and was commissioned in the rank of Temporary 2nd Lieutenant on 6 December 1917, at the age of 18½. He qualified as a pilot and went to France in 1918, where he was posted to a fighter squadron, flying the SE 5a.

As my readers will have gathered, my parents must have liked what they saw of each other, when my father could eventually persuade my mother and her sister to stop! They were soon engaged, married, and moved out of London to live in the delightful village of Brasted, near Westerham in Surrey. There they started a family.

My elder brother, Geoffrey, was born on 29 January 1922 (christened, like many small boys at that time, after a relative killed in the war, whom he had never known). Shortly after Geoffrey had been born my parents had to move back into town so that my father could be nearer to the company's showrooms in Croydon. So I was born in the rather grim and forbidding 105 London Road, a few hundred yards from the offices of the Allen Bennett Motor Company, on the Ides of March 1923. The following year Rodney was born on Derby Day in June 1924. With a gap of only 14 months between myself and Geoffrey, and 15 months between Rodney and me, we were a close-knit little family. Throughout the twenties and the thirties we enjoyed a happy upbringing and childhood.

Before leaving those early days I should perhaps mention that my mother came from a Roman Catholic family. She, herself, was a Christian and had a great faith, but never sought to press her belief on others. She was just a lovely person in every sense of the word.

After Geoffrey was born, she was visited by the local Catholic priest to ascertain that her baby son was going to be brought up in the Catholic faith. Certain documents were produced, confirming the manner of the little boy's upbringing, to which my mother was asked to put her signature. The long and the short of it was that she refused to do so and took the, then, very brave step of leaving the Catholic Church. As a consequence, we were all brought up in the Church of England, in which she found comfort and peace throughout the remainder of her life. I have always admired her bravery and been grateful to her for taking that decision.

The highlight of those days was that, for a period, Lawrence of Arabia used to come to my father for his motor-bikes. He used to arrive at 105 London Road very early in the morning, go off with my father to the showrooms, where they would choose two of the Brough Superior bikes (for which my father had the agency) and roar off around the empty streets of Croydon, testing them out, probably swopping round at the half-way stage.

Then they would return to breakfast, prepared by my mother; we three would be brought down in our pyjamas to meet Lawrence and then he would depart as quickly and as silently as he had arrived, hopefully, from my father's point of view, on his new BSA. Later, when I read about him and the various steps which he took, on his return to England from Arabia, to avoid publicity (by enlisting in the RAF under a false name), I remembered those early morning visits and the three bewildered little boys being wakened from their sleep and paraded downstairs to shake hands with 'Lawrence'.

More on our level, and very much a part of the scene at 105 was 'Florry Ford', an ancient company van, in which we were allowed to play on Sunday mornings! There were endless happy hours spent shifting around in her cab and taking turns to 'drive', push on the accelerator pedal and haul on the old-fashioned brake lever. Whatever childhood pressures we put on 'Florry Ford', we never succeeded in moving her an inch.

At the beginning of the thirties the business folded. It may have come about because of the great slump at that period, or it may have been that one partner (my father) looked after the sales side of the business and the other (Cyril Bennett) looked after the accounts – and that they were not as close as they should have been. Whatever the cause, after nearly seventy years, it matters not, and the outcome was beneficial in other ways.

As a direct result of the closing down of the Allen Bennett Motor Company, my father had to give up the sporting side of the motor-cycle business in which he had been a notable contender. The days of the London to Land's End Rallies, the Hill Climbs and the Speed Trials along the Front at Brighton and Worthing were gone for ever.

Apart from being able to ride a motor-cycle, my father remembered that he could also pilot an aeroplane. He returned to flying and spent the rest of his life in civil aviation, in one form or another.

Initially he joined Henley's, the prestigious motor dealers, whose base was in Piccadilly, and working for Frank Hough he opened up an Aviation Division at Heston Aerodrome, just to the north of present-day Heathrow. With an agency from Roy Dobson of A.V. Roe & Co. Ltd, the aircraft designers and manufacturers of Manchester, he set about selling Avro Avians and Tutors, in addition to the other light aircraft on the market at that time.

He spent a lot of time away from home, attending the various air displays around the country, contacting potential customers, taking them up and demonstrating the aircraft, often with quite dazzling flying displays of his own! In the mid-thirties he moved across to Croydon Airport, where he started up the Brian Allen Aviation Company, continuing to buy and sell a variety of light aircraft.

He also undertook charter work, and secured contracts with some of the newspapers for taking aerial photographs of major disasters, incidents, fires, etc. This meant having a Cessna on standby with a panel cut away from the side of the fuselage, out of which the cameraman would hang precariously, whilst my father or one of his pilots orbited the burning building, or whatever the incident was, at as low a height as possible! Everything was done at a rush, then back to Croydon as quickly as possible for the precious photos to be loaded into a fast car for the journey to Fleet Street and a deadline for the morning editions to be met, on pain of death!

Then in 1938 it was away from Croydon to Hanworth Aerodrome, near Feltham, and into light aircraft manufacture. The Tipsy, designed in Belgium by E.O. Tips and manufactured in association with the Fairey Aviation Company, was a low-winged light aircraft, powered by a single 62 h.p. Mikron engine and a selling price of c.£550.

When the Tipsy Aircraft Company of Great Britain (commonly known as 'Tipsy's') was formed, a factory was built at Hanworth and my father was appointed Managing Director. The Tipsys were soon rolling off the production line for their test flights, frequently undertaken by my father. Within a year war had broken out, all civil aircraft production had come to a halt and Tipsy's went over to sub-contract work for the Fairey Aviation Company, which, like the other big aircraft manufacturers, was controlled by the Ministry of Aircraft Production, and part of the defence industry.

The thirties were still the era of the pioneering long-distance flyers. Amy Johnson, Scott and Black, Kingsford-Smith, Amelia Earhart, Parmentier and Moll, Jimmy Mollison and many others. During his time at Heston, Croydon and Hanworth my father came across most of them. In particular, he and 'Smithy' became close friends. Smithy was actually Air Commodore Sir Charles Kingsford-Smith KBE, AFC, the great Australian pilot, who made the first crossing of the Pacific in *The Southern Cross*.

When he was in England preparing for one or other of his record-breaking flights, Smithy used to keep his aircraft in my father's hangar at Heston, working on it himself and coming back each night to stay with us at our home in Twickenham. When he went missing, somewhere over the Indian Ocean, flying a Lockheed Orion, we could not believe it and felt certain that he would turn up. His loss remains one of the mysteries of the air.

Probably my father's greatest friend was Leslie Irvin, the American parachute designer who had come over to England to build on the successful business which he had already started in the States. He built a factory at Letchworth in Hertfordshire and set up in production, buying a beautiful house close by. He was a pilot himself and rented a field just off the Baldock–Royston Road, from which he flew – in and out – in his splendid Stinson Reliant (you can still see his old hangar 3–4 miles on your left, as you head north from Baldock). The Stinson was the 'Rolls-Royce' amongst the smaller aircraft of the day.

My father made several trips to America with Leslie Irvin and secured the Stinson agency for Brian Allen Aviation in Great Britain. As boys, we were frequent visitors to Letchworth and twice we sailed out of Southampton for weekend cruises on his ocean-going yacht, the SY *Velda*, which he had named after his wife.

When the Second World War broke out Leslie Irvin elected to stay in England and run Irvin Airchute Ltd in Letchworth, rather than taking the easier course and returning to the parent company in Buffalo, New York. Thousands of parachutes were made at Letchworth for the RAF and the Allied Forces during the War. As early as 1922, when Lieutenant Harold Harris, a young United States Army Air Corps test pilot, saved his life with an Irvin parachute baling out of a Loening monoplane (which had faulty ailerons), Leslie Irvin had made a pledge.

He said that he would donate a small gold tie pin in the shape of a caterpillar to every person, anywhere, who saved his or her life in an emergency with a parachute of his design. The parachute canopy was of silk, and so was the tiny thread on which the silkworm safely lowered itself to earth from its leaf. What better symbol for those who had saved their lives by floating down to earth beneath a silken canopy, after jumping from a stricken aircraft?

Thus was the famous Caterpillar Club born, and on 20 October 1922 Lieutenant Harris became Caterpillar No. 1. The numbers grew steadily throughout the twenties and thirties, as the parachute came into wider use and as it was adopted by the air forces of the world. When the war ended in 1945, the Letchworth branch of the Caterpillar Club was 27,000 strong. Twenty-three thousand had been wartime enrolments.

Leslie Irvin, with the brilliance of the original inventor and the wisdom of an Indian Chief, is a name unknown in this country – except to those who owe their lives to one of his parachutes and by those who have worn them. He is, surely, one of this country's unsung heroes? No official recognition from the British Government ever came his way but, being the man he was, his satisfaction came from saving lives. Rodney and I were privileged to know him as Uncle Leslie. I was one of the many who wore an Irvin parachute for years but, fortunately, never had to use it.

After the Germans started to drop anti-shipping mines from a low altitude (attached to parachutes), the Ministry of Defence approached Leslie Irvin with the request that he should design a parachute which could be attached to an aerial mine. They wished to repay the Germans in their own coin! They ran into unforeseen trouble, to say nothing of the simple humanity of the man who held the key to their problem. Irvin is said to have replied quietly, '. . . I don't know about that . . . I have always designed my parachutes *to save life*, not to take it.' I believe he wrestled with his conscience for some days before acquiescing to 'the Men from the Ministry', and only gave way under the exigencies of war. One does not meet many people in one's life who possess genuine wisdom. I have met only three, and he was one of them.

The low point for the Allen family in the thirties occurred in 1934, not long after we had moved from Croydon to Strawberry Hill (to be nearer to Heston Aerodrome). My elder brother, Geoffrey, died of a mastoid a few days after his twelfth birthday. A first operation was followed by a second. Rodney and I were taken to see him in the hospital at Twickenham, and a few days later – it was on a Friday evening I remember – our parents came back from the hospital to tell us that he had died.

It was just before the age of penicillin and the antibiotics, and there was nothing anybody could do for him. I remember when Rodney and I returned to school a few days later, walking across the yard at the Mall School and all the other boys were staring at us, not knowing what to say. No one ever knew what Geoffrey's death cost my mother. Shortly after the war broke out 5½ years later, when Geoffrey would have been 17½, she said quietly to me, one day, 'You know, he might have found this all rather difficult, he was such a gentle little boy.'

Conversely, the high point was my father's solo flight from England to Abyssinia during the Italo-Abyssinian War! He took off early one morning from Croydon in 1935, flying a DH Leopard Moth. His destination was the Abyssinian capital, Addis Ababa. A week before, one of his pilots (a chap called Griffiths) had set out on the same route, but had crashed at Avignon in southern France. The purpose of Griffiths's flight was to go to Addis Ababa and send back reports and photographs of the war for a newspaper syndicate in London.

The syndicate which had given this commission to Brian Allen Aviation Company Ltd comprised the *Daily Sketch*, *Daily Telegraph*, *Daily Express*, Associated Press and Paramount News. When Griffiths crashed my father decided that he must go himself. In front of me – as I write – is one of the few remaining pieces salvaged from the ruins of our home in 1944. It was smashed at the time, but I had it restored to its former glory. It is a silver cigarette box. On the top are the initials 'B.A.', and on the front is the following:

WELL DONE! BRIAN ALLEN.
Thanks for your Abyssinian flying.
From D.S. D.T. D.E. A.P. and P.N.
1935

When he got to Addis, my father had some hair-raising drives over the mountainous passes surrounding the capital – sent back outstanding reports and photographs to the syndicate in London – was invited (as a famous World War pilot!) to inspect the few ramshackle old planes which passed for the Abyssinian Air Force – and had two audiences of the Emperor, Haile Selassie! In modern parlance, he had himself a ball!

Before leaving these halcyon days I should mention that his purpose, in going to the palace, was not strictly on business for the syndicate. He sought audience of the Emperor in order to try and sell him some aeroplanes, which could be of use in the war against the Italians! Brian Allen was nothing if he was not a salesman. But in this instance, I don't think he was successful, the war was too far gone in favour of the Italians.

Returning to England, flying a Percival Gull, he himself crashed. Coming into Wadi Halfa at dusk, he hit a *donga* crossing the boundary of the aerodrome, and wrote off his undercarriage. Unhurt, but stranded halfway between Khartoum and Cairo, he ended his adventurous journey by flying home, in comfort, on Imperial Airways.

This then was the world in which Rodney and I were brought up. The thirties were the heyday of civil aviation, and our father was very much a part of the scene. He first took us up in 1931, when I was eight years old, in an Avro Avian flying from Heston. We spent all our spare moments at Heston from then on, either in his office or, more likely, in the hangar where his aircraft were parked and serviced. We cadged a flight whenever we could, but we had strict instructions not to go up with anyone else, unless our father knew who they were, and was satisfied with their skill as a pilot.

It also has to be said that Rodney and I spent quite a few hours outside the bar, in the clubhouse at Heston, fortified with a mineral water (a rather different liquid to the 1980s designer item) and a packet of Smith's crisps, waiting for our ebullient parent to emerge and take us home! Throughout those sometimes stormy years our gentle mother soldiered quietly on, keeping the home going and finding solace in her garden. She hated the atmosphere of the clubhouse and cordially disliked the 'hail fellow, well-met' attitude of many of my father's friends. To say nothing of the lounge lizards who were too often invited back to our peaceful and modest home for a party.

From 1931 onwards both Rodney and I wanted to be pilots when we grew up and I don't think we ever seriously considered any other way of life.

In the summer of 1936, having sat the Common Entrance Examination, I left the Mall School. In the September, I went off to boarding school in Sussex where, at St John's College, Hurstpierpoint, a whole new world began to open up in front of me.

By the spring and summer of 1939, I was enjoying Hurstpierpoint and life in general. I had made some good friends in Ken Lock and John Eeles, I'd got my full House colours and Colts XV colours, I was no longer a Junior, so no more 'fagging' for the House prefects. I was even starting to enjoy the Officers' Training Corps!

We had fun shooting off the .22 ammunition on the 25-yard range in the school grounds, and then got down to the serious stuff with the .303 at the 250- and 500-yard range set in a cleft of the South Downs near Wolstenbury Tor. One year, I made it to Bisley! However, after a week's camp at Bordon under canvas, in the summer of 1938, I came to the conclusion that, if ever there was a war or anything like that, there must be an easier way of serving one's country (and more importantly, one's self!) than marching for miles in full kit – crawling around at night in muddy ditches – and having earwigs *et al.* dropping from the roof of the tent, down the back of your neck, when you are trying to sleep!

After all one had to think about such things because there had been that 'happening' last winter called the Munich Crisis, when hefty members of the 1st and 2nd Rugby XVs had been summoned from their classrooms, given large spades and other rustic implements and sent to dig a line of trenches in South Field! We were not sure whether the trenches were to be used as air-raid shelters or to be used in case of invasion.

But we enjoyed the few days' break from our books! Anyway, it had all passed over, Mr Chamberlain had come back to Heston Airport waving a piece of paper and declaring that it was '. . . Peace in our time . . .' We had reluctantly trickled back to our classrooms, and war, in that summer of 1939, seemed pretty remote to us, pursuing comfortable and privileged lives, as we worked (and more often played!) our way up the school!

By the autumn, I was cycling seven miles to the factory and working on the shop floor of a large aircraft company as an apprentice and cycling the seven miles back home at the end of the day. My life – and that of many others – had changed irrevocably within a few short months.

Mr Chamberlain's hand had turned out to be 'a busted flush', Adolf Hitler was on the march again and England was at war with Germany. Visions of playing in the 1st XV and becoming a prefect had vanished for ever! I now had to concentrate on getting up early each morning and (after the cycle ride!) hammer away, all day, making cowling-clips on the turn-buckle bench along with the other apprentices. In the evenings – three nights a week – I cycled on to Southall where I commenced studying for the Ordinary National Certificate in Mechanical Engineering. It was then ten miles to cycle home.

It had been envisaged for some time, by my father, that as I wanted to become an aeronautical engineer I would have to leave Hurstpierpoint earlier than those planning to go on to university. However, I had not expected to do so in quite such dramatic circumstances: it was a rude awakening! The most cruel cut came at the beginning of the Winter Term.

I had left in the July in possession of a mediocre School Certificate and 'Cert. A' from the OTC to signify my prowess as a soldier! My brother Rodney was going back and I travelled down in the car (from Ashford) to Hurst, to keep my mother company on the homeward journey.

A few miles away from the school we caught up with another car. In it were John Eeles and his younger brother. He saw me and immediately thought, 'Great! Michael hasn't left after all! He's coming back for another term and we'll both be able to try for the 1st XV.' When we stopped outside the school to unload Rodney's trunk I had to tell John that I wasn't coming back. (Postscript: John did make the Rugby XV and was awarded the colours that we had prized so much. Having survived the war, in the Navy, he married, had two children, and started to build a successful post-war career in industry. He was killed in the early fifties in a motor-car accident. Such is life.)

In those weeks of change my parents had moved from South Croydon to Ashford in Middlesex and rented a house in Clarendon Road. It did boast a name, Westwick, but it was really No. 60 Clarendon Road. It was not a bad house and it had about a quarter of an acre for the garden. Ashford, in those days, was little more than a village and a pleasant place in which to live. It was not far from Hayes (for my work). Heathrow Airport did not exist! There was a local golf course and an active and friendly cricket club. It was on the morning of Sunday 3 September 1939 at 60 Clarendon Road after listening to Mr Chamberlain's broadcast to the nation, that my father opened a bottle of sherry. He poured my mother a glass, then poured out one for me and one for Rodney. The four of us stood in the drawing room, facing out onto the garden, and drank a toast to 'Victory!' in the war against Germany which had just been proclaimed by a desolate Prime Minister.

My father and mother were 40 and 41 respectively. I was 16½, still too young to join up, and Rodney had just turned 15, so likely to be at school for several years to come. Things didn't look too bad for the Allen family.

By one of the ironies of war and, indeed, of life in general, I was to survive nearly four years of flying on operations, whilst our father and mother were to die, in the room above the drawing room, as a result of enemy action. Rodney was to lose his life in a flying accident after the war was over.

None of us knew or could have guessed, because no such weapon as the German A-4 rocket existed then, the significance of the move to 60 Clarendon Road on the lives and fortunes of the Allen family . . . and I am sure that this was just as well for all of us.

Amongst the flood of changes which overran our lives was that the Tipsy Aircraft Company, at Hanworth Aerodrome four miles from Ashford (of which my father was the Managing Director), ceased building light aircraft. They went over to making component parts for the warplanes being built, now in ever increasing numbers, by the Fairey Aviation Company at Hayes, with whom I had just started my apprenticeship. My father, whose company already had a close working relationship with Fairey's, put the half-assembled Tipsy aircraft into storage for the duration (as it was called), and secured a variety of sub-contract work to keep the factory and its workforce going, whilst making a substantial contribution towards the War Effort.

My mother, apart from continuing to run our home, took in a couple of our friends who needed temporary accommodation and then took up some war work herself. At a diesel engine company in Staines, she drove a motor-van all over Middlesex, Surrey and London, picking up spares and components which had been made and assembled for the main factory. Wherever my mother went she commanded respect, admiration and friendship from those around her and at every level. People just loved her for the wonderful person she was.

I was an apprentice at the Fairey Aviation Company for eighteen months before I broke my indentures to join the RAF. I worked at Hayes from September 1939 to 13 March 1941 (two days before my 18th birthday). What happened was that the war with Germany broke out just before I was due to sign my indentures. These would bind me for the term of my apprenticeship, i.e. five years. In those days it was a very serious matter to break your indentures: it could mean that your career was in ruins before you had really started in life and that the whole of your future could be in jeopardy.

On the other hand I had always planned to join the Royal Air Force Volunteer Reserve (RAFVR) when I was eighteen and learn to fly over the weekends in conjunction with my apprenticeship. Not surprisingly, my father had encouraged me in this aim! But the outbreak of war changed everything. I now had a problem and it was a serious one.

My problem was this: working in industry on tanks, ships, aeroplanes and other weapons of war was now designated as a 'reserved occupation'. Employment was controlled, workers could not move at will, freely, from one job to another. Also, there were special restrictions placed on them joining the Armed Forces. All this was absolutely right and as vital to the successful prosecution of the war as was the manning of the three Services. You could not have, in time of war, skilled workers chopping and changing their jobs and still hope to maintain the essential production programmes needed to supply the weapons of war.

In short, if I signed my indentures and started work at Fairey's I would be held there until the end of the war. It is sometimes said cynically that '. . . it ain't what you know, but who you know'. My father *did* know the right people at Fairey's and he went to see them! He came back with an assurance that when I was eighteen, if I still wanted to join the RAF, they would allow me to break my indentures with no penalty. They would not raise an objection with the Ministry of Labour (who controlled all movement of labour at that time) about me leaving a reserved occupation. Fairey's only laid down two conditions for agreeing to release me. Firstly, the arrangements must remain entirely confidential between the board and my father (if it got out, other apprentices would also want to go). Secondly, if I left, I must never darken their doorway again!

With this assurance and with this secret – held back from my fellow apprentices – I signed my indentures, got on my bike and started work.

My father, who in some ways never quite grew up from his early years in the Royal Flying Corps in World War I, was very sensible about some things. Firstly, having missed out on a full apprenticeship himself, he was anxious that I should have one if I was going to go into the aircraft industry. But when, due to the fortunes of war, it seemed unlikely that I would complete my technical training, he was still concerned that I 'should know what it was like to do a real day's work' and have 'some of the corners' knocked off me before I went into the Air Force. I have always been grateful to him for that. Years later, when I went into the Personnel field, I found it useful to be able to say that I too had started on the shop floor. To say nothing of the experience that I gained, long before the well-organised Apprentice Training Schools of the aircraft industry emerged in the fifties and sixties.

As already mentioned, I started on the turn-buckle bench and along with the other apprentices I must have made thousands of them because I did nothing else for the first nine months! These turn-buckles were, in reality, cowling clips, and they were used to hold the stressed-skin metal panels on to the framework of the aircraft of those days: in our case the Fairey Swordfish and, later, the Fairey Albacore which was used extensively by the Fleet Air Arm. There was really no proper training. I just started with the various pieces for the turn-buckle on the bench in front of me, a hammer in my right hand and a steel punch in my left! At the end of the 49-hour working week, I was fifteen shillings better off and had a ring of scars and bruises on the top of my left hand where I had missed!

And so life continued during the first winter of the war. Except that I did not miss the punch so often and my left hand slowly recovered from the battering which it had received. Sometimes, as I got a little quicker, I used to make a bit of bonus and a few more welcome shillings appeared in my wage-packet. I did my best to put all thoughts of the RAF out of my head, but I do remember worrying about whether I would really get out of Fairey's when the time came and if they would keep their word and the promise which had been given to my father . . .

There were no air raids that first winter of the war, and in France the 'phoney war' on either side of the Maginot Line took its misleading course. I continued my daily cycle ride from Ashford to Hayes, and back at night, little knowing that when I turned north off the old Great West Road at the Champion Plug Factory to head for Harlington and Hayes I was riding over the very centre of the future London Airport of Heathrow. Fairey's did have a small grass airfield there, pre-war, from which they did some of their test flying. In fact, I saw my father demonstrate a Tipsy there one day and carry out certain manoeuvres which *Monsieur* Tips, the designer, had not designed it to do!

But in May 1940 the Germans started to move: the 'phoney war' came to an abrupt end as the *Panzers* went into top gear and across the Low Countries, and Anthony Eden, the Foreign Secretary, made his famous speech. He called over the wireless one night for volunteers for the defence of our homes and our country as, within weeks, the Germans were looking across the Channel from Calais at the White Cliffs of Dover – from a range of 22 miles.

I joined 'Dad's Army' alongside my father and thousands of others. Although in the early days it was called the Local Defence Volunteers and we wore a khaki armband with the letters L.D.V. emblazoned on it, on our left sleeve. It was not renamed the Home Guard until some months later, when the first potent threat of invasion had passed and Hitler had – luckily for us – turned away from the West and attacked his erstwhile allies, the Russians.

We went along to the Ashford Cricket Club the night after Anthony Eden's broadcast. The scene which ensued was not unlike that depicted in the opening of the TV series *Dad's Army*. All the retired colonels and 'old sweats' from past wars and skirmishes, back to the Crimea, seemed to be there, signing on for the LDV. But there was no mistaking the enthusiasm of the volunteers and the feeling of patriotism which abounded in the cricket ground that night. It was the only time I saw such a mass feeling of patriotism during the whole of the war.

As I remember it, we all started off as members of the Ashford (Middlesex) Company, but later my father (who I think became a captain) transferred to the Air Force to serve with the Air Training Corps, and was commissioned into the RAFVR as a flying officer. I also transferred, to the company formed at the Fairey Aviation Company, and on the strength of my three years experience in the OTC at school, I was soon promoted! I was made a Section Leader, with the rank of lance-corporal, and put in charge of eight old 'sweats' from the 1914–18 War.

I suppose I was closest (to those in the TV series) to 'Young Pike', the butt of much of Captain Mainwaring's wrath! I do have one vivid memory. I was patrolling up and down on one of the catwalks on the roof of the factory and heard a rifle shot go singing past my ear! At the other end of the catwalk the veteran (from the Boxer Rebellion!) with whom I was sharing my watch was looking ruefully at his equally ancient firing-piece and muttering to himself '. . . there must have been one up the spout . . . !'

During that long hot summer of 1940 there was not much enemy activity over Hayes, considering there was so much industry in the area. However, one day a Junkers 88 *did* dive out of the clouds and dropped four bombs, some of which hit the factory. It was a mercy that the alarms went too late for us in the LDV to take up our posts on the catwalks and other strategic places of defence, otherwise I and the old warrior mentioned above might not have survived the day. And in August 1941, Harry White might have had to look elsewhere for an AI operator!

The reason? I forgot to mention that all we had to defend ourselves (and the factory) was a Canadian Ross rifle, a steel helmet, a pouch full of ammunition (similar to something worn by Lord Kitchener's Army of the Sudan fifty years earlier) and a bayonet. Not exactly the most appropriate weapons with which to repel an attack by low flying aircraft!

Too late to get up on the roof, I made tracks for the fire which had started in one of the main stores. Because of the close-fitting racks and narrow walkways it was proving difficult to get the fire under control and to get at its source. Somehow I found my way round onto a staging several feet up from the ground and where three or four people were playing a hose onto the fire. I helped them to hang onto it and we called out for another length of hose so that we could get a bit closer to the heart of the blaze. I must have been more of a hindrance than a help, because I hadn't a clue what I was supposed to be doing.

Then, in typical 'Dad's Army' style, we watched as the hose we had been holding was detached from our nozzle . . . and attached to a hose held by somebody else! I now found myself holding onto the waterless and useless nozzle and much nearer to the flames erupting from the burning store than was either prudent or sensible. I felt like that unfortunate boy who stood upon the burning deck 'when all but he had fled'!

So much for my efforts to defend the factory or become a firefighter. I think I was eventually pulled back out of the smoke by an electrician pal of mine. He took me to his home which was close to the factory, where he and his wife gave me a cup of tea and set about cleaning me up. As Captain Mainwaring would have said, '. . . you stupid boy!'

Before we leave the summer of 1940 I might mention that when new acquaintances hear that I was in the RAF, the question is invariably, 'Were you in the Battle of Britain?' When I reply to the effect that I was working in a factory at the time, their interest wanes rapidly.

The summer of 1940 brought other changes and I learned about something called 'overtime'. In May, when Mr Chamberlain found out to his horror that Hitler 'had *not* missed the bus', he resigned as Prime Minister and Mr Winston Churchill took up the reins of government. Amongst his early appointments was Lord Beaverbrook – the Canadian newspaper magnate – as Minister of Aircraft

Production. Within a short while everyone in the aircraft industry felt the irresistible driving force of 'the Beaver', from the highest to the lowest!

At our level, we apprentices felt it because with the call from the Fleet Air Arm (FAA) for more and more aircraft, the factory at Hayes was put on full overtime, and it was the same picture right across the country. In short, for a period of eight weeks from June to August, I worked the normal working hours of 7.30 a.m. to 5.00 p.m. from Monday to Friday and 7.30 a.m. to 12.00 noon on Saturdays. Plus an extra two hours Monday to Friday from 5.15 p.m. to 7.15 p.m. and Saturdays from 7.30 a.m. to 5 p.m. And the same again on Sundays. If my father wanted me to find out what it was like to do a day's work, I certainly found out that summer!

But as every student of history knows, the aeroplanes were produced and the RAF and the FAA were not kept short of machines in 1940 by any lack of effort on the part of the aircraft industry. However, it might just be mentioned, that there were some strikes in the industry during the war as a result of militant action by the Trades Union movement, notably at A.V. Roe & Co. Ltd in 1943. I learned the details of this deplorable incident when I went to work at AVROs in Manchester after the war. Even in 1940, when the country really was fighting for its survival, there was always some subversive activity going on somewhere, if you knew where to look for it.

At Fairey's there was a magazine called *The New Propeller* circulated 'under the bench'. It was very 'Red', against the war, against the Government, against the Royal Family and against just about everything it could think of! It was certainly Communist inspired. The shop steward who brought it round used to wave it under the noses of the apprentices, muttering something to the effect that he didn't expect that any of them would buy one. I always did. *The New Propeller* was certainly an eye opener for me!

By contrast, and on a happier note, when the King and Queen paid an official visit to the Fairey Aviation Company to mark the successful attack on the Italian fleet in the harbour of Taranto by Fairey Swordfish from the Mediterranean Fleet, the workforce came from all over the factory to see them! Before the visit, I heard quite a number of the fitters and electricians say that they weren't going to bother to try and see the King and Queen when they would be walking the length of the main assembly shop, and they didn't mince their words over what they thought about the Royal Family.

But, when the day *did* come and Their Majesties *did* walk slowly down the main gangway, where the Swordfish were being assembled, it was a different story. Fairey's employees came from far and near, climbing onto the benches and to any other vantage point they could find, just to catch a glimpse of them. It was the second time I experienced the intangible magic and mystique of the Royal presence. The blasé feeling up to a few minutes before they come and then that indefinable change that takes place when they are there. You feel different and you can't help yourself. There was to be a third time.

I think it was May – before all the overtime started – that I first procured 'four wheels'. I went with my father to buy my first car. It was a 1938 Ford 8 Saloon, second-hand, and with only about 10,000 miles on the clock. It cost £50. My father paid half and I paid half! It was black, almost the only colour available in those days, and from then on, I drove to work in style!

There were no driving tests to worry about during the war; as soon as you turned 17 years you just got in a car and drove! I think that I had one lesson from my father and one from my mother, and that was it. Of course the great thing was that, during the war, there was very little traffic on the roads because, apart from there being fewer vehicles licensed 60 years ago, there was petrol rationing.

The restrictions were so tight that many people took their cars off the road altogether and laid them up in their garages. The battery was removed and the car was jacked up on bricks to help to preserve the tyres. I did manage to obtain a small monthly ration of fuel coupons to get to Fairey's and back but that was about it. Later, in the Air Force, I was able to draw petrol coupons to go on leave.

All in all, the roads were much safer during the war than they were to become in the post-war years. When driving at night all headlights had to be screened because of the blackout, there were no street lights and all buildings had blackout curtains. One drove in almost total darkness but at slower speeds, which kept the accident rate down. Garages were hard to find, and a spare can of petrol in the boot was a wise precaution. Tyres were the real worry, you just could not buy them. I remember having to mend four punctures – between West Raynham and Ashford – when coming on leave in 1944. Still, in May 1940 it was marvellous to be able to ditch my bicycle and drive to and from work, particularly when the overtime started in June.

When I had been on the turn-buckle bench for about nine months I was transferred to the main assembly shop to work under a fitter. I helped him to put a number of fittings into the rear cockpit of the Swordfish. When the new Albacores started coming onto the line he had the important task of fitting the sliding Perspex canopy onto the two channels either side – and above – the pilot's head.

I enjoyed working on the assembly line where the aircraft started to take shape and were moved gradually along the floor and final assembly before being put on the 'Queen Marys' (articulated trucks with trailers, 60 feet long) for transport to Fairey's aerodrome. There the wings were attached to the fuselage and the test flying programme began. I assisted in fitting the sliding-roof and I learned a lot from the fitter with whom I was working, but I remember thinking – even then – what happens if the roof jams in the 'shut' position when the pilot needs to get out in a hurry and free himself from a stricken aircraft? Little was I to know that in a few years' time I was to find myself trapped in a burning Mosquito . . . even though in that case, I had been able to jettison the Perspex canopy over our heads without any trouble.

It must have been in the winter of 1940/41, when I was only a few months away from my 18th birthday and making plans with Ken Lock for joining up together in London, that I nearly wrecked everything! I have already said earlier that we did not have any proper training, and indeed we were not even shown how to handle our tools, i.e. we just used our hammers, screwdrivers, soldering irons, etc. in any old fashion. Quite simply, I was using a screwdriver one day and nearly put my right eye out!

I was bending too far over the component on which I was working – screwing away with the screwdriver – my right hand slipped – and in a split second I had twisted the tool up into my right cheek, where it went in just below my right eye.

The injury was not severe, no damage was done to my right eye and I was quickly patched up in the surgery by the industrial nurse. But I can remember, as if it was yesterday, breaking out into a cold sweat when I realised what I had done and how near any chance of joining the Royal Air Force and learning to fly had come to disaster.

Apart from the daylight attack on Fairey's and the ensuing fire, the nearest I got to the Battle of Britain was in late August when, together with my mother and father, we slipped off for a week's holiday in West Sussex. We stayed at the Spread Eagle Hotel in Midhurst, just to the north of the Downs, and my father and I used to go off to play golf at Goodwood.

There on that wonderful course, just below the Trundle, on the south-facing slopes of the Downs, he and I got away from it all. Sometimes my mother would walk round with us; the course was practically empty, so we could pause when we felt like it and look to the south, where the spire of Chichester's cathedral dominated the surrounding countryside. We could look beyond to West Wittering, where our childhood summer holidays had been spent in the twenties, and then to the jutting tongue of Selsey Bill and the Channel. Over to our right lay the Isle of Wight, Southampton Water and Portsmouth.

But, to the left of our view, my father could point out where the RAF aerodrome of Tangmere lay. It had recently been the target for a strong daylight attack by the *Luftwaffe* using its terrifying dive-bombers, the Junkers 87s. He remembered it from his RFC days. In little more than a year from that moment, when I was standing on the 5th fairway with a number 4 iron in my hand, I was to be posted there myself.

Chichester too was to figure largely in my life during the period 1941/42: the pubs and dance halls were to see our first youthful, and mostly innocent, escapades in the Air Force and the cathedral was to see us bury our dead.

One day during that magical week, when we were playing, an air battle developed over our heads. There were plenty of vapour trails high up in the sky above us, the sound of turning and wheeling aircraft and the noise of machine-gun fire. Further to the south we could see that there was dark smoke over to our right where lay Portsmouth and the Naval Dockyard.

I do not remember seeing any aircraft come down, but empty cartridge cases and a few other bits and pieces seemed to be spattering onto the hallowed ground of Goodwood Golf Club. Sure enough, as the battle moved away and after we had played our second shots, I spotted a piece of metal lying on the side of the fairway which looked unfamiliar! I picked it up and found it to be a square panel, about three to four feet across, with the centre pressed out on the outer side, which was sprayed a duck egg blue.

The four corners were broken, where the panel had been ripped off an aircraft – and it had a funny smell to it (that distinctive smell that I was to sniff when examining a captured Messerschmitt 110, several years later). I picked it up and we carried it home in triumph, attached to our golf-bags! I think it was a wing-panel, possibly off an Me 109, removable from over the breeches of the guns when they were being rearmed – and the broken-off corners had held something with which I was personally familiar: no fewer than four turn-buckles assembled by one of my opposite numbers working in an aircraft factory somewhere in Germany!

We bore our trophy home to Ashford at the end of the week and I hung it up in my bedroom, where it stayed until the house was destroyed in October 1944. I don't remember seeing it again after the V2 rocket had fallen.

Before leaving these treasured memories of 'Glorious Goodwood' and that wonderful view from the course, there was a small village in our foreground which was, and still is, special to me. It was the village of East Lavant.

At East Lavant was Ken Lock's home, Church Farm, and around the village lay the many acres of the Goodwood Estate farmed by Ernest Lock, his father. When we had been at Hurst together I had been to Church Farm many times on our *exeats* from the college, and I had grown to love the farm and his parents.

Ken was somewhere down there as my father and I paused on our round of golf. He would soon be 18 but he would wait for me to attain that great age before we would join the Air Force together on the Ides of March 1941, both hoping to become pilots, but all too soon to be posted on our separate ways. Lavant, where John Eeles (the third member of our trio in Fleurs-de-Lys House at Hurst) also came to stay and where the three of us played cricket for the East Lavant XI on the village green, although only Ken Lock could really play – he was a natural batsman and played for the 1st XI at school at an early age. But the memories of the fun we had conjure up thoughts of all that was best in England before the Fates took a hand in our destinies.

Our week's holiday in Sussex soon came to an end and it was back to the bench at Fairey's with a 6 a.m. start to the day . . . more overtime . . . night school at Southall . . . LDV duties to be carried out . . . and each evening the black-out curtains and screens having to be drawn a few minutes earlier with the approach of winter.

In the autumn of 1940, as I mentioned earlier, the *Luftwaffe* failed to gain ascendancy over Fighter Command during the hours of daylight. They then changed their tactics and started to launch their attacks on our towns and industrial centres at night. These night raids soon became known as the 'Blitz' and, with the change, the Germans were soon inflicting serious damage to the war effort and disruption amongst the population.

So, like many others in England that winter, when I got home from work I spent the night in the air-raid shelter in our garden. With my parents and with Rodney, when he was home from school, I listened to the ominous sound of the German bombers. That distinctive, intermittent, but unforgettable, sound of their desynchronised engines as they flew overhead every three or four minutes on their way to some target in the Midlands or further north.

As many of the stories of the 'Blitz' reveal, there was always a lighter side to the upheaval of having to carry one's bedding and treasured possessions down into the shelter each night (to say nothing of the loss of much needed sleep). Our evening's entertainment usually began with the spectacle of watching my father trying to climb into his hammock. If he had called at The Green Man on his way home it was even better.

Although only a few stray bombs fell on Ashford, one on the house of a friend of mine which I went to 'gawp' at, I did have a second experience of fire. It could have been in November, when the telephone rang for my father just when we were thinking of going into the shelter (we could hear the sound of a raid not too far away). The call was from Hanworth Aerodrome, where it will be recalled that Tipsy's had their factory. The message for him was that Tipsy's had not been hit, but another factory assembling Horsa gliders and carrying out major servicing on Hawker Hurricanes had suffered a direct hit and was well on fire.

He and I got dressed again (we usually all got into our pyjamas before going out to the shelter), drove over to Hanworth and spent the rest of the night helping to haul and drag the Hurricanes and the half-built Horsa gliders out of the burning hangar onto the airfield, where they were safe enough until morning.

Strictly speaking, this was my third close experience of fire because when I was about six and standing in our nursery at our home in Croydon, I had watched in horror whilst a towel – suspended across the fireplace by a piece of string – had dropped at one end, fallen into the fire and caught alight. Within seconds the flames were going up the wall. Not knowing what I was doing, I grabbed at the other end of the towel and thrust the whole lot back into the fire. Then Nanny Evie must have heard my yells, came into the nursery and the situation was soon restored.

As we shall see, my attendance at the fire at Hanworth Aerodrome that November night in 1940 was not to be my last experience of this truly terrifying element.

And so, the winter of 1940/41 wore on, now with two or three nights a week at Night School in Southall where I had started on the first year of the Ordinary National Certificate course in Mechanical Engineering. This added to the basic week of 49 hours at Fairey's. My commuting from Ashford to Hayes was some-times disrupted by air raids and several times I did not get back to Ashford at all.

I remember being flagged down on my way home by the police or an air raid warden and ordered to get into the nearest air raid shelter as quickly as possible, and the worry of not being able to get to a telephone and let my mother know where I was. All the time my eighteenth birthday, and consequently the day when I would be able to leave Fairey's and join the Air Force, was drawing near. By December Ken Lock turned 18 and I had only three more months to go, but would I still be allowed to go? That was my constant fear!

I was careful to hang onto my secret when I was with the other apprentices. But nobody else had left to join up since I had started at Fairey's at the begin-ning of the war, nearly a year and a half earlier. As the New Year came, I continued to wait in fear and trembling as the days passed.

I did learn one other valuable lesson at Fairey's before I drove out of the gates at Hayes on 13 March 1941 (not knowing that it was to be the last time ever). The lesson was – and I pass it on to young men with girl friends – don't ever say in boastful tones, 'Oh, I can easily get that mended for you!' when she wails over some broken but treasured heirloom. I think her name was Marnie – or was that her nickname? Anyway our friendship was very decorous (most of them were, when we were in our teens, how fashions change!).

One day she showed me a small dish, shaped like a champagne glass which was broken in two. The stem was detached from the bowl and she asked me if I could mend it as she knew I worked in a factory. I'd been shooting a line about the work I'd been doing and now was going to pay the price for my folly! The little dish was made out of bronze and I, knowing nothing about welding, thought it would be easy enough to have the two pieces welded together.

After a cursory look at the treasured heirloom I said airily, 'Oh, I've got a pal in the welding shop, he'll soon fix this for you.' A day or so later I gave it to him and forgot all about it. The weeks went by and Marnie started to ask about the little dish and how I was getting on with it? I thought that the time had come for me to chase it up and then bear the restored treasure back to her in triumph. So, one morning during the tea break, I sauntered up to the welding benches to see my friend, a bit surprised that he had not brought the dish back to me as soon as he had welded the two pieces together.

I soon found out why! After an awkward silence and a guilty look he pulled open the drawer under his bench. Lying in the bottom of the drawer was Marnie's family treasure – still in two pieces – but with an enormous hole burnt through the dish! I gazed at the two blackened and twisted relics in horror.

He muttered some technicalities about one piece being bronze and the other copper and that it was difficult to braze the two together. But I wasn't listening, as I gazed spellbound at the two burnt offerings in the drawer; I was only thinking of what I was going to say to Marnie and how I could account for the destruction of the precious dish which she had entrusted to my care. At this point, memory escapes me except that the scene which took place at her home in Hampton, a few days later, proved to be the end of a beautiful friendship! After all, we had once had an hour and forty minutes on the phone together . . . at my father's expense. Anyway, the episode taught me a good lesson about making rash promises to girls.

*   *   *

When I got home from work on Thursday 13 March, two days before my eighteenth birthday, my father was waiting for me. He said 'Do you still want to join the Air Force?' I replied in the affirmative. He then said, 'It's OK then, I've "fixed" it for you. You can join the Air Force on Saturday.' He went on to tell me that he had got confirmation from a member of Fairey's board that I could break my indentures and leave the company. Fairey's would make no representation to the Ministry of Labour to hold on to me under the 'Reserved Occupations' Laws which were, rightly, being enforced during the war to keep people in jobs vital to the war effort.

I was already getting excited when my father said, 'Hold it a moment. Fairey's have laid down three conditions for your release!' Firstly, I must not return to the factory. Secondly, I must not communicate with any of the other apprentices (a number of my pals were wanting to join up and were being turned back at the Recruiting Offices) and lastly, I was never in the future to 'darken their doorways' again.

I was a bit taken aback at the severity of these conditions and replied to the effect that I would have to go back to Hayes to pick up my tool box and, in any case, the following day was Friday when I would need to collect my wages. My father vetoed this immediately. He said, 'Under no circumstances are you to go into Fairey's in the morning or, indeed, ever again!'

He told me that he would arrange for my tool box and my wages to be collected, and eventually they would reach me; all this duly happened and I never did darken the doorways of Fairey's again. In retrospect, Fairey's conditions for my release may seem rather hard but, at the time, with many apprentices throughout the aircraft industry – and indeed, the whole of the armaments industry – wanting to join the Armed Forces, it was fully justified.

Fifty-two years later I found myself, quite by chance, in contact with a former Fairey Aviation apprentice who had been at Hayes at exactly the same time, having started in September 1939. Peter Beechey, who now lives in Spain, served in the RAF and subsequently went into civil aviation and flew as an airline captain for thirty years. Peter also wanted to join the Air Force in 1941 and he, evidently, did not have a father who could 'fix' things. If I may say so, there were not many people who could be quite so persuasive as Brian Allen, when he put his mind to it.

Peter was not so lucky, and I can quote directly from his letter of 10 January 1993 in which there is a hilarious description of some of his experiences at Fairey's. His attempts to get out were neither funny nor successful.

'Like you, I continued day part-time release at Southall Tech (Au. I only went to night school!) but also went to a pre-Air Crew school in Coldharbour Lane twice a week in the evenings. I got as far as attestation at Weston-super-Mare in 1941 and then got sent back to Fairey's. It was September 1942 before I was accepted and there then followed exactly one year of deferred service.

Thereafter is another story, one more remarkable coincidence. I am wondering if I was your replacement on Daly's Section when you left? I remember being told that an apprentice had left for the RAF – I was furious, of course, having been trying to get out myself!'

Although I lost my training and potential career as an aeronautical engineer, I am ever grateful to Fairey's for letting me go in March 1941. Although, in the post-war years when I found myself dealing with apprentices and their re-instatement rights after National Service, I did occasionally find myself wistfully thinking whether I had any reinstatement rights in my own right!

Looking back, I would not have had things any different, and there was, also, something else for which I was always grateful to Fairey's. On the shop floor I gained a view of life which I would never have had otherwise. Which is, I think, why my father was so keen on me going there in the first place.

On my eighteenth birthday I went up to London to join the Air Force, and Kenneth Lock, forsaking his father's farm at East Lavant, came with me to join up as pilots as we had planned soon after the war broke out. We went to the Recruiting Office close to Euston Station and volunteered as 'u/t pilots', i.e. Pilots under Training. We filled in forms, were medically examined, wrote one or two test papers and were interviewed by various officers, some of whom wore the wings which we so coveted.

I thought that one of them was not too impressed when he learned that I had been working for the Fairey Aviation Company. I remember thinking that perhaps he had been on Fairey Battles in France in the spring of 1940 – when the Germans broke through the Maginot Line – and the squadrons in the Advanced Air Striking Force (AASF) on Battles had such fearful losses over Maastricht and elsewhere. However, the incident passed and at the end of the day we were told that we had passed everything successfully and could go home.

We were summoned back for more tests two weeks later. Again, all went well but we learned that there would be a third series of interviews in a few days time for final selection of aircrew categories before returning to our homes to await our call-up papers which would, apparently, come three months later. When Ken Lock and I left Euston for the second time our spirits were high and we could already see ourselves (like Danny Kaye's 'Walter Mitty') with our pilot's wings up and shooting down 'Jerries' from all angles.

Years later, I heard the great Leonard Cheshire say that one of the things which the war had taught him was that 'Just when you thought that everything was all right . . . things started to go wrong'. He was referring, in particular, to one of his remarkable low-level marking trips over Munich, or some other target.

Flying a Mosquito, he was leaving the maelstrom of the target area and remarked to his navigator, 'I think we're clear now!', i.e. after the flak and search-lights. But the next minute, Cheshire said, all hell broke loose. The searchlights came on and held them. The flak opened up again and it was another ten minutes of weaving, climbing and diving – with nonstop heaving on the control column before they could escape into the darkness of the night and safety.

Leonard Cheshire added – with some feeling – that he had found that this lesson held good for many of the things which had happened to him in the post-war years!

So it was for Ken and I, and our hopes of going on and taking our pilot's training together – and for my hopes of following in my father's footsteps. The memory of one of the worst days in my life is with me still.

Halfway through the third round of interviews and medicals I was called back by one of the Medical Officers. He looked apologetic, muttered something about there being astigmatism in one of my eyes (which I did not quite take in), and then the next moment I heard him say that I would have to go into the Air Force as an observer and not as a pilot. I would be called up as a u/t observer and not as a u/t pilot.

The shock and disappointment of that MO's words, when my ambition to fly and become a pilot (held since I was eight years old) disintegrated, has never gone away. My little world fell apart and, in a way, has stayed apart.

Subsequently, on my particular roller-coaster through three score years and ten of life, and in the light of the incredibly good luck which came my way as an observer, it seems as if I am being ungrateful to the Gods to lay so much stress on my failure to go through into the Air Force as a pilot. As with many aspects of life, only those who have been through a similar experience can really appreciate one's misery, but ungrateful to 'Dame Fortune' who has watched over my 'roller-coaster' and given me fifty-four bonus years of life – that I can never be . . .

Ken tried hard to comfort me as we left Euston for the last time, and I tried hard to comfort myself with the thought that there was nothing really wrong with my eyesight. The whole thing had simply come about because the Air Force had happened to want more observers on that day. The story about the astigmatism from the MO was just to fob me off and, as soon as I got into the Air Force, I would set about transferring to a pilot's course. My obvious assets and suitability for pilot training would be apparent to all. Little did I know that I was just kidding myself . . .

Nevertheless, on the way home, there was a small incident which reveals the fragile state of my composure. I had to change trains at Clapham Junction, to get to the Windsor Line, and somehow, getting out of the carriage, I got in a bit of a tangle with another passenger, who was trying to get in. It was practically nothing at all but I have a vivid memory of possibly bursting into tears or alternatively punching the man straight in the face. Remember, I still had to break the dreaded news to my mother and father, when I finally got back to Ashford, that I had been turned down as a pilot. Of course, I need not have worried. When I told them what had happened my parents were just as considerate and understanding of my disappointment, as they always were, with all their children.

I was called up to join the Air Force on 13 June 1941 and amongst my papers was a railway warrant from Ashford to Stratford-on-Avon, where I was to report to No. 9 Receiving Wing. But, before describing the send-off my parents gave me, I must fill in the three months gap from the time I left Fairey's so precipitously to the middle of June.

I went to work for my father at the Tipsy Aircraft Company as a progress chaser based on the factory at Hanworth Aerodrome. Immediately on the outbreak of war, the production lines had been closed down and Tipsy's, in common with many other factories and workshops all over the country, went over to sub-contract work for the Ministry of Aircraft Production.

In turn Tipsy's sub-contracted work on small components, many of them to garages in the West London area. Every garage owner with a couple of lathes, a few pin-drills, a fly-press and perhaps the odd milling machine could get sub-contract work to replace the servicing of cars and commercial vehicles which had made up his livelihood in peacetime. These vehicles were now mainly off the road due either to petrol rationing or to their owners being otherwise engaged on war work or in HM Forces. And so the orders went out from the Production Planning Departments for 10,000 screws here; 5,000 bolts there; 1,000 bushes somewhere else.

There was a deadline on them all to match the production schedules at Tipsy's, and in turn for Tipsy's to deliver their ammunition boxes and other component parts to Fairey's. Fairey's could then, in their turn, complete the sub-assemblies and ultimately, the final assembly of the Swordfish and Albacores at Hayes. From there the aircraft would be transported the short distance by road to Heathrow – where Fairey's had their own airfield long before the Jumbos took over at what became London Airport.

In those days aircraft companies employed 'internal progress chasers' to expedite the detail parts being made in their own factories, and 'external progress chasers' to go out to the smaller sub-contractors. They would chase up the orders and, where possible, load the completed parts into their cars, bring them back to the parent factory and book them in at the 'Goods In' section of the stores.

With extra petrol coupons for war work, I started with Tipsy's soon after Ken and I had first gone up to the Recruiting Office. I had changed my overalls for a sports jacket and flannels and in my button-hole I sported proudly the little silver and blue RAFVR badge that we had all been given when we took the King's shilling. It signified, in a way, that we were awaiting our call-up papers and were not dodging the column.

In those three months I drove all over the outlying suburbs to the west of London: Acton, Hammersmith, Brentford, Richmond, Twickenham, Kingston and many others. I had some knowledge of what I was doing, acquired during my time at Fairey's and felt it was useful work. I thoroughly enjoyed the independence and the freedom of the job after being cooped up in the factory at Hayes for eighteen months.

Furthermore, my father had put me on a reasonable salary, which seemed like a fortune after my basic fifteen shillings a week (plus bonus!) which I had been bringing home as an apprentice. Also, living at home, I was able to save a bit because I knew things would take a downward turn when I became an Aircraftman 2nd Class in a few months' time!

Whilst at Tipsy's, life was not entirely uneventful, and the Gremlins – sensing a prospective candidate – started to lay their mischievous fingers across my path. I gave out an incorrect order for some straps for the ammunition boxes (mentioned previously) and thereby was the cause of a substantial quantity of valuable leather having to be scrapped. I had a mild flirtation with one of the girls in the office, which did not go down well at home or with my father, and I was caught by the police for exceeding the speed limit in a 30 m.p.h zone in Brentford.

I suppose I was lucky not to have been trapped more often because I was always moving fairly rapidly from one workshop or garage to the next. I thought

I would have a good excuse, but a friend of mine, who had recently been caught for the same offence, persuaded me to plead 'Guilty'. I duly appeared before the Magistrates' Court in Brentford, pleaded 'Guilty' and was fined ten shillings. When I was at the court I saw why my pal had advised me not to contest the charge.

An elderly man pleaded 'Not Guilty' – again for a speeding offence – and took up ten minutes of the court's time complaining about the injustice of the charges against him. He had apparently spent a lifetime promoting safety on the roads, belonged to every motoring organisation under the sun and had served on every committee you could possibly think of which was involved with motoring. The magistrate listened – with some irritation – to his diatribe and fined him four times as much as the rest of us miserable sinners who had pleaded 'Guilty'. So, at the cost of a precious 'ten bob' another lesson was learned, i.e. if you are going to take up the court's valuable time, you are going to have to pay for it!

If I was called up and set off for No. 9 Receiving Wing (RW) on 14 June, what happened to Kenneth Lock? He, much to my chagrin, had been accepted as a u/t pilot, whereas I had not! Kenneth, the farmer's son, who had only really decided to join the Air Force because I was doing so . . . the irony of it tortured my mind at the time, but in the end 'Dame Fortune' chose to smile on me and not on Ken.

He was called up about the same time but went to a different Receiving Wing. I was only to see him once more and that was towards the end of the year when Harry and I were on the Havoc 'Turbinlite' Flight at Tangmere. You may recall, this was only three miles east of East Lavant and his home at Church Farm.

He actually came up with us – illegally – in the back of a Havoc, and we took him over Church Farm so that he could see it from the air, along with the village cricket green mentioned earlier!

Ken was at home on leave and waiting for a boat to take him to the United States for pilot-training under the Arnold Scheme (a scheme whereby, prior to the States coming into the war in December 1941, the USAAC trained a large number of RAF pilots). Ken was to be awarded his wings in 1942. He must have passed out with an Above Average rating and done extremely well on his course, because he was retained as a flying instructor and he did not manage to get off instructing and return to the UK until 1944. I can't imagine it was ever his choice to become a flying instructor because, like the rest of us, he had only one aim – and that was to get onto ops.

But as many people have found before Ken and me, and after us, that once in the Services you do as you are told until you have got a lot of pips on your shoulder or rings on your arm! There are always a few exceptions to every rule – thank God – as we shall see, but not many! Ken was only back in England for a brief period and – stationed in Norfolk by then – I did not manage to see him.

The next thing I heard was that he had gone out to the Far East and was 'somewhere in Burma' on a photographic reconnaissance squadron. He had made it onto ops at last, flying either Hurricanes or Spitfires.

2 The School for Secrets

– and how I came to 'crew-up' with Harry White

To return to June 1941 and my call-up papers. When they arrived I left Tipsy's and my job as a progress chaser and spent a few days seeing friends and saying goodbye, including a trip to Oxted, where my grandparents lived. Grannie Allen and I did not see eye to eye, we never had! Only a few weeks before she had had a go at the morals and behaviour of young people (even as I do now), and I had responded by blaming the older generation – her included – for allowing the war to start anyway! She, in turn, accused me of being a Communist! My parents arranged a farewell party at the home of Tom and Joan Wesson for the day before I was due to leave for Stratford-upon-Avon.

The Wessons lived at Laleham three miles down the road from Ashford and almost on the river. Tom Wesson had flown for my father in the pre-war days at Croydon (with Brian Allen Aviation Ltd) and was a very experienced pilot with two to three thousand hours in his log-book. He had been on the Reserve and had been called up immediately on the outbreak of war. He was in his thirties and was now a flying instructor at White Waltham. I think he was already a flight lieutenant. Tom was a rotund and cheerful soul and the nicest of persons but, when it came to flying, he took things extremely seriously and my father thought a lot of him. I understand that he was a very good instructor and I looked up to him, hoping one day to be like him.

Joan Wesson was a sweet person and a great friend of my mother's. They had a little girl named Judith, who must have been about two years old. Tom got home each night from White Waltham, and I think they must have been a very happy little family. I remember they gave me a great evening on my last night in 'civvy street'. A week later, Tom was dead.

It was one of those freak accidents that just happen. Tom was killed whilst instructing on a Tiger Moth, and his pupil survived. I recall my father telling me that the Tiger Moth was one of the safest aeroplanes ever built. Thousands of pilots had learned – and were to learn – to fly on it. It was one of those accidents that nobody could believe had happened and especially to such an experienced pilot as Tom Wesson.

I was told that the pupil had got the Moth into a flat spin, that Tom could not get it out and gave instructions to the pupil to bale out. The pupil being either unable, or unwilling, to jump, Tom decided that he could not leave the aircraft as long as his pupil was still in it. They continued to lose height and, on impact, the pupil was thrown clear – with Tom Wesson dead in the wreckage.

I got the news of Tom's death at the end of my first week in the Air Force and just as a batch of us – now in our blue uniforms and forage caps, with the white flash inserted round the front denoting to the world at large that we were training to become aircrew – were entraining for an ITW (Initial Training Wing) on the Welsh coast. It did not seem to bode very well for my own future, and suddenly life in the Royal Air Force took on a more serious note.

But we must go back once more in time, this time only one week! It was on the afternoon of the Saturday – the day following my party at the Wessons' – that I arrived at Stratford-upon-Avon with quite a few others (I had noticed the RAFVR badges in their lapels) by train from London, with orders to report to the Shakespeare Hotel. Earlier that day my parents had taken me to lunch at an old haunt of my father's – Hatchett's (long since gone) in Piccadilly, then, with the atmosphere getting more strained by the minute, we headed for Paddington Station.

My last sight of them, as the train steamed out, was a vivid picture of my father (who by then had recovered his normal boyish humour – he was only 42 and still flying himself) leaping up and down on the platform like a dervish indicating that he wanted to come too! As an old RFC pilot it was almost too much for him. My mother just stood there quietly. It was 18.25 on Saturday 14 June 1941.

Stratford-upon-Avon Railway Station (was it the LMS in the good old days of the railway companies, or was it GWR 'God's Wonderful Railway'?) was a busy place in those days. It seemed as if the trains were coming in – and leaving – every few minutes. Almost all the seats were taken up by young men. Those arriving were in civilian clothes – those leaving were wearing brand new uniforms of a light blue colour and lugging along two heavy and unwieldy white kitbags. They wore a white flash in the front of their forage caps.

Those of us getting out at Stratford were mostly carrying a small suitcase as we tumbled out onto the platform (no hold-alls or shoulder-bags then) and crowded out into the forecourt. I can't remember whether we piled into buses to be taken to our billets or whether we were marched into the town, but I duly arrived at the Shakespeare Hotel as required on my call-up papers. Once at The Shakespeare we quickly learned that we would only be at Stratford for one week.

We were only going to be at No. 9 Receiving Wing (RW) long enough to undergo further medical examinations; to be inoculated against all sorts of horrible diseases (and hope that we didn't pass out as we watched the needle plunge into the arm in front of us); to attend a few lectures, to get kitted out, including our flying clothing; to do a bit of 'square-bashing' (so that, when we got our uniforms, we could go out into the town without bringing the Royal Air Force into disgrace); to have our photographs taken for our identity cards; and to draw our first week's pay!

Then, in exactly seven days' time (if all went well) we would be returning to the railway station and on our way to an ITW 'somewhere in England'.

Of the Shakespeare Hotel: I have never forgotten that the titles of the most famous plays were inscribed on the bedroom doors: *Romeo & Juliet*; *Macbeth*; *Twelfth Night*; *The Tempest*; *As You Like It* and so on but inside there was none of the luxury that greets today's visitors when they are shown into their rooms! In 1941, the bedrooms were jammed with as many iron bedsteads as could be got in and as little furniture as possible! In which room did I sleep?

Did the title on our door bode for laughter or for tears? Triumph or tragedy? I do not remember and – in all faith – we were an uninhibited lot. Would-be pilots, navigators and gunners did not indulge themselves in introverted and unhelpful self-analysis in those days; how lucky we were in that regard. Downstairs in the hotel was – I think – given over to an extensive canteen and messing area, but I could be wrong. Certainly those entering the well-appointed and luxurious reception area of today would have a shock if the clock in the foyer were turned back 58 years!

Of Stratford: I know that one or two of us went to the theatre, which was still functioning even in the middle of the war. I think we saw *Twelfth Night*. I had been brought up on Shakespeare at Hurstpierpoint College, and once, as 'an Officer', had had three lines to speak in *Hamlet*. The performance was marvellous and I remember thinking quite clearly that one day – when the war was over – I would come back to Stratford and come back to the Shakespeare Theatre.

It took me forty-seven years to realise that particular ambition! I also remember that some of us went on the river and tried our hands with a punt-pole! The results were far from satisfactory and some of the locals on the bank were quick to point out that, unless we could make a better job of piloting and navigating our aeroplanes, our chances of survival would be slim indeed!

I have one sore memory. As soon as we were issued with our uniforms we sallied forth to buy masses of boot polish and button-cleaning material but we returned with rather wry faces and much lighter pockets. The prices charged by the good merchants of Stratford reflected the old fashioned laws of supply and demand, and (knowing that the new recruits for the Air Force had money in their pockets, on leaving home) were extortionate. I guess, that with the war, they had lost out on the tourist trade and – that year – we were their harvest.

Of friends: We of No. 9 RW were hardly there long enough to make any, although some of us went on to the same ITW at Aberystwyth in Wales. I remember two chaps, Horrocks and Connolly, who went into the night-fighter business who were there. The former was also at the Operational Training Unit (OTU) in Yorkshire where I went in August; but I then sadly lost touch with him; Ralph Connolly was posted direct to a squadron (No. 141) at the end of his spell at No. 3 Radio School, enjoyed a successful career in the 'business' with a number of E/A (enemy aircraft) destroyed to his credit, retired after the war as a squadron leader and resumed his career in the Civil Service. Happily we met again in 1993, after a gap of over fifty years, and have been able to resume our friendship in our dinosaur years.

By the following Saturday I was amongst the crowd of those who were departing from Stratford and *en route* for Aberystwyth, and most important of all I had, in my forage cap, one of those white flashes which denoted that Aircraftman Second Class Allen M.S. 1388889 was u/t aircrew. Of course the thought that I was a 'u/t navigator' still rankled but, never mind, I would soon be able to get a transfer onto a pilot's course, now that I was in the Air Force . . . or would I?

Aberystwyth in June is a pleasant place to be! Those of us who had come from Stratford, and other RWs around the country, to No. 6 ITW had the prospect of six weeks there. Billeted at a hotel looking out over the sea front across Cardigan Bay with the Welsh mountains behind us. Six weeks, during which we were going to study mathematics; navigation; aircraft recognition; armaments; meteorology; the Morse code, with a few other funny ones like Air Force Law, hygiene and gas thrown in for good measure. Six weeks, for us to sort ourselves out after the flurry and scurry of the RW at Stratford, and – of course – six weeks for our instructors to sort us out and decide who was fit to go on to AONS (Air Observers Navigation School) and the serious business of becoming an observer.

An observer. The title was just changing to 'Navigator' – who would probably be destined for Bomber Command and the task of guiding a heavy bomber across the vivid night skies of Germany to its target and even more importantly, from the point of view of his fellow crew members, back home again to its base.

In between our classes we did early morning PT on the Front, much to the enjoyment of the local populace; stood guard outside the hotel at night and wandered round the shops in the town in our brief off-duty moments. Whilst engaged on the latter, I had one of those brief encounters that stay with us for the rest of our life. It was not with a girl, but with an old lady.

Together with Horrocks (who had also come on from Stratford), I went into a milk-bar. In those days, a visit to a milk-bar was almost the zenith of our ambitions! We went up to the bar counter and were trying to decide whether to have a strawberry milk shake or one of the other more exotic concoctions, when there was a rustle just to our right and a little old lady (dressed in black and not appearing to be very well off) reached up to the counter and said quietly, so quietly that we could hardly hear her, 'There, let that pay for your drinks' . . . and was gone.

She was virtually out of the milk-bar and halfway up the street before we could gather our wits and say 'Thank you'. When we had recovered from our surprise we looked at the counter. On the counter was a shining new half-crown which had not been there before. We ordered our milk shakes, both too moved to say very much. You could buy quite a lot with half a crown in 1941.

For eight of us, at Aberystwyth, it was not to be six weeks. We did not know it but we were about to be launched into the world of Jules Verne. The world of the scientists, the world of radar.

About two and a half weeks after the course had begun, some twenty of us had a funny sort of interview with one of the officers, who talked vaguely about a trip to London – and some tests there – to see if we would be suitable for a transfer to another kind of aircrew training. Everything was very 'hush-hush' and we mustn't talk to anybody else about it – were we interested?

I can remember him asking me a few questions about what I had done at school (which wasn't much anyway except for a Credit in Mathematics in School Certificate and a bit of Rugby), in any case, a free trip to London sounded too good to miss; so I volunteered . . .

A few days later, armed with our railway warrants and some overnight kit, some sixteen of us set off for our two-day visit to London and a happy release from running up and down the Prom in the early hours of the morning. Our destination was a block of flats near to the Lord's Cricket Ground at St John's Wood. But our hopes of beating up London – discussed on the long train journey from Wales via Whitchurch and Crewe – were soon dispelled! For the whole of the two days we were interviewed and given tests in an atmosphere of the greatest secrecy. For a job the details of which were not, initially, disclosed to us!

Many of the tests involved looking at a diagram showing two circles, side by side, and each about 4 cm in diameter. In the right-hand circle was a picture which resembled a Christmas tree with a long thin trunk, and some of the roots, just visible at its base. In the left-hand circle was a similar 'Christmas Tree' but, in this case, the tree was lying on its side, with the top of the tree pointing to the left. As far as I can remember these diagrams were in black and white.

About three-quarters of the way up the trunk of each tree there was a diamond-shaped blob. On the vertical trunk, in the right-hand picture, the blob showed up more on the right than on the left. Whereas, in the left-hand picture, where

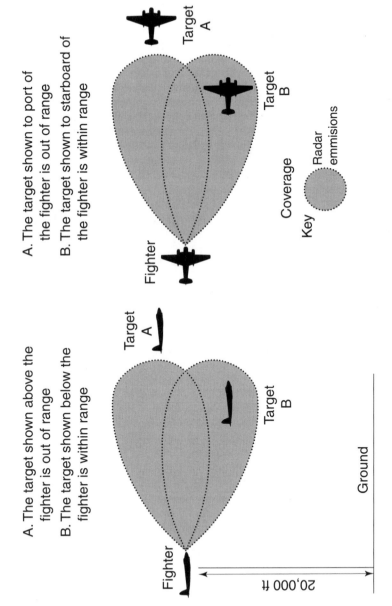

Mk IV AI – Range & Coverage (in front of fighter)

A. The target shown to port of the fighter is out of range

B. The target shown to starboard of the fighter is within range

A. The target shown above the fighter is out of range

B. The target shown below the fighter is within range

Target A

Target B

Fighter

Coverage

Key

Radar emmisions

Azimuth – Plan view

Target A

Target B

Fighter

Ground

20,000 ft

Elevation – Side view

the tree was lying horizontally, the blob was showing rather more above the line of the trunk than below it.

We would then be shown two or three other diagrams, in quick succession, each with the same two Christmas trees, one vertical and the other horizontal. But the diamond-shaped blobs on the trunks were shown to be in different positions and at different distances along them.

The officers in charge of the tests busied themselves with asking us to assess when the diamond-shaped blobs on the trunks were off-centre, and by how much they were off-centre. They also wanted to know how far the blobs were from the roots at the base of the tree (in relation to the whole of the long thin trunk showing below the main branches of the tree).

Little was I, or my colleagues, to know that we were looking at representations of a then modern scientific wonder. That the pictures were of the cathode-ray tubes of a Mark IV Airborne Interceptor (AI) set, currently being installed in the new British night-fighter aircraft – the Bristol Beaufighter Mk 1.

Great Britain was hastening to shore up its night defences after the attacks by the *Luftwaffe* in the winter of 1940/41 and before an even heavier Blitz was launched in the winter to come, as the hours of darkness started to lengthen.

We were not to know that the pictures represented what the observer (or more accurately, the AI operator) would see on his AI equipment – seated under the Perspex cupola of the Beaufighter – and the means whereby he could guide his pilot towards the enemy bomber to intercept it. With a running commentary over the intercom the operator could hope to bring his pilot in behind the target aircraft and to within visual range, i.e. anything between 800 and 200 feet, according to the blackness of the particular night. On moonlit nights pilots could spot the target at much greater distances – providing they knew where to look!

A *visual* meant that the pilot could see a silhouette of an aircraft in front of him – and hopefully he would have been brought in by his AI operator 10–15 degrees below it so that he could, for a moment or two, formate on the other aircraft whilst identifying whether it was friend or foe. Once the pilot had identified the target as a bandit he could plan his attack and, hopefully, shoot the other aircraft down.

The Christmas tree on the diagrams in front of us at St John's Wood represented the signals picked up from the ground by the Mk IV AI set and were called the 'ground returns'. The trunk was the time trace and the diamond was the echo from the target aircraft – known as a blip – which was picked up on the receiver aerials on the wings of the Beaufighter.

These signals were modulated and reflected on to the cathode-ray tubes in the viewing unit of the set. The AI operator peered into the viewing unit – rather as we used to peer into one of the machines on Brighton Pier trying to see 'what the butler saw' or as we now look at our television sets!

I and my colleagues were being assessed on our ability to estimate the angle off of the blip, i.e. when it was larger on the right than on the left of the time trace. Was it 10 degrees to starboard or 15, or could it be as much as 20 degrees off? When, on the left-hand picture, the blip was larger above the line, was it 20 degrees above or was it more? If so, how much more? As the tests continued we were shown a sequence of diagrams with the blips changing in position and changing in their distance – on the time trace – from the ground returns. These changes represented the changes in position of the two aircraft in relation to each other in the air: in other words, as they flew on converging (or diverging) courses.

We were asked to describe what was actually happening and what directions we would give to our imaginary pilot in order to bring him in behind the target aircraft and slightly below it so that he could obtain the vital visual and shout, 'OK I've got it!'

Above all, we were being assessed on our ability to look at two tiny television screens – shimmering with green lines and mush, pick out the all important blips from the rest of the signals on the cathode-ray tubes – whilst being bumped and bounced around in the back of a Beaufighter in the middle of the night. From the movement of the blips across the face of the tubes we were then supposed to estimate the course, height and speed of the target in relation to our own aircraft. Then relay that information quickly and clearly to our pilot and, by a series of directions intermingled with a running commentary, bring him into a position whereby he could see it. If it was 'for real' a Heinkel 111 or a Dornier 217, he would attack it and shoot it down!

All this must be accomplished without the AI operator suffering the mortification of seeing the precious blip disappear off the face of his cathode-ray tubes and have to report to his pilot, over the intercom 'Sorry, I've lost contact!'

We were told by our examiners, who seemed to be a strange mixture of Air Force officers and civilians, that speed was of the essence, that the AI operator only had a few seconds in which to react when a 'CONTACT' appeared on his tubes. If the target was on a rapidly converging course to the pursuing night-fighter or was approaching head-on, his reactions had to be immediate and his assessments of its movements instantaneous. Nothing else was acceptable.

For example: if the blip showed up on the starboard side when the contact first appeared on the time trace and the operator looked at it quickly and shouted to his pilot '*Contact – turn starboard!*' when the target was crossing in front of them from starboard to port they would quickly be following diverging courses! The hapless AI operator would see the blip move rapidly across his Azimuth cathode-ray tube from starboard to port and then slide quickly up the time trace (as the range increased) and disappear into the ground returns. Note: The AI range of the fighter was dictated (on the early airborne radar) by the height of the fighter above the ground.

Assuming the fighter was flying at 15,000 feet above the ground, the time trace on the cathode-ray tubes, on which the blips could be seen and assessed, was roughly 3 centimetres. Once two aircraft were on diverging courses it did not take long for the blip to vanish off the tubes as quickly as it had appeared!

It was rather a chastened party that left St John's Wood for the return journey to Aberystwyth. We did not know whether we had passed or failed the tests. We had no idea where we stood and we did not know if we wanted the job of 'AI Operator', even if we were selected! This was hardly surprising because we had only just been introduced to the concept of night-fighter operations and its marvellous equipment. Two days earlier we had no idea of its existence!

Back at Aberystwyth we were told to carry on as if nothing had happened and, above all, we were told not to discuss our visit to London with anyone. We were again advised that the whole thing was 'TOP SECRET' and the penalties for any loose talk would be severe; apart from disqualifying us from any chance of selection that we might have.

So, rather bewildered, and unable to say, in our letters home, anything of our recent doings, we carried on and tried to put out of our minds all thoughts of defending 'our Island Home', during the perilous night hours and shooting down innumerable Heinkels and Dorniers. We tried hard to catch up on the two days we had lost from our studies of navigation, mathematics and the rest! We also returned to the dubious pleasures of guard duty and running up and down the prom in the early hours.

In the event, it was only a day or two before eight of us were sent for, by the Flight Commander, told that we had been selected for this new job . . . and asked if we would like to volunteer for night-fighters and the course for Observers (Radio) – as they were rather grandly called.

I do not remember if anyone turned the offer down in favour of remaining at Aberystwyth and continuing with the straight observer's course. I only remember (like a few others, so I learned later!) thinking that my maths was not quite as good as it might appear from my exam results and that I might run into a spot of bother as the navigation course progressed; this seemed to be a convenient way of putting off the evil day!

Anyway, I was still fooling myself that somehow I could get a transfer onto a pilot's course. I argued to myself that, as I did not want to be an observer of any description, I might as well volunteer for this Observer (Radio) job as anything else!

Within twenty-four hours the eight of us (we never heard anything more of the other eight who had been on the London party) were on our way from Aberystwyth to Scotland! We were whipped straight off to No. 3 Radio School at Prestwick without being allowed to finish our six weeks' ITW course, and I never did do any more serious studies of the art of navigation!

Radio School? Most of us could barely tune in the family wireless set! What on earth were we doing going off to a Radio School? It all sounded absolutely nuts and we began seriously to wonder what we had let ourselves in for.

We began our worrying as the evening train puffed its way out of Aberystwyth on its journey across Wales to Crewe. We were still talking about it when we finally steamed into Crewe at about 10 p.m. and found that we'd got nearly three hours to wait for the connection to Glasgow, which was scheduled to leave Crewe at 1 a.m. the following morning.

The junction at Crewe (immortalised in song with 'Oh, Mr Porter, what shall I do', etc.) became famous for its delays and general atmosphere of confusion. It was wet and miserable on the platform at midnight and we debated seriously whether we would have done better to have stayed where we were and finished our ITW course properly, rather than plunging off into the unknown. It is one of the interesting aspects of life in the Services that loyalties to units and one's colleagues are quickly formed and anything which occurs to break those ties is viewed with suspicion and – subconsciously – resented.

I remember climbing the steps of an old iron bridge over the lines, walking out into the road and finding an all-night café a few yards from the station. We each had our two kitbags, one for our clothes and personal things and the other stuffed full of our flying kit; boots, Sidcot suit, inner lining, helmet, etc., and we had to lug them with us up to the café (where we managed to get a cup of tea), and then back down to the platform, whilst we tried to kill time until the arrival of the train from London. We were informed that we would arrive in Glasgow in the early hours of the morning and change onto a local train for Prestwick.

When the train eventually pulled in, just after 1 a.m., it was full. I don't mean just that all the seats were taken, but the corridors were full too! You could not get into the train! It was crowded from end to end with servicemen and women in every attitude you could imagine and all of them prepared to guard their precious few inches of space with their lives!

Eventually, with the whistles of the guard and the platform staff starting to warn of the train's impending departure and after struggling, with our heavy kit-bags, past three or four bulging coaches, we found that we could open the door of a guard's van located in the middle of the train. We fell in, literally as the train started to move, pulling our accursed kitbags in after us. Once inside the guard's van and on our way, we turned to survey our capture! It was piled high with luggage and there was barely any floor space on which to sit down.

In one corner, however, I spotted a pushchair which I promptly comman-deered, and it was where I spent the rest of the night! We reached Glasgow at about 6 a.m. – not having had much sleep – and were parked in a siding before being shunted into the station an hour and a half later. By then, we were *certain* that we had made the wrong decision!

All that I can recall of the short journey out to Prestwick on the local train is the number of golf-courses which caught my eye, the filthy taste in my mouth and the need for some sleep on a bed which was not clattering across the points and bumping from side to side! I must have dozed off before we were bundled out at Prestwick for the last stage of our journey. We clambered into a bus and were driven off to a remote country house. Adamton House was surrounded by extensive grounds, screened by woods and heavily guarded by Security Police.

It became known as the School for Secrets and after the war, when a film was made about the invention of radar it was given that title. In 1941 it was the home of No. 3 Radio School, located some three miles from Prestwick Aerodrome, where we would undergo our practical training in the air. We found on our arrival that the intake for the new course was made up of airmen from other ITWs, and there must have been about thirty-five of us altogether.

So there I was, having been in the Air Force for little more than a month, about to start technical – and flying – training for a job I knew nothing about; and if truth be told, held scant interest. I still yearned to be a pilot. I did not realise that every step I took now was taking me further away from my ambition.

We were at Prestwick for three weeks. At the School for Secrets we were lectured on the new science of radar and radio location. We learned the mysteries of cathode-ray tubes; diodes and anodes; modulators; viewing-units and other 'black boxes'. We saw our first AI equipment – the Mk IV AI as it was known – set up in our classrooms (which were more like laboratories), and we saw our first pictures on the cathode-ray tubes.

Immediately we recognised the pictures from the diagrams which we had seen at St John's Wood. There was the Christmas tree on both tubes (the one on the left lying on its side, as before), there was the trunk and there was the small diamond at the bottom of the trunk – lying dead centre. All the signals on the tubes showed up in green; they were shimmering and sometimes they were a bit fuzzy. There were a variety of knobs and switches on the sets, and we were shown how to tune and focus the quivering green lines, so that we would be able to get a good picture when we tried it for real in the air in a few days' time.

When we had learned all our instructors could teach us about the equipment and how to set up for ourselves, they introduced onto the time trace spurious echoes (called blips) to represent target aircraft on which we had to carry out mock interceptions, i.e. assessing the course, height and speed of the enemy and giving a running commentary to our imaginary pilot on what was happening until the chase was completed, the blip brought to minimum range in front and slightly above and a visual obtained.

We also learned about night-fighter operations: the theory and practice of intercepting aircraft at night and also in weather when it was too bad for the day-fighters to take off. We learned about the Ground Controllers at the GCI stations – now dotted all round the country – from which both day- and night-fighters were vectored onto the track of the enemy bombers.

We were taught about 'Mother'. And further, we were taught about another 'black box' which enabled night-fighter crews to identify whether the target they were chasing was friend or foe. There seemed to be no end to the miracles which had been achieved by our scientists. Last, but by no means least, on 22 July 1941 we got airborne and attempted to put all the theory we had learned into practice.

I and half a dozen of the other students were taken by road to Prestwick Aerodrome where, two or three at a time, we were taken up – with an instructor – in ancient Bristol Blenheims. For some, it was their first flight ever! The pilot was a Flight Lieutenant Saunders – the Blenheim 1 was L8672 – and we were up for one hour and ten minutes.

Hunched up in the fuselage and taking it in turn we had our first sight of what the AI pictures looked like in the air. And we were shocked! The clear signals shown up on the test sets in the laboratory were gone. What we saw was a pulsating, blurred and flickering green mass on the cathode-ray tubes that defied the imagination. This, together with being bounced around in the back of the old Blenheim, seemed to us to nullify our chances of ever seeing the blip of an enemy raider, let alone being able to guide our future pilots onto it, even before we had begun! We staggered out of the old Blenheim – after we had landed – wobbly at the knees and feeling very depressed.

My Observer's and Air Gunner's flying log-book shows that I carried out two more flights at No. 3 Radio School – spent a total of four hours in the air – and that my actual time operating the AI set was recorded as two hours and fifty minutes. This figure was rather optimistic, I thought, because the time spent on the AI set was never much more than twenty minutes because the instructor had to get through three students. Not least, the aircraft had to get up to c.9,000 feet and down again. So a total of 2.50 hrs operating time (entered on my certificate and pasted into my flying log-book) was a bit of wishful thinking on someone's part.

In my log-book is a certificate giving the result of 'Preliminary Observer (Radio) Training'. It states that I had passed the course and been assessed as 'AVERAGE'. It is dated 1 August 1941.

On the evening of 4 August I flew, for the first time, at night, but a lot had happened over that August Bank Holiday Weekend. On Friday 1 August, at our secret country home, the news came through that those of us who had passed were to be posted to an Operational Training Unit (OTU) in Yorkshire. Here we would undergo further training and crew up with a pilot, before going on from there to a squadron. Such was the urgency to provide the night-fighter squadrons with AI operators that some of the students from our course were to be posted direct to squadrons, where they would be expected to pick up the rest of their knowledge and gain their experience as they went along!

The grim news was that fifteen of those at Prestwick had been failed and presumably were returned to their units. Thirty-three of us were on the train at 19.12 hrs the same day, facing another overnight journey, *en route* for the No. 54 OTU at Church Fenton.

I still have some brief diary entries which can be used to describe what proved to be an epic week in my life. It also put paid, finally and for all time, to my hopes of becoming a pilot. However, the compensations for this loss turned out to be beyond my wildest dreams . . . and to this day, can never be measured! Let us turn to the fading entries (written in pencil) of my 1941 diary:

Friday 1st August

At last the news has come through and I have been posted to No. 54 O.T.U. at Church Fenton with Teddy. 15 have been failed Gosh! Left Prestwick on the 19.12 train with 33 others after having a drink and getting my hair cut. Very hot night.

Saturday 2nd August

Travelled all night down to Leeds where we had three hours to wait so we slept in a carriage and then had a wash and a shave arriving at Church Fenton about 9 o'clock. After some trouble we at last managed to put up in the Sergeant's Block and get our kit from the Guard Room.

Sunday 3rd August

I had an interview with Flying Officer Ellis which shook me a good deal because I made rather a mess of it. In fact I thought I might be slung out on my ear. In the evening Teddy and I went into Tadcaster and had tea and dinner at the Londesborough Hotel.

No. 9 Course for Observers (Radio) at No. 54 OTU, Church Fenton, Yorkshire. (I am in the middle row, fifth from the left.)

Monday 4th August

Spent the morning in going over to 'D' Squadron to see what we could do about teaming up with a pilot and found Joll over there who was pretty decent. Then I later fixed myself up with a Sergeant Pilot called White instead of the P.O. which Joll put me in touch with.

Tuesday 5th August

Went flying last night and did two details and almost a third, only the kite was u/s. Grand trip and I think Harold and I are going to hit things off OK. But while I was sitting up in the front I was eating my heart out to be flying the kite instead of being merely a passenger. Weather good.

Wednesday 6th August

Did not fly last night because of gale so went to lecture at 11 o'clock on Morse which developed into a gen talk. Lectures in the afternoon and this is an amazing course one moment you are up and the next you are right down. Have just got over Sunday, food not too good. But parcel from Mum arrived.

Thursday 7th August

Flew again last night making nearly 8 hrs. N.F. A beautiful moonlit night and there was a Hun floating about. He took a pot at an Oxford but missed. We stooged for 3 hrs before it was clear. Had photo taken then went onto Link for half a hour. Am now bankrupt.

Day 1 – of what proved to be such an epic week in my life – was Friday 1 August when we left Prestwick and has already been described; so I will pick up the story again on Day 2, the Saturday, and put some flesh on the brief entries in the diary.

The day began at 04.00 hrs on Leeds Railway Station with most of us trying to catch up on our sleep in a disused railway carriage. It ended with us being allowed to sleep in the sergeants' barrack block at Church Fenton and hauling our kit there from the guard room! Earlier in the day we had run into trouble there – nobody was expecting us or knew where to put us! The problem was that most of us were still airmen and, quite rightly, could not be allowed to use the sergeants' mess.

We had to feed in the airmen's mess but they could not very well put us into the airmen's barrack blocks when we were going to be night-flying and would need all the sleep we could get during the day, i.e. when the other airmen would be coming and going on their normal daily tasks. So they compromised and let us sleep in the sergeants' barrack blocks, but as we shall see, for me that was not the end of the matter and it was not an auspicious start for the four weeks we were supposed to be at No. 54 OTU.

Day 3, the Sunday, was no better. As can be seen from my diary, I made a hash of an interview with Flying Officer Ellis, one of the instructors, and thought that I might be thrown off the course! I apparently sought a little light relief in the afternoon when I went into Tadcaster, the nearest town, with Teddy. That was Teddy Horrocks and his name crops up several times in my diary. We had been together since Stratford and Aberystwyth, had been up to London, been selected for the Observer (Radio)'s course and had then both got through No. 3 Radio School at Prestwick. By this time we were firm pals. We were posted to different squadrons a few weeks later and, sadly, I never heard from him again.

Somehow, when Day 4 dawned, I was still there. It was August Bank Holiday and I had been told by Flying Officer Ellis that I had to see if I could find a pilot and crew up with him. That is, a pilot who was undergoing training as a night-fighter pilot and who was currently without an AI operator. It seemed as if this crucial stage, this 'marriage' with the person with whom we would fly on operations against the enemy, was to be left to us! To say that I had no idea how to go about crewing up with a pilot, and to say that I was worried, was putting things mildly!

My diary entry talks about '. . . going over to "D" Squadron . . . finding a chap called "Joll" and then meeting up with "a Serg. Pilot called White".'

What actually happened was this: After breakfast I was told that I had to report to the Flight Commander at 'D' Squadron and tell him that I was looking for a pilot. 'D' Squadron was located in some dispersal huts located on the far side of the aerodrome, so I set off from the barrack block, to walk round the perimeter track. The dispersal huts must have been the best part of 2½ miles away and I had to be careful when crossing the end of the main runway, as there were aircraft constantly taking off and landing on training exercises.

Eventually, I came to a number of Bristol Blenheims like the ones in which we had flown at Prestwick, and arrived at a hut marked 'D' Squadron. I still had no clear idea of what I was supposed to do and thought the prospects of any pilot wanting me as his navigator were zero. I had been in the Air Force for just 47 days and had precisely four hours' flying experience. Things were, once again, at a low ebb.

I found a clerk sitting in the outer office, was told that the Flight Commander was in, knocked on his door and walked in. I found myself looking at a tall flight lieutenant in an immaculate uniform and wearing pilot's wings. Even as I saluted him I realised that I knew him! It was Ian Joll, a former prefect from my old school, Hurstpierpoint College. We had even been in the same house, the Fleur-de-Lys. Joll had already done a tour on the well-known No. 604 Squadron of the Royal Auxiliary Air Force in the early days of night-fighting (during the time that John Cunningham and Jimmy Rawnsley were making a name for themselves) and he was now 'on rest' as an instructor.

After asking me what I was doing, and hearing that I was looking for a pilot, he said that my problem was easily solved, because he knew of a pilot officer who was looking for a navigator! Joll went on to say that he would be seeing him in the officers' mess at lunchtime. I was to come back to 'D' Squadron at 14.00 hrs and he would introduce us, he was sure that we would get on well together.

He then started asking me about the school as he had left three years before me and wanted to catch up on the news! For two or three minutes we had an animated discussion about 'Hurst' in which the disparity between our ranks was completely forgotten. Eventually, Ian Joll said that he must reluctantly bring our conversation to an end, as he had another navigator to see. I thanked him very much, saluted smartly and retreated out of his office, promising that I would be back promptly at 14.00 hrs.

I started off on the perimeter track, heading for lunch hugging myself at my good fortune. The 2½ miles back to the barrack block, where I would collect my 'irons' and set off for the airmen's mess, did not seem nearly so far. My problem was solved; I was walking on air! I had got a pilot!

The last sentence in my diary for 4 August reads: '. . . then later (i.e. after I had met Ian Joll) I fixed myself up with a Sergeant-Pilot called White instead of a P/O which Joll put me in touch with . . .'

It was a significant entry, the effects of which were to change the whole course

Aircraftsman 2nd Class H. E. White, u/t pilot who joined up 'under age' at 17. He received his 'Wings' in spring 1941, at Kidlington.

Collision over the intersection of the two main runways at No. 54 Operational Training Unit, Church Fenton in July 1941. Sergeant H.E. White, taking off in an Airspeed Oxford, hit a Bristol Blenheim (landing on the wrong runway) at a height of 50 feet and both aircraft were destroyed. The wreckage of Harry's Oxford is in the foreground and the heap beyond is that of the Blenheim. Both pilots walked away unharmed.

of my life. It also meant, even as early on as that, the difference between life and death . . .

Sergeant-Pilot Harold Edward White had come to Church Fenton (I think some time in June) after obtaining his Wings at the Service Flying Training School at Kidlington in Oxfordshire. He now had about 120 hours' flying experience. He had joined up a year under age in May 1940 and when I first met him he was 18¼ and I did not realise that he had managed to get into the Air Force when he was only 17 years of age.

God knows how he did it, because he looked as if he should still have been at school when I first saw him! I also did not know that for some reason he had failed to pick up a navigator from the previous batch of AI operators to arrive at Church Fenton. Likewise, I was also unaware that a few days earlier he had survived a serious crash when taking off – in daylight – in an Airspeed Oxford.

A Czech flight sergeant pilot had been landing in a Bristol Blenheim – but on the wrong runway. They met, over the intersection of the two runways, at a height of 50 feet above the ground. There was a loud bang and the wreckage of the two aircraft fluttered to the ground. There was no fire and both Harry White and the Czech pilot walked out of the debris – unscathed.

When I reached the barrack block it was about midday and I was ready for an early lunch. I felt a bit footsore, but was well pleased with my morning's work. I was still unable to get over my good fortune and the coincidence of meeting someone from my old school, who was also in a position to help me crew up with a pilot. I was anxious to get my lunch quickly, knowing that I had to walk back round the perimeter track and be at 'D' Squadron for 14.00 hrs. At the door of the block I was stopped by a sergeant-pilot. I made to go past him but he moved to bar my way.

He was shorter in height than I was, a fresh-faced stocky figure but with a distinctly aggressive manner. I was asked, in no uncertain tones, what I thought I was doing going into the senior NCOs' barrack block and didn't I know that I had no right to be there? I had an uncomfortable feeling that it would not have been a good idea to tangle with him, even if he had not had three stripes on his arm. My mental roller-coaster, so high only a few minutes before, was heading downwards at an increasing rate of knots!

I gave him my name and the number of my course and assured him that we had been told that we could use this block until, hopefully, we became sergeants ourselves! He seemed slightly mollified but when I asked if I could go, he said 'No, I want to talk to you. We had better walk out onto the perimeter track, it's easier to talk outside.' So back out onto the perimeter track I had to go, with thoughts of lunch rapidly receding!

We exchanged names and the length of time we had been at Church Fenton and our last station – the usual opening gambits. Then he said abruptly: 'I'm looking for a navigator!' I hastened to inform him of the events of the morning and of my date at 14.00 hrs with Flight Lieutenant Joll to clinch the deal. He was not impressed. His features hardened again and he took up the belligerent stance – and the abrasive attitude – he had adopted at the door of the barrack block. I repeated my story and said that I would be flying with the pilot officer that Ian Joll from my old school had found for me.

Sergeant White (because it was indeed he) then proceeded to be very rude about Flight Lieutenant Joll. Very rude about my old school. And very rude about the poor inoffensive pilot officer, my prospective pilot! We were on the perimeter track, somewhere out by the Watch office, when he finished off his tirade by saying: 'You're flying with me!'

All my protests were in vain; he went on to add: 'I'm on the flying detail tonight – SEARCHLIGHT HOMINGS – and you're coming with me!' Then the awesome figure in front of me threw out another bomb-shell: 'Oh! and you'd better go and tell Joll that you're flying with me!'

We finished up back at the barrack block, with me still vainly protesting. The time was now 13.00 hrs. Still with no lunch I duly set off once more around the wretched perimeter track. I just had time to get back to 'D' Squadron by 14.00 hrs. I was frightened by the prospect of having to tell Joll what had happened but I was even more frightened of facing the stocky figure of Sergeant White in full flow!

When I arrived back at 'D' Squadron and went in to see Flight Lieutenant Joll, he had the pilot officer waiting outside. He was not at all pleased, to say the least. In fact he was livid and I was faced with the second tirade of the day when I told him that I had met a sergeant-pilot – since seeing him in the morning – and we had decided to fly together.

When he had calmed down a bit he enquired, in icy tones, for the name of the sergeant-pilot. All traces of us having been at the same school together had gone! When I said 'It's Sergeant White, Sir' he said 'You don't mean it. He is the one who had that crash last week. He and a Czech pilot nearly wrote themselves off. White couldn't get a navigator from the previous intake and now nobody will fly with him!'

When I then told him that I had arranged to fly with Harry that very night, the reply was, 'Good God, you must be mad!' He finished up by implying that, apart from letting him down, I was letting down 'the Old School' by behaving in such an appalling manner! Rather grumpily, when I had apologised, Ian Joll said, 'All right, if you are determined on it, but you two won't last three months!'

My decision to fly with Harry, rather than with the pilot officer, had a grain of commonsense in it – quite apart from Harry's forceful way of putting things! Because it had quickly occurred to me that, assuming I passed the course *and* assuming I was then promoted to sergeant, it would be better for us, as a crew, to be sharing the same mess. If I crewed up with an officer, he would be in the officers' mess and I would be in the sergeants' mess, so we would only meet up in the dispersal hut and when we went flying. The idea did not appeal to me.

If, and at that stage it was a mighty big 'if', we managed to stay together we might in the dim and distant future be considered for a commission. Then there was a chance that we could be commissioned at the same time, *then* we would go into the officers' mess together. Little did we know that, within nine months, this is exactly what would happen.

There is another postscript to the above story: the pilot officer, who I never did meet, crewed up with another navigator and they were both killed in a flying accident within three months.

In retrospect I cannot remember how any of the other u/t navigators on our course met and crewed up with their pilots. I have no reason for not thinking that many of them came together by chance, just as Harry and I did on that August Bank Holiday Monday, fifty-eight years ago. Our meeting was typical, not exceptional. And, as my diary entry for 5 August (Day 5) shows, the mutual loyalties between two strangers were immediate.

'I think Harold and I are going to hit things off OK.' I had no possible way of being able to judge whether Harry was a good pilot or a bad one! And, *vice versa*, he had no way of knowing whether I was going to make the grade as a navigator. If a crew survived this instant loyalty, in the main it lasted for ever. If they died, or if one of them survived and lived on, it is safe to say that their loyalty to each other remained unaffected and that they would not have had things any different.

Whether they were a successful crew, or not, very often made no difference. When a pilot did eventually go to his CO to say that his navigator was losing too many contacts or, more rarely, a navigator to complain about his pilot's night landings(!) and a change was made, success and survival were by no means certain to follow. All too frequently death, in a flying accident or on operations, proved that their chances of staying alive either way, were not dissimilar, if they kept at it for long enough.

One thing is certain, and this is true of all members of a crew, whether in a night-fighter or the larger crews of Bomber and Coastal Command – 'death did not them part'. Even though, like Harry and myself, they came together by luck, fate, chance, or call it what you will.

August 6 & 7 (days 6 & 7 in that momentous week in my diary) show that Harry and I flew again on the Wednesday and how my morale was still up one moment and down the next, as the course progressed.

The remainder of the week has been recorded in my diary (see pages 45–6). The entries show that Harry and I did some more night flying; the course still had its ups and downs, even though I had now got myself a pilot; the Germans were using 'intruders' over our airfields (one day the positions would be reversed!); and they finish with the alarming statement about my financial affairs, '. . . am now bankrupt'.

After 4 August, Harry and I did ten flights in daylight between the 8th and the 20th. We carried out various AI exercises with another Blenheim acting as target – twice with an instructor – but mostly on our own. On 19 August we made our first complete interception, from obtaining the initial contact to a position just behind the target aircraft and 10 degrees below it. At night it would have been a visual, for Harry. We were up for 2 hours and 10 minutes. On 20 August I had my final test, with a Pilot Officer Patston on board to check me out. My log-book records that I spent 1 hour and 10 minutes on the AI set and '. . . CARRIED OUT TWO INTERCEPTIONS, HOLDING MINIMUM RANGE, AND HOMING ON "MOTHER".'

My log-book also certifies, on the opening page, that '1388889 Sgt. Allen M.S. has qualified as OBSERVER (Radio) with effect from 20.8.41.' The entry was signed by a Squadron Leader George Budd (of whom there will be more anon) and was dated 21.8.41.

If it were not for this entry – still there in my first log-book – I might have difficulty in believing that it all happened. There I was, rushing off to the Stores to get my sergeant's 'tapes' and a flying badge with the letters 'RO' on it; after being in the Air Force for exactly sixty-seven days!

This is not quite all the story of Church Fenton. Harry and I put in a number of other trips at night, as we had on the day we met. He wanted to get in as many hours at night as possible, before going on to a squadron. We managed twenty-five hours in all, proudly entered into my log-book in red ink, to denote night-flying, to be put alongside the twenty-four daylight hours I had acquired at No. 54 OTU. Together with the four hours at Prestwick, I had a grand total of fifty-three flying hours when, on 9 September 1941, Harry and I reported to No. 29 Squadron.

There was, however, a snag to all the nice red-ink entries in our respective log-books. There were no facilities at Church Fenton for AI training at night! We did plenty of 'SEARCHLIGHT HOMINGS', 'VECTOR ORDERS' and 'R/T HOMINGS' in the night skies over Yorkshire; so all the time Harry was gaining invaluable night-flying experience but I rode as a passenger! Never once in those thirteen exciting flights, in what was to be our new habitat, did I touch the AI set. Never did we fly with a target aircraft on which to practise our new trade! It follows that, along with all the other new crews joining night-fighter squadrons around the country, Harry and I joined 29 without ever having carried out an interception at night!

Looking back on our days at Church Fenton I guess it would have been too dangerous to put up two u/t crews at night to practise intercepting each other, turn and turn about. The object on each run was to close in on the target to a range of 600–400 feet. It was very easy to overshoot the target if one's approach speed was too fast, and therefore the chances of collision were not inconsiderable! In any case, the losses at the OTUs in aircraft and in men were already quite high enough. Harry's course had experienced several crashes (apart from his collision with the Czech pilot!) and we saw a Blenheim 'go in' when we were walking round the perimeter track to fly on one of the night details.

We heard an aircraft in the circuit and Harry could tell immediately that the pilot was having engine trouble. We could see his navigation lights at the far end of the aerodrome as he came in through the funnels on his approach to land. Then, as we stood and watched, the lights came on up the runway towards us and the speed of the aircraft – as far as we could judge – was much too fast, as the pilot held it a few feet above the ground. A few seconds later it was past us and over the boundary fence of the aerodrome, where it crashed and immediately blew up!

There was nothing anybody could do to save the pilot (a Pilot Officer Okell), who must have been killed instantaneously. Harry and I, having stopped to see if we could help, walked on round to the dispersal hut and a few minutes later we were in the air ourselves. I imagine that those who were responsible for getting night-fighter crews quickly to the squadrons felt that the young and inexperienced pilots at OTU had enough to do on their night trips without the hazards of flying close to other aircraft in the darkness. I am certain that the instructors would have had their reservations about flying with 'sprog' pilots to check us out. It was bad enough for them during the daytime!

Harry's comments (made many years later) were:

> 'On the training at Church Fenton at that time all I can say, now, is that the blind were leading the blind. No one knew much about night-flying and even less about asymmetric flying (flying on one engine). A lot of crews were killed during my three months at Church Fenton, a high proportion at night, and several because of engine failure. Those who got there were almost lucky to survive. The Pennines too collected their fair share of wreckage as people improperly let down through cloud to try to establish their position.'

I am sure the authorities were right. We had enough on our plates and once we got to a squadron we could be sent up at night in company with an operational crew, and the practice interceptions would be under the control of an experienced GCI Controller.

In September, soon after Harry and I had left Church Fenton and joined No. 29 Squadron, my mother wrote to her sister-in-law, Joyce Garlick, in South Africa. My father's elder sister Joyce, née Allen, had met her husband, Donald Garlick, when he came over to England with the South African contingent, during the 1914–18 War.

She went out to South Africa and lived in Cape Town, where the Garlick family owned a large store (probably the South African equivalent of Harrods), with branches in the Provinces. Joyce Garlick was very fond of her sister-in-law, and must have felt cut off from her brother, and her parents, living in wartime England. My mother wrote to bring Joyce up to date with the activities of the family and, in doing so, gives an overall picture of our lives, as the war entered its third year:

'WESTWICK
Clarendon Road
Ashford, MIDDX.
Tele. Ashford 2747
September 23rd. 1941

Hello Joyce,

Thought you might like to have a letter from me. First of all, thank you very much indeed for the parcels, we have had four up to date. They were marvellous. [My mother is referring to the food parcels my aunt sent to us throughout the war, to augment our somewhat sparse 'rations', restricted by the wartime ration cards.]

We are all very well and very busy – I have been managing for the past two months with only a morning help in the house, so do not get any time for my garden, which distresses me – I would far rather work in the garden.

I send you a snap of my own private Air Force. I expect Mother has told you that Brian has a Commission in the R.A.F.V.R., Air Training Corps, gives lectures in the evenings and parades with the boys on Sunday mornings. ['Mother' here is my father's mother, living in Oxted.] This is voluntary.

Rodney is a Corporal in the same Squadron and about to get his Sergeant's stripes; he has just passed his first Air Ministry Exam and has obtained his Proficiency Star, which he now wears on his left sleeve. I went over on Sunday to see these Stars presented. Rodney has been placed in charge of the Recruit Squad and was pulled up by his C.O., who was standing with the U.C. Major who was to present the Stars, for not doing something or other, and his reaction and the way he handled his men rather impressed the U.C. Major for, when he was addressing the whole Squadron afterwards, he congratulated Corporal Allen and spoke very highly of him . . . I was thrilled . . .

Michael is now a full blown Sergeant Radio Observer and has been posted to a Squadron. He now wears one wing up since I took this snap. He rang up on Sunday and informed us that he had already been on his first night op. He has been able to take his Ford with him as now he is a Sergeant he can afford to run it. I am afraid he will not be happy until he has another try at being accepted as a Pilot.

I am meeting Mother in London tomorrow, we so rarely get down to Oxted now-a-days . . . Sandy McKay [the Cairn terrier that my father had brought back from Scotland, as a puppy, some years before] is still going strong and I was astonished to find the other day that he was nine years old last May. He badly misses his old pal Mr. Scott [a delightful mongrel terrier, of dubious origin!] did you know that he had to be put to sleep – in the early part of this year? The eye that had been hurt with a ball got worse and I did not like the idea of having an operation and the eye removed, as they told me this is what should be done. I shall not get another dog until the War is over . . .

Hope you and Don are well and that you are getting good news from Neil. [Neil, her son, was serving with an artillery battery in the South African contingent – in the Western Desert.]

With love to you all
from
Kathleen.'

My aunt kept this letter amongst her personal treasures, and after her death in 1977 my cousin, Neil, found it and thoughtfully returned it to me. Happily, when I was living in South Africa between 1966 and 1982, I was able to stay with Aunt Joyce at her lovely home, Chilterns, looking out over Constantia, on a number of occasions. She was always extremely kind and generous to me, though I was rather frightened of her! I did manage to get to know her better in the last years before her death – thanks to my wife Pam, of whom she became extremely fond; they got on like a house on fire.

3 Learning Our Trade with the Aid of an Airborne Searchlight

– and how we then became a Ferry Crew

Although Harry and I, and other crews from 54 OTU, joined our first squadrons without ever having attempted an interception at night (let alone having carried it out successfully!), there were other u/t AI operators who never even went through the OTU.

Apart from Ralph Connolly, Lewis Brandon went straight from No. 3 Radio School to 141 Squadron at Ayr and learned his trade 'on the job' along with the air gunners, as the squadron re-equipped with Beaufighters. Number 141 Squadron, equipped with the Boulton & Paul Defiant, had been slaughtered one awful day during the Battle of Britain and converted to night-fighting. The priority, as I mentioned earlier on, was to get new crews to the squadrons as quickly as possible before the night Blitz was resumed by the *Luftwaffe*. 'Brandy' – as we knew him – went on to make a name for himself and together with his pilot, 'Ben' Benson, had a distinguished career, both of them winning the DSO and the DFC & Bar.

Harry and I did six operational patrols on 29 Squadron, including the one in which we compromised the colours of the night. With that particular episode we sealed our fate so far as 'Two Nine' was concerned. Six weeks after having joined it with such high hopes, we were on our way, having been sacked by Guy Gibson. The moral here is that if you are going to be sacked, it is better to be sacked by 'the best in the business'! There is also little doubt that by having us posted away to the down-market Turbinlite operation, Guy saved our lives and at the same time gave us the opportunity to learn our trade properly.

So we exchanged our Bristol Beaufighters for the American-built Douglas Boston and arrived at Tangmere in the middle of the mock gas attack on 21 October. By the 23rd we were airborne in Havoc Y 904 for one hour fifteen minutes to gain type experience. Havoc was the name given to the night-fighter version of the Boston, a medium bomber.

When we joined 1455 Flight, we not only changed the type of aircraft but we went on to a completely different kind of tactical operation from that being carried out with increasing success by the Bristol Beaufighters. The Havocs of the Turbinlite flights had no guns . . . we found that we had exchanged our cannon and machine-guns for an airborne searchlight!

Looking back, of course, being 'fired' from 'Two Nine' gave us the chance to redeem our debit balance in HM King George VI's Aircraft Accounts Book when the bomber support operations started in the summer of 1943.

Although Harry and I were to be on these strange aircraft for fifteen frustrating months, we owed a lot to 1455 Flight at Tangmere because it was there we did our real apprenticeship in the craft of night-fighting. It was in the lumbering ugly Havoc with a searchlight in the nose, 48 batteries weighing a ton (literally!) stowed in the bomb-bay and no guns, that we learned our trade.

The airborne searchlight was the brainchild of a certain Wing Commander W. Helmore and was designed and developed when any project which might help to repel the German night-bombers was given serious consideration. This included aerial mines and lengths of steel cable suspended from balloons and hung in the anticipated path of the incoming raiders! The concept of the 'Turbinlite', as Helmore's light came to be known, was that there might be certain weather conditions and, on occasion, extremely dark nights when the pilots of the Beaufighters might not be able to get a visual even when their AI operators had brought them in to under 500 feet behind the target aircraft, and that this problem could only be overcome with some form of illumination!

The device, which emerged by courtesy of the General Electric Company and their laboratories at Wembley, was truly worthy of a future Member of Parliament! The Helmore Turbinlite consisted of the most powerful searchlight in the world and it was mounted in the nose of a Havoc I, or II.

The Boston – as it was – would have had the standard nose, used to carry a navigator/bomb aimer, hack-sawn off; this would be replaced by a para-elliptical reflector and the Mk IV AI set (together with the AI operator) would be housed in the rear cockpit (inhabited for bomber operations by a rear gunner). The forty-eight 12-volt batteries would be stowed in the bomb-bay and they were capable of discharging in 120 seconds! GEC were responsible for the electrics and designed a remarkable lamp unit, with mechanically fed carbons and a small frontal area. The power of the Turbinlite may be gauged from the current consumption. Against the 150 amps of the standard Army, Navy and the later Leigh Light, it used 1,400 amps!

The reflector projected a horizontal sausage-shaped beam of 300 degrees divergence, 950 yards wide at one mile range. As the French would say, *formidable*! There was, however, one snag from the operational point of view. By the time these modifications had been carried out the weight of the Havoc was such that it could not carry any guns or ammunition and there was no room to put them, anyway! The midwives of the Turbinlite concept did not allow this minor inconvenience to worry them. The answer would be that a single-seater fighter would be sent up with the Turbinlite Havoc and, when the light was put on, the pilot of the fighter would see the enemy bomber lit up in the middle of the beam and go in and shoot it down! QED.

Discerning airmen of all ages will be quick to see that it was not quite as easy as that! It is necessary to go into the full details of the Turbinlite operation if it is to be properly understood. . . .

Number 1455 Flight was one of ten such flights located in 11 and 12 Group of Fighter Command. They were, in effect, 'half-squadrons' and were mostly based on airfields where there was already a night-fighter squadron equipped with Beaufighters and, in one case, Havocs with AI and armed with twelve .303-in machine-guns but – no light!

The flight was commanded by Squadron Leader J. Latimer DFC and the Czech Military Cross – rather a remote figure, of whom I have no recollections at all. He was replaced a month or two after Harry and I went to 1455 by Squadron Leader George Budd DFC – formerly, like Ian Joll, of 604 Auxiliary

Squadron – the same George Budd who had signed my log-book, when I completed the course at No. 54 OTU; his AI operator was Flight Sergeant George Evans DFM (one of the former air gunners who had transferred to AI operator. Like many of them he proudly hung on to his 'AG' badge!). They had shot down several enemy bombers in the winter of 1940/41 and were an experienced crew.

On nights when there was a likelihood of enemy raiders coming in over the South coast, 1455 Flight's main task was to mount standing patrols, throughout the night or until stood down by the Duty Controller, on a line from Selsey Bill to Beachy Head and the reciprocal track to Selsey Bill. The patrols lasted between an hour and a half and two hours and were carried out at a height of about 15,000 feet. We had with us a single-seater fighter, usually a Hawker Hurricane. As we flew up and down between Selsey Bill and Beachy Head our attendant fighter was provided – albeit reluctantly – by the pilots of No. 1 Squadron.

Having said earlier that it was, generally speaking, not practical to fly in formation at night, I must now describe how the Turbinlite operation provided one of the exceptions to that rule. It did prove to be possible for two (or even three) aircraft to fly in formation on operations at night for a limited period and under limited tactical and weather conditions. The Germans also tried it later on, when defending their country against our raids, but for a different reason. It was a cumbersome and complex operation with plenty of room for errors to creep in, and it went like this:

When we were ready to taxi out round the perimeter track Harry would call up the Hurricane pilot to follow us towards the runway in use (according to the

No. 1455 Flight, Tangmere: the Airborne Searchlight known as the 'Turbinlite' in a Douglas Boston with a modified nose-section, re-named a 'Havoc'. This is a Havoc II, showing clearly the 'sawn-off' nose (housing the reflector and the carbon arcs for the light). Also shown, beneath the port main-plane, is the white strip – illuminated at night – used by the attendant Hawker Hurricanes to formate on the Turbinlite Havoc and shoot down the enemy aircraft (once the interception had been completed and the beam of light, illuminating the E/A, had been switched on).

wind) and both aircraft would taxi out together and wait by the runway for clearance from Flying Control. When this was given by the Flying Control Officer we would turn on to the runway; the Hurricane would follow and take up the normal No. 2 position, i.e. just behind the tail-plane and on the starboard side of the Havoc; both aircraft would have their navigation lights on.

With a brief word over the VHF to the pilot of the Hurricane, Harry would open his throttles and the Havoc would start to move down the runway. In the back, I would be watching the lights of the Hurricane starting to move forward to keep in formation with us as we increased our speed. He would probably be just airborne as we came 'unstuck' and lumbered into the air. From there the two aircraft would climb away from Tangmere and up to 12–15,000 feet over Selsey Bill to start our patrol. The difference was that the Hurricane pilot – from the moment he started to trundle forward – had one eye on his instrument panel and the other on an illuminated white strip on the underside of the Havoc's black starboard mainplane! He had to formate on that white strip for the duration of the patrol, because navigation lights were then switched off. If he lost the strip and with it, sight of the Havoc, then the mission had to be aborted.

At the end of the patrol, both aircraft would usually stay together until the Hurricane pilot had spotted the flashing beacon at base, knew he was within sight of Tangmere and then broke away to land independently. That was the drill for a straightforward patrol and with no target to attack. If there was an interception under the control of the GCI Controller at Durrington and a target to be chased, then that was another matter entirely. Once the Havoc pilot started to receive directions and new courses to steer, the Hurricane had to follow him through every move, every change of course, height and speed.

If, and when, the AI operator in the Havoc got a contact then the alterations of course, height and speed would continue – sometimes more violently – as the Turbinlite aircraft closed in on its prey, which, in its turn, might be taking evasive action, making it still more difficult for the Hurricane pilot to stay in formation.

The aim of the AI operator in the Havoc was to bring them in 2,000 feet behind the target, dead ahead and on the same level – different tactics from the normal night attack. Once he had achieved this, he would immediately tell his pilot, who would then expose the light! The special batteries gave the searchlight a maximum duration of 2½ minutes, so there was not much time to waste. Apart from the obvious fact that, if there was a German gentleman caught in the beam, he was not going to wait around to be shot at! So the theory was that just before we, the Havoc crew, were ready to switch on the light, Harry would warn the Hurricane pilot that the searchlight was about to come on and the enemy aircraft would be right there in the centre of the beam!

The Hurricane pilot would immediately push his stick forward, open his throttle and dive to a point roughly halfway between the Havoc and where he presumed that the target would be! He would then be ready, as soon as the beam came on, to pull the stick back, get his sights on the enemy bomber, make his attack and shoot the raider down . . .

This happy fairy-tale ending to the Turbinlite story is dependent on two things – if not more! Firstly, the Hurricane pilot's ability to maintain his position in formation with the Havoc, through every manoeuvre in the book (on a dark night, remember!) and to get into the right position when the light comes on. Secondly, that the target does not evade the light almost immediately, to disappear under cover of darkness. It was extremely difficult for the Havoc pilot to find the target again by manoeuvring his aircraft and, as it were, waving the light around as if it were a hand torch.

Additionally, unless the AI operator is spot on with his commentary and directions for his pilot, they would never get to 2,000 ft dead astern and on the same level as the target, particularly if the enemy aircraft is taking violent evasive action and making for home with his nose well down. In certain circumstances it is quite possible to conjure up a picture of the Havoc finally exposing his searchlight – with the target right there in the centre of the beam – but with no Hurricane to shoot it down! I know of a number of chases which had to be broken off because the Hurricane was unable to stay with the Havoc, and indeed, this was one of the inherent faults of the whole concept of the Turbinlites.

Although we completed 49 defensive night patrols and practices – any of which could have been turned into an operational flight, if the need had arisen – we never saw so much as the exhaust flame of a German bomber. Thus by the time we were posted, in January 1943, back onto Beaufighters, Harry and I had been together as a night-fighter team for eighteen months – and never seen a shot fired in anger. For most of that time (on Turbinlites) we had had no shots to fire anyway! However, we must not race too far ahead, there is more to tell yet concerning the Turbinlite story, and it becomes even more complicated when describing the way in which we had to practise these operations.

During the whole of our fifteen months at Tangmere the German night raids became fewer in number and more isolated, e.g. the haphazard *Baedeker* Raids. The Germans had gone to Russia and the pressure on the British Isles was relaxed. Indeed, against all expectations the heavy night Blitz of 1940/41 was never to be resumed – and the young inexperienced British night-fighter crews like Harry White and myself were left more or less in peace, to complete our training. The few German bombers which did try their luck in the winter of 1941/42 found the Beaufighters ready for them. We in the cumbersome and unwieldy Turbinlite formations were not needed.

With the lack of real German bombers on which to practise we, on 1455 Flight, needed target aircraft in the same way that we had done on 29 Squadron. There, two Beaufighters went up on patrol over Kent and the area of the Channel, and the GCI Controller (providing there were no incoming German raids) used one as the defending fighter and the other as the bandit or hostile aircraft. One or two practice interceptions were carried out and the two Beaus would then change places, so that both crews could keep their skills and their interception techniques on the top line.

Again, it was No. 1 Squadron – and later on No. 43 – who provided the answer, in the shape of another Hurricane! Our radio call sign at the time was, rather inappropriately, 'WODAN'. So let us call the second Hurricane 'WODAN RED 3' and follow a typical night practice flight such as that recorded in my log-book for Monday 3 November 1941, when Harry and I took off in Havoc E 413 at 22.05 hrs:

Duty	Remarks	Duration
Turbinlite	Took up two Hurricanes from No. 1 and carried out two successful exposures. Weapon satisfactory but elevation N too G.	1.05 hrs

We were 'WODAN RED SECTION' and our call sign was 'WODAN RED 1'. When we were ready to leave Dispersal, Harry called up both Hurricane pilots briefly to check that they too were ready to go. We then taxied out round the perimeter track, as before, but this time with two Hurricanes following along behind – all with our lights on. When the time came for us to turn onto the main west/east runway, RED 2 took up the position on our starboard side and RED 3 waited just off the runway. We took off with RED 2 and did a slow climbing turn to port over the South Downs, on to a reciprocal course.

As soon as we had got well down the runway, RED 3 turned on to it and took off to follow us. He could see our lights still turning to port, and by making a tighter turn, he could cut off the corner and join up with us in formation. By the time we had turned 180 degrees and were coming back over the Downs – in the vicinity of Goodwood – and to the north of Tangmere, both Hurricane pilots would glue their eyes to the illuminated white strips on the underside of our wings, nav. lights were switched off and the whole of our 'flying circus' would climb up to patrol height together.

Once we were up to 15,000 ft over Selsey Bill and heading east, Harry sent RED 3 off on a diverging course – up to a range of 2/3 miles away. I picked up the contact and carried out a practice interception with RED 2 still in formation. When we had got the Hurricane dead ahead, on the same level and at a range of 2,000 ft, Harry gave RED 2 a quick call on the R/T. The Hurricane pilot pushed his stick forward, opened his throttle to close the gap between him and the target and about 15 seconds later Harry switched on the light!

There, sure enough, was RED 3 right in the centre of the beam and Harry sat back to watch RED 2 make the mock attack. When RED 2 had made his attack, broken away and called us up on the R/T to say that he was clear from RED 3, there followed what may well be called *pièce de résistance*! All three aircraft in WODAN RED SECTION switched on their nav. lights, re-formed and turned back onto 270 degrees for the second leg of the patrol. Navigation lights were then switched off again and this time we sent RED 2 off to act as target; carried out our second interception and used RED 3 as the attendant fighter, so that he too could gain experience of making an attack with the aid of the Turbinlite beam.

If we were still some way from base when RED 3 had completed his attack we would once again have switched on our navigation lights and gone through the hairy manoeuvre of re-forming our circus. But if we were safely back over Tangmere both Hurricane pilots would have been happy to break away and land independently after the strain of trying to follow that little white strip. Harry and I would have been pleased to let them go and relax. Formation flying at night is a severe constraint on the pilots and the fear of a mid-air collision is never far away.

It will now be seen how vital it was, for the operation of the Turbinlite concept, to have an accurate interception by the Havoc pilot and his AI operator. With the attendant fighter in close formation there must be a minimum of steep turns and changes of speed during the interception and absolute accuracy at the culmination, i.e. just before the light was switched on. The enemy bomber had to be visible in the beam immediately the Havoc pilot pressed the button and the Hurricane pilot had to be able to make his attack before a hail of bullets was directed – by the rear gunner in the Heinkel or Dornier – at the source of the light and the hapless crew of the Havoc!

Furthermore, if, worse still, the enemy aircraft was *not* in the beam, the hail of bullets would still come. But from the cover of darkness! The Hurricane pilot would see nothing in the beam above him and would have no idea where, in the darkness, to look! In fact, he would be no better off than his forebears who had gone up so bravely at night without AI in September 1940.

The further one goes into the details of the Turbinlite operation the more it becomes clear that – in practice – the idea was too complicated to work, except under ideal conditions. For the GCI Controller, it was better to use a patrolling Beaufighter than to call up a Turbinlite Havoc and its attendant fighter. Even with the limits of the Mk IV AI at minimum range, it was rare for the skilled AI operator not to be able to give his pilot a visual at 400–500 ft on the darkest of nights.

There was yet another feature of the Turbinlite operation. If there was a lot of cloud about, the difficulties – for the Hurricane pilot – of keeping formation climbing up and whilst on patrol are self-evident. It was all too easy for him to lose sight of the white strip on the wings of the parent aircraft. Again, the mission would have to be abandoned. There was yet another snag (there seems to be no end to them as the memory of those flights comes back). If when driving a car in mist or fog at night – or sometimes during the day – you attempt to use your headlights in order to see better and to penetrate the gloom, the result is that the light tends to be thrown back at you. You find you can see rather less than if you use only your sidelights! So it was with the Turbinlite. On occasion, when Harry switched the light on, there was just an opaque whitish glare in front of him and it was quite impossible for him – or the Hurricane pilot – to distinguish if there was another aircraft in the beam, or not, let alone for the Hurricane to make an attack on it!

When we had been at Tangmere for some months, a party of us were invited to the GEC Laboratories at Wembley for a tour of the factory and a visit to the Experimental Department where the Turbinlite had been developed before being put into production. They had a prototype of the Helmore invention with reflector, lamp unit, carbons, etc., and our hosts asked us if we would like to see a demonstration under laboratory conditions! Of course, we all replied in the affirmative, then wished that we had not done so!

When the device was switched on, both the noise and the heat of the arc were fearsome! Smoke and flame seemed to engulf the whole contraption and the thought of this witches' cauldron boiling up a few feet in front of the pilot's cockpit brought on the twitch to every Turbinlite pilot and AI operator in the party!

(Note: in the air we were spared most of the noise of the carbons burning, but we could see the glare and the smoke emanating from the light and that was frightening enough when airborne at 15,000 ft!)

As I have said, Harry and I owed a lot to the Turbinlites and to 1455 Flight because the legacy that we took with us in January 1943 was fifteen months of training in night-flying and learning how to make accurate night interceptions, and I had another 300 hours' flying in my log-book. This was when we really learnt our trade.

The most notable development on the war front which occurred in the winter of 1941/42 (as mentioned briefly above) was that the anticipated resumption of heavy night raids against England never materialised. Adolf Hitler started a war in the East before he had finished the War in the West, and this country, its people, its resources and its young inexperienced night-fighter crews were let off the hook. Only the latter were disappointed!

In June 1941 Hitler launched Operation 'Barbarossa' against Russia, his temporary allies, and in the autumn took a large number of German bombers away from the Channel coast to support the land assault on the Soviet Union. Although sporadic raiding of all kinds (from hit-and-run daylight attacks on some coastal towns of no military value, to intruding into our returning bomber stream) continued until the end of the war, the Heinkel 111s, Dornier 217s and Junkers 88s never again came in strength. Of those that did come, many were intercepted and shot down by our improved night defences, and the score of those crews lucky enough to be put on to them by the GCI Controllers mounted slowly but steadily. But for the majority of us – whether we were on Beaus or Havocs – this was the period, frustrating though it may have been at the time, when we learned our trade.

Harry and I were among the lucky ones to have the opportunity to put this prolonged training to good use, but not on Home Defence and not on the German bombers. As we settled into 1455 Flight at the end of 1941 these were only dreams . . .

Christmas came and went with an enormous sit-down meal for the airmen served, in traditional style, by the officers and senior NCOs in one of the hangars that had been badly damaged during the Battle of Britain, but now cleaned up and partly restored.

In 1455 we had a very popular Flight Commander, Flight Lieutenant Dudley Hobbis DFC – a brilliant pilot and a gay character (when that word did not mean what it does fifty years on). Dudley really enjoyed life whether in the air or on the ground. He was one of those happy warriors who worked hard and played hard. The airmen had their menus that they wanted us to sign. Everybody had had a few drinks and the party was really getting going. In front of Dudley Hobbis was a pile of menus waiting for his signature.

Amongst them, one optimistic airman had slipped a leave pass, reckoning that 'Hobby' (as they all affectionately referred to him) would not notice it with the fun and games going on all around him. Eventually they got his attention and he sat down and started to work his way through the heap of menus. Anxious eyes were watching him and an anxious airman was holding his breath as Hobby came to the leave pass. Without batting an eyelid Dudley Hobbis signed the leave pass 'Santa Claus' and passed on to the next menu!

Later that day the officers came across to the sergeants' mess for a drink before going back to their own mess for their Christmas meal.

A few days into the New Year I had the opportunity of seeing the Flight Commander at closer quarters. On 5 January I had to fly with him and have my abilities as an AI operator checked out. This was not funny at all. I became very worried whether I could manage to carry out a successful interception with him in the front seat and not with the now familiar Harry White. All my old fears and doubts, which I had experienced at Church Fenton, returned and once more there were visions of being thrown out!

In the event, I nearly was. I flew with Dudley Hobbis twice that day and the first time I made such a hash of two interceptions that I came down and told Harry that I was almost certain to be grounded. On the second trip, all went well and I carried out two near-perfect interceptions, so I was saved again. On the same day Flt Lt Hobbis sent his AI operator Flt Sgt Terry Clark up with Harry so the long-suffering White would have the opportunity of seeing how an interception was carried out by an experienced operator! I would have to look to my laurels in future!

Happily – 58 years on – Terry, who lives in York, and I, are still in touch. On 5 January each year, we have a telephone call to toast our two pilots, Harry White and Dudley Hobbis, who have 'reached the stars before us'.

Three days later Harry and I carried out four successful interceptions during a night flying test, and taking off at 22.45 hrs we managed three successful exposures in a trip which took 1.55 hrs.

Some of the code words used over the R/T would give a lot of amusement today. For example, when we in the Turbinlite Havoc were ready to expose the light on the target aircraft Harry would call up the Hurricane pilot to get into position (i.e. to make his attack) with the word 'BOILING!'. If my AI set had failed at the crucial moment when we were making the interception, as it sometimes did, Harry would have to call up the GCI Controller and say 'MY WEAPON IS BENT!' Conversely, and equally suggestive, was the message over the R/T if the AI was all in order (for all the world to hear), 'MY WEAPON IS FLASHING'.

Whilst we were stationed at Tangmere, Harry and I became frequent visitors at Church Farm – Ken Lock's home, only three miles north of Chichester. Mr and Mrs Lock took to Harry and became as fond of him as (I like to think) they had been of John Eeles and myself, since we first started to spend some of our *exeats* from school there in September 1936.

The dinner-table at Church Farm was always a sight for sore eyes, when food rationing was the order of the day. We knew where we would be welcome if there was any shortage of commons in the sergeants' mess. After dinner we would all sit round and play whist, with Frank Lock (Ernest's brother) frequently dropping in with his wife to join the party. We had a Tiger Moth on 1455 Flight. Harry and I used to take it up about once a month for a bit of relaxation, and usually he gave me some dual instruction. Before returning to base, we would set course for Church Farm.

Harry would take over the controls and we would make one or two low passes over the farm buildings to be told, on our next visit, that they knew it was us and that we had stopped the chickens from laying! By this time Ken was in the States on a pilot's course . . . lucky man!

Looking at my log-book entry for 28.1.42 I find that we took off in a Havoc II at the unearthly hour of 02.15 hrs on an altitude climb to 20,000 ft and our 'time up' was 1.25 hours. In the 'Remarks' column I wrote: 'Port Azimuth still u/s, but 20,000 was reached O.K. and it was B. cold up there.'

I also wrote, courtesy of Longfellow:

> 'The heights by great men reached and kept
> Were not attained by sudden flight,
> But they, while their companions slept,
> Were toiling upward in the night.'

Whenever possible we carried out AI practice – during the day and at night – and by the end of February my total flying hours had topped 200, including 73.15 hours at night.

At some time in March 1942, Harry and I were asked by Squadron Leader George Budd – who had taken over from Squadron Leader Latimer as CO of

1455 Flight in January – to apply for commissions. We were both sergeants at that stage and had been crewed together for eight months. I had just turned 19 and Harry was still 18. George Budd had known us for a couple of months and I don't think that he gave either of us a formal interview, but in April we both had an interview with the Station Commander, Group Captain Appleton DSO, DFC.

The interview did not last long but I always remember it because, when he had finished he said, 'All right Allen, I'm going to recommend you'. I walked out of his office knowing exactly where I stood and as I found out, later in life, that is a rare occurrence . . .

Then we were ordered to attend at RAF Uxbridge to be seen by the AOC himself, Air Vice-Marshal Trafford Leigh-Mallory CB, DSO. It was an experience to go to Uxbridge, but the atmosphere in and around the huts and the parade ground (as we crossed it) was oppressive and we were glad to get back to Tangmere. I nearly forgot, my interview with Leigh-Mallory lasted no more than two minutes and when I left his office, I did *not* know where I stood!

My mother's 'Private Air Force': I had just been promoted to Flight Sergeant, my father was a Flying Officer and Rodney was a Flight Sergeant in the Air Training Corps. Note: She referred to her 'Private Air Force' in her letter to her sister-in-law, quoted in the narrative.

Harry was granted a commission back-dated to 26 March 1942 and mine, three weeks later, was dated 17 April. So in future, when I came to enter up my log-book, I would have to remember that I was now flying with Pilot Officer White! We both, in turn, shot off up to London to order our new kit, and I remember going to Horne Brothers in the Strand, which is happily still there today.

We returned to Tangmere as pilot officers, moved out of our billets in Tangmere Village into Shopwyke House (which became the officers' mess after the old mess on the airfield was almost destroyed during the Battle of Britain) and carried on at 1455 Flight where we had left off. There was no question of going off on an officer's training course, or anything like that!

Two other things of note occurred just before our commissions came through. On 2 April, the whole of 1455 Flight took to the air (9/10 Turbinlite Havocs) and flew from Tangmere in the evening up to Hunsdon, a night-fighter station just north of Harlow in Essex. The following day, we all flew back to Tangmere. The reason? The Dieppe raid was scheduled to take place on, I think, 4 April and we had to get out of the way, to make room on Tangmere for the day-fighter squadrons who would be using it as a temporary base while flying many sorties across the Channel in support of the Landing Forces and the Royal Navy.

As we heard afterwards, the raid was cancelled and then took place later in the year on 19 August, with disastrous results. Rumour had it that there had been a security leak in April which contributed to the tragedy which took place on the beaches at Dieppe in August. In August we in 1455 Flight again took off – like a gaggle of frightened geese – and took refuge at Heston, feeling once more, very much out of things.

The second thing which occurred was that although my commission did not come through until three weeks after Harry got his, I was promoted – much to my astonishment and to his chagrin – to flight sergeant. He had been a sergeant for some months longer than I had but never got the coveted crowns!

I have mentioned – when describing night-fighter operations – the need for the night-fighter pilot to identify the target clearly once his AI operator has brought him to within visual range. I have also hinted that sometimes mistakes occurred and British fighters fired on their own aircraft. There were instances of this so-called 'friendly fire' both at night and in the daytime. One such incident was now to occur on 1455 Flight.

Harry and I were not on the flying detail that night so we were not involved in the incident which is about to unfold. Just as well, or our careers might have come to a full stop there and then and this book would never have been written. Being released, we went into Chichester to celebrate my promotion. The arrival of my crowns, after only being in the Air Force for ten months, could not be let pass without partaking of a little liquid refreshment!

That night six Stirlings of No. 218 Squadron flew a long and hazardous trip to bomb the Skoda Works at Pilzen. By contrast, S/Ldr Ashworth and crew, also of 218, carried out a nice safe Nickel (leaflet dropping) op to Lyons in southern France. When safely, as they must have thought, over Sussex *en route* for their base further north, the most hazardous part of their trip was about to occur.

At the same time and in the same area at about the same height, an enemy force was bent on attacking Portsmouth. The scene was set. Enter S/Ldr George Budd DFC and his AI operator, George Evans DFM, on patrol with their attendant Hurricane in the vicinity of Selsey Bill. Number 1455 Flight was about to claim its first, and only, success.

No. 1455 Flight, Tangmere: Harry and myself, newly commissioned, in the gardens of Shopwycke House, Oving, Chichester. The former preparatory school was used as the officers' mess after the old mess at Tangmere was severely damaged in August 1940 during The Battle of Britain.

I heard all about it when I encountered George Evans on my return to the NCOs' billets at about 1 a.m. that night. He said, 'We got one.' 'What was it George?' I asked, excited by the news. 'It was a Stirling!' he replied lugubriously. I have no recollection of my reply.

The GCI Controller told George Budd (over the R/T) that there was a bandit in his vicinity and gave him a new course to steer. Within a few minutes George Evans got a contact on his AI set and completed the interception. It was a bright moonlit night and George Budd got a visual on the target at a range of 2,000 feet. He didn't even need to use the light as he could see the aircraft in front of him so clearly and there was no point in advising the enemy of his presence before the Hurricane went forward to carry out the attack.

George Budd closed in and identified the target as a Heinkel 111; the Ground Controller again confirmed that it was a bandit, and the Hurricane pilot (still formating under the Havoc's starboard wing) was given the order to go in and make his attack . . .

George Budd could see the Hurricane as it opened fire with its four 20-mm cannon and watched with satisfaction as flames sprouted from the starboard wing of the aircraft in front of him and it started to lose height.

It was at that moment that the Controller on the ground had a change of heart. Something must have aroused his suspicion about the identity of the aircraft which was now going down in flames. So he called George Budd up on the R/T, saying, 'HELLO WODAN RED 1. CONTROL HERE. WE THINK THIS MAY BE A BOGEY' (i.e. unidentified friend or foe). George Budd replied in his fruitiest tones, 'HELLO CONTROL! WODAN RED 1 HERE. WELL . . . IF IT'S A BOGEY – THEN BY GOD, IT'S A DEAD BOGEY NOW!' as he watched the burning aircraft go down in front of him. By the time he landed back at Tangmere he was a little more contrite, but he and George Evans were comforted by the Station Commander, who said, 'Don't worry George, remember I got a Wellington a few months back!'

There were similar incidents on the Beaufighter squadrons, and the attack on the Stirling, mistaken though it was, bears no particular reflection on the Turbinlite operations as such.

After all, the problem of identification is as old as war itself and there were a number of cases (on both sides) of friendly aircraft being shot down in daylight – let alone at night. If the fighter pilot is repeatedly told that he is chasing a bandit, and the other circumstances of position, course, height and behaviour seem to bear out that the target is hostile – then he has already half identified it before he actually sees it. The rest is done by self-suggestion and in the heat of the moment, coupled with the fear of being seen to let a hostile aircraft get away, he sees it as a hostile and opens fire. I am told that, even with the sophisticated equipment of the fighter aircraft of today, the problem is still there – as natural as war itself.

Squadron Leader Ashworth and his crew all parachuted safely to earth from the Stirling, before it crashed at Gatehouse Farm, Lurgashall in Sussex. After they had been rounded up from various fields and trees in Sussex we had the five NCO members of the crew in the sergeants' mess – and we of 1455 Flight had to face them over the breakfast table! They were at Tangmere for a week, waiting for the Court of Inquiry, so we saw quite a lot of them. At first, they were only too relieved to be alive. But, after seven days of waiting around the station, they were beginning to let us know what they thought of 1455 Flight and all those who might have the slightest connections with it! One couldn't blame them.

In June we did six patrols – up and down the line of Selsey Bill to Beachy Head – but although we carried out a number of successful practice interceptions, we were never used by the GCI Controller to chase any of the few German bombers that came over England during the spring and summer of 1942.

The most exciting incident of the month, looking back through my log-books, took place at Hendon where I had gone, in pre-war days, with thousands of other aircraft enthusiasts to the great RAF Pageants, there to marvel at the Royal Air Force Aerobatic Team and the rest of those wonderful air displays.

Harry and I had a brief to go up to Hendon and pick up the CO, who had been having a few days leave in London. We took a Boston 1 which we had on the flight. The nose had not been sawn off to turn it into a Turbinlite, so it had a navigator's compartment in front, in a Perspex canopy right over the nose-wheel. I thought it would make a change to sit in front, where you had an unimpeded and exciting view of everything that was going on.

We got up to Hendon in fine style but, when we looked at the runway on which we were to land, coming in over the railway embankment it looked woefully short. In the days of the Air Pageants the aerodrome had always seemed so big, with masses of aircraft parked all over it and many more in the air above. Now, in a Boston which came in on the approach at 140 m.p.h. and 'over the fence' at 120, it looked about the size of a postage stamp. Nothing daunted, Pilot Officer White did a low circuit (looking at the closely built-up area, compared with the open fields around Tangmere, was enough to make me – sitting exposed in the nose – wish that I was in my normal seat in the rear cockpit!) and in we came, conscious that the CO would be standing outside the old clubhouse waiting for his 'taxi' back to Tangmere and watching our performance.

In we swept over the embankment, giving me a worm's eye view of the main-line to Scotland, bang down on the runway, jam on the brakes – and watch horrified as the fence at the end rushed up to meet us! Harry still on the brakes – no reverse thrust in those days – and with smoke rising from the tortured tyres on the main wheels we finally ground to a halt, the nose of the Boston, with me inside it, a yard or two short of the fence. We, and the aircraft, were all in one piece when Harry clambered out and I released myself from the Perspex nose. Unfortunately, that is more than could be said for the tyres!

They were completely shredded. The Boston had to be towed ignominiously back to the Watch Office, and George Budd had to wait another day for his taxi home. Ken Matthews (a pilot with the most marvellous night-vision) had to fly up the following day, by which time S/Ldr George Budd was 'smoking' as much as our tyres!

Chichester was only three miles west of Tangmere and as we all had bicycles – either issued, or pinched – a number of us used to cycle into town when we had a free evening. There was Charlie Aindow, 'Old Greg', Dougie Gillam, Jimmy Cleall, Terry Clark, George Evans and an ex-air gunner whose name was Forbes amongst the AI operators, and Clive Barber and Harry amongst the pilots. Earlier in the year we were all NCOs together and we had a lot of fun.

We used to go to a cinema and then on to a pub for a few drinks. Sometimes it was to Kimbell's Restaurant in North Street for a dance, then late on in the evening we would mount our machines and steer an erratic and wobbly path back to our billet (for several months in the winter of 1941/42 some of us were billeted in a requisitioned private house near to Westhampnett).

The Sussex constabulary watched over our comings and goings with leniency and care but, every now and then, they felt they had to clamp down a bit on our lack of attention to the need for having lights – front and rear – on our bikes or some other local bye-law which we had chosen to ignore. So it was one night – when weaving our way out of East Street on the way home – we found that our long straggling line of bicycles was right in the middle of a police trap, and there were a number of constables, with their torches flashing us down, spread out along the road.

For once, I managed to come to my senses quicker than usual and realised what was happening. I was cycling with Harry and when we were stopped by an officer saying 'Ere, Ere!' I said 'All right officer, you are busy here, I'll go on to the next constable . . .' Having said this I put my foot down and cycled on smartly to where I could see the next constable, waiting to take my name and address. When I reached him I said politely 'Good evening, officer . . . I've just had my name taken by the constable down the road!' He told me – rather reluctantly – that I could go, and I cycled happily on my way. When Harry, having duly had his name and address 'took' caught up with me, he was distinctly put out!

On another occasion I had gone into 'Chi' in my car and we were all at a dance at Kimbell's, when I had an unusual evening, to say the least of it, and it had nothing to do with any police traps. At some time, late on in the evening, Sergeant B . . . (who was married) came up to me in the throng of people on the dance floor and shouted, above the hub-bub of noise 'I'm fed up and I'm going home. You've got a car, you take my wife home when you come . . . she doesn't want to come now!', and before I could protest, had disappeared into the crowd. They'd got digs somewhere out between Tangmere and Fontwell and all would have been well – if I had not run out of petrol . . . !

When the dance finished I found Sgt B . . .'s wife looking a little forlorn but not in too bad shape, considering that her husband had run out on her, and we went to look for my Ford 8 in the car park. We set off all right, although I was a little bit worried about the level of the fuel gauge. In 1942 fuel rationing was pretty tight and our source of free petrol from the bowsers, which refuelled our aircraft, had dried up.

Sure enough, just past the entrance to Tangmere, I ran out of petrol and there I was stuck – in the middle of the night – with Sgt B . . .'s wife. My situation bore no resemblance to the many jokes that have been made over the years about errant Casanovas deliberately luring some wretched girl into their car with ulterior motives and then announcing (having reached some shady nook), 'I'm so sorry my dear . . . but I've run out of petrol!' So, leaving the car forlornly by the side of the road, we set off to walk the 3–4 miles to her home and her husband.

At some point on the main Chichester–Arundel road she announced that her feet were killing her (she only had thin dance shoes), and she walked the rest of the way back to their digs in her bare feet. When I finally got her home we found her husband in bed cuddled up with – the family dog. To say she was not pleased is putting it mildly, and although she offered me a bed on the sofa I decided I would be better off walking the four miles back to my billet than remaining in their tiny home, where the atmosphere was deteriorating at the rate of knots. Lord knows at what time I got home!

Whenever my wife and I go back to Chichester now and I stand in West Street, in front of the Dolphin & Anchor opposite the cathedral, I am reminded of another little incident which took place in that much-loved city. It all happened at the bus stop outside the Dolphin, a few weeks after I had been commissioned.

I had been on leave, and having returned by train from London, I had walked up South Street to catch a bus out to Tangmere. It was pouring with rain and by the time I reached the bus stop I was pretty well soaked. The buses ran every half-hour and I was relieved to see that there was one there with people climbing aboard. Unfortunately, by the time I reached the steps of the bus it was 'FULL UP' and the conductor waved me back. I was then left standing as the bus pulled out and headed off round the Market Cross on its way to Tangmere and Arundel. I had thirty minutes to wait in the rain, but at least I was now at the head of the queue.

By the time the next bus pulled in I was really wet and I climbed in gratefully and sank down onto one of the side-facing seats just inside the door. The rest of those who had been waiting in the queue behind me piled on and the bus was soon full up. When all the seats had been taken they started standing downstairs, and the line of those who had missed out on getting a seat stretched back to the door in front of me. There, immediately facing me, was an old lady hanging onto one of the straps above her head. I got up from my seat, gallantly offered it to her and she sat down, thanking me profusely. Then the conductor got on. He took one look at the line of people standing on the bottom floor of his bus and exploded! He said there were far too many people standing up and the last four who had got on would have to 'Get Off!'

I was, to all intents and purposes, amongst the last four to get on! I contemplated, for a second or two, whether I should argue the toss, but quickly realised that I would finish up in the middle of an undignified fracas if I were to do so. I got off the bus and walked the three miles home in the rain.

There was a sequel a few days later. I was again on a bus jammed pack full but, this time, I had a seat to which no one had contended my right! I overheard two women who were standing just behind me and one said to the other (in an awful complaining sort of voice) and directed at my back, 'I say, dear, it seems to me the age of chivalry is dead in Britain now!' I was sorely tempted to tell the good lady what had happened to me on the last occasion when I had tried to use a little chivalry and emulate Chaucer's 'true and perfect-gentle knight'. However, for the second time, I decided that discretion was the better part of valour and stared fixedly out of the window.

As the shortest day came and went, so the AI practice NFTs and standing patrols – back and forth along the Sussex coast – continued and our hours slowly mounted. By the end of July, I had over 300 flying hours and Harry and I had been crewed up for a full year. But, of real operational flying and contact with the enemy, we saw nothing at all. Sometimes, as summer turned to autumn, and Bomber Command started to penetrate deeper into Germany and also right down south over the Alps to Turin and Milan, we used to have diverted Lancasters, Halifaxes and Stirlings putting down at Tangmere. Sometimes they had wounded crew members on board and we met up with pilots, navigators and gunners in the mess. Their world seemed very far removed from our safe existence. Harry and I felt guilty and uncomfortable in their presence.

Down at the flight we continued practising AI interceptions. No. 1 Squadron left Tangmere and was replaced by 43 Squadron, whose pilots, like their prede-

cessors, were not pleased when they learned that they had to take their turn with
our flying circus and patrol the coastline between Selsey and Beachy Head
formating on a Turbinlite Havoc. Sometimes we were able to write 'PATROL'
into our log-books:

25.6.42	02.45 hrs	Havoc III D	P/O White PATROL 01.25 hrs Weapon OK. All quiet. No joy. Weather wizard. Base Beachy Head.	01.25 hrs

and again

27.7.42	00.55 hrs	G	P/O White PATROL 01.20 All OK. Full Moon. Perfect night. 43 had finger out. Patrol Selsey–Beachy.	01.20 hrs

and again!

28.7.42	00.40 hrs	D	P/O White PATROL All OK. Usual Patrol line Z. Weather perfect but as usual no Hun	02.00 hrs

These standing patrols went down in our log-books as 'operational', but we
knew that they were very far removed from the hazards and risks experienced by
the bomber crews flying over Germany. We felt guilty when we reflected that we
were enjoying all the privileges of being operational aircrew without any of the
drawbacks.

On 27 July we flew three times: a ZZ practice, a night flying test and a patrol
(taking off at 00.55 hrs on a perfect night with a full moon). The ZZ practice
referred to a Radio-Controlled Approach System for use in bad weather. We had
to fly in towards the runway at Tangmere from about 20 miles out – and change
direction, height and speed according to the Ground Controller's instructions to
Harry, given over the R/T.

That afternoon the weather was good and we could see the Channel on our
starboard side and the line of the South Downs on our port, as we came in north
of Portsmouth and approached Tangmere from the west. Gradually losing height
down to about 500 ft as we passed the spire of Chichester Cathedral to starboard,
at this stage the Controller started to give us a change of course, turning onto
080 and then 060 degrees. Soon, with another turn to port, we were heading direct
for the South Downs! We flew low over them – just to the east of Goodwood –
Harry pulling the nose of the Havoc up at the last moment. He then called up the
Ground Controller on the VHF and told him that the Havoc had crashed into
the Downs with the loss of all on board.

The Controller was not pleased and by the time we landed he had rung up the
Flight Commander, Ken Matthews (soon to be promoted to Squadron Leader
and appointed CO of 1455 Flight), to complain about us and Harry's language
in particular! Ken – when he heard our side of the story – rang the Controller
back and contributed further to his discomfort!

It must have been sometime during the war years that I saw 'Nothing to Report
– A Recollection' in *Punch*. It still seems appropriate for Harry and me, during

the period we were on the Turbinlite Havocs at Tangmere, although we had to wait for our first glimpse of 'The Rhine, a pallid streak and lightly thrown across the blue-grey plains . . .' until the July of 1943!

Nothing to Report
A Recollection

'You had no joy?' he asked. 'No luck at all,
We didn't see a thing. No joy.' we said.
No tale of death flung down on those abed
From our unfeeling hands; of foe's long fall
To earth and flaming pyre, by stealth struck down.
No death – no joy. But yet no word we told
Of moonlit seas' shot silver, touched with gold;
The Rhine, a pallid streak and lightly thrown
Across the blue-grey plains, with shadows patched
Where lay the woods; untouched in all by signs
Of man's uneasy life, save where the lines
Of bare high road stretched white. That peace unlatched
The door and let us glimpse true beauty's face –
But no report of this we made at Base.

Published in *Punch*

We also had to wait until July '43 to experience the feeling of seeing '. . . foe's long fall to earth and flaming pyre, by stealth struck down . . .', but it was worth waiting for!

As it was, when the Dieppe raid was laid on again, in August, and Tangmere became a hive of activity, we were shipped off out of the way to Heston and took off like a flock of frightened geese in our ungainly aircraft, leaving the real action to someone else.

We were only just into August when things started to happen 'for real' for us, and continued to go that way until the end of the year, when the ten Turbinlite flights around the country were finally disbanded. It was not the longed for enemy action which caused our several tragic losses of men and machines, but a series of flying accidents, all of which took place during the hours of daytime. We continued with our complicated and inherently dangerous formation flying at night without losing anyone.

On 4 August Harry and I had lunch at Shopwyke and then cycled to the aerodrome and on round to our dispersal on the south side of the east/west runway and at the eastern end of it. Harry had to go off on a course to West Malling and one of the other crews were going to take him across. I was to have a few days with nothing much to do. I hung around the Flight Office for a bit, then got on my bike and pushed off back round the perimeter track to return to the mess, with a nice quiet afternoon in front of me.

I had not stayed to see who was going to ferry Harry over to West Malling, so, when I saw a Havoc taxi out and take off, I had no idea if he was on it or not. I stopped and watched as the Turbinlite took off east to west and then, turning port and climbing slowly to about 2,000 ft, headed back east some three miles south of the aerodrome.

As I looked, the black wing suddenly banked sharply and the aircraft dived straight into the ground. It blew up with an awful *wumph* as it hit the field, into which it had fortunately fallen, and a column of smoke and flame rose into the air to a height of 2–3,000 ft above the wreck. I realised that neither of the crew could have got out and that both must be dead.

Then I thought 'Christ, was Harry on it?' I got back on my bike and set off in the direction of the pillar of smoke. I cycled down several farm tracks and over the main railway line from Barnham Junction to Chichester and eventually reached the field in which the burning remains of the Havoc lay. I knew there was nothing anybody could do for the crew, but I had to go up to the aircraft to see if there was a third body in it. If so, it could well be that of Harry White.

I went right up to the crumpled and smoking wreckage of the front cockpit and found the blackened and shrivelled remains of the pilot. I could not recognise who it was. I then went to look into the rear-cockpit. To my great relief there was only one body in it. The AI operator lay broken and twisted beyond belief and, again, he was unrecognisable. But as I walked away, my heart was soaring there was no passenger on the aircraft, only the unfortunate pilot and his radio observer. Harry was not on it and some other crew must be ferrying him across to Malling.

When the fire engine and the 'blood wagon' arrived I quietly slipped away and cycled back to the 1455 dispersal, just to check and make sure. When I got to the Flight Office I found that it was Pilot Officer Leader who was the pilot of the crashed Havoc – a relatively new arrival on the flight. Sadly he had taken with him 'Old Greg', Flight Sergeant Gregory – a married man in his thirties and one of the former air gunners who had retrained successfully as an AI operator. He was an experienced navigator and an extremely genuine person. As I had surmised, Harry was now safely on his way to Malling with one of the other crews.

On 22 September at 18.00 hrs Flying Officer Michael Winter flew into the hills near Liphook on a Havoc, killing himself and his AI operator, Flight Sergeant Jimmy Cleall. Unfortunately he *did* have a passenger on board who also died in the crash. This was Pilot Officer Lindley – commissioned in the Administrative Branch – who had just gone along for the ride. As if this was not enough for a small unit to cope with, two days later on the 24th at 16.00 hrs Flight Sergeant Jardine, a Canadian and one of our Hurricane pilots, lost his life.

On the evening that Michael Winter and Jimmy Cleall were killed, I received a telephone call late on from a WAAF corporal in the Operations Block on the airfield. She said that one of the WAAFs there was Jimmy Cleall's girl friend. The girl was inconsolable and none of them could do anything with her. Somebody had said that I was one of Jimmy's friends and would I come down to the Operations Block right away and see what I could do to comfort the girl.

I drove to the aerodrome and found the situation was just as the corporal had described it. The girl (whose name I don't remember) was distraught and upsetting all the other switchboard operators. I do remember that the poor girl did not want us to call the MO or any of the WAAF officers, but it was obvious that she could not be allowed to remain in the Operations Block in that state.

I really hadn't a clue what to do with her, I was completely out of my depth! In desperation, I took her outside and started to walk. The time must have been somewhere after midnight when we set off and somehow found our way onto the perimeter track, with me hauling the half-demented girl along by the arm. We walked all the way round the Tangmere perimeter track (some two or three miles?) until we arrived back at the operations block, footsore and weary beyond belief.

For the second time within a few weeks I found myself out on my own in the middle of the night with a young and attractive girl. For the second time, the situation was anything but romantic. I don't remember much of what we said, but I do recall that she thought that she was engaged to Jimmy – which made things rather worse.

I also recall – about halfway round – that it dawned on my thick skull that if I could make her physically tired, then her mental reactions might be weakened and she might sleep. In the event, that is what happened and by the time we had completed the circuit all the way round the perimeter track, she was out on her feet. I delivered her back into the hands of the WAAF corporal and they had no difficulty in putting her to bed. I think she was asleep before her head hit the pillow. Once again, I have no idea what time I got back to the mess and my own bed.

This was not to be the end of the story. I was the only officer amongst the AI operators, so I got the job of going through Jimmy's kit before it was cleared from the station and his personal belongings were returned to his family. I still remember doing it. Some of its contents revealed that there may have been other contenders for Jimmy's hand apart from the distraught girl in the Operations Block. All that matters, these many years later, is that Jimmy Cleall had a good life, was a good AI operator and although he only had a short life, he enjoyed it.

Things were still not over and I became involved in some of the arrangements for Jimmy's funeral. I went into Chichester to a flower shop in South Street to order a wreath from 1455 Flight, newly designated No. 534 Squadron.

I had already been informed by Station Sick Quarters (SSQ) that Jimmy's body had been brought back to Tangmere prior to the burial, which would take place at Brookwood Cemetery (near Woking). When I had collected the 1455 Flight wreath the following day I brought it back to the aerodrome and went along to SSQ. There I was directed to the mortuary at the rear of the building. I walked round to the mortuary and opened the door with some trepidation. When I had done so, I stood in the doorway and froze in my tracks.

As mentioned above, two days after Michael Winter and Jimmy Cleall had been killed, one of our Hurricane pilots, the Canadian Jardine, crashed in a wood near Arundel attempting to make a forced landing. The aircraft was completely destroyed and Jardine was killed outright. I should mention that, at this stage of the Turbinlite operations, we had had our own Hurricane pilots posted in and could dispense with the services of the Hurricane squadron based at Tangmere, much to their satisfaction. Poor Jardine's body was brought back to Tangmere and taken to the mortuary.

When I opened the door, with my wreath in my hand, I turned towards the little chapel on the left and walked through to place my wreath on Jimmy's coffin. As I did so, I glanced round to my right and there – on the slab in the centre of the mortuary – lay the body of Flight Sergeant Jardine. I gulped, paid my silent tribute to Jimmy, and left the awful building as soon as I could get my legs to work again . . .

I had *still* not quite finished. On the following day, I took a small party to

Barnham Junction Railway Station where we put Jimmy's coffin into the luggage van. I pinned the instructions, for the guard, onto the lid of the coffin and then we stood back on the platform and saluted as the train pulled out.

By contrast, Michael Winter's funeral was held in Chichester Cathedral. His father, Canon Winter, had made the request of Bishop Bell, and six of us bore his coffin, draped with the Union Jack and with his service cap on the top, the length of the cathedral and laid it gently on the bier. I do not recall what happened in respect of poor little Pilot Officer Lindley, our Adjutant, who just went along for the ride.

Sadly there were to be two more of our Hurricane pilots killed in flying accidents, before the Turbinlite units were disbanded at the end of 1942. The worst part, apart from the sad loss of all these men's lives, was that we had nothing to show for it in the way of German aircraft shot down. It was a miserable period down at the 534 Squadron dispersal hut sited in the south-east corner of the aerodrome.

Fortunately for me, I was not involved with the losses of Sergeant Davies and Sergeant 'Nobby' Bardwell (on 21 October and 29 December respectively), but we were all glad when 1942 came to an end with the prospect of better times ahead.

Two VIPs came to Tangmere during the autumn, which made for a little excitement. One was Lord Trenchard, 'the Father of the Air Force', and the other was HRH the Duke of Kent. The former provided us all with a short, but memorable, talk and the latter was, I am afraid to say, something of a disappointment.

I will mention the Duke's visit first. Prince George at that time held the rank of Air Commodore and spent a lot of his time diligently visiting RAF stations at home and abroad. When he came into our drab little dispersal hut, escorted by George Budd, he went all the way round, shaking hands with each of us. He, poor man, only had two questions, 'How long have you been in?' and 'What did you do before you joined up?' One of our chaps enlivened the proceedings (as the Duke made his doleful way round the hut) by telling him that he had been in 'the insurance racket'.

He noticed George Budd's DFC and asked George how many he had shot down to which George replied (in his best Auxiliary Air Force voice), 'Five, Sir'. The Duke inquired, 'What, all in one night!?' And I can remember George replying, in slightly mortified tones, 'No Sir, in my career'.

It is necessary to state that all George Budd's successes had been obtained whilst he was on No. 604 Squadron, based at Middle Wallop with George Evans as his AI operator, before they came to 1455 Flight.

In September all the Turbinlite flights were granted 'Squadron' status, and we suddenly became 534 Squadron but nothing else changed and the days of the Turbinlite Units were obviously coming to an end anyway.

As far as I can recall, no mention was made, during the Duke's visit, of the shooting down of the Stirling a few months earlier. Sadly, the poor lugubrious-looking Duke was himself due to die a few weeks later in the wreckage of a Sunderland flying boat on a Scottish hillside.

The other VIP was a 'bird of a different feather'. Marshal of the Royal Air Force Lord Trenchard – long known as 'Boom' Trenchard – came to the dispersal hut of the resident Beaufighter squadron on the southern part of the perimeter track, and we went across to join the Beaufighter crews. None of us had ever seen a Marshal of the Royal Air Force before and Trenchard was then an elderly man, recently retired after his stint with the Metropolitan Police Force, but now actively employed by the Air Board to go round the stations to talk to the aircrew and encourage them with short impromptu 'pep' talks.

I can still remember him today, and some of the things he said to us, he was terrific! He could really talk to aircrew people and we had a great regard for him. I recall him turning to the Squadron Commander and saying, 'He's the person you want to listen to now, I'm only an old man, you don't want to bother with me!' and there he was standing next to the wing commander who was twice decorated and he, Trenchard, had about seven rows of ribbons, to say nothing of the rings which went halfway up his sleeve! He encouraged us in flying the night defensive patrols and we all felt better for his visit as we returned to our unshapely Havocs.

Throughout 1942, on our many practice flights, we did not often land away from Tangmere, but I do remember taking an old Boston up to an aerodrome near Walsall in the Black Country for disposal. As we approached Birmingham we could navigate our way round it to Walsall by the pall of black smoke which hung over the city. There were no such things as smokeless zones in those days!

The runway at Walsall, like that at Hendon, was very short but this time we managed to avoid bursting the tyres and landed safely. Harry and I had to make the return journey by train via London, lugging our parachutes and flying kit with us. People were looking at us as if we had just crashed somewhere and it was an uncomfortable and tiring journey back to Tangmere.

The other trip away from home was more pleasant. We flew up to Upavon, on Salisbury Plain, to have lunch with my father and Wing Commander Donaldson (one of the famous Donaldson brothers who had served in the Air Force since the pre-war days, with great distinction). We lunched in style at Upavon and returned to Tangmere with the feeling that life was definitely looking up for White and Allen!

When I was on leave, at about this time, I experienced a gesture which (like the one I had had in Aberystwyth, when the old lady had paid for us in the milk bar) has stayed with me throughout my life. It concerned our dentist, Mr Greatrex, whose surgery was in Richmond. Although we had long since moved away from Twickenham, where my mother had first taken us to see him in 1933, I still tried to go and see him twice a year for a check-up, as the journey by car from Ashford was only five or six miles. Somehow I never quite fancied the RAF dentists at West Malling and Tangmere, although I had no good reason for steering clear of them.

So, once more, I found myself in the well-remembered surgery and chatting away to Mr Greatrex. When he had finished, and all was well with my molars, I said (as I always did): 'How much do I owe you?' I did not think it was fair to run up a bill in case, in a few weeks time, I was not around to pay it! His reply, and the warmth with which he said it, I can hear now: 'Michael, I treat the boys in the Air Training Corps "for free". How can I possibly charge you anything?', and, for the rest of the war, he never did.

In October it was, if I remember rightly, that Harry and I were sent on a week's rest course and stayed at a large country house, somewhere in Essex (or Hertford, was it?). The name of the place was Dudbrook House and it was owned by an elderly wing commander (whose wife was, I think, a radio personality of the day, residing under the stage name of Mrs Feather!). The house and grounds were at our disposal and I think there were about twenty other members of aircrew there besides ourselves, kicking their heels and playing games. Supposedly whilst we recovered after our strenuous tour of operations!

Harry and I didn't think much of Dudbrook House and as we hadn't 'done anything' as yet we didn't see why we had been sent there anyway! It was all very innocuous and probably did us no harm, but by the end of the week all of us had coined a rude name for the place, referring to it as Dudf**k House. Harry and I were glad to get back to Tangmere.

Shopwyke House had been made into a very comfortable officers' mess. A former preparatory school, to which use it was returned after the war, there were pleasant grounds surrounding the main building and even a small swimming pool. When the Americans arrived in the autumn, apart from playing poker-dice on the floor of the bar, they monopolised the swimming pool! One of their chaps was supposed to have swum the 'Golden Gates' and somebody laid a bet that he couldn't do 'umpteen' lengths of the tiny pool at Shopwyke. I recall seeing the pool surrounded by a crowd of the 'Yanks', yelling their heads off as their champion threshed his way up and down the pool – with their chaplain holding the stakes!

In our quarters, Harry and I experienced the services of a batman for the first time. We thought this was terrific but, when he started waking Harry up with an early morning cup of tea and the greeting, 'Good morning, Mr Allen!', Harry, who liked to sleep on a bit, did not take such a good view of our new acquisition! It was about this time that people started to get us muddled up and asking for me when they wanted Harry and vice versa!

Throughout the autumn and into the winter months the training went on and Harry and I continued with our 'apprenticeship' on 534 Squadron. As we learned our trade, our flying hours mounted slowly and by the end of November I had over 400 hours in my flying log-book, 142 of them at night.

All thoughts of trying to remuster to a pilot's course had disappeared. Indeed they had vanished from the moment I had crewed up with Harry in August of the previous year. As I have said at the beginning of this story, loyalties are quickly formed in the Services and are not easy to break. Soon after we flew together on 4 August 1941 such a loyalty was formed between us. We wanted to stay together as a crew, we wanted to prove ourselves and we wanted, above all, to shoot something down!

At Tangmere, during the period that Harry and I were there, from October '41 to December '42 there was a Hurricane squadron (No. 1 and later No. 43), a Beaufighter squadron (No. 219 and later 141), ourselves on 1455 Flight (later rechristened 534 Squadron) and another unit, of which so far, I have made no mention. This was No. 161, Special Duties Squadron, which was not actually based at Tangmere. Their home was at Tempsford, just to the north of Bedford, but a few of their aircraft used to arrive quietly at Tangmere at the beginning of each moon period. These were the Westland Lysanders flown by men like G/Capt. Charles Pickard, F/Lt Hugh Verity (with whom I had flown once on 29 Squadron) and F/O McCairns, but we never saw them.

When they came, they stayed away from Shopwyke House and the mess. They were lodged remote and away from the life of the station, at Tangmere Cottage, opposite the main gates of the camp. They were securely guarded and no one had access to them. When the moon was up Tangmere Cottage became the secret operations centre for 161 Squadron, and from there agents awaited transit to France by Lysander into German-occupied territory.

Charles Pickard, with an operational record second to none and later to lose his life in the Amiens raid (18 February 1944), and his pilots were the experts in the dropping and picking up of SOE (Special Operations Executive) and other agents; and the rescue of persons with qualities or information of value to the Allies.

They were also involved in dropping supplies to groups of Resistance workers pursuing their dangerous vocations throughout Western Europe. Sometimes, in the middle of the night, when we were cycling back round the perimeter track, after flying one of our innocuous defensive patrols up and down the coast, we would catch a glimpse of the outline of one of 161's Lysanders and maybe the shape of a large and mysterious-looking limousine. Dim figures could be spotted climbing in and out of the rear cockpit, whilst armed security guards formed a cordon allowing no access closer than 150 yards.

The Lysander pilots, in any case, never used either the perimeter tracks or the main runways. They took off and landed on the grass, somewhere, in front of the Watch Office. If we tarried for too long, one of the guards would materialise out of the dark and without too much ceremony order us to 'Move On!' It was exactly like something out of a James Bond film, long before one saw a James Bond film!

There was one spin-off as a result of 161's connection with Tangmere, in the shape of Flight Lieutenant McCairns DFC**, MM, as he became later in the war, before he too lost his life. One day all the aircrew from all three squadrons were called into the briefing room and were addressed by the Station Commander. Group Captain Appleton DSO, DFC took the stage and intro-duced an officer standing beside him, in a foreign-looking uniform.

This was the then Flight Sergeant McCairns MM, who on one of his oper-ations had become stranded in German-occupied territory, had evaded capture and had made a home run, for which he received a well-deserved Military Medal. McCairns was going round the various stations talking to aircrews about Escape and Evasion in the hope that, if we ourselves were unfortunate enough to be shot down over 'the other side', we might be able to profit by his experiences. He gave us one of the most marvellous talks I have ever heard, but first he explained why he was wearing the German uniform!

It was his practice – when going to a station where he was due to give one of his talks – to change into a uniform of the German *Luftwaffe*. He would march in through the main gates . . . present himself to the guardroom . . . state that he was a Polish or a Czech Officer, or perhaps another nationality amongst our Allies(!) on transfer to that station . . . and see how far he could get into the camp, past the security procedures and guards! Only the Station Commander was in on the plan and the date of his visit.

He told us how easily he had walked into Tangmere that morning and how – at most of the stations he visited – the story was the same. The lesson, for us, when he reversed the picture was that when evading capture in German-occupied territory, one could allow for similar laxity on the part of the enemy!

We sincerely hoped so, and his talk was an eye-opener for everyone. You could have heard the proverbial pin drop whilst he was speaking. This was particularly the case for those of us immured on 534 Squadron on our hum-drum and uneventful operations.

Some random entries in my log-book help to tell the story of our lives at Tangmere late in 1942:

16.11.42	17.35 hrs	Havoc E	P/O White N.F.T. A.I. Set as above but serviceable. Weather hazy.	00.40 min
16.11.42	20.05 hrs	E	P/O White BULLSEYE Took 1 Hurricane and got 2 Wimpeys and 1 Beau. All OK and weather better. .5 moon.	01.15 min
19.11.42	17.25 hrs	E	P/O White N.F.T. Weather duff again and we have now reached rock bottom as we have 1 kite only.	00.15 min
28.11.42	17.15 hrs	G	P/O White N.F.T.	00.30 min
28.11.42	20.20 hrs	G	P/O White Turbinlite Did 2 Runs. 1st OK 2nd 100 ft. below. A.I. V.G. Thin layer of cloud, very dark.	01.20 min
28.11.42	02.20 hrs	G	P/O White G.C.I. Did 2 successful Runs. All OK. Mother off colour. Weather now clear.	01.20 min
12.12.42	17.00 hrs	G	P/O White N.F.T. & A.I.	01.50 min
12.12.42	19.55 hrs	I	P/O White BULLSEYE 5 Interceptions and 4 Visuals of Wellington. Watery cloud. Visuals at 800 ft. H & S too high.	01.45 min

Then the last night trip with 534 Squadron!

| 22.12.42 | 23.20 hrs | E | P/O White G.C.I. 2 Interceptions on Beau and 2 Visuals at 4500 ft. Harry did a CATSEYE OK. Bags of joy. | 02.05 min |

But the days of the Turbinlite Units were now definitely numbered and rumours abounded that all the Turbinlite squadrons were to be disbanded at the end of the year and their crews posted to one or other of the night-fighter squadrons, some of which were being re-equipped with the de Havilland Mosquito.

Harry and I wanted to get back onto Beaufighters and try to pick up where we had left off on 29 Squadron in October '41, but this time without making so many mistakes.

I can't remember the Christmas of 1942 at Tangmere but I do remember the New Year! Many of the aircrew from the stations around Arundel were invited by the Duke of Norfolk to a New Year's Eve Party at Arundel Castle! It was a splendid party, with at least one Observer (Radio) toppling off the battlements and finishing up in the Royal Sussex Hospital in Chichester. Happily he soon recovered, to continue a distinguished career!

On 29 December 1942, I was attached to the Fighter Interception Unit at Ford, where I completed the Navigator Radio Leaders' course on 9 January. By the time I got back to Tangmere the Turbinlite squadrons were being disbanded and some of the crews of 534 Squadron had already been posted away. I found Harry waiting with bated breath to see if and when we would get a posting and, above all, where would we be sent after our prolonged apprenticeship.

The Turbinlites could finally be consigned to history because, for the second winter running, the German *Luftwaffe* had not resumed the nightly Blitzes of 1940/41: it was busy in Russia. The few raiders that had crossed the English coast had been intercepted, and many shot down, by the Beaufighter crews. There had been no need for the GCI Controllers to call in the clumsy flying circus of one of the Turbinlites on standing patrol. Admittedly, there had been one or two successes (apart from the Stirling got by 1455 Flight!), notably by Squadron Leader Charles Winn DFC and his AI operator, Flying Officer R.A.W. Scott (Scotty), flying from Hunsdon with No. 538 Squadron. But that was all . . . they were, in truth, long past their 'sell by' date.

I have not set out to denigrate these strange aircraft deliberately but I have sought to give the facts about a little-known operation which must have sounded better to its authors in 1940 than it does to us – with hindsight – over fifty years on.

But, for the moment it was only good news that Fighter Command had decided that the experiment of flying one aircraft around the night skies with radar to find the enemy and a searchlight to illuminate it, plus a second aircraft to shoot it down, was not a viable proposition.

So we on 534 Squadron were redundant and how delighted we all were! Hopes rose anew, for Harry and me, that we might be able to get back onto a Beaufighter squadron – and make a fresh start. We had now been in No. 11 Group, in the south-east corner of England where any fighter action was most likely to take place, for sixteen months and we had never even fired the guns on the air-to-ground firing range, let alone at the enemy! And so it was – with joy in our hearts – that we heard that we had been posted to 141 Squadron, which was based only a few miles to the east of Tangmere, at Ford close to the coast and due south of Arundel. We would be back where we had started sixteen months before with 29 Squadron at West Malling – still on Home Defence – but with a much better chance of catching the GCI Controller's eye, if and when enemy bombers entered our sector at night.

By the middle of January 1943 we had settled in with 141 which was commanded by Wing Commander J.R.D. 'Bob' Braham DSO, DFC & Bar, who had been a Flight Commander of 'B' Flight on 29 Squadron when we were at West Malling in the autumn of 1941. He and his AI operator, Flying Officer W. 'Sticks' Gregory DFC, DFM, had already made a name for themselves in the night-fighter world. Before the war ended, they were to become a legend.

Harry and I hoped that the CO would not remember *too* much about us and our various misdoings which had resulted in Guy Gibson booting us out after seven weeks! We were put into 'A' Flight and our Flight Commander was Squadron Leader Joy. On 20 January I flew with him so that he could show me their NFT procedure and to gain experience of a later version of the Mk IV AI set, the MK VII AI, which I had not seen before.

Harry and I flew nearly every day until the end of the month. He soon got used to the Beaufighter again and we carried out a number of practice interceptions. We flew two trips at night and got 'visuals' on our targets. Two entries in my log-book for 23 January tell their own story:

23.1.43	14.40 hrs	Beau 7848	F/O White N.F.T. All OK. 1 Freelance and Jinking. Weather wizard.	01.15 min
23.1.43	24.00 hrs		F/O White G.C.I. Four Runs and two Visuals on Beau. Perfect moonlight night. All OK.	2.45 hrs

This was a different ball-game from our incompetence at 29 Squadron when we were straight out of OTU and as green as they come. We were determined that there would be no repetition of the miserable events which had taken place at West Malling this time: White (now promoted to Flying Officer!) and Allen were going to make it!

We were looking forward to being made operational at an early date. Then the blow fell! At the beginning of February we were called into the Orderly Room to see the Squadron Adjutant, Flight Lieutenant 'Dickie' Sparrowe, to be told that we were to be attached to the Overseas Aircraft Delivery Unit (OADU) based at Lyneham in Wiltshire! Furthermore, we would be engaged indefinitely on ferrying new Bristol Beaufighters to the Middle East! Dickie Sparrowe said it was only an attachment and hopefully he would see us back on 141 one day . . .

Harry and I were completely shattered. We had been on 141 for less time than we had been on 29 Squadron. What had we done to deserve this? This attachment onto a non-operational 'stooge' job might last for months once they got their hands on us. We might never get back to 141 and never get onto any real ops. We left Ford for Lyneham with our spirits at an all-time low.

By 11 February we had picked up a brand-new Beaufighter from Bristol's factory at Filton and were flying it round the Irish Sea on a fuel consumption test. This lasted for 5.05 hrs and we then took it back into Lyneham, to prepare for our departure to the Mediterranean! Collecting the Beau from Filton was rather like buying a new car – without having to pay for it! At Lyneham we learned that we were going to fly Beaufighter V8646 out to Cairo as part of the reinforcement programme for the Beaufighter squadrons in the Middle East.

Our route out would start at Portreath on the North Cornish coast and then via Gibraltar; French North Africa; Libya (recently liberated by the 8th Army!); Cyrenaica and on to LG 224 at Cairo. We would probably be going in company with four or five other Beaus, although not in formation.

Apart from our disappointment at being whisked away from 141 so quickly, there was another worry on our minds (or should I say, on my mind, because I don't think it ever bothered Harry for one moment). There we were, faced with taking one of His Majesty's brand-new aeroplanes to a remote and foreign place that, hitherto, had only figured in my mind in stories like *Ali Baba and the Forty Thieves* and I had never done a navigation course!

It will be recalled that – on being transferred to AI Training in the summer of 1941 – I had gone straight to the 'School for Secrets', then to an Operational Training Unit and from there to 29 Squadron. I had not even finished the elementary navigation lectures being given at the ITW at Aberystwyth, such was the rush to train night-fighter crews!

I did not even know what an air plot was – let alone how to work one out! How to do that in the cramped rear quarters of a Beau over the hostile Bay of Biscay or the North African Desert (when our lives might depend on my navigation) made my blood run cold and it stayed that way! In the event, I spent two days in the navigation room at Lyneham learning how to work out an air plot, and then off we went to Cairo!

It was about this time that the reality of the war was brought home to me for the first time when I heard that Jimmy had been killed. Jimmy Tolkien had lived next door to us at Strawberry Hill in the early thirties, when we were both about ten years old. He had red hair, almost copper-coloured, and although we didn't go to the same prep schools, we became very close friends. He was an only child of rather retiring parents. We must have joined up at about the same time. We had left Strawberry Hill in 1936 and I had somewhat lost touch with him because I heard from him, in 1942, that he had got his wings and become a sergeant-pilot and envied him his good fortune. Late in the year I had heard he was in Carlisle doing an OTU course and spent part of one leave travelling up there to see him for a couple of days. That was the last time I ever saw him.

Later, he was posted out to the Middle East, where he joined a Hurricane squadron and was engaged on low-level ground-strafing operations, in support of the 8th Army, when he was lost. In due course 'MISSING' was replaced by 'KILLED IN ACTION'. It hurt horribly.

On my next leave (after I got the news that Jimmy was missing) I went back to Strawberry Hill. Back to 14 Waldegrave Gardens (we had lived in No. 12) to see his parents. They were in their little home when I called but I had one of the worst half-hours of my life.

I had always been vaguely aware that Jimmy's father had dabbled in spiritualism but I didn't really know anything about it. On the day that I walked in – I walked into the middle of a seance. Mr Tolkien was holding the seance, poor little Mrs Tolkien was beside him and terribly distressed. They were trying to get in touch with Jimmy. In other words, when poor old Jimmy went 'MISSING' they turned towards spiritualism in their distress, as a source of help, quite naturally and without thinking twice about it! Mr Tolkien was in effect already fully operational on this emotive and somewhat frightening activity. Frightening, that is, to most of us, but apparently not so for those who follow and practise this pursuit.

The curtains were tightly drawn and the atmosphere was what I, in my ignorance, always had imagined it would be, but I can remember little else before I fled from the room in terror, never to return.

I remember vividly Mr Tolkien, who was a kind and gentle man, saying to me 'Michael, Jimmy is flying in your aircraft with you, he will be watching over you . . .', and a few more things like that, before I somehow managed to quell my rising panic, got up out of my chair and with a few mumbled farewells, bolted from that awful room.

Outside once more, but with my nerves in shreds, I found that – for the first time in my life – I *had* to have a drink (I was 19) and I legged it for the nearest pub. I ordered a whisky, although I normally only drank beer in those days, and I may have had two! They nearly choked me but I felt more myself and then I left Strawberry Hill. I never saw either Mr or Mrs Tolkien again.

We left Lyneham on 19 February in V8646 and headed south-west for Portreath on the North Cornish Coast. At 08.05 hrs on the following morning we set off for Gibraltar. With a good met. forecast we passed over the Scillies and turned south across the Bay of Biscay for Cape Finisterre. My log-book reads:

> 'Hit Finisterre on the dot and then plain sailing i.e. flying down the Portuguese Coast, outside Territorial Waters and turning Left, when we got to the Mediterranean. All of us landed within 10 minutes of each other.'

Our flying time was 5.40 hrs.

We had a day in Gibraltar, feeling very important and cocky having made it and completing the first 1,000 miles of our journey to Cairo without any hitches. On the 22nd we took off from the strip at Gibraltar and set course for the French North African Coast and a place called Blida; I wrote as follows: 'Met. w/v – given to us at GIB – not so good. P.P. on Tenes, then saw Algiers before going in. What a BL**DER of a place.' Flying time 2.55 hrs.

In the afternoon we strolled around, trying to avoid the small urchins who were pestering anybody in the Services for cigarettes with the cry, 'No fumé – for Papa!' We had some sort of a meal at an awful café. I can only remember that the proprietor was a bit short of cutlery and produced a clasp knife out of his hip-pocket to make up the deficiency. He opened it, wiped it on his trousers and handed it to me with much ceremony. We did not stay in Blida for longer than one night and much to our relief we flew on the following morning.

We climbed up over the Atlas Mountains and, although our destination was the recently captured Italian airfield at Tripoli, we had to fly a 'dog-leg' out over the desert. This was to keep us and our new aeroplane clear of the fighting which was still going on, as the 1st and 8th Armies advanced to squeeze the Germans out of Africa.

Our route lay via Touggourt and Ghadames to Castel Benito, but I don't recall seeing either of these two places. The trip took us 4.55 hrs, but there is no mention in my log-book of the struggle I had with the sheaf of maps I had picked up at Gibraltar and my efforts to distinguish a second-class camel track from a first-class camel track as we cruised at 8,000 ft over the Sahara Desert . . . and thought perhaps we should have joined the French Foreign Legion with Beau Geste and his brothers rather than the RAF. I should mention, for the uniniti-ated, that a first-class camel track was shown on our maps with two dotted lines, whereas the other had only one dotted line. They looked fine on the map, but when I looked down from my cupola in the back of the Beau, I saw neither tracks nor camels!

Our main worry, as we flew on, was that we should not turn onto a north-east course for Tripoli too soon. If we were to do so, we would find ourselves in the Mareth Line with the possibility of an Me 109 obstructing our quiet little ferry trip to Cairo! If we left it too late to alter course for the Libyan coastline, we would have some doubt whether to turn to port – or to starboard – for Castel Benito.

As we headed for the mythical Ghadames which was our turning point we were feeling increasingly lost. Visions of finishing up at some remote outpost (perhaps Fort Zinderneuf?) started to fill my mind. A silence fell over the aircraft and the conversation between Harry and I over the intercom became somewhat strained. I thought we were lost and I knew that he knew that I thought we were lost!

Neither of us wanted to put it into words. To have done so would have only confirmed our worst fears!

It was about this time that Harry coined a phrase that was to stand us in good stead, on numerous occasions in the future, when things were going awry. We had fallen into the habit of addressing each other as 'Boy' and after a long and tense silence I heard his voice on the intercom saying, 'Look Boy, when there's nothing to say, *don't say it!*'

Our worst fears were not realised, and when we hit the Libyan coast we could pin-point our position on the map and turned port for Tripoli and the aerodrome at Castel Benito. It was a good airfield and we were put into comfortable quarters for the night. We saw the wreckage of German and Italian aircraft lying about everywhere and felt we were getting nearer to the war at last.

My log-book entry records that we took off at 08.20 hrs on the following day and headed east along 'the Desert Road' over which the 8th Army had fought its way westwards only a few weeks earlier. The 'Remarks' column shows: 'Hedged-hopped down the road. Most interesting part of the trip and three cheers for the 8th Army.'

We landed at Marble Arch after 1.40 hrs in the air, that monstrosity, built by Mussolini, in the middle of nowhere. It was supposed to be the triumphal arch through which he would ride – on a white horse – *en route* for his conquest of Egypt!

Marble Arch was a staging post between Tripoli and Cairo, an outpost in the desert. We refuelled and, anxious to be on our way, we took off after only 1½ hours on the ground. The next entry picks up the story: 'Lost an air filter taking off so had to start again, both praying hard so on to Alex and Cairo.'

The special air filters were vital for flying over the desert, where there was always the danger of sand being sucked into the engines – with the obvious disastrous results. When we lost one on take-off we had visions of being stuck indefinitely at Marble Arch.

Harry had taken a picture of Marble Arch as we approached it at low level and he did the same as we flew towards the Pyramids. I still have these photos and I remember how we looked down and marvelled at the sudden break in the line of the desert, as it meets the green of the land immediately bordering the banks of the Nile. We landed at LG 224 (Cairo West) after 4.05 hrs flying, and immediately found we had another short hop to make to 108 Maintenance Unit on the Faiyum Road – where we would finally take our leave of Beau V8646, according to my log-book: '. . . looking a little battered, especially round the port air filter. Then to El Amaza and the S.S. Egypt'.

Our first ferry trip had taken us five days (18.10 hrs' flying time) and we had safely delivered our new Beaufighter to its destination. But what did the reference to El Amaza and the SS *Egypt* mean? Thereby hangs a tale that does not appear in my log-book.

When we and the other crews had handed over our Beaus at 108 MU we were conveyed, in the back of a truck, to our lodgings for our first night in Cairo. There was Joe Cooper and Ralph Connolly, 'Hutch', Johnny, 'Dunc', two or three others and Harry and myself. Our destination was a camp sited in the desert a few miles out of Cairo and it was called El Amaza (my father landed there in 1936). Once there we were allocated some tents and little else. To say that we were appalled is to put it mildly, as we appeared to be stuck there until our return flight to England, when we would be required to fetch out more aircraft to the Middle East.

There was sand everywhere and we spent a most uncomfortable night, not only physically, but also mentally, worrying about how we were going to get ourselves out of El Amaza. There was worse to follow in the morning! As Harry and I peered out round the flap in our tent we saw – the time was only about 07.00 hrs – a column of Air Force personnel being marched up and down, with the dust and the sand swirling about them. Worse still, when we looked, we saw that they were all aircrew, they all had a flying badge! We heard later that they were surplus pilots, navigators, air gunners, etc. who were awaiting postings up to the squadrons in the desert. In the meantime they were being held in this infamous transit camp and drilled by non-flying NCOs.

By nightfall on the same day we, the newly arrived ferry crews, were all ensconced on one of Thomas Cook's houseboats, moored on the Nile, to the south of Cairo near the Abasse Bridge . . . and living in the lap of luxury. The boat was called the SS *Egypt* and the scene was straight out of Agatha Christie's *Death on the Nile.*

This radical change in our fortunes was solely due to guile and the personality of one 'Joe' Cooper. Harry and I were to meet up with him later on, when he and his navigator, Ralph Connolly, joined 169 Squadron for the Bomber Support operations: the same Ralph that I had met as far back as the RW at Stratford-upon-Avon in 1941. But Joe was never to be of such vital interest to our well-being as he was that day at El Amaza.

Joe was quite a bit older than most of us. He was a good pilot and very much the man about town. Most important of all, Joe was a Squadron Leader. He would forgive me for saying so, but Joe had also got something else – he had style. He reminded me of 'the Saint', that suave good-looking gentleman adventurer, with something borrowed from Robin Hood. Apart from a Ronald Coleman moustache on his upper lip, Joe *was* the Saint. I am as grateful to Leslie Charteris for his famous character as all of us were to Joe Cooper that day.

Joe was not used to the cavalier treatment that had been meted out to us after we landed at 108 MU. He was not used to it at all. After a miserable breakfast in a large tent Joe muttered something under his breath and disappeared. Shortly afterwards he reappeared with a light truck and a driver and said to the rest of us, 'Get your things together – we're leaving here – and make it sharp!'

We set off in fine style but with no idea where Joe was taking us. I then heard him order the driver to take him to GHQ, and we drove straight into the centre of Cairo. Once there, I saw Joe brush his way past the sentries and disappear into the building which seemed to be teeming with high-ranking staff officers entering and leaving. After about half an hour Joe emerged from General Headquarters, looked into the truck and said, 'It's all fixed up, chaps, there's been a mistake. We weren't meant to be at El Amaza at all. We're off now to one of Cook's houseboats, where we shall be for the rest of the time we're in Cairo!'

So off we drove back through the city to where the SS *Egypt* was moored on the Nile. As we stopped by the gangplank servants ran forward to take our kit and we were shown to our cabins as if we had been guests arriving for a million-aire's cruise down the Nile to the tombs at Luxor. As we had driven out of El Amaza we saw, looking back, the dusty columns of aircrew marching up and down outside the sea of tents but, for us at least, our worries were at an end and we settled down to enjoy ourselves. Only the thought of our return flight to England in the bomb-bay of a Liberator, in a few days' time, gave us any qualms.

To this day I don't know how Joe managed to commandeer the truck and the driver, let alone how he fixed it for us to be billeted on board one of Thomas Cook's magnificent houseboats, with a full peacetime crew to look after our smallest wants, but that was Joe Cooper.

It was 5 March when, after seeing the sights of Cairo and having our young eyes opened at places like 'The Bardia' and other night-spots, we were picked up from our comfortable home on the SS *Egypt* and were on our way back to England. Not before some of the others, under Harry's guidance, had held me upside-down over the rail and threatened to drop me into the river. I remember that my chief concern was that if you went into the Nile, you would need about twenty-odd inoculations to counter the hundreds of germs living in the river!

I have diverted, where were we? We were being picked up by bus and then taken back to LG 224 (Cairo West) for the return journey to the UK. When we got to the aerodrome about twenty-four of us, all pilots or navigators, climbed aboard Liberator AL616 for the night flight to Gibraltar. There was no seating, but the bomb-racks had been removed and there we settled down, wrapped in Irvin jackets to keep warm. We were laid out in the bomb-bay, twelve either side and packed in like sardines. We were ready for our 11½ hour flight to Gib. and it was 22.10 hrs when we took off and left the lights of Cairo behind us.

The Eastern Mediterranean around Sicily and Malta was still hostile so most of the route west towards Gibraltar had to be covered before daybreak. An unarmed Liberator in those areas, in daylight, would have provided the *Luftwaffe* with a tasty morsel and a rich dividend in the consequent loss of thirty aircrew. The pilot of the Lib. was a Czech, whom Harry had known at Church Fenton, then a sergeant pilot, now a flight lieutenant. Prchyl was one of a courageous band of Polish and Czech pilots who had escaped from Eastern Europe when the Germans overran their countries, made their way to England and joined the Royal Air Force. Many of them were experienced pilots, with hundreds of flying hours to their credit.

Nevertheless, as we heard the engines open up and felt the aircraft starting to move along the runway, there were none of us in the bomb-bay who did not look surreptitiously at our watches to count the seconds until the heavily laden Lib. started to come unstuck and lifted off the ground. I had a specially long look at my watch. It was a new one, bought in Cairo – shockproof, sandproof and waterproof, with a flashy white strap. I was inordinately proud of it! But, as we shall see a little later on, pride always comes before a fall.

We slept fitfully for most of the way, but awoke as daylight came into the few small windows in the rear of the aircraft. We had been already about eight hours in the air. After several more hours and some scratch rations for breakfast, the time came when we calculated that we should be starting to lose height for our landing at Gibraltar. But still the Lib. droned on in a westerly direction . . . and droned on. Holed up in the bomb-bay, we were getting restless. Then much to our surprise and concern we felt the Lib. turning, and it kept on. By the time it straightened up, we could tell by the sun that we were on a reciprocal course and heading back east!

We eventually landed safely at Gibraltar, two hours overdue after 13 hours 20 minutes in the air. We were not amused. The explanation? Prchyl had had a new 2nd Navigator on board, who had made a mistake in his calculations. We had overshot Gibraltar on our westerly course, and by the time the crew realised that something was wrong the Lib. was about 200 miles out over the Atlantic and heading for America! In the 'Remarks' column of my log-book: 'Packed like sardines in the bomb-bay. Pilot wizard. Navigator b***** awful.'

We had a day in Gibraltar – some of it spent at the Bristol Hotel – then back to the Lib. for another night take-off. This time it was off the strip that is like a large aircraft-carrier, i.e. with the sea at both ends! Algeciras Bay to the west and the Mediterranean to the east. Once more the twenty-four watches in the bomb-bay were carefully consulted as Prchyl opened the throttles as we lumbered along the runway and up into the night *en route* for England. Although the met. report at Gibraltar was bad, we 'found England bathed in sunshine, much to our relief'. The flight, this time, was uneventful and we landed at Lyneham after being 8.15 hrs in the air. Our first ferry trip was safely over.'

There is a sad postscript to add to the story of our return flight. A few months later Flight Lieutenant Prchyl was again taking off from the strip at Gibraltar that had got us – in the bomb-bay – so worried. This time he had General Sikorski, Chief of the Polish Armed Forces, and some of his staff on board. The Liberator just cleared the end of the strip before crashing into the sea. The General and almost all of those on board were killed and only Prchyl and one or two others managed to scramble out of the front hatch before the aircraft went under. It was a sad loss for the Allied cause.

On 19 March, after a few days' leave, we went back to Bristol's and picked up another new Beau. This time it was V8703. A WAAF driver had taken us over from Lyneham and done her best to kill us on the way. There were the two Canadians, 'Dunc' and 'Dalt', Harry and I and another crew, crowded into the back of a small pick-up truck.

I got the idea that she was trying to show off and she was certainly driving much too fast. We were going along a fairly narrow country road, somewhere in the vicinity of Colerne, when she spotted some orange cones in the middle of the road. I also saw that there was a workman painting in new white lines in the centre of it. The WAAF, now fully into her stride, started to zig-zag between the cones (she would show these aircrew people a thing or two!). The road-mender saw her coming and leapt for the hedge on our offside.

Unfortunately, he chose the wrong way to jump for safety, and her zig-zag to the right missed him by a whisker. Years later, when I think about it, I still don't know how she missed him. We were glad to get to Filton in one piece and it was the only time I ever felt like putting someone on a charge.

On 20 March, Harry and I tried to kill ourselves! We went off from Lyneham on the usual 'consumption test' which was mandatory for all new aircraft. We flew the same course up to the Wirral, out over the Irish Sea and back over Cumbria, the Midlands and return to base, just south of Swindon. We got lost on the second half of the route – over Cumbria!

The weather was not good and there was a lot of thick cloud about. We foolishly let down to see where we were, thinking we were still over the Irish Sea. I got my first view of the Lake District when we dropped out of the bottom of the cloud and saw Great Gable only a few hundred feet below us! The view did not last long as Harry pulled the stick back and we soared up into the cloud again, two very chastened flying officers.

On 22 March we left Lyneham for Portreath and our second ferrying trip. My log-book entry, 'The two stooges off again', sums up our mood. Things followed much the same pattern as on our initial trip. Except that we were held up at the start by bad weather. Portreath became crowded with an accumulation of aircraft and crews waiting for a break in the weather. Much to our annoyance, we had to move out and fly back up the Cornish coast to a small aerodrome by the name of St Mawgan. It is said that 'it is an ill wind that blows nobody any good', and so it proved at St Mawgan.

When Harry and I landed there on 26 March they had not seen an aeroplane for months; unless you count a few target-towing aircraft! When we let down in our brand-new Beau the Station Commander came out in his car to meet us! They then proceeded to lay out the red carpet and to make our enforced stay as comfortable as possible.

The officers' mess was a dream: it was a farmhouse with the cows and chickens still fully operational. There was fresh milk and eggs every day, chicken in every conceivable form – and no work to do! On the station, both officers and airmen were living the life of Riley with every indication that the Air Force had forgotten their existence and, with luck, they would see the war out in comfort and without interruptions!

After two days of bliss, the weather over the Bay of Biscay cleared up and the logjam of aircraft at Portreath started to move. We were summoned back and left for Gibraltar on 29 March. At St Mawgan they were sorry to see the Beaufighter crews leave: for all I know, they may still be there!

I have omitted to mention that on our way down to Portreath I had been map-reading, full of confidence after our first trip to Cairo, and announced our arrival over Portreath. When we had landed and taxied up to the Watch Office, I got out only to learn that we had landed at the wrong aerodrome, it was some dump called Perranporth! I clambered back hurriedly and we took to the air again for the five-minute hop to Portreath. The gentleman in the front cockpit was not at all pleased.

However, worse was to come, at Gibraltar, when we came to hand in the maps which we had used on the flight out from England. When handing them in, the navigators were supposed to draw a fresh set of maps to cover the route on to Cairo. When we were in the air and heading for Blida on 30 March (the flight out from Portreath had gone well on the previous day), I opened up my green navigation bag to look for the map of the North African coast, only to find that I still had all the maps covering the route from the UK to Gibraltar and none of those for the route to Cairo. Inadvertently I had muddled up the two sets of maps at Gibraltar.

Try as I would, all I could find in my beautiful navigation bag was an Admiralty chart of the Mediterranean which told us how deep the sea was – in fathoms. This useful bit of information for mariners was just about the last thing Harry and I wished to know!

At Marble Arch, where we stayed overnight, I managed to break some of the furniture in our tent and on the way home I got a dose of 'gippy tummy' in Gibraltar. All that I can remember of that awful day – by then it was 24 April – is that I spent it on my back in our room at the Bristol Hotel, whilst Harry and the others went on a visit to an aircraft-carrier (I think it was HMS *Implacable*) which was in the harbour. There was one other thing. I recall that, as I staggered out of my room down the corridor to the lavatory, my eyes were riveted on the small panel set in the door. If the sign said *Libre* I was OK but if it was turned to *Occupé*, then I was in dead trouble.

When we were hanging about in Cairo for three weeks, after delivering our second Beau there on All Fools' Day, Harry and I tried to get a posting to Malta as there was a night-fighter squadron there, but nothing came of it. Then there was a rumour that we were going to be split up and I was to be sent off permanently to some ferry unit, equipped with very ancient aircraft. When we got back to the UK Harry did a delivery flight to Rabat with another navigator.

It was not a good time for White and Allen and our chances of ever returning to 141 Squadron seemed to be slipping further and further away . . .

We only did the two trips to Cairo. After we arrived back at Lyneham on 27 April I was not airborne again until 12 June. I don't know what happened to May, because there are no entries in my log-book for the whole of the month. It was during that period that Harry was sent off to Rabat, in Morocco, to deliver a Beau X, equipped for Coastal Command work and anti-shipping strikes and with another navigator.

All my old fears about us being split up one day returned with a vengeance. With them came the thought of becoming a spare navigator without a pilot and at the beck and call of any pilot, according to the whim of one's CO. Heaven knows, there was no particular reason why White and Allen should be kept together as a night-fighter crew. By May 1943 they had been flying as a team for nearly two years and there was precious little to show for it on the credit side. Their sum total was forty-five innocuous standing patrols on Home Defence and a couple of Beaus delivered to the Middle East. On the other hand, there was quite a lot on the debit side of their personal balance sheet with His Majesty King George VI. The 'red ink' entries were:

Machine		Value
1 Airspeed Oxford	Destroyed	(shared) £7,500
1 Bristol Blenheim	Destroyed	£10,000
1 Miles Magister	Damaged	£2,000
1 Bristol Beaufighter	Destroyed	£10,000
Total		£29,500

Plus! Compromising the secret colours of the night by discussing them over the intercom with their VHF transmitter left switched ON, whilst flying over the English Channel in October 1941 within range of the German monitoring posts in northern France. Damage to the Allied cause? Cost incalculable!

The only thing which is surprising, on reflection, is that HM auditors of such matters had not consigned White and Allen to the penal service battalions months before . . .

So what, if anything, had Harry and I learned from our brief excursions overseas? We'd seen a bit of the world. Not much, but a bit. On our second trip we had got stuck in Cairo for three weeks before we could get on a flight back to the UK, so we had visited the Pyramids and went inside the Blue Mosque but, in truth, we had spent most of the time at the Gezira Sporting Club, swimming and lazing about round the pool – it was a great life!

We had learned that we could get around with a minimum of navigational skills but this had been in daylight and might only have given us a false sense of security. We had no idea that we would shortly be asked to wander about over Germany in the dark and that they would not be ferry trips! Like others, we had returned home suitably laden with watches and silk stockings – plentiful in Cairo, absent from the scene in wartime England. The latter were for our girlfriends or mothers, and Harry and I only purchased a modest few pairs. But I do remember one of our party, a potential entrepreneur, filling an enormous bag, the contents of which were clearly not destined for his nearest and dearest. I am sure he did well in civvy street!

There was one pleasant social call that we made whilst we were in Cairo and that was to see the Curator of the British Museum, Dr (or was it Professor?) Engelbach. One of the great characters on 141 Squadron was a chap called 'Paddy' Engelbach. 'Angels' (as we always knew him) had been up at Oxford before the war and compared with the rest of us he was 'educated'! When Angels heard that we were going out to Cairo he said, 'That's where my father lives, you must go and see him!' Harry and I politely inquired what his father did in Cairo and how we might find him. To which Angels replied, 'Oh! He's the Curator of the British Museum and his job is to keep the mummies warm!' We were glad to be able to give Dr Engelbach first-hand news of his son, whom, if I remember rightly, he had not seen since the outbreak of war.

4 Operation 'Serrate'
– night-fighter versus night-fighter

My log-book is a complete blank for the month of May (as I have said), but there is an entry for Saturday 12 June that tells us that Harry and I flew Beaufighter V8900 from Filton to Lyneham and that can only mean that we were about to set off on our third ferry trip to the Middle East. Three days later, on the 15th, we were manning another Beau and flying from Wittering, an aerodrome near Peterborough, to Drem just South of Edinburgh. Once more there had been a change in our fortunes and luck, fate, chance, or call it what you will, had taken a hand in our affairs. This time there were some trumps in our hands, if only we could grasp them.

Over that weekend we got a telegram to report back to 141 Squadron. By Tuesday 15 June we were at Wittering and by 18.00 hrs we were in the air, heading for Scotland. One hour forty minutes later we landed at Drem.

Whilst we had been away from 141 – it was four months since we had left Ford so precipitously for our attachment to the Overseas Delivery Unit at Lyneham – the squadron had not been idle. They had moved twice, first to Predannack in Cornwall and then, more recently, to Wittering. Although still in Fighter Command, they had been taken off Home Defence and the standing night patrols along the South Coast as the number of enemy raids had continued to diminish during the winter of 1942/43.

At Predannack, they had been put onto 'Night Ranger' ops over Brittany and SW France. Also, by day, 'Instep' patrols over Biscay and the Western Approaches, to attack enemy shipping whenever and wherever they could find it! They had gone over to the offensive and Harry and I had missed out on all of it, whilst languishing by the pool at the Gezira Sporting Club. Now, with the move to Wittering, they had been chosen to pioneer a new and top secret Intruder operation over Germany and Occupied Europe, using a device called 'Serrate'.

Most of the crews had already been through a week's training at Drem and returned to Wittering to commence the Serrate operation by the time we got there . . . we had to catch them up!

Here, belatedly, something must be said about the man who had brought about this startling change in the squadron's fortunes. The Commanding Officer, Wing Commander J.R.D. 'Bob' Braham DSO, DFC & Bar – whom Harry and I had first seen when he was a Flight Commander on No. 29 Squadron – had taken over 141 late in 1942. One of the youngest officers in the Air Force to hold that rank, he was barely 23(!), he had already made a name for himself during 1941/42 as a brilliant night-fighter pilot.

Together with his AI operator, Flying Officer W.J. 'Sticks' Gregory DFC, DFM, they had destroyed a number of enemy aircraft, with others 'probably destroyed' or 'damaged'. They were an exceptional crew in every way. Before the end of the war, Bob Braham had flown over 300 operational sorties against the enemy and his claims totalled 29 German aircraft destroyed.

He was ultimately shot down in June 1944 when flying on a 'Day Ranger' over Northern Germany. He effected a crash landing on the Danish coast, and both he and his navigator (thankfully, not 'Sticks') survived to become prisoners-of-war for the final year of the European struggle. He was the only man ever to be awarded three DSOs and three DFCs, a unique collection of decorations which is, by the nature of things, unlikely ever to be rivalled. A number of senior RAF officers, who are more well versed in such matters than I am, have expressed the view that Wing Commander Braham should have been awarded the Victoria Cross.

On the day that Harry White and I returned to 141, 15 June, our Squadron Historian recorded the award to W/Cdr Braham of a Second Bar to his Distinguished Flying Cross; and quotes from the official citation:

> 'This officer is a fearless and determined leader, whose impressive qualities have inspired the Squadron he commands. Wing Commander Braham has destroyed 13 enemy aircraft, whilst his most recent achievements include a damaging attack on a U boat and another attack on a motor torpedo-boat which was set on fire. His fine fighting spirit and keenness have set a praise-worthy example.'

'Johnny' Johnson, the legendary day-fighter pilot, has said, of Braham, in one of his books, 'He was one of the finest fighter pilots ever to strap an aircraft on his back!', and 'J.J.' ought to know.

Bob Braham's name has figured in countless publications since the end of the war, but today, in so far as the general public are concerned, he is virtually unknown. To those of us who served under him and who flew with him, and others who were in the night-fighter world of the Second World War, plus a handful of military historians and researchers, his legend will live on.

His story was published in a book entitled *Scramble* in 1961, but it does not begin to do justice to his incomparable record. Sadly, he himself died in his early fifties, in Canada, where he emigrated with his family after the war. There is an unpublished biography of Group Captain Braham (as he became) researched and compiled by the devoted 141 Squadron Historian, and thankfully, a copy may be found in the archives of the Royal Air Force Museum at Hendon. Perhaps one day due recognition may be accorded to the finest night-fighter pilot this country has ever seen.

These few lines must serve, for the moment, as an introduction to the Commanding Officer of 141 (Special Duties) Squadron, as we were now labelled. He had been singled out from amongst all the leading night-fighter pilots in Fighter Command to pioneer the new High-Level Intruder operations in support of the increasingly heavy raids being mounted on Germany by Bomber Command. He was to lead the single squadron of Beaufighters allocated to Operation 'Serrate' in May 1943.

Harry and I travelled up from London by train to Stamford, where we were picked up by station transport and driven the three miles to Wittering and past the beautiful grounds of Burghley House which lie just to the north of the aerodrome on the old Great North Road. We reported to the Squadron Adjutant that we were back and 'Dickie' Sparrowe asked us briefly about our ferrying trips to Cairo. We in turn made it clear to him how glad we were to be rejoining the squadron when, only three days before, we had been about to set off on our third delivery flight.

The elderly flight lieutenant then sat back in his chair and uttered some prophetic words which I have never forgotten. He knew aircrew well and he knew how disappointed we had been when we were attached to the Ferry Unit and sent off to Lyneham after only nine days on the squadron. He said quietly, 'Well, I think you two have fallen on your feet this time', and then he started to outline the new operations to be undertaken in support of the heavy bombers of Bomber Command.

The first Serrate operations had actually commenced the previous night, when five Beaufighters had taken off in support of a raid on Oberhausen in the Ruhr and W/Cdr Braham had claimed the squadron's first success over the other side destroying a Messerschmitt 110, which crashed in flames eight miles north of Staveren in Holland. Dickie told us that the essence of Operation 'Serrate' was that 141 would be flying freelance High-Level Intruder sorties, over Germany and Occupied Europe to try and find and destroy the German night-fighters who were themselves trying to find and destroy the Lancasters, Halifaxes, Stirlings and Wellingtons of Bomber Command.

There were different tactics to be learned. Sometimes we would be flying near to the bomber stream, sometimes over the target area, sometimes with a spoof raid attempting to draw the German Home Defence *Staffeln* away from the main target, etc. For the immediate future, Dickie told us, we must get up to Drem and complete the special training necessary on Serrate interceptions as quickly as possible. Then, all being well, within a few days of returning to Wittering we would become operational and have the opportunity of putting our years of training into practice. That night we were on our way to Drem, feeling that strange mixture of elation, anticipation and fear that comes before the start of all worthwhile human activities . . .

Before we take the story on – and to appreciate the work on which we in 141 were to be engaged – we must go back to the autumn of 1942 to find the origins of Operation 'Serrate'. It is a good story and perhaps, one day, someone will make a film about it – and dedicate it to the memory of Wing Commander 'Bob' Braham.

To resume with the story of Serrate and its origins: Don Aris wrote in his history of 141 Squadron;

'In order to counter the ever increasing losses of Bomber Command from mid 1942 onwards, caused mainly by enemy night-fighters, a wide and complex range of measures were investigated and many implemented.

Some of these were; the streaming of the bomber force and concentrating aircraft in a shorter period over the target area to swamp the defences; indirect routes to and from targets; increased electronic intelligence; radio counter measures, both air & ground, to jam the enemy's defences; spoof raids to divert enemy night-fighters; the dropping of "Window", strips of metalized foil, from the night of 24th/25th July 1943, to confuse ground and air radars; light bombers to attack enemy night-fighter airfields; low-level night-fighters, without A.I. radar, to patrol those airfields at night; high-level bomber support by A.I. radar-equipped night-fighters. Synthetic oil plants and aircraft manufacturing factories were increasingly targeted by the bombers to try to reduce the number of enemy aircraft and the fuel to fly them.'

In October 1942, the C-in-C Bomber Command, ACM Sir Arthur Harris, had suggested to the C-in-C Fighter Command, that Mosquito night-fighters be mixed in with the bomber stream. At that time Fighter Command was against this, as the Home Defence night-fighter squadrons had been reduced, many being sent overseas. Mosquitoes, in short supply and great demand, were needed for any renewed attacks on this country and there was the fear that the AI radar equipment would fall into enemy hands if operated over enemy territory. There was also the problem of telling friendly bombers from enemy fighters at night.

Don Aris continues:

'Early in 1943 the Telecommunications Research Establishment at Malvern developed a receiver or homer which would pick up the impulses from the German night-fighter's A.I. radar, this was code named Serrate [see Appendix 1B] due to the display looking like a serrated herring bone. Serrate indicated direction at ranges up to 80/100 miles, however, it did not indicate the exact range of the target . . . and for this the A.I. radar was needed. The Serrate signal would also indicate that the target was an enemy.

In the Spring of 1943 a decision was made to allow the use of the old and, by now, superseded Mk IV A.I. radar over enemy territory. One Squadron, No.141, then in Fighter Command, was chosen to carry out the first high-level bomber support operations over enemy territory using Beaufighter Mk VIs equipped with the new Serrate homer, Mk IV A.I. radar and Gee navigation equipment.'

So we see that the concept of Operation 'Serrate' came about due to the growing threat posed by the German Home Defence *Nachtjagdgeschwadern* to our heavy bombers. Our opposite numbers! Throughout the winter of 1942/43 the weight of bombs dropped on Germany and Occupied Europe increased, as the raids over England decreased. The work of the defending Junkers 88s and Messerschmitt 110s increased as the 'trade' for the Home Defence Beaufighters and Mosquitoes decreased. The key to the new operation lay in the Serrate homer.

This was an additional 'black box' with which the Beaufighters of 141 were to be equipped. As Don has said, this new receiver would enable the AI operators, seated in the back of the intruding Beaus, to pick up a serrated herring-bone signal on their cathode-ray tubes when in the vicinity of the emissions from the German *Lichtenstein* AI radar. The Serrate homer was developed by TRE at Malvern by the 'boffins', the British scientists who matched up the frequency of the Serrate receiver with the frequency used by the Germans for their *Lichtenstein* FuG 202, FuG 212 and FuG 220 AI radars.

Thus when the 141 AI operators switched over from their Mk IV receiver they could see on the same cathode-ray tubes the azimuth and elevation time-traces which, if a *Lichtenstein* AI was transmitting within their range, would be covered by a pulsating, yet quite distinct, herring-bone pattern. To our greater advantage there was no ground-return interference!

With these long-range signals we could guide our pilots to within the lesser range of the Mk IV AI, then, switching back to the normal Mk IV display, pick up the contact at maximum range to complete the interception to give the pilot a visual. What is more, the identification was made that much easier for the pilot, who could be 99.99% certain that the target was a German aircraft and not a British bomber, bearing in mind that the bomber support fighters would be operating in close promixity to several hundred friendly bombers. Remembering the story of how the Stirling was shot down by one of our Hurricanes from Tangmere, this was the priceless bonus provided by the Serrate 'black box'. (See Appendix 1B.)

In October 1942 when the first discussions were taking place between the Chiefs of Bomber and Fighter Command, the frequency which the Germans were using for their *Lichtenstein* AI radar was not known to the British scientists. It would be remiss to proceed with the account of the Serrate operations without filling in an essential gap in the story. Prior to 3 December 1942 the scientists did not know the frequency of the *Lichtenstein* AI radar. *After* 3 December, they did know it. How did this information, vital to the whole concept, come into their hands?

On 6 January 1943, a citation was presented by the Air Minister, Sir Archibald Sinclair, to His Majesty the King. The awards were for three of the six crew members of Wellington Mk Ic DV819 'DT-G' built at the Vickers factory at Chester. The aircraft, which made its own contribution to the events which took place on the night of 2/3 December, had served on Nos 57 and 109 Squadrons before being transferred to the strength of No. 1474 Flight.

The only sure way to find out the frequency of the emissions from the transmitter aerials in the noses of the German AI night-fighters was to take a radio set, with a wide frequency band, put it in front of a Junkers 88 (or a Messerschmitt 110!) and ask the radio operator to tune . . . and retune . . . and retune again, until he had found the *Lichtenstein*'s signals and identified them as coming *from* the German night-fighter! This is what the crew of the Wellington were asked to do.

Pilot Officer Edwin Poulton, the pilot, took off with Pilot Officer Harold Jordan as the Special Radio Operator, Flight Sergeant William Bigoray and the other three members of his crew. They flew out in the bomber stream as if they were taking part in one of the many raids on Germany at that time. Their mission was to make sure that they were intercepted by an enemy fighter! They did so. Pilot Officer Jordan found the frequency of the *Lichtenstein*'s transmissions . . . they returned home . . . and the necessary information was duly passed on to the scientists at TRE in Malvern. We know the rest of the story. But do we?

Before Pilot Officer Jordan, a schoolmaster in civilian life, could be sure that he had all the information that the scientists needed to develop the Serrate homer, the Wellington was subjected to 10 or 12 attacks by the Junkers 88 which had obligingly taken their bait. Four of the crew were wounded and the aircraft was severely damaged.

They crash-landed on Walmer Beach on the morning of 3 December. An attempt was made to recover the Wellington, but the damage which it had sustained was altogether too severe and the aircraft was written off Category E. 'DT-G' had done its duty and Operation 'Serrate' was on!

If ever there was a suicide mission, this was it. The award of medals is never easy and it can never be done completely fairly, but it is hard to understand why all six members of this gallant crew did not receive some recognition.

And so the High-Level Bomber Support operations commenced in June 1943 and continued, with many variations, until the end of the war in Europe, in May 1945. Harry and I were fortunate enough to be involved, first in Fighter Command and later in Bomber Command, in this, the most satisfying of night-fighter operations, throughout the whole of these two years. From now on it would be a case of dog eat dog or night-fighter v. night-fighter! Up to this point, dog-fighting had been a strictly day-time occupation.

For us, personally, the period from June 1943 to May 1945 was to change our lives significantly and afterwards things would never be quite the same again. The intangible element of luck was never far away and 'the slings and arrows of outrageous fortune' were part and parcel of our lives, often in our favour, sometimes not!

It will be recalled that on 15 June, the day after our return to 141, we were on our way to Scotland for a week's training on the art of using the Serrate homer for freelance interceptions. Drem was located a few miles east of Edinburgh and we spent only two days flying with, and intercepting, a Beaufighter fitted with a radar transmitter emitting pulses on the same frequency as the *Lichtenstein* AI used in the German night-fighters.

Drem had been chosen because it was thought to be located beyond the range of the German monitoring units sited 450 miles away in northern France. Those same units who had picked up our unscheduled VHF transmissions of the secret colours of the night (when on 29 Squadron in 1941) would have been delighted to intercept British transmissions on the same frequency as their AI!

Harry and I flew three times on Wednesday and four times on the Thursday. Each time, in the 'Duty' column of my log-book I entered simply 'Ex.', which was short for 'Exercise 15'. This operation really was TOP SECRET. Our time in the air, spent somewhere over the North Sea and off the east coast of Scotland, was solely occupied in getting in as many practice interceptions as possible on the target aircraft, using the Serrate homer initially and closing to visual range on the Mk IV AI. More detailed descriptions of AI Mk IV and Serrate are at Appendices 1A and 1B.

I found that I could pick up the herring-bone pattern of the mock Serrate signals when the target was fifty to sixty miles away. Harry and I were most impressed. For the last flight on the Thursday I went up with Squadron Leader Esplin, CO of the special Training Unit, for a test. I must have passed because on the Friday Harry and I were on our way back to Wittering! We had seen nothing of Drem, 'Auld Reekie' or anywhere else in Scotland: that would have to wait till 50 years later!

I remember the flight back because from the time we took off at 11.05 hrs and climbed up into the 10/10ths cloud lying across Scotland, until a few minutes before we landed at Wittering (300+ miles to the south), we never saw the ground again. We were able to travel almost the length of England on 'Mother', the radar homing device which was sited at all the night-fighter bases, each transmitting its own easily identifiable Morse code signal. We dropped out of the cloud base about three miles east of Wittering and touched down marvelling at what were then the miracles of science.

Back with the rest of the squadron we learned that a number of Serrate sorties had been flown in support of Bomber Command's raids. Successful interceptions using the new homer had been carried out and visuals obtained on Junkers 88s and Messerschmitt 110s. Claims of German night-fighters destroyed or damaged, were starting to come in and 141's score was beginning to mount! For the remaining week in June Harry and I flew seven more 'Exercises 15' and two cross-country flights.

On the latter I learned how to use our new navigational aid, the 'Gee box'. In the months to come Gee would be of help in checking our point of entry over the enemy coast and again, on our way out but, once over the other side, the Germans were able to jam it effectively as the radio and radar countermeasures war became more intense.

By the end of June our Flight Commander, Squadron Leader Frank Davis, reported to the CO that White and Allen could be considered 'Operational'. We were nearly there at last.

On 1 July we flew Beau VI V8713 for the first time and carried out a night-flying test lasting 1.40 hrs. There was no major raid on that night. It was the same pattern again on 2 July. The Squadron Historian has recorded that:

> 'On the night of 3rd/4th July, Bomber Command carried out a raid on Cologne, Germany by 653 aircraft with losses of 30 aircraft. 141 Squadron operated on Serrate Bomber Support on this night, and 6 aircraft flew to the forward base of Coltishall from Wittering for this night's operations . . . amongst them were Flying Officer White and Flying Officer Allen.'

Before leaving for Coltishall where we would refuel, be given the latest met. reports and wait until our appointed take-off time, the six crews down for ops had attended a briefing in a small and closely guarded hut in a remote corner of Wittering aerodrome.

There, Wing Commander Braham and the Squadron Intelligence Officer, Flying Officer 'Buster' Reynolds, had explained the details of the raid planned on Cologne, including the bombers' route, the time of the attack, the pathfinder tactics and types of marker flares and our own patrol areas. 'Buster' Reynolds was destined to become one of our dearest friends.

Harry and I took off from Coltishall on what was our first real operation at 20 minutes to midnight and landed at Wittering three hours and twenty minutes later. On our return we were debriefed and both of us had, in time-honoured British fashion(!) to fill in a form. The contents of Harry's form are taken from Intelligence Form 'F' and Personal Combat Report and marked 'SECRET'.

Mine was a Special Report on the AI Serrate and Gee box: how they functioned, what the pictures on the cathode-ray tubes looked like, in fact, a minute account of the whole of the time I had spent crouched over my AI set! These 'TOP SECRET' forms were whisked away and we never saw them again. But one of the interesting things about the following Combat Report is that no mention is made anywhere in it, of how we intercepted our Messerschmitt 110 that night. The details were too secret to be included even in a SECRET report!

The report simply says: ' . . . we sighted a white tail-light of an aircraft 500 feet above and 300 yards ahead . . .' That statement is true. But we saw the tail-light only *after* I had picked up the tell-tale herring-bone pattern of the Serrate signals on my cathode-ray tubes, matched them up with the blip on my Mk IV AI set, and completed the interception, with some slight assistance from the occupant of the front seat of 8713, by bringing us up behind the E/A and close enough for Harry to pick out the white tail-light. Then he obtained his first visual on what proved to be a Messerschmitt 110.

The blurred shape in the night sky in front of Harry gradually resolved itself into a silhouette which, in turn, became the shape of one of the models and posters which adorned the ceilings and walls of the crew room back at Wittering. The moment for identification had come at last and I heard him shout 'IT'S A 110!'

Our Combat Report reads as follows:

'We took off from Coltishall at 23.40 hours on 3rd July, 1943, in Beaufighter VI on Intruder Patrol to Eindhoven. Crossing coast in at 00.20 hours and set course to Eindhoven. Patrol area until 01.15 hours when we sighted white tail-light of aircraft 500 feet above and 300 yards ahead. Investigated and identified as Me 110. Opened fire at 200 yards dead astern, with a 2 second burst. Strikes were seen on starboard engine nacelle and wing root. Range closing rapidly to less than 100 yards. Gave E/A second burst of m.g. and cannon but no strikes observed, shower of small pieces hit our own aircraft. Beau dived violently to avoid collision and overshot, breaking away to port. E/A was not seen again. Patrolled area for another 15 minutes but nothing further was seen. Set course for Dutch coast which was crossed at Knocke at 02.00 hours. Over English coast 02.30 hours. Landed Wittering 03.00 hours.

Weather: Visibility very good, small amounts of high cloud and low patches over the coast.

UP: 23.40 hours. DOWN: 03.00 hours.

Enemy Casualties; ONE Me 110 Damaged. Our Casualties: NIL'

Note: It will be recalled that people were starting to mix up the two of us. The report, which commenced with our names, read as follows: Navigator: F/O H.E. ALLEN. Pilot: F/O M.S. WHITE.

Harry saw the Me 110 all right and attacked it but we only damaged it. What actually happened was that I messed up the closing stages of the interception. I did not see, in our excitement, that the range of the target from us was diminishing far too rapidly! In the back of the Beau, as we overtook the Messerschmitt I could hear the thudding noise of the four cannon firing and the lighter, quicker, fire of the machine-guns. I could also smell the cordite . . .

Then I felt V8713 shaking and yawing as Harry 'pulled everything back' and wrestled with the controls in his attempt to avoid colliding with the twin fins of the Me 110, looming ever larger in his gun-sight. Jounced around, under the cupola in the rear of V8713, I had still got my head stuck into the viewing unit of the AI set and was peering at a large blip, disappearing inside minimum range. The Combat Report says, 'Range closing rapidly to less than 100 yards.' – and that's close! We came in too fast, did not give ourselves time to steady up and put in an accurate burst of four or five seconds, and then had to break off the attack. We let 'a sitter' off the hook.

Whilst the Combat Report continues sedately: 'Patrolled area for another 15 minutes but nothing further was seen', what was happening inside the Beau was quite another story! Harry was cursing his head off, because he knew that we would only be able to claim a 'Damaged' and I was desperately trying to pick up the lost contact so that we could make another interception and finish the job we had started. The blip had, as we broke away to port, shot out of minimum range, up the time trace and disappeared into the ground-returns.

That meant he was already more than two miles away from us and when I switched back to the Serrate frequency, which would have enabled me to pick him up at a greater range, I could find no trace of the revealing herring-bone pattern . . . he was gone. Much chastened and disappointed we set course for home, where we landed without further incident.

When we taxied in and Harry had switched off the engines, we climbed down. We were greeted excitedly by our ground crew. They could see, by the light of their torches, that the canvas patches which normally cover the gun-muzzles (to keep out dust and dirt) had been blown away. This could only mean that we had fired our guns, and I heard shouts of 'Did you get anything?' and 'What did you get?' We had to tell them that we had only got a 'Damaged', but they seemed pleased enough and were happy for us that we had got something on our first trip. We were lucky to have the same ground crew for many months and – no matter what hour of the day or night it was – they always gave us tremendous support and encouragement.

Flight Sergeant 'Chiefy' Stanley – the senior NCO i/c the 'B' Flight ground crews – once said to me, whilst looking at V8713: 'You know, Mr Allen, we would never let you and Mr White go if there was anything wrong with her!' It was the same later when we converted to Mosquitoes . . . and they never did.

Harry and I walked back to the crew room, dumped our parachutes and the rest of our kit and headed for the Intelligence room and debriefing, to say nothing of the form-filling mentioned earlier on! When we got there and looked around, it seemed as if everyone was in a good mood; there was a general air of excitement in the room! For a moment we thought that the squadron must have had several successes and that one or two of the other crews had been able to claim 'One Destroyed'; the excitement could not be accounted for by our meagre efforts.

When our IO, not 'Buster' Reynolds on this occasion, sat down and started to write, at our dictation, I looked across the table and saw that he was solemnly writing down 'One 110 damaged a white Messerschmitt', and seeming to be pleased with his efforts, he looked up at Harry and me for confirmation. Then the penny dropped and we remembered that there was a big mess party on that night and we had been disappointed to miss it. It was clear to us now, that the Intelligence Officer hadn't!

As mentioned above, they succeeded in mixing up our initials, when typing out the Combat Report, but Harry really liked the 'White Messerschmitt' touch. Pilot Officer Hair quickly recovered his normal and universally respected composure, the reports were completed and Harry and I went over to the mess to join the party. We were pleased to have made a start but were still reliving those vital seconds when we had let the 110 get away.

Before leaving our first sortie 'over the other side' there must be a word said about navigation, that thorny subject which had been so noticeable by its absence in my training in 1941. I don't remember what the other AI operators did in this regard on the Serrate sorties, but I do remember that Harry and I decided at the outset that I should 'keep my head in the box' (i.e. the AI set) for virtually the whole of the trip and certainly for the whole of the time that we were over Germany or any part of Occupied Europe.

Only by doing this could we be sure that we would not miss the chance of investigating any aircraft that came within range of our radar equipment and which could be a hostile. Harry would look after the navigation! At briefing, Harry would mark out the track to our patrol area and the track of the bomber stream, to and from the target, on a Captains of Aircraft map. He would then, with a red crayon, put in the defended areas, i.e. the Ruhr and all the major cities of Germany, add the time of 'H' Hour over the target, fold his map up and stuff it into the top of his right flying boot and off we would go! It was there, handy in his boot, if needed when we were wandering about over the Third Reich in a few hours' time!

Sometimes, in the early days, I would take the Gee charts and take a fix as we crossed in over the enemy coast (and again on the way out), and although the Gee box was effectively jammed over Germany it could be used for some 70/80 miles inland over northern France if a crew really didn't know where they were. Personally, I always resented any time which I had to spend away from the AI set in case we were to miss the chance of upsetting some German night-fighter crew's evening.

Our first patrol had been spent more in the vicinity of Aachen on the German border with Belgium than over Eindhoven airfield, and several miles to the north-west of the night's target at Cologne. But these patrols were loosely defined, and providing you found a German night-fighter somewhere on your travels nobody was going to worry too much where you found him . . . In his book, *The Peenemünde Raid*, of which there will be more anon, Martin Middlebrook was to refer to our 'wandering Beaufighter' when, in August, 141 flew in support of the raid on the Rocket Development Station at Peenemünde.

On 5, 6 and 7 July we carried out NFTs, but did not operate. We had a Serrate target Beau on which the squadron could carry out practice interceptions in the daytime, and Harry and I were assigned to this chore the day after we had damaged the 110. It consisted of flying up and down between Loughborough and Leicester at a height of 7,000 ft, hopefully below the height at which the German monitors would be able to intercept the Serrate-type emissions being sent out into the Leicestershire air! The mock homer was installed in Beau 8284 and we stooged up and down over the prescribed patrol line for one and a quarter hours whilst our colleagues intercepted us and followed up with a mock attack on our undefended rear quarters!

Then, on the 8th, we took the 141 Tiger Moth up to Loughborough where we landed on a small airfield to be met by – of all people – my father! At that time the Brush Electric Company was involved in various types of sub-contract work which included the servicing and maintenance of a number of de Havilland Rapides. My father was up there doing the test flying of these aircraft after they had come out of final inspection. He took us out to dinner and we stayed the night, returning to Wittering the following morning.

Of course he was interested in hearing that we had now gone over to the offensive, but because of the nature of Operation 'Serrate' and the secrecy surrounding it, there was very little that we could tell him. However, it was good to see him looking fit and well at 44 and still flying! Both he and my mother knew Harry well by this time, as he had often come back with me to Ashford to spend two or three days of his leave with us. Later on – and for reasons which will be described in due course – 60 Clarendon Road became almost a second home to him.

Returning to the Squadron History, Don Aris writes:

'On the night of the 9th/10th July Bomber Command carried out a raid on Gelsenkirchen, Germany by 418 aircraft and 12 were lost. 141 Squadron operated on this night on Serrate Bomber Support. Five aircraft operated and they were unable to use either Coltishall or West Malling as forward bases as the weather had clamped in on these airfields. It was therefore decided to operate from Wittering and cut short the patrol time over enemy territory.'

We were amongst the five crews. After an NFT of 50 minutes and the visit to the remote briefing hut on the aerodrome at Wittering, we took off for the heavily defended industrial area of the Ruhr, known to the bomber crews as 'Happy Valley', at twenty minutes to midnight. In the 'Remarks' column of my log is the brief entry: 'Serrate Gelsenkirchen. No Joy. 10/10ths at 16,000 over Target.'

The trip took us 3.35 hrs and we must have been over Gelsenkirchen but we never saw anything of it except for the dull glow of the fires, because the whole area was blanketed with 10/10ths cloud. Don reports that we patrolled 'uneventfully' and crossed out over the enemy coast at 02.10 hours.

The bad weather must have deterred our opposite numbers in the Junkers 88s and Messerschmitt 110s because the losses in Bomber Command for the night were only 2.9 per cent, whereas in the raid on Cologne on 3 July the figure of 30 lost out of the 653 aircraft taking part represented 4.59 per cent. The patrols of the other four crews of 141 who flew that night were equally uneventful.

Don Aris notes that on 15 July an Air Commodore Lee MC, the temporary AOC of No. 12 Group, Fighter Command, visited Wittering and spent some time with 141 Squadron during the morning. The air commodore wrote a book after the war which was called *Special Duties*. In his book he says that 'In a lifetime of flying and being among flying people, the one that stood out most prominently was W/C J.R.D. 'Bob' Braham, 141's present C.O.' He also said that he 'had never met a man with such quietly determined cold-blooded courage as him'.

He goes on to say that, had the Victoria Cross been awarded to airmen for a long succession of acts of deliberate courage as well as for single acts of desperate courage, then Braham should have had that ribbon also on his tunic to go with the three DSOs and the three DFCs. Lee, an Air Vice-Marshal when he wrote the book, had perhaps forgotten Group Captain Leonard Cheshire VC, DSO**, DFC, whose VC was awarded, in effect, for four years of sustained courage rather than for one single act.

As I have observed in an earlier paragraph, medals and decorations are difficult forms of recognition to award fairly and can, if one is not careful, become a subject of controversy for the individual rather than one of pride for his squadron or regiment, which is what they should be. Staying with the Squadron History, there are further entries for 15 July, starting with:

> 'On the night of the 15/16th July Bomber Command carried out a raid on Montbeliard, a suburb of the French town of Sochaux where there was a Peugeot motor factory. 165 Halifaxes were used and 5 were lost. 6 aircraft of 141 operated on this night and F/O White with F/O Allen destroyed an Me.110. They flew from Wittering to operate from the forward base of West Malling.'

So, on St Swithin's Day 1943 we flew south to West Malling, the home of No. 29 Squadron where, nearly two years before, we had been sacked by the man who, since the raid on the Dams by 617 Squadron two months previously, had become a legend in his own lifetime – Wing Commander Guy Gibson VC, DSO & Bar, DFC & Bar – before taking off in support of the raid on Montbeliard.

As we clustered round the Watch Office with the other five crews, who were operating that night, we were both, I think, conscious of this and hoping to do better. The material part of our Combat Report reads:

> 'After patrolling Juvincourt without any sign of activity from 01.33 hrs. to 01.55 hrs. we flew South East. When we were about 8 miles South East of

Rheims at 02.00 hrs. we saw an Me. 110 3000 ft ahead of us flying straight and level at 10,000 feet. We were 2000 ft. above flying South East in the same direction as the E/A, so we at once dived down to get dead astern and slightly below. Opening fire at 750 feet we slowly closed to 600 feet, in a 2 second burst of cannon and machine-gun. There were strikes on both engines and on the fuselage and a moment later the whole aircraft exploded in flames, splitting into 2 burning pieces, one of which was blown right behind us. We watched both pieces strike the ground, where they continued to burn, and then, as we were not too well off for fuel, made for the French coast.'

We will pause there and go back to the interception. As we have seen, from the Combat Report, we patrolled the Juvincourt area for about twenty minutes without any sign of activity. We then went off in a south-easterly direction wandering over northern France to see what we could find. Sure enough, I very soon picked up a strong Serrate signal, and the herring-bone pattern on the two cathode-ray tubes was getting stronger by the minute! I switched across to the Mk IV AI and there was the blip on the tubes.

Switching back to the Serrate and then again to the Mk IV AI there was no mistaking it. The signals on the Serrate were coming from a *Lichtenstein* AI and, as the blip was already well down the time trace, it showed that we were within a couple of miles of a German night-fighter. The weather was fine and there was 'excellent visibility in bright moonlight with small amounts of high cloud'. This accounts for the fact that, once we started to close in and reduce the range, Harry first spotted the silhouette when the E/A was still 3,000 feet (over half a mile) in front of us.

There is no mention in our Combat Report of the dog-fight on AI that followed before we could get into a position to make our attack. As we closed in the E/A turned sharply, the blip on my tubes started to move back up the time trace, the range began to increase and it looked as if he might get away. I managed to give Harry a running commentary of what was happening and, for several minutes, we chased our elusive opponent around the night sky – almost as if we were day-fighters!

The German crew were now obviously using their *Lichtenstein* AI to try to get behind us . . . while we were doing our best to get behind them! Fortunately, as we have already seen, Harry and I got there first and he was easily able to identify it as a Messerschmitt 110. I think the German crew were still wondering where we had got to when we opened fire.

We had evidently learned something from our abortive combat on 3 July, because we did not come in to the attack so fast that we had to pull away to avoid a collision and without Harry having been able to take aim and deliver an accurate burst of fire: 'Opening fire at 750 feet we slowly closed to 600 feet.'

This time, as we watched the Me 110 go down in two burning pieces and hit the ground, there was no need for me to 'keep my head in the box' and look for a missing blip that had vanished off my tubes. And, when we got back to Wittering, our ground crew would really have something to celebrate!

According to Martin Bowman in his book, *Confounding The Reich*, the pilot of the Me 110 which we destroyed on 15 July was Major Herbert Rauh of II/NJG 4. I do not know any other details about him or his crew, but it would seem that he was an experienced pilot and this would account for the violent chase and evasive action which ensued before we succeeded in making our attack.

He and his crew were just unlucky but the net result was that they would not be around to seek out and destroy a British bomber the following night. That was the essence of Operation 'Serrate'.

I have talked optimistically about giving our ground crew something to celebrate but the night was not over yet and – watching the 110 go down – we were not yet back at Wittering! Our report continues:

> '. . . and then, as we were not too well off for fuel, made for the French coast. As we flew over Dreux a searchlight came on and tried unsuccessfully to pick us up, and there was a good deal of heavy flak, far too accurate for comfort.'

The trouble was that after the 110 had gone down and hit the ground our faithful Beau V8713 was virtually left to fly itself, whilst we were busy telling ourselves how clever we were and what a superb crew we made together, etc., etc. After all, we had had to wait for nearly two years before being able to claim any fruits for our nocturnal labours!

We had used up quite a lot of fuel in the chase after the 110 and we did need to set course for home, but we were not in any trouble. What was it that the great Group Captain Leonard Cheshire used to say? 'Just when you think everything is all right . . . something else goes wrong'. The Fates allowed Harry and I just about one minute of self praise, before the searchlights started to look for us and the flak opened up! Full of elation at our victory we had allowed our attention to wander and had flown straight over a defended area close to some of the German night-fighter bases.

We were brought back to reality (and nearly to the ground!) with a bump as the accurate bursts of heavy flak rocked the Beau and the probing fingers of the searchlights reached out into the night to find and hold us. We got back safely to Wittering and landed at 03.50 hours. It looked as if we had still got a lot to learn . . .

By the time we had taxied in and Harry had switched off the engines, we had calmed down a bit, but we were still excited and, once again, our ground crew could see that the canvas covers were missing from the gun muzzles. The shouts went up 'Did you get anything?' and this time we were able to say 'Yes, we got a 110!' When we went across to the Intelligence room for debriefing all was quiet and respectable – no mess party on St Swithin's! and this time there was no more talk about White Messerschmitts!

'Buster' Reynolds was on duty and took down our story of the night's events with all the smooth efficiency of a good solicitor, which is what he was in civilian life! The following morning we learned from the Armaments Officer that Harry had only used 30 high explosive incendiary and 30 semi-armour piercing/incendiary 20 mm cannon shells and 84 armour-piercing and 84 incendiary 0.303 inch machine-gun bullets to destroy the Me 110; whereas, on the earlier attack of 3 July (when we had only been able to claim a damaged) he had used 180 20 mm cannon shells and 330 machine-gun bullets. He was coming on!

Many years later I was invited to give the address in Chapel, on Remembrance Sunday, at my old school, Hurstpierpoint College, in Sussex. Trying to find a bridge across the generation gap and suggesting that the boys themselves would have experienced similar feelings and emotions to those we had experienced during the war, I recalled a letter written, during the 1914–18 War, by a young tank corps officer to his mother and trying to describe for her what it was like out in France in the unbelievable horrors of trench warfare. He wrote: '. . . the

excitement for the last half hour before an attack, is like nothing on earth. The only thing that compares with it are the few minutes before a big School match.'
I continued:

> 'The question you want to ask (as I did, when I was at the School in 1936) is, "What was it like? What did it feel like to go out on operations?" I believe that we all experience the *same* feelings and emotions before – and after – any big event in our lives. Whether it be in our everyday life, or in time of war. Beforehand, we feel a mixture of excitement, anticipation and hope – sometimes these feelings are laced with a measure of fear! After the event is over, our emotions are governed by the results. Satisfaction, joy and relief if things have gone well. Disappointment, misery and a return of all our fears, if things have gone badly for us. Sometimes we try and console ourselves with the thought that "we were just unlucky". I suggest that there isn't anyone here who has not experienced these sensations from their earliest childhood.'

Thus it was for Harry and me in the days following St Swithin's Day. It also happened to be my mother's birthday and I always thought, to myself, of it as a birthday present for her. Although I wasn't sure it was in too good taste! After two years of trials and tribulations, to say nothing of endless practice interceptions, Harry and I had been able to make our first real claim and we had enjoyed every minute of it! Satisfaction, joy and relief (i.e. that we could do it) were all ours and already we were starting to think about the next one.

For the record, and for those who, in this day and age of changing fashions, concern themselves with such things, I can say that neither Harry nor I ever lost any sleep over those we might have killed or wounded . . .

I remember a film, from bygone days, when someone observed that, 'Hunting was a great sport and the hunting of man was the greatest sport of all.' I doubt if I would have reacted in the same way if I had been on the ground and someone had been chasing after me with a rifle and bayonet, but 'each man to his own last' and, fortunately for me, ours was an impersonal kind of warfare . . .

After the excitement and fun of St Swithin's Day things settled down a bit and Harry and I did not operate again until 27 July. There were a number of Serrate patrols being flown, nearly all the crews in both 'A' and 'B' Flights had got three or four trips in but somehow the squadron's score of 'Destroyed' and 'Damaged' did not seem to be rising as quickly as we had hoped and there were too many early returns due to failure of the radar/radio equipment for the CO's liking. Harry and I did a number of NFTs and we also practised single-engined landings against the day when we might lose an engine due to enemy action or straightforward mechanical failure.

Encouraged by watching the superb airmanship of 'Bob' Braham when demonstrating single-engined approaches and landings, we carried out a number of them ourselves on 22 and 24 July. It was a bit 'hairy' because, at that time, the Beaus on 141 did not have fully feathering props and I remember watching with my heart in my mouth the port prop milling round, causing a lot of drag, as we lurched over the Great North Road and across the boundary fence, with the starboard engine going full bore and plenty of opposite rudder! It will perhaps be remembered that we AI operators spent much of our time facing aft and often only rotated our seats, to face forward, when the aircraft was on the approach. In the event, we never had to 'return on one' whilst we were flying the sturdy and robust Beaufighters but we had reason to be grateful for the time we spent practising single-engined landings when, later on, it came to flying the 'Wooden Wonder' – the Mosquito.

It is rational to think of the High-Level Bomber Support operations, during the period October 1942 through to May 1945, in seven phases. If the initial concept of mixing our fighters into the bomber stream to oppose the growing threat of the *Nachtjagdgeschwadern*, the suicidal sortie by the Wellington crew on 3.12.42, and the development of the Serrate homer by the boffins was the first phase, then the choice of Wing Commander Braham to lead a single squadron of Beaufighters, the delivery to 141 of their Beau VIs plus the installation of the new Serrate homer and the training of her crews at Drem, was the second phase.

By the end of July 1943 (Operations had commenced in June) we at Wittering were in the middle of the third phase, which was to last until the end of September of that year. Somehow, the anticipated results, in terms of German night-fighters shot down, were not forthcoming. During the month of July the squadron operated on ten nights and set off on 66 Serrate patrols. Their claims only amounted to one E/A destroyed and two damaged and yet plenty of Serrate signals were being picked up by their AI operators. Something was going wrong somewhere.

To return to Don Aris's History:

> 'On the night of the 27/28th July, Bomber Command carried out the second of its four major raids on Hamburg, Germany over a 10 day period 787 aircraft took part and only 17 were lost, again showing the effectiveness of "Window". This was the night of the firestorm which caused such enormous destruction, mostly to residential areas, some books say that approximately 40,000 people died, others say 20,000 dead with 60,000 injured. 141 Squadron operated on this night on Serrate Bomber Support, after the usual servicing, inspections and night flying tests in the afternoon, 5 aircraft flew from Wittering to the forward base of Coltishall.'

Harry and I took off from Coltishall at 23.55 hours to patrol an area of the north coast of Holland where several German night-fighter bases were located, including that of IV/NJG 1 at Leeuwarden and I/NJG 3 at Vechta. We flew around over the former, then we went off to Vechta, and then we returned again to Leeuwarden. I could not pick up any Serrate signals anywhere. We had no chases but on our way back skirting the Dutch islands of Ameland and Terschelling and out over the North Sea, Harry spotted a light on the water. My log-book records: 'Hamburg. No joy and no chases. Gave "Mayday" for types in Dinghy.'

The dawn was starting to break and, as we were steering a westerly course for home, Harry's attention was attracted by a tiny light on the sea. We lost height and went down to have a look. Then we saw the rubber dinghy, with several figures in it. We circled round and transmitted a 'Mayday' call on the VHF in the vain hope that the Air-Sea Rescue people would come out and find them, before they were spotted by the Germans and taken prisoner. We had no idea of the outcome of our distress call, as we heard no more after we had returned to base. One can only hope that they were picked up, if not by us, then by the Germans. It was a funny feeling leaving them there, as we turned back onto 270 degrees and headed for home. We landed at Wittering after 4.20 hours in the air.

Don mentions the use of 'Window' in his preview of the night operations and this code-word now needs some explanation. Window was the code-word that was used for strips of aluminium foil that were dropped by our bombers over Germany as a countermeasure to the German ground and airborne radar equipment. These Window strips were *c.*30 cm long and 1.5 cm wide. The aluminium foil was stiffened by black paper backing and the shiny side was blackened, so that it would not show up in the searchlights.

The strips were put up in bundles, like small parcels. We (the AI operators on 141) were given some and I used to chuck them out of the flare chute, when I could spare a minute! For the bomber crews it was a much more serious matter and they were briefed to release the bundles at correctly timed intervals. The slowly descending clouds of these strips jammed the German equipment and rendered most of their radar sets ineffective, except for the *Freya* long-range sets used mostly for the detection of the incoming British bombers when they were still well out over the North Sea.

Window strips had been in existence for some time and it was thought that they could prove an effective way of helping to reduce the increasing losses of aircraft and crews in Bomber Command. But they had been held back by request from those responsible for Home Defence who feared that the device might be taken up by the Germans and used by *their* bombers to swamp the British ground and airborne radar, with disastrous results for London, Manchester, Plymouth and other vulnerable targets. With hindsight, Window might well have saved the lives of more British aircrew – if it had been released earlier – than would have been lost among their civilian countrymen on the ground, in view of the greatly reduced number of raids on England after the winter Blitz of 1940/41. But, of course, everything is simple with hindsight!

Window had been used on the first of the big raids on Hamburg, which took place on the night of 24/25 July, but the bomber support crews did not operate. We were cancelled at the last moment. Harry and I had done an NFT and flown over to Coltishall at 20.35 hours. When we had refuelled and got the latest met. report and were all ready to go, the op was cancelled. At 00.35 hours the following morning we, and the other crews, got into our aircraft, grumbling the while, and flew back to Wittering.

Whenever ops were cancelled at the last moment, there was a feeling of anticlimax. It happens to everyone, if they are keyed up for some big event, and it is a natural feeling. One's feelings are in fact, mixed. On the one hand people are glad that they did not have to go out and 'prove' themselves. On the other, they rather wish that they *had* had to!

In our case, and in the case of the 'bomber boys', the feeling of relief was short-lived, for the cancellation of a trip was only putting off the evil day! When we awoke the following morning we would not be waking up with the pleasant thought that the number of ops to complete our tour (of 30 trips) had been reduced by one – and we would still have to be prepared to go the next time that ops were on.

In describing the meaning and use of Window, I have omitted to include our Historian's summary of the bomber support efforts on the night of 27/28, although earlier in this chapter I have suggested that 'something was going wrong somewhere'. It will be remembered that five Beaus flew to Coltishall and Don's comments are as follows:

'This had been a very disappointing night for 141 Squadron, three aircraft had returned early due to radio trouble, this was almost certainly the radar, one had returned early for lack of oxygen and only one, White/Allen completed the operation.'

We ourselves were certainly to experience failure of our AI set shortly and to discover the feeling of failure, when having to return early. On 30 July we did an op in support of a raid on Remscheid in Germany. We flew around in the area of Venlo in Holland and landed after only 3.05 hours in the air. I picked up no Serrate signals and the trip was entirely uneventful. When we taxied into our dispersal area the canvas patches were still in position over the gun muzzles and our ground crew had nothing to get excited about. We could feel their disappointment.

On the last day of the month I had a real shock to my system. Harry and I had slept late after landing back from the Remscheid op at 02.30 hours on the 31st and getting to bed, after debriefing, at about 4 a.m. We wandered down to the flights after lunch, expecting a nice quiet afternoon and an evening off. I was horrified to hear the CO, who had just come into the 'B' Flight office, saying to Frank Davis (our Flight Commander) '"Sticks" is going to have some leave. I think I'll take Mike with me tonight!' and turning to me said, 'OK Mike, we'll do an NFT later on, and then those who are on tonight will go over to Coltishall after briefing.'

My reply stuck in my throat, but I think it was something like '. . . *GLUG!* Sir.' Harry did not seem exactly overjoyed at this turn of events, nor did Frank Davis. The only one full of bonhomie and cheerful as a cricket was Bob Braham as he contemplated doing yet another op. There is no doubt that the drug of the excitement and challenge of operational flying had bitten deep into his soul . . . 'Sticks' Gregory, the CO's incomparable AI Operator, had been operating continuously with Bob Braham for three years with virtually no break or rest period. They had been flying together since the days of the Battle of Britain and were already a legend in the night-fighter business.

I had first met him in September 1941 at 29 Squadron, when he was a flight sergeant and the two of them were just starting to make a name for themselves with their early kills on Home Defence. Sticks had, at the beginning of July, been awarded a Bar to his DFC (he already held the DFM), but he was an older man than Bob and he was simply worn out. Bob had already got another experienced AI operator lined up to fill Sticks's outsize shoes, but 'Jacko' hadn't yet been released from No. 51 OTU at Cranfield.

The more I thought about it, the less I liked it! What if I was to get a Serrate contact and lose it? Or fail to find 'Mother' and get us safely back to Wittering? I would be finished on the squadron and another navigator would be posted in to fly with Harry! How could I, with only one success to my name, hope to match the exceptional standards set by Bob and Sticks?

I had recently seen a film called *The Life of Emile Zola*, in which a French officer, Captain Dreyfus, is stripped of his uniform and his badges of rank (right down to his sword-knot) and drummed out of his regiment. In my mind's eye, I could already see the squadron drawn up on the parade ground to watch whilst I was stripped of my flying brevet and drummed out of the Royal Air Force!

At 17.10 hours we went up in the CO's Beau 8147 (otherwise known as *Betsy*) for an NFT but we were down on the ground again in 15 minutes, without me even having had time to check the AI set properly! At 20.30 hours we and the other five crews scheduled to fly in support of another of the big raids on

Hamburg took off for our advanced base at Coltishall. I turned round in my seat, as the CO and I taxied out, to see the forlorn figure of Flying Officer White standing on the perimeter track. On the way over to Coltishall I remember Bob Braham saying cheerfully, on the intercom, 'Mike, if we can't find anything high up tonight, we'll go down and see if we can find anything to "shoot up" on the ground!' I think my reply was the same as before, i.e. 'Glug! Sir.'

At around 10 o'clock we were at Coltishall and were all ready to go when the op was cancelled owing to bad weather. I breathed one deep sigh of relief. However, there is still something to be told, before the night was over and I got to bed at Coltishall. Bob told the other five crews to find some beds, get some sleep and return to Wittering in the morning. He then said to me that he had to be in his office at 8 a.m. and we would take off immediately and try to fly back to Wittering, even though the weather report was bad across Norfolk to King's Lynn and Wisbech, where lay our route. The storm centre, moving slowly east, which had been the cause of the op being cancelled, lay between us and home! In the 'Remarks' column of my log-book there is the following succinct entry: 'A very enlightening trip which finished back at Coltishall.'

After exactly one hour of hair-raising flying, during which Bob tried everything he knew to get round (or over!) the great banks of cumulo-nimbus cloud which lay across East Anglia, and I was thrown around in the back of *Betsy* like a pea in a drum, we found ourselves back on the ground at Coltishall. When Bob eventually gave up the attempt to get home, the lightning was still flashing around us like Dante's Inferno although the dangers of us being struck were not nearly so risky as an unscheduled entry into one of the turbulent black clouds which, at times, seemed to surround us.

That would probably have been too much even for Bob Braham's exceptional airmanship. I could see the Wittering beacon flashing its welcoming Morse-code signal on my cathode-ray tubes whenever I could keep my head in the visor of the viewing unit for more than a few seconds, but the storm clouds which lay in our path went up to over 30,000 feet, so we could not go over them. They spread out for miles either side of us and we certainly couldn't go through them. I heard Bob's voice over the intercom, 'OK Mike, we've had it for tonight. Get the Coltishall beacon and we'll go back there.'

As we yawed round to the east, the turbulence on the fringes of the storm was still throwing the Beau all over the sky, and I heard the CO say 'Mike, I can see a hole in the cloud . . . we're going down. Better put your parachute on.' I did and we literally fell out of the sky, to get through the transitory hole in the clouds before it had closed over and blotted out our escape route.

Navigators in the Beaus wore a parachute harness, which had two large hooks on the front, the 'chute itself being too bulky to wear, when one had to move about the aircraft. It was like a small canvas attaché case with four handles, and we parked it in a stowage, close to hand. If there was an emergency you grabbed one of the handles, hooked the 'chute onto your chest and prepared for the worst.

I found the Coltishall 'Mother' on the AI, we got through the hole in the cloud, flew back below the cloud base and landed safely just after midnight on Sunday 1 August. We got to bed at about 1 a.m., slept for a few hours and returned to Wittering first thing in the morning, without further incident. On reflection, it might have been less nerve racking to have gone on the op! I never flew with the CO again and I had an idea that Harry White, although he would not have said so, was quite glad to see me back.

It must have been about this time that my new 'waterproof' watch from Cairo was put to the test. The watch was a large showy-looking affair, which resembled an outsize medallion rather than a wrist-watch. I could hardly raise my arm, it was so heavy! The whole thing was affixed to my wrist by a flashy white strap, which indicated to the cognoscenti that one had been overseas and thus carried with it a certain prestige over the lesser persons who had not left the shores of Albion. It was of course – according to the proprietor of the shop where I bought it – shockproof, dustproof, waterproof and s***proof, etc. For a few piastres I had obviously got a bargain.

Well, back with those suspicious types on 141, I flaunted this hideous watch and its attributes to anyone who would listen. Until the day came when I shot a line once too often about my new acquisition and its awful white strap.

In that exciting summer of '43 at Wittering we, in 141, enjoyed the comfort of a pre-war mess when we were on the station and, when we felt like going out, there was plenty of local hospitality. Just down the road to Stamford lay Burghley House, surrounded by its magnificent park and we were welcome there whenever we had a free morning or afternoon. In Burghley Park was a lake in which it was quite safe to swim. The rest of the story is quickly told. A party of us were down by the lake on a hot July afternoon, disporting ourselves as the Duke's guests, when – egged on by Harry – someone said, 'I wonder if Mike's Cairo watch really is waterproof?' From there on it was all over bar the shouting.

I was hoisted aloft and with a 'ONE! TWO! THREE!' from my so-called friends was cast into the air over the lake! I did not remain airborne for long and when I eventually surfaced, spluttering and gasping for breath, I was not the only one full of water. I think that, when I was restored to dry land, there were more bubbles in my watch than there were in me! After that, there was no more talk of waterproof watches and the white strap was conspicuous by its absence.

No. 141 Squadron, Wittering: group photo taken in August 1943 during the pioneering stage of the High-Level Bomber Support operations. The Commanding Officer, Wing Commander J.R.D. 'Bob' Braham DSO, DFC is seated in the centre; the Station Commander, Group Captain Legg, is on his right. (Harry and I are in the middle row, fifth and sixth in from the left respectively.)

Fortunately, about this time, we navigators were given a Government Issue watch. I went to the stores to draw a handsome replacement for my waterlogged and misguided Middle Eastern purchase. It was fabricated by a gentleman named Longines and it did not have a white strap.

August began with more AI practice, camera-gun attacks and single-engined landings. Then it was our turn to experience the frustrations of radar failure and the cancellation of operations at the last minute. On the 2nd, Bomber Command carried out the last of its four major raids, within ten days, on Hamburg. Of the 740 aircraft which took part 30 were lost, showing that the Germans were quickly implementing their countermeasures to Window. Seven 141 aircraft flew from Wittering to the forward base of Coltishall, including us, to take part in the operation.

Coltishall was as far as Harry and I got that night; on the way over the transmitter on the Mk IV AI went u/s. At Coltishall I worked for two and a half hours, with the help of two radar mechanics from No. 68 Squadron, to change the transmitter and the modulator, but eventually we were unsuccessful. In the end we had to return to Wittering as the other six aircraft were taking off to support the Hamburg raid.

Two days later we – and three other crews – got as far as the advanced base of West Malling. Operations were cancelled at the last minute due to bad weather and we all flew back to Wittering. On 6 August, Flight Lieutenant 'Jacko' Jacobs DFC arrived on the squadron from No. 51 OTU at Cranfield, where they were training night-fighter crews, to take Sticks Gregory's place and fly with the CO. Jacko was an exceptional AI operator and had flown with Bob Braham on some Home Defence operations in 1942 when the latter was on 29 Squadron at West Malling. They had destroyed a Junkers 88 and damaged two other E/A.

He was now to have a successful spell on 141 during the remainder of the CO's time on the squadron. I was quietly relieved because Jacko's arrival would mean that there would be no more rides for me in *Betsy*, no more talk of 'going down low to see what we can find to shoot up'. Braham had attacked a U boat, when the squadron had been at Predannack earlier in the year. With me on board on 31 July, he might have gone for a cruiser in Bremen dockyard, for all I know! Jacko was a popular figure and he was to play a prominent part in the events which happened later in the month, when 141 supported the great raid on the German Rocket Development Station at Peenemünde.

On 9 August Harry and I did another trip, flying from Bradwell Bay on the Blackwater Estuary. We took off at 01.40 hours the following morning in support of a raid on Mannheim. We landed back at Wittering just before 5.30 a.m. but, whatever action there was that night, we did not succeed in finding it. Don's 141 History records that we set out to patrol the German night-fighter airfield at Venlo and that we crossed the French coast NE of Dunkirk at 01.59 hours:

> 'They patrolled the target area without seeing any sign of activity so they flew South. There was a visual Lorenz on at Florennes airfield but no other activity. They recrossed at Dieppe at 04.25 hours where they came under considerable heavy flak and three searchlights which failed to illuminate them.'

Once more our ground crew were disappointed as they waved us in, on our return to Wittering, and saw, in the light of their torches, that the canvas patches were still in place over the gun muzzles. Taking off earlier, the CO – with Sticks in his usual place and doing one 'last' trip – got an Me 110 south-east of St Trond. Their success, as the 110 went down in flames, was seen by Thornton and Ron Mallett, another 141 crew patrolling in the vicinity. This was Braham's 16th victory and his fourth with 141 Squadron.

Sadly, the month had already been marred by the loss of one of our crews, Flight Sergeant Frost and his Navigator/Radio Sergeant Towler, who crashed whilst on an NFT in broad daylight not many miles away from Wittering. Don's History records the accident:

> '. . . [they] took off at 14.15 hours in Beaufighter VIF V8702 . . . approximately 25 minutes later their aircraft crashed in a ploughed field on the side of a hill about two miles South of Braunston in Leicestershire. So far as could be gathered from rather conflicting evidence, the aircraft broke cloud in a dive and the pilot was unable to pull out before crashing. The Beaufighter exploded on impact and debris was strewn over an area 600 yards by 400 yards. Both crew must have been killed instantly.'

This was a sad business because in July they had damaged a German night-fighter, after a successful Serrate interception, and their exploit had featured in the national press. They were an 'Above Average' crew and might well have gone on to get more.

When we had operated on 9 August there had been a gap of one hour and 25 minutes between us taking off from Bradwell Bay and the first four (which consisted of the CO, Thornton, Anderson and 'the Major' (otherwise known as F/L L.J.G. Le Boutte). The Squadron History records that:

> 'Even though the reports say only that the patrols were to German night-fighter airfields, the 141 Squadron aircraft on their way to their target area, usually flew on the fringes of the bomber stream and the splitting of the Squadron aircraft is (He says) best explained by W/C Braham in his book *Scramble*.'

Braham writes:

> 'Our practice was to send half our available fighters out with the stream to fly as far as they could. The rest took off later during the night to meet the returning bombers, again as far out along the return route as possible. This wasn't very satisfactory. It split our small effort in half, but it was the best we could do. In discussing the problem with Staff Officers at Fighter Command, I requested that our Beaus should be replaced by the longer range Mosquitoes. This they promised to look into, but they could do nothing immediately. They still weren't prepared to send Mosquitoes, with the latest A.I., over enemy territory.'

The first Serrate operations had only started on the night 14/15 June but it was already apparent that a single squadron of Beaufighters was inadequate for the task.

On the night 10/11 August Bomber Command attacked Nuremberg, Germany, with 653 aircraft and lost 16. Seven crews of 141 operated in support, four using the forward base of Bradwell Bay and the other three going on to West Malling for their final met. report and topping up of their fuel tanks. Harry and I set off again for Bradwell Bay and took off from there on the op at 22.45 hours. Don's entry against our name for that night, which was again a failure, reads:

'F/O H.E. White with his Nav/Rad F/O M.S. Allen in Beaufighter VIF V8744 took off from Bradwell Bay at 22.45 hours on an Intruder Patrol to the German night fighter airfield of Juvincourt, France. They crossed the enemy coast NE of Dunkirk at 23.05 hours. At 23.59 hours they saw four lines of tracer going into a bomber 10 miles S. of Namur, the bomber blew up at 7000 feet and came down in burning pieces. They could not find the enemy aircraft so they patrolled the target area without any sign of activity. They had a fleeting glimpse of an unidentified enemy aircraft with two green lights believed on tail, 4000 feet ahead near Courtrai, Belgium at 01.15 hours but were unable to engage before enemy aircraft dived out of sight into cloud. They recrossed NE of Dunkirk at 01.30 hours and over the British coast at Bradwell. They landed at Wittering at 02.30 hours.'

That night, as so often in the months ahead, when we were equipped with Mosquitoes and could range further into Germany, we saw, or rather Harry saw, as my head was firmly rammed into the viewing unit of my AI set, a British bomber attacked and shot down, without us being able to do anything about it. And later we had the frustrating experience, common to all night-fighter crews, of catching a fleeting glimpse of an E/A and yet being unable to complete the interception. We flew back into Wittering disheartened.

It was about this time that I heard the CO deliver himself of a remark that I have never forgotten. His remark, made viciously and without any reservations, has for me always spelt the lie to the trite phrase that is often used to describe the emotions of men like Braham who have an exceptional record of front-line service. The phrase to which I refer is: 'Of course, he didn't know the meaning of the word Fear.'

The story of this remark appeared in a short profile of Bob Braham which I wrote for one of the many notable and exciting books written by 'Laddie' Lucas and first published in 1989. It was entitled *Thanks For The Memory – Unforgettable Characters in Air Warfare 1939–45*.

We were down at one of our advanced bases, I think it was West Malling, and waiting to take off in support of a raid somewhere in southern Germany. There were three crews there and we were standing by the Beaufighters and close to the Watch Office, just waiting for the word to take off on the op. In the twilight of a beautifully soft autumn evening the Kentish countryside looked marvellous – particularly to those of us who were about to leave it!

There was Bob Braham, the CO, and Sticks Gregory who had been operating together for three years and were already highly decorated. There was Harry White and myself, who had been around for some time but had very little to show for it, and there was a new crew, the pilot, a young flight sergeant and his navigator, a sergeant.

The 'pre-match' tension was building up, as we walked a few paces, yawned and walked back, or as one of us disappeared behind the adjacent hangar for a last-minute relieving action. The new pilot felt someone ought to say something. Turning to Bob Braham, he managed, despite his dried-up throat (which I certainly had also!), to blurt out: 'I suppose it's all right for you, Sir. I don't expect you feel anything?'

Even Harry and I were taken aback by the vehemence of the CO's reply. He swung round and almost snarled out: 'Don't be such a bloody fool'. The remainder of his words were of an Anglo-Saxon origin and unknown to the young flight sergeant. He followed this up by saying, in slightly kinder tones, 'Of course I do – and it gets worse every time.'

Whilst the first half of the lesson that Bob Braham was trying to pass on to the new crew was brutally administered, the second half was totally reassuring for the two sergeants. Their legendary CO had admitted that he was prone to exactly the same feelings before an op as they were! Further, after his many operations, he felt the twitch (as we called it) even worse than they did. Only an exceptional man – and leader of men – could have spoken in such a manner and at such a time. Here, the words of our highly regarded and irrepressible Intelligence Officer 'Buster' Reynolds got to the heart of the matter, when he said 'Bob Braham's 100 per cent dedication and commitment to the task, whatever it might be, set him apart from other people and lesser mortals.'

Flying Officer Buster Reynolds, married with four children and much older than the rest of us, sometimes flew on operations with the CO, although he had no call to do so. In fact, it was strictly illegal for him to do so! If they had been shot down over the other side and he had been made prisoner-of-war, he would have been given a hard time at *Dulag Luft* (the Interrogation Centre for Air Force prisoners, located at Frankfurt) because he had a lot of 'TOP SECRET' information which would have been of the utmost value to the Germans.

However, he told the CO that he did not think he could do his job properly, particularly the debriefing of returning aircrews, if he did not go and have a look for himself and see what things were like over Germany. I think also, on reflection, that he might have given his interrogators a few problems before they got any information out of him! Under a bright and breezy exterior Buster had thwarted many a confident prosecutor. There were 'no flies on him', none at all. He was, in fact, very sharp. In later years he was hardly recognisable to us as Alderman Cedric Hinton Fleetwood Reynolds JP, but when you talked to him in the bonus years of his long life, the old Buster – and the man who had flown with Bob Braham – was never far away!

There are other stories to be told – which can only add to his reputation – to say nothing of the night when, after a party in the Mess, he had gone to bed but had to emerge shortly afterwards to attend to the call of nature. On his return journey he opened the door of what he thought to be his room and climbed into bed with the Roman Catholic padre.

Buster, who was a 'penguin' and wore no flying badge, went flying and as a result he was totally admired and respected by everyone on the squadron. He was one of the great characters of 141 and I do not know what we and the CO would have done without him.

On 12 August Frank Davis, our Flight Commander, with his Nav/Rad Jimmy Wheldon shot down a Junkers 88 over northern France and we – in 'B' Flight – were all pleased for him. Frank again was older than most of us and a very experienced and skilled pilot, but he had come into operational flying late on in his career and, like other pilots with many hours of flying instruction behind them, found that life on a squadron was a very different kettle of fish. Men like Frank Davis were gallant gentlemen and the morale of 'B' Flight got a good boost with his victory.

On the night 15/16 August Bomber Command attacked Italy with a raid on Milan for the second night running. Eight aircraft of 141 went down to Ford (our old station) on the Sussex coast, which was used as a forward base when the bomber's target was in southern France or Italy. On this night, the squadron's aircraft were not split into two sections and the eight of us took off with only 40 minutes separating the first and last aircraft. There were no claims and one 141 crew, F/Sgt M.M. Robertson and F/Sgt D.J. Gillam, were reported 'MISSING'. Harry and I took off at 22.05 hours and 'Robbie' and 'Dougie' went off ten minutes behind us. They didn't come back.

It was not until nearly fifty years later that I met up with Dougie again and heard the full story of hazard and adventure which, in many ways, exceeded the experiences of those of us who survived on the squadron to complete a tour of 30 trips. They were shot down over northern France . . . baled out of their burning aircraft . . . were captured and became prisoners-of-war. They were interrogated at *Dulag Luft* . . . and then sent to *Stalag* IV B in Eastern Germany.

Both Robbie and Dougie received their warrants, whilst in the camp, and were promoted to Warrant Officer before being released and returning to England in May 1945. They played a courageous and leading part in the life of *Stalag* IV B and, in the post-war years, they followed one another as President of the *Stalag* IV B POW Association, a considerable honour and one which reflected the regard in which they were held by their fellow POWs. Robbie was a dour, but very likeable, Scot and I did not know him that well, but Dougie Gillam had been with Harry and me on the Turbinlite Havocs at Tangmere throughout 1942.

Dougie was a gentle little man but dogged and full of determination. They were both a loss to the squadron. He has continued to overcome all sorts of trials and tribulations with courage and humour beyond the call of duty. He has achieved many successes in his life and, happily, today I am privileged to number him among my closest friends.

We must now return to our own sortie of that night. It will be recalled that Harry and I took off from Ford ten minutes in front of Robbie and Dougie to patrol the German airfield of Châteaudun. Don's History records yet another failure:

> 'They crossed the French coast at Fecamp and continued towards target area but owing to radio (radar) failure they patrolled short of target area and Paris area.'

We landed back at Wittering at 00.20 hours and before we got to bed learned that Robbie and Dougie were missing and nobody had made any claims of E/A destroyed or damaged. One of our eight aircraft, flown by Charles Winn, with 'Scotty' as his navigator, was hit by return fire from a friendly aircraft, when they were investigating an AI contact. It proved to be a Wellington whose crew were, quite rightly, taking no chances over Occupied Europe! 'Winnie' (as Squadron Leader C.V. Winn DFC, OC of 'A' Flight, was affectionately known) lost his hydraulics and the VHF and had to make a belly-landing at Ford on his return. To add insult to injury, he was fired on by the aerodrome's ground defences, but fortunately both Charles and Scotty survived these 'slings and arrows' without any injury to their persons. One way and another, it had been another depressing night for the Serrate fighters of 141.

On the 16th Harry and I did a X-country up to Scotland and back via Drem and Dallachy. I can't think why: it must have been another attempt to improve my navigation! We took off at 15.05 hours and landed back at Wittering four hours later.

Looking back through the Squadron History for the night 15/16 and the patrols flown by the 141 aircraft, there was, after all, one bright spot on the horizon. The inimitable CO – with Jacko in the rear cockpit – found no joy, at high-level, so went down and shot up Melun airfield near Paris with cannon and machine-gun and strafed the hangars! He wrote in his log-book '. . . chased Hun around Melun airfield and machine-gunned aerodrome . . .' Braham said that he 'awakened the defenders and they filled the sky with streams of flak.' He thought that it was all great fun!

There was another crew on 141, Flight Lieutenant H.C. Kelsey and his Nav/Rad E.M. Smith, who were starting off on a distinguished career in the night-fighter business. Howard Kelsey was already an experienced pilot when he came to 141, but both he and 'Smithy' were new to the game. They were among the rare night-fighter crews who, on coming from OTU to a squadron, achieved immediate success, and prior to 16 August they had had several combats and claims. On the 16th, over northern France, in the area of Châteaudun (where Harry and I had been on the previous night) they found three German night-fighters in a close V formation. This was a most unusual and delectable sight!

The formation was very close, less than a span apart, consisting of a Junkers 88 in the centre, a Messerschmitt 110 on the starboard side and a second Ju 88 on the port side. Howard Kelsey wrote in his report, 'We saw no lights on the enemy aircraft who appeared so preoccupied with their formation flying that they did not see us'. He opened fire and managed to make an attack on all three aircraft. He and Smithy claimed the leading Ju 88 destroyed, the Me 110 probably destroyed and the remaining Ju 88, on the port side, as damaged.

After all that was written in the chapters on the Turbinlite operation – and the difficulties of flying in formation at night – this was a most interesting development and we were left wondering exactly what new tactics were being developed by our opposite numbers in the *Luftwaffe*. Needless to say, Harry and I were envious of Howard and Smithy's good fortune when we heard all about it on the morning of the 17th. Later on, we ourselves were to find two Me 109s in formation but generally, like ourselves, the Germans fought the war at night on a single aircraft versus single aircraft basis.

We must now turn our attention to one of the great raids of the war – the Peenemünde raid and the small, but significant, part played in it by 141 Squadron. On the night 17/18 August 1943, 600 aircraft bombed the German Research and Experimental Station of Peenemünde, located on the Baltic coast. Here, under a tight blanket of secrecy, Hitler's so-called secret weapons were being designed, developed and test flown. In particular, they were the Flying Bomb, a pilotless aircraft known as the V-1 (later nicknamed 'the Doodle Bug') and the A4 long-range rocket, designated the V-2.

When the photographic reconnaissance aircraft returned to base with their pictures after the raid, it was deemed to have been successful. The development and production of these weapons were considered to have been set back by several months. The price? 40 bombers and their crews, nearly 300 aircrew, was not thought to be excessive. Supporting the raid, 141 Squadron shot down four German night-fighters without loss.

The Peenemünde raid ranks as one of the five best known raids carried out by Bomber Command during World War II. The others are the first 1,000-bomber raid on Cologne, the Dams raid, the Hamburg raid of 27/28 July 1943, the Nuremberg raid on 30/31 March 1944 and the raid on Dresden in February 1945.

The outstanding book on Peenemünde was *The Peenemünde Raid.* (*See* Bibliography.)

Turning to the Squadron History:

> 'On the night of 17/18th August 1943, Bomber Command attacked the secret German experimental research establishment at Peenemünde situated on a peninsula on the Southern Baltic Sea coast in Northern Germany. It was here that the V-1 pilotless flying bomb and the V-2 rocket, were being developed and it was vital that it be destroyed to avert heavy attacks by these new weapons on England. A force of 596 bombers were dispatched made up of Lancasters, Halifaxes and Stirlings. They dropped 1,924 tons of bombs and they suffered the loss of 40 bombers, 6.7% of the force. The attack was carried out on a moonlit night in order to ensure bombing accuracy and – for the first time – a Master Bomber was used to control the raid.'

> . . .

> '141 Squadron operated on this night and put up the best effort yet on Serrate Bomber Support by operating 10 Beaufighters. Their small force was split into two halves in order to give support to the bombers as they went out over the North Sea, and similarly, as they returned after attacking Peenemünde.'

> . . .

> 'W/C Braham with F/L Jacobs destroyed two enemy aircraft and F/O White with F/O Allen claimed one destroyed and one damaged, but post-war research has amended that to two destroyed. This total of four enemy aircraft destroyed in one night, with no losses, was the best overall success that 141 Squadron had in World War II.'

Before the ten Beaus took off from Wittering we had the usual briefing in the remote hut on the airfield, when the CO and Buster introduced us to the name of Peenemünde, of which no one had ever heard. The bomber track looked an incredible distance as it stretched out across the North Sea, on over Denmark and then still further on into the Baltic, until it was just past Rostock. The target must have been all of 600 miles away. It was pointed out to us that it was an exceptionally important target and success was vital.

The story we were given (remember that prior to 17 August the discovery of the V-1 and V-2 rocket sites was 'TOP SECRET' and for obvious reasons!) was that Peenemünde was a special site, chosen by the Germans, because it was remote from attack by British bombers, where they were manufacturing night-fighter aircraft. The bomber crews could not have been given any more cogent reason for pressing home their attack! There was no mention of the flying bombs and the rockets. . .

There was one other ominous piece of information delivered by Wing Commander Braham himself, before the briefing was ended, and I never heard it at any other briefing right through to the end of the war. He said, with more seriousness than usual;

> 'I have been instructed to tell you, and this instruction is going out to every crew taking part in tonight's raid, that if the attack is not successful, you will go again tomorrow night . . . and if it is not successful tomorrow night, *you will go every night until it is successful.*'

There was quite a hush in our small briefing hut. God knows what it must have been like in the larger briefing rooms of the bomber squadrons . . .

The plan was that we, in our Beaufighters, should patrol to the north of the Frisian Islands, thus positioning ourselves between the German night-fighter bases in Northern Holland (and NW Germany) and the bomber stream, as it passed on its way across the North Sea heading towards Denmark. Similarly, on its return journey after the bombing of Peenemünde. It was anticipated that once the bombers were picked up by the *Freyas* (the German long-range radio-location equipment) the waiting Me 110s and Ju 88s would be scrambled by the Ground Controllers from Leeuwarden and elsewhere and ordered to fly north to intercept them.

Our small force was split into two: five Beaus taking off from our advanced base at Coltishall (at five-minute intervals) between 10.00 and 10.26 hrs, to be on patrol when the bombers were heading for Denmark; the other five taking off at the later times of 23.45 to 00.07, with the aim of being over the Frisians when the returning bombers were over Denmark. They could then escort them on the long seaward crossing back towards their bases in East Anglia, Lincoln and Yorkshire. All ten Beaufighter crews were hoping that they might be able to come between the defending German fighters and their prey. Harry and I were amongst those on the second wave, and we took off at one minute to midnight.

Bomber Support Operations: the Bomber Stream shown flying out at dusk, over the North Sea as darkness closes around them. The 'loose gaggle' closed up as the stream neared the target area. Nobody ever attempted to fly in formation in the dark, but the concentration of heavy bombers over Germany was generally supposed to bring greater protection from flak and night-fighters.

The entries in my log-book, for the night's work, read:

Tues. 17th 18.40 hrs	Beau 8713 F/O White To Coltishall	00.25 hrs
Tues. 17th 23.59 hrs	Beau 8713 F/O White Ops Peenemünde 1 Me 110 DAMAGED at Groningen. 1 Ju 88 DESTROYED at Lingen	04.00 hrs

The entry was decorated with a swastika, such was the fashion of the times!

Harry wrote an account of our trip which was published in 1985 by 'Laddie' Lucas in his book *Out Of The Blue, The Role of Luck in Air Warfare 1917–1966*. It will be seen from Harry's account, under the heading 'Strangers in the Night', we had a fair amount of luck, ourselves, that night. Introducing Harry's story, 'Laddie' wrote: 'With all the sophisticated radar equipment which the Allies could now employ, night intruding by our fighters was becoming an important factor in support of Bomber Command's offensive. It made the *Luftwaffe* crews, bent on stalking our bombers, feel very uneasy.'

Harry liked to call his account of the night's happenings by another title and, in reproducing it in full here, I shall use the title which he favoured of 'One Up – Two Down'.

> 'Four lines of yellow tracer streaked just over our canopy and, almost simultaneously, we heard the rattle of his cannons.
>
> A shout from my navigator, "Some bastard's firing at us!"'

No. 141 Squadron, Wittering: the Beaufighter Mk VI with which the Squadron was equipped, when the first High-Level Bomber Support operations – code-named 'Serrate' – were flown in June 1943.

"I know." I had already pushed everything – stick, rudder throttles – into the "bottom right-hand corner".

Bomber Command's attack that night, 17/18 August 1943, had been on the German V-1 and V-2 experimental rocket base at Peenemünde on the Baltic coast.

As night intruders our Squadron's role in Fighter Command was for one flight to escort the Lancasters out as far as the limited range of our Beaufighters would allow. Our other flight was, later, to meet the returning bombers as deep into Germany as possible and escort them home. Our targets were the enemy night-fighters which ranged along the bomber's route that night.

Mike Allen, with whom I shared four years of war, and I took off from our forward base at Coltishall in Norfolk at midnight and, an hour and a half later were approaching Hamburg at about 16,000 feet on a clear moonlit night. Mike had picked up a contact on his radar and we set out to investigate. Normally we would know from the type of our radar contact whether it was hostile or not. This time we did not. I suppose, looking back, that was why I was less alert than I should have been. I presumed it would be "one of ours".

Using our radar we closed rapidly from two to three miles and had to lose height to put our target slightly above so I could identify it visually against the slightly lighter sky. Going "down hill" we had built up a fair overtaking speed.

Bomber Support Operations: the defending German night-fighters (equipped with airborne radar) were the Junkers 88 and the Messerschmit 110. This photograph of a captured Junkers 88 clearly shows the cumbersome aerials of the Lichtenstein AI. *These unwieldy aerials detracted from the performance of an aircraft which proved itself to be one of the most efficient and versatile machines of World War II.*

I saw a dull black shape emerge from the darkness just above the horizon about 1,500 feet away, closing fast. At 500 feet I realised this shape was a Messerschmitt 110, a twin engined German night-fighter.

I swore.

I was closing too fast to open fire. I eased back the throttles. I dare not snap them shut. If I did there would be sheets of flame from our exhaust. We would be seen.

To help lose speed I turned hard port and then back to starboard. It was at that precise instant that we became the target. The Me 110 must have seen this Beaufighter slip out from underneath him and then, slowing down, turn to port and starboard in front of him. A gift . . .

If it hadn't been for that instant glimpse of tracer I would not have had that split second lead which I needed to get the hell out of it. If he hadn't used tracer – and only some German night-fighters did – he would have had time to correct his aim before I knew I was being attacked. He would, perhaps, have written this story: not me.

But the night was still young.

Chastened, breathing deeply, but having evaded, we climbed back to our operating height. Neither Mike nor I were in a mood to let matters rest there.

Twenty minutes later, using our radar, we were closing slowly on, this time, a known enemy aircraft. Even at full throttle it took an age. Our opponent was obviously on his way towards our returning stream of bombers. Mike read off the range –

"1500 feet."

I acknowledged. Black; still very black out there.

"1200 feet."

I could see a faint blur.

"1000 feet."

It looked like another Me 110.

"900 feet."

It was an Me 110.

"Still 900 feet."

And again, "Still 900 feet."

Even at full throttle we couldn't close the range further.

I took aim. 900 ft is not an ideal range, even on a light night. I opened fire with our four cannons and six machine-guns. There were strikes, like fireworks; flecks of flame; flashes; a dull red glow and the Messerschmitt dived steeply. We followed. I lost sight of the blur. It merged with the inky blackness of the ground below. We would claim one enemy aircraft damaged. It might have been destroyed but we couldn't be sure.

Back up to operating height again. Re-set course to meet our returning bombers. On we went; eastwards. Shortly, another enemy radar contact. Again, even at full throttle, slowly, laboriously brought to within visual range.

"It's a Junkers 88, Mike."

My navigator grunted and looked up from his radar.

"Fix him properly." he said. "Don't bugger about this time."

Slowly I closed to 700 feet. I took careful aim. I gave him everything. The first three second burst started a fire in his starboard engine. The fire flashed through the fuselage. It engulfed the port engine. The Ju 88 was well alight. I gave it another three-second burst of cannons and machine-guns. There was a blinding flash. The Ju 88 spiralled down shedding burning pieces and minutes later blew up as it hit the ground. One enemy aircraft destroyed.

With fuel now critical we set course for base, landing two hours later. We had made a hash of one attack and had only survived to make two successful attacks that same night because our attacker had – by chance – been armed with visible tracer ammunition. That had to be the chance of a life-time. For Mike and I that tracer had been the difference between life and death. But that is not quite the end.

Forty years later, as part of his research for his book on the Peenemünde raid, Martin Middlebrook found and interviewed a pilot of a Messerschmitt 110 who had been attacked and shot down at the precise time and place of our second encounter on 17/18 August 1943. He had been burned and had baled out that night.

The real score that night was One Beaufighter frightened; One Messerschmitt 110 and One Junkers 88 both destroyed. One Up; Two Down.

HEW

28 Oct 1984.'

We were certainly lucky that night and I will always be grateful to 'Laddie' for including 'One Up – Two Down' in his collection of unbelievable stories about 'The Role of Luck in Warfare'.

Apart from the swastika that I entered in my log-book, the morning after Peenemünde (rather like getting a 'star' in one's class book at infant school!) I inserted a quotation from Rupert Brooke – which will be mentioned later.

Our Combat Report says:

'We took off from Coltishall at 23.50 on an intruder patrol to Leeuwarden and crossed the English coast three minutes later. The Dutch coast was sighted at 00.30 hours and crossed at 00.37. At 00.50 an enemy aircraft was sighted 500 feet below crossing port to starboard.'

This was the Me 110 that – a few seconds later – caused me to shout out to Harry 'Some bastard's firing at us' and which caused him to take such violent evasive action.

Our Combat Report continues:

'We turned in below and closed rapidly to 400 feet where enemy aircraft was identified as Me 110. Beaufighter overshot and turned to port then hard to starboard to regain visual. Messerschmitt fired short burst of tracer from above and behind, Beaufighter peeled off undamaged.'

As we have seen from Harry's account, written for 'Laddie' many years after the event, which commenced, 'Four lines of yellow tracer streaked over our canopy and, almost simultaneously, we heard the rattle of his cannons'.

What really happened was that, soon after we had skirted the Dutch island of Terschelling, I saw a contact on the Mk IV AI but thought it was too soon for us to be picking up any German aircraft. I thought it must be one of ours and I never bothered to intercept it properly! I thought it could be one of the other Beaufighters operating in the area or even a stray British bomber off track! Harry never had a chance.

At the last minute I saw that the range of the blip on my tubes was decreasing rapidly and that we were on a converging course with the other aircraft, which would mean that we would pass within close proximity of each other and at completely the wrong angle for us to take a good look at him. The blip disappeared into minimum range on my AI and Harry got the fleeting glimpse of him as we overshot and he slipped in behind *us*. We both thought afterwards that, as we passed in front of him, the pilot of the Me 110 was too close behind to get his nose down properly without the danger of ramming us. Thus when, as Harry says, he was presented with 'a sitter' and opened fire, his tracer went over the top of our canopy and we were belatedly made aware of his true identity!

He must have been close, because both of us heard the sound of his cannon above the noise of our own engines. The quotation in my log-book, to which I referred earlier, comes from a piece of Rupert Brooke's and reads, 'And then you suddenly cried, and turned away!'

I thought it was rather apt for the moment when I drew Harry's attention to the four lines of tracer going over our heads with the Anglo-Saxon observation to the effect that some bastard was firing at us and he replied 'I know' as he pushed everything into the bottom right-hand corner and 8713 fell out of the sky.

In our first encounter of the night we lost a lot of height as we peeled off and out of the way of the unpleasant attention of the gentlemen behind us. We must have been down to about 10,000 feet before Harry decided it was safe to pull out. We clawed our way back up to about 18,000 feet and almost immediately I found an AI contact. I switched across to the Serrate frequency and there was the distinctive herring-bone pattern pulsating away strongly with every indication that the enemy night-fighter was in front of us and only a mile or two away.

Sure enough, when I switched back to the AI time trace there was the blip which, in azimuth and in elevation, matched up with the Serrate signals. We had only to finish off the interception carefully . . . bring him to minimum range . . . obtain a visual . . . and we would have him. And thereby, we would be able to atone for the earlier fiasco.

At this point, it may well be asked, 'Why didn't you use your Serrate frequency to check on your first contact of the night? If the Me 110 had been using his *Lichtenstein* AI you could have identified him for Harry straight away . . . carried out a successful interception . . . and saved yourselves a lot of trouble!' I have wrestled with that problem, over the intervening years, and I honestly don't know the answer to it. Finger trouble, I suspect, is the solution!

To return to our Combat Report and our second contact:

> 'At 01.10 a second Me 110 was sighted ahead and on the same level at 1500 feet; range was closed very slowly at full throttle to 900 feet and three second cannon and machine-gun burst fired as Me 110 dived steeply, several strikes and a red glow was seen. A further three second burst was fired, no further results observed. Claim Me 110 damaged.'

What happened was that the Me 110 was faster than we were. With full throttle pushed right through the 'gate', we simply could not catch him. Eventually Harry was forced to open fire at very long range – 900 feet – where he could hardly be sure of hitting him; let alone doing enough damage to make sure he went down. As Harry said '. . . There were strikes, like fireworks; flecks of flame; flashes; a dull red glow and the Messerschmitt dived steeply. We followed. I lost sight of the blur. It merged with the inky blackness of the ground below. We would claim one enemy aircraft damaged. It might have been destroyed but we couldn't be sure.'

Already it has been observed that the Serrate operations were not going as well as might have been hoped. And mention has been made of the relatively short range of the Beaufighter. We only had fuel for a sortie of about five hours and this imposed severe limitations on our ability to support the bombers properly. On the night of Peenemünde we could only mount patrols over the Dutch Islands and the north-west tip of Germany, although the main action by the German night-fighters was, inevitably, going to take place over the target, the Baltic and Denmark.

Harry and I had now had personal, and frustrating, experience of the second major limitation on the chances of success against our opposite numbers. The Me 110s and the Ju 88s were too fast for us and our Beau VIs could not catch them if the interception developed into a lengthy stern chase. Apart from reducing the chances of destroying them, it meant that we were spending too much of our time and fuel chasing one E/A around the sky (as with the second Me 110 we met) instead of being able to make a quick kill and go looking for the next.

The CO with Jacko got the other two kills on the night 17/18, as we shall see shortly, and they destroyed two Me 110s within the matter of a few minutes. We must return once more to our Combat Report and to our third encounter of the night:

'Patrol continued until 01.55 when a Ju 88 was sighted slightly above and to starboard. Enemy aircraft was followed visually for five minutes at full throttle as range slowly decreased to 250 yards. A three second burst was fired from dead astern, strikes were seen and a fire in the starboard engine spreading through the fuselage to the port engine. After another three second burst a blinding yellow flash blotted out everything. Enemy aircraft was still burning, spiralling down leaving a track of burning pieces and blew up on hitting the ground North of Lingen at 02.00 hours. Claim one Ju 88 destroyed. Recrossed Enemy coast at Spiekeroog at 02.30, English Coast East of Coltishall at 03.30 and landed Wittering 04.00.'

Our third combat came about through another Serrate interception and, as will be seen from our Combat Report, we again had difficulty in overhauling our target and bringing it within firing range. Harry's account in his piece for 'Laddie' Lucas picks up the story '. . . Back up to operating height again. Re-set course to meet our returning bombers. On we went; eastwards. Shortly, another enemy radar contact. Again, even at full throttle, slowly, laboriously brought to within visual range. "It's a Junkers 88, Mike".' It was at that stage of the proceedings that I apparently grunted to him over the intercom, and told him to 'Fix him properly', and added, for good measure, 'Don't bugger about this time'. As he said '. . . I took careful aim. I gave him everything . . .'

When we landed back at Wittering and taxied in, our ground crew saw that the patches over the guns were gone and that this time there was cause to celebrate . . .

There were two sequels to our sortie on the night 17/18 and for both of them we are in the debt of Martin Middlebrook. When he was carrying out his research for *The Peenemünde Raid*, I happened to be on leave in England (my wife and I were living in South Africa at the time) and had the good fortune to meet him. Charles Winn and his wife Sue kindly invited Pam and I to lunch at their lovely home outside Huntingdon and Martin Middlebrook came down from Lincolnshire to join us.

Charles had flown on the Peenemünde trip but had had no joy. So, after lunch, he left me alone with Martin. I quickly learned that he knew far more about what had been going on that night than I did! He was painstaking and precise in his questions and I acquired a deep regard for his work as a military historian and for the humanity of the man himself.

Martin told me that our third contact had also been with a Messerschmitt 110, not the Junkers 88 which we had apparently identified in error, but fortunately not attacked in error, i.e. it might just have been one of our own Beaus. Greg and Steve had taken off from Coltishall only minutes after us! Further, Martin went on to tell me that the E/A had been flown by *Hauptmann* Wilhelm Dormann of III/NJG 1, a pre-war *Lufthansa* pilot and a veteran night-fighter who had been sent up from Twente to patrol a local box. His fighter control officer kept vectoring him on to 'stray British bombers' which was, in fact, the wandering Beaufighter. In other words – *us*! The view of events, from our opposite number *Hauptmann* Dormann, is related in Martin Middlebrook's book:

> 'My radar man kept on obtaining firm contacts but none of them led to a visual sighting. The bombers were flying faster than we were. They knew this area well and were diving through it fast. I was sent higher so that I, too, could dive on the next contact, but that didn't work either.
>
> Then my operator got another contact on his screen. I went after it, but the next thing that happened was that we were hit by well-aimed defensive fire from its rear gunner. My plane started burning and the rudders wouldn't work. We were going straight down. I couldn't contact the radar operator because the intercom had failed. I was pulled out of the plane by strong suction. I made a hard landing and lay in a field until a farm worker found me next morning.'

Martin goes on to say that *Hauptmann* Dormann suffered severe head injuries and burns and never flew operationally again. He was most interested to be told, nearly forty years later, that there never had been a bomber and that he had been shot down by an intruder. The body of his radar operator, *Oberfeldwebel* Friedrich Schmalscheidt, was found near his half-opened parachute.

The second piece of information that Martin had for me was that the Me 110 which Harry and I had not been able to catch, and had only been able to claim as 'DAMAGED', was in fact 'DESTROYED', and Don Aris in his 141 History records that the Me 110 came from IV/NJG 1 based at Leeuwarden in northern Holland. Of the crew, the pilot, *Leutnant* Gerhard Dittman, and *Unteroffizier* Theophil Bundschuh were both killed when they dived away from us and crashed into the sea, just north of their own airfield.

It will be recalled that we all took off that night in ignorance of the futuristic weapons that were being developed at Peenemünde. For me personally, there was no hint that I might be flying in support of a raid on a target from which was to come – in the shape of a V-2 – the destruction of my own home and the death of my father and mother. Perhaps, here, the Germans had the last laugh after all?

But on the morning after one of the great raids of the war, the Germans were not laughing, as they surveyed the ruins of their rocket development station. Back in England the news filtered through to the bomber stations that the raid had been a success and that there would be no need for the crews to go, again, to Peenemünde.

This news was soon followed by the announcement that there would be no ops that night and all Squadrons were stood down until the following day. The briefing hut at Wittering and the briefing rooms throughout Bomber Command were silent and empty on the evening of 18/19 August.

At the beginning of the Peenemünde story we have already learned that W/Cdr Braham with F/Lt Jacobs destroyed two enemy aircraft. The CO and Jacko took off with the first wave at 22.00 hours and an hour later he was shooting down the first of his two Me 110s! Fifteen minutes after seeing it catch fire and fall into the sea, he was attacking the second one!

Jacko had picked up Serrate contacts as they flew up the line of the Dutch islands and past Ameland to Schiermonnikoog, matched first one and then the other to the blips on his AI tubes and Bob Braham, seeing the E/A early, in the good weather conditions, had done the rest. In *Scramble* Bob related how he nearly collided with the second 110.

> 'Above me in a tight turn was another Me110 and, at the speed we were travelling, looked as if we were going to ram him. I eased back the stick, put the sights on him and fired at the point-blank range of about fifty yards. There was a blinding flash as the Me exploded in my face. Our Beau. rocked violently, threatening to flick over on its back. My windscreen was flecked with oil from the exploding wreckage which hurtled seawards. "God, that was close." was all Bob Braham could say.
>
> Then, by the light of the moon, he saw a parachute floating down. He called up Jacko on the intercom and said ". . . One of the bastards must have been blown clear, I'm going to finish him off." As Bob banked round to come in and open fire on the figure dangling from the shrouds of the parachute it was Jacko, who shouted out "Bob, let the poor blighter alone."'

The CO pulled away and let 'the poor blighter' go. He told us all the story, when we got back later to Wittering. The life of that airman – at least at that minute – was saved by a Jew. Jacko was of that race which had the least cause to show any humanity towards the Germans but, apart from being an exceptional AI operator, Jacko was just a wonderful bloke.

There was an interesting sideline to this story for Harry and I. It looked as if we weren't the only crew to come in too fast and overshoot in the closing stages of an interception!

Don's History states:

> 'The two Me 110s shot down by W/C Braham came from one of the most successful German night fighter units, IV/NJG 1 based at Leeuwarden, Holland. They were part of five Me 110s that had taken off under *Leutnant* Heinz-Wolfgang Schnaufer to intercept what they thought were bombers.'

Leutnant Schnaufer had to abort his sortie on account of engine failure which, in the light of his subsequent career, was a pity. He went on to become the most successful German night-fighter pilot, claiming the destruction of no fewer than 121 British aircraft, the majority of which were the four-engined heavy bombers. If he had not had engine failure that night he might have come up against Bob Braham. Who can tell what the outcome would have been? But Schnaufer was only at the beginning of his brilliant career and, biased in Bob Braham's favour, it makes for wishful-thinking to ruminate on the chance that 121 British bomber crews might have lived a little longer.

As it was, both the CO's victims – *Feldwebels* George Kraft and Heinz Vinke

– were experienced night-fighter aces, with some 35 successes between them. Vinke survived to carry on operating and had a total of 54 victories before he was finally shot down on 26 February 1944. One of our victims, *Hauptmann* Dormann, was also a veteran night-fighter pilot, with 14 victories.

When I wrote, in one of the earlier paragraphs about '. . . the small but significant contribution made by 141 Squadron . . . to the Peenemünde raid', this was one of the aspects I had in mind, whilst never forgetting that the worst casualties amongst our bomber crews were being suffered east of Denmark and beyond the range of the Beaufighters.

Leutnant Dittman and his crew who went down in our damaged Me 110 crashing to the north of Leeuwarden also came from IV/NJG 1, so as Martin Middlebrook observes: 'This made three aircraft lost and five men killed from this elite *Gruppe* which had spent most of the night chasing 141 Squadron's Beaufighters instead of flying in the more profitable operations at Peenemünde.'

So what about the other eight Beaufighter patrols, four – apart from the CO – on the early shift and four – apart from Harry White – on the late shift? What sort of luck did they all have? Sadly, from the point of view of many unnamed bomber crews the answer was 'None'. Although the other eight crews picked up a number of Serrate signals which were followed up, there were no other claims. So the squadron's score for the night remained at four E/A destroyed. Although, as already pointed out, at the time 141 had to settle for three destroyed and one damaged.

A full account has been given of the part played by 141 Squadron in the Peenemünde operation. It probably did not make much difference in Bomber Command's losses for the night, which amounted to 40 aircraft, but the account does give a clear illustration of what the squadron, and other squadrons, might have been able to achieve if they had been equipped with faster aeroplanes, capable of flying further into Germany.

Shortly after we on 141 started to pioneer the Serrate operation we began to receive visits from the recently formed Operation Research Section; we might think of them as the logistical boffins.

They questioned us carefully on our return from operations (in addition to the normal debriefing by Buster Reynolds) and took away all the radar/radio reports filled in by the AI operators. They carefully analysed the results of the Serrate operations and their reports must have played a significant part in the developments which were to take place later in 1943 and heralded the start of Phase 4 of the radar countermeasures which were all aimed at reducing the losses among the bomber force.

As I have already recorded, when discussing the operations of 9/10 August, the CO was very much alive to the problem and had, for weeks, been badgering 12 Group and Fighter Command for 141 to be re-equipped with the faster Mosquito, which also had a much longer range. If we had Mosquitoes, we could get to Berlin 550 miles away across the North German Plain and would stand a chance of overhauling the 110s and 88s which had been pulling away from us to safety.

The Operational Research Section produced a 'MOST SECRET' Synopsis of the Serrate Operations carried out on the night of the Peenemünde raid, although I did not see it until many years after the war. The synopsis is an important document, not only because it was covering the night of 17/18 August 1943, but because it paints such a clear picture of the nature of the Serrate operations overall during the pioneering days of High-Level Bomber Support and in what I have classified as Phase 3. By the middle of August Phase 3 had only a few more weeks to run.

After Peenemünde, Harry and I must have gone on nine days' leave because apart from a night flying test on 19 August, my log-book reveals nothing until the 30th, and then an uneventful op in support of a raid on Berlin on the last day of the month. It seems trite to refer to any raid on Berlin as being uneventful but it will be remembered that at this stage, with the limited range of our Beaufighters, the 141 patrols were stopping far short of 'the Big City'. We were only briefed to wander about the German airfields in Belgium and Holland. We were not going out to our aircraft at Coltishall to face the deadly defences of the Third Reich over the Fatherland, potent from the ground in the shape of masses of 88 mm anti-aircraft guns with myriads of supporting searchlights, and potent from the air with the single-engined 'Wild Boar' fighters, now backing up the radar-equipped 88s and 110s, over the target area.

Whilst Harry and I were away on leave, another story was added to the many which have been collected, treasured and handed down concerning the CO, and this time it involved two of the elderly non-flying officers who served 141 Squadron, and Bob Braham, so well.

At least, one of them was supposed to be a non-flying officer, but he had already shown earlier in the year (when the squadron was flying Instep patrols and Rangers at night over the Bay from Predannack) that he did not think he could do his job properly, unless he did go on operations himself.

This was, of course, our irrepressible Intelligence Officer, Flying Officer Cedric 'Buster' Reynolds. The other was Flight Lieutenant 'Dickie' Sparrowe, the Adjutant of 141, who was also of mighty assistance to the CO by virtue of relieving him of all unwanted paperwork, which, for Bob Braham, really meant all!

On the night 27/28 August the CO with his Nav/Rad F/Lt Jacobs flew on a sortie in support of a raid on Nuremberg. He took with him, as a passenger, Buster Reynolds, but not before Dickie Sparrowe had made Buster sign a 'blood chit' absolving the Air Force of all responsibility, should things go wrong! So here we had a man, well into his thirties, married with four children, a solicitor in private life, who had no call to go flying – least of all on operations – cheerfully signing away any chance of a pension for his widow (if he was killed) and compensation for his four children, the whole signing process being carried out by a gloating wing commander and his adjutant, both prophesying the worst! If books could be written about Bob Braham, one could certainly be written about Cedric Reynolds.

The three of them took off from Coltishall at 21.30 hours on an Intruder patrol to the German night-fighter airfield of Florennes, Belgium, with Buster standing just behind the CO and immediately over the pilot's escape hatch. It must be emphasised again that the Intelligence Officer had no business to be airborne and setting out over Occupied Europe. Anyway his fate, if he had become a POW, has already been mentioned in an earlier chapter. Buster had his own helmet and head-set, so that he could hear all that passed over the intercom between Bob and Jacko and speak to either of them – should the occasion warrant it! He also had a portable oxygen set, which had been specially fixed up for him by the Engineering Officer; so he was well set up for his trip although he was unlikely to take a stroll down the fuselage to see Jacko, because that would have meant clambering over the ammunition-drums which fed the four 20 mm cannon in the belly of the aircraft.

Reading Don Aris's History covering this sortie we see that:

'They crossed the English coast at Lowestoft at 21.38 hours and the enemy coast at Vlissingen at 22.07 hours. There was intense but inaccurate flak from Brussels. There were large orange ground lights in unusually large numbers in clusters, lines and irregular shapes all the way from the coast to the target area. At Florennes the visual Lorenz NE/SW was on continually, the floodlight switched on several times but no sign of enemy aircraft. On the way out there was some flak from Brussels, and they recrossed the enemy coast at Walcheren, Holland at 00.05 hours. Just after doing so the starboard engine threw out sparks and finally burst into flames, possibly through flak. The fire was put out by extinguisher after five minutes but the propeller was in "fully fine" and the port engine was running badly.

W/C Braham set course for base on one engine and the other running badly and found it impossible to maintain height. He was dropping rapidly from 6,000 feet, so course was altered to Bradwell Bay on the Essex Coast . . . and he was down to 1,500 feet when he got there. He made a perfect landing at 00.55 hours. It had been thought at first that the engine had been hit by flak but closer examination proved it to be a technical fault.'

We all got the full story, at the time, of the conversation which had ensued over the intercom as the Beaufighter steadily lost height over the Channel as Bob made for a single-engined landing at Bradwell Bay. Many years after the war, when I used to call on Buster at his home in Totteridge and we would reminisce about Bob Braham, this was one of his favourite stories.

As they struggled back, with one engine out and the other running badly, Braham started a conversation with Jacko, telling him that they could no longer maintain height and that he had better start looking around to see what was 'movable' and could be jettisoned to lighten the aircraft. Jacko made quite a thing of pretending to look around and made one or two suggestions back over the intercom to an apparently carefree and relaxed Bob Braham sitting up in front – with an anxious Buster behind him and peering out over his shoulder at the defunct starboard engine.

In point of fact, there was very little which could be jettisoned from a Beau. It was not like a large bomber, where the gunners could wrench their guns from their mountings, throwing them and the ammunition belts out, thus making a material contribution to reducing the aircraft load and giving it much-needed extra height. Additionally, if the navigator were to prise open either his own hatch in the rear, or the pilot's hatch over which Buster was standing, they would cause extra drag which was the last thing the pilot needed at that moment.

Although the exchange between Bob and Jacko was apparently light-hearted, the situation was, in fact, deadly serious for all three of them. A Beau VIF, with one engine out and the other running badly, was not a happy aircraft. Only a few weeks later we were to lose F/Lt Ferguson when he went into the sea just off the French coast, in very similar circumstances. Fortunately, his navigator, Roger Osborn, was saved by the Air-Sea Rescue Services.

However, Bob and Jacko continued to build up the story. Including Buster in their conversation they asked him what he thought should be thrown out of the labouring Beau which, by now, looked as if it was headed for a ditching with a long row home for its crew! Eventually Bob Braham said to Buster, when none of them could think of what ought to go, something like, 'Jacko and I might just make it on our own . . .' and then, a few minutes later: 'Buster, I'm terribly sorry to have to ask you, but I think you've got to go . . . !'

I could never get out of Buster his answer to this monstrous suggestion (made with Bob and Jacko restraining themselves from laughing with some difficulty), but thankfully, Buster was still with them when they landed safely at Bradwell Bay.

When we got back home from leave, apart from that story, we found that the 'Yanks' had moved in and it was rather like Tangmere '42 all over again. Plenty of poker-dice played on the floor of the bar and plenty of lively repartee, on both sides!

The third squadron of the USAAF 20th Fighter Group, the 55th, had arrived at Wittering on 27 August. They were equipped with P-38 Lockheed Lightnings and were under the command of Major D.R. McGovern who had had some operational experience in the Pacific. He was a first-rate Commanding Officer and he and Wing Commander Braham became firm friends. Major McGovern flew with Bob and Jacko on 29 September (the CO's last op with 141), as a passenger, and witnessed Braham destroy an Me 110 and damage a Ju 88. Buster Reynolds was rather put out when he learned about it, because in all his various sorties with the CO he had never had the satisfaction and fun of seeing a German aircraft shot down.

In the mess, the Americans were irrepressible but, along with their Commanding Officer, they quickly formed a deep respect for the CO of 141. A story went round that, when a new arrival was having a drink in the bar he spotted Braham over in the distance and inquired of his neighbour the identity of the young wing commander. His companion said 'Oh, that's Wing Commander Braham, the great night-fighter ace'. Looking at the CO's ribbons, beneath his pilot's wings, the newcomer, who like many of them had a number of ribbons already on his tunic, observed in deprecatory tones that Braham had only *two* . . . surely that could not be the great ace? The other American assured him that he was. So the new boy looked again, more closely, and then said 'Well, he's only got two but they sure are riveted on!' It is true that Wing Commander Braham *only* had two medal ribbons at this time; but they were the DSO and the DFC and both had the silver rosettes of the bars to these decorations, stitched to the centre of the ribbon.

Before the end of the war, they were both to be 'riveted' on even more securely, with two rosettes on each. The honour of being awarded three DSOs and three DFCs has been awarded to no other officer in Her Majesty's Forces, before or since.

Don Aris summarises the squadron's activities for August, in his History, as follows:

'During the month of August 1943, 141 Squadron at Wittering and using the forward airfields of Coltishall, Ford, Bradwell Bay and West Malling, carried out 104 Serrate Bomber Support operational sorties, on 13 nights, all with Beaufighter VIFs using Serrate and Mk IV A.I. radar. They had 24 early returns, of which 20 were due to what the records say was radio trouble but was in fact radar and four due to R/T and intercom failure. The Squadron gave what support it could during, among others, three important Bomber Command raids in the month, Peenemünde, the Hamburg firestorm and the start of the first phase of the Battle of Berlin.

It was a successful month with seven enemy aircraft shot down, two by W/C Braham/F/Lt Jacobs, one by W/C Braham/F/Lt Gregory, two by F/O White/F/O Allen, one by S/L Davis/F/O Wheldon and one by F/Lt Kelsey/Sgt Smith. Also one was probably destroyed and another damaged also by F/Lt Kelsey/Sgt Smith.

Two Beaufighters were lost, one in a flying accident resulting in the deaths of F/Sgt Frost and Sgt Towler and one shot down on operations with the crew, F/Sgt Robertson and F/Sgt Gillam, becoming P.O.W.s.'

The squadron records make frequent reference to an enemy airfield as 141 Squadron's patrol area. Why, then, were these airfields not attacked when no enemy aircraft were encountered in the air? The main reason for this was that attacking airfields was not our task: there were low-level intruder squadrons to do this. Our task was to destroy or deter enemy night-fighters attacking our bombers in the air. Accordingly, as indicated in our combat reports, we operated at the same height as the bombers, that is between 10,000 and 22,000 feet, far above enemy airfields.

In these early days of bomber support, our Beaus did not have the range to accompany the bombers all the way to most of their targets. We were given the enemy night-fighter airfields for patrol areas as the most likely places to contact the enemy. But we were freelance and we usually flew with the bomber stream towards their designated target either just below, just above or to one side of the bomber stream. We were using our Serrate and AI radar sets as soon as we left the English coast and were over the North Sea and the same on our return flights to pick up enemy aircraft operating over the sea.

Harry and I were looking forward to another profitable month in September, but there was a downside to the figures quoted in the above summary. This was the worrying figure of 24 early returns – of which 20 were due to faulty radar equipment and four to R/T and intercom failure – out of a total of 104 operational sorties, i.e. 25 per cent. Even allowing for the experimental nature of our Serrate equipment (the Mk IV AI installation in the Beaufighter was well proven by the autumn of 1943), it was a matter for concern that we AI operators had been responsible for aborting 21 per cent (the pure radio faults being excluded) of the squadron's operational patrols during the month of August.

If there had been a similar percentage of crews returning early on one of the heavy bomber squadrons, their Group Commander would have been asking some awkward questions of some of his squadron commanders and they, in turn, would have been asking some even more awkward questions of some of their crews! The shadow of doubt about a crew – and their concern about carrying out the operations for which they had been briefed – did not take long to ferment into an unpleasant suspicion, if they had three or four early returns. It made for a difficult situation for the CO of a squadron. He was faced with the question of whether these were due to genuine technical failure or a reluctance to face the enemy.

Harry and I had now had three aborted trips owing to AI set failure and we were just as likely to find ourselves under scrutiny as anyone else. There is no doubt that on 141 the majority of early returns were genuine. The Mk IV AI sets and the Serrate homer were prone to failure, particularly at the height at which we were operating, i.e. up to 22,000 feet. Our friends, Howard Kelsey and Smithy, Robbie and Dougie (before they went missing), John Forshaw and Frank Folley and the others in 'B' Flight (whom we knew best) were all just as fed up as we were, when having gone through all the preliminaries of NFT, briefing and flying to an advanced base, the Nav/Rad had to tell his pilot that the vital signals – which might lead him and his pilot onto an enemy night-fighter – had disappeared off his cathode-ray tubes.

Furthermore, we were briefed to come home at that stage and not to run the risk of losing the Serrate aircraft by coming down and attempting to operate as a low-level intruder. If we had remained wandering about the skies at high level we would have been only a danger to ourselves and in no better situation than the early night-fighters over England, milling around with no radar. Only a Bob Braham could afford to ignore such orders, and he *did*!

Before leaving the subject of early returns, there was another possible cause to be considered – incompetence. It was at about this time that Frank Davis came to Harry and I and said 'I'd like you to take "the Major" (F/L Le Boutte, our very popular 40-year-old Belgian pilot) with you on ops. He would like to stand up behind Harry, listen to you both on the intercom and see, at first hand, how you carry out a sortie.' Frank was our Flight Commander, so what he said went and when we were next on, 'the Major' sat with us at briefing and watched our preparations for the trip.

We were slightly worried by the idea of having to take a passenger and risk his neck as well as ours and particularly such an experienced pilot as 'the Major'. In the event our Beau was reported as being unserviceable by our ground crew, at the very last moment as the three of us walked out to the Beau, with our helmets in our hands and ready to go.

The corporal i/c told Harry, apologetically, that the port exhaust manifold was cracked and they could not possibly get the aircraft ready in time for us to fly on operations that night. In the event we never did have the opportunity of taking 'the Major' with us, and it would have made for an entertaining evening. It was only years later that I learned from Buster Reynolds that W/Cdr Braham had been worried about Le Boutte's AI operator and wanted 'the Major' to see how another crew operated – and then the two of them would make a decision on whether F/O P . . . seated at the AI set in the back of Le Boutte's Beaufighter was doing all in his power to engage the enemy more closely! Although the Major did not have to listen to Harry and me shouting at each other over the intercom, F/O P . . . did not remain on the squadron.

There was, however, an occasion at Wittering when I came face to face with the emotive and contentious subject of what was known throughout the Air Force as 'Lack of Moral Fibre', or LMF for short. It came in the shape of one of our Nav/Rads, a P/O P . . . who was also, as it happened, flying with another of our Belgian pilots. He came to me one day, when we were standing out on one of the dispersal bays and said that he did not think he could carry on. He was worried about going on ops.

I don't know why he came to me. I wasn't the Navigator Leader of 141, or his Flight Commander, for that matter. I can still remember much of what he said and I found it an uncomfortable twenty minutes but, in essence, he said that he was going to go to W/Cdr Braham and ask if he could be taken off ops. I tried, with no success, to point out what the consequences of such action would be. He was adamant that he could not face any more ops and a few minutes later he was in the CO's office. Within 48 hours he was off the station.

I never heard what happened to him, but one's first thought was and still is, 'there but for the grace of God go I'. Most of us would have done anything rather than face a man like Braham and say 'I'm sorry Sir, but I can't face up to going on ops tonight'. It takes a certain brand of courage to do so and it is a brand which most of us do not possess. The thought of having 'Lack of Moral Fibre' stamped across what would then be the last page of your flying log-book, being isolated from one's peers and being summarily dispatched to an ominous-sounding 'reselection centre' would, for most of us, rule out such a course of action.

You would also be instinctively aware that a decision like that would stay with you for the rest of your life. For the vast majority of us, all of whom had volunteered for aircrew duties, the fear of being seen to be afraid was greater than that of *being* afraid, and in the post-war years, Lord Moran's book *The Anatomy of Courage* made these things clearer to us than they were at the time.

There were all sorts of stories circulating about LMF, some of which were true and some of which were false, but whilst you did hear of some poor air gunner in Bomber Command being unfairly made LMF after surviving half-a-dozen or more terrible trips over the heavily defended targets like Berlin, Frankfurt, Munich, Stuttgart and, of course, the Ruhr, by and large the difficult decisions involved in taking a man off ops were fairly taken and fairly administered. There is no doubt that, once the decision had been taken, a man must leave the squadron. If he could not continue on ops, he had to be off the station immediately. Such a thing is contagious.

In conclusion, and within my own experience, P/O P . . . had not done very many trips, nor had he experienced a particularly rough time on any of them. He was just one of those people who had slipped through the aircrew selection net and was not suited to the business in which he found himself. He may have done well in another sphere of action: I hope that he did.

In the meantime Harry and I had been on leave, he to stay with his widowed mother in her flat in North London, and I to Ashford to see my parents . . . play a little golf at Ashford Manor Golf Club . . . and take Betty Sessions out to the films in Staines. It was quiet at home because Rodney, my younger brother, was now in America on a pilot's course. He had gone into the Air Force soon after his 18th birthday (4 June 1942) via the Short University Course, which was a mixture of academic study and initial RAF training. He had had a year up at Cambridge, as a member of Clare College.

Once, during the winter of 1942/43 (I think it must have been while Harry and I were still at Tangmere on the Turbinlites), I had gone up to Cambridge to see him, spending a couple of nights at the Garden House Hotel. I enjoyed the atmosphere of Cambridge and was somewhat envious of my brother, both on account of the university life and that he had been selected for a pilot's course.

If I had given more thought to the former, I might have made a better choice of careers in 1946, when it came to leaving the Air Force, but, in the immortal words of J.M. Barrie, 'You never can tell'. By September 1943 Rodney was at No. 3 British FTS at Miami, Oklahoma and well into his Initial Flying Training Course on the PT-19A Stearman.

It was about the time of this spell of leave that my mother remarked that it would be nice, after the war was over, when I could tell them what I was doing!

I could only tell her, and my father, that Harry and I were now operating on 'Intruders' over Germany and Occupied Europe and that we had had one or two successes. The Serrate operation was still 'TOP SECRET' and I could say nothing about it to my parents. In the event, I was never able to tell them . . .

At Wittering, on 3 September our Squadron Medical Officer, an irrepressible Irishman, Flight Lieutenant James Dougall MB, BCh, found himself before a general court martial. 'Doc' Dougall was the finest sort of Medical Officer that an operational squadron could have and, like Buster Reynolds, he used to fly sometimes with the CO on operations. He was foremost in all the parties, when we had something to celebrate, and his hangover tonics were without parallel! His ridiculous court martial became part of squadron history.

The charge (if it can be believed, in this day and age) was stealing a bicycle, for which he was to be tried under Section 41 of the Air Force Act. Starting with the President of the Court Martial, a Group Captain, there were no fewer than eight officers spending their day on this charade, including Doc's Defending Officer. It all came about because a party of us had gone down to 'The George' in Stamford to celebrate the squadron's recent victories . . .

At the end of a convivial evening, we all set off back to Wittering in our cars, without realising that we had left Doc behind! In short, he 'borrowed' a bicycle and it happened to belong to a member of the landlord's family. The latter did not see the funny side of the matter, took umbrage and went to the police, who, in turn, went to the Station Commander at Wittering, G/Capt. R.J. Legg.

The whole affair was not the farce it would now seem to us 50 years after the event. Firstly Doc Dougall could have lost his commission if he had been found guilty. Secondly, he might have found himself in trouble with those whose task it is to govern the medical profession and its members. There were, and still are, strict rules of conduct laid down for medical practitioners, and their 'lords and masters' do not like to hear of them gallivanting about town and bringing the profession into disrepute. So the charge against the Doc was more serious than it looked at first sight, from the point of view of Dr James Dougall's future career.

The Court found that F/Lt Dougall was 'Not Guilty' of the charge and he was acquitted. Notwithstanding this verdict Doc Dougall was posted away from 141 and away from Wittering to, of all places, Balloon Command! Happily, Don Aris learned that the Doc was soon posted off to India and Burma as a Medical Officer, where he must have enjoyed himself, as well as livening things up for his colleagues.

After the war, he left the Service and resumed his medical career with no problems arising from his untimely and unnecessary court martial. But how was he acquitted, when he so obviously *had* stolen the child's bicycle? He had ridden it back to camp, albeit with some difficulty, and parked it by Station Sick Quarters. Who saved the day for him and, possibly, even saved his commission?

Once again, in 141's History, it is F/O Cedric 'Buster' Reynolds's name which crops up! It will be recalled that our Intelligence Officer was a solicitor in private life. It was he who undertook the apparently hopeless defence of our erring Medical Officer. It was, after all, 'beyond reasonable doubt' that the Doc had taken the bicycle and ridden away on it, so he must surely be guilty?

But underneath his cheerful and breezy exterior Buster was a shrewd and clever solicitor. He entered a plea of 'Not Guilty', made mincemeat of the evidence produced by the local 'bobby', got the charge thrown out and finished up reprimanding the demoralised representative of the law in Stamford for ever having brought the charge against Flight Lieutenant Dougall in the first place! All in all, when we heard about it in the bar afterwards, it must have been a masterly performance, and, thanks to Buster, Doc Dougall walked out of the court martial a free man!

September saw the continuation of the more serious business of Serrate operations for the squadron and for Harry and I. On both the 2nd and the 3rd we carried out NFTs and practised more single-engined landings. On the 3rd we flew to Coltishall with five other crews in support of a raid on Berlin. Again, the best that 141 could do was to wander about over northern Holland whilst the major air battles of the night were taking place over the North German Plain and 'the Big City'.

Our own trip was uneventful but before it was over my AI set went u/s when the modulator packed up. There were no claims made by any of the six 141 crews who operated that night but of the 316 Lancasters who took off to attack Berlin, 22 were missing, a loss rate amounting to nearly 7 per cent. Each night of operations it was becoming even more plain that, so far as bomber support operations were concerned, a single squadron of Beaufighters was totally inadequate for the job.

Three days later Harry and I did another op, which, this time, was more successful, and to set the scene, we must return to Don Aris's History:

> 'On the night of 6/7th September 1943 Bomber Command carried out an attack on Munich, Germany with a force of 404 aircraft with the loss of 16. 141 Squadron operated on this night and seven aircraft flew from Wittering to the forward airfield of Ford for operations that night. Unfortunately two developed trouble and were unable to operate from there. The small force of 141 aircraft was again split to cover the outward and the return route which was, apparently, over Northern France again F/O White with his Nav/Rad F/O Allen destroyed a Ju 88 on this night.'

Harry and I took off from Ford at 20.45 hours and we were only away for 2.50 hours, before landing back at Ford, to refuel and go on home to Wittering. We were briefed to wander about over the Rheims area and in the vicinity of Juvincourt, a German night-fighter base. At about 22.05 hours I got a strong Serrate contact, which I was soon able to match with a blip on my AI tubes. We completed the interception and at 22.10 hours Harry saw four very bright exhausts of an otherwise unseen aircraft flying away east of Rheims at 17,000 feet and turning to port. We followed and, turning in behind as we closed the range, Harry identified it as a Ju 88.

It will be recalled that on the night of the Peenemünde raid we had identified a Me 110 as a Ju 88. Although, it must be said, that Harry White had never quite accepted Martin Middlebrook's researches in that regard! This time it really *was* a Ju 88 and I remember glancing up from my AI set and turning round to take a good look at it. I could see the tail-fin, rudder and tail-wheel all quite clearly, and the large swastika emblem on the former. Our Combat Report continues with the story:

> 'The enemy aircraft was doing about 160 ASI and was evidently quite unaware of our presence. Throttling back and getting immediately behind on the same level we gave a two seconds burst cannon and machine-gun from 600 feet, closing gently to 550 feet. There were many strikes on the fuselage and on the

starboard engine, which burst into flames. Burning petrol came streaming back and small burning pieces came away in showers. Streams of glycol covered our windscreen. We gave enemy aircraft another two seconds burst with all guns from the same range and there seemed to be strikes all over it. Enemy aircraft climbed steeply, straightened out and then dived steeply enveloped in flames. We watched it strike the ground, where it could be seen through the haze burning fiercely, and continued our patrol.'

Looking at the Armament Report, Harry used, of cannon ammunition, 90 high explosive and 90 semi-armour piercing shells. From the six machine-guns, 360 armour-piercing and 360 incendiary bullets.

This sortie on the 6th was satisfactory and good fun all round for us but the trouble was that we and the other crews on 141 were not achieving this sort of result frequently enough to make any serious inroads into the fast-growing strength of the German night-fighter *Staffel*. Not only that, our Ju 88 only went to level the score with that of the previous night . . . when 141 had lost a Beau and its crew, somewhere over Occupied Europe.

On the night of 5/6 September six crews had operated out of Ford, intruding into northern France, in support of a raid on Mannheim/Ludwigshafen, Germany. Our Deputy Flight Commander in B, Flight Lieutenant 'Dave' Maltby and his Nav/Rad F/O W . . . took off at midnight, to patrol in the vicinity of the German night-fighter airfield at St Dizier, and neither they nor their Beau were ever heard of again.

On 16 June we had lost Douglas Sawyer and Albert Smith; there was some indication that they might have gone down in the North Sea, but throughout July and August, at least on ops, the Gods had smiled on us. Emphasising, once more, that the shallow penetrations over 'the other side', determined by the limited range of our Beaufighters, made our job many times safer than that of the bomber boys.

The Squadron Operations Record Book states 'The Squadron mourn the loss of a very good crew and an excellent Deputy Flight Commander.' The bodies of Dave Maltby and F/O W . . . were never found, and their names, like those of 'Tommy' Sawyer and his navigator, are commemorated in the cloisters of the Royal Air Forces Memorial at Runnymede. There, on Coopers Hill above the historic site where the Magna Carta was signed, are to be found the names of over 20,000 airmen who lost their lives flying from the United Kingdom over Europe and who have no known grave.

The loss of Dave Maltby and his navigator was always something of a mystery. As the Squadron records state, they were 'a very good crew' and the navigator was an experienced AI operator who had flown a number of operations with a former CO of 141, whilst the squadron was on Home Defence duties. He had brought his pilot to within visual range of several enemy bombers marauding over England. Combats had resulted . . . claims had been put in . . . and in due course recognition, in the shape of an award, came through – but only for the pilot, nothing came through for F/O W . . . and I think he nursed something of a chip on his shoulder in this regard.

There was also another worrying feature, when we came to look back, after he and Dave were reported missing. When they had been operating over a German night-fighter airfield at Florennes in Belgium, on the night of 8/9 July they had, as recorded in the Squadron Operations Book:

'. . . lost their way returning (from Florennes) and finally came out (of Northern France!) via St Malo, France and Guernsey in The Channel Islands. They experienced flak from Guernsey but were not hit. They were finally homed by searchlights from Plymouth and landed at Exeter at 04.55 hours.'

That night their navigation had been an awful long way out and they might easily have been shot down anywhere along the way. We started to wonder: had their navigation let them down again? There was something else, in the aftermath of their disappearance from the squadron, which I think can now be told without bringing hurt to anyone.

Flying Officer W . . . was living out with his wife not far from Wittering and it was the CO's sorry task to have to get into his car and drive off to where they had taken accommodation, to break the news to Mrs W . . . that her husband had not returned from the night's operations. When the door was opened and Bob Braham started to disclose his miserable news, the lady who had answered his knock stopped him short by saying 'Thank you very much for coming to tell me, but I am not Mrs W . . . .' When this unwelcome news came back to us Harry and I remembered how, on several occasions during July and August, F/O W . . . had gone to Frank Davis (the 'B' Flight Commander), when he found he was on the list for ops, with a plea to be taken off the list because his wife was not at all well. We had all commiserated with him and on at least one occasion Harry and I had offered to take their place on the night's programme. Well, they were gone and 'there was a war on'! We soon put it behind us.

*   *   *

On the same page of my flying log-book in which I recorded the destruction of the Ju 88 over Juvincourt, there is another entry: 'HARRY AWARDED D.F.C. 8/9/43.'

Harry's decoration does not appear in the Squadron History until 24 September, where it is recorded as follows:

'Flying Officer Harold Edward White, a pilot with 141 Squadron was awarded the first of his three DFC's as announced in the *London Gazette* Serial No. 36183 of the 24.9.1943.

Citation:
   This officer has completed numerous sorties over enemy territory and has displayed great skill and determination throughout. In July 1943, he shot down a Messerschmitt 110, while during another sortie in August 1943, he engaged 3 hostile aircraft in separate combats. In the latter engagement his opponent's aircraft was seen to spiral towards the ground in flames and explode on impact.'

In the same issue of the *London Gazette*, the CO was awarded a Bar to his Distinguished Service Order, and his title and style thus became Wing Commander J.R.D. Braham DSO & Bar, DFC & two Bars. His decoration was given in recognition of the destruction of 'a further five enemy aircraft' and his leadership of 141 Squadron during the pioneering days of the High-Level Bomber Support operations. He was 23 years of age.

The official announcement of Harry's award may not have come through until 24 September, but soon after we got the news on the squadron there was another party down in Stamford! Harry and I went in Roger Osborn's car, a Ford 10 as I remember it, and we all finished up at a pub somewhere in the Square. Amongst the highlights of the evening was the sight of Harry turning green after being persuaded to smoke one of Charles Winn's fearsome cigars . . . myself being chased round the emergency fire-water tank, in the middle of the square, by one of the 'ladies of the town' . . . and later, in his car, Roger and Harry in the front, hearing my plaintive shout (from the back) 'She's bitten me!'

Although I was not similarly decorated until 5 November, perhaps this is an appropriate time to discuss awards in general and mine in particular, because it had some significance for the other Nav/Rads on the squadron. The story, which came out later, was that Wing Commander Braham had put both Harry and me up for an award at the same time, conscious, as he was, of the part played by the Nav/Rads in the Serrate operations. When nothing came through for Harry's navigator, the CO was extremely put out because of the detrimental effect this might have if other navigators on the squadron felt that there was little chance of their efforts being recognised in a similar manner to those of their pilots.

Buster Reynolds the Intelligence Officer (who actually drafted the citations for awards, for the CO) told me, years later, that Wing Commander Braham got onto 12 Group Headquarters and made this point to the AOC, with happy results for me in November and for other navigators in due course.

Awards and decorations are funny things. All of us could cite a case where someone deserving, in our opinion, of recognition was unlucky and maybe another, in reverse, whereby we had seen a man decorated who, as we saw it, did not merit an award. It is a surprisingly difficult, complex (and sometimes embarrassing) area, and honours which should afford nothing but pleasure and pride can become the subject of a distasteful acrimony. I would like to think, looking at some of the photographs of German aircrews, that we never took medals quite as seriously as they did, or even the Americans for that matter!

When I had the privilege of giving the address to my old school, Hurstpierpoint College, on Remembrance Sunday in 1995, I included a word about 'Unsung Heroes'. I warned the boys never to make the mistake of thinking they could judge a man by the medal ribbons that he wore on Remembrance Sunday or, more likely, did *not* wear!

In 141, none of us have ever forgotten Warrant Officer 'Lofty' Hamer, who was recommended for the award of the Victoria Cross, in late '42. The award would have been a posthumous one, because he lost his life in saving that of his navigator, after they had shot down a Heinkel 111 in the Channel, just south of the Isle of Wight. Lofty had been hit by the return fire of the enemy gunner and he was sorely wounded. He flew the Beaufighter back over dry land, enabled F/Sgt Walsh to bale out safely, then, being unable to get out himself, went in with his damaged aircraft.

In those days, the only awards which could be made posthumously were the VC and a Mention in Dispatches. Six months after the recommendation for Lofty's Victoria Cross had been turned down twice, the *London Gazette* contained the announcement of a 'Mention' being awarded to a member of 141 Squadron. The name of the recipient was Warrant Officer R.C. Hamer.

In the Squadron Records for 5 November 1943 there is the following entry which, as I have included Harry's, should be added to conclude our happy and profitable six months at RAF Wittering, due to come to an end in December:

'Flying Officer Michael Seamer Allen (120723) R.A.F.V.R. of No.141 Squadron was awarded the Distinguished Flying Cross, announced in the London Gazette Serial No. 36235 dated 5th November 1943.

Citation:
    As observer, Flying Officer Allen has undertaken many sorties at night and has assisted in the destruction of 3 enemy aircraft. This officer has displayed exceptional keenness, skill and determination.'

I suppose that Guy Fawkes' Day was quite appropriate, when you come to think about it! And let us hope that this attempt to put awards and decorations in their right perspective will have met with some success.

On the 9th, we made another fruitless trip across to our advanced base at Coltishall but the op was scrubbed due to the weather and we all flew back to Wittering later the same evening.

On the night of 15/16 seven Beaus took off from Ford to patrol in the vicinity of various German night-fighter airfields, in northern France. With the CO and Jacko still operating, we were supporting a raid on the Dunlop rubber factory at Montlucon in central France. It was a good night for Bomber Command, except for the three crews that were lost; they had sent out 369 aircraft. These figures illustrate vividly the difference for the Lancasters, Halifaxes and Stirlings in flying over Occupied Europe and operating over the heavily defended Third Reich.

The CO, finding no activity at high level (for some reason, there was virtually no reaction that night by the German night-fighters), went down low and shot up a train on the Dieppe–Paris line! He had a lot of his own particular type of fun – the engine of the train exploded – but he went down so low that he hit some trees on the railway embankment and came back to Wittering with a hole in *Betsy*'s bottom. Fergie and Roger Osborn did not come back.

Flight Lieutenant R.W. Ferguson with his Nav/Rad F/O R.W. Osborn had taken off from Ford at 22.10 hours to patrol in the Chartres area, and the Squadron History tells the story, which is interesting because the CO heard Fergie on the VHF radio call up to say they had engine trouble. From the record:

'At 00.57 hours F/Lt Ferguson was heard to call up, saying that one engine was unserviceable and that there was oil pressure trouble with the other. W/C Braham, who was in the vicinity, immediately called up and gave instructions for the crew to bale out if they had sufficient height. This order was acknowledged by F/Lt Ferguson at 01.03 hours and he gave a Q.D.M.S. [magnetic course to steer with zero wind] as 335 and 300 but no fix was obtained.'

Note The CO was fully aware that our Beaus were a tricky proposition on one engine, without fully-feathering props, let alone if there was also a problem with the remaining engine. He therefore had no hesitation in breaking R/T silence over enemy territory to warn one of his crews to bale out rather than to fly the damaged Beau back across the Channel to England.

What happened was this: Fergie and Roger limped back over northern France and crossed out over Fécamp, losing height as they went. A few minutes later, and about five miles out from the enemy coast, Fergie, too low now for them to bale out, ditched the Beau in the sea. A ditching at night is a hazardous affair and the Beau was a heavy aircraft. Roger, in the back, had got his hatch (the Perspex cupola over the navigator's crew position) open before they struck the water and he was out quickly, with his parachute harness off and his Mae West inflated, as soon as the Beau struck. As the Beau started to go under, he saw the aircraft dinghy released from its stowage in the port wing and started to clamber into it.

The nose of the Beau was already dug deep in the water. Fergie may have been knocked out when the aircraft hit the sea but Roger heard and saw nothing of him and there was no way that he could have got round to the front cockpit to try and help his pilot. Fergie went down with Beau V8803 and his body was never recovered.

Roger, much older than the rest of us and already in his thirties, was a tough, resourceful and extrovert character. He spent the next 36 hours in the aircraft dinghy before being spotted by the Typhoons of No. 486 (NZ) Squadron, returning from a day sweep over France. He was picked up by a Walrus seaplane of No. 277 (Air-Sea Rescue) Squadron and returned to Wittering a few hours later, rather sun-scorched but otherwise little the worse for the experience.

He told us that their trouble had started when they were hit by flak. Both engines sustained damage and, from then on, they were always going to have trouble in getting back to base. He said that, when daylight dawned, he found he was only about four miles off the French coast! He was worried that he might drift closer in, be spotted by the Germans and they would put a boat out to pick him up. It was towards the end of a long day in the sun, sitting in his dinghy, that he was spotted by the pilot of one of 486's Typhoons. But, by then, it was too late, with dark falling, to send out the Walrus to land on the water and collect him.

He spent a second cold and anxious night in the dinghy with the knowledge that he had been seen by the Typhoons and the hope that he would be rescued when daylight broke. But, when the dawn broke and the sun came up, Roger was appalled to see that he had drifted even nearer to the shore during the night and was now so close in that he could hear, across the water, the sound of the cows mooing as they waited for the morning milking.

An hour or two later and, without further incident, the Walrus seaplane arrived – escorted by the faithful Typhoons – and effecting a very gallant rescue, landed and picked him up, still in full view of any watcher on the coast!

When they had got Roger safely back on British soil the Walrus crew let him in on a secret. He had been floating around 'close to an enemy minefield'. The Air-Sea Rescue crews were among the largely unsung heroes but Roger Osborn never forgot that they had saved his life – at the risk of their own.

Harry and I had operated that night, patrolling an airfield at Coulommiers, France, but with no joy. We got back to Wittering at 01.55 hours on the morning of the 16th, to learn that Fergie and Roger were missing. Rather irreverently – at such a time – I remembered that I had lent him my squash-racket a few days previously. This was serious because, shortly, the Adjutant would arrive to lock and put a seal on the door to Roger's room. This was standard practice, as soon as someone was reported missing.

I was in a dilemma. On the one hand, I wanted my squash-racket back, but, on the other, it was a serious matter to enter the room and take away something from it – even if it was your own property! A charge of stealing from the dead was more than on the cards, if one was caught. In the end I thought 'The old bugger won't mind!', took a chance and retrieved my precious racket!

A few days before Roger and Fergie went down we had had a memorable evening in the mess with my father and, on 16 September, he wrote a long letter to his sister, who lived in South Africa. As mentioned, he was up at Loughborough in the autumn of 1943 doing some test flying for the Brush Electric Company, and he flew into Wittering on a DH Rapide. Before coming down to dinner, he used the room occupied by Harry and myself to change into uniform, and I had the pleasure of entertaining him in the mess.

He was able to meet many of the pilots and navigators on 141 which, with his pilot's wings and First World War ribbons, was fun for him and for them. He felt at home in their company and they treated him with affection and respect. In due course I was able to introduce him to the CO, whose own father had also been an RFC pilot.

A few years ago, when I had returned to South Africa for a visit, I was in Cape Town and staying with my cousin, Neil Garlick, who had served with distinction with the 8th Army in the Western Desert and in Italy. His mother had been dead for several years and amongst her papers he had found the letter of 16 September 1943 written by her brother. He himself had known my father well, from his school-days in Britain in the nineteen-thirties, and he asked me if I would like to have the letter back. Having very few things, after the house in Ashford was destroyed in 1944, belonging to my parents, I accepted gratefully.

The letter beginning 'My Dear Joyce . . .' is beside me now, as I write. Telling his sister the family news he says:

'. . . Rodney has made good progress in the R.A.F. and is now at Miami, Oklahoma, U.S.A. undergoing his flying instruction and we get most cheerful letters from him . . . he will be quite a little man when he returns. Michael is on night-fighters at a station not far from here. I flew over to see him the other evening and spent the night there. His Commanding Officer is a charming man with a DSO & Bar, DFC & two Bars. He told me how pleased he was with Michael and said he would do all he can to help him in his career. To date, he has three Huns destroyed and two damaged. He has just had seven days leave which he spent with Kathleen [my mother] . . .'

My father's visit to Wittering evidently gave him a lot of pleasure but, after Harry and I waved him off, in his Rapide, the following morning, it proved to be almost the last occasion on which I saw him.

On 20 September I went up in a Mosquito for the first time. My log-book tells me that I flew in Mosquito D HJ870, 'local flying' for 35 minutes. There were no other remarks, so it can't have made much of an impression on me! Furthermore, for some unaccountable reason, 'Joe' Cooper (the same colourful character who had rescued us from the desert camp of El Amaza, during our ferrying days to the Middle East) was the pilot! He was attached to 141 to learn about the Serrate Bomber Support operations and would shortly be going to join 169 Squadron as a Flight Commander. (Rumours were starting to filter through that there were to be two more Serrate squadrons formed, one of which would be 169.)

Joe was to crew up with an old friend of mine, Ralph Connolly, whom I had met as far back as my first week in the Air Force at Stratford-upon-Avon. Ralph had gone straight from 'The School for Secrets' to a night-fighter squadron (141) in August 1941, when the rush was on to get the new AI operators onto the squadrons before the anticipated winter raids began.

On the 21st, Harry and I flew to a heavy bomber station, Woolfox Lodge in Leicestershire, where there was a squadron of the ungainly (and rapidly becoming obsolete) Stirlings. Our task was to fly a 'fighter affiliation' with one of their crews, carrying out mock fighter attacks, to give their gunners practice in fighting us off and their pilots practice in the corkscrewing technique, which was used by most of the bomber pilots to ward off attack from the German night-fighters. Harry and I, having already seen some of their number, i.e. the Stirlings, shot down, were only too happy to oblige.

On 22 September the word 'Serrate' is mentioned in the Operations Record Book for the first time. This entry, coming three and a half months after these operations were commenced, is a further indication of the tight security which had surrounded us since the inception of these specialised high-level intruder sorties. To quote from the ORB:

> '. . . So far these activities have resulted in the destruction of 13 enemy aircraft, the probable destruction of one more and the damaging of six. This operation is known as "Serrate". It is hoped that with the re-equipment of the Squadron with Mosquito aircraft, their additional manoeuvrability and range will produce even better results. It has been necessary to observe the utmost secrecy with regard to these operations, and it is still so, as it is hoped that the enemy still have little or no idea of the methods employed.'

Harry and I started out on another op on the 23rd, taking off in support of a raid on Mannheim, Germany – this time from Bradwell Bay, on the Blackwater Estuary. We were supposed to patrol in the area of a German airfield at Florennes, Belgium, but once again my AI set went u/s. This time it was the Serrate switch motor and all that I could record in my log-book was another 'early return'.

Harry and I didn't contribute any further to the squadron's activities in September, but our astonishing CO went happily on his way having, in his own words, 'bags of fun'! His time as Commanding Officer of 141 Squadron was rapidly drawing to a close but, even in its dying moments, he made sure that it was not him and Jacko who were going to die!

He had been almost continually on operations for three years, and despite a direct appeal to Air Vice-Marshal Roderick Hill, his days at Wittering were now numbered. He ended his time with us in a blaze of glory, destroying (on his last two trips) a Dornier 217 and a Messerschmitt 110 and damaging a Junkers 88. All these combats resulted from AI contacts, and Jacko had done the impossible. He had stepped straight into the man-sized shoes of Sticks Gregory and matched the latter's incomparable performance.

During the month of September 1943, 141 flew 56 sorties on 11 nights, out of which they had 11 early returns. They destroyed only three enemy aircraft and lost two Beaufighters in doing so. In relation to Bomber Command's efforts, and their mounting losses, this attempt at giving them some sort of support by British night-fighters was totally inadequate, verging on the derisive. On the night of 27/28 September, when six Beaus flew out from Coltishall in support of an attack on Hanover, Germany (and Bob Braham got the Dornier 217, mentioned above), Bomber Command's losses were 38 aircraft out of a force of 687, i.e. 5.6 per cent. Most of the losses took place beyond the range of the Beaufighters and many of the four-engined bombers and their seven-man crew fell to the guns of the German night-fighters. Re-equipment with Mosquitoes and the formation of further Serrate squadrons, already hinted at, could not come soon enough.

But, for Braham, the end of September spelt the end of his ten months as 141's CO. Even in his closing victories (until he was to pop up again, like some demon king, in 1944 – in 2 Group) he was still showing us how it should be done. The pilot of the Messerschmitt 110 he destroyed on the 29/30th was a *Luftwaffe* ace, *Hauptmann* August Geiger of NJG 1, who had 53 victories, all RAF aircraft as far as is known. He held the Knight's Cross with Oakleaves, the third highest German decoration, and one can only conjecture how many more of our heavy bombers he might have shot down, if he had not fallen to the guns of Wing Commander Braham. Once more, this victory was at the very core of the Serrate operation which Braham had so successfully pioneered over the previous three and a half months.

The Squadron ORB – for 1 October – pays a glowing and heartfelt tribute to its departing CO, as does the Squadron Historian Don Aris in his mammoth work, tracing Bob Braham's illustrious operational career to the date when he leaves 141 as the Ace Night-Fighter Pilot, having topped (with his last victory) John Cunningham's score of enemy aircraft destroyed.

It would be wrong to close this part of the Bob Braham story without briefly relating the tale of how he went to Bristol to give a pep-talk to the workers employed at the Bristol Aeroplane Company. They were manufacturing the Bristol Beaufighters, on which he had scored so many of his successes, firstly against the incoming German bombers and, latterly, against men like *Hauptmann* Geiger. Essentially a modest man, Braham hated this sort of thing and, indeed, this humility, which he displayed from the time his name first came to the attention of the media, is one of the reasons why the memory of him and his prodigious record is so little known to the general public of today.

However, a personal invitation from the Managing Director of Bristol's was not to be ignored, so off went Braham taking along with him, for moral support, his Intelligence Officer, the inimitable Buster Reynolds. He managed the speech to the workers without any problems and they gave him a marvellous reception. He and Buster then repaired to one of the major hotels in the city and set off to have a night on the town. After several adventures, including a brush with a posse of American Service Police and visiting several of the local hostelries, they returned to their five-star hotel in good spirits!

They then learned, rather late in the day, that although the gallant wing commander had been booked into the Presidential Suite (by courtesy of the Directors of the Bristol Aeroplane Company), no accommodation had been arranged for his Intelligence Officer! However, at that time of night, a little problem like that was unlikely to daunt them. The CO said 'Don't worry, Buster . . . there's plenty of room in my suite!' and, without more ado, they headed for the lift and the Presidential Suite.

In the morning, Braham was up bright and early, despite the party they had had the night before. He ordered early morning tea and set about getting dressed. Things were not quite the same with his older companion, the Squadron Intelligence Officer, who, in his own words to me, was still 'out for the count'. A few minutes later there was a knock at the door and the maid came in with a tray of tea things. As she looked round the magnificent bedroom of the Presidential Suite she saw first the young handsome Wing Commander getting dressed . . . and then her eyes swung round to the massive double-bed. There she saw Buster's head on the pillows at one end . . . and his boots sticking out of the covers at the other!

As he admitted later he had, on this occasion, gone to bed fully clothed. The horrified maid took one more look at Bob and with a screech of 'You dirty buggers!' dropped the tea tray and fled from the room. Bob Braham thought this was quite the best part of the whole weekend in Bristol, and Buster 'dined out' on the story for the rest of his life.

So with the posting of Wing Commander Braham to HQ Fighter Command the Squadron came to the end of an era . . . and to the end of Phase Three of the Serrate operations. As I wrote in my notes for a seminar at the RAF Staff College, in March 1993, on the High-Level Bomber Support operations:

> 'So with a single Squadron of Beaufighters operations were commenced (in June 1943) – 141 roamed about over the Occupied countries and sometimes into Germany – Me 110s and Ju 88s were homed onto using the "Serrate" Black Box and the A.I. – stalked and shot down – tactics were worked out as they went along by trial and error (e.g. like White/Allen, getting in front of the target instead of behind it) and they found that the otherwise admirable Beaufighter was limited in speed and range for the task in hand. Notwithstanding these serious limitations the "Serrate" operation was proved to be a success, e.g. on the night of the Peenemünde Raid in August four German night-fighters were destroyed.'

Writing in his book, *Scramble* (of his leaving 141) Wing Commander Braham said: 'My association with my first love, 141 Squadron, was now broken for good; and with it comradeship such as I have never known since.'

In his flying log-book he wrote: 'The end of very happy and exciting days with 141 as CO.'

It was indeed an end of an era for him, as well as for the squadron.

5 The Development of the Bomber Support Operations

– and the price paid for equipping the Serrate Squadrons with 'worn out' Mosquitoes

The loss of our inspirational CO was tempered by the prospect of being re-equipped with the de Havilland Mosquito. With its greater range we would be able to reach Bomber Command's targets deep inside Germany and, with a higher speed than our Beaufighters, we would have a better chance of catching the Ju 88s and Me 110s, when we found them. With the news of two more squadrons being formed, all three being equipped with Mosquitoes, and the whole Serrate operation being transplanted into a new radar-countermeasures Group (No. 100) being formed in Bomber Command itself, hopes were running high! Phase Four was about to begin.

In the event, there was anticlimax for the crews of 141 (and those of 169 and 239, the two new squadrons). The Mosquitoes which were delivered to us were Mosquito NF IIs. They were old, worn out and much used aircraft from Home Defence night-fighter squadrons, which were now being equipped with the latest marks of Mosquito and AI radar. Ultimately they all had to be re-engined, but only after several crews had been lost and others had crawled home on one engine. There was also an initial problem with the fitting of Serrate and 'backward-looking' AI aerials on the wings of the Mosquito, which virtually grounded us for three and a half months (it was not sorted out until 13 January 1944). Meanwhile, the squadron still struggled on with its ageing Beaufighters.

This sorry turn of events spelt disaster for many of the bomber crews. In short, at the height of Bomber Command's losses, in that terrible winter of 1943/44 – when the Battle of Berlin was proving so costly – the British long-range Serrate Mosquitoes, the only hope of combating the German night-fighters, were absent from the fray. There was no bomber support, of any measurable proportions, from October 1943 to the end of January 1944. Phase Four of the Serrate operations, which should have reaped a rich harvest of Ju 88s and Me 110s cut down (and bomber crews and their aircraft saved, in consequence) proved to be an unmitigated failure.

On a personal note, during this period Harry and I took off only seven times on operations, four times on a Beau and three on a Mosquito. On three occasions the radar became unserviceable and on only one trip – on 28/29 January 1944 – was the outcome successful, when we destroyed an Me 109 over Berlin. Even then, all the radar failed before we returned to base! In the following month, we lost the port engine over Kiel when we were chasing a target and only 3,000 feet behind it.

To return to the situation at Wittering at the beginning of October 1943. Harry and I went up together in a Mosquito for the first time on the 1st of the month, to act as target for Serrate practice homings. We stooged up and down between Leicester and Loughborough for just under two hours. Significantly, before we landed, the intercom went unserviceable! We did several more daylight trips for type experience before the end of the month, but no operations.

We did do two operations, both on our faithful Beau VI V8713, one over Juvincourt in northern France and the other to an area just short of Bremen. Neither was of any significance, and on the former, the gain control on the AI failed. I am ashamed to see that, when I look back at my log-book, I only flew 19.50 hours in the whole of the month. In the meantime, Bomber Command was attacking targets deep in Germany with ever increasing losses, such as when 569 aircraft attacked Kassel on 22/23 October with the loss of 43 aircraft.

Our Squadron Historian has recorded that, on 2 October, Sir Archibald Sinclair, Secretary of State for Air, visited Wittering. He was accompanied by the AOC 12 Group, Air Vice-Marshal Hill.

He inspected 141 Squadron and talked for some time to the aircrews and congratulated the squadron on its recent successes. He also said he would do all possible to expedite the fitting and delivery of Mosquito aircraft. So writes Don Aris, but I regret to say that I have no recollection of Sir Archibald's visit at all! As the month went by a distinctly downward trend in our affairs was felt by us all.

There was some good news on the 21st of the month when we heard that Jacko, Flight Lieutenant H. Jacobs DFC, had been awarded a Bar to his DFC. It will be recalled that Jacko had flown with Bob Braham as his Nav/Rad during the latter part of his time as CO of 141. He had assisted Bob in the destruction of four enemy aircraft and the damaging of another. He had stepped manfully into Sticks Gregory's outsize shoes and was an exceptional AI operator in addition to being a most delightful person. We were all pleased that his contribution to the CO's successes had been recognised by this award.

In his summary of the month of October Don Aris supplies the facts which were underlined by our feelings! The squadron carried out only 49 Serrate patrols and operated on only nine nights. Three of these patrols were carried out by Mosquitoes and the remainder by our rapidly ageing Beaus. There were no fewer than 15 early returns. One aircraft was lost, with both crew killed, and there was nothing to show for it on the other side of the balance sheet: no German night-fighters shot down or even attacked! Admittedly, the weather was bad during October and we operated whenever Bomber Command were operating, but with 141 still the only Serrate squadron operational, it was a very serious situation and one which was to deteriorate still further.

For the first time my log-book, signed by Frank Davis ('B' Flight Commander), was countersigned by Wing Commander Roberts AFC. Ken Roberts had considerable flying experience and he came to us from No. 151 Squadron. They were a Mosquito squadron, based at Middle Wallop, on Home Defence, but much of his service had been spent in Flying Training Command and he must have found it a tough job to be posted as CO of a long-range night-fighter squadron engaged on operations of a rather specialised nature; let alone the task of trying to take over the mantle of Bob Braham (who, along with John Cunningham, had already become a legend in the night-fighter business). Harry and I felt a bit sorry for him, as well as feeling concerned about the future of the squadron.

He tried his best to keep things going during this difficult period in which our

Beau VIs were being phased out and the Mosquito IIs were being delivered. For example, on 20 October he put himself on the night flying programme and took off in Mosquito F II DD666 to do an NFT (with his Nav/Rad F/O Joyce), but they came back with engine trouble and were unable to take it on ops that night. Ken Roberts certainly could not be blamed for all the second-hand Mosquitoes which caused us so much trouble in the ensuing weeks, and it is charitable to say simply that he was unfortunate to take over 141 at that particular time. It was not long before he was posted.

Mosquito FII DD666 which the CO tried to use on 20 October provides a good example of what both the aircrew and our ground crews had to face from October onwards. Referring to Don Aris's Squadron History, we find the following entry on page 292:

> 'DD666 Mosquito FII fitted with Merlin 21s was manufactured at Hatfield by De Havillands. Taken on charge by the RAF on 14.6.42 and then transferred to the Royal Aircraft Establishment at Farnborough on the 30.6.42 . . . it then went to 264 Squadron on 12.7.42. Whilst on 264 Squadron it was twice classified as Category AC in flying accidents which meant that it was so badly damaged that it had to be repaired by a Central Repair Organisation. It then went to 307 Squadron until it came to 141 Squadron. It was therefore over 15 months old and had hard use with two operational Squadrons; as well as being with the R.A.E.'

No. 141 Squadron, Wittering: this was an official photograph taken in November 1943, just after the award of the DFC. I was a Flying Officer at the time. (Imperial War Museum)

In the early months of 1944 nearly all Mosquitoes had to be re-engined due to having so much trouble with them, and it would seem that even these replacement engines were reconditioned ones! There is an entry in the squadron records for 27 February 1944 stating that all the reconditioned engines were to be returned, and while stocks lasted only new Merlin Mk 22 engines were to be fitted. This is interesting, because it was only three days after Harry and I returned the 350 miles from Kiel 'on one', after the port engine had packed up. (I wonder if Mosquito FII 712 had only re-conditioned engines to keep us in the air on that dim and far-off night?)

Don writes another telling paragraph about this period in which he outlines some of the difficulties it made for the ground crews. As well as for the aircrews, with the extra danger of an engine failure, he says that those most affected were the engine fitters, who were constantly having to change the engines at all hours of the day and night, also, the radar mechanics, who had a great amount of trouble with both the AI Mk IV sets and the Serrate homer as installed in these Mosquitoes. I remember well the problems with the aerials because Harry and I flew a number of the test flights demanded by our Radar Officer, Flying Officer Pollard. 'Polly' was an Electronics Engineer of the highest quality, and he it was who finally solved the problems of the aerials, but not until 13 January 1944.

On 3 November we did our first trip in a Mosquito over the other side. We took Mosquito FII DZ290, having tested it – including a cannon test, in which we fired off all the guns – in the afternoon. Although we had no joy, it is perhaps

No. 141 Squadron, West Raynham: re-equipped with Mosquitoes to replace the ageing Beaufighters. This photograph, taken in the Navigator/Radar Operator's seat (to the right of his pilot), shows the Viewing Unit of the AI set and the visor – which the Navigator used to peer at the signals on his cathode-ray tubes, hoping to see the blip of an enemy aircraft!

worth including the extract from the Squadron Operations Record Book. On this night Bomber Command attacked Düsseldorf with a force of 589 aircraft, and lost 18. There were some minor operations and a diversionary raid on Cologne. Number 141 Squadron operated with three Mosquitoes flying direct from Wittering and three Beaus (still having to use an advanced base) flying from Coltishall. We took off at 17.52 hours, pleased that we no longer had the inconvenience of setting off for the advanced base earlier in the afternoon, and flew to the Bocholt/Lohausen area of Germany. The report continues:

> 'They crossed out over Lowestoft at 18.25 hours and over the Dutch coast at the Hague. They saw a visual Lorenz E/W with a canopy of three searchlights at Deelen airfield, Holland, through a break in the cloud. They patrolled the target area uneventfully. They saw a bomber shot down, by a direct hit from flak, over the Ruhr at about 19.45 hours. They crossed out over Holland just South of the Hague at 20.35 hours and in over Lowestoft at 21.00 hours and landed at Wittering at 21.35 hours.'

In my log-book I wrote 'Intruder to Düsseldorf 3.30 hours', and this time we really had been there. We had no problems with the Mosquito – enjoyed the extra speed and range – and I liked being able to see what was going on up front which had been impossible in the back of the Beau. We had also had our first good look at the target area during, and after, a major attack. In short, the centre of Düsseldorf looked, for all the world, like the stories one was told, as a child, about Dante's *Inferno*.

Last but not least, when we woke the following morning and learned that Bomber Command's losses had only amounted to three per cent we started to cheer up, with the promise of better days to come. Little did we know that this was premature thinking of the most dangerous kind. Our opposite numbers in the German *Nachtjagdgeschwadern* had a lot more in store for the 'bomber boys' and for some of us . . .

On 7 November we did an NFT on the same Mosquito and actually flew down to Ford to operate but ops were scrubbed at the last moment and we returned to Wittering. On the 13th I flew up to Church Fenton with Johnny Forshaw. His navigator was a mercurial little character named, aptly, Frank Folley, and for some reason he was nowhere to be found! Flight Lieutenant John Forshaw was also quite a character. In fact, both he and Frank were members of the acting profession and had known each other pre-war. Anyway, I quite enjoyed going back to the scene of my attempts to crew up with a pilot and my first meeting with Harry. I think we must have been getting rid of one of our old Beaus to a Home Defence squadron. Harry duly arrived to pick me up and we flew back to Wittering in Mosquito DZ270 in style, in 25 minutes.

We did four NFTs in the first half of November, but each time operations were cancelled because of poor weather conditions. Then, on 15 November, we had one of those tragedies that happened all too frequently throughout one's flying days and we lost a crew from 'B' Flight in an accident at our home base.

At Wittering there are two runways: one exceptionally long, east to west, but the south to north is short, barely 1,450 yards. Derek Welsh and Bill Ripley walked out of our dispersal hut just before 2.30 p.m. for an NFT. The wind was in the north, so they were faced with taking off on the short runway. With the prevailing westerly winds, we hardly ever had to use it, and 1,450 yards was barely enough to get off in a fully loaded Mosquito II.

In the crew room we heard them open up and take off. Then, a bang and a *Woomph* was heard – and they were not very far away. We all leapt to our feet and rushed outside. There, on the far side of the airfield, was the pillar of smoke and flame, which told us all that we needed to know . . .

I jumped into my car and, with two or three others bundling in, I drove fast round the perimeter track to the north side of the airfield and stopped just short of the blazing wreckage. Derek and Bill were lying on the grass – and they were alive! Thanks to the prompt action of a Naval rating and a 141 pilot, F/O C.B. Thornton, who were nearby when the Mosquito failed to gain height and crashed on the boundary at the end of the runway, both pilot and navigator had been pulled out of the burning wreckage. The Squadron Record gives further details which we only heard later:

'The rescue party led by LAC Robertson of the AFDU did an extraordinary fine piece of work, at considerable risk to themselves, as the wreckage caught fire – and ammunition was exploding in all directions. Two Naval Ratings, AB Howard and AB White, showed a total disregard for their own safety. The former, with the assistance of Flying Officer Thornton, who had by then arrived on the scene actually extinguished the flames on F/O Welsh whilst still within a few feet of the burning wreckage, afterwards removing the injured pilot further from the scene of the crash.'

I spoke to both Derek and Bill, as they lay on the ground, and they answered me. I said to Bill, who did not look as if he had been too badly hurt, something like 'You'll be OK, Bill' as he was lifted into the ambulance, and he acknowledged what I had said. I thought that they would be OK when they were taken off to Stamford Infirmary a few minutes later. They both died at about 07.00 hours on the following morning. Their injuries and shock proved to be worse than we had thought and, although the cause of the crash is not given in the Squadron Record, it was thought by a former 141 aircrew member to be engine failure on take-off.

The aircraft, Mosquito FII DD266, was one of the first Mosquitoes to be delivered to 141 and the loss of a crew in a flying accident was always a miserable business. They had only been on the squadron since 1 September and I remember hearing that Derek Welsh had already survived a ditching in the North Sea and three/four days in a dinghy before being picked up by the Air-Sea Rescue Services.

Bill Ripley was an experienced Navigator/Radio, who had been on 604 Squadron at Middle Wallop in the early days of Home Defence night-fighting in 1940/42. He had flown with Squadron Leader 'Rory' Chisholm DSO, DFC & Bar (who was shortly be appointed as SASO to the new radar-countermeasures Group in Bomber Command, for which the Serrate squadrons were destined). He had shared in Rory Chisholm's successes and been decorated with the DFM before being commissioned. He and Derek Welsh stood every chance of becoming a successful crew on the Serrate operations if the wind had not been blowing in the wrong direction that day.

All those involved in the rescue were recommended for awards, and in the Squadron Record for 21 March 1944 is announced an MBE for Flying Officer Thornton to mark his gallantry on 15 November 1943.

We reverted to our old Beau for two trips on the 18th and 19th respectively.

The former was another early return with the radar going u/s just inside the Dutch coast; the latter, although giving us no joy was written up in the Squadron Record and is of more interest in relation to a general description of our operations at that period:

> 'F/O H.E. White with his Nav/Rad F/O M.S. Allen in Beaufighter VIF V8713 took off from Bradwell Bay at 17.35 hours on an Intruder Patrol to the night fighter airfield at Bonn/Hanglar and its area. They crossed the Belgian coast at Knocke and they had 2 Serrate contacts on the way to the target area, they chased but had no AI contact. They had about 8 Serrate contacts in the target area and again chased without AI contact. There were 3 vertical searchlights 15 miles South of Leverkusen, Germany, running SW/NE and spaced 2 and 3 miles.
>
> The SW searchlight flashed three TSs and then the other two flashed TS simultaneously while the first doused, followed shortly by the dousing of the other two. This was repeated continuously, F/O White could not be certain of the middle and NE searchlights characteristic owing to intense heavy flak and searchlights in the Leverkusen area. There was moderate inaccurate heavy flak from Lille on their way back. They crossed out at Le Touquet, France at 20.35 hours and in over Dungeness at 20.55 hours and landed at Wittering at 21.35 hours. F/O White's impression was that enemy night-fighters were mainly grounded and that flak was given a free hand.'

This report also indicates that Harry was taking more notice of the general progress of the raid and what was going on around us, now that we were becoming acquainted with conditions over the other side. In the morning, Harry's impressions were confirmed when we learned that a force of 266 bombers had attacked Leverkusen and the losses were only three aircraft.

On the last day of the month we did an NFT on Mosquito FII 758, hoping to take it on ops that night. We were up for only 15 minutes, before finding that the Serrate was u/s, and this was to be the story of our life until the middle of January, by which time we would have changed our comfortable quarters and 5-star mess for the harsher climes and icy winds of Norfolk.

It was on 27 November that we heard that we were to move from Wittering to West Raynham, in the middle of Norfolk and located about 16 miles NE of King's Lynn. We were to be absorbed into Bomber Command and become the first operational unit in the new No. 100 (Special Duties) Group. The new Group would be commanded by Air Commodore E.B. Addison (later to be promoted Air Vice-Marshal) and the move would take place on Friday 3 December.

However, before leaving Wittering (to which I was not destined to return until 50 years later) we must consult Don Aris's summary of the month of November and follow the squadron's downward path and our own:

> 'The month of November 1943 was another unsatisfactory month for 141 Squadron, they carried out only 33 Serrate Bomber Support operations on only 8 nights . . . 19 with Beaufighters which had 7 early returns . . . and 14 with Mosquitoes which had 6 early returns they had no successes against the enemy and suffered the losses of 2 Mosquitoes and 1 Beaufighter in accidents and on operations, all six crew were killed; and there was also the loss of another Beaufighter, where the crew baled out.'

The Squadron Operations Record Book makes no better reading:

'A very disappointing month from the operational point of view. The weather has been generally unsuitable and considerable trouble is still being experienced with the Special Equipment in the Mosquito aircraft. It is hoped, however, that the technical troubles will be overcome and the closer co-operation which will become possible with the Squadron actually in Bomber Command will lead to more successes in the future.'

Our personal record for the month also reflects the situation. My log-book shows only a total of 22.05 hours, of which just 9.35 were operational. There is also a note on the 18th, when we took V8713 to advanced base at Bradwell Bay to operate in support of a major attack on Berlin, saying 'Awful shambles owing to Gen being late', and then, when we did eventually get off the ground at 17.55 hours, the AI became unserviceable and we had to abort the trip.

All this was happening whilst 884 heavy bombers were battling their way to Berlin and another target at Mannheim/Ludwigshafen and losing 32 aircraft (which meant the corresponding loss of c.250 aircrew). That was also the night we lost one of our Belgian pilots, F/O Renson, with his Nav/Rad, F/O Baldwin.

They took off from Bradwell Bay, four minutes after us, in a Beaufighter, and nothing further was ever heard of them. Leonard Florent Renson's body was found, buried at first in Germany and later repatriated to Belgium. Ken Baldwin's body was also found and he lies buried in the Reichwald Forest War Cemetery, Germany. He had been the replacement for the Navigator/Radio, P/O P . . . (who had come to me to say that he could not face any more ops, and was soon off the squadron). He had been with us for less than a month.

Harry and I flew across to West Raynham in our old Beau V8713 on 4 December. As things turned out, we were to spend the rest of the war stationed in Norfolk, although not all of our time was to be at Raynham. Norfolk worked its own peculiar magic on me and I always felt at home there, especially up on the North Coast around Burnham, Overy, Staithe and Holkham. I could live there any time!

But, looking back on our days at Wittering I find that I have been remiss in forgetting to give a mention to the catering arrangements that we enjoyed there in our 5-star officers' mess. There was nothing to match them anywhere! In charge, and very much in charge, was one Sergeant Renaldi, and the answer was, in peacetime Renaldi was one of the head waiters at the Savoy and he ran the officers' mess at Wittering just as if he was still at the Savoy!

Wartime food rationing and shortages did not seem to figure in his calculations. When he was charged with laying on a big mess party, the spread of food (and drink!) was as good as pre-war days! Renaldi was a jewel, and when the war was over he returned to the Savoy. Any former member of 141 who, in the days of the 'Five-Shilling Dinner', ventured into the imposing foyer of that great hotel, could always be assured of a warm welcome by Renaldi, who had swopped his sergeant's stripes for an impeccable tail coat. To say nothing of a very modest account slipped quietly to him at the end of the evening! He treated us as if we were millionaires! Perhaps I should explain that five shillings was the maximum that any establishment could charge for a meal in those days of austerity, but it was usually supplemented by a cover charge.

With a few more quick fragments from the Wittering days, we must make the move out of Fighter Command and over to Norfolk to transfer our allegiance to

Bomber Command and its indomitable leader, Air Chief Marshal Sir Arthur Harris.

There was the time when Harry and I, going on leave by train, hitched a lift into Peterborough in a passing jeep – and wished we hadn't, because the Yanks drove so fast that we never seemed to have all four wheels on the ground at the same time!

Then there was the station defence exercise! Don says it took place on 16 August and it involved all personnel on the station, including aircrew! I can remember very little of the evening, because – as part of the attacking force whose objective was to penetrate the boundary defences of the airfield – we were not due to move off until 22.20 hours. Prior to the forthcoming military manoeuvres, we had taken the precaution of fortifying ourselves at one of the local pubs, somewhere south of Stamford!

Bob Braham refers to the exercise in his book *Scramble*, which confirms that he took part in it. He says that not only was it good fun but it taught us some useful lessons! For me, it was just like being back in the OTC at Hurstpierpoint, as we crawled towards the barbed wire entanglements strewn along the airfield boundary, in the pitch dark and laden with rifle, bayonet and blank ammunition weighing a ton! I have one vivid memory of collapsing across the wire and various of my friends stumbling over me with heavy boots – and encouraging me to stay where I was, so that they could get over more easily! Then the effect of the beer that I had consumed took over and I remembered no more!

One night we had a party and with thunder flashes being poked down the chimney of the ante-room we nearly set the Mess on fire . . . and, last but not least, when Harry and I had a mild celebration, I kissed a very attractive red-headed WAAF in the dining room as she served me with the soup! I suppose, today, that would be called harassment and I would be court martialled for not treating the red-head as a man! But then she seemed to have no objection to me treating her as a woman . . . how fashions change!

As the Adjutant, Dicky Sparrowe, had said to us when we returned to the squadron in June, from our Egyptian ferrying, 'I think you two boys have fallen on your feet this time!'

And at Wittering – so it was . . .

*   *   *

Don Aris records that on 1 and 2 December there were no operations by Bomber Command, although I can see from my log-book that Harry and I did an NFT in Beau 8744. I noted 'ALL OK' and we were back on the ground after an hour in the air and ready to operate if need be. On the following day the squadron records say: 'Still no operational flying' and, with the advanced party having left Wittering for our new base at West Raynham, the squadron continued packing for the move. Whilst we were so occupied the 'bomber boys' whom we should have been protecting went to 'the Big City' with a force of 458 aircraft – and lost 40. We were still some way away from the real war.

The main party of 141 Squadron moved on 3 December, by road to West Raynham. On the same day HQ 12 Group gave authorisation for the wearing of the ribbon of the 1939/43 Star or the Africa Star: one could not, at that time, have both! Harry and I learned that we had operated for sufficient time to qualify for this medal. They were sort of campaign medals really, and the authors of them probably had in mind the 1914/15 Star introduced in the 1914–18 War. The

1939/43 Star meant something when it was first promulgated and we all pushed off happily to the stores to pick up a little strip of ribbon (in the colours of the three Services!) and take it round to the station tailor to have it sewn on. After all, many of the recipients had, by December '43, been operating for three or four years, without anything to show for it. This particularly applied to the air gunners and WOP/AGs in Bomber and Coastal Command.

Post war, in the shambles perpetrated by the new Labour Government designing and allotting campaign stars and other medals to mark the 1939–45 War, the 1939/43 Star was irrationally replaced by the 1939/45 Star. This hybrid was then dished out to all and sundry, including many people who had only been in for a few months and had seen hardly any action at all! Thus was the 1939/43 Star debased and its value, in our eyes, spoilt.

On the night of 3/4 December 1943, Bomber Command carried out an attack on Leipzig, Germany, with a force of 527 aircraft, and 24 aircraft were lost. 141 Squadron did not operate.

Because Harry and I were to be posted three times to West Raynham in the ensuing two and a half years, and because, like Wittering, this station was to play a significant part in our lives, it is worth turning back to Don's History for a picture of our new 'home'.

Our new base was, and is, situated in a lovely part of north-west Norfolk. It is isolated, and the nearest town, Fakenham, is eight miles away (and in 1943 Fakenham was a very small town). Swaffham is eight miles south of the airfield; and King's Lynn, the nearest large town, is 15 miles to the west. The coast – that magic Norfolk coastline – is 15 miles to the north. However, in 1943, the nearest railway station, East Rudham, was just over a mile away and from here the single-track line connected with the main line at King's Lynn (and beyond that, Peterborough).

Almost everything required by West Raynham came via the railway to East Rudham station and its small sidings: personnel, equipment, stores, bombs, ammunition and the thousand and one things necessary to keep an operational station going in time of war. The railway line through East Rudham and on to Fakenham, of which John Betjeman would have so much approved, has long since been closed down.

The station, officially opened on 8 April 1939 under No. 6 Group of Bomber Command, was soon transferred to No. 2 Group Bomber Command and became operational as soon as war broke out on 3 September. Originally it was a grass airfield but, in May 1943, it was closed to flying and the construction begun of two concrete runways. No. 1 runway, the main and longer was NE/SW, and No. 2, the shorter, was E/W. In order to construct the runways, more land was commandeered and another country lane closed and removed to allow for the western end of the E/W runway.

The station had fine brick messes and buildings and four large 'C' type permanent hangars. The squadron's aircraft were not dispersed far away from the hangars and the main site and, as far as we know, this was the first time that the squadron had not used dispersal bays (spread out around the perimeter track). One can only assume that, at this stage of the war, it had been decided that the advantages of not having the aircraft dispersed outweighed the possibilities of enemy air attacks.

The Squadron Servicing Echelon, No. 3059, soon to be re-numbered No. 9141, took over No. 1 hangar, the end and most southerly of the four hangars. Built onto either side of each hangar were offices and workshops and these on No. 1 hangar were taken over by the squadron for the CO's office, Adjutant and orderly room, flight offices and workshops for the various trades. 'A' Flight aircraft and the CO's aircraft were parked on the grass in front of No. 1 hangar and 'B' Flight's aircraft were round the corner of the hangar. Here – in the 'B' Flight crew room – Harry and I were to play out much of our remaining time together, and here at West Raynham, many years later (in April 1989), we were to spend our last evening together . . .

However, Don tells us that there was very limited accommodation for the ground crews due to the large number of personnel on the station. No. 239 Squadron, and its Servicing Echelon, joined No. 141 Squadron at West Raynham on 9 December. Additionally, there were all the headquarters staff of the newly formed 100 Group, who had to be accommodated at Raynham until they could be transferred to Bylaugh Hall (a small, and not very stately home) a few miles away. By the end of December there were 1,740 personnel on the station!

Our ground crews' main barrack block (similar to the one where I had first met Harry at Church Fenton – and to which he had refused me entry!) was No. 104. But Don and the others had to put up with double-tiered bunks down either side of each room in the barrack block, in order to double up on the number of men in each room. There were, however, no extra ablution or toilet facilities for the extra airmen. But Don recalls that, as far as he can remember, there were few complaints because they were warm and dry for the winter and they knew that they were far better off in comparison with being on a dispersed Nissen-hutted camp!

In the officers' mess – situated near to the main gate of the camp – we found it was just like home from home (compared with Wittering) with one important exception: there was no Sergeant Renaldi and no Savoy-style catering! West Raynham became the home of 141 Squadron for the rest of the war and only moved from there after the war on 3 July 1945. On 4 December 1943 Harry and I moved happily into Room 13.

Resorting once more to Don Aris's History of the Squadron, it is necessary to give some background to the business in which we, in 141 and the other bomber support long-range fighter squadrons, were to be engaged until the end of the European war. The general public, at least the older citizens, have some idea of the operations carried out by the day-fighters, mainly from stories of the Battle of Britain, and also of night bombing, from films such as *The Dambusters.*

Also, when they do give a thought to poor old Coastal Command, they can probably visualise the Sunderland flying boats bravely patrolling above the convoys of ships crossing from America, far out over the Atlantic. As observed earlier in this book, general knowledge of night-fighter operations does not usually extend beyond cats' eyes and carrots! Knowledge of night-fighter 'Intruder' offensive operations is precisely nil.

At Wittering, 141 Squadron had been in No. 12 Group, which had its Headquarters at Watnall, Notts. When 141 moved to West Raynham on 3.12.1943 it became the first squadron in the recently formed No. 100 Group and became part of Bomber Command. Number 100 Group was formed on 8.11.1943 at Radlett, Herts. under the command of Air Commodore E.B. Addison, and Group Headquarters moved to West Raynham on 3.12.1943. The

Group was formed to bring together, under one control in Bomber Command, the few units already operating on bomber support, electronic countermeasures, electronic intelligence and other highly specialised tasks.

Once formed it expanded rapidly with more squadrons and units engaged on these activities. The Group's principal aim was to give direct support to night bombing, or other operations, by attacking enemy night-fighter aircraft in the air; or by attacks on airfields or installations on the ground. It employed ground and airborne electronic countermeasures equipment to deceive, confuse and jam the enemy radio navigational aids, enemy radar systems and wireless communication signals. It also helped to deceive the enemy as to the actual bombing target by carrying out diversions and spoof raids.

The Group had close affiliations with the Telecommunication Research Establishment at Malvern and its airfield at Defford, Worcs., and helped to develop new electronic equipment under operational conditions. The larger aircraft of the Group, particularly the Fortresses and Liberators, used some 32 different devices for jamming. Some produced electronic 'noise' intended for disrupting German radars and others produced audio interference on R/T communication channels, and yet others were used for jamming German early warning radars. All had various code names.

So there we were, poised to take the profits from 141's pioneering efforts between June and September and offer the beleaguered crews of the heavy bombers some real support by rooting out and destroying as many of the German night-fighters as we could find. All that we needed were some new Mosquitoes and some serviceable AI and Serrate equipment. We had neither . . .

There were no major operations by Bomber Command on the night of 4/5 December 1943 and neither were there any for the next 11 nights. Therefore 141 did not operate during this period and the remission gave us time to settle into our new base.

On 8 December our New Zealand Radar Officer, F/O Pollard, was given permission by the AOC No. 100 Group to have the complete use of a Mosquito aircraft for 'experimental purposes'.

The records also state that a Mr E.J. Smith from ORS (the Operational Research Section) at Headquarters Air Defence of Great Britain (the misguided and temporary title bestowed on Fighter Command!) to assist Flying Officer Pollard. It was hoped that within a fortnight, their efforts would bear fruit! In other words, Polly was told, in no uncertain terms, that he must get on and solve the problem of the faulty radar equipment on the Mosquitoes as top priority and every means available would be put at his disposal.

My log-book records that Harry and I flew Mosquito 712 on 8, 9, 10 and 11 December and each time it was on a radar test. These formed some of the trials initiated by Polly and my brief notes were, respectively: 'Spurious echoes' – 'MK IV O.K.' – 'SERRATE u/s' and 'SERRATE Elevation u/s'. It was to be another month before Polly was able to solve the problem.

In the meantime Harry and I were to meet some people whom we never forgot. We spent two days with No. 35 Pathfinder Squadron at Graveley, located a few miles to the west of Cambridge. It had been decided that some information about the High-Level Bomber Support operations and Serrate should be passed on to the heavy bomber crews. This was evidently not before time, because one of the first things we were jokingly told (when we got to 35 Squadron) was that when, at briefing for a raid, it was announced that it would be 'SERRATE,

TONIGHT!' some of the crews thought that the Briefing Officer was referring to a new type of wind!

Harry and I were looked after by the 'A' Flight Commander, Squadron Leader Julian Sale DSO & Bar (to which he was to add the DFC) and his navigator, Raich Carter DFC (to which he was to add a Bar).

We were flown down from West Raynham to Graveley on 16 December 1943, by Warrant Officer Pugsley, in the Oxford (the Squadron runabout), and he picked us up to fly us home, on 18 December. In Don's History there is an entry which could have had a lot of significance for Harry and me, if 35 (Pathfinder) Squadron had been flying Lancasters and not the Halifax III. The connection may not immediately be clear but when the story of our two days at Graveley is continued, the reader will see how near we came to being caught up in 'Black Thursday' (as it became known in Bomber Command thereafter). The entry reads as follows:

> 'For a period of 12 nights from the 4th December not one heavy bomber had operated, due to a combination of full moon and bad weather . . . and this was the reason why 141 Squadron had not operated. On the night of 16th/17th December, Bomber Command resumed operations with an attack on Berlin by a force of 483 Lancasters and 15 Mosquitoes. On the raid itself they suffered the loss of 25 Lancasters and then had further losses of 34 Lancasters on their return to England. Very bad weather conditions (back at their bases) caused collisions, crashes and some crews having to bale out due to running short of fuel. This became known as "Black Thursday" and Bomber Command suffered its worst bad weather landing casualties of the war. There was therefore a total loss of 54 aircraft.'

When 'Pug' flew us down to Graveley on the afternoon of the 16th the weather was already looking pretty murky and there seemed to be the chance that fog was somewhere in the offing. As already mentioned, Julian Sale took Harry under his wing and Raich Carter looked after me and, soon after we had landed, they told us that ops were on and they were about to do their NFT. They asked if we would like to come with them! Briefing was at 17.30 or 18.00 hours (I can't remember which), the weather was closing in fast . . . so there wasn't much time.

We set off, at the high rate of knots, in a truck with the other five members of Julian's crew out onto the perimeter track and off in the direction of 35 Squadron's dispersal bays, but by the time we found the Flight Commander's Halifax III the fog had rolled in and we could hardly see our hands in front of our faces!

All this while (since we had landed at Graveley) Harry and I had been trying to come to terms with the awful truth: that we might actually have to fly with Julian Sale and his crew, not only on the night-flying test but also on the op!

We were actually starting to climb up into the Halifax when word came through that NFTs were being 'scrubbed' and Julian and his merry men, plus Harry and I, clambered back into the truck. As we drove away and headed for the briefing room Julian observed, quite casually, 'That's no problem, we'll take her without an NFT. OK with you, Harry?' It may well have been 'OK' with Harry. I rather suspect he was looking forward to it . . . another new experience! It was anything *but* OK with me! The thought of going off in that Halifax on ops over Germany (we didn't, at that time, know the target) as a surplus navigator was enough to give me the idea of going 'LMF' on the spot!

Apart from anything else, I couldn't get it out of my mind that I had never done a navigation course and was not a proper navigator! Raich Carter wore the 'O' on his half-wing – the sign that he had completed a full observer's course. I wore an 'N', but that was only a 'cover up' to replace my 'RO' (when we had started to operate over Occupied Europe in June). What would happen if Raich were to be wounded – some time on the trip – and Julian Sale were to ask me to navigate the Halifax back to base at Graveley!

We got to the briefing room and I went in with Raich Carter, trying to assume an air of indifference and still without having had the chance to voice my fears to Harry. I suppose he was calmly working out how he would fly the Halifax home, if Julian was the one to be hit! Worse was to come! When the curtain was drawn by the Station Commander and the target revealed, we saw that the tapes went all the way out to – Berlin, and there was a groan from the crews massed in the briefing room. It was going to be 'the Big City' (code-named 'WHITEBAIT'), and the weather report was just about as bad as it could be, with thick cloud right across northern Germany – up to 18,000 feet – and then low cloud and fog over England forecast for the time that we (*c*.700 aircraft) would be attempting to land back at our bases.

There was quite a lot of muttering going on, because the crews knew that they would have the greatest difficulty in getting their Halifaxes up through the front of bad weather which lay across the North German Plain. Suddenly, a messenger arrived on the platform and passed a note to the Briefing Officer, who paused in mid-sentence, then 'OK, chaps – ops are scrubbed for all Halifax squadrons, the Lancs are still going . . .' There was a mighty cheer! We didn't care about the Lancs and any problems *they* might have as long as *we* didn't have to go!

The Lancasters could climb up over the front, good luck to them, but we were on remission, and with the tension broken the crews, including our own, started to break up and leave the briefing room. The potential horrors of the night were relegated to the back of our minds and, not having to go, we could all be brave again! Then, whilst I was still trying to recover my nerve, a small incident occurred which I have never forgotten. I heard Julian Sale saying, apologetically, to Harry, 'I'm sorry, Harry, but I'm going to have to leave you. I've got a touch of flu and I am running a temperature. I'm going to take myself off to bed. Raich will look after you and Mike . . .' and off he went.

As long as ops were on Julian Sale was going to go. Only when they were cancelled did he think of declaring himself to be unwell, and going to bed. He was that sort of man. We learned, during the 17th, which we spent on the squadron, that he had been shot down earlier in 1943 and that both he and Raich Carter had evaded capture and returned to the squadron to continue their tour. He was the sort of man Chaz Bowyer had in mind when he wrote *Bomber Barons*. Bowyer was talking about some of the great bomber captains who had given their lives getting their crews to safety, before going down with their aircraft. He said that, sometimes, this selfless regard for their crew members resulted in them escaping death, and cites the following example. He said it occurred in the early morning of 21 December 1943 at Graveley airfield. (*Note* Just three days after we had left Julian Sale, sick with the flu!)

'A Toronto-born Canadian pilot, Squadron Leader Julian Sale, had piloted Halifax HX328 to Frankfurt the previous evening as a Primary Visual Marker for the 600-plus main force. Over the target thick clouds at low heights obscured Sale's view of the intended aiming point and he made five circuits at succeedingly lower altitudes attempting to identify the target to no avail. Releasing his high explosive bomb load, he retained his target indicators and returned to Graveley.

On reaching base, and as he circled the field prior to landing, one of the TIs in the bomb bay detonated, setting the rear turret and a wing on fire. Climbing away from the airfield in a full-boost climb to 2000 feet, Sale levelled out and ordered his crew to bale out. He then trimmed the Halifax to stay (hopefully) in level flight as he prepared to take to his parachute and follow his crew – only to find Flight Lieutenant Bob Lamb, his mid-upper gunner, standing by the pilot's seat, holding a burned out parachute pack.

Sale immediately forgot his own intended escape, radioed Graveley to clear the runway for an emergency landing, and flew the blazing Halifax down quickly, taking it at full speed as far as possible away from the main buildings. As the burning aircraft slowed down, Sale and Lamb leapt out, still in full flying gear, and raced as fast as possible away from the bomber. Just 200 yards were covered before the Halifax exploded and burned out, flinging both men onto the ground by the force of the blast, but both then stood up uninjured.'

I even recall that, after he and Raich had evaded capture once, they always flew wearing their escape clothing, in case the same thing should happen to them again. They did so even when we went out to fly the NFT with them on the 16th. They were an outstanding combination.

Chaz Bowyer goes on:

'Julian Sale's luck had been stretched over a long period of operations. On the 1st May 1943 he had been shot down on a sortie, but evaded capture, returned to England and became commander of 35 Squadron's "A" Flight before the 20th/21st December sortie, already described. In the interim he was awarded a DSO and Bar, and a DFC, but on the 19th February 1944, during the outward leg of a raid against Leipzeig Julian Sale's luck ran out.

Attacked from below by a Wunstorf based Junkers 88 night-fighter, Sale was wounded and one of his Halifax's fuel tanks erupted in flames. Ordering his crew to take to their parachutes, the wounded Sale managed to follow suit shortly after. Tragically, his wounds proved fatal and he died on 20th March in captivity.'

On the 17th we also learned of the heavy losses sustained by the Lancasters trying to land back at their fog-bound bases in the early hours of the morning and thanked our lucky stars that our trip from Graveley had been cancelled. Some of the Lancs had tried to use the newly installed FIDO system to get in at Graveley itself, but four had crashed around the airfield attempting to make a landing off a normal circuit, instead of flying out on a reciprocal to the runway (once they had got over the airfield) and carrying out the normal blind-approach procedure. The welcoming glare thrown up through the fog by the oil-burners set out along the runway was too tempting for some pilots and they were loath to leave it, even though it was much safer to do so. Rumour had it that there were 27 bodies in the station mortuary.

When 'Pug' came to pick us up on the 18th to fly us back to West Raynham, he found two rather chastened and thoughtful members of 141, not acting at all like the usual Harry White and Mike Allen with whom he was familiar.

Harry and I had met some of the 'bomber boys' whom we were trying to support and came away from Graveley conscious of the relative safety of our own operations, when compared with theirs. And feeling even guiltier that more was not being done by the bomber support squadrons to assist them, and by the under-employed Home Defence squadrons too, for that matter. We had plenty of food for thought.

I have never forgotten those two days at Graveley. Raich Carter survived the war, married the brave French girl who helped him to evade capture and has lived happily in France ever after.

A few years ago we exchanged letters and memories. It was a privilege to know Julian Sale and Raich Carter – even for only 48 hours. They set a standard which most of us could not match.

Before Harry and I went down to Graveley the Station Commander at West Raynham, Group Captain E.T.T. Nelson, called a full parade of all station personnel and gave what was commonly called a pep talk, i.e. he stressed the importance of everyone giving 'of their best work' in the hope that this would help to shorten the war. It must be said that this sort of approach did not go down particularly well with operational aircrew. Station Commanders, and Squadron Commanders who had themselves done a tour, or more, on operations were closer to the aircrews and did not usually indulge in such fruitless pastimes.

At Tangmere in 1942, I remember hearing a Wing Leader, he was a South African, encourage his pilots, as they raced out to their Spitfires, with the single phrase 'BUTTON "B", YOU BASTARDS!' He was of course referring to the VHF channel that they were to use, but that was all he said to them as they took off for a daylight sweep over northern France!

Group Captain Nelson was one of those unfortunate regular officers who had been too young for the 1914–18 war and were now too old to take an active part in this one. I remember him only as a rather remote and stiff little man, although I did not really know him well enough to pass an opinion.

Once again, Harry and I felt sorry for him and regretted that we did not have a former bomber captain in charge at West Raynham, off whom we could have learned more about Bomber Command and the tactics used by its crews over Germany.

On 16 December, when Harry and I were away at Graveley, 141 operated with two Mosquitoes and two Beaufighters and claimed an Me 110 as damaged. This partial success was gained by Freddie Lambert and Ken Dear and their Combat Report indicates that they had a violent dogfight with two German night-fighters who chased them all over the sky! Freddie was only able to get off 20 rounds (from each cannon) and had to open fire at 900 feet, after they themselves had been fired on three times by the E/A!

It was something, but as Don Aris said: 'This was another poor showing by 141 Squadron, of the four aircraft operating only two reached the target areas, and one of these when the rear hatch blew open! Even Ken Dear's AI went unserviceable at their end of the dogfight.'

On 20 December 1943, we were going to take V8713 on ops, in support of a raid on Frankfurt (the same night that Julian Sale saved the life of his mid-upper gunner), and everything was on the top line when we did our NFT. But later, as we walked out to take off on the op, we were informed that the Beau was unserviceable.

When the Beau was ready again and ops were on for the 31st, the weather was bad and our trip was scrubbed once more. All this time the losses among the heavy bombers were growing. On the 20th (when we could not go to Frankfurt) they attacked with a force of 650 aircraft and lost 41.

Just before Christmas Howard Kelsey and Smithy cheered us all up when they shot down a Ju 88, when supporting a raid on Berlin. They had made an outstanding contribution to the Serrate operation in the early days, and this was their fourth success, as well as having 1 PROBABLE and 1 DAMAGED to their credit. Later, we were to lose them from 141 when they were posted, first to 169 and then to 515 Squadron (another new fighter squadron in No. 100 Group). They continued operating with great success until the end of the war, Howard Kelsey having been awarded the DSO & DFC and Bar, and Smithy (with whom I am happily still in touch) the DFC and Bar & DFM.

On Christmas Eve, Harry and I flew up to Castle Bromwich and then back to Raynham. I suspect it was to take someone on leave but the only comment in my log-book is 'Nearly spent Christmas on a balloon cable'. So I guess that we did not do our homework properly before taking off for Castle Bromwich, that the balloons around Birmingham suddenly loomed up out of the murk and we only spotted them at the last moment!

The down side to Howard Kelsey's success (as it would be called nowadays!) was that we lost Joe Gunnill and Hanson, his Nav/Rad. They went off on the 23rd, in support of a raid on Berlin, flying Beau VIF V8402, and were never heard of again. They lie in adjoining graves in the Schoonselhof Cemetery at Antwerp in Belgium.

No bombing raids were carried out by Bomber Command on either Christmas Eve or Christmas Day, so 141 Squadron did not operate. Don reports that there was a 'fun' football match in the morning between the officers' and sergeants' messes, and at 12.45 hours the officers and sergeants formed up outside the officers' mess and, led by Group Captain Nelson, marched down to the airmen's mess, and served Christmas dinner to the airmen and airwomen. Afterwards we were entertained in the sergeants' mess, before returning to the officer's mess to have our own dinner. I don't remember much of these proceedings, although I was certainly there!

Perhaps, along with Roger and Andy, Johnny and Frank, Angels and Ron and the others – I dined not wisely, but too well? Three out of these six were to be lost in 1944, and Angels would be spending his next Christmas in a POW camp. So I am glad we had a good 'thrash'! The entry in 141 Squadron's Operations Record Book for the Boxing Day is enough to put all thoughts of Christmas out of one's mind. It reads: 'All Mosquitoes have been temporarily grounded until modifications are completed by De Havilland workmen. Experimental work is still proceeding with the Mosquito aircraft and most difficulties have been, or are being, solved.'

It is only when I came to read through Don Aris's entries for the period October '43–January '44, during the preparation of this book, that the full tragedy of what occurred came home to me. He recorded that in the last major raid of 1943, on Berlin on the 29th December, 141 could only put up two Beaufighters:

'The Mosquitoes were temporarily grounded with constant engine and radar problems and most of the Squadron's Beaufighters had been transferred to other units with the assumption that it would be able to operate the old Mosquitoes. No wonder this was the most dispiriting time Squadron had experienced since the tragic Defiant losses during the Battle of Britain in 1940.'

Just before the end of the month Johnny Forshaw and I went in a Beau, to have a look at Woodbridge, near Ipswich, which was one of the three emergency landing grounds, laid out to take returning bomber (and other) aircraft, badly damaged – possibly with wounded men aboard – and likely to have difficulty in making it back to their own base. The other two were Manston, in Kent and Carnaby in Yorkshire. All three were situated on the coast. They were 3,000 yards long, with a grass 'overshoot' at either end of 1,000 yards, and the width was such that those in Flying Control could bring in three aircraft, at any one time!

Johnny orbited Woodbridge three times, whilst we took a good look at it, both hoping that we would not have to use it, but very glad to see it there! Again, I don't know where Frank Folley, Johnny's elusive Nav/Rad, had got to but there was a rumour that (like my mother-in-law, of later years) Frank did not 'do very many miles to the bottle'. I am sure this was false, because they were proving to be an above average crew, and were an asset to the squadron. This gives me the opportunity of saying that, although in our off-duty hours some of us managed to imbibe a fair quantity of war-time beer, I never came across any case of pilots or navigators drinking when they were on duty and likely to have to fly.

There were no bomber operations on New Year's Eve and so we saw out the year 1943, which had had its fair share of triumph and tragedy. If we had any wish for 1944 – other than hoping to stay alive until 1945 – it was that the problems which dogged our Mosquitoes would soon be solved, and we could play our full role in trying to support the men like those whom Harry and I had met at Graveley.

The final word for 1943 must be that Harry and I did not operate on any night throughout the month of December.

The year 1944 opened with two heavy raids on Berlin, in the course of which Bomber Command lost a further 55 Lancasters. All that 141 could manage in support was two Beaufighters on the second of the two raids and neither Ken Pamment nor 'Greg' met with any success. Then, on 3 January insult was added to injury, when two Avro Ansons were loaned to the squadron for practice interceptions and AI training, so we were soon hurtling around the skies over Raynham at 120 knots with Harry trying to out-turn the Anson in front of us and me yelling encouragement to him over the intercom! When we landed, we went to see Buster Reynolds in the Intelligence room, to put in a claim for one Avro Anson – DAMAGED!

We even did one AI practice in an Anson at night! The trip was recorded in my log-book: 'Full moon. 1 visual on Anson which would not play. G.C.I. solid.'

This entry meant that we were disappointed that the pilot in the other Anson was not prepared to have a dogfight with us and secondly, that we did not think very much of the GCI Controller! Harry and Johnny Forshaw shared the 'driving' and we were up for 1.40 hours, our first night trip for nearly two months!

Between 10 and 13 January, Harry and I played an active part in testing out Polly's modifications to the AI and Serrate equipment on the Mosquitoes. We flew Mosquito 644 and found, to our delight, that, with new aerials, everything worked properly and then we carried out four radar test flights on Mosquito 712, all of which were OK. On 13 January there is the following entry in my log-book: 'All O.K. Operational Again'.

It was tremendous news and I managed to pluck out of my memory a suitable quotation from the Bard, to mark the occasion. At the top of the page I wrote: 'It works! Thou hast done well, fine Aerial!' from *The Tempest*, and alongside it, in more plebeian style, 'Good Old POLLY!' Subsequently Flying Officer Pollard was awarded a richly deserved MBE for his work as Radar Officer on 141 Squadron.

It is disappointing to see from my log-book that, after becoming operational again, we did not fly again until the 23rd, so presumably we went off on ten days' leave! Something was wrong somewhere. After all, we hadn't done anything for three months! It is always easier to sort out other people's problems – and easier still with hindsight – but surely the CO should have postponed all leave for the aircrew as soon as the squadron was classified as being operational again? Surely Harry and I should not have gone on leave, at that stage of the proceedings?

After the 13th, there were three Mosquitoes which had been installed with the modified radar equipment (including 712, which Harry and I had tested), one for 141, and one for each of the two new Serrate squadrons, 239 and 169.

On the 14th, Bomber Command went to Brunswick with a force of nearly 500 aircraft – and lost 38 Lancasters. Our squadron put up two Mosquitoes (787 and 712). The former, with Freddie Lambert and Ken Dear, lost the port engine and landed back at Coltishall making a successful single-engined landing. The latter, with Frank Davis (the 'B' Flight Commander) and Jimmy Wheldon, found some Serrate signals, made one AI contact and were chasing after it, when the intercom failed! So the nadir of 141's fortunes was to continue into 1944.

In the meantime, a farewell dinner (and then a cocktail party!) was being held in the officers' mess at West Raynham to speed the headquarters staff on their way – to Bylaugh Hall, their not-so-stately home! Surely, such festivities had no place at Raynham when the catastrophe of the Mosquitoes was still unfolding before the eyes of the new AOC? We were not sorry to see them go!

Whilst we were away, on leave, we missed out on a talk given by a squadron leader from Pathfinder Force (PFF) outlining the marking procedures they were using, although we had picked up this information whilst we were with 35 Squadron at Graveley. We also heard, when we got back, that Howard Kelsey and Smithy had been to talk to 239 Squadron (now well settled in at Raynham) about Serrate bomber support operations. There was no crew better qualified to do so, and indeed 239 became a successful and efficient squadron, as conditions gradually improved in the spring and summer, eventually gaining the edge on 141, before the year ended.

Whilst we were still away there was yet another major raid on Berlin in the course of which 35 bombers were lost out of an attacking force of 769 aircraft. Six Mosquitoes were got ready by the over-worked and over-strained ground-crew of 141 but, in the end, only two took off in support of the bombers. Four were found to be unserviceable, mostly with AI radar and Serrate problems. On the same night the two new Serrate squadrons, 239 and 169, commenced operations each putting up a single Mosquito.

The following night 648 bombers went to Magdeburg and lost 57. No. 141 Squadron operated with four Mosquitoes and Snape and Fowler claimed a Ju 88 damaged to the south of Brandenburg. Two of the other crews had chases via Serrate contacts which they were unable to bring to a visual, and the fourth, W/Cdr Roberts and F/O Joyce, were an 'early return' after their AI equipment became unserviceable.

It is virtually certain that the Ju 88 damaged by F/Sgt Snape and F/O Fowler was flown by the then top-scoring German night-fighter ace, Major Prince zu Sayn Wittgenstein, who was shot down and killed that night. The death of the Prince, whose score was then thought to be either 83 or 84 victories has (like that of Baron von Richthofen in an earlier war) always been shrouded by controversy and is mentioned in a number of publications concerning the air war of 1939–45. The Prince had already shot down four Lancasters, and some well-respected military historians hold that his Junkers 88 was hit and destroyed by the rear-gunner of his fifth victim.

Snape and Fowler were themselves to be posted missing in February, with the news reaching us later that Fowler had survived to become a prisoner-of-war. Sadly, this meant that Snape never lived to know that he had shot down one of the greatest of the German night-fighter aces and, thereby, probably saved countless unknown bomber crews.

On both 27 and 28 January 1944, after a break of five nights, the Allied war of attrition against the German capital city was resumed with the aircraft in the two forces totalling just under 1,200 bombers. They lost a total of 79 aircraft, which amounted to a figure of 6.6 per cent for the two nights' work. As a rough guide, any figure over 5 per cent for the bomber losses was reckoned to be prohibitive.

Harry and I operated on both nights (each time in Mosquito HJ941). On the 27th our trip was abortive: my AI set became unserviceable at a height of over 18,000 feet and we returned ignominiously to base after 1.45 hours in the air. On the following night, we got a Messerschmitt 109 right over the target area and the fruitless spell since September was broken at last! The bomber stream was routed to come in towards Berlin from the north-east and return, after bombing in a north-westerly direction, to the east of Denmark, cross out over the coast, and then turn east and fly back to England across the North Sea.

Our route was direct from West Raynham to Berlin, due east on 090 degrees! Our tactics were to arrive over Berlin as the bombing was coming to an end and as the last of the Lancasters and Halifaxes were getting out of the glare of the fires, and the searchlights, into the blessed cover of darkness. We hoped that some of the German night-fighters, not knowing exactly what time the bombing was due to finish, would still be hanging about in the area.

As we headed east we had no trouble with our navigation: we could see the glow of the target area from our height of 22,000 feet from up to 100 miles off! With a tail wind of c.90 mph we covered the 550-odd miles to Berlin in about 1.30 hours and on the way past Münster, Osnabrück, Hanover and Magdeburg, into the target area, we had to ignore a number of Serrate contacts away on our port side and some which appeared on the starboard.

Our fuel would allow for us getting to Berlin and back (hopefully!) and up to half an hour hunting around in the target area itself. We could not afford either the time or the fuel to divert to the north-east of our track, where the German night-fighters were probably starting to get into the bomber stream and seek their first victims, although it was very tempting to do so. Once over the target area, we again found ourselves looking down at Dante's *Inferno*, but I wasted little time outside the visor of the AI set in front of me, and at this stage we should, for continuity, revert to our Combat Report:

> 'On reaching target at 03.40 hours an A.I. contact was obtained 20 degrees to starboard and 500 feet below at 18000 feet range. Mosquito was then at 22,000 feet. Mosquito chased this enemy aircraft for two minutes, closing the range to 2000 feet, when a second A.I. contact was observed 2000 feet astern. Our aircraft orbited hard to port, losing both contacts.
>
> At 03.42 hrs another backward looking contact was obtained 5000 feet astern. Mosquito orbited and obtained another head-on A.I. contact at 11,000 feet (height 23,000 feet). At the same time Pilot obtained a visual from this range (roughly two miles) of a green light on an enemy aircraft's starboard wing. Mosquito turned in behind enemy aircraft, which appeared blissfully ignorant of our aircraft's presence, and took no evasive action beyond a gradual loss of height to 18,000 feet. Our Pilot closed the range to 600 feet identifying the enemy aircraft as a single engined aircraft (probably an Me 109). He then opened fire from astern and below, giving a five second burst. Enemy aircraft burst into flames and exploded and was seen to dive vertically, still burning through haze. The time was then 03.45 and the height 18,000 feet. Claimed as one Me 109 Destroyed.'

We fired 70 rounds from each cannon and there were no stoppages, but as soon as we opened fire my AI set became u/s. This was distinctly annoying, because I always kept my head 'in the box' during a combat, in case the E/A should peel off and get away! As we ourselves had done, in front of an Me 110, on the night of the Peenemünde raid.

If this was to happen I would see the blip of the E/A emerge from minimum range and move away up the time trace as the range increased and also spot – from the elevation tube – if he was diving away from us. This was the most likely evasive action that he would take, once we had opened fire on him. There was then the chance, if I was quick about it, that we could follow him, intercept him for the second time and regain the visual which we had lost. Fortunately, on this occasion, Harry had hit the 109 first time and he had exploded in front of us.

There was a navigational problem that cropped up occasionally, and we took a routine precaution against it. The firing of the four 30 mm cannon and four .303-inch machine-guns could disturb the compass, by inducing a powerful magnetic force. Harry turned on to a northerly heading and fired a 'compass corrector' burst of 1½ seconds on the guns, to (hopefully) counteract any previous induction.

We turned for home at 03.50 hours but the night was not quite over:

> 'At 10 degrees East (over Hannover) one Serrate contact was obtained astern to port and below at 30 miles range. The E/A closed the range in a chase to the Dutch coast. Serrate was then line astern and trace faded at this range when over the Zuider Zee.'

This probably meant that one of our opposite numbers had been vectored onto us, but without any forward-looking AI it would have been fruitless to turn round to try and find him, even if we had had sufficient fuel, after our chases over Berlin. The rest of my radar equipment proceeded to pack up as we made our way home to West Raynham on a steady course of 270 degrees! At 9 degrees E the backward-looking AI failed and at 4 degrees E, after I had obtained a Gee fix over the Dutch coast, Gee and Serrate failed.

We had crossed out over the Dutch coast on track (south of De Kooy) at 05.20 hours at 20,000 feet and landed back at base at 06.00 hrs.

When we clambered out of 941 our ground crew were excited about the destruction of the Me 109 and encouraged to think that the squadron was fully operational again, and on entering the Intelligence room we heard the good news that 239 Squadron had obtained their first success on a bomber support operation. Neil Munro and Hurley had got an Me 110, also over Berlin. Then came the bad news, a crew from 239 were missing. It was John Brachi and old Angus MacLeod.

John and 'Mac' had joined 141 at the same time as Harry and I (in January 1943). They had taken part in the daylight 'Instep' operations down into 'the Bay', when the squadron was based at Predannack, and had been one of the crews to pioneer the Serrate operation. They were an above-average crew, who had completed a considerable number of ops without having had the success which they deserved.

Mac was married and, at 37, older than the rest of us. He had volunteered to become an Observer/Radio when he might easily, and with full respect for his age, have sat the war out in some ground job. John Brachi was a committed Christian and a gentleman, in every sense of the word. When I visit the Air Forces Memorial at Runnymede, where his name is inscribed on Panel No. 201, I think of him and how he did not take kindly to the business of war and did not mix easily with the rest of us, who did not have his scruples and were rather enjoying ourselves.

Nevertheless, John did his duty on 141, before he and Mac were transferred to 239 as an experienced crew, to assist them when they commenced bomber support operations. They were definitely among 'the Unsung Heroes', of whom there were many in Bomber Command. When I am standing in front of Panel No. 201 at Runnymede and looking up at John's name, I find myself hoping that when things got rough on the night of 28/29 January 1944, his religion gave him comfort. Mac's body must have been washed up on the Dutch coast, because he lies in Zouteland General Cemetery, Holland, in the lasting care of the Commonwealth War Graves Commission, but John was never found.

John and Mac had taken off about forty minutes before Harry and I and had also been briefed to patrol over Berlin. As Harry and I waited in the Intelligence room news came through that John (flying Mosquito FII HJ935) had called up Flying Control to report that their starboard engine had failed whilst they were over enemy territory, and that they had turned round to make the journey back to base on one engine.

John said over the R/T that after flying for one and a half hours the port engine had started cutting out and finally failed. They were over the North Sea and he gave their position as 5148N–0247E. Mac must have been using Gee right up to the last moment to plot their course accurately as they struggled back with the crippled Mosquito. John then told Flying Control that they were both baling out at this position. It was a dark winter's night and there was no chance of ditching the Mosquito successfully in the North Sea.

Harry and I were debriefed, grabbed a meal and a few hours' sleep, then went back to the crew room to find that aircraft from both 239 and 141 were out looking for John and Mac. As soon as Jock Murray and George Bliss got down in HJ712 we had it refuelled and took off to join in the search. We flew down to the area of John's last known position which was about halfway between the Essex coast and the estuary of the River Scheldt. We searched, flying just below the cloud base, for two hours, but saw nothing. Air-Sea Rescue trips are just about the most soul-destroying sorties you can ever make, particularly if the people 'in the drink' are your own people!

Each time you have flown up one line of a square search and seen nothing, doubt creeps into your mind that you may have missed scanning some part of the limitless ocean and that maybe they are there. Should you not retrace your steps and look again?

Then common sense prevails and you realise that, if you break down the routine of the square search you will soon be wandering to and fro across the sky. You will likely be gazing at the same piece of sea without realising it, until your fuel runs out and you have to return to base. Although we (who still regarded John and old Mac as being very much a part of 141) and his new colleagues in 239, as well as aircraft from other squadrons, carried out an extensive Air-Sea Rescue search, we found no trace of them. My log just says: 'Air-Sea Rescue Search – for John Brachi and Macleod lost on previous night. No joy.'

As Don writes: 'Their deaths were solely due to the failure of both engines on the old Mk II Mosquito that was one of those issued to Nos 141, 239 & 169 Squadrons at this time.'

John was perfectly capable of getting himself and old Mac home if one of the engines had only kept going. Little did we know that, in three weeks' time, Harry and I would also be struggling home on one engine for the same reason, but our luck was in, and the other one kept going!

On the evening of 29/30 141 threw a party in honour of our old CO, Wing Commander Braham, during the course of which he was presented with a model of *Betsy*, Beaufighter V1F X8147 TW-A, which had been made by the Bristol Aeroplane Company. In *Betsy* Bob had shot down seven enemy aircraft and damaged a further two. The only other thing I can remember about the party was that he had flown up to West Raynham in a Gloucester Gladiator, which he had 'borrowed' from RAE at Farnborough! It was a gesture completely typical of the sort of man he was.

I think Harry and I must have left the party early; we were pretty tired, having only got back from the Berlin op at 06.00 hours and then going out on an Air-Sea Rescue search to look for John and Mac. In fact, I can recall that we started singing to try and keep each other awake whilst we were peering out of the cabin to try and spot the dinghy, which we felt must be there somewhere . . . The noise of our singing was worse than the fear of dropping off to sleep, so we soon gave that up!

On 30/31 January there was yet another big raid on Berlin. A total of 534 aircraft attacked and the losses were 33 heavy bombers. The good news was that a new crew on 141 – Graham Rice and Jimmy Rogerson – shot down an Me 110 on their first operational sortie! And on 169 Squadron our old friend from the Middle East ferrying days, Joe Cooper, opened this squadron's score with an Me 110 shot down near Berlin. Joe's navigator was still Ralph Connolly, with whom I had joined up at Stratford-upon-Avon and gone on to ITW and later to No. 3 Radio School for AI training.

The bad news was never far away, but this time, it came in a rather unexpected form and it was not the loss of another crew. All five 141 crews operating that night had taken off quite early and our newly found friends, Johnny Forshaw and Frank Folley, the latter recently commissioned, left the ground at 18.05 hours. Some three hours later, shortly after 21.00 hours, I received a call from 'Chiefy' Stanley (who was the highly competent senior NCO i/c the ground crews of 'B' Flight) asking me if I would come down to 'the Flight' because he had a spot of bother! When, after leaving the nice warm mess, I arrived at 'B' Flight I asked the nature of the problem confronting a very capable flight sergeant, who was not usually baffled by anything!

Chiefy said that his problem was with Flight Lieutenant Forshaw, who had just landed. He knew that the flight lieutenant was a friend of mine, so he had rung me up, to see if I could sort the matter out! I recall clearly saying: 'For goodness sake, what on earth is wrong? If they've landed safely, and they are both unhurt – what on earth is all the flap about?'

Flight Sergeant Stanley said: 'Well, it's like this . . . Mr Forshaw won't leave the cockpit and when anyone comes near him he starts swearing at them and telling them that he is going to stay just where he is! We can't simply leave him there for the night, so we thought of you!' I thanked him in good old Anglo-Saxon terms, pulled on my Irvin jacket again and stepped out into the cold night air to see what all the trouble was about.

When I got to the spot where Mosquito FII DD758 was parked, one of the ground crew shone his torch up into the cockpit and there were Johnny and Frank still sitting in their seats, completely unscathed, but with the former swearing like a trooper at all and sundry!

I quickly learned what had happened, but it was still quite a long time before I could persuade John to push Frank out down the steps and leave the aircraft himself. The language he was using was new to me and even to some of the ground crew, who had gathered round to watch the proceedings!

Johnny and Frank had, somewhere in the Hanover area, completed a classic Serrate AI interception . . . closed into minimum range . . . obtained a visual . . . identified the target as a Messerschmitt 110 . . . John had then pressed the trigger to open fire – and nothing had happened . . . none of the four cannon fired! They had had to break off the attack and return to base, with the bitter feeling of having had a German night-fighter at their mercy and being forced to let him get away. All the frustration which they felt, had built up on their way home and, by the time that he had landed and parked the Mosquito back at 'B' Flight, all John's emotions had boiled over. He was beside himself with vexation, disappointment and the sense of anticlimax.

Remembering the profession from which both of them had come (the theatre), it was not surprising that John went momentarily over the top. I felt desperately sorry for him and for Frank as well, who after all had done his stuff in completing the interception and obtaining 'the visual' for his pilot. Eventually, I succeeded in coaxing them both out of the Mosquito and across to the Intelligence room for debriefing, Johnny taking a last longing look at the four fabric patches over the gun-ports, which should not have been there . . .

There is an entry in the Operations Record Book for 31 January which summarises the situation as the month ended:

'Special equipment on Mosquito aircraft is gradually becoming more reliable, thanks chiefly to the experimental work of F/O Pollard, the Squadron Radar

Officer but, unfortunately, the state and age of the aircraft allotted is such that endless trouble is being caused by mechanical failures.'

Howard Kelsey and Smithy operated that night and had a number of Serrate and AI contacts without being able to bring any of them to a successful conclusion, showing that even when the aircraft and the equipment were serviceable, and in the hands of an exceptional crew, during High-Level Bomber Support operations it was difficult for the Nav/Rads to pick out which Serrate contact to follow and which AI contact to select when several appeared on the time-trace at the same time. The nearest might appear to be the most tempting, instructions to the pilot would be suddenly changed and off they would go chasing a target which might be flying too fast for them to catch.

The confusion on the AI tubes when operating close to the bomber stream, or crossing through it, had to be seen to be believed. The Serrate contacts had no indication of range, other than the size and strength of the herring-bone pattern on the azimuth and elevation tubes. If there were several on the tubes at the same time, it was always a gamble which one was selected for the chase. One must also remember that the German night-fighters were themselves not generally flying a straight course with a steady airspeed, which would make for an easy interception. They were under the direction of their GCI Controller and being continually vectored onto different courses to intercept the British bombers. The 'Wild Boar' single-engined fighters, which were not equipped with radar, were a different proposition. Once they had been ordered into the target area they were left to freelance in the glare of the fires and the searchlights.

It is worthwhile taking a closer look at Howard Kelsey's sortie of 30/31 January, which provides us with a good example of these difficulties:

'F/L H.C. Kelsey DFC & Bar with his Nav/Rad F/O E.M. Smith DFC, DFM in Mosquito FII DD717 took off at 18.35 hours on Serrate Bomber Support to Berlin. They crossed the enemy coast South of De Kooy at 19.39 hours. No contacts until 20 miles from target at 20.30 hours, when about three Serrates appeared on each side. [Note: Three Serrate signals were seen by Smithy, showing that the German night-fighters were on their starboard side. Although, of course, they may have been crossing from starboard to port and three were on their port side].

Their range was 20/30 miles, and all were from the Berlin area. As target area was approached, Serrate were seen to be coming from North of the target. Over the target area they chased six or seven Serrate contacts at heights varying from 22,000 feet down to 6,000 feet. [Note: That's low over Berlin, very low! That's up to Leonard Cheshire and Mickey Martin's standards . . . or should I say down to their standards!] It was impossible to close any of these nearer than about one to two miles as a stronger blip would repeatedly occur, leading to another chase only to be interrupted by a further Serrate.

After 30 minutes over target A.I. began to develop a "squint" so they set course for base. They had several A.I. contacts on their way to the Dutch coast and a few weak Serrates. Their Mosquito was chased for some time by an enemy aircraft showing an A.I. but evaded by gaining speed to 220 A.S.I. Recrossed out at Den Helder at 22.15 hours and landed at West Raynham at 23.00 hours.'

Howard and Smithy were at that time the most experienced and successful crew operating on bomber support, and although the radar did eventually start giving trouble, that was one occasion when even their skill could not bring them any success, although there were a number of German night-fighters in their vicinity.

In January the bomber support operations by the three Serrate squadrons started to 'turn the corner'. The number of sorties began to mount, the radar equipment in the Mosquitoes was proving to be more reliable and, most important of all, four (possibly five) E/A had been shot down. It would have been six if Johnny Forshaw's guns had not failed at the crucial moment.

But, out of the 24 sorties carried out by 141 on the Mosquitoes there were no fewer than eleven early returns, eight of them with engine failure. The loss of John Brachi's aircraft with their tragic double engine failure is not, of course, included in these figures. Although the disastrous Fourth Phase of these operations was coming to an end, there was still some way to go, as we shall see, when we come to look at the month of February!

Early in the month we flew one of the Ansons back to the OTU at Ouston. There is an odd note in my log-book which says: 'Perhaps the most unpleasant trip to date!'

I seem to remember that I was suffering from a hangover and, as the old Avro Anson wallowed on its way up to Church Fenton and then on to Ouston, I felt worse and worse! When Harry asked me to wind up the undercarriage, the task was almost beyond me! On the old Anson, the undercarriage was operated manually and had to be raised (and lowered) by turning a massive handle! The number of turns, if I remember rightly, was at least 120 before the 'undercart' was safely locked up or down. I know that after we took off from Raynham I got about half way, with sixty or seventy turns and then I couldn't remember which way I was going and started to wind it down again! I think I finally got the wheels fully retracted when it was time to start putting the undercarriage down again, so that we could land at Church Fenton, with Harry laughing away in the pilot's cockpit at my discomfort.

There were only minor raids by Bomber Command during the first week of February. But on the 8th the Squadron Record shows that I accompanied Ken Roberts, the 141 CO, and Paul Evans, 239's CO, to a conference at No. 100 Group Headquarters at Bylaugh Hall. The only reason that I can think of why Harry did not also go was that he was suffering from a bad dose of flu, which had kept us on the ground for two or three days. I have no recollection of what was discussed at the conference but it must have centred around the Serrate operation, our aircraft, equipment and most probably, our tactics.

The weather had been poor for almost all of the first two weeks in February, but on 15/16 the attack on Berlin was resumed once more. The target was attacked by 891 aircraft and the losses were 41 bombers. Five Mosquitoes operated from 141 and three from 239 Squadron. Howard Kelsey and Smithy were again operating, but had no luck. Johnny Forshaw and Frank had a hectic chase in the Brandenburg area, with the enemy aircraft weaving violently in front of them – as if it was aware of their presence. Their Combat Report reads: 'A visual was obtained at 1,000 feet range and positive identification of a Ju 88 obtained at 300 feet. As enemy aircraft was turning to starboard, F/Lt Forshaw opened fire with a two second burst at 300 feet, 30 degrees off to starboard.'

The enemy aircraft turned hard starboard, increasing the range to 600 feet, and

F/Lt Forshaw gave another four-second burst. Strikes were observed and streams of sparks came from the enemy aircraft's port engine and it immediately peeled off to starboard and went vertically downwards with sparks still coming from the port engine. They followed and got in another two-second burst with unobserved results before the enemy aircraft disappeared into cloud and haze below. They claimed a Ju 88 damaged.

At least, this time, Johnny's guns worked for him . . . but he and Frank would have been disappointed that they were not able to finish the Junkers 88 off and claim it as destroyed.

Harry and I planned again to get to the target area as the last of the bombers were leaving. We were flying Mosquito FII DZ726 (Z) and took off from West Raynham at 19.20 hours. We arrived much too early but were lucky enough – in the vivid shambles which was taking place in the skies over Berlin – to see a navigation light on an aircraft about one mile in front of us. It turned out to be a Heinkel 177, which we destroyed. Our Combat Report gives an overall picture of the scene and of the night's work:

> 'We crossed the enemy coast at 20.10 hrs, and three Serrate contacts – at extreme range to port, North and below were seen from 06.00'E, 08.00'E and 10.00'E, on their track, each lasting 3–5 minutes, but were not chased, according to instructions. The target area, Berlin, was first seen dead ahead from a distance of 70–80 miles, illuminated by concentrated red and green Pathfinder Force skymarkers at Zero – 3. The attack developed above, and presumably below, 10/10ths cloud as Mosquito approached, arriving at the target seven minutes early i.e. Zero + 13. There were few Serrate fighters about, but a considerable number of fighter flares; stationary searchlights also helped to illuminate the cloud top.
>
> Bombers were approaching from the North and turning, after bombing run,

A model of Mosquito DZ726 in which we destroyed an He 177 in February 1944 and a Ju 88 in May 1944.

onto a Westerly heading thus providing a right angle of concentrated activity. "Window" was much in evidence both aiding the identification of friendly bombers – and adding to the general confusion on the AI tubes. Several of these contacts were followed, but chases were abandoned because of "Window" identification or other contacts (unidentified) appearing at close range behind.'

As will be seen, Harry had a grandstand view, of everything that was happening as we approached Berlin but once we got there, we were soon

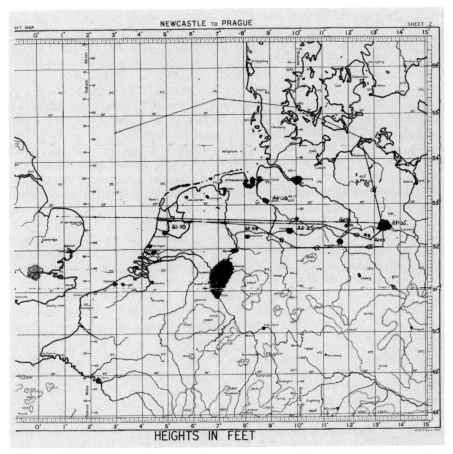

No. 141 Squadron, West Raynham: a 'Captains of Aircraft' map was carried by all bomber support pilots (usually in a fold of their flying book). On it they drew in their tract – and that of the bomber stream – and marked the heavily defended areas along the route in red crayon (to remind themselves not to overfly the ever-menacing flak and searchlights of the German ground defences). This particular map is a copy of the one Harry used on the trip we flew to Berlin on 15/16 February 1944, when we destroyed an He 177 over the target area.

experiencing the same sort of difficulties that had hampered Howard Kelsey and Smithy on 30/31 January.

The report continues:

> 'After patrolling the target area for seven minutes, a white light was observed ahead, crossing on the same level and crossing gently to starboard. This light was followed through a gentle turn and range closed at full throttle, because E/A appeared to be drawing away, to 500 feet, where E/A believed identified as Heinkel 111. Navigator had meanwhile obtained contact on this aircraft closing from 7,000 feet. Mosquito was closing much too fast to open fire [navigator not guilty] so we throttled back, turned hard starboard 45 degrees and hard port until contact regained at 3,000 feet and range closed gently to 800 feet.
>
> Pilot opened fire from dead astern with a three second burst, placing the only part of the E/A visible, namely the tail light, in the centre of the sight, range obtained from Navigator. Strikes observed in fuselage and starboard engine, resulting in a fire. Second burst was fired as E/A gently turned to starboard, this increased the volume of flames and E/A now clearly seen to be an He 177. E/A spiralled down enveloped in flames, followed to 12,000 feet by Mosquito. E/A disappeared into cloud. Pilot used the speed accumulated, 420 I.A.S. to regain height as soon as possible. Several other A.I. contacts were chased at heights from 20/23,000 ft. but again identified by "Window".
>
> A corrector burst was fired on due North, camera not used, and course set from the target area at Zero + 40 [21.57 hours]. Several fighter flares were dropped along the return route but only negligible distant Serrate noticed. Navigation was aided by D/F on the bomber stream. Apart from the target area no flak was experienced, though moderate amounts were seen on the return journey as far as 09.00'E, to North and South of our track.
>
> The Dutch coast was crossed at Texel, where our first Gee fix was obtained on the return journey, Coltishall A.I. Beacon, had, only a few minutes earlier, been obtained on a "second" time base, at a range of 170 miles. Course was set for base where we landed at 23.45 hours.
>
> The only unserviceablity experienced came from our port inner cannon, which had jammed after firing 30 rounds, due to a fault in the ejector chute. The Met conditions experienced and winds used were, within narrow limits, as predicted.'

Don's History records that we had used 306 rounds of 20 mm cannon shells, 92 from each of three guns and 30 from the one that jammed. He goes on to say that the Heinkel 177 was a large heavy bomber that was being used by the Germans to drop fighter flares in the target areas – in order that the 'Wild Boar' s/e fighters (such as the Me 109, that we had found over Berlin in January, and the Fw 190) could freelance above the target and pick off the bombers as they were on their bombing run where they were, of course, most vulnerable. The He 177 had not proved to be successful as a heavy bomber, so it was down-graded to the secondary task of flare-dropping in support of the enterprising night-fighter force defending the Third Reich so successfully. This was rather like the ill-fated Avro Manchester, before Roy Chadwick's genius intervened and turned the ugly duckling into the Lancaster.

After each major raid the Operational Research Section at 100 Group compiled a synopsis of Serrate operations. It outlined the plan for the various patrol areas; précised the crew's reports; gave the statistics related to the Serrate sorties; discussed the night's operations in the light of the tactics used by the enemy and the results achieved by 100 Group. It concluded with a report on inter-ference/jamming experienced and any technical trouble with the AI and/or the Serrate.

I have only had the opportunity of seeing these reports in the post-war years and, although I may be mistaken, I have no recollection of them being made available to us at the time, let alone having the opportunity of a profitable discus-sion from which we could all have learned something!

From the synopsis for 15/16 February we can see that Flying Officers White and Allen collected 'a bit of a rocket' for arriving in their patrol area too early! On page 4 of the synopsis one finds that:

'Of the Serrate aircraft patrolling in the target area, 141/Z [that was us!] clearly arrived much too early (22 minutes before the final bomb was dropped). The Heinkel 177 was reported shot down before the end of the bombing. Such early arrival at the target is not a tactic that is likely to be successful very often.'

The researchers were quite right and their criticism of our premature arrival at Berlin that night is valid. The most interesting part of these reports is the account of the direction of the German night-fighter Groups and the instructions sent out to our opposite numbers, in their Ju 88s and Me 110s, as the bomber stream penetrated even deeper into the skies above the Fatherland.

On the night in question, there was clear evidence that the Controllers were trying to get their fighters into the bomber stream on its approach to the target; directing them to avoid Berlin itself because of the flak and wait until the bombers had left the target, before attempting to intercept them on the first part of their journey home.

Note: I would presume to think that these instructions did not apply to the 'Wild Boar' fighters, for whom our friends in the He 177 were dropping their flares!

As so often, there was bad news to counteract any successes we may have had on 141. 'Jumbo' Gracie, CO of 169 Squadron, was killed when his Mosquito was shot down in the Hanover area, although his navigator, Wilton-Todd, survived to become a PoW. Wing Commander Edward John Gracie DFC was a colourful character and a popular figure wherever he went; we had had him on 141 as a supernumerary to learn the ropes of the Serrate operation, before he went to Little Snoring to take over the command of 169.

He was one of those irrepressible characters thrown up by the RAF from time to time and he had made a name for himself as a successful day-fighter pilot during the Battle of Britain and later over Malta. His claims were a substantial mixed bag of E/A destroyed, probables and damaged. In March 1942 he led a flight of Spitfires which were to be delivered to Malta, as reinforcements to the beleaguered island. This task entailed flying them off the aircraft carrier, HMS *Eagle*, when the ship was within range of the island! He subsequently repeated this hazardous type of operation, leading 601 and 603 Squadrons to Malta – after taking off from the US Carrier *Wasp*.

Rumour had it that on one of these trips Jumbo, having got the whole for-mation safely off the deck of the carrier, was heading away from the island until an observant sergeant pilot noticed that they were flying on a reciprocal course to that for which they had been briefed! Word was duly passed to Jumbo, they all turned round and just made it to Malta before they ran out of fuel! When he was with us he was heard to ask Ken Roberts if he could have a few airmen from 141 whom he could order about as he was getting fed up with having nothing to do! He was a sad loss, both to the Group and to the Air Force.

On the 17th and 18th we carried out NFTs, both times finding that the AI was u/s, the weather at the time being cold and snowy. On the night of 19/20 February Bomber Command switched from Berlin to Leipzig and attacked with a force of 823 aircraft. They suffered the very heavy loss of 78 bombers. Although 14 Mosquitoes operated in support, none of the crews had any success, whilst the German night-fighters had yet another rich harvest amongst the hapless British bomber crews.

Don Aris has once again recorded a precise and telling summary of the overall strategy being pursued by the AOC (working in accordance with the policy laid down by the War Cabinet) and its effects – on both sides:

> 'The very heavy losses suffered by Bomber Command during the attacks on Berlin and other Northern German cities, due to the long routes over Holland and Germany had caused Sir Arthur Harris to abandon his Battle of Berlin, except for one last major raid on Berlin on the 24th/25th March 1944. Although causing heavy damage and casualties to the enemy, he had not destroyed Berlin. He therefore decided to attack targets in Southern Germany where routes to the South, over France, could be taken.'

During the afternoon of 20 February Harry and I did an NFT: all was OK except for the weather, when we found ourselves icing up, in cloud at a height of only 1,500–5,000 ft. We took off in Mosquito FII HL941 (X) late in the evening in support of a raid on Stuttgart but it was a fruitless trip and we had no joy. We were part of a spoof raid to the north, planned to draw the German night-fighters away from the bombers heading south for Stuttgart. We carried out our 'blip-less' trip around Kiel and the Hoya area and landed back safely at 02.25 hours on the following day. The good news was that the Command attacked with 598 aircraft and lost only nine bombers, which was the thing that mattered!

Two days later we tested Mosquito 941 X and found the aircraft and the AI to be OK, but once again ops were scrubbed owing to bad weather. Mosquito 941 was the one in which we had gone to Berlin at the end of January and found the Me 109, which was almost certainly one of the 'Wild Boar' fighters operating without AI and freelancing over the target area. When we had the Beau VIs at Wittering, we had our own aircraft, V8713, and we never had any engine trouble, at any time. The Mosquitoes were proving to be so unreliable it was impracticable for the Flight Commanders to allocate any particular aircraft to one crew, and it meant that each time we went on ops we had to take a different machine. Every crew who you ever met preferred to have their own aircraft, with which they were familiar; we hated having to chop and change.

The previous day we had learned that the CO, Ken Roberts, was posted away from the squadron to an OTU in Warwickshire. There was a rumour that Frank Davis, our Flight Commander, in 'B' Flight, was to be promoted to Wing Commander and become 141's new Commanding Officer. The change was not entirely unexpected, although the many problems encountered in the re-equipping of the squadron with Mosquitoes and its poor showing in the previous four months could certainly not be laid at Ken Roberts's door, and he had simply done his best under very difficult circumstances.

Looking back, I think Ken was the fall guy. Someone's head was probably demanded by Air Commodore Addison, and Ken was selected to carry the can for the débâcle of Bomber Support in that cruel winter of 1943/44.

On the 24th we switched to Mosquito 712 (R). We did a long NFT of 01.2 hrs and the remark in my log is: 'ALL O.K.' We took off at 18.20 hrs, in 712, in support of a raid on Schweinfurt, Germany. Out of 734 bombers attacking the target 33 were lost. Schweinfurt had been bombed on the previous day by the Americans and had come to prominence in August and September of 1943 when the USAAF had suffered disastrous losses, whilst attempting to destroy a ball-bearing plant thought to be vital to the German war effort. The bombers were going south and deep into the heart of Germany, so 100 Group's efforts were mainly directed to the north, in order to try and draw off the German night-fighters and persuade their Ground Controllers that the attack was once more directed at Berlin.

Harry and I were briefed to fly out across the North Sea over Denmark and patrol in the Kiel, Kattegat and Little Belt area. At 19.55 hrs and when we were at 20,000 ft I picked up an AI contact at maximum range crossing to 20 degrees starboard. We were heading north at the time, so we turned starboard to come in behind the target aircraft. We found that it was flying straight and level and heading east, very fast, at 25,000 ft. We climbed to 24,000 ft and closed the distance to 3,000 ft with the target still 1,000 ft above us. We had been flying at full throttle for about 10 to 12 minutes in a long stern chase when Harry shouted that the port engine was overheating, running roughly and the temperature gauge was showing 145 degrees. We were left with no choice but to abandon the chase and let the presumed enemy aircraft get away.

Cursing and swearing Harry feathered the port engine and we turned for home. The target was still flying straight and level as we banked round onto a reciprocal. I watched helplessly as the range increased and the blip disappeared up the time-trace and into the ground returns. We were somewhere in the Kiel area at approximately 54.12N–09.50E and we were a long way from home. Heading W across Denmark and keeping well clear of Sylt and Heligoland we gradually lost height down to 12,000 ft. We left the Dutch Islands well to port and flew on out over the North Sea.

When the engine temperature had dropped to 90 degrees Harry unfeathered the propeller but, in a few minutes, it shot up to 140 degrees! There were considerable sparks coming from the port engine and it was still running very roughly. Harry had no alternative but to feather the propeller once more and carry on as best we could, hoping that the starboard engine would keep going.

Somewhere to the north of Terschelling and at about 05.00'E we made contact with another 141 aircraft over the VHF and asked them to pass on a 'MAYDAY' call, giving base our position and saying that we were returning on one engine. Shortly afterwards we managed to get a reply from Sector Control and then Harry gave vent to our feelings. We had only just left the enemy coast behind us, and we still had about 150 miles to reach West Raynham.

Harry never had much time for Ground Controllers, and although it was a WAAF's voice which came over the R/T asking if we needed any help, Harry showed her no mercy . . . With the history of engine failures over the past few months on all the Serrate squadrons and several crews having gone missing without a trace, we were anxious to let those on 141 know *exactly* what had happened to us! Harry did not mince his words! He switched the VHF over to

'TRANSMIT' and let fly! He said (to the wretched girl on the other end, who was only trying to help anyway): 'THIS IS CREEPER 24 HERE. RETURNING ON ONE ENGINE AND YOU CAN TELL THE BOYS IT WASN'T ANY F*****G FLAK OR BASTARD FIGHTERS THAT GOT US! LISTENING OUT.' I can still remember thinking, quite clearly, 'That'll be a marvellous line if we get back!'

The AI was still serviceable and I had picked up 'Mother' at base, the starboard engine was holding out so we continued on course for West Raynham and resisted the temptation to put down at Coltishall. But we were not the only 141 crew to be in trouble that night; shortly after we had sent our own 'MAYDAY' call we heard Creeper 43 (Snape and Fowler) twice send out a call for 'MAYDAY' to Manlove Control.

Their distress calls came from the vicinity of the Dutch island of Texel and were sent out at 21.00 hours. They had been briefed for the same area, around Kiel, as ourselves but nothing more was ever heard from them. Harry and I continued on our way and landed safely at West Raynham at 21.55 hrs.

Newly commissioned Pilot Officer Desmond Snape and his Nav/Rad, Flying Officer Ian Fowler, were the crew who may have shot down the German nightfighter ace, Prince zu Sayn Wittgenstein, when they claimed one Ju 88 damaged, on the night of 21/22 January. Desmond was a very nice Australian and Ian came from Canada. Together they made an above average crew and they were a sorry loss to the squadron. Ian survived to become a POW and was repatriated to Canada when the European war came to an end in 1945. Desmond was killed and is buried in north-east Holland.

I have never discovered whether the loss of Snape and Fowler was due to engine failure or to some other cause, but apart from ourselves, Graham Rice and Doug Gregory also returned to base with engine trouble! Graham's starboard engine started to overheat. Doug experienced engine vibration from the moment he took off! The squadron operated with five Mosquitoes on 24 February and only one crew completed their sortie as planned.

On the following night the dismal story of bomber support – or the lack of it – from West Raynham was continued. Bomber Command attacked Augsburg in southern Germany with 594 aircraft and lost 21. From West Raynham seven Mosquitoes (from the two squadrons) set out to support them. Three went from 141 and all three had early returns with engine and AI failures. The other four were from 239, of which two completed their patrols, one was missing and the other crashed on return, killing both the crew. The tragic and profitless Fourth Phase of the High-Level Bomber Support operations was still, obviously, far from over . . .

It is reported that there were no operations by Bomber Command or by 141 Squadron on 27 February but official confirmation was received that Squadron Leader F.P. Davis had been promoted to Wing Commander and was the new Commanding Officer of No. 141 Squadron, in succession to Wing Commander K.C. Roberts AFC.

Harry and I had got to know Frank Davis quite well since we had rejoined the squadron in June and gone into 'B' Flight. He had been a successful, and helpful, Flight Commander and he was a very experienced and skilful pilot. Many years our senior in age, Frank had, like Ken Roberts, been a flying instructor but, unlike Ken, he seemed to have found it more easy to settle into the life of an operational squadron. He and his navigator, Jimmy Wheldon, had been with 141 at

Predannack and flown some of the adventurous sorties, led by Bob Braham, down to the French coast and into the Bay. He had done a number of Serrate sorties in the Beaus from Wittering and claimed at least one E/A destroyed. We were all pleased – on 141 – to keep it in the family and wished Frank well in his new responsibilities. He immediately had some reassuring news for us and, after the spate of engine failures we had experienced, it was certainly not before time!

On the day his appointment was confirmed, Frank Davis went to 100 Group HQ at Bylaugh Hall and returned with the news that all reconditioned Merlin XXII engines in the Mosquitoes were to be returned and, in future, and while stocks lasted, only new engines were to be fitted when replacements were required. When a comment was made, in the Group's Report for February, it was stated, with regard to the 17 early returns through engine failure by the three Serrate squadrons, 141, 169, and 239: 'It is hoped that by fitting new engines, the position will be eased considerably.'

Remembering the loss of John Brachi and Angus MacLeod and our own 350-mile haul back on one engine (three nights before!) Harry and I, and the rest of our friends on the three squadrons, must have all breathed a sigh of relief at this news.

To finish off the month, I did an air test on Mosquito 704 with John Forshaw, to check for engine vibration! From my log-book, I see that the aircraft was: 'N.B.G. and the starboard prop would not feather!'

Once again, where was Frank Folley? And why did I let myself in for gallivanting around the sky with strange pilots, when I had a perfectly good one of my own?

Don Aris's Summary for the month of February records that the three Serrate squadrons claimed four E/A destroyed and two damaged. All three suffered losses of aircraft and crews, and all three had many early returns from engine and radar failure. Anyone, writing of operations at this period, must return continually to the tragedy that was unfolding around us. The heavy bomber force urgently needed every bit of help possible to mitigate their enormous losses, almost all of which were due to the unrelenting efficiency of the German night-fighter arm.

Nearly all of the German twin-engined night-fighters were, by now, fitted with the 'Window-proof' FuG 220 SN-2 AI radar, and these aircraft were scrambled to orbit various radio beacons, as soon as a raid was detected by the long-range *Freya* radio location units, sited all the way round the coast from Denmark to the Brest Peninsula. They were then directed into the bomber stream, both along the route to the target and on the bombers' return journey. They used their new radar equipment to locate the bombers, the aces sometimes claiming five or six kills within a matter of 30 minutes.

Many of the Ju 88s and Me 110s were now fitted with two upward-firing cannon. This armament enabled them to manoeuvre into a position directly underneath the Lancasters and Halifaxes without having to run the risk of being seen, either by the rear-gunner or the mid-upper gunner.

The skilful German pilots, who were getting plenty of practice after all, could formate on the visual of the large bomber 2–300 feet above them, take careful aim for the fuel tanks in the wings, and then open fire. The bomber crew would never know what had hit them and, unless they were extremely lucky, would be on fire with their aircraft disintegrating around them, already too late to take avoiding action. That is, if it had not exploded as the first cannon shells ripped into it . . .

Such were the 'Tame Boars', and Window, which had been launched with such success at the start of the raids on Hamburg in July of 1943, was no longer any protection. The 'Tame Boar' and 'Wild Boar' systems enabled more enemy aircraft to be used for night-fighting and allowed inexperienced crews to operate as well. All this resulted in even greater losses for Bomber Command.

The attack on Leipzig on 19/20 February by 823 aircraft cost the Command 78 heavy bombers, i.e. 9.47 per cent with seven aircrew in each Lancaster and Halifax, which added up to 546 trained aircrew lost in a single night. None of the seven supporting British night-fighters had any success, and worse was still to come at the end of March.

Of course, some of the crew members would have survived, to be taken POW but it was not easy to extricate oneself from a gun-turret or a bomb-aimer's compartment, in a stricken Lancaster, spiralling down from 18,000 feet and out of control. What opportunities were lost by the bomber support squadrons whose crews were virtually grounded by engine and radar problems? Four enemy night-fighters destroyed and two damaged in February was of no use whatsoever.

There should have been six squadrons, with Mosquito VIs and serviceable AI and Serrate equipment, fully operational by the beginning of November 1943, after the initial pioneering work had been carried out successfully by Wing Commander Braham. (He personally accounted for seven E/A destroyed and one damaged, even though he only had a Beaufighter and was only flying on Serrate operations for four months.) It could have been done.

There is not a shadow of a doubt that too many experienced night-fighter crews (who were flying new Mosquitoes) were retained – kicking their heels – on the Home Defence squadrons, long after the menace of further heavy night raids on England had disappeared. It was a tragedy of the highest order . . .

6 One Party in Ashford – and Another Over Frankfurt

– and how Harry White received a kiss . . .

Early in March 1944, Bomber Command was under orders from the War Cabinet to change its policy from strategic bombing to tactical bombing, and started to attack a variety of targets, particularly those affecting rail and road communications, in northern France and Belgium. These attacks were designed to prepare the ground for the Invasion which was to be launched somewhere along the French coast, later in the year.

The Invasion itself was a remarkably well-kept secret, right up to 6 June when the fleet set sail for the Normandy beaches. In March we knew nothing, except that a switch to the 'soft' targets, just across the Channel, meant a reprieve for the heavy bomber crews, although the toll for the month was still to be exorbitant, culminating in the ill-fated raid on Nuremberg on 30 March. In a raid on Trappes a few days later 267 aircraft successfully laid waste to the massive railway yard and, unbelievably, none were lost! Harry and I did an NFT in HJ941 and then I read in my Log: 'All O.K. Ops cancelled bad weather. Off on 7 days and my 21st . . . and Harry's 48 hours.'

I went down to Ashford for my leave and celebrated my 21st birthday at home, three years, to the day, since I had volunteered to join the Air Force. Harry broke his own leave to join me for the big party held on Wednesday 15 March, at 60 Clarendon Road, thrown by my parents. The house was packed full of people and I can't remember just how many slept there, when we finally called it a day in the early hours of Thursday morning.

I know that Harry was 'well away' and insisted on telling some New Zealand pilot about all the trips that he and I had done on the bomber support stuff since July '43! We had found the New Zealander somewhere and invited him into the party and to stay the night so he didn't seem to mind! Many of the Sessions family were there, as were my father's friends from Ashford Manor Golf Club. There was only one absentee and that was my brother, Rodney, who was still in America.

The splendid news was that we had just heard that he had been awarded his pilot's wings and commissioned as a Pilot Officer. My father was as pleased as Punch to think that Rodney had followed in his footsteps and we all stood up and drank his health. It was a never to be forgotten evening, so far as I was concerned, and in the light of what happened later in the year, I have always been grateful that I was vouched that one marvellous day – in the middle of the war – to celebrate my birthday and be at home with my family.

Harry and I returned to Raynham together on the 17th to find that the serviceability of both the aircraft and their radar equipment was improving, more ops were being flown and there had been plenty of Serrate and AI chases but no one seemed to have had any luck, resulting in a kill.

Three days after my 21st, on Saturday 18 March, my log-book has two entries, and the first told its own story! '11.25 MOS HJ710 F/O White N.F.T. Wizard kite, all on top line but crew pretty ropey after nine days leave. 01.15hrs.' and the second: '20.50 MOS HJ710 F/O WHITE OPS Frankfurt. 890 Bombers. Flak and S/Ls over Köln. Two Ju 88s destroyed. One – 15, miles north of target and the other in Target Area. Crossed Southern Ruhr on way out. All O.K. Except for R/T. 03.35hrs.'

'Crossed Southern Ruhr on the way out.' *Wow*! that was a bit stupid! It looks as if – for a second time (remembering 15 July 1943!) – our successes over Frankfurt went to our heads and we forgot to take care, when we were on our way home! We must have forgotten to allow for magnetic variation (or something?), for no one in his right mind flew back 'across the Southern Ruhr'.

The Ruhr Valley – or 'Happy Valley', as we knew it – with its widespread industrial complex, was just about the most heavily defended area in the whole of Germany! Once more, our luck must have been in, and our ground crew were over the moon when we landed back at West Raynham and they learned that we had 'got two'.

For the full picture, we must return to the Squadron History before looking at our Combat Report, because this night's operation is an example of what we – and all the crews on the three Serrate squadrons – were trying to achieve. But did not manage to do it often enough to make any serious inroads into the hundreds of Ju 88s and Me 110s now being used by the Germans to counter the massive raids being launched by Sir Arthur Harris on the Fatherland:

> 'On the night of the 18th/19th March 1944, Bomber Command carried out an attack on Frankfurt, Germany with a force of 846 aircraft and suffered losses of 22 bombers. There were also diversionary and support operations and among them 98 aircraft carried out mine-laying in the Heligoland area. Eight aircraft from West Raynham operated, six from 141 Squadron and two from 239 Squadron. Five of 141's and one of 239's aircraft supported the Frankfurt raid and one from each Squadron supported the mine layers to Heligoland. All eight aircraft completed their missions and 141 Squadron shot down three Ju 88s, two by F/O White with F/O Allen and one by F/Lt Forshaw with P/O Folley.'

Johnny Forshaw and Frank Folley landed shortly after we had got back and we soon learned that they had got an 88. We were delighted for them (and so were the rest of the squadron); they were a colourful and popular crew. They were also an above-average crew, who had already claimed an 88 damaged and then experienced the frustration of losing another when (as already related) they had a 'sitter' in front of them, and their guns failed.

On this occasion they were so keen to see their Ju 88 hit the ground, after seeing a large explosion and watching 'pieces of aircraft falling away' that Johnny stalled the Mosquito as the E/A spiralled down out of control, and then had to pay attention to getting themselves back in one piece!

The synopsis of Serrate operations produced by the Operational Research Section states: 'The losses of the bombers on this night were comparatively small (2.7%) and it is not quite clear why the enemy fighters did not achieve more success. Weather may have been a contributory factor.'

The report goes on to comment on the use of 'assembly' beacons by the German night-fighters. I am indebted to Martin Streetly's *Confound and Destroy – 100 Group and the Bomber Support Campaign* for a clear and concise explanation of these beacons. His book is a quite exceptional technical treatise on the bomber support operations, covering in detail the technicalities of the British aircraft and their radio/radar equipment, together with those of their opposite numbers. The ground control systems, equipment and tactics used by the Germans on 'Home Defence' are equally well covered and the text is supported throughout with photographs, diagrams and appendices that puts the book in a class of its own.

When the '*Kammhuber* Line' with its *Himmelbett* system was rendered ineffective by the use of Window at the start of the Hamburg raids (24 July 1943), the Germans had to develop new tactics to counter the ever increasing numbers in the bomber stream. One of these tactics was designed to bring more radar-equipped *nachtjaeger* into the bomber stream before it reached the target area and to keep the Ju 88s and Me 110s there for as long as possible. This came to be known as *Zahme Sau* (as different from *Wilde Sau*; which was the placing of non-radar-equipped s/e fighters i.e. Me 109s and Fw 190s, over the target area). Martin Streetly (on pp. 220/221) says:

> '"Zahme Sau" aircraft were controlled by means of a running commentary broadcast over the Y-system. Giving the night-fighters details of the bomber streams composition, altitude and heading.'
>
> Aircraft were scrambled from all over Europe and navigated by radio beacons to a designated stacking beacon where they were concentrated ready to meet the oncoming bomber stream. When the order came to leave the stacker, around which as many as 50 aircraft might be flying, the fighters received the latest information on the bombers and made off in their direction.
>
> When the fighters made visual or radar contact with the enemy, they reported the exact position of the stream back to the operations centre and then went into the attack. In this way, the Germans could feed all available night-fighters into the bomber stream with which they would stay until forced down by lack of fuel.
>
> If the bomber stream changed course and passed out of the area of one control centre, another would take over, and so on as the bombers proceeded across Reich territory.'

As the operations of the fighter squadrons in 100 Group developed, and the monitoring services produced more and more information concerning the German defence systems, these 'assembly' or 'stacking' beacons began to figure increasingly in our plans. What an attractive honey pot they were, if only a few of our Mosquitoes could get in amongst the 40/50 E/A waiting to be vectored into the bomber stream! There were a number of successes using the ploy of flying direct to the area of these radio beacons (which were known to us) but never the harvest that was there for the picking.

Returning to the ORS Report for the night 18/19 March we find:

> 'The main beacons used by the [German] fighters were Q, Philip (probably), O, and Kuli, "I" was also used. The majority of interceptions reported by the bombers occurred in the target area and South of the target. A larger number

of interceptions than usual was reported at the enemy coastal area, mostly on the way in.'

Of our own trip the report comments:

'141/T (F/O White and F/O Allen) who patrolled from 22.15 to 22.35 hours did not report a large number of contacts, but resulting from one, a forward A.I. contact, at 22.25 hours (Z + 25), a Ju 88 was shot down. 141/T also shot down another Ju 88 en route to the target. This combat, which resulted from an initial back A.I. contact, took place in the region of beacon I, and it is possible that the fighter was waiting there, although the intercepted traffic would indicate that the fighters had been sent from I towards the target earlier on.'

On further examination of the report, I note that there were four different patrols planned for the 13 Serrate fighters that night. Patrols (b, c & d) were briefed to fly direct to one or other of the stacking beacons. Patrol (a) on which we set off was designed as follows:

'Plan
    To patrol over target area for 35 minutes to intercept enemy fighters orbiting target after the bombers had left the area. No contacts to be chased until target was reached then all A.I. to be investigated.
    Four aircraft were planned for this patrol to arrive at the target Z + 20.'

Johnny Forshaw and Frank were, like us, also briefed to go straight to the target area and shared in the successes of the night. In the event, none of the nine crews sent to the stacking beacons had any joy!

I trust that if I now return to our own Combat Report the events of that night will be clearer to the reader and, as already mentioned in the ORS Report, we were flying Mosquito II – 141/T (HJ710).

'Mosquito took off from West Raynham at 20.50 hrs., crossed enemy coast in at 21.30 hrs. and obtained first Serrate contacts at extreme range on the starboard side five minutes later. These Serrates continued for 10–15 minutes growing slightly in intensity, then faded from the tube. At 50.45N–07.30E, at 23,000 feet when approaching target area at 22.10 hours, five minutes ahead of E.T.A. and slightly North of track, an A.I. contact was obtained on the backward looking A.I. at 10,000 feet range, height of Mosquito 23,000 feet.

    Mosquito orbited to starboard and obtained contact 8,000 feet ahead on forward A.I. Range was closed gently to 1,200 feet and a visual obtained on a Ju 88 showing four white exhausts, silhouette could be seen quite clearly; navigator confirmed identification before fire was opened at 600 feet. Three, two second bursts were fired as the range was closed gently to 300 feet. The first burst resulted in considerable strikes in fuselage and starboard engine causing a small fire, two other bursts added to conflagration. As enemy aircraft slipped by under starboard wing, it was seen to be burning furiously in both engines and fuselage. Enemy aircraft spiralled down and exploded when it hit the ground. The enemy aircraft was flying due East and took no evasive action.

    Course was set for the target area where we patrolled for ten minutes. At 22.25 hours, two miles SE of target, an AI contact was obtained at 14,000 feet ahead on port side and crossing port to starboard. Range closed rapidly to 5,000 feet as enemy aircraft crossed in front. Mosquito turned starboard and range closed to 1,000 feet where visual obtained on a Ju 88 again showing four white exhausts, again seen by Navigator. Pilot opened fire at 800 feet with a two second burst resulting in strikes in both engines and a small fire in fuselage. A second two second burst increased area of flames considerably. Enemy aircraft began spiral to port so a third two second burst was fired, range 600 feet allowing 20 degrees deflection. Strikes were again seen and several pieces blew off enemy aircraft which dived down to ground and exploded. Height of combat 23,000 feet. No return fire experienced throughout. Claim two Ju 88s Destroyed.

Armament Report: 165 rounds 20 mm fired from each cannon, no stoppages and camera exposed.

Weather: Medium cloud over North Sea breaking to 3/10ths. inland. Visibility moderate with considerable ground haze off from West Raynham at 20.50 hours.'

The plan for those crews on Patrol (a) included the clear order that 'No Contacts to be chased until target was reached' and we had been briefed to fly straight to the target area. It would appear that the temptation of that first AI contact – a good 40/50 miles to the north west of Frankfurt – was too much for us! Happily, when that contact led to the destruction of a Junkers 88, no one was going to argue too much about where and when we got it!

In their summing up of the night's happenings, the ORS people said that '. . . the target area after the bombing proved to be a good bet.' They also said that the beacons chosen for the patrols were the ones used by the enemy, but that the timing of the enemy fighter movements had not been anticipated correctly.

There was one other worrying comment, to the effect that: 'Certain of the patrols at the beacons should have contacted (enemy) fighters, according to intercepted traffic, but they did not do so.'

Lastly, they noted that in none of the three combats of the night (our two, and Johnny Forshaw's one) did the enemy aircraft take strong evasive action during the approach, indicating that they had no warning of the fact that they were being stalked from behind, i.e. they had no backward-looking AI equipment at that time, and this, of course, was good news for us! The other piece of good news – apart from the figure of only a 2.7 per cent loss rate for the bombers – was that out of 13 Serrate sorties, only two were early returns.

As Phase 5 of bomber support operations got underway, we were slowly turning the corner, and each of the three Serrate squadrons were starting to build up their claims of German night-fighters destroyed or damaged, as the serviceability of both aircraft and radar equipment improved during the month of March.

On 19 March Harry and I received a summons to attend at Bylaugh Hall for an interview with the Senior Air Staff Officer, Group Captain Roderick Chisholm. When we got there he took us in to see the AOC, Air Vice-Marshal Addison, and I still remember how he introduced us! 'Good afternoon, Sir, these are the two chaps who have been busy – putting round holes into square heads!'

The AOC said one or two kind words about our trip the previous night and the destruction of the two Junkers 88s and then told us that he would like us to go and talk to the new night-fighter crews being trained at No. 51 OTU.

Number 51 OTU was located at Cranfield, near Bedford, and the idea was that Harry and I should fly down there and give a talk on the Serrate operations, in an endeavour to obtain volunteers, who would join one or other of the 100 Group fighter squadrons when they had finished their training. The date had already been fixed for 23 March!

On leaving the AOC we were taken back to Rory Chisholm's office, where he asked us a number of questions about the tactics being developed, now that the serviceability of the aircraft and equipment was at last showing signs of improvement. Rory Chisholm was a remote and austere character to us, as junior officers, and very much in the vein of other distinguished members of the Royal Auxiliary Air Force. But he had been on No. 604 Squadron at Middle Wallop, with Charles Appleton, John Cunningham, George Budd and others who were in at the beginning, when the night Blitz started in earnest, in September 1940, and he knew his stuff.

He had a number of claims to his credit, most of them with Bill Ripley as his AI operator (Bill, whom we had seen killed with Derek Welsh at Wittering in November). After leaving 604, Rory Chisholm took over the Fighter Interception Unit (FIU) at Ford where he carried out a number of intruder sorties. He came from there to 100 Group as the SASO. His promotion was amongst the most rapid ever seen; he went up from being a Flying Officer (Auxiliary Air Force) in 1940 to Air Commodore in 1944! He was an exceptional man and we were lucky to have him as SASO. After the war, when he returned to one of the big oil companies in Persia, he wrote a small but outstanding book covering his war years, with the title *Cover of Darkness*. Before then, and as 1944 unfolded, Harry and I were to see more of him.

On 23 March we were flown down to Cranfield in the Oxford by Howard Kelsey and duly spoke to a number of the new crews who were undergoing similar, but more comprehensive, training to that which we had carried out at Church Fenton, more than two and a half years earlier.

A number of the pilots and navigators were instructors, 'on rest' after completing a tour on a Home Defence night-fighter squadron. When we had been at Bylaugh Hall, Rory Chisholm – in his briefing – had said that he was particularly anxious to get some volunteers for 100 Group from amongst them; their experience would be invaluable on the Serrate squadrons.

Harry spoke first and, having outlined the history of Serrate, described the operations on which we had been engaged for the past eight months and the tactics which were still being developed. I then took over and, with the use of the blackboard and copious drawings of both the Mk IV AI and Serrate pictures, tried to convey to the navigators in the audience what their job would be if they decided to volunteer for one of the bomber support squadrons. I think it was the first time that I ever had to stand up and speak in public; it was not to be the last!

Both Harry and I emphasised the point to the audience that flying in support of the heavy bomber crews, in their desperate defence against the almost overwhelming odds posed by the German night-fighter force, was the most worthwhile job in the whole of the night-fighter business. I have no idea how successful our trip to Cranfield was in terms of recruits for Serrate but many years after the war (at a reunion of Mosquito aircrew) someone came up to me and said 'I remember you and Harry White coming to talk to us at Cranfield!' I was strangely gratified, because by that time Harry was dead and my heart warmed to anyone who remembered him. Amongst the mass of useless material that I suspect we are all guilty of keeping (to the frustration of our wives!) I still have the notes which I scribbled out for the talk I gave over 50 years ago!

A few days earlier Bill Murray DFC, DFM had been posted to Group and John Forshaw had been promoted Acting Squadron Leader to replace him as 'A' Flight Commander. Although he had only been on the squadron a few months and had, to my knowledge, no previous operational experience, he and Frank had had three or four combats and had destroyed one Ju 88 and damaged another – to say nothing of the one they lost, when their guns failed them at the crucial moment.

John was tall and lanky with good looks and a charming manner. He looked every inch an actor in the Jack Buchanan/1930s style. I met him once or twice in London, when our leaves coincided, and he showed me some of the pubs in and around Piccadilly frequented by members of his profession. I remember one called The Captain's Cabin where we had an uproarious evening with some of his actor friends. We didn't know that, within a month, he and Frank Folley would be posted 'MISSING' . . .

By the middle of the month we thought that things had turned the corner and that life – in real terms – would become a bit easier for the crews of the heavy bombers. By the end of the month they had suffered two of the worst disasters of that dreadful winter of 1943/44, one over Berlin and the other over Nuremberg. On the night of 24/25 March there was a major attack on Berlin by 811 bombers. Unusually high winds from the north scattered the bomber stream across northern Germany and many missed the target. On the return journey, some were blown off course, taking them over heavily defended areas, some even finishing up over the Ruhr itself, with flak claiming more victims than usual. It was the last of the sixteen major raids on Berlin.

The cost of the campaign since August '43 was 625 aircraft, with the deaths of 2,690 bomber crews and 987 airmen made prisoners-of-war. The percentage loss on 24 March was 8.87. All that the two West Raynham Serrate squadrons had to show for it was one Fw 190 destroyed by Howard Kelsey and Smithy, and one Mosquito from 239 Squadron 'MISSING'. Bomber Command was most certainly, in Leonard Cheshire's terms, not in the clear yet . . .

On the following night we, in 141, lost one of our Belgian pilots, F/O Van den Plassche. His navigator was F/O Mamoutoff who, I think, was of Russian extraction. Two months later, on 21 May, Van den Plassche walked into the mess and subsequently continued his tour with the squadron. His story is one of the minor classics of the war and one of the major classics of 'Escape'. Starting with the fact that after he had baled out of his Mosquito over northern France, he landed in the middle of a German aerodrome, one or two miles west of Chambry and some 580 miles from the Spanish frontier. Oh, yes, the aerodrome was being used for night-flying operations at the time!

Once safely on the ground, Van den Plassche's story starts off, 'I packed my Mae West, harness and parachute together, hid them under some bushes, and headed west across the aerodrome – later passing between two woods SE of Chambry . . .'

It ended when, after many miles of walking and frequent use of the trains, as he travelled through France and crossed the Pyrenees into Spain, he arrived back on British soil in Gibraltar, on 27 April, five weeks later. Sadly, there is not the space to include the full story of his remarkable journey, during which he was not assisted by any organisation (i.e. the French Resistance) on any part of his journey. In his own words: '. . . I did not have any identity papers in my possession. I am a Belgian and was able to travel easily, as I speak fluent French.'

But approaching the Demarcation Line between German-occupied and Vichy France not far from Toulouse, and being without any papers, Van den Plassche had to jump off a moving train, resulting in wounds to his face and body. He was helped over the Demarcation Line by some French railway workers. He used the money from his 'escape box' to buy his several railway tickets, although he said that it was insufficient.

He used the silk maps with which we were also provided, plus a compass, to cross the Pyrenees and make his way down into Spain. He lived on water and bread during the whole of his journey the length of France. He was flown back to England from Gibraltar on 2 May and turned up in the officers' mess at West Raynham three weeks later, looking none the worse for wear!

The Belgians awarded him the *Croix de Guerre* and the Officer Cross of the Order of Leopold with Palm. The only award he received from the British Government was a Mention in Despatches. This seemed a bit mean – surely he had deserved either an MC or the MBE, which were given to a number of those who escaped from the prison camps; or, like Van den Plassche, had evaded capture altogether? Once again it is easy to see how some people came to view decorations and awards with a certain degree of scepticism.

George Mamoutoff (Van den Plassche's navigator) was not so lucky. Aged 20, the son of Vladimar Mamoutoff and Rolly Mamoutoff, of St John's Wood, London, lies buried in Choloy War Cemetery in France. They had had one chase and then Van den Plassche found that the port engine was losing oil pressure. Starting for home, it soon dropped to zero. The engine would not feather and then it caught fire. The fire-extinguisher was used, but without success. Whilst still at 19,000 feet, Van den Plassche told his navigator to bale out.

The report that he made to the Belgian Government (resident in London) was that the Mosquito was on fire and that he did not, himself, get out until they had lost height down to 1,640 feet. It was never known exactly what happened to George Mamoutoff after he had baled out or how he met his death. What we did know, when Van den Plassche rejoined the squadron, was that once more we had lost a friend and a valuable aircraft, due to being re-equipped with second-hand and worn-out Mosquitoes.

On the other hand one of our contingent of Belgian pilots had proved what resolute and resourceful men they were. All of them had made their escape from Europe in hair-raising situations after the German advance swept through Holland and into Belgium, then on into France. The fact that Van den Plassche was prepared to repeat the performance so that he could return to the squadron, and carry on the fight, was a marvellous example to us all . . .

On 26/27 March, Bomber Command attacked Essen, in the Ruhr Valley, with 705 aircraft and, marvellous to relate, lost only nine bombers. Harry and I went off again in 941 X and were briefed to patrol Beacon 'L'. We ought to have got at least one, if not two, more to add to our claims. In the event we were only able to claim one Ju 88 as damaged, and there is a fairly caustic comment in my log-book! It reads as follows: 'F/O White OPS. Essen. A.I. Practice with Johnny over Osnabrück. Ju 88 DAMAGED near Essen. Very dark night. Harry going on a course to St Dunstans. 04.40 hrs.'

The reason why I wanted Harry to be sent to St Dunstan's (on a course for the blind) is that, although we got a visual on the '88', he just could not see it properly, particularly when he came to open fire, as will be seen in an extract from our Combat Report:

'Several Serrates, 5–20 miles, were now showing, of which one was selected at 22.10 hrs. and chased for 2–3 minutes, heading West towards the target at 23,000 feet. This was converted to an AI contact at 12,000 ft. and range was closed gently to 800 ft., 190 Indicated Air Speed, when pilot obtained a visual on enemy aircraft, 20 degrees port, 10 degrees above, showing four very dim exhausts, provisionally identified as a Ju 88, still burning Serrate.

These exhausts could not be seen from line astern. Pilot, finding it very difficult to retain visual, closed range to 500 ft. line astern and opened fire with a one second burst; but no results were observed and visual was lost momentarily due to the glow from the cannons. A second very short burst was fired from the same range and strikes were observed in starboard engine and wing root resulting in a small explosion, and a few small pieces were seen to blow off the enemy aircraft. The enemy aircraft dived steeply with the Mosquito following and a large explosion on the ground, which occurred at this time, lit up enemy aircraft now clearly identified, from 30 degrees above, as a Ju 88. As the explosion died down the visual faded. Pilot turned 45 degrees starboard and back to port hoping to regain contact as enemy aircraft emerged from minimum range.

Unfortunately the negative "G", applied as we dived, had unhooked the Navigator's visor, resulting in his eyes becoming full of dust and adding to the general confusion in the cockpit.'

On looking back, it seems as if Harry was not the only one who could not see properly that night over Essen! But we bitterly regretted losing the '88' and only being able to claim it as damaged. Johnny Forshaw and Frank took off 10 minutes after us and, mentioned in my log-book but not in our Combat Report, somewhere near Osnabrück I picked up an AI contact, we completed the interception and got a visual – on a Mosquito!

A brief – and strictly illegal – call over the VHF, established that it was Johnny and Frank! Johnny was not too pleased to find us sitting there behind him, and in a position to open fire if we had been a Junkers 88! Although the losses that night were mercifully only nine bombers, there were 13 Serrate aircraft out and nine of us reported picking up Serrate signals. Which indicated that there were a number of German night-fighters airborne in the vicinity of our patrol areas.

Once again and with serviceable aircraft and equipment (there were only two abortive sorties) we had failed 'the bomber boys'.

I have referred to the worst disasters to befall Bomber Command in the winter of 1943/44, one of which was the loss of 72 aircraft on 24/25 March in the last major attack on Berlin. The second was about to take place on 30/31 March 1944.

There are certain names and phrases which can still – after more than 50 years have passed – bring a change of expression to the faces of those who flew in Bomber Command in World War II. Prominent amongst them you will find the phrase 'LMF' and the names of Nuremberg, 'The Big City' (Berlin) and 'Happy Valley' (the industrial complex in the valley of the Ruhr). On the night of 30/31 March a force of 795 aircraft attacked the German city of Nuremberg and lost 95 bombers.

Harry and I were not on the battle order that night and I have always felt a sense of guilt that we were not there . . .

There were a variety of reasons which were put forward to account for this tragedy, when 12.07 per cent of the force were lost. But, perhaps with the superbly efficient German night-fighter Groups now swarming over the Fatherland in ever increasing numbers, a victory for them on this scale was always just around the corner anyway.

The definitive account of the Nuremberg raid has been given by that gifted and caring military historian and writer, Martin Middlebrook, in his book of that title, published by Allen Lane. I had the privilege of meeting Martin when he was researching for a similar book on the Peenemünde raid, and I conceived the warmest regard for his work and for the man himself.

I will simply quote three paragraphs from his summary of the cost of the Nuremberg raid. For the rest, one must read his book for oneself. When I do, it shakes me to the core.

The Cost

'The Nuremberg Raid has been described by historian Alfred Price as "the greatest air battle of all time", and it is certain that the intensity of the aerial carnage between the German frontier and Nuremberg, when eighty heavy bombers and possibly ten night-fighters (German) were destroyed in the hour and-a-half after midnight, has never been surpassed.

The damage caused by the bombs dropped was – minimal. In Nuremberg, one factory was half destroyed and three others suffered lesser damage. It is impossible to calculate the exact effect of this on Germany's war effort but clearly it was no more than a pinprick. The accidental bombing of Schweinfurt again hardly affected production of the vital ball-bearings. This, and the unconfirmed destruction of ten German fighters, was a poor return.

If the secret operations Halifax and the Intruder Mosquito that had been shot down are now included, the total loss in aircraft numbers 108. It cannot be stated with absolute certainty how each of these met its end but the following table is reasonably accurate:

Crashed on take-off	1
Shot down by night-fighter	79
Shot down by flak	13
Hit by both night-fighter and flak	2
Collision	2
Shot down by "friendly" bomber	1
Crashed or crash-landed in England	9
Written off after battle damage	1
Total:	108 '

Harry and I had been sent for by Rory Chisholm and were over at 100 Group Headquarters for another discussion on tactics . . . would that we had been elsewhere. Whilst at Bylaugh Hall we were shown the target and the route for the ill-fated raid and, like others, we commented adversely on the outward route. It was too long and too straight!

So it proved to be, for it was on the 'Long Leg' (as it became known) where most of our casualties occurred. They were on an easterly course, south of the Ruhr, then north of Frankfurt for over 200 miles. This, together with the short southerly course into the Target, was where our opposite numbers had their 'field day'.

Oberleutnant Martin Becker of 1/NJG 6 with his crew, flying a Messerschmitt 110, from Finthen airfield near Mainz, shot down three Lancasters and four

Halifaxes in just two sorties; others were not far behind. We were to learn later that Air Vice-Marshal Bennet, the AOC of the Pathfinder Force, had protested vigorously against the 'Long Leg' but, tragically, he was overruled.

Apart from the hazards of the outward route there were two unusual weather conditions conspiring against the cover of darkness which, as we have seen throughout this narrative, was so essential for the safety of the night-bomber in the Second World War. There was a considerable degree of moonlight and due to certain atmospheric conditions the bombers flying below 19,000 ft were leaving in their wake vapour trails, such as are commonly seen from modern passenger jets!

These condensation trails marked their progress for any German night-fighter to complete the interception, whether *Zahme Sau* or *Wilde Sau*. The débâcle of Nuremberg was of course not as simple as that: it was a combination of many factors, and only a close study of Martin Middlebrook's *The Nuremberg Raid* will reveal the full and awful details of what was arguably the greatest air battle of all time.

If it *was* the greatest air battle, the Serrate Mosquitoes of 100 Group could hardly be counted as amongst those present. Only 17 of them reached the vital area where the attacking force was being decimated and only two of these fired their guns. One solitary Ju 88 was destroyed by a crew from 239 Squadron. On the 'Long Leg' the Lancasters and Halifaxes flew head on into 200/250 German night-fighters . . .

Words still fail me, when it comes to sum up this tragedy, which came to symbolise much of the failure of the Bomber Support operations up to the time of Nuremberg. So perhaps we should refer for the last time to Martin Middlebrook, whose comments, on p. 44 of his book, are more objective and more charitable than mine:

> '100 Group was to do great things in the last year of the war but at the time of the Nuremberg Raid was not fully effective. It had three Serrate Mosquito Squadrons equipped with ancient aircraft and out-of-date radar sets (an ordinary radar was needed as well as the Serrate equipment). These were achieving a trickle of successes but, for example, to the end of March 1944 No.239 Squadron had shot down only three German night-fighters but had lost six Mosquitoes on operations or in training.'

The 'last year of the war' was too late for many bomber crews . . .

Whatever the last word may be on the March disasters of Berlin and Nuremberg, there can be no doubt that these two raids were a watershed for Bomber Command, in terms both of strategy and of tactics. Fortuitously, the nights were getting shorter and deep penetrations into Germany would no longer be possible during the hours of darkness anyway. Secondly, the Strategic Bomber Forces of both our Command and that of the US 8th Air Force were required for the softening up process needed before the Invasion of Europe by the Allies, planned for June, could take place.

By the time the nights lengthened again in September, and strategic bombing was resumed, D-Day had seen a successful landing on the Normandy coast and the Allied armies had pushed up through France into Belgium. Although targets like Chemnitz, Leipzig, Potsdam, Dresden, etc. were still to be attacked, the conditions for the bomber crews operating in the winter of 1944/45 were infinitely more favourable than those faced by their predecessors, such as Julian Sale and his crew on 35 PFF Squadron whom Harry and I had met at Graveley and never forgotten.

From April onwards the bomber crews found suddenly that they might even survive to finish their tour of 30 operations, although 214 aircraft were lost that month, and losses of that order continued to be borne by the Command until August. The 'soft' trips to northern France and Belgium were sometimes not so soft.

Back at West Raynham, March had been a better month for 141 and 239 Squadrons, and 169 had also started to score successes. But the 37 sorties carried out and the six E/A destroyed must be reckoned against the broader back-cloth of the losses incurred by the heavy bombers on the major attacks, such as we have seen on Berlin and Nuremberg. Bomber support operations, undertaken by the long-range Mosquito fighters, had now turned the corner. But nothing could hide our failure during the crucial nine months just ending.

As spring came and the weather, which had caused so many operations to be scrubbed in the winter months, started to improve, Harry and I began to explore the Norfolk countryside and its pubs! I still had my 1938 Ford 8 and with the petrol coupons issued when we went on leave, augmented with the odd gallon from a friendly farmer, we were not badly off for fuel, although filling up from the petrol bowsers with 100 octane, whilst our Mosquitoes were being refuelled, was no longer on the cards! As others who kept their cars on the road during the war will remember, it was tyres and spare parts which were in such short supply.

When driving the 130 miles home to Ashford, or any other long journey, it was always advisable to carry a can (usually a 'jerrican' in the boot with three or four gallons of petrol in it), because many garages had closed down 'for the Duration'. Fakenham, about seven miles to the east of West Raynham, was, in those days, a quiet country town, and of its many pubs, *The Crown* soon became the favourite for 141 aircrew and many a happy session was enjoyed there.

Then some of us ventured further afield and found the Norfolk coast between Hunstanton and Wells – the area around Burnham Overy Staithe and Holkham, with its beaches and the many small waterways running into them. The 'Peter Scott' countryside teeming with bird life had its own magic. And at Hunstanton itself there was always the *Le Strange Arms* the doors of which seemed to be open to members of 141 at any hour of the day or night!

Not far from the aerodrome was Raynham Hall, the family home of Lord Townshend of Kut. One day Harry and I went exploring, and in the grounds of the park we found Raynham church. Adjoining the church was a typical country graveyard, with its mouldering tombstones overhung by willow trees of equal antiquity. Many years later, when I saw the film *The Eagle Has Landed*, in which much of the action took place around a Norfolk country church, I was immediately transported back to that churchyard at Raynham . . .

As we stood there, drinking in the peace and quiet, we heard a voice behind us and, turning round, saw a little old lady standing in the porch of the church. What followed was sheer magic. We greeted her, said we were just having a look round and remarked how peaceful it was in the churchyard, when we were so close to the airfield. We were both in battledress and, in response to her polite enquiry, confirmed that we were stationed at West Raynham.

She then said, 'I don't know whether you know it, but we have three German airmen buried here.' We said that we did not know that. She then continued,

'Yes, you know a German aeroplane came down near Holt and the three men were killed. The vicar of Holt said that he was not going to have them buried in *his* churchyard! Then, our dear vicar said the poor men must lie somewhere and that he would have them in this churchyard, here at Raynham. You can see the graves over there.' And she pointed to the very far corner of the little cemetery.

The kindly vicar had had the three German airmen buried as far away from the rest of his departed parishioners as was possible! The little old lady, seeing us looking with some surprise at the wide open space between where the Germans were laid and the other graves, went on: 'Yes!' she said, 'He thought it best for them to lie over there and he also arranged for an extra heavy stone to be put on the top, so that there would be no chance of them causing any trouble . . . !'

Quite what sort of trouble she had in mind we never found out. Instead, we thanked her for her kindness and wandered over to look down at the graves of our opposite numbers, each of us with our own thoughts.

For the first few days of April the weather was again bad, and there were no operations. Charles Winn, now a wing commander at 100 Group HQ, sent out a letter to all Night-Fighter Operational Training Units to encourage pupils to volunteer for the Mosquito Serrate squadrons.

An extract from his letter, entitled 'Special Duty – Bomber Support', describes our operations and the standards for which he was looking:

'Since the commencement of large scale attacks on Germany by Bomber Command, the enemy has used many varied types of defensive weapons, of these, his night-fighters have proved by far the most effective against our Bomber Force. A means of combating this menace had to be devised:

Serrate: The object of this operation is to destroy enemy night-fighters whilst they are endeavouring to intercept our bombers over enemy territory. The equipment used is a normal A.I. night-fighter equipped with Mark IV A.I., "GEE" and an extra Radar device to identify enemy aircraft. The standard of crew training for these squadrons is essentially high, both in A.I. and navigation. The Pilot has to rely entirely on his Navigator Radio, quick decisions having often to be made during frequent dog-fights with ground controlled enemy night-fighters of equal speed and manoeuvrability to themselves. It is therefore essential that both the Pilot and the Navigator Radio have complete confidence in one another and both have the offensive spirit and that they have the opportunity of volunteering for these duties, rather than be posted into them, when they maybe totally unsuited. The operation is planned to have certain aircraft over the Target itself, whilst other fighters patrol near the bomber stream on the inward and outward routes. This type of operation has proved by far the most fruitful of any A.I. method of interception. Crews do not carry out uninteresting patrols in the hope that one day an enemy aircraft may come in their vicinity, but go out to the area where they know they have a reasonable chance of being in the vicinity of twenty or more enemy night-fighters.

In considering crews for these duties with No.100 (SD) Group, Instructors should bear in mind the offensive spirit required and the high degree of skill needed in the use of Mk IV A.I. and other radar equipment.'

Charles Winn also made reference to 'Flower' operations, which were the Low-Level Intruder operations designed to harass the German crews when taking off and landing at their airfields. It had been pioneered way back in 1941 by 23 and 605 Squadrons, to say nothing of No. 1 Squadron at Tangmere, which I have already mentioned.

As with our talk at Cranfield, I have no idea how successful the letter proved to be in gaining recruits for 141 and the other Serrate squadrons. Perhaps Harry and I might be permitted a quiet laugh on reading Winnie's remarks concerning the need for '. . . both the Pilot and the Navigator Radio to have complete confidence in one another . . .' He should have heard Harry shouting at me when I had lost a contact or, vice versa, me bawling that he ought to be sent on a course to St Dunstan's, when he couldn't see a Ju 88 when it was 300 ft in front of him!

There is an entry in the Squadron Record for 6 April which reads as follows:

> 'Signal received from Headquarters Bomber Command that His Majesty The King on the recommendation of Air Officer Commanding-in-Chief has approved the immediate award of first bar to the D.F.C. to Flying Officer Harold Edward White and Flying Officer Michael Seamer Allen.
>
> These awards are mentioned in the records of RAF Station West Raynham on the 1.4.1944 and also on the 23.4.1944 that they have been gazetted.'

It was a good feeling for both of us that, this time, our awards had come through together. To be treasured were the telegrams we both received from Air Chief Marshal Sir Arthur Harris himself, the C-in-C Bomber Command, and signed by him. It seemed marvellous to us then that the remote figure, whom we never saw but who controlled all our destinies, should be able to find the time to sign, and have sent, the POSTAGRAM which was dated the day after the fateful raid on Nuremberg. It was headed (superbly) from 'The Commander-in-Chief, Bomber Command' and said: 'My warmest congratulations on the award of your First Bar to Distinguished Flying Cross.' It was signed 'A.T. Harris Air Chief Marshal'. It is beside me today, as I write. I only hope that Harry's next-of-kin have his safely.

We did NFTs on 1 and 8 April without operating, although we did some AI practice on the latter night for an hour and a half, and from my log-book I see we got 'Three Visuals in Full Moon'. That sounds as if we were cheating a bit, because we could not normally rely on that sort of celestial assistance when over the other side! Nuremberg had, as we have seen, been the tragic exception. On 9 April, whilst some of the squadron were supporting a raid by 225 bombers on a railway yard near Paris, Harry and I went north to the Flensburg area to support a mine-laying operation in the Baltic off Gdynia and Danzig.

We picked up no AI or Serrate contacts and the only thing we had to show for our trouble, when we landed back at West Raynham at 1 a.m. the following morning, were some flak holes in the tail unit caused by some unfriendly ack-ack gentlemen in Kiel. Incidentally, the 225 bombers that went to the Villeneuve-St-George marshalling yards suffered no losses.

The following night over 900 bombers were involved in attacking various rail targets in France and Belgium, and they lost 19 aircraft. Neither of the West Raynham Serrate squadrons operated, but Johnny Booth with Ken Dear had an unpleasant experience whilst on a training flight. One engine of their Mosquito caught fire. Ken baled out and made a safe landing but Johnny, one of the most colourful characters on 239, brought the aircraft to make a magnificent landing, with the engine still on fire! So, well into April, the problems concerning the reliability of our engines had still not been solved.

There was a light interlude on the 10th, which was Easter Monday, and Don Aris reports it as follows:

'The 10th was Easter Monday and after practice flying and with no operations, a comic soccer match was held at 17.00 hours between the Officers' and Sergeants' Messes. As they did on Christmas Day, all the players turned out in a weird assortment of garments and the game was started off with piano and trumpet accompaniment, and interrupted at intervals by thunder flashes and Very lights. The final touch was added when a whiff of tear gas was wafted over players and spectators alike. When the gas cleared the game resumed and, despite a smoke screen adding to the general confusion, the Sergeants won by 2 goals to 1!'

The next day we operated in support of a raid by 352 bombers on Aachen, which is just over the German border and south of the Ruhr. It was a shallow penetration and the bombing force only lost nine of their number. We had no joy, but our report is of some interest, as it refers to Serrate signals which I was picking up from the ground:

'. . . [We] crossed the enemy coast at 21.55 hours and had no airborne Serrate indications on way to target [Aachen itself] In target area at 23.00 hours an A.I. contact was obtained hard starboard, [We] closed the range to 5,000 feet when the blip disappeared. At 22.30 hours at 50.43N–07.22E at 23,000 feet we homed to a position 4/5 miles South of Beacon "I" on a bunched Serrate signal picked up on 505/508 Mgcs. Signal was definitely radiated from the ground. In target area at 23.05 hours at 23,000 feet another strong bunched Serrate signal on 492 Mgcs was radiated from the centre of target area, definitely from the ground. We recrossed the enemy coast at 23.45 hours and landed at 00.35 hours.'

Nobody from 141 found any E/A, but Neville Reeves, on 239, with that wonderful character (and brilliant Nav/Rad!) Mike O'Leary, got a Dornier 217. This time it was Howard Kelsey and Smithy who had to return when their port engine became unserviceable. They even took off a second time after it had been repaired but once more had to return to base, on finding that the trouble had not been cured.

Then Harry and I went down to Manston, an airfield in Kent, with Flight Lieutenant Wright from 239 (and his navigator) to get information on Low-Level Intruder work. I think we must have visited 605 Squadron, but I kept no notes of the trip, and cannot recall what Frank Davis had in mind, when he sent us down there! We did eventually do some low-level work, but not for some time and, as will be seen, there were still plenty of German night-fighters to be had at the higher levels. We returned to Raynham on the 15th but I am not sure that we were much the wiser because, when we tried returning from our next op at low-level we finished up at Scarborough and I was nearly 'fired' again!

Whilst we were away, Wing Commander Braham (supposedly 'on rest') at 2 Group Headquarters dropped in with 'Sticks' Gregory in tow and on his way to carry out a daylight Ranger patrol to Denmark. He had borrowed his Mosquito from 305 Squadron. The ground crews, delighted to see their much loved and respected former CO, turned to and checked over his aircraft whilst it was refuelled and Bob took off at 13.39 hours with almost all of 141 Squadron waving him 'Good Luck!'

On that trip he was to destroy a Heinkel 111 and a Focke-Wulf 58, and escape the attentions of two Messerschmitt 109s who opened fire on him, by violent evasive action, pulling his Mosquito over onto its back and then up into cloud cover.

These were his 25th and 26th victories and, with the drug of operational flying deep in his veins, he would continue until his luck finally ran out. Even then, he was to escape with his life from the attentions of a Focke-Wulf 190 and finish the war in a German prison camp. There was nobody quite like him.

On 17 April we went 'air firing'. Number 1694 Target Towing Flight towed a white drogue (on a long cable!), and with our cannon loaded with ball ammunition (not high explosive, incendiary or armour-piercing!) we went charging off to the firing ranges, out at sea beyond the Wash, and let rip! I'm not sure that it did my esteemed pilot much good, because two nights later we were to fire three times at a beautiful Junkers 88 – and miss it each time!

Harry's promotion from Flying Officer to the dizzy rank of Flight Lieutenant came through on 14 April, two years after he had been commissioned as a Pilot Officer in the far-off days at Tangmere. 'Paddy' Englebach was similarly promoted about the same time. Paddy, or 'Angels', whose father we had visited in Cairo, had been on the squadron for well over a year and his Nav/Rad at the time was George Jones.

Angels had had mixed fortune, which had included a spell of illness, when he was off flying but he was struggling on with great courage and he would shortly be crewed up with Ron Mallett, one of the older navigators on the squadron and an experienced AI operator, who was later to get a Fw 190 destroyed, whilst flying with Graham Rice (Jimmy Rogerson being sick at the time). Perhaps Angels's luck would change when Ron joined him. Who could tell?

We had a frustrating trip on the 18th, again escorting 168 minelaying aircraft who were operating in Kiel Bay, Swinemunde and off Denmark. This was the night we tried to come home low-level and finished up crossing back in over the English coast at Scarborough, a little matter of 100 miles north of where we should have been! During the trip we had twice had our hopes raised.

Approaching the Danish coast – just to the west of Esbjerg at 20,000 feet – I picked up an AI contact to starboard at maximum range. We closed the range to 8,000 feet and followed the target through a starboard orbit. We closed in further to 5,000 feet – 'IT' was only a mile away – and then the blip faded out. A few minutes later, NE of Esbjerg, I got a second AI contact also at maximum range, this time to port. We closed the range to 8,000 feet and the target began to weave violently. The range was closed to only 2,000 feet, but, for the second time that night, the blip faded out. I must have made a mistake in reading the elevation tube; Harry was not pleased!

Graham Rice with Jimmy Rogerson were also briefed for the same area but that night it was their turn to suffer engine failure. Crossing the North Sea, at 19,000 feet, a steady flow of white sparks sprayed out over the top of the wing from the starboard engine. Graham was an exceptional pilot, later to become an airline captain and one of British Airways' senior pilots, and he brought Mosquito 732 'S' back safely to West Raynham – for us to fly on ops two nights later!

Bomber Command were continuing their attacks on the transportation systems in Belgium and northern France, mixed in with some industrial targets like Aachen and Cologne, which were only just over the German border and could be reached safely in the steadily reducing hours of darkness. On the night

20/21 April 1944, the astonishing total of 1,155 sorties were flown (379 to Cologne and the rest to various railway yards) for the total loss of 15 bombers. Harry and I had quite an exciting night (in Mosquito 732 'S'!) but, sadly, 239 lost one of their Flight Commanders when S/Ldr Kinchin with his Nav/Rad, F/Lt Sellors, did not return.

Seventeen Serrate Mosquitoes operated from West Raynham and there were only three early returns. But although things were looking up, 'kills' were few and far between, and although the Serrate operations were not very dangerous, compared with those of the heavy bombers, we seemed to miss many of our chances to do more damage to the enemy. Harry and I were about to miss two of ours!

Our remit on the night of 20th/21st was to float around in the St Trond–Florennes–Juvincourt–Le Bourget area in support of attacks on three marshalling yards near Paris and see what we could find. Taking off at 22.45 hours and setting course when we had reached 6,000 feet, the trip was uneventful until we got over northern France and picked up our first Serrate contact. It was to starboard and below, crossing to port. Our Combat Report takes up the story of an op on which we had some disappointments and quite a lot of fun:

> 'We gave chase going "down hill" and obtained an A.I. contact at 12,000 feet range which was found to be jinking considerably. Height was decreased to 12,000 feet and range closed to 1,500 feet when Serrate and A.I. contacts faded. We turned starboard and back to port hoping to regain contact – no joy. Enemy aircraft switched off Serrate as we broke away. Throughout this interception our elevation was behaving most erratically and it is believed that the enemy aircraft was directly below us at 1,500 feet when contact faded, the usual reason for fading blips.'

NB: That was one lost.

As time went by, Harry's accounts of our trips became more expansive, and his natural sense of humour began to surface:

> 'The gyro having spun during the interception, I had little idea where this interception had taken me, so set course towards the estimated position of Paris, which I hoped shortly to see illuminated, and fix my position. At 00.20 hours various contacts were obtained on the bomber stream leaving the Paris area, Window was much in evidence.
>
> At 00.25 hours an A.I. contact at 15,000 feet to port and below was obtained a few miles West of the stream and chased. We decreased height and followed contact through gentle port and starboard orbits reducing height to 12,000 feet and eventually closing range to 600 feet where I obtained a visual on four blue-white exhausts, later positively identified at 300 feet as a Ju 88. For five minutes I followed enemy aircraft patiently through gentle port and starboard orbits at 200 indicated air speed, eventually opening fire, still turning, at 500 feet with a 1 second burst allowing 5 degrees deflection, no results. Enemy aircraft, completely clueless, continued to orbit.
>
> Apparently clueless also, I tried again with a 1 second burst, again no results. A third burst was fired as enemy aircraft peeled off to starboard and disappeared from view. I have no idea why I continually missed enemy aircraft and can only attribute it to the dot dimmed out from the gun sight and gremlin interference.'

NB: It looks as if we both 'had our fingers up' that night. That was No. 2 lost!

At one o'clock in the morning, whilst close to the bomber stream during its second attack in the Paris area, we got another Serrate contact. It was to starboard and below. We followed it for three minutes and tried our luck again:

'This Serrate momentarily faded and enemy aircraft was presumed to be orbiting, at least turning. This was confirmed in a few seconds by a head-on A.I. contact at 15,000 feet range and well below us. We turned behind and closed rapidly to 600 feet, and there obtained a visual on four quite bright blue exhausts, identified from 300 feet as a Dornier 217, now flying at 10,000 feet. Enemy aircraft was now turning very gently port and was followed for 5 minutes, not wishing to repeat above. At 450 feet only the exhausts could be seen, though these, unlike the Ju 88, quite clearly. Not wishing to approach closer I opened fire at this range with a 2 second burst and was gratified to see enemy aircraft explode with a blinding flash and disintegrate. Several pieces were flung back at us and I instinctively ducked as they spattered over the windscreen and fuselage. Apart from two broken Perspex panels, which were causing more noise than worry, we appeared to be O.K., but visions of damaged radiators caused some concern for the first few minutes. We had no trouble in that respect and returned uneventfully to base.'

Bomber Support Operations: a badly damaged Mosquito of 100 Group, Bomber Command. The damage including the paint burned off the fuselage was caused by the debris thrown back from a German night-fighter, which the crew had just destroyed. The art of a night attack is for the attacker to come in 'behind and below'. Then, when hits are registered on the enemy aircraft and pieces start to break off it, the debris flies back over the top of the attacker . . . and not into his machine and the radiator grilles of his engines.

There had been several cases of Mosquito crews opening fire, whilst flying on the same level and dead astern of their target, and then finding that the debris blown back (from an exploding enemy aircraft, like our Dornier) was sucked into one, or both, radiators with disastrous results! A few minutes later, whilst probably still celebrating their success, they found that they were in serious trouble themselves, as one or both of their engines chewed up the fragments from the E/A! A great friend of mine (who actually also came from Ashford, Middlesex), John White, with his pilot Bob Bailey, had this problem. They were on 239 and went missing in May. Both baled out safely and we learned some months later of what had happened.

To return to our Dornier 217, although the Germans were using the Ju 88s and Me 110s for their radar-equipped night-fighters, there were a few of the old Dornier bombers which had been converted and pressed into service as night-fighters.

As Harry observed, the noise (and the cold air!) coming into the cockpit from the broken Perspex panels sounded worse than it was and we scuttled swiftly back to West Raynham, as will be seen by my log-book entry:

'F/Lt. WHITE OPS. 03.50 hours.

Paris and Brussels marshalling yards. 1 Ju 88 rendered L.M.F. and 1 Dornier 217 left in a lot of small pieces. Slight damage to our A/C so home sweet home *trés vite.'*

So No. 3 did not get away – and we got home safely for our faithful ground crew to pick up some of the fragments from the Dornier that had blown in, and repair the broken window panels. I remember that when I went down to 'the Flights' late on the 21st I was presented with a broken ammunition-link, with German markings on it, which one of our fitters had found on the floor below my AI set.

There is still a little more to come from our Combat Report, and Harry had some helpful remarks about tactics to pass on to other crews and 100 Group HQ:

'Three separate target areas, although one briefly illuminated, aided navigation considerably, particularly after long chases with unappreciative gyro. The fact that we were routed in at 18,000 feet, well above the bombers, enabled us to use our height advantage to close the range on Serrate contacts and rapidly turn them into something more mature. Such a height advantage has seldom been obtainable previously. At briefing the exact heights at which the bombers were operating was not known. Such information is of great importance. First, to know how much height you have in hand and, secondly as a possible means of identification.'

Our report concludes by mentioning that Harry and I had seen the remains of the Dornier burning on the ground; also that neither of the two German aircraft we had seen had shown any lights and we had experienced no return fire.

There were even a few comments about the weather for the Met. men so that they could check up and see how accurate their forecast had been on conditions over France! I must record that, usually, at briefing when the Met. man took the stand and produced his charts, there was a round of 'horse laughter' and a sceptical look was prominent on many faces!

Theirs was a difficult task in those days and – with no satellites circling in space to provide all the answers – they did a good job within the limits of their equipment and the information sent back to them by the courageous crews of the 'Met. Flights', far out over the Atlantic. They also operated over Germany and occupied France.

Harry and I didn't fly again that month and, when we got back from leave at the beginning of May, we found that Johnny Forshaw and Frank Folley had been posted missing. The Squadron History for the night 26/27 April tells the story:

> 'S/L J.C.N. Forshaw, "A" Flight Commander of 141 Squadron, with his Nav/Rad P/O F.S. Folley took off from West Raynham at 23.24 hours for a Serrate patrol to Essen. They did not return from operations and were posted as missing and the following is the entry in 141 Squadron's Operations Record Book:
> S/L Forshaw with P/O Folley up at 23.24 hours but nothing further has been heard of them and they are presumed missing. S/L MacAndrew with F/O Wilk, however, whilst chasing a right-hand orbitting A.I. contact in the Osnabrück area at 00.52 hours at 24,000 feet, heard on the R/T "BOGEY – GET AWAY" in a voice like that of S/L Forshaw. One and all regret the loss of a very fine crew and an excellent Flight Commander and two of the most popular members of the Squadron. It is hoped that news may be received of their having successfully crash landed or baled out.'

Don Aris was unable to find out if they had been shot down, or what had happened to them but, from the Commonwealth War Graves Commission, he discovered that John and Frank are buried in joint graves in Germany, so it can be assumed that they were over Germany when they came down. They were both very good friends of mine so I am, on this occasion, including the bare and sombre details that Don obtained from the CWGC, that most excellent and efficient body that continues to keep faith with us and with 'Them':

> 'S/L John Charles Noel Forshaw. 111102 RAFVR. Age 29. Son of George Alfred and Enid Mary Forshaw. Buried in Rheinberg War Cemetery, Germany. Plot 9. Row B. Joint Grave 24–25. Register Germany 2.'

and

> 'P/O Frank Smith Folley. 170237 RAFVR. Age 28. Son of Percy Smith Folley and Margery Folley and nephew of Doris Haighton of Caernarvon. Buried with S/L Forshaw in Joint Grave 24–25.'

Don Aris noted that the cemetery at Rheinberg is only about 45 kilometres from Essen, where Johnny and Frank were heading on the night of 26/27. Over 900 bombers were operating, with the targets at Essen, Schweinfurt and a marshalling yard in northern France and their losses were 29 aircraft. With Johnny, the Command lost 30.

I've often wondered about the faint R/T call heard by Ronnie MacAndrew and Lionel Wilk, whilst chasing an AI contact near Osnabrück, 'Bogey – Get Away' What did Johnny mean? If it was Johnny's voice? Was he thinking that he had got another Serrate Mosquito behind him and chasing him round the sky as Harry and I had chased after them the month before? Also, as it happened, over the Osnabrück area? Was it an attempt to get a friendly Mosquito off his tail? Or was it, in reality, one of our opposite numbers who had turned the tables on the hunter, and behind Johnny and Frank – on stage, for their last act – was a deadly

Junkers 88 about to open fire and its pilot calling '*Horrido*' to his Ground Controller? We shall probably never know, but of the many of my friends who 'ran out of luck' Johnny Forshaw is still, after more than fifty years, one of those whom I miss the most . . . I wrote his name, and Frank's, in my log-book and, underneath them: 'Lest We Forget.'

That was not all. The following night the squadron lost another crew. Vic Lovell with Bob Lilley did not come back. They were a very experienced crew and had been in the night-fighter business for a long time. They had had several claims whilst flying with 89 Squadron, in the defence of Malta, and both held the DFC. In fact, they were on 29 Squadron in September 1941, when Harry and I arrived green and raw from 54 OTU at Church Fenton and were given such short shrift by Guy Gibson!

Vic and Bob were flying in support of an attack on Stuttgart/Friedrichshafen and, after they took off from Raynham at 04.00 hours, nothing more was ever heard of them. Only that day Vic Lovell had been recommended by Frank Davis for the vacant post as 'A' Flight Commander, to replace John Forshaw, and promotion to Acting Squadron Leader. They are buried in a joint grave in Heverlee War Cemetery, about 25 kilometres from Brussels.

There is a note in the Squadron Record that the CO, Frank Davis, was becoming concerned that, 'With sickness and the large number of crews who will soon become "tour expired", new personnel must be asked for immediately.' I don't remember any great degree of sickness, nor were Harry and I thinking about coming off ops. We were enjoying every minute of our life at West Raynham and were – in modern parlance – finding a lot of Job Satisfaction out of the work on which we were engaged!

*   *   *

Whilst I was on leave, Rodney was also at home at Ashford. Fresh back from the United States as a pilot officer, with his wings. It was marvellous to see him. Little did he know that he was in for a frustrating year before he could get to an OTU and finish his training. He was one of a large number of air crew – of all categories – who were returning to the UK, keen to get on ops, but surplus to the immediate requirements of the three operational Commands (Fighter, Bomber and Coastal). Many of them, including Rodney, were never to make it to a squadron until after the war in Europe had come to an end in May 1945.

I was still seeing Betty Sessions when I was on leave in Ashford. She was the youngest of a family of six (three boys and three girls, and lived a quarter of a mile from us at Dencliff House. Her mother, widowed early in her married life, was a stoic and courageous lady. Having been well off when her husband had been alive, she had to 'turn to' when he died, and with the help of 'Old Aggie' in the 'back premises', she had kept her home going by taking in lodgers. Throughout the week Harriet Sessions worked like a slave and scrimped and saved to make the pennies go round. On Sunday afternoons she sat in her drawing room and Aggie, using the best china tea service, brought her tea into her. She was a very great lady and, before 1944 was out, Rodney and I were to find out just how great she was.

Her three sons (I had been at prep. school with Teddy, the youngest) were all in the Air Force and when we happened to be on leave together we used to meet up at the King's Head, just round the corner from the church! Sally and Betty were working (the former, in London) and Mary was already married to a doctor, serving in the RAMC. I was fond of Betty and we had some lovely days together, but both of us had other boy and girl friends and somehow we never let things between us become too serious.

It was a little earlier in the year that Harry had told me the story of Joan and what an incredible tale it proved to be. Harry – from the time we first met in August 1941 – had never mentioned having a girl friend nor showed much interest in any of the womenfolk that we met at the mess parties, or at one of the local hops. This is the tale which he unfolded, with some emotion from a man who rarely showed his inner feelings. He had attended Bearwood School, near Reading, which was a school run on Merchant Navy lines. It was attended by boys and girls whose fathers were serving in – or had served in – the Merchant Navy. Harry's father had been a First Officer in the MN, but had sadly died at a relatively early age, leaving his widow with four little boys to bring up and educate on a pension verging on a pittance. Mrs White buckled down to the task and brought up her four sons with little help from the State or from anyone else. But, in doing so, like other mothers – before her, and since – she became fiercely possessive.

I think Harry's two elder brothers also went to Bearwood but, although one was in the RM and the other in the RAF, I never got to know them as I did his younger brother, Gerald. He was certainly at Bearwood with Harry in the mid-thirties and – following in his father's footsteps – went on to enjoy a successful career in the MN, rising from Cadet, when I first met him in 1942, to Master and to be a Member of Trinity House.

Both the boys and the girls wore a uniform akin to that worn by MN cadets and although, in those days, they were kept strictly segregated, Harry's eye fell on a sweet little Scot whose name was Joan Crombie. It is true to say that his eyes never left her until the dreadful day, twenty years later, when she died in his arms following a road accident in Singapore.

Harry having made his way up the school, excelling at swimming and boxing, it is equally certain that her eyes fell on him, and liked what they saw. When they left school they wrote to each other and kept in touch.

In 1939, Harry joined a City firm as a shipping clerk and in May 1940 – putting a year onto his age – he volunteered for the Air Force at 17. How he convinced the Recruiting Officer that he was 18, no one will ever know! When I met him, over a year later, he still looked as if he should have been at school. Nine months on he was awarded his wings and passed out from his SFTS as a fully blown sergeant-pilot, with over a hundred hours in his flying log-book – and quite a few of them 'on twins'.

About that time, I think it must have been early in 1941, he was told to take some embarkation leave as he would shortly be going overseas. At the end of this leave he went, accompanied by his mother, to Victoria Station, to catch the train back to his unit. Presumably he would not be home again for some time. Joan was also there to say 'Goodye!' and wish him luck. As the porters were starting to close the doors – and the Guard's whistle blew – Harry bent down to kiss his mother. Joan then stepped forward and also kissed him . . .

Harry climbed up into the carriage and the train pulled out but the damage had been done!

Harry didn't go overseas: his posting was cancelled. In the meantime, his mother had only seen that there was an intruder on the horizon of her precious family and that she might be about to lose her beloved third son, not for months overseas, but to Joan Crombie.

She wrote to Harry and, unbelievably, banned him from ever seeing Joan again or having any further contact with her. There was, in the whole 'make up' of Joan Crombie, nothing to which any potential mother-in-law could have taken exception. Rather, the reverse, for she was a sweet person. It was a cruel and unjustified sentence on both of them.

Harry, strong character though he was, also knew his duty towards his mother. As he grew up he learned to have a deep respect for the hardships and sacrifices she had endured in order to educate and care for him (and his brothers) after his father's death. He accepted the ban.

Throughout the remainder of 1941, through 1942 and well into 1943 he kept his word to his mother and neither saw nor wrote to Joan. But, equally, he never looked at another girl! The essence of Harry White, in that regard, was that he was a one-woman man.

I think it was towards the end of 1943 that one of their mutual friends wrote to Harry and mentioned how much Joan, now serving in the Wrens, would like to hear from him. After wrestling with his conscience for some days (he told me) he wrote to her and they resumed their correspondence. Nobody will ever know what it cost him, to break his word to his mother. Subsequently, they met and it was not long before Harry asked her to marry him. They were indeed childhood sweethearts in the best possible use of the term.

He related to me how, when he broke the news to his mother, 'the wheels came off'. In her agony of losing Harry, as she saw it, she told him that she would not have Joan in the house and she did her best to disown him. From that time, Harry quite often came back with me to Ashford, when our leave became due. There, my mother and father made him feel welcome in our home and gave him the support which was no longer forthcoming at his mother's flat in North London. It was during April that Harry told me that he and Joan were planning to get married in June and asked me to be his Best Man.

Back on the squadron, Graham Rice was promoted to Squadron Leader and given the twice vacant post of 'A' Flight Commander to replace the luckless Vic Lovell, and before him, Johnny Forshaw. It proved to be a good choice by Frank Davis. Together with his Nav/Rad, Jimmy Rogerson, Graham survived to destroy several more E/A, make a good Flight Commander and, with Jimmy, be awarded a DFC at the end of his tour.

At the end of the month a detailed report, comprising some 30 pages covering the period of December 1943 to April 1944 ,was produced by No. 100 Group (SD) Headquarters. It stressed all the problems suffered by the three Serrate squadrons. It also reported on the activities of the other squadrons and units in the Group and the various countermeasures on which they were engaged, everything being aimed at causing as much murder and mayhem as possible amongst the German air and ground defences.

Most of the points appertaining to the Serrate operations have already been gleaned from Don Aris's definitive Squadron History, but something can be added to the dismal story of the unserviceability of our Serrate homer, which had been the source of many of our troubles when we converted from the Beaufighter to the Mosquito. The relevant extract follows:

'RADAR: At the time when 100 Group was formed in December 1943 three Squadrons of Mosquito Mk II Serrate fitted aircraft, Nos. 141, 169 and 239, were transferred from Air Defence of Great Britain (ex Fighter Command).

The Serrate canister-type aerial system in these aircraft were found to be unsatisfactory due to ambiguity of D/F. It was therefore decided to replace the aerials by the old type Serrate aerials as fitted on the Beaufighters. An extensive programme of aerial modifications was therefore undertaken at West Raynham. Twenty-eight aircraft were refitted with Beaufighter-type Serrate aerials, the canisters were removed from the leading edges and the mutilated edges made good.

Fitting of backward looking A.I. Mk V transmitter, modulator and aerial system were also undertaken. This modification was later introduced at 218 M.U. Colerne, so that all Mosquito II aircraft being delivered to 100 Group would arrive complete with the modification. In the early months of the year, 1944, a period of bad radar serviceability was encountered, this largely being due to faulty switch motors and the secondhand condition of the A.I. aerial installation which came complete from A.D.G.B. A considerable number of wing tip aerials also broke off in flight. Here, the trouble was due to fatigue of aerials that had seen considerable service before transfer to 100 Group. Action was taken to improve the design of the switch motors, install new aerials and to overhaul completely all connections, junction boxes and plugs in the aircraft.'

I wonder if the loss of some of these aerials, in mid-flight, may have been the cause of some of our fading blips and lost contacts? Amongst the concluding paragraphs is the following:

'It is remarkable that with all the problems with engines, radar and secondhand machines, resulting in so few serviceable aircraft, that the three Serrate Mosquito Squadrons shot down 27 enemy aircraft, 10 by 141, 9 by 239 and 8 by 169 Squadron.'

With a degree of cynicism, and all the benefits of hindsight, it is difficult not to conjecture whether this report had not been initiated for the purpose of 'whitewashing' some of those who had been responsible for the débâcle. I could find no accompanying paragraph stating how many of our own aircraft and lives the destruction of 27 E/A had cost . . . or how many of those were caused by engine failure . . . or again, any estimate of how many Ju 88s and Me 110s we might have 'hacked down' if we had been properly equipped in the first place.

THAT WAS APRIL 1944, THAT WAS!

*   *   *

There were one or two memorable parties in the mess at Raynham, notably 'BOSTICK NIGHT'! Earlier in the year when we had a number of representatives from various companies – starting with de Havilland's – assisting our Engineer and Radar Officers to modify the worn-out Mosquitoes: some of them stayed in the officers' mess. One of them was from the company which made an aircraft glue called by the trade name of 'BOSTICK', and its adhesive qualities have never been bettered!

Like all good reps this chap had his bag of samples and one night, in the middle of a party, someone on 141 unearthed this bag – from the cloakroom or somewhere – and brought it triumphantly into the bar. It took only a second or two to open the bag and remove some of the samples . . . it took much longer, and in some cases, weeks (for those of us who were daubed with the wretched stuff) to get it out of our hair and, in some cases, our clothing! As a substitute for hair-cream, 'BOSTICK' was not an outstanding success, but we had a great party!

Looking back through my log-book for May I see that Harry and I carried out 16 NFTs but only operated on five nights. Looking at the Squadron History I see that we were now to be called 141 (BS) Squadron, along with the other squadrons in 100 Group. The 'BS' stood for 'Bomber Support'. Since the early days of Serrate we had enjoyed the prefix of '(SD)' which stood for 'Special Duties', but this nomenclature was no more to be used.

I am sure these changes pleased somebody, but I cannot recollect that we worried much about that sort of thing. More important was the fact that the Command continued with its attacks on railway yards and factories in northern France and, on 1/2 May, 801 aircraft operated on a variety of targets and lost only nine. They were supported by 10 Serrate Mosquitoes from West Raynham and, for once, there were no early returns. On the night of 8 May Harry and I did a rare practice trip, combining an exercise with the local GCI Controller, and a X-country – being up for 3.5 hours.

I think we must have been getting pretty blasé by that stage of the proceedings, because there is a caustic comment in my log:

'F/L WHITE X-COUNTRY & G.C.I.
G.C.I.s I'VE HAD THEM! NEVER AGAIN, LOW LEVEL X-COUNTRIES, I'VE HAD THEM TOO! THEY STINK'

Evidently I must have lost an AI contact from the GCI Controller and Harry probably got lost – flying at low level somewhere over England! I suppose that, looking back, we fancied we should be on ops all the time and whenever we flew at night! And that is how accidents happen . . . we were getting too 'cocky' . . .

In the meantime, on 3/4 May, there had been another disaster for the Command, and the comfortable pattern of raiding northern France (in preference to the Third Reich) and only suffering minimal losses was rudely upset. There was a total of 598 sorties; but the losses were 50 bombers and many of these were incurred by a force of 360 aircraft which attacked a German military camp at Mailly-Le-Camp, France.

The attack has been the subject of numerous reports and, apparently, there was some delay in marking the second aiming point. As the attack was being carried out in bright moonlight, this delay was very dangerous and the Germans were able to concentrate all their fighter squadrons (allocated for the defence of northern France) on Mailly-Le-Camp.

Many bombers were seen to be shot down in the target area; and the serious thing about it, from the 100 Group point of view, was that neither 141 nor 239 Squadrons were on operations that night! Harry and I had actually done an NFT on Mosquito 717 for 1.20 hours but surprisingly, the squadron records say that 'operations were cancelled due to bad weather'! (*NB:* In the post-war years controversy has continued to rage over Mailly-Le-Camp and there has even been a suggestion of a breakdown in security, that news of the raid was 'leaked' to the enemy.) In general, I am always amazed, when I look back, that with so few obvious security arrangements, compared with today, there were not more 'security leaks.'

At about this time our well-liked and well-respected Adjutant, Dickie Sparrowe, was posted to the Tactical Air Force, after serving 141 faithfully for eighteen months. Together with Buster Reynolds, the Intelligence Officer, and as an older man, Dickie had rendered sterling service to Bob Braham, when the latter had arrived in December 1942 – as a very young wing commander – to take over the squadron.

Bob did not greatly enjoy paperwork anyway, and only wanted to be in the air. Dickie and Buster made it possible for him to do so. We had particular cause to remember Dickie and were very sorry to see him go. He, it was, who had welcomed us back to the squadron (after our Middle East ferrying interlude) with the words: 'Well, I think you two have fallen on your feet this time.' How right he was!

From time to time we had to carry out Dinghy Drill. On 9 May a coach load of us set off for Cambridge, about one and a half hours' drive from Raynham. There, in that beautiful city where I was to live for seven happy years in the early sixties, our first destination was The Leys School. The Headmaster had kindly granted the RAF permission to use the school swimming baths, to let aircrew train in the cold and difficult task of trying to scramble out of the water into a water-logged dinghy – having first jumped off one of the diving-boards in full flying clothing!

I found it a hair-raising experience and always told Harry that (as an experienced and qualified life-saver) I expected him to tow me home, if we ever had to come down in the drink! After a hilarious, but not very reassuring, afternoon in the school baths we repaired to the *Eagle & Child, The Blue Boar, The Red Lion* and numerous other hostelries in Cambridge.

I remember the *Eagle* was so crowded that I had to crawl to the bar on my hands and knees in order to buy a drink. At around 10 p.m. we foregathered in the Market Square, before climbing into our coach and heading for West Raynham. In the event, it was some time before the coach left, because somebody – full of *joie de vivre* and Cambridge beer – had thrown Harry's cap up onto the first-floor balcony of one of the buildings on the east side of the Square, and there it had stuck!

I think we made one or two half-hearted attempts to climb up and retrieve the cap but without success. However, we were not going to leave without the cap and we proceeded to set up a demonstration in the street with shouts of '*No cap! No ops!*' This plea, made with all of us sitting along the pavement and refusing to '*Move along, please Sir*' (from the local constabulary) caught the sympathy of the crowd which had started to gather! The idea of us all sitting in the street and refusing to fly on any more operations until we had got the missing cap back has remained an enduring memory over the years. I know that someone went off and found a ladder and that Harry climbed up to retrieve his cap. With much ceremony, he replaced it on his head and climbed down. We heard, a few days later, that the Chief Constable had written in irate tones to the 'Wingco', Frank Davis, to the effect that 141 were no longer welcome in Cambridge!

Two nights later we were 'on ops' and the targets were in Belgium and France: more military bases and more railway yards. The attacks were made by 725 heavy bombers from which 16 aircraft were lost. Six crews from 141 operated, there were no early returns and 239 Squadron did not operate on this night. Two successes without loss were achieved by 141. In my log-book there is the following comment:

'MOSQUITO 726 (Z) F/L WHITE OPS. TARGETS IN BELGIUM
AND FRANCE
Ju 88 DESTROYED N. OF AMIENS AFTER A.I.CHASE
THROUGH STREAM.
ONE FOR JOHNNY. 3.25 hours.'

The last sentence 'One For Johnny' reads like something out of the 1914–18 War, when our forebears were flying their flimsy machines above the trenches and dog-fighting with the Red Baron and other German gentlemen, i.e. revenge for a comrade shot down the day before. There must have been something in it, because Harry and I definitely had it in mind that night to get one for Johnny Forshaw if we could – all these years later it sounds rather melodramatic. It did not seem that way on 11 May 1944.

The 100 Group Report for the week ending 13 May 1944 remarks that the destruction of six enemy aircraft was a 'very satisfactory result . . .'. I think that statement is debatable. When one comes to read through the Crew Reports (for 141 Squadron, alone) and, as a one-time AI operator, one cannot help being struck by the number of Serrate and/or AI contacts which either we failed to follow up, or lost! It is, however, interesting to note that our Ju 88 was probably one of the '. . . enemy aircraft coming from the East before and during the bombing . . .' and that the patrol areas for the night were well planned at 100 Group HQ.

Harry and I took off from Raynham at 22.12 hours in Mosquito HJ726 Z (which we had used when we got the Heinkel 177 over Berlin in February) but, as will be seen, we were still having to chop and change our aircraft, flying a different Mosquito on almost every op. I also see from the squadron records that I had been promoted to the rank of Flight Lieutenant at the beginning of May. I had now been commissioned for two years and this was simply a routine promotion. Our Combat Report picks up the story:

'This sortie was entirely uneventful until we reached a point about 50 miles S. of Brussels at 23.50 hours when weak indications of Serrate were seen North of us. Some fires were seen on the ground due presumably to previous Bomber activity.'

We were just able to D/F on these Serrate indications so turned onto 055 degrees and headed in their general direction. No improvement was noticeable by 00.10 hours when an AI contact was obtained at 12,000 feet range on the starboard side, our own height being 15,000 feet. This contact, flying on a westerly course at Zero Hour for the Brussels area target, was believed to be a Hun, so we turned in behind and followed as E/A turned south, at an IAS of 200 mph, an even better indication that it was a Hun.

We closed gently to minimum range but Harry could not get a visual so we throttled back and came in again from 2,000 feet, with the E/A flying at a height of 11,000 feet. We repeated this four times during which we had the frightening experience of flying through the bomber stream, with us trailing along behind him at a distance of 1,500 feet. Whilst we were passing through the stream, and sometimes being rocked by the slipstream of the bombers, the time trace on my cathode-ray tubes was almost blotted out with innumerable blips moving down and up it, as the ranges decreased and then increased again. It was impossible to take avoiding action because one could not D/F on any single blip long enough to be able to tell if the Mosquito was going to hit – or miss – the other aircraft!

In any case, I was trying to hang on to our elusive target, keep him at a range of 1,500 feet and then hope to deal with him, when we got clear of the bomber stream. The target was not burning Serrate and appeared to be blissfully ignorant of his position relative to our bombers! As Harry said '. . . he was definitely considered to be LMF!' Eventually, my tubes cleared to indicate that we had passed through the last of the bombers and there was the one precious blip, still at 1,500 feet in front of us. We closed to 800 feet where, at last, Harry could see the silhouette of our target, and going in to 500 feet, although there were no exhausts visible, he identified it as a Junkers 88.

Returning to our Combat Report:

> '. . . as it was a very dark night we flew on – waiting for the E/A to turn into a lighter part of the sky. Unless he was completely unaware that there were such things as British bombers, he must shortly turn North; this he did, after seven minutes. We were flying just through the tops of 3/10ths thin broken cloud momentarily losing sight of the Ju 88, Harry eventually opened fire from a range of 250 feet and 10 degrees below the enemy aircraft and gave it a four second burst. The Junkers exploded and fell away in two burning pieces, both of which we saw hit the ground – where they continued to burn.'

Our closing comments fit in well with the ORS Report mentioned earlier and read:

> 'This route, which circumscribed the target areas, is considered a very good one. It enables a crew to turn off towards the target areas, from any point, at the first indication of activity and places the Serrate fighters between the target areas and the lines of approach of the German night-fighters enabling all AI contacts, outside the NE and S sides of the rectangle, to be chased as probable E/A.'

We also reported that because I had been able to pick up the 'Mother' radar beacons from Beachy Head–Martlesham Heath and Manston on the second time-trace of the AI, these had proved to be a valuable aid to navigation when we were operating well inside France, where Gee fixes were unobtainable.

When we got back to Raynham and into the Briefing room there was great excitement because another 141 crew had also shot down an 88: it was none other than 'the Major', Flight Lieutenant Lucien Le Boutte, the most senior of our several Belgian pilots, and nearing the end of his tour. Flying with him as AI operator was another 'old stager', Flying Officer Ron Mallett. It will be remembered that Ron, a very experienced 'blip basher' from the early days in 1941, had recently helped Graham Rice to destroy a Focke-Wulf 190, when Graham's own navigator (Jimmy Rogerson) was off sick. It will also be recalled that Wing Commander Braham had wanted 'the Major' to do a trip with Harry and I, because he was not entirely happy concerning the navigator with whom he was then crewed up . . .

'The Major', well over 40 and a lifetime of flying behind him, was ecstatic over his success, and could hardly contain himself! Trying to describe what happened when his Ju 88 burst into flames and blew up in front of them, he meant to say 'It was amazing!' Instead, he had us all in fits, when he came out with 'I was amazing!'

He was an amazing man – old enough to be the father of many of us, with hundreds of flying hours behind him – he was normally quite imperturbable. Never seen without a cigarette drooping from his upper lip, in true continental fashion, from the time he came down to breakfast in the morning, to the moment when he climbed into his aircraft: then, the minute he had landed, he was lighting up again. Like most of his countrymen he had escaped in hazardous circumstances from Belgium following the German *blitzkrieg* of May 1940, and it took a lot to shake him. One of the many stories about him which I liked was that one night, earlier in 1944, he had been on ops (in a Mosquito II) supporting a raid on Berlin and the weather had turned bad. On the return journey, back across the North German Plain, he, along with many of the bombers, had been blown south by unpredicted winds coming from the north and he, like them, was running short of fuel. As he came out over the estuary of the Scheldt and headed across the Channel, 'the Major' could hear, over the R/T, several aircraft calling up and asking for emergency landings at Manston. This was the specially long strip on the Kent coast, designed for aircraft returning to England but in serious trouble and unlikely to be able to get back to their own airfields. Flight Lieutenant Le Boutte had the same idea in mind!

When he got over Manston he called up Flying Control and asked for permission to land. The Controller called him back and said that there were a number of other aircraft in the circuit, some of them with battle damage, and he would have to get them down first; was Creeper 14 (or whatever his call-sign was) quite happy? 'The Major' called back, 'Quite 'Appy, Thank You. Creeper 14 Listening Out.' By then the weather was closing in, he was running short of fuel and he himself had had an engine failure, and was 'flying on one'! Under the circumstances to reply to Flying Control, when he had just been told that he might have to remain airborne for another 10/15 minutes, telling them that he was 'quite 'appy, thank you', spoke volumes for the man and set a standard that most of us could not match.

But on the night of 11/12 May, almost at the end of his operational career, he had not only destroyed a German night-fighter but he had shot it down over his native Belgium and only 30 miles south-west of his home in Brussels. For once, in that briefing room, he really showed his emotions and old Ron Mallett (who had brought him his success) was not far behind him. It was marvellous to see them . . .

The following day there was more excitement. The irrepressible Bob Braham (supposedly 'on rest' at No. 2 Group HQ) had again 'borrowed' a Mosquito VI from 107 Squadron and with Sticks had set off from West Raynham on his own, on a daylight 'Ranger' over Denmark.

A Ranger operation to Wing Commander Braham meant that he could go looking for trouble, anywhere he could find it! It also meant that he was pitting himself, in his Mosquito, against the German day-fighters, i.e. the Fw 190s and Me 109s (*NB:* I am reminded of one of my mother's dictums when, as children my brothers and I were attempting anything particularly hazardous, 'It will only end in crying!') Eventually, for Bob Braham, it did!

Having been debriefed ourselves, Harry and I got to bed in the small hours of 12 May, sleeping through the morning. We had had lunch and strolled down to 'the Flights'. There we learned that our former Squadron Commander had gone off on a Ranger operation and we thought (once again!) he must be mad to chance his arm by going out over Denmark, on his own, in broad daylight. Then the telephone in the Flight Commander's office rang . . .

The last paragraph of the report of the incident, in the Squadron History, reads as follows:

> 'When W/C Braham's "May Day" call had been relayed to West Raynham, 141 Squadron stood by to carry out a search plan and when news of the intended ditching was received about 14.00 hours, two 141 Mosquitoes were airborne within five minutes of his pin-point being given.
>
> Five other Mosquitoes were running up prior to joining in the search when news was received of him and F/Lt Gregory being picked up safely from the sea.'

Harry and I were one of the two Mosquitoes airborne within five minutes, and my log reads: 'F/Lt White Air-Sea Rescue for Bob Braham and "Sticks" Ditched N.W. of Cromer. Both O.K. and picked up by H.S.L. from Grimsby. 00.25 hrs.'

As will be noticed, we were only airborne for 25 minutes. We had just got out to the search area and started to look for the ditched Mosquito, and fearing the worst, when we were recalled to base, with the news that they had been picked up and were safe and sound! When we landed everyone was celebrating and telling the amazing story that had started to filter through.

It has to be told here, even if it means diverting from the main theme of our life on 141 Squadron in the weeks leading up towards D-Day.

> 'W/C Braham and F/Lt Gregory took off from West Raynham at 08.13 hrs on a daylight, lone aircraft, Ranger operation over Denmark. After being fired on by flak from a ship, W/C Braham saw and pursued a Fw 190 near Aalborg, during his pursuit he was attacked by an Me 109 which hit his Mosquito both aft and in the port main-plane and petrol started to leak from a tank.
>
> Despite this, W/C Braham continued his pursuit of the Fw 190, which in trying to escape him, flew very close to the ground. W/C Braham opened fire and the Fw 190, after parts exploded and bits flew off, did a violent stall turn and almost came down on the Mosquito. The Fw 190 then hit the ground and blew up. There was no sign of the Me 109 after its attack and W/C Braham made course for home. He stopped one engine and feathered the propeller in order to try and conserve fuel, lost from the leaking tank.
>
> He then saw that the tips of the propeller were curved when he had hit a mound on the ground during his extremely low level attack on the Fw 190. They were hit again by flak on crossing out of Denmark and realising, when halfway across the North Sea, that they would not make the English coast, he informed Coltishall Control that ditching would be necessary and sent out several "MAY DAY", requests for help, calls.
>
> When about 70 miles from Cromer they saw three Naval Minesweeping trawlers and W/C Braham ditched half a mile ahead of one of them – as his fuel gauges were reading zero. They got out of the top hatch, got into a dinghy and were rescued by a boat from one of the minesweepers. They were later transferred onto a Naval Motor Torpedo-boat which made for Grimsby, when halfway there, they were transferred to an RAF Air-Sea Rescue launch. They landed at Grimsby and spent the night at a nearby RAF bomber Station.'

And people wonder why we, of 141, revere the name of Bob Braham.

When I next saw Sticks Gregory he said, 'You know Mike, Bob never even got his feet wet! He told me to get the (aircraft) dinghy round, and he simply stepped into it! A few minutes later, we were picked up by a boat from one of the minesweepers – I was completely soaked!' If ever a navigator deserved his medals, Sticks did!

The following days, ops were once more scrubbed due to bad weather after we had tested 732 twice and found all well on the second attempt (it was in 732 that we had got the Dornier 217 in April).

On 14 May, F/O John Watkins and his Nav/Rad, F/Sgt Thomas Pantry, joined 141. Two days later, on the 16th, they were lost. It was another of those in-explicable and unsolved mysteries of the air. They were transferred to us from 85 Squadron, along with another crew, where they had been on Mosquitoes, so they were not a completely 'sprog' crew. At 13.50 hours they took off from Raynham in Mosquito FII DD726 (Z) (in which Harry and I had operated successfully, five nights earlier) for a one-hour AI and Serrate practice.

They were to carry out a full NFT in the Spalding–Peterborough–Boston area and they had petrol for four hours' flying. No further trace was ever heard of this aircraft, or of its crew. It was daytime. The weather wasn't bad. They were familiar with the aircraft. They simply vanished into thin air. They are still listed as 'MISSING' in Air Force records and their names are commemorated on the Royal Air Force's Memorial at Runnymede, amongst over 20,000 others who have 'No Known Grave'. To this day, there is nothing to show what happened to them. There was one other odd thing that I do not think has been previously recorded. It was only a slight incident – and it seemed like a joke at the time . . .

About two hours after Watkins and Pantry had taken off, we were starting to get a bit worried as to where they had got to, but we were still not overly concerned when Harry got out of his chair and walked up to the blackboard, on which were chalked up the names of all the pilots in 'B' Flight. The board was used to record 'TAKE OFF' and 'LANDING' times and the nature of the flight, i.e. NFT, X-COUNTRY, OPS or whatever it might be. There on the board was 'F/O Watkins' and the time of his take-off, 13.50 hours. Harry took a piece of chalk and drew a line across the name of F/O Watkins and through all the other details, saying, as he did so: 'Oh well, we won't see them again!'

We never did.

On the night of 19/20 May Harry and I operated and I missed two more AI contacts. Although we did not know it, D-Day and the invasion of Europe was less than three weeks away. Bomber Command sent out over 900 sorties and, miraculously, lost only seven bombers. There were some minor targets in Germany, but mostly the attacks were on railway yards, coastal gun positions and a radar station, scattered from Boulogne to Amiens and Tours to Orleans. Fifteen Serrate Mosquitoes operated out of West Raynham and there were no early returns!

The relevant part of our disappointing trip was as follows, and our patrol was in support of an attack on a marshalling-yard at Tours:

'At 00.20 hours at 16,000 feet they [i.e. us!] had a weak Serrate contact too distant to chase. They reached target area at 00.55 hours at 16,000 feet and the bomber stream was contacted. They set course for Orleans following a distant Serrate contact. At 01.15 hours at 47.30N–01.15E at 16,000 feet a medium strength Serrate signal was seen dead ahead and followed for three minutes with signal strength increasing. Head-on contact obtained, range 12,000 feet and to starboard.

They turned starboard about, decreasing range to 5,000 feet. Contact was then lost and not regained. At 01.20 hours at ORLEANS at 16,000 feet they had an A.I. contact port at 12,000 feet. They turned port and attempted to close, but they could not engage F.S. blower and range was closed very slowly at 250 I.A.S. to 1,200 feet. A fleeting visual was obtained on a single green exhaust of jinking target but visual was not maintained and range again closed on jinking target to 1,200 feet in a tight orbit to port. Target peeled off to starboard going down to ground level. Target took no evasive action until they closed to 3,000 feet, when target commenced to jink violently. Contact was eventually lost in the PARIS area. This chase lasted 20 minutes. No further contacts were had on the return route.'

In my log I wrote:

'F/Lt White   OPS   IN SUPPORT OF RAID ON TOURS.
NONE MISSING NO JOY BUT DOG-FIGHT WITH PRESUMED
E/A ENDING OVER PARIS. COMPRESSOR U/S i.e.
CANNONS NO GO! 03.50 hours'

There is no mention of the compressor going u/s in the Squadron Operational Records, but if I wrote that into my log-book it can only mean one thing. If, after chasing all round the night skies over France, we had been able to hold the visual – identify the target as an E/A – and Harry had then pressed the gun-button to open fire . . . the cannons would not have worked anyway!

Oh Dear! Oh Dear! what were we all playing at?

It was on the 21st that our 'missing' Belgian pilot F/O Van den Plassche returned to the squadron and told us of his fantastic journey of evasion across France. We were all delighted to see him and to congratulate him, but sorry to hear that Mamoutoff, his navigator, had been killed. There was a nice little touch to his return. Don Aris can remember that he went in search of the WAAF parachute-packer who had packed the 'chute which had saved his life, and presented her with a bottle of French perfume!

We operated again that night, flying HJ941 (X) (which we were starting to regard as our own aircraft). We had needed to carry out two NFTs, because I found the AI was unserviceable. We thought we had got it right when we did the second NFT after lunch, but we were proved wrong.

We set off for a Serrate patrol to Duisberg, in the Ruhr. But, soon after we crossed the enemy coast, the azimuth tube on the Mk IV AI became unserviceable, and we had to pack up and come home.

On the way we saw plenty of tempting Serrate signals to chase, if we had had the means to do so. To add insult to injury, we had to make our way back to base through the oncoming bomber stream and without a workable AI set to give me some clue where they all were! Worse was to come; we learned the next day that of the 532 aircraft which attacked Duisberg, 29 were lost. It just seemed that whenever the 'bomber boys' really needed us, we were not around. Three days later 'the Major' and Ron Mallett were both awarded the DFC.

Lucien Le Boutte had been operating with 141 since August 1942, including the daylight 'Insteps' from Predannack early in 1943, and right through the pioneering days of the Serrate operations, on the Beaufighters at Wittering.

Ron Mallett was now on his third tour as an AI operator on night-fighters, and had brought his pilots a number of successes. 'The Major' was shortly to leave us and be promoted to the highest ranks of the Belgian Air Force.

Ultimately, he became Chief-of-Staff, in the rank of General, and an ADC to the Belgian King. Those of us from 141 who had the chance of spending a few days in Brussels (in the post-war years) were always assured of a warm welcome.

Ron Mallett was shortly to die when he and Paddy Engelbach were shot down whilst operating over Germany. What a pity it was that Ron could not have crewed up with 'the Major' earlier on and then have finished their tours together. But, as is often said, 'if wishes were horses, then beggars would ride' . . .

On 24/25 May Harry and I tried again and once more took HJ941 (X), giving it a good NFT (lasting an hour and twenty minutes) and finding that everything, including my AI set, was 'on the top line'. At 21.50 hours we took off on a Serrate patrol to Aachen, which was just across the German border, and south of the main industrial complex of the Ruhr. It was only a shallow penetration and there was no need for us to go wandering about in 'Happy Valley' where the natives were always distinctly hostile. Unbelievably, our Mk IV AI failed us again, or perhaps the blame lay on me, for not having tested it properly during the NFT; after all this time, who can tell anyway and what does it matter? My log entry shows:

'F/Lt White   OPS   FIGHTER SWEEP IN SUPPORT OF
RAID ON AACHEN TOOK OFF IN DAYLIGHT. BAGS OF JOY
LATER AT BUT COULD NOT COPE WITHOUT FRONT A.I.
CHASED OUT. LANDED 1.40 HOURS LATE! 04.30 hours'

For the details of yet another disappointing night we turn once more to the Squadron History and pick up the story at 23.00 hours, as we steered SE across Belgium (having passed over the enemy coastline 20 minutes beforehand). We had one chase after a Serrate contact, but my opposite number in the E/A switched off his AI when he was still more than five miles away from us and our ground returns restricted me from getting an AI contact on my Mk IV set at our height of 20,000 feet. Then as the official report said: 'At 00.25 hours their forward A.I. became unserviceable but they continued their patrol.'

We were so fed up when the forward AI went u/s that we decided to carry on and home in on any Serrate signals I could pick up, on the offchance that I could bring Harry in close enough to the target for him to get a visual. It will be remembered that the herring-bone pattern of the Serrate signals, showing on the Mk IV AI cathode-ray tubes, covered the whole of the time-trace on the azimuth and elevation tubes. Also that the pulsating edges of the herring-bones did not give a very accurate indication of how many degrees the target aircraft was to starboard or to port, or above, or below, in relation to the position of the pursuing fighter.

The whole concept of the Serrate operation was that the A.I. operator would pick up the herring-bone signals of the *Lichtenstein* AI sets, in the Ju 88s and Me 110s, at long range, and using only ragged definitions of azimuth and elevation, plus the strength of the signals, bring their aircraft within range of their Mk IV sets. Then with the far more accurate blip showing up alone on both time-traces and the range measured in feet (rather than miles!), an interception could be concluded and a visual obtained, which would hopefully turn out to be an aircraft with swastikas painted on its tail! Although Harry and I spent nearly two hours trying, it was too difficult for me that night, as we can read from the report:

'. . . They had no contacts on their North/South flight so they patrolled East/West from 23.50 hours during which they chased a Serrate contact for 10 minutes which was lost when the target switched off. A few miles South of Brussels a weak Serrate contact was chased which became strong over 10 minutes and F/L Allen is sure A.I. contact would have been made on the enemy had his forward A.I. been working. This Serrate was also lost when contact switched off his A.I. 4 Serrate contacts were chased in the Aachen area, but all were inconclusive because they had no A.I. forward. South of Rotterdam at 01.35 hours at 20,000 feet they had a backward A.I. contact at 6,000 feet range, they orbited and got behind the enemy but this was lost when enemy switched off his A.I. They had one final Serrate contact a few miles West of Aachen but after 5 orbits they were able to confirm it came from the ground. They recrossed out over Overflakee at 01.50 hours and landed at 02.20 hours.'

To comment further on this sortie would be only a repetition of what has been said earlier, to the effect that the efforts of the long-range fighters in 100 Group to support the heavy bombers were still, at this late stage, being severely hampered by the poor serviceability of our radar equipment.

The next day we were briefed for operations in support of a raid on Mannheim, but the trip was scrubbed at the last minute due to the weather.

With D-Day growing ever closer it is interesting to refer to the Squadron History and the outline of Bomber Command's operations for the night of 27/28 May: 'They attacked military camps at Bourg-Leopold, Belgium . . . railway yards at Aachen, Germany and Nantes, France, the airfield at Rennes and on five coastal gun batteries on the French coast, plus other minor operations and minelaying. There was a total of 1,111 sorties with losses of 28 bombers.'

This gives a clear picture of the tactical use of the heavy bomber force by Air Chief Marshal Sir Arthur Harris – and the variety of targets chosen for destruction by the planners – which would serve to reduce the opposition faced by the Allied Armies and the Royal Navy on 6 June. The report continues:

'. . . 7 aircraft of 141 Squadron supported the raids on Aachen and Bourg-Leopold with one "Early Return" and F/L White with F/L Allen destroyed an Me 109, their 11th victory and they had damaged two other aircraft, all with 141 Squadron. F/L White had just assumed, the previous day, the responsibilities of Officer Commanding the Station Flight as well as his normal operational duties with 141 Squadron.

No.239 Squadron at West Raynham also operated this night with eight aircraft on Bomber Support and S/L Reeves with P/O O'Leary destroyed an Me 110 but they had one crew "MISSING", F/O Bailey and F/O White.'

I haven't any recollection of Harry being put in charge of the Station Flight at Raynham. In any case it was no great shakes, because it only comprised a couple of Airspeed Oxfords, the odd Tiger Moth and a handful of ground crew! However it was his first command and the forerunner of many more!

I was concerned when we got back at 4 o'clock on the morning of the 28th and learned in the Briefing room that Bob Bailey and John White of 239 were missing. John, it may be remembered, lived in Ashford, Middlesex, close to our house in Clarendon Road, and we had played in the local cricket team together.

More serious was the fact that he had recently got married to a very nice girl, named Hazel, who was stationed – not far away – at Bircham Newton, and serving in the WAAF. Some weeks later we heard that both Bob and John had baled out of their stricken Mosquito and were safe, but not before Hazel had bravely accepted their wedding present from the squadron (239), not knowing whether John was alive or dead.

My log entry is succinct and describes the events of the night in five lines:

'F/Lt White   OPS   Aachen and Bourg-Leopold.
A.I. Jamming and no Serrate. Me 109 DESTROYED
N.E. of Aachen. Harold Blinded, I saw second 109
slip by. Weather bad at base, just made it. Most
unpleasant trip. 03.15 hours.'

We saw the first Pathfinder Force flares going down over Bourg-Leopold and although I was not picking up any Serrate signals, there was some jamming on the AI tubes which would make any interception difficult. We patrolled the target area for about 15 minutes without contacting anything, but we saw (or rather Harry saw, because my head was firmly 'in the box' and staring at my AI tubes) three bombers shot down in five minutes.

As there were still no Serrate signals to be found, we set course for Aachen – which, being further inland, might mean that the jamming showing up on my AI tubes would be less intense. We would then have a better chance of carrying out a successful interception on any tempting blip that might appear on the two shimmering green lines in front of me.

From 02.25 hours we patrolled the target area for 10 minutes, and watched (on the AI by myself, with a running commentary to Harry) as the bomber stream set out on its homeward journey. Towards the end of our patrol the jamming was switched off altogether and I had, at last, two clear tubes.

At this stage of the proceedings it will be beneficial to look at Harry's Combat Report:

'... At 02.35 hours, a little to the West of Aachen, two A.I. contacts at 14 and 12,000 feet were obtained on the starboard side, crossing starboard to port flying N.E. on the same level, well above bombing height. At a range of 8,000 feet these two contacts merged into one and Mike (F/L Allen) remarked that a bomber was about to be shot down in front of us at any minute.'

NB: We were once again in HJ941 (X) and this time the AI was working perfectly. What I was actually seeing was not one of our bombers with a German night-fighter behind it, but two German 'Wild Boar' single-engined fighters moving into a closer formation! Harry's report continues:

'Still crossing, we turned to port behind this one contact and at 1,200 feet, obtained a visual on two white exhausts. We had not increased speed as range was closing quite rapidly. But as we assumed the line astern position, the exhausts faded from sight and range increased to 8,000 feet before, at full throttle, we were once more able to decrease the range slowly to 1,200 feet again, where we obtained a visual on two white exhausts. We closed to 600 feet where I was able to identify the target as an Me 109. I closed further to 300 feet and opened fire with a 2 second burst from 15 degrees below.'

What happened then was that the Me 109 blew up with a colossal flash, right in front of Harry's eyes, and blinded him for about a minute and a half. He then started to shout at me to read his instruments for him so that we could keep on an even keel, because he couldn't see a thing and we were in grave danger of falling out of the sky, unless he could quickly regain control!

But the flash of the 109 exploding had made me look up (from the visor of my AI set) and as my head came up, I saw – through the window on my side of the cockpit – an Me 109 slip by, just under our starboard wing. This must have been the second of the two 'Wild Boar' fighters which I had seen merging together on my AI.

My immediate reaction was that we must try to get the second 109 which, by now, had vanished from view so I got my head quickly back into the visor of the AI. As the blip (from the Me 109) emerged from minimum range behind us, I started with my running commentary to Harry. We would shortly decide when to execute a rapid 360 degree turn to port and arrive up behind him!

So there we were, somewhere over enemy territory, with the pilot blinded and shouting to the navigator to help him control the plunging Mosquito. Meanwhile the navigator was trying to carry out the interception of a known enemy aircraft, all on his own, not taking the slightest notice of the yells from his pilot or realising that there was no response to his instructions! Incidentally, the enemy aircraft was, now, directly behind them! For the outcome of this shambles, we must go back to Harry's report:

> '. . . with head now well in the box, Mike commenced reading off the range as this enemy aircraft emerged from minimum range behind. But even the best Navigator cannot carry out an interception with the help of a blind pilot and the range had increased to 6,000 feet astern before I could even see my instruments. We turned hard port but contact went out of range at 14,000 feet. Enemy aircraft is presumed to have turned starboard as we turned about; throughout we had been flying at 18,000 feet with our target flying about 240 I.A.S. There were no further signs of activity so we set course for base.'

Looking back, I think we must be grateful for small mercies, because in the few moments when Harry's vision was completely blotted out, things could have gone horribly wrong. Of course, after it was all over, I could picture myself leaning across my blinded pilot, grabbing the stick . . . flying us back to West Raynham . . . and, having somehow got Harry out of his seat . . . making a safe landing and saving his life! In practice, it didn't quite work out like that and the night was not quite over anyway.

As we crossed the Channel and flew back over East Anglia, the weather was closing in and the cloud base got lower and lower. When we finally got into the approach Harry (who by this time was fully recovered) could hardly see the funnel lights or the runway lights. Somehow we just managed to crawl in and put 941 down as the mist closed in around us. The next aircraft following us in to land at West Raynham – I think it was Greg and Steve – had to pull away and fly on to our old base at Wittering, where the weather was still clear. As I concluded in my log, it was a 'Most Unpleasant Trip'.

The Operational Research Section's Report for the night 27/28 had some interesting comments:

> 'A significant point about the Bourg-Leopold and Aachen escort, where the Serrate aircraft were detailed to cross and recross the bomber stream, was that only a few Serrate contacts were obtained although the bombers had fairly

heavy casualties. In fact one Serrate aircraft reported seeing six bombers shot down on the way home [Note, we saw three] but obtained no Serrate contacts [Note, neither did we!]. The intercepted traffic indicates that the main opposition to the bombers on these raids was the Medium Range Benito controlled night-fighters, and it is possible that only a few enemy fighters were responsible for the majority of the bomber losses.'

We were glad that Neville Reeves and Mike O'Leary, of 239, had got an Me 110; they were an exceptional crew and we would have been pleased to have had them on 141 in the early days of Serrate . . . There is one other postscript to the night's operations . . . this time it was the turn of Flying Officer Gallagher (with W/O McLean) to have engine failure – when they were chasing a presumed E/A – and have to 'return on one' . . .

We did two more NFTs – prior to operations – before the end of May, but on both occasions ops were scrubbed on account of bad weather. One can realise how worried the D-Day planners must have been with the poor weather conditions continuing right through the spring of 1944 and the softening-up raids for the invasion having to be cancelled time and again. The period of 5/6 June, when they must 'GO' or else face a long and dangerous postponement, was now only one week away!

The 141 CO, Wing Commander Frank Davis, of whom there has been little mention, was – like Ken Roberts before him – not having a very easy ride. Frank had also had to face the loss of a number of crews; as well as the ongoing problems with the Mosquito IIs and the poor serviceability record of our AI and Serrate equipment.

In April there had been the loss of two Flight Commanders on successive nights, and earlier in May there had been the disappearance of Flying Officer Watkins and his navigator, in daylight – on a practice flight – without a trace. Now Frank, who like 'the Major' was getting on in years, was going to have to face another blow, on top of the unmistakable feeling that our rivals at West Raynham, in the shape of No. 239 Squadron, were starting to turn in rather better results (i.e. for E/A destroyed) than we were, on 141.

Warrant Officer Potter with his Nav/Rad Flight Sergeant Gray had joined 141 on 18 May. Eleven days later, whilst on a training flight, and having taken off in a Mosquito II just after noon, their aircraft appeared to explode in mid-air. They crashed a few miles west of King's Lynn and both of them were killed outright. The Court of Enquiry, which was held on the station three days later, determined that the crash was due to loss of control, but were unable to discover whether it was due to structural failure or a high speed stall due to the inexperience of the pilot. The morning after they had gone in Frank sent for Harry and me and said that he had to drive up to the crash site. Understandably, he seemed to be very cast down by this latest disaster and he asked us if we would go with him, as he did not want to drive all the way there and back on his own.

We duly went with him and the three of us drove across to the village of Clenchwarton, and found the site on North Farm. It was a bit depressing. All that there was to see – in an expanse of fen land – was a large crater and a lot of very small pieces of aeroplane. We drove away in silence and lunched in King's Lynn on our way back to West Raynham.

During May, the squadron carried out 62 Serrate sorties, with only five early returns, but we only succeeded in destroying three enemy aircraft at the cost of two of our own (due to accidents), and 239 had now shot down a total of 19 E/A (10 of them in May!), to our 13.

This now meant that 239 Squadron led the three Serrate Mosquito squadrons in the number of enemy aircraft destroyed on bomber support in 100 Group, 19 to 239 Squadron 13 to 141 Squadron and 12 to 169 Squadron at Little Snoring. The figure of 13 for 141 does not include our successes whilst we were at Wittering and still in Fighter Command. This was the period June–December 1943.

We must have gone on leave at the beginning of June, because I can find nothing in my flying log-book until the 11th of the month when we did an NFT on our Mosquito II HJ941 (X) lasting one and a half hours. We repeated the process the following day and flew an op to Gelsenkirchen, in the Ruhr, but had no joy. The day after that, Harry and I were posted from 141 Squadron.

Thus we missed out on the D-Day operations – news of which I remember hearing on the radio and reading in the press, whilst safely at home in Ashford. It was a bit of an anticlimax. Although there was not much reaction from the German night-fighters (and therefore no 'trade' for us) it would have been fun to be there and to have seen something of the masses of shipping in the Channel which comprised the Invasion Fleet!

'What did you do on D-Day, Grandpa?'
'Well, Richard . . . actually I was on leave!'

Oh well, Harry and I had been able to make a minute contribution towards the softening up process during the preceding three months, which was something.

We also missed the departure of Howard Kelsey and Smithy, who were posted to the Bomber Support Development Unit at Foulsham, Norfolk. They had been on 141 since April 1943 and, without having had any previous experience in the night-fighter game, they started to score in the pioneering days of the Serrate operation and maintained their successful record throughout their tour. They made a very real contribution to the ultimate success of bomber support operations and continued to operate until the end of the war in Europe.

By that time they had increased their claims of enemy aircraft to nine destroyed, one probable and two damaged. Howard Kelsey later became the CO of 515 Squadron, with Smithy as his Navigator Leader. He led that squadron with distinction, being awarded a DSO to add to his two DFCs that he had won on 141; whilst Smithy, who had gained first the DFM and then the DFC with us, was awarded a well-deserved Bar to the latter. They were an exceptional crew and two nice people. Happily, 50 years on, I am still in touch with Smithy.

We also missed seeing Lucien Le Boutte leave the squadron at the end of his tour, when he was posted to the staff of the Belgian Inspector-General in the rank of Wing Commander! Later in the month he would return to West Raynham where, at a ceremonial parade, he would be presented with his recently awarded DFC by Air Commodore Addison, the AOC 100 Group. Various high-ranking officers from the Belgian Air Force and many other VIPs attended the parade but sadly, by that time, Harry and I had left Raynham for pastures new!

As a matter of passing interest, Harry and I had still not received our awards, although they had been gazetted some six month before 'the Major' was awarded his DFC. Another year was to pass before we were to have the honour of attending an investiture at Buckingham Palace.

On 3 June 1944 Frank Davis, the CO of 141, was posted to 100 Group

Headquarters and Charles Winn, an experienced night-fighter pilot and a former Flight Commander, who had been in at the birth of the Serrate operations, took over the squadron. Frank Davis had been with 141 since January 1943 and the Squadron Record states: '. . . that he was guide, philosopher and friend of all the Squadron, and one of the few remaining links with the Squadron's earliest days.'

He was our Flight Commander before he became CO and Harry and I had a lot to thank him for. We had also become good friends and later on, when his wife gave birth to a daughter, he did us the honour of inviting us to be joint god-fathers to the little girl!

Charles Winn was a completely different character! Winnie, as he was widely known, was an exuberant and happy extrovert, apart from being a successful night-fighter pilot who already had two tours behind him. Additionally, he had now had six months' invaluable experience on the planning staff at 100 Group Headquarters. His posting was a most popular one with both the aircrew and the ground crews. He was still in command of the squadron when Harry and I returned to 141 in the February of 1945.

Although, as already mentioned, Harry and I took no part in the D-Day operations, the following short extract from the Squadron History for 5/6 June cannot be left out of the story:

> 'This was the eve before D-Day, the invasion of Normandy, France. 946 aircraft of Bomber Command, with only 3 losses, carried out attacks on various Normandy coastal batteries and at least 5,000 tons of bombs were dropped during the night of 5/6th June 1944. There were numerous other operations . . .'

When we got back from our leave we were regaled with accounts of the invasion fleet and the activities of that night, much to our chagrin! And, to make matters worse, 239 Squadron had managed to chalk up two more successes!

Amongst the crews on 141 who welcomed the events of 6 June, more than most, were our two Frenchmen, F/Lt 'Bunny' D'Hautecourt and his little navigator, P/O Kocher. They had been on the squadron since February, had done a number of trips and were a very popular crew. Two days after the invasion they took off on a Serrate operation over northern France at 22.55 hours. Four hours later they crashed at Ford (141's old base on the Sussex coast), attempting a single-engined landing, and they were both killed.

Whether one engine was put out by combat, or by flak damage, or by engine failure is not stated in the squadron records. There was an added hazard to landing on any of the airfields along the coast at that time. They were full of aircraft supporting the Normandy operations, parked in every available space, including either side of the runways. If an aircraft swung off the runway, when landing, they were in trouble. Bunny D'Hautecourt, coming in on one engine, touched down on the runway, could not, with his crippled Mosquito, correct the swing and ran off the concrete onto the grass at high speed. He hit two fighter aircraft which were parked there and caught fire. Although they were rescued from the wreckage by some very brave men, the two Free Frenchmen died a few hours later. It was one of the saddest tragedies of the many we saw . . .

The two fighter aircraft with which Bunny d'Hautecourt collided were Spitfires from No. 442 (RCAF) Squadron. A ground crew servicing commando, who was warming up one of the Spits at the time, was also killed.

We even missed a change of Station Commander! Group Captain Nelson

AFC, was posted to neighbouring Great Massingham to take command there; and Group Captain L.C. Slee DSO, DFC became the new CO of West Raynham. He had had a distinguished career as a bomber captain and Commanding Officer of No. 49 Squadron in 5 Group of Bomber Command. Number 5 Group – with its outstanding AOC, Air Vice-Marshal Cochrane – was considered to be the élite Group amongst the 'Main Force' Groups in Bomber Command.

On 17 October 1942 5 Group carried out a hazardous daylight attack on the Schneider-Creusot armament factory in southern France, with 94 Lancasters flying in a loose formation and led by the CO of No. 49 Squadron.

The attack was deemed to be successful. The CO of 49 was Wing Commander Slee. Harry and I were only under his command for a few days, so we did not really know him and he did not stay at West Raynham for very long. We heard a rumour that he was suffering from ill-health but not before we also heard that he was a formidable character!

On 11 June 1944, three days before Harry and I were posted – supposedly 'tour expired' –, there was another accident on 141 and again it was a new crew, who had only been a short time on the squadron. Don Aris, with his meticulous research of the Squadron Records, has put together this horrifying, but feeling, report:

> 'F/Lt P.A. Riddoch 121206 with his Nav/Rad F/O C.S. Ronayne 152497, were on a training flight from West Raynham on the afternoon of the 11th June. At 17.30 hours their Mosquito HJ916 (Y) (which had been flown an hour earlier by Roy Marriott) appeared to explode and disintegrate in mid-air two miles South of Chippenham village, between Mildenhall and Newmarket, Suffolk.
>
> One report says this was due to the structural failure of the port wing. F/Lt Riddoch was blown out of the aircraft and his parachute was accidentally pulled – saving his life. He suffered from a dislocated right shoulder, a fractured jaw, and lacerations to his face and eye-lids. He was taken to the White Lodge E.M.S. Hospital in Newmarket. His Navigator, Flying Officer Ronayne, who was aged 33, was found dead from multiple injuries with his parachute covering him. He is buried in the churchyard of the lovely little church of St Andrew at Little Massingham. It is close by Great Massingham airfield and near to West Raynham. I visited his grave in 1990 . . . it is in a most peaceful and quiet situation.'

Perhaps I might be forgiven, as our time on 141 came to an end, for saying that latterly it was sometimes referred to as 'One Four-White Squadron', which was a marvellous tribute to Harry.

7 Life with The Boffins and Death at Home

– and how we nearly lost our lives on Mosquito MM797

This may be the moment for a brief summary of the overall situation in relation to the bomber support operations involving the Serrate fighters; but excluding the other airborne and ground-based countermeasures carried out against the enemy prior to, and since, the formation of No. 100 Group within Bomber Command.

I have suggested that these operations fell into seven phases, we were now coming to an end of Phase Five. Although Phases Six and Seven are still in the future, it seems appropriate to include a brief description of all seven phases here:

Phase One: Oct 1942–April 1943

The concept of using British night-fighters over enemy territory to counter the growing threat of the defending German night-fighters was born. The frequency used by the German AI radar was discovered and a 'homer' was designed and developed, which would enable the British long-range night-fighters – using also their Mk IV AI sets – to home onto and identify the defending German night-fighters.

Phase Two: April 1943–June 1943

During which No. 141 Squadron, under its commanding officer, Wing Commander J.R.D. Braham, was chosen to pioneer the 'Serrate' operation. The squadron was moved into No. 12 Group, Fighter Command, and relocated to Wittering, Northants. It was re-equipped with Beaufighter VIs, the Serrate homer was installed and training commenced (in Scotland).

Phase Three: June 1943–Sept 1943

Operations were commenced in support of raids by the heavy bombers of Bomber Command on Germany and Occupied Europe. The Beaufighters of 141 stalked the defending Ju 88s and Me 110s using the emissions from the German AI to find them and completing the interception on the Mk IV AI. They flew free-lance patrols, working out their own tactics as they went along, and proved that a success could be made of the Serrate operation. A number of German night-fighters were attacked and shot down, notably on the night of the great raid on the German rocket station at Peenemünde in August when three Me 110s and a Ju 88 were destroyed by the squadron.

Phase Four: Oct 1943–Jan 1944

The Beaufighters had insufficient range and speed for the task and the need for them to be replaced by the latest mark of Mosquito night-fighter became paramount. The whole Serrate operation was transferred into the newly formed (radar countermeasures) No. 100 Group and became part of Bomber Command. Number 141 Squadron – with two new Serrate squadrons – were to be re-equipped with Mosquitoes. All three squadrons then experienced serious problems with the Mosquitoes and with the AI and Serrate radar equipment, which severely hampered the entire operation.

Phase Five: Jan 1944–June 1944

The three Serrate squadrons were equipped with worn-out Mosquitoes from the Home Defence night-fighter squadrons. They were in no way suitable for operations over Germany and Occupied Europe. There were frequent engine failures – at one stage all the Mosquitoes were grounded – and a number of crews from 141 and the two new squadrons, 169 and 239, lost their lives. There was also a serious problem with the aerial system for the Serrate equipment on the Mosquitoes. The net result was that the Serrate operation and the vital harassment of the German night-fighter force was not available when it was needed most. Many crews of the heavy bombers were lost in the winter of 1943/44 as a result. During the latter two months of Phase Five, the serviceability of both the Mosquitoes and the radar equipment showed some improvement and a number of E/A were shot down by all three of the Serrate squadrons.

Phase Six: June 1944–Dec 1944

Two more squadrons of Mosquitoes – 85 and 157 – were moved across to 100 Group from Home Defence, and with two others – 23 and 515 – specialising in low-level intruding, there were now seven night-fighter squadrons operating in No. 100 (BS) Group. A Training Unit and a Development Unit had been formed and the Group's fighter arm was at its peak, and it was a more profitable period for the Serrate squadrons. But these improvements came too late to enable the Serrate squadrons to make a significant contribution to the Strategic Bomber Offensive, which was coming to an end as the Allied Armies moved across Occupied Europe towards Germany. In a sense, after D-Day, 'the ball was over'. Tactical daylight bombing (in which Bomber Command's fighters could play no part) was reintroduced. Thanks to the extent of the Allies' air superiority, deep penetrations to heavily defended targets became fewer than in the previous winter.

Opposition in the air and on the ground was starting to crumble and, by September, that 'Happy Valley' in the Ruhr was much nearer, even if it was still to be feared. Going low level when they could find 'no trade' at 20,000 ft, the Mosquito's claims continued to mount (one crew got four E/A destroyed, in one sortie). Above all, and this is what really mattered, Bomber Command's losses continued to drop in comparison with the awful winter of 1943/44.

Phase Seven: Jan 1945–May 1945

Now the Ball was definitely over for all but the unlucky few – there were a handful of deep penetrations but the bomber losses were minimal: for example, only two lost on Leipzig on 10 April. Our opposite numbers in the German *Nachtjagdgeschwadern* were overtaken by events and 100 Group's fighters ranged over Germany at will. Now often at low level, with bombs, cannon and napalm, they went for anything they could find. They also started to wonder what it would be like flying against Japan.

Harry and I were to see out Phase Six on the Bomber Support Development Unit (BSDU) with a few 'excursions' back to 141, before finally rejoining the squadron in February 1945. Some explanation of the work of BSDU is therefore required before our story can continue.

'The Secret War' in which Harry and I had now been involved for nearly three years involved a wide range of electronic and radar equipment, and to date we had merely been attempting to use some of it on operations against the enemy. Now we were to participate in the development and flight-testing of new and untried 'black boxes'.

Their identity was hidden by some weird and wonderful code-names, such as Monica; Mandrel; Airborne Grocer; Jostle; Perfectos. In general, we were involved in testing out a variety of radar homing devices, backward-looking AI Sets, and jamming equipment (to counter the enemy's airborne and ground radar defences).

The task of BSDU was to undertake the development and experimental work on the newly designed equipment; firstly by airborne trials over England, and then by taking it on operations over Germany. Reports would then be made out and a decision taken on whether modifications were needed before a final assessment was made regarding the operational value of the new 'black box' when, if the answer was affirmative, a production order was put in hand.

The unit had a fleet of nine Mosquitoes (of various marks) and was commanded by Wing Commander Rupert Clerke DFC. Additionally, there were two or three civilian scientists attached to BSDU who had specialised in the design and development of radar equipment, and with whom we – the half-dozen flying crews on the unit – worked in close co-operation. In other words, we had our own private boffins who supervised the work of the radar mechanics and checked that the new 'boxes' were working properly before we took off.

When we landed to make our reports, they were there and sometimes they had the offending piece of 'the gubbins' removed immediately to their workshop where, with soldering iron in hand, a few bits of wire and a resistor or two, they would effect a miraculous repair, and we would be back in the air, to test 'the George box' out. This was a good term to use, because our favourite boffin was George Bailey.

A distinguished academic, holder of three or four degrees and a brilliant scientist, George Bailey was the most delightful of men. He rendered great service to his country – as did other scientists – for which he was ultimately awarded the OBE. To be with him in his workshop for half an hour was an education in itself, and it was never too much trouble for him to explain to Harry and I what he was doing, although he must have found us pretty clueless at times! The other thing about George Bailey was that – like the legendary

Barnes Wallis – he was always concerned for us, the pilots and navigators, who had to take off with his inventions and try them out over Germany. Harry and I learned to have a deep liking and a great respect for him – feelings which have not diminished with the passing of the years.

BSDU was one of two new units formed soon after 100 Group made its appearance in Bomber Command. The other one was the Bomber Support Training Unit (BSTU) where night-fighter crews coming onto the Serrate squadrons were given a few weeks' training, before joining either 141, 169 or 239 Squadron. Both the instructors for the Training Unit (located at Great Massingham) and the crews for the Development Unit were being found, in the main, from tour-expired aircrew off the Serrate squadrons. At first there was a rumour that Harry and I would be going to the Training Unit, because Howard Kelsey and Smithy, who had finished their tour a few weeks before us, had gone to BSDU.

A switch must have been made, because they moved over to Great Massingham and we went to Foulsham. I've got a nasty feeling that Harry went to the SASO (Rory Chisholm) and said something like 'Mike and I would like to keep on operating, if that's at all possible, Sir; can't we go to BSDU instead of to the Training Unit?' He was speaking for himself!

I would have greatly preferred to have a nice peaceful six months off ops at BSTU! I would have liked to do some instructing! *Except!* I would have not enjoyed being flown around East Anglia by young and inexperienced pilots . . . particularly at night! Anyway Harry had now got the bit firmly between his teeth, and the drug of operational flying – as with Bob Braham – had worked its way deep into his system. So, off to BSDU we went, with him trailing his reluctant navigator behind him!

I have no strong memories of RAF Foulsham. Still in Norfolk, it was a wartime airfield and a hutted camp. It lay further to the east than West Raynham and about 15 miles to the north-west of Norwich. In any case, we were only to be there for a few months before the BSDU was moved to Swanton Morley. There was another reason why I did not spend many of my off-duty hours at Foulsham! Through the good offices of Rupert Clerke I found myself in the pleasant village of Aylsham. Here I met, first, the daughter of the local midwife, and then the daughter of the local doctor – of whom, more anon. Aylsham was only 10 miles from Foulsham.

Predictably, our first flights went down in my log-book as 'Radar Tests'. Unpredictably, we found ourselves flying a later Mark of Mosquito than we had had – and suffered – on the squadron! We were not that pleased to learn that the Development Unit had Mark VI and Mark XIX Mosquitoes on its strength, whilst poor old 141 was still struggling with its clapped out Mark IIs.

But we did not really have time to settle down in our new surroundings before we were off on leave again. This time we had an important date to keep: Harry's wedding to Joan on 23 June, with me as best man. We set off from Foulsham on Thursday 22 June. It was an epic journey, in more ways than one. Our destination was Aberdeen, but first we had to go to Scarborough.

We could not attempt to drive all the way to Scotland (without stealing a lot of petrol coupons!) so we went courtesy of the old London and North Eastern Railway, the LNER, starting from East Rudham on the single-track line through King's Lynn due west across to Peterborough. Then north to York, where we changed trains again, and on to Scarborough, which we reached late in the evening.

On Friday 23rd Harry and Joan were married. She was in her Wren's uniform and supported by a small group of friends from her unit, and I was about the only other person present. After a short reception party, the three of us set off for the railway station where we caught a train back to York and, picking up the mainline train from London to Scotland, we settled back for the rest of the long journey to Aberdeen!

Once more we arrived late in the evening and there, on Aberdeen Station, the bride and groom (on their first night of marriage) went their separate ways: the former to her home with her mother . . . the latter to a hotel, with his best man! On the following day, 24 June, they started all over again and – with a traditional family wedding – Joan was married in white which was what she had so much desired.

The reason for the two weddings? Because Joan – by virtue of serving in the Wrens – had not spent the required period resident in her own parish (or the Scottish equivalent!) she could not have a white wedding unless the knot had been legally tied beforehand – elsewhere! After yet another reception party and plenty of wee drams I caught a taxi to the station, and round about midnight (having seen Harry and Joan safely on their way at last) I crawled onto The Aberdonian to head back towards London, and the start of my own leave. The journey was relieved by the presence of a naval lieutenant in the compartment, who was good enough to share a bottle with me. But whether it contained whisky, gin or brandy I had – by the time we reached King's Cross on Sunday the 25th – no idea!

When we met up again, at the beginning of July, the first thing that Harry said to me when I asked him politely 'how married life was suiting him' was to reply, with great force: 'Look Boy, getting married isn't going to make the slightest difference to what you and I are doing and we are going to press on just the same as we have always done! If you ever see that it is starting to make a difference, you are going to bloody well tell me!'

Needless to say, getting married made not the slightest difference to the way in which Harry approached his flying. I never had to encourage him to press on, as the saying was, in those days. Rather, the reverse! As the weeks started to go by without any operational flying (our new equipment at BSDU was not yet ready to take on ops) he broached the idea that we might take a night off, go back to West Raynham, 'borrow' a Mosquito from 141, and do a trip with them! This was another of those bright tricks specially thought up to frighten navigators, one that he had picked up from our irrepressible former CO, Bob Braham! I remember gulping several times before saying: 'Yes, chum – a jolly good idea!' (whilst my inner man was saying 'don't be such a bloody fool!')

To make matters worse (for navigators with 'press on' type pilots), one of the first things we heard when we got back to Foulsham was the news that W/Cdr Braham was missing. He had taken off on yet another daylight Ranger operation in a Mosquito and set out for Denmark to look for trouble – he found it. Pitting his skills against the single-engined day-fighters, once too often, he was attacked and shot down by two Fw 190s.

How he got his crippled and burning aircraft down on the shore at Ringkobing Fiord, Denmark – and saved his own life and that of his navigator – no one will ever know . . . but he and F/Lt Walch DFC survived to be captured, becoming prisoners-of-war and released in May 1945, when the war in Europe came to an end.

It took several weeks for this story to filter through, during which aircrew and ground crew alike on 141 were plunged into gloom. Our only cause for relief was that he did not have Sticks Gregory with him, when he took off on his 15th operation whilst 'on rest' on the Headquarters Staff of No. 2 Group. Rumour had it that he had just picked up F/Lt Walch, who had been quite comfortably sitting in the mess, reading and enjoying a break, after a strenuous tour of operations and who really had no idea what he was letting himself in for! Twenty-four hours later, after a nightmare dogfight, the Mosquito on fire, a crash landing on a foreign shore, and he found himself sitting out the rest of the war in a German prison camp!

When we, of 141, heard that Bob was POW we were relieved on two counts. Firstly, that he was alive, and secondly, that he was safely tucked away in *Stalag Luft 3* at Sagan, in eastern Germany. We all knew that if he had gone on – as he would have done – flying lone sorties in daylight over enemy territory, his luck would have run out and he would have killed himself. Now, hopefully, and with all due respects to John Cunningham and Branse Burbridge, the greatest night-fighter pilot ever produced by the Royal Air Force (with over 300 operational sorties to his name) would survive the war.

The news that W/Cdr Braham was missing was not the only bad news from West Raynham that we heard when we returned to BSDU at Foulsham, from our sortie to Scarborough and Aberdeen. Angels, F/Lt Paddy Engelbach, had gone missing on the night of 27/28 June, flying in support of attacks on flying-bomb sites, railways and communications in northern France, by over 1,000 heavy bombers. (*NB:* Three weeks had now passed since the successful D-Day Landings in Normandy, and Bomber Command – still operating in a tactical role – was employing maximum effort to support the Allied armies as the soldiers fought their way inland from the beaches.) Sadly, we also heard that Angels had taken Ron Mallett with him.

Ron, who had recently flown with Graham Rice and 'the Major' – helping them both to destroy a German night-fighter apiece – and awarded a well-earned DFC, was on his third tour. He had been on operations for the best part of three years, having been one of the many air gunners who remustered to become AI Operators as their gun turrets were converted into Mk IV AI sets. Older than most of us, having come up the hard way, he was an extremely nice man and an exceptional Nav/Rad.

When we heard later that Angels had baled out of their stricken Mosquito, landed safely and been taken prisoner, we were distressed to learn that Ron had been killed, probably as their aircraft disintegrated and broke up . . . he was a great loss to the squadron. He lies in Eindhoven (Woensal) General Cemetery, not far from one of the old German night-fighter airfields. Angels wrote up a report of what happened to them, when he was released from captivity in May 1945, and returned to the squadron.

It is well worth reading because it shows how the German night-fighter crews were attempting to turn the tables on the Serrate fighters. For some time – probably since the pioneer operations in June/July/August of 1943! – our pilots' nerves were set on edge by a shout (over the intercom), as we peered into our AI sets, of 'There's Something Behind Us!'

It will be remembered that the Mk IV AI sets had a short coverage behind the fighter of *c.*2–3,000 feet. A tell-tale sign that another aircraft might be behind you was when you suddenly spotted a blip – fainter than a contact picked up in front, hovering at about 2–3,000 feet, and then seeing the range starting to decrease. At

that point, it became necessary to draw one's pilot's attention to the matter . . .
the hunter had become the hunted!

I am certain that – on many occasions – I panicked too quickly, when I saw a
stray blip at a range of 2,000 feet. Often, I am sure, it was another aircraft passing
harmlessly on its way, and not out looking for us at all! All I was doing mostly,
when I yelled out to Harry that there was something behind us, and he had to
take evasive action, was to worry him unnecessarily and waste precious hunting
time. I strongly suspect that many of my fellow 'knob twiddlers' did the same!

Behind Angels and Ron, in the early hours of 28 June 1944, was a hunter – and
it was no stray blip. Behind their Mosquito was a Heinkel 219, one of the latest
German night-fighters, with a performance infinitely superior to that of
the Mosquito FII. Angels's report, which is included in Don Aris's History of
141, made out nearly a year after the event, reads as follows:

> 'After patrolling North Holland for 1 hour at 20,000 feet, Navigator gave order
> HARD ABOUT but then reported there was nothing there. He then reported
> that we were being heavily predicted. I turned South, there was three/quartered
> moon, extremely clear visibility and bright Northern Lights. Cloud eight/tenths
> at 3–4,000 feet. Suddenly the Navigator ordered "HARD ONTO THE
> RECIPROCAL!" as I threw the aircraft over I asked if there was anything
> behind.
>
> The answer was a series of judders as my tail was shot off and I went into a
> spin. I pulled the aircraft out of the spin but was immediately hit again. At
> about 2,500 feet the aircraft disintegrated and I was thrown out through the
> canopy. I opened my parachute after a long search for it, and my fall was
> broken at about 1,200 feet, and I landed unhurt. The Navigator was killed. The
> Germans said that the aircraft which shot me down was a Heinkel 219.'

One of the last things that poor old Ron Mallett must have seen was that faint
blip disappearing into minimum range, and then, as the Mosquito went into a
spin, he may not have had time to find his parachute and clip it onto his harness,
before the aircraft broke up. Angels, with his pilot's 'chute attached to him when
he was thrown clear of the stricken Mosquito, was more lucky.

There was a short postscript to an earlier entry in Angels's flying log-book,
which was added at the same time; and it typifies his approach to life and his
sense of humour, which was always lurking just below the surface. Two days
before he was shot down himself, Angels had been amongst the crews who had
been engaged on the Air-Sea Rescue search out over the North Sea, which
had been set up when W/Cdr Braham was reported overdue on his last daylight
Ranger operation.

As already known, they did not find him. Angels had entered the ASR search
– he had been up for 2 hrs 35 mins, when he landed. He was now, a year later,
able to enter the remark 'Found him in *DulagLuft*!!' (*DulagLuft* was the
Luftwaffe interrogation camp, near Frankfurt, where all prisoners were taken
after they had first been shot down and captured.) They spent two/three weeks
there being questioned and harassed by the specially trained Intelligence officers,
before being transferred to a permanent POW camp. Bob Braham, shot down
on 25 June, was already there!

There was a touch of irony here, because Bob had done a lot for Angels, when
Paddy first came to 141, and as a new pilot struggled hard to master the little
tricks which the Bristol Beaufighter was apt to play on unsuspecting and inex-

perienced pilots! Bob admired courage in any form and he persevered with Flying Officer Engelbach when many other COs would have considered a posting such as that meted out to Harry and I by Guy Gibson, when he threw us off 29 Squadron.

But Angels had great courage and Bob kept him on 141, where he developed into one of the great personalities of the squadron, completing a large number of sorties on both Beaufighters and the Mosquitoes when the latter came into service.

He was always good company and I can remember one day, in the mess at dinner, he was reproved by the Station Chaplain for using the word 'bastard'. Never at a loss for an answer, Angels replied, in his smoothest tones, 'Oh, I don't know Padré . . . these days, if you call someone "an old bastard", it's really more a term of endearment than anything else!' And with this disarming reply, the padré, who was pretty remote from the aircrew anyway, was completely floored!

Whilst he was a POW Angels wrote some poetry. It will be remembered that he had spent two years up at Oxford before the war and, like Richard Hillary, added to his education by flying on operations against the enemy. Richard Hillary, recovering from his burns, wrote his unsurpassed book *The Last Enemy*. Angels, in a German prison camp, put together half a dozen poems which are unknown, except to his widow, Helena, and a handful of his close friends. He showed me these poems, when he rejoined 141 at Little Snoring in August 1945, and I immediately asked him if I could have them copied. I have always treasured them, and they are beside me now, as I write. Angels himself is long since dead, killed in a tragic post-war flying accident, having decided to stay on in the Air Force.

Two of his poems appeared in *Out of the Blue, The Role of Luck in Air Warfare 1917–1966*, edited by 'Laddie' Lucas and published by Hutchinson's in 1985. One of them was this sonnet, which was clearly written with the recent experience of being shot down over Holland very much in his mind:

'SONNET'

I have been near that state which men call death,
And given up my life ere now as lost.
In fact I have, with truth, been known to boast
That once I thought I'd breathed my final breath.
Yet cabin-trapped, or hanging underneath
A silken billow above a hostile coast,
I cannot say what thoughts were uppermost
In my mind, I did not feel my teeth
Begin to chatter, or the tightening cord
Of panic bind my brain, and seemed to miss
The awful stab of late contrition's sword.
The next time may be different but this
I know, that as you go to meet your Lord
A strange, warm comfort calms you with its kiss.

P.S. Engelbach.

Squadron Leader P.S. Engelbach, Commanding Officer of No. 23 Squadron, was killed, while flying a DH Venom at night, 15 February 1955. I hope, with all my heart, that he again found that 'strange, warm comfort that calms you with its kiss' . . .

Before picking up the story of our frustrating seven months on the Bomber Support Development Unit time must be spared to see how my brother, Rodney, was faring in his attempt to complete his training and get into ops. We left him, in April, along with hundreds of other 'surplus' members of aircrew, kicking his heels at Harrogate. Although the RAF's losses had been severe enough (the Battle of Berlin alone had resulted in Bomber Command losing 2,690 aircrew dead and another 987 out of action as POWs), the enormous success of the Empire Air Training Scheme had produced more qualified aircrew by the summer of 1944 than the three operational Commands could absorb.

It is important to note that these men, although qualified as pilots, navigators, WOP/AGs, etc., had not been through an OTU; so they could not be posted to a front-line squadron. The OTUs were only located in England and there was a long queue of desperately keen young men trying to get into them, becoming more and more downcast as the war started to pass them by. The word 'anti-climax' doesn't even begin to describe their feelings.

At the same time, the powers that be were desperate to find something for them to do, other than sending them on almost indefinite leave! There were also, in wartime Britain, some other jobs where labour was in short supply: could the two

A group of RAF Officers at the Running Sheds of the old London and North Eastern Railway at Peterborough in the summer of 1944. They had been asked to volunteer for duty as 'Second Stokers' on the railway until they could get a posting and complete their operational training. At this time there were a large number of 'surplus' aircrew at Harrogate (and elsewhere) who could not finish their training and get posted to an operational Squadron. My brother, Rodney, was one of them... and he can be seen, second in from the right, holding a long-handled shovel, which is bigger than he is! The only caption for this unbelievable photograph is 'Anti-climax'.

be matched together? The following extract is taken from Rodney's diary for 29 May 1944 (one week before D-Day). It has not previously seen the light of day, and for once the word 'unbelievable' may be used in its true sense.

At the top of the page is a large arrow pointing towards the words 'Volunteers for Firemen'.

'At 17.00 hrs F/Lt Holford came in to announce a special parade for pilots and WOP/AGs. Much speculation as to subject. We all paraded in field after dinner at 19.15 hrs and as expected a Groupie from H.Q. arrived and began to talk. He made to us what must surely be one of the most extraordinary proposals ever made to Officer Aircrew saying that due to the surplus of pilots for fighters and bombers, we should have nothing to do for months. He was asking for volunteers to become Firemen – on the Railways, for three months, to fill a very urgent need for Stokers!

All were flabbergasted! Everyone just laughed. After some talk and a show of volunteer hands, the parade was dismissed. All just talked about the proposal, it left all of us astounded, I then went for a walk to a nearby pub to get a drink. It was closed so I went on to one about 3½ miles from camp, where I had some cider with some of the boys, all going "CHUFF! CHUFF!".

In Camp later, a demonstration took place which was very funny. A hand-cart, rigged as a locomotive with a tin boiler and funnel stuffed with paper, flaming up the funnel, with whistles blowing and shrieks of laughter, the "engine" was pushed about and onto the parade ground. A parody of battle drill – as for engine driving "FALL IN" was done. As for engine driving number, "I AM NO.1 FIREMAN, I CARRY A SHOVEL etc SIR!" All permanent staff came out to watch and laugh. One of the best "rags" I am ever likely to see.'

We must leave Rodney and his friends there for the moment and return to BSDU. We may have had a few problems in getting used to our new role testing out the 'black boxes', but they were nothing compared to those of the frustrated men at Harrogate being asked to volunteer as stokers on the London and North Eastern Railway!

In the account of the raid on the night of 27/28 June, when Paddy Engelbach was shot down, there is mention of the bombers attacking flying-bomb sites, and in my log-book the first entry (for a 30-minute radar test) includes a brief comment on our leave: 'Mosquito VI 181 F/Lt White RADAR TEST. Back from wizard leave with Harry now a married man. Self spent week avoiding Doodlebugs.'

About a week after D-Day the Germans had launched the first of their so-called secret weapons, the Flying Bomb, commonly called the 'Doodlebug'. These weapons – pilotless aircraft – were launched from sites, looking rather like ski ramps, on the French coast and, in the main, they were aimed at the London area where the Germans thought that (lacking any accurate guidance system) they might do the greatest damage and affect the morale of the war weary citizens of the Metropolis.

Like other servicemen, I only encountered the Doodlebugs when on leave and spending time in or near London although, later on, Harry and I were to fly two or three sorties against them as they came in across the Channel. There is no need to remind anyone who was in London at the time of the sound they made, like a two-stroke motor-cycle, 2–3,000 feet up in the air, and coming nearer all the time and then the awful silence, as the motor cut out, and you knew it was falling to earth somewhere close. You hoped, not too close.

I was glad to get back to the safety of Norfolk! The V-2s were the second of the two secret weapons which were being developed at the Rocket Station at Peenemünde, raided by Bomber Command in 1943, and it is generally accepted that the attack of 17/18 August delayed the deployment of these weapons until after the invasion of Europe had successfully taken place. We carried out a number of local flights during July, testing out various pieces of radar equipment, sometimes with lengths of wire hanging out of them, where George Bailey and his colleagues had not had long enough to tie up all the ends . . . and time was pressing.

We even took part in a camouflage test to ascertain whether glossy or matt-finished aircraft were more easily seen in a searchlight beam. Halifaxes of 4 Group acted as our targets, and it was found that the glossy aircraft were more difficult to see.

Towards the end of the month we carried out two 'buzz-bomb' patrols (this was yet another name for these pilotless aircraft, which were really weapons of the next war rather than being likely to have any significant effect on 'our' war). Both trips were abortive. The first time we were informed, when we were just off the Suffolk coast, that the cannon were on 'Safe' – we were not amused. The second effort to get ourselves a 'buzz-bomb' ended, after we had seen someone else shoot one down, by a total failure of all our electrical equipment and we crawled back into Foulsham muttering such words as 'It was never like this on 141!' and others, less polite.

Twice we went over to West Raynham, with the intention of borrowing an aircraft from the squadron and doing an op with them: each time the night's operations were cancelled due to the weather; and we had to return empty handed to Foulsham. The third time we were lucky.

My log for 28 July reads: '23.50 Mosquito 11 713 (R) F/Lt White OPS. 141 B Flt. 600 Heavies on Stuttgart. 40 Missing. 2 Ju 88s Destroyed S.S.W.Metz. Greg and Steve got another which we saw go down. No Serrate, 490's HAD IT. 13.40 hrs.'

It was just like old times, and Chiefy Stanley and the rest of our old ground crew were over the moon including my faithful Canadian radar mechanic, John Kendrick. Apart from Greg and Steve's 88, which we saw going down in flames (they also saw one of ours!), the CO with Scotty claimed a 'Damaged', also a Junkers 88, so it was a good night for 141, who operated with 10 Mosquitoes, and there were no early returns. Nine aircraft of 239 Squadron also operated, but on this particular night they did not add to their score.

The Synopsis of Serrate Operations No. 53, for the week ending 28/29 July 1944, issued by the Operational Research Section at No. 100 Group Headquarters, had the following general comment: 'Support has been given to bomber operations on five nights during the week. 107 sorties were dispatched and 97 carried out a patrol. One aircraft is missing. 6 enemy aircraft have been destroyed, and one damaged, all from initial A.I. contacts.'

The ORS Report gives the overall picture of the operations which took place on the night 28/29 July. It provides a clear illustration of the way in which the high-level Serrate fighters were being used during the period following D-Day and as the Allied armies started to break out of the Normandy beach-head and move eastwards across northern France. Whilst the heavy bombers were continuing to give tactical support to the troops on the ground (and as the autumn nights started to get longer), they resumed the strategic bombing of major industrial targets in Germany. The report also provides the background for the trip that Harry and I made that night, when we went back to West Raynham and were third time lucky!

'Night of 28th/29th July, 1944.
The main attacks on this night were on Stuttgart and Hamburg and attacks were also made on a Pas de Calais target. The Mandrel Screen was used in the North Sea and a Bullseye and a Window diversion flew towards North Holland.

The Serrate aircraft were divided between escort of the Hamburg bombers, escort of the Stuttgart bombers, and patrols at Beacons in North Germany (Hummer, Quella and Puma) and at Beacons in France and Southern Germany, including Kuli.

Both the Hamburg and the Stuttgart bombers lost heavily on this night, and it is clear that the enemy night-fighters were not seriously diverted from these attacks by the "Spoofs".

On the Stuttgart raid the enemy fighters carried out interceptions over a considerable part of the bomber route. Beacon Kuli appears to have been the main assembly point, for interceptions carried out near the target.

The Serrate aircraft in the North reported very few suspicious A.I. contacts, but obtained two Serrate contacts, one near Heligoland and one near Emden, which were followed for some time before being lost.

The Stuttgart escort reported no Serrate contacts, but obtained several A.I. contacts, presumably on enemy aircraft. A visual on an Me 110 was achieved, but this was lost after the A.I. had gone U/S.

Three Ju 88s were destroyed following initial A.I. contacts near Beacon Kuli by aircraft on Beacon Patrols, two by 141/R (F/Lt White and F/Lt Allen) and one by 141/Y (P/O Gregory and P/O Stephens). These three aircraft were destroyed between 00.35 and 00.52 hours, and were probably aircraft heard ordered to Kuli from the North at about 23.54 hours. 141/A (W/C Winn and F/Lt Scott) obtained, in the Trappes area at 00.47 hours, a visual on a Ju 88 with a white light in its nose, crossing 50 feet above them. At this time the observer was examining some interference. This aircraft was attacked and is claimed as Damaged.

Discussion.
The main points of interest during the operations of the week considered are:
(1) There has been an increase in the number of Serrate contacts reported, although this number is still very small. Three Serrate contacts have been chased for 20 minutes or more.
(2) The Beacons still provide a profitable patrol for the Serrate aircraft. On the 28/29th July three enemy aircraft were shot down near Beacon Kuli.
    100G/TS.4025/1/ORS
    16th August, 1944'

There are one or two words of explanation needed for a better understanding of the ORS Report:

1.   *The Mandrel Screen* was provided by Nos 171 and 199 Squadrons of 100 Group, flying Halifaxes (earlier it had been Stirlings), carrying electronic jamming equipment – for the purpose of jamming the enemy's *Freya* radio-location units and their other GCI systems, thus impeding their task of detecting the incoming heavy bombers.

2.   *Bullseye Operations* were a force of bombers, made up with a number of aircraft from the OTU, which would fly off from England in a completely different direction from the main attacking force, in order to divert the attention of the German Controllers, in the hope that they would send off their fighters on a wild goose chase after the spoof raid. The spoof raiders had instructions to turn back (and head for home!) soon after crossing into enemy territory, or just before they reached it!

3.   *Escort*, as used in these reports, is somewhat misleading. It gives the impression that the Serrate fighters were formating on the bombers and flying a close escort in the manner of day-fighters. This is quite incorrect (for reasons given in earlier chapters). The Serrate fighters were flying individual freelance sorties, sometimes in the vicinity of the bomber stream, sometimes many miles away! The word 'patrol' also needs an explanation. For defending fighters – whether day or night – working under a GCI Controller, a fairly accurate patrol line is usually laid down. We, the long-range fighter crews of 100 Group, working without the assistance of a Ground Controller, gave a broad interpretation to the word 'patrol', roaming far and wide above the Third Reich in the hope of finding, and upsetting, one of our opposite numbers.

4.   *Beacons* are the radio beacons used by the German Controllers to assemble their night-fighters before vectoring them into the bomber stream. We ourselves did not have the necessary equipment whereby we could home onto these beacons: life would have been easier if we had! We simply knew the locations of these assembly beacons through the intelligence services, and would set course accordingly. When, by DR, we reached the general area where they were supposed to be, there was nothing we could see, or hear, and we would wander about in the hope that we navigators, with our heads firmly in the box, could pick up either a Serrate or an AI contact.

5.   The reference in the report to aircraft being 'heard ordered to Kuli' stems from electronic intelligence. The RAF's first electronic intelligence, or Elint as it became known, was the Wireless Intelligence Development Unit. It had its listening equipment installed in aircraft as well as in the ground stations. It was from Elint that ORS learned of the messages sent out to the gathering Ju 88s and Me 110s who were, in turn, sent speeding towards Beacon Kuli as we steered SE across Germany to meet them. I wish we could have heard them, too!

6.   *Serrate Contacts.* Lastly, it will be noted that the successful claims came from AI contacts, rather than from Serrate contacts. In the spring and summer of 1944, as the sorties mounted by the Serrate fighters slowly increased and more attacks were made on the defending fighters, the Germans realised that we were homing in on their AI, and changed the frequencies and their AI equipment. Although this had been anticipated by the British scientists and modifications were being made to our equipment, the net result as the weeks went by was that 141, 239 and 169 picked up fewer and fewer Serrate contacts. The problem was mainly solved

by a change of tactics and, in the latter part of the year, by new aircraft with more advanced AI sets.

With this background, we can turn at last to Harry's report of our night out with 141!

'We took off from West Raynham at 23.00 hours and climbed to 20,000 feet. Course was checked on "Gee" and A.I. gun-defended area, interference, believed to radiate from Gilze/Rijen and Eindhoven A/Fs. This sortie was quite uneventful till at 00.35 hrs. (five minutes after E.T.A.) we reached the estimated position of "KULI" though no lights on the ground indicated the position of a beacon.' ["Kuli" was sited in the area of Metz and Saarbrücken, and was over 100 miles NW of Stuttgart.]

It was at this time that A.I. contact was made with a bomber stream a few thousand feet below, being identified by Window activity, and presumed to be the "spoof" force detailed to attack Frankfurt. A few seconds later, now flying North at 17,000 feet a head-on A.I. contact was obtained at max. range. Range closed rapidly to 5,000 feet, when Mosquito turned hard port about, and found target to be orbiting port, at about rate 1½ (turns).

Contact was maintained, through three gentle port orbits, between 2/3,000 feet away and slightly port and, as near as we could judge, on the same level. Target straightened out on a vector of 210 degrees Magnetic and we closed gently to 1,200 feet and there first obtained a visual. Closing further to 300 ft., where I identified A/C as a Ju 88. I asked Mike what he thought it was, no exhausts being visible, and was shocked to hear him reply "Me 110!". (I feel, however, that some allowance must be made for these poor harassed navigators' night vision).

I dropped back to 500 ft, waited for a minute or two till E/A obligingly placed himself with a patch of cirrus cloud, illuminated by the moon, as a background – and opened fire with a two second burst, causing in order of appearance, strikes in both engines and fuselage, pieces to blow off and pass overhead and, at end of burst, a sizeable fire in port engine and fuselage.

E/A dived away to port in flames and continued to jink violently, alternating steep dives with very steep climbs till, just above ground level, it exploded and was seen to continue to burn on the ground. Although I could see E/A clearly all the way down, A.I. contact was maintained in case a second burst would be found necessary; it just wasn't – time 00.42 hrs.

We had now lost height to 12,000 ft. and had only just regained 16,000 ft., still heading 210 degrees (M), when our second A.I. contact was obtained at max. range ahead, quite indistinct and Mosquito had to be manoeuvred carefully at full throttle at the best angle off, 30 degrees port. Range was closed very slowly to 7,000 ft. and there for a moment or two, it remained, although we were flying at an I.A.S. of 275 mph. Pushing the nose down we lost a precious 1,500 ft. and increased speed to 300 and closed gently to 1,200 ft., where I obtained a visual, climbing as best we could as range decreased, and closing further to 200 ft. identified A/C as a Ju 88.

Fortunately there was no argument in the cockpit this time, so no further time was wasted. Dropping back to 500 ft. I opened fire with a two seconds burst, everything seemed to be going well, but when I stopped firing the fires just went out. Two further one second bursts were fired as range closed slowly, at the end of each burst I had to remove my head from the gun-sight to regain my visual. Each of these bursts scored direct hits, again blowing off several pieces, but the fires started each time, just would not continue to burn. At last it appeared to have dawned into the thick German skull that there was, possibly, someone behind – and he whipped up his starboard wing, preparing to "peel off" to port. With 90 degrees of bank, presenting me with a target 10 degrees off, and no more than 300 ft. away, very slightly below, I fired a fourth burst, of two seconds.

The fires resumed their sizeable proportions and this time continued to burn, while E/A slipped smartly into the ground dead below Mosquito, where it exploded. Having had ample warning of our presence and he, himself, being in such a favourable position at the beginning of our 4th burst, I was quite surprised to experience no return fire from the opposing "Crystal Gazer", cum "Air Gunner", – perhaps he was already exploring heights of the order of 60,000 ft. plus! Time 00.52 hrs

[Then we saw Greg and Steve's Ju 88 go down. They had done two tours without a break; and now, nearing the end of their second tour they were claiming a number of successes. We were delighted for them. Au.]

Knowing ourselves to be at least 60 miles SSW. of "Kuli" we set course NNE and at 00.57 hrs. (approx) were gratified to see another A/C going down in flames to the NE knowing that 141/Y was operating in this area. Shortly afterwards, flying North through the bomber stream, navigator's twitch set in; but even when the mass of A.I. contacts had faded from the tube, considerable interference remained, to make the Mk.IV Set unusable for several minutes.

By discussion on the ground later, it is believed that this interference radiates from "Mandrel" aircraft in the stream, thus making any escort of the stream impossible. [I have already mentioned some of the other reasons why any close escort of the bomber stream was impossible at night.]

Between 01.05 and 01.12 hrs. two other A/C were seen going down in flames to the East, and by the size of the explosions and the various coloured lights, dropped from both, were assumed to be bombers. Obviously a number of fighters must have found their way into the stream, South of beacon "Kuli". [This is borne out by the ORS Report.]

At 01.20 hrs. we set course for the estimated position of KULI and returned uneventfully to base, picking up West Raynham A.I. BEACON on the second time-trace, while crossing out at Ostend (145 miles).'

Harry then felt free to add one or two more comments on the trip, whilst I was completing the Special Report Form, which all Navigators had to fill in at de-briefing. He continued:

'The success of this operation, it is felt, was due primarily to the excellent positioning of the Serrate fighters at a reasonable distance North of the stream, about 30 minutes before the bombers were due to pass through, thus giving adequate scope for a brief patrol round the beacon and for quite lengthy chases (i.e. 10 minutes) before the stream could interfere. The orbiting of the first Ju 88 destroyed on this sortie is not considered as evasive action, but is attributed to his position over, or quite close to, beacon Kuli.'

It is interesting to see how closely Harry's report, dictated immediately after we had landed, compares with the ORS Report, which was published two weeks later.

In the morning we flew back to Foulsham in great spirits, and that night I took the daughter of the District Nurse, Ursula Jenner, to the village hop in Aylsham. It was in the Foreword and Dedication to his book *Enemy Coast Ahead*, that Guy Gibson said, contrasting the lives led by soldiers, sailors and airmen during the war – and suggesting that their loved ones cannot see the former doing their jobs:

> 'Peace and war are vastly different. But the atmosphere our crews live in is shared by their next of kin.
>
> One moment they are together living their own lives and happy. A man and wife walking hand in hand down a country lane may in a few hours be separated, perhaps for ever. Picture peaceful England on a cool spring evening. The flowers are blooming, the hum of serenity is in the air. Suddenly there is a snarl of four motors, and a few hours later your airman is fighting the hell of flak and destruction over the target. At home they wait, brave and patient, asking the same questions again and again: "I hope he gets back all right; when are they due?"'

Ursula and I were not man and wife, and Harry and I did not have four motors – but that is the way it was for the relatives and friends who lived close to England's wartime airfields.

Throughout August we were airborne nearly every day testing the various 'black boxes', which were cobbled together so skilfully by our boffins. There was the tail warning device, code-named 'Monica', which was particularly needed in aircraft equipped with some of the new marks of AI, which had only forward coverage.

It will be remembered that the Mk IV AI (with all its limitations of range and clarity) did have a rearward coverage of 2–3,000 feet, which gave us some protection against any predatory Ju 88 turning the tables on us! Then there were the various homers, including an audible Serrate homer, as compared with the visual signals that we had been picking up from the German *Lichtenstein* AI sets since the inception of the bomber support operations.

As the radio/radar countermeasures war continued, the Germans, like us, were constantly changing their equipment and the frequencies which they were using. It was our scientists, men like George Bailey, who were occupied, throughout the war years, in keeping us one step in front of them. Harry and I were privileged to see them at work and to help them with the various development trials which were carried out at BSDU.

We did three ops during the month, one against the flying-bombs, and two bomber support trips. Both the latter were from West Raynham, one to Russelheim and the other to Kiel. We had no joy on any of these sorties. It was on the 7th that we flew our third and last 'Diver Patrol' (the official code name for the V-1s). The idea was to patrol up and down the French coast, between Calais and Le Treport at a height of 7–8,000 feet, looking down to try and spot the bombs when they were launched from the 'ski ramps'.

At night, and we had taken off at 22.15 hours from Foulsham, one could see the flame from the VI's motor making a trail, as it levelled out at *c.*2,000 feet – its course set for the south-east corner of England! The idea was, once you had spotted the tell-tale flame, to use your height and dive down on the thing at 300–400 m.p.h., hoping that you would arrive up within firing range by the time you had levelled out! You hadn't got long, because if you overshot you would have to break away and lose speed, and if you undershot you would never catch the flying-bomb in a stern chase before it had crossed the Channel and was over land.

The plan was to try to knock them out, if possible, whilst they were still over the sea. Once over England the task of destroying them was allocated to the ack-ack batteries. We saw one, dived down on it, and loosed off a six-second burst. We must have been out of range, because there was no satisfying explosion and the wretched thing went happily on its way. The weather then packed in across East Anglia, and we were diverted to Ford.

There were some skilled exponents in the business of shooting down the flying-bombs; 34 pilots were credited with destroying ten or more bombs, and one, Squadron Leader J. Berry of No. 501 Squadron, shot down 61½. He was awarded the DFC and 2 Bars, but sadly did not survive the war. Even though there had been many attacks on the launching sites, the scale of V1 flying-bomb attacks, which started on 13 June 1944, can be judged by the fact that some 8,000 were launched, causing 6,184 civilian deaths and 17,981 civilians seriously injured.

As the armies fought their way across France they overran the launch-sites on the coast, and for a short period the *Luftwaffe* took over, launching them from Heinkel 111s flying in – at low level – over the North Sea, when they were about sixty miles from the east coast. These attacks did not last for long, and the Home Defence night-fighter squadrons (notably No. 25), who had been starved of 'trade' for so long, accounted for a number of the lumbering old Heinkels.

But the Germans are nothing if not persistent, and after the flying bombs there came forth another product, which had also started life at the Rocket Development Station at Peenemünde. This time, as will be seen, the Germans had cleverly managed to produce a weapon against which there was no defence . . .

On 25 August 1944, we took a Mosquito VI on the strength of BSDU and went across to West Raynham to operate with 141. We also had on board the new SN II homer with which we had carried out a number of test flights during the month. This was the audible homer designed to replace the visual Serrate homer, which we had been using since June 1943. We took off from Raynham at 22.10 hrs, crossed the enemy coast 45 minutes later, and headed for the area of the Kuli beacon where we had had so much fun the previous month. We had no AI or Serrate contacts on the way. After about 20 minutes I got a head-on AI contact and we tried to turn in behind it. I must have made a bosh of it, because the next thing we knew was that I saw a blip appearing 3,000 ft astern!

For the next 15 minutes we orbited, first to port and then to starboard, after what we thought must be an enemy aircraft. When Harry at last got a visual, it turned out to be a Halifax! We thought we had been orbiting a little to the north of the bomber stream, and above it, and that the contacts had come from that source.

We were carrying drop tanks on the extremities of both wings, each containing 100 gallons (thereby extending our range). We now jettisoned the two tanks in order to be ready, if we got any more chases (the drop tanks tended to affect the manoeuvrability of the Mosquitoes). Unfortunately the starboard tank hit our AI elevation aerial and broke it off, thus rendering the Mk IV AI set u/s! On top of this disaster we found that the oxygen system was leaking and there would be insufficient for us to stay on patrol anyway.

We headed back to West Raynham, in not the best of tempers, and landed after 3 hours 50 minutes in the air. Having not got to bed until around 4.00 a.m. we slept through in the early afternoon. When we got down to the briefing room we found that ops were on again that night. So we quickly flew back to Foulsham for a new AI elevation aerial for 337, which we did not even have time to check properly, and were back at West Raynham again at 18.15 hrs, in time for briefing, for a trip to Kiel. My log entry shows that everything was not sweetness and light when we landed back at Foulsham in a hurry because we wanted to operate again that night. The Remarks Column reads: 'In mad rush back, had not time to test new elevation aerial in fact, no time even for tea. Greeted at Foulsham by thoughtless bods – nearly told them to fly it themselves.'

Kiel was attacked by 382 heavy bombers, of which 17 were lost, and we found that the SN II audible homer, from which we were hoping to pick up the 'dots' and 'dashes', signifying that we were in the vicinity of the German night-fighters, spent most of its time picking up signals from the *Freyas* (the ground radio-location stations), which were using the same frequency!

Trying to find the Ju 88s over Kiel with only the use of our old Mk IV AI set was futile, and the need for us to be re-equipped with one of the later marks of AI was becoming ever more urgent.

To add to our misery we ran into some bad weather, with the storm clouds rising to 26,000 ft. We landed back at Raynham at 1.30 a.m. and my last entry for these hectic two days reads: 'Sun 27th 15.30 F/Lt White Ret Foulsham. Both pretty done up, after fighting two battles; one here, and the other over the other side. 00.05 hrs.'

The following day we spent an interesting few hours at the Royal Aircraft Establishment at Farnborough. On 13 July a German night-fighter, a Junkers 88, landed intact at Woodbridge, the emergency landing strip on the east coast. Some said that the crew had landed in England by mistake, others were of the opinion that it was all pre-planned and the crew knew exactly what they were doing. Whatever the truth was, and the Germans think of the pilot as a British agent, the aircraft was fully equipped with the new SN II radar! We had been presented with a priceless gift and the opportunity to study and evaluate both the Ju 88 and its AI. My log reads: 'Mosquito F/Lt White Test with 337 Ju 88 to hear the audible Serrate for ourselves. Range dead astern is 5 miles. Also tested backward range of Ju 88 with W/C Jackson. Found it nil – YIPPEE!'

We had been vouched the fascinating opportunity to test our SN II homer on the real thing, an actual German night-fighter and, incidentally, to learn that our opposite numbers had, on this equipment, no backward-looking coverage. So, we might continue to approach them without their Nav/Rads being able to see us on their cathode-ray tubes.

However, the down side was that we did not seem to be able to pick up the audible signals from more than five miles away, not much more than the range of the Mk IV sets at a height of 20,000 ft, whereas the original Serrate signals, presented visually on our AI tubes, with their distinctive herring-bone pattern, had been received from ranges up to 20, 80 or even 100 miles away. We also had to consider, when intercepting the enemy night-fighters, that they would almost certainly have a separate tail warner tuned to a different frequency from that of the SN II. So it would still not do to be too complacent when stalking them over Germany!

Then there was the thrill of seeing the enemy – which we had spent much of the past twelve months chasing – in the flesh! The crews of the destroyers and corvettes, hunting the wolf packs across the North Atlantic, must have had a similar feeling when they forced a U boat to the surface, and saw their enemy clearly for the first time!

Admittedly, the swastikas (of which we had sometimes caught a glimpse, just before opening fire) had been painted out and replaced with RAF roundels and the German crew had long since been removed to spend the rest of the war in a prison camp.

The W/Cdr Jackson who was operating the SN II in the Ju 88 was Wing Commander Derek Jackson, the Chief Airborne Radar Officer in Fighter Command. Derek Jackson had been one of a select group of scientists working at the Cavendish Laboratory in Cambridge under Rutherford, in the years preceding the war. Derek was a remarkable man, among several remarkable men!

He had ridden in the Grand National, had an Oxford DSc., and switching his many and varied talents to the RAF saw active service as an AI operator (with several successful claims on Home Defence night-fighter operations), picking up the OBE, DFC, AFC on his rapid way up to his important appointment at Fighter Command. He played a considerable part in the countermeasures war, and was a great character; it was fun to meet him and something of a privilege to work with him.

Amongst the other notable events in quite a busy month, we visited Defford (where the Telecommunications Research Establishment based at Malvern carried out its airborne trials); Radlett, where BSDU had a workshop and we had lunch with Dr Calvert who was developing Perfectos, a device for interrogating the German IFF (Interrogation Friend or Foe); testing out a new gyro gun-sight; going to a 141 'B' Flight party at West Raynham; and flying a certain Mosquito XXX No. 797 for the first time, in which we did an altitude test and clawed our way up to 30,000 feet in 30 minutes.

When we were at West Raynham we were sorry to learn that our old Mosquito FII HJ941 (X), on which we had done a number of ops and had several combats, had been lost when Robin Hampshire and his navigator, Alan Melrose, went missing in June. They had joined 141 just before Harry and I left, and had only been on the squadron a month. They were both killed (although our Historian has been unable to ascertain how they were brought down) and lie buried in adjoining graves in Belgium.

Before we move on into September, which was the month of the ill-fated 'Market Garden' operation, the airborne landings at Arnhem, we must see how Rodney and his fellow surplus aircrew fared after the astonishing suggestion that they should volunteer to be railway stokers! At the end of July, the nightmare became a reality and his diary for Wednesday 26 July 1944 reads as follows: 'Visit to Peterborough. In morning I went [from Grantham] by the 10.27 to Peterborough (the L.N.E.R. Running Sheds) to meet the R.A.F. types there and find out their working hours and conditions, waited for them to turn up after lunch. The Staff were very good, re tea and soap etc.'

And some extracts from the days that followed: '. . . after hearty if late breakfast arrived at Depot at 09.15. Went, to my surprise on shift as Shed Shunter's Mate. There was little work to do . . .' '. . .I spent most of the afternoon making out a compromise rota under which six people will be on Spare Fireman Shift each week; the 9 remaining will do 3rd Man trips as before . . .' '. . . Signed on at 2.00. I spent the afternoon quite pleasantly on a shunting engine, No.4278. At 6.30 Knowles came over and said, "You're on Leave!"'

This unbelievable and degrading detachment to the railways only lasted two/three weeks and then it was over. Frequently, when the RAF officers turned up for their shift at the depot, as Rodney recorded in his diary, there was little work for them to do. I cannot conclude this soul-destroying period in Rodney's career in the Air Force without mentioning that, when he was going on leave and my parents had arranged to meet him at King's Cross Station, they waited on the platform opposite to where they had been told the 1st class coaches would stop. The train drew in but they could see no sign of Rodney stepping out of the carriage. Then they heard a shout, and, looking up towards the engine, they saw their son saying goodbye to the driver and fireman as he stepped off the foot-plate, wearing coal-blackened overalls, topped by his RAF officer's cap!

Rodney and his fellow 'stokers' returned to Grantham and resumed their efforts to get a posting to an Operational Training Unit.

Early in September, 1944, Harry and I did an altitude test, in daylight, in the Mosquito XXX No. 797, and I recorded 'Climbed to 37,000 ft. Highest yet and high enough'. At that height, in an unpressurised cabin, we felt distinctly un-comfortable – and the aircraft was wallowing about and threatening to fall out of the sky. We were glad to get down.

Then I went off to Twinwood Farm for a week's course on the Mk X AI. The Mk X (or 720) centemetric AI was a great advance on our old Mk IV AI sets, and had been in use by the Home Defence night-fighter squadrons since the previous year. Now, with the end of the war in sight, the Mk X AI could be used over enemy territory without any danger of its secrets being developed, and used, by the Germans against us. Indeed, earlier in the summer the 100 Group fighter strength had been augmented by the arrival of two more squadrons, Nos 85 and 157. Both these squadrons were equipped with Mk X AI and the latest night-fighter version of the Mosquito. They also had a number of highly experienced crews, some of whom (like Harry and I, before we commenced the bomber support operations) had spent many months on the Home Defence squadrons, waiting for the German bombers that never came, but all the time honing their skills during the interminable practice interceptions.

No sooner had they arrived at Swannington in May (belatedly, as far as we were concerned!), than they were whisked away in June to go and chase the V-1s, but they were soon back in 100 Group, after successfully destroying a number of flying-bombs. The Mk X AI had been developed in America by the Massachusetts Institute of Technology and produced by the Western Electric Company. It had a wavelength of 10 cm and a frequency in the region of 3 GHz. At most altitudes, the set had a range of 8 to 10 miles (12,800 to 16,000 m) in an arc terminating in an 80 to 100 degree angle to the transmitter.

In the vertical plane, the set could 'see' up to 50 degrees above the aircraft's centre-line and between 15 and 30 degrees below it. The restriction of our range, by the height of our aircraft above the ground – with which, on the Mk IV AI we had lived for so long – was suddenly removed! We could roam, at will, round Germany, high level or low level, and still pick up possible targets 8 to 10 miles away! For bomber support operations, even the need for a homer to pick out and identify the German night-fighters was diminished. The other 'old' Serrate squadrons were not immediately re-equipped with Mk X and had to soldier on with their old AI sets. Numbers 85 and 157 Squadrons proceeded to reap the fruits and both enjoyed a highly successful period of operations in 100 Group, which continued through the last winter of the war to 17/18 April 1945. I'm afraid we of 141, 239 and 169, who had had to battle on with old aeroplanes and old AI sets for so long, were more than a little jealous. But let us not do anything to diminish their achievements, which, led by Branse Burbridge and his navigator, Bill Skelton, were considerable.

Branse and Bill quickly ran up a score of 20 E/A destroyed, which included the shooting down of four enemy aircraft in one night, three Ju 88s and one Me 110. Others, like Jimmy Matthews (we were at Hurst together) and Penrose, and Jim 'Ben' Benson and 'Brandy' (with whom I had trained at Prestwick) were not far behind them.

The week's course at Twinwood Farm consisted of some ground instruction and four daylight flights in a Wellington, each of about two hours' duration. Several navigators were taken up in the 'Wimpy' at a time and we took it in turns to operate the Mk X AI. The target was a Hurricane, the pilot of which threw his aircraft about the sky with great abandon, making our task of intercepting him as difficult as possible. He was probably fed up with having to do a stooge job anyway!

I made an awful hash of my first attempts to use the Mk X but eventually settled down and 'pulled my finger out'! Thoughts of what Harry would say, if I failed the course, were a powerful incentive, and I duly collected a pass, pinched a night at home in Ashford, and returned to Foulsham.

On 15 September we took a BSDU aircraft fitted with Monica VI across to West Raynham, for an op to Kiel. This was because briefing facilities, etc. were still not available at Foulsham to enable us to operate from there. A trip to Brunswick, which might have been more profitable, was scrubbed, so we supported the 500 heavy bombers who went to Kiel. Attacks on other targets were made by 356 aircraft and, happily, the Command only lost 11 all told.

Our opposite numbers must have been having a night off. We didn't see a thing. I lost one head-on contact and we got shot at by some rather ropey flak in the area of the Kiel Canal. We thought it was coming from some rocket guns. Anyway they missed. We came home with the Monica VI and the R/T un-serviceable, landing after 4 hrs 10 mins in the air.

We then proceeded to do one of our rapid turn-arounds! We flew back to Foulsham, had our radar and radio sets repaired, and flew back to West Raynham to operate again on the Saturday night. I had had a date with Ursula (who at the time sported the splendid nickname of 'Raindrop'!), which necessitated a quick and circumspect telephone call, that is marked in my log by the following entry: 'Poor Raindrop, she's had me for tonight.'

The trip itself is of some interest, because it was the night before Operation 'Market Garden', the airborne landings at Arnhem and Nijmegen. My log entry reads: 'Sat 16th 21.40 Mosquito XIX F/Lt White Ops 100 Lancs on tactical A/Fs. In preparation for A/B invasion of Holland. We nearly joined them 'cause starboard engine packed up. 3.50 hrs.'

It will quickly be realised that the 100 Lancasters were being used to bomb – and hopefully put out of action – the German airfields in Holland, from which the defending day-fighters might be expected to take off, when the airborne armada flew out on the Sunday morning. We, along with some of the other night-fighters in the Group, were briefed for a high-level patrol of the same areas, in case the Germans decided to come up; in the event the shallow penetration by only a handful of British bombers (in comparison with the big raids on major targets) did not provoke any significant reaction.

Harry and I played a completely undistinguished role in the airborne invasion of Holland, which was launched on Sunday 17 September 1944 and, even to this day, remains the object of much criticism and controversy. After wandering about fruitlessly for about an hour and a half seeing only a few flashes as the bombs burst four miles beneath us, the oil pressure dropped 'off the clock' on our starboard engine! Harry had to feather it immediately to avoid the hazard of it catching fire and we were faced with another single-engined return. We duly fled ignominiously from the arena that was being prepared for the morrow and landed safely back at Raynham.

It will have been noted that no mention has been made of operating with 141 that night and, when we got back, we learned that they were destined for more exciting things! But as we heard further details about the operation and how the paratroopers and the gliders would be landing, within a few hours, in the very areas where our starboard engine had packed up, it dawned on Harry and I that if we had had to bale out, the chances were that we would have landed plumb in the middle of the dropping zone (hence the remark in my log about nearly joining them!).

Charles Winn had other plans for 141 that night – or rather for the early hours of Sunday morning! Due to take off at 05.00 hrs, with five other Mosquitoes, his objective was a low-level dawn attack on the German airfield of Steenwijk, in Holland. Of course, as soon as Harry got wind of this, he wanted to go too! Only the combined efforts of 'Winnie' and myself managed to talk him out of it.

The raid on Steenwijk airfield was a great success and, although four of the Mosquitoes were damaged by flak, they all returned safely to Raynham.

When we had had a few hours' sleep we got up and went down to 'the Flights' to inspect 638 and assess the damage. Much to our annoyance, having carefully nursed it back home, there was more damage than when we had landed! An engineer officer (who shall be nameless!), ignoring the report that Harry had left for him to the effect that there was no oil in the engine, insisted on the engine fitters starting the starboard engine and running it up! The result was predictable – a large hole in the side of the crank-case!

Most of the rest of the day (as far as I can remember!) was spent at the Crown at Fakenham, where we repaired, to join the crews who had been to Steenwijk, in an uproarious mid-day session. Having no Mosquito in which to return to Foulsham, Harry and I were ferried home in an Airspeed Oxford, both a trifle woozy.

We didn't operate again until the following Saturday, and then it was not in direct support of the airborne landings, which, by then, had run into serious trouble. Indeed the poor weather conditions, which prevailed in the days following the landings, severely hampered the day and night operations – laid on by the RAF – in their efforts to assist the soldiers fighting against mounting odds on the ground. I sometimes think (from my armchair!) as I read the various accounts of the battle at Arnhem, that insufficient attention has been given – by the military historians – to the part played by the capricious weather conditions in this tragic operation.

Before going on an op to Münster on the 23rd I flew with Neville Reeves on a 'Perfectos' test and Harry and I put in some practice on the Mk X AI. The attack which we were supposed to be supporting was by 135 aircraft of 5 Group, on the

Dortmund–Ems Canal; they lost 14 bombers. We hadn't got a clue as to what was going on that night (and I said as much in my log-book when I filled it in, the following day), but judging by the results, neither had the rest of the 100 Group fighters. Although 22 bombers were lost, out of the 923 which attacked the various targets, no enemy night-fighters were claimed by the bomber support Mosquitoes.

I think it was whilst we were at Foulsham that I went down with 'Saturday night paralysis', and I found myself lying in a bed in the RAF hospital at Ely! It happened this way: I woke up one morning after a not particularly hectic party and found that I could not move my left arm. I managed to get myself dressed, but at breakfast I could not hold my fork in my left hand to cut up my bacon and egg!

Harry and our other friends found it all highly amusing, as both bacon and egg finished up on the floor. I realised that it was time to go and see the Medical Officer! He said: 'I think I know what you've got. You've got Saturday night paralysis, you should be all right in six/seven days, but I'd better send you across to Ely – just to make sure.' And so it was that I found myself lying in a ward – surrounded by gallant members of aircrew, who had been wounded in action – whilst I was reaping my just rewards, for having succumbed to the evils of Bacchus! I couldn't get out of Ely fast enough, my left arm rapidly thawed out, and I was back with BSDU in two days – fortunately, none the worse for wear.

By the end of September my flying hours had risen to 993.25 in a little over three years. Looking back, an average of $c.300$ per annum does not seem very much, and one may well ask 'What did you do with yourselves for the rest of the time?' I've sometimes wondered! But we certainly had a liberal ration of leave, which for operational aircrew was 9 days, every 6 weeks, and Harry and I were off again on leave at the end of September.

I feel sorry for our opposite numbers, when I hear stories to the effect that they had no such prescribed periods of leave. They more or less stayed with the *Gruppe* until they were killed or worn out!

*   *   *

We should now take a quick look at Don Aris's Summary for the end of August in order to keep in touch with the general situation and its effect on the work of the Serrate squadrons. The following notes are extracted from it:

> 'During the month of August 1944, 141 Squadron carried out 107 Serrate Bomber Support operations and operated on 11 nights, and all from West Raynham. The first operation with a new Mk FVI Mosquito was on the 7th August and throughout the month further Mk FVIIs became operational – and of the 107 operations, 54 were by Mk FIIIs and 53 by Mk FVIIs. There were 8 early returns, 4 due to radar, two due to generators and one each to icing and electrical problems. Only one enemy aircraft was shot down, an Me 110 by W/O Lampkin with F/Sgt Wallnutt and an Me 110 was damaged by F/L Thatcher with F/O Calvert.
>
> However, during the month, the fellow Mosquito Squadron at West Raynham, No. 239, destroyed 3 enemy aircraft and damaged one, thus keeping them well ahead of 141 Squadron in the number of enemy aircraft shot down from West Raynham, 38 by 239 Squadron and 24 by 141 Squadron. The poor results were due, as has already been explained, to the fact that almost all

German night-fighters were now equipped with the new SN-2 A.I. radar which made the Serrate equipment practically useless. It will have been seen that the few Serrate contacts now picked up all radiated from ground sources. Also the old Mk IV A.I. radar in the Mosquitoes was being jammed and so many A.I. contacts were being lost due to interference. [It was at this time that Harry and I on BSDU were involved in carrying out flight trials on new homers to replace the Serrate equipment.]

During the month concern had been expressed as to what would become of the Squadron (i.e. if the High Level Patrols, using only Mk IV A.I. radar, continued to give such a poor return). Much practice had taken place, including 'low-flying' in order to prepare the Squadron for any new role. The amount of this practice is shown by the fact that a record of over 900 hours of flying had been done in the month, 350 on operations and 550 on practice flying. As will be seen in the forthcoming month of September, the Squadron would make a start on other types of operations. No casualties were suffered during the month of August.'

In the event 141, as already mentioned, carried out the first of a number of low-level operations when six Mosquitoes, led by Wing Commander Winn, attacked the German airfield at Steenwijk in Holland, on 17 September, in support of the airborne landings at Arnhem and Nijmegen.

The net result of the loss of being able to home onto the German AI was that apart from the occasional combats by the three original Serrate squadrons – 141, 169 and 239 – only the new additions to 100 Group – 85 and 157 Squadrons – with their Mk X AI radar (and AI operators experienced in its use) were properly equipped for both High-Level and Low-Level Bomber Support work. It was rather galling for the squadrons at West Raynham and 169 at Great Massingham that by the time their clapped out Mosquitoes (which had been the cause of so many casualties in the first half of the year) were finally replaced by better aircraft, their radar equipment was out of date! At Swannington, 85 and 157 were able – with their Mk X AI radar – to pick up interesting contacts at ranges of 8 to 10 miles, irrespective of altitude, and go exploring at high and low level. They had many successful encounters and they had some high-scoring crews, reflecting much credit on aircrew and ground crew alike.

We had some leave at the beginning of October. Harry set off for Scarborough where Joan was still stationed with the Wrens and I drove down to Ashford and spent the nine days with my parents. When I returned to BSDU I wrote in my log-book on 7 October: 'BACK FROM "BEST EVER" LEAVE . . .'

So things must have gone well! Perhaps I saw more of Betty Sessions than on previous occasions? Doubtless there were several convivial evenings spent at the Ashford Manor Golf Club, in company with my father!

Rodney was also at home for part of my leave (he was still trying, in vain, to get a posting to an OTU and get into ops). He came home with the news that he and some of the other surplus pilots might have to remuster for training as glider pilots! At this time the Defence Chiefs would be thinking about the Rhine Crossings and had of course lost a number of glider pilots in the abortive 'Market Garden' operation which had failed to achieve the breakthrough into Germany which might have brought about an end to the war in 1944.

Additionally, we had Joan Wesson – Tom Wesson's widow – staying with us at the time (it will be remembered that Tom had met an unlikely death in 1941, whilst instructing on a Tiger Moth, a few days after I had departed for No. 9 Receiving Wing at Stratford-upon-Avon). My mother was very fond of Joan, who had been left with a little girl, Judith, who must have been about five or six years old in the autumn of 1944. So, all in all, it was a cheery household and none of us could have envisaged that 'the slings and arrows of outrageous fortune' were about to descend on the Allen Family – literally, and from the skies.

There was another cause for celebration at 60 Clarendon Road at the beginning of October. Just before we went on leave Harry and I had been informed that we had both been awarded a Second Bar to our DFCs.

It will be remembered that Harry was awarded his DFC about six weeks in advance of mine being gazetted on 5 November 1943. It was an added source of satisfaction to us that both our subsequent awards came through on the same date. However, the initial disparity between the dates of our first awards did have one unfortunate consequence. When eventually we were to have a letter from the Central Chancery of the Orders of Knighthood (in the summer of 1945) advising us that 'The King will hold an Investiture at Buckingham Palace at which your attendance is requested' we saw that they were for different dates. Thus we did not have the satisfaction of going to the Palace together.

By July 1945 I also had reason to be disappointed because there was an unavoidable delay of some 20 months between the date of the award and the date of its presentation; although, of course, we had been able to wear the ribbon from the day we learned, from the CO, that we had been lucky enough to receive an award.

The delay was nobody's fault. From 1942 onwards a considerable number of decorations had been awarded, some of which were presented 'in the field' (or on an RAF station), and there was a limit to the number of recipients who could be invited to the investitures held by His Majesty at Buckingham Palace. By the end of the war at the time of VJ-Day in September 1945, the backlog was stretched to over two years! In the end, some recipients of awards for gallantry were sent their medals through the post, in a small cardboard box! Harry and I were amongst the fortunate ones to receive a summons to the Palace.

At the time – for us it was in 1943 and 1944 – you never saw the citation for your award and generally, you did not know if you had been put in for a decoration. You might make a few guesses, but the whole sequence of events was conducted with the utmost decorum – and in an air of confidentiality – by the Squadron CO, the Adjutant and the Squadron Intelligence Officer. Sometimes there were a few lines in the *London Gazette* (from which the media would draw on, for use in the press or on the radio, often after they had embellished the basic facts, more than a bit!) There was, of course, no television. I never saw the full citations until many years after the war, when a kind friend secured copies from the Public Record Office and sent them to me.

It may be of interest to follow the recommendation for Harry's third award through its various stages. The following letter was sent by Wing Commander Winn, the Commanding Officer of No. 141 Squadron to Group Captain Slee, the Station Commander at West Raynham:

'FLIGHT LIEUTENANT HAROLD EDWARD WHITE (119508) D.F.C. & BAR. PILOT – ROYAL AIR FORCE VOLUNTEER RESERVE.

Flight Lieutenant White joined No. 141 (BS) Squadron on the 18th January 1943, and on the 9th September, 1943 was awarded the Distinguished Flying

Cross, and on 31st March, 1944 he was awarded a bar to the Distinguished Flying Cross. He had at that time, destroyed five enemy aircraft and damaged a further two, all over enemy territory in support of the Bomber Forces.

Since being recommended for the Bar, Flight Lieutenant White has had seven combats over enemy territory as follows: On March 19th, 1944 he was approaching Frankfurt when he obtained a visual on a Ju 88 which he destroyed after three short bursts. On reaching Frankfurt he obtained a visual on a second Ju 88 which he also destroyed with three short bursts of cannon fire. On 26th March, 1944 whilst on patrol in support of the raid on Essen he obtained a visual on a Ju 88. He fired two short bursts and observed pieces falling off. The Ju 88 then dived away steeply, and visual was lost. The enemy aircraft was claimed as damaged.

On 20th April, 1944 he obtained a visual and destroyed a Do 217 with one two second burst. He also gave two bursts at a Ju 88 without observing any results. These combats took place whilst on patrol in support of the attack on Batignolles.

On May 11th, 1944 whilst on patrol near Brussels, he intercepted a Ju 88 which he destroyed with a four second burst.

On 27th May, 1944 whilst patrolling near Aachen, he obtained a visual on a Me 109 which he destroyed. Enemy aircraft blew up immediately in front of him with such brilliance that it completely blinded him for some minutes. His Navigator took over the controls and obtained a visual on a second Me 109 under the starboard wing. Pilot was unable to see it, and the enemy aircraft had disappeared when he regained his normal sight.

Flight Lieutenant White has now completed his operational tour with this Squadron, having completed thirty one sorties. Prior to joining this Unit he carried out three ferrying trips to the Middle East and nineteen sorties as a Defensive night-fighter.

In view of the above and the magnificent example he has been to the remainder of the Squadron, Flight Lieutenant Harold Edward White is strongly recommended for the award of a second Bar to the Distinguished Flying Cross.'

Group Captain Slee, when he received this letter, added his own remarks in support of the recommendation:

'REMARKS OF STATION COMMANDER.

Flight Lieutenant White has now completed his first tour of operations to a total of thirty one sorties, during which time he has been instrumental in the destruction of 12 enemy fighters.

He has shown throughout his entire tour, skill of no mean order and determination of the required quality. By his successes and his conduct on operations he has set a most excellent example to the aircrew of his Squadron and this Station.

Though he has completed only eight sorties since the date of his last award he destroyed three enemy aircraft during this period, and I recommend the award of second bar to the D.F.C.

Date:16th July 1944'

Air Vice-Marshal Addison, Air Officer Commanding No. 100 (SD) Group, when he received Group Captain Slee's communication, supported the citation and added his own remarks before sending the recommendation forward to the Air Ministry:

'REMARKS OF AIR OFFICER COMMANDING:

Since F/Lt White was last recommended for a decoration he has destroyed five more German aircraft on Bomber Support operations, and damaged a further one. His skill as a night-fighter pilot is of an exceptionally high standard and he has well maintained his fine offensive spirit. I strongly recommend him for a second bar to his D.F.C.

Date:- 26th July, 1944.'

In due course the recommendation for a non-immediate award was approved by the Air Ministry early in October.

Whilst producing this fair copy of the documentation of Harry's third award, it has not escaped my notice that there are several discrepancies between the three letters . . . but I have no intention of pursuing them, after this passage of time!

It will be seen here that there is a clear difference for an end-of-tour award and one given for specific action(s), i.e. in the case of our first two awards. There was a subtle difference in those days, although this may no longer be the case. The rules governing the award of honours and decorations have been changed significantly since our war. The three Service Crosses (the DSC, MC and DFC) can now be given posthumously although, in previous days, it was thought that such a practice could lead to these decorations being given in sympathy for the death of the recipient, rather than for his deed.

Then the medals, previously awarded to other ranks (the DCM, MM, DSM and DFM), much prized by those who won them, have been scrapped and now all ranks are eligible for the Service Crosses!

These changes appeared to be simply a political ploy, by the party in power, to win votes on the theme of doing away with outdated social distinctions and class differences. It is arguable whether this sort of tinkering with tradition in the name of political correctness elevates a selected few, or cheapens the whole system.

Soon after I had written in my log-book 'BACK FROM "BEST EVER" LEAVE . . .' we did an op to Bochum on 9/10 October 1944, testing out the latest Monica tail-warner (sadly, the equipment again went u/s), but happily only five aircraft were lost out of a force of 450 bombers. The following night we experimented (over England!) with removing the flame dampers from the exhaust manifolds on 797 – to see the effect. We soon had them put back as the engines gave off far too much flame without them, which would be seen from astern by any inquisitive Ju 88 or Me 110.

Four nights later, and after a false start on the NFT owing to a u/s boost control and oxygen gauge, we took 797 to Brunswick. Once more the equipment failed us: this time it was the oxygen supply, the fault which we had found on the NFT had not been properly rectified – and we had to make another early return. On our way back, crossing the North Sea at below 10,000 ft, we saw two V1s shot down and a third 'go in' (somebody was having some joy).

A consumption test was needed on 797, although why we set off to carry out this fuel test at night is beyond my recollection, but the decision to go nearly proved to be our undoing. The weather was bad and neither of us was very keen to fly that night. I can't tell you why, but all aircrew had the odd night when they just felt uneasy. Sometimes the emotion was stronger, and a man felt that if he took off that particular night he would get the chop.

Eventually, and my log-book for 18 October says 'After much argument on both sides', we took off at 19.05 hrs and headed west in the direction of Peterborough. Fifty-five minutes later we were back on the ground again – but not at Foulsham, having been scared out of our wits! We had climbed the Mosquito XXX up to about 32,000 ft when the rev. counters started to alter rapidly, up and down, indicating that both engines were surging by 300–400 revs. We could feel the loss of power, and the aircraft became unstable.

One moment we had been sitting up there relaxed because we were – for once – not over enemy territory . . . and the next, poor old 797 was wallowing all over the night sky above Cambridgeshire, with Harry fighting to control her! He quickly detected that both engines were suffering from fuel starvation and the sooner we could lose height and find an airfield – any airfield – and put the Mosquito down, the better it would be for all concerned. He said, over the intercom, that if the engines did not pick up on the way down we might have to bale out and leave 797 to its own devices.

When it came to the unpalatable business of abandoning one's aircraft the pilots were better off than we were! In most World War II fighter aircraft, including night-fighters, they had seat-type parachutes. If they had to bale out they could be reasonably sure that their chute would be attached to them when they did so.

Navigators wore only a harness, and the all important canopy was in a separate pack. It was carried out to the aircraft like a weekend bag or a going-away case which, of course, sometimes it proved to be! It was stowed away in the dim recesses of the fuselage. I always parted with mine reluctantly – if we had to bale out in a hurry, I would be certain to forget some part of the drill for abandoning aircraft – what if I should leave my going-away case behind?

I had taken a quick glance at the wildly fluctuating rev. counters when I had first felt the Mosquito starting to go out of control, as the engines died, restarted, and died again. This, I thought, was it! Remembering my precious bag, I searched surreptitiously for it in the darkened cockpit, found it and, with a sigh of relief, clipped it onto the two hooks on the front of my harness.

As we clawed our way through the now unfriendly night sky, the air speed indicator slipped back, nearer and nearer, to the point of stall . . . Seconds later Harry's cool voice came over the intercom saying: 'Don't panic, but put your parachute on!' I've often wondered if he believed me, when I replied: 'I'm not panicking – but I've got it on!'

We sent out, over the VHF, a MAYDAY call for an emergency homing and spiralled gently down to a lower altitude. The surging slowly started to even out and the engines picked up. We were about 25 miles north of Cambridge when the Sector Controller brought us straight in for an emergency landing at Molesworth (a few miles to the north of Huntingdon). We were concerned to land off our first approach, not knowing if the engines would cut out once more if we had to open up and go round again. Harry made a good landing and, having taxied the Mosquito round the perimeter track, we parked it by the Watch office and vacated the cockpit, thankful to be down in one piece.

We soon found ourselves in the officers' mess, but not with a glass of beer in our hands. Molesworth turned out to be an American bomber base with part of the US 8th Air Force and I found myself sampling a 'Planter's Punch' for the first time! The Americans proved to be extremely hospitable and I tried the Planter's Punch again, just to make sure. I think I tried it a third time, and what promised to be a fairly riotous night was only cut short because our hosts had been briefed that they would be operating the following day. The 'Yanks' attended to our every want and we slept well.

In the morning we were invited up into the Watch office to watch the B-17s taxi out and take off on a daylight raid to Germany – we wished them luck. I remember that the take-off was somewhat delayed because one of the Flying Fortresses caught fire, and in another one of the crew-members could not find his flak-jacket!

When all the 'Forts' had taken off – facing a laborious climb and up to two hours of orbiting, over East Anglia, as they picked up their full formation before setting course for Germany – Harry and I walked across to 797, to see if it could be flown back to Foulsham. We climbed in and Harry started the engines. He ran them both up to full power, checked for a magneto drop and throttled back. No trouble at all, and no sign that there had been any problem with the engines the previous night! We signalled to the ground crew that all was well – and waved the chocks away. We taxied out round the perimeter track, took off with our hearts in our mouth, and Harry flew 797 gingerly back to Foulsham, where we landed twenty minutes later, without further incident.

Again, when we got to BSDU the engine fitters could not find anything to account for the fuel starvation we had experienced the night before!

In the afternoon we tested a Mosquito XIX 638 and at seven in the evening, took off and flew to Nuremberg in support of a raid by 200 Lancasters of 5 Group on a special target. We were busy trying out a new Monica (tail-warner) but had no joy in finding any of our opposite numbers. The Lancs only lost two aircraft on this trip, one of which we saw shot down.

As the Allied Armies fought their way across France, through Belgium and into Holland, the Germans started to lose their early-warning' radar installations, their Home Defence systems started to crumble and they were having to worry about the fuel supplies needed to keep their day-fighters and night-fighters in the air.

Since June Bomber Command had been able to return to daylight bombing, escorted by single-seater fighters, to augment the work of the American 8th Air Force. With the front line now close to the borders of Germany neither we, nor the Americans, had to spend so much time over enemy territory, and our losses fell accordingly. At this time Bomber Command were losing an average of only one to two per cent of its crews on each sortie, compared with between five and ten per cent in the dreadful winter of 1943–44.

However, there were still plenty of Ju 88s and Me 110s about, flown by brave and resourceful men like Heinz Rökker of 1./NJG 2, to say nothing of the new Heinkel 219s and Ju 188s. Whether it was that Harry and I were having to concentrate too much on testing our 'black boxes', or had gone stale, I don't know, but even allowing for the frequent unserviceability of both the aircraft and the equipment on BSDU, our ops seemed to be in the doldrums.

Since getting the two Ju 88s on the Stuttgart raid, at the end of July, we had set off on eight operations and, beyond our test reports, we had nothing to show for it. In the meantime, 85 Squadron and 157 Squadron with their Mosquito XIXs and their Mk X AI radar were making a killing! On 4/5 November Branse Burbridge with Bill Skelton got four in one night, destroying some of the E/As at high level and some at low level on their way to a total tally of twenty! A marvellous performance by an exceptional crew, who were also two exceptional men in every other way.

And the victories of these squadrons (later re-equipped again, with Mosquito XIXs) were not confined to the aces. A number of crews shared in the fun. We were both a bit fed up with our lot during this period and missed the adrenaline we had found on 141 Squadron, where one's sole objective, for eleven months, had been to find the enemy and destroy him . . .

*   *   *

In the meantime, on 12 October, Rodney had arrived at West Raynham, of all places! Still at Harrogate, some of the surplus pilots had been offered a short posting to various operational stations as an 'Aerodrome Control Pilot'.

After the débâcle of being asked to volunteer as stokers on the railways this was a great improvement! Rodney looked at the list of postings available and saw that West Raynham was one of them, and to quote from his diary: 'After much uncertainty volunteered for A.C.P. at West Raynham and regretted it almost at once, then later on finding that three others were going felt quite O.K. again.'

That was on 10 October. His entry for 12 October read as follows:

> 'Up early for journey to West Raynham. Left by 8.17 train, had coffee in Leeds, snack lunch at Peterboro, journeying with F/Lt John Bulling, ex Anson Instructor and P/O Pete Sherman of 18 Course. Arrived East Rudham [It will be remembered that this was the station for West Raynham], mid wind and rain at 18.45. Dark. Rang for transport. Dinner in the v. comfortable Mess and phoned Michael who seemed much more pleased than I had expected . . .'

I was of course at Foulsham with BSDU when Rodney got this posting to Raynham. Rodney was soon using his time at Raynham to full advantage and Harry and I were soon using the Tiger Moth to go across from Foulsham to see him. His diary continues: 'Monday, October 17, 1944. Went to Speke in afternoon with Johnny Bulling, was shown how to work Gee on way up by Nav whom we dropped there . . . on way home flew thru' cloud and I brought us home by navigating Gee while Johnny flew. Night landing in thunderstorm. Michael and Harry in Mess for joyous evening, with their second Bar up.'

Rodney did not record the aircraft type, but I think it must have been an Avro Anson, belonging to the Station Flight.

Rodney's happy and useful few days at Raynham were shattered and the following abrupt entry in his diary gives the reason: 'Tuesday, October 24, 1944. Selected for Gliders. Signal ex H'gate. Four days Embarkation Leave.'

Now, after all the waiting about and six months of frustration trying to complete their training and get onto ops, Rodney and some of the other pilots were told that they were to be re-trained – as glider pilots. It was, of course, only a few weeks after the abortive 'Market Garden' operation, when a number of glider pilots had been either lost or captured, and the Air Ministry must have had in mind the possibility of further airborne operations, i.e. the Rhine Crossings; but it did seem a bit hard on these young pilots who, for so long, had had their sights fixed on flying fighters, or bombers or perhaps going to Coastal Command, anywhere, as long as they were flying on operations.

Admittedly, they might be operating once they had been trained to fly a glider, but the idea of being towed into battle in a lifeless, powerless craft on a one-way ticket, behind a Halifax or a Stirling, was abhorrent to most of them . . .

Once more Rodney's morale sank as he set off home for his four days' embarkation leave. I never actually heard where they were being sent for their training on gliders. His diary entries for the first three days were brief, what could he say? 'Wednesday, October 25, 1944. Came Home on Leave.' 'Thursday, October 26, 1944. A Lazy Day.' 'Friday, October 27, 1944. Went skating in Morning at Richmond with Paul Marsh, who is now home as a P/O Pilot and is going on Gliders.'

Thus it was that by a quirk of fate (his sudden and unexpected posting onto gliders, and his four days embarkation leave) that Rodney came to be at home on the night of 27/28 October. His diary entry for the fourth day was somewhat longer . . .

*   *   *

Harry and I did three more NFTs before the end of the month. Each time ops were cancelled at the last moment. On Friday 27 October we were going to take Mosquito XIX No. 638, and test out the Perfectos equipment, designed to interrogate the German IFF. When the news came through that ops had been scrubbed once more, Harry and I went back to the mess for a quiet evening and turned in early. In the bar, in some messes, they hung up a dice when ops were on, changing it to a scrubbing-brush when ops were off. Anyway, we had an early night . . .

We were woken up by our batman at about 8 a.m. next morning, Saturday 28 October. When he came into the room he had a telegram in his hand. The telegram was for me and when I opened it I saw that it was from the police in Staines, Middlesex. Staines was three miles to the west of Ashford, which had, in those days, no police station of its own. I read:

HOUSE DAMAGED. PLEASE RETURN HOME IMMEDIATELY.

It gave the name of the superintendent in charge at Staines. I had barely had time to consider the meaning of it, before our batman was back with a second telegram. This one was from my brother and read:

HOUSE DESTROYED. AM AT DENCLIFF HOUSE WITH MRS. SESSIONS. PLEASE RETURN IMMEDIATELY. RODNEY.

I remember quite clearly saying to Harry that in neither of the telegrams was there any word of my parents. I said further that, because there was no mention of them having been injured, it looked as if the worst had happened, i.e. that the house in Clarendon Road had been destroyed and that they had both been killed . . .

Trying to absorb the implications of the two telegrams I then said to Harry '. . . what you and I have been doing for the past three years will help me to deal with whatever has happened down at Ashford'.

I rang Rupert Clerke, who was most concerned and said that of course I must leave immediately for Ashford. Harry did not say much: as he was to write in a letter to me, later on '. . . the time that we have spent together means that the interplay of words, between us, is unnecessary'.

I threw some things into an attaché case, grabbed a quick breakfast and was in my car, driving out of the camp past the guard room by 9 o'clock.

Driving down the old A1 into Hendon, round the North Circular Road and then onto the Great West Road, I reached Ashford just before 2 p.m. Rodney had indicated that he was at Dencliff House, the family home presided over by Mrs Sessions, so I drove straight there . . .

I found Rodney and Joan Wesson there, shocked but unhurt. He immediately told me that our father and mother had been killed instantly, when a German V-2 rocket had landed in the garden of 60 Clarendon Road in the early hours of the morning. He and Joan were trapped by the falling wreckage as the building collapsed but were miraculously unhurt. They were both rescued by a team made up of courageous ARP and AFS men, who were quickly on the scene.

The V-2 had fallen at about 5.00 a.m. when everyone was still asleep. My father and mother's bedroom overlooked the large garden to the side of the house. The rocket landed about twenty yards away from the house – and blew up. The blast from it swept into their room and killed them outright, as they slept.

Rodney and Joan, sleeping in rooms at the front and rear of the house respectively, were sheltered from the blast, and the sturdy construction of the house ensured that, although it collapsed, it was not completely demolished. Apart from swallowing a lot of dust, as the house collapsed around them, they were found uninjured when the rescue teams reached them.

As soon as they had been brought out of the wreckage Rodney asked that he and Joan should be taken straight to Dencliff House, where he knew that Mrs Sessions and her family would give them refuge. He was not mistaken. Mrs Sessions gave us a home, which lasted well into the fifties.

Walking in the garden of Dencliff House, Rodney and I did not say much. Considering what he had been through, a few hours earlier, he was very brave. Neither of us cried. I do remember saying that if we could both stand up to what had happened, then all our friends would stand with us but, if we lay down under it, then nobody would be able to help us. Looking back, over half a century later, that is roughly how things worked out . . .

Rodney even had the courage to write up his diary for the fourth and last day of his embarkation leave:

> Saturday October 28, 1944
>
> FATHER † MOTHER
>
> 'At about 05.00 hrs. a V-2 fell in garden demolished house killing Mother and Father. Mother, I think instantaneously. I heard Father, spoke to him, he responded, probably died after about two or three minutes. Joan Wesson and I saved, and O.K. Went to Sessions. Telegraphed Michael. Returned about 08.00. By which time death was certain. Bodies recovered. Michael arrived at 14.00 hrs., Slept fitfully. Fearful brick dust in throat. Visited by G/C Donaldson and wife Sue.'

And the following day: Sunday October 29 1944. 'Everyone was very helpful. Many offers of shelter. W.F. Fuller v. helpful. Drove over to see Granny. She was v. brave.'

Later in the afternoon (of Saturday) I drove round to Clarendon Road, to see for myself. I learned that two or three other properties had been damaged, and

I think one other person had been killed. It was amazing that the damage and the casualties were so slight, considering that the V-2 had fallen in a heavily populated area.

With Rodney and the police officer in charge I went over, and looked down into the crater. It was about 30 feet across and only about 10 feet deep. When the missile exploded, it was the shallowness of the crater which had served to increase the force of the blast.

As I looked down I saw that there were a number of twisted components and fragments of the rocket lying embedded in the earth. These were later salvaged and removed for examination by the authorities. It was early days in the V-2 offensive and there was little known about their equipment at this stage.

Whilst we were standing there I saw a car stop and an RAF group captain got out. I went across, saluted, and immediately saw that it was Group Captain Donaldson, one of the three brothers, all of whom had seen distinguished service in the Air Force. I had last met him in 1942 when Harry and I had flown over to Upavon in a Boston from Tangmere to have lunch with him and my father. He and my father were old friends from pre-war flying days, and a few days before, he and his wife, Sue, had been invited over to tea by my parents. They had arrived at 60 Clarendon Road only to find a heap of wreckage . . . then had taken themselves off for half an hour and had learned what had happened. They said the right things to Rodney and myself and discreetly departed the scene.

When Rodney and I got back to Dencliff House we found Betty, the youngest of Mrs Sessions' six children, of whom I was very fond, still hard at work, trying to get the dust and dirt out of Rodney's uniform and Joan's clothes. I had some telephoning to do . . .

I telephoned Harry and told him what had happened. I asked him to put me through to the CO, and I told Rupert, asking for two weeks' compassionate leave, to enable me to sort things out. This request was immediately, and kindly, granted. Rupert then said that Harry could have the same time off, so that he could come down to Ashford, and give me a hand. Harry arrived on the Monday, and Mrs Sessions put him up as well! I then had to think who else should be notified of my parents' death.

We were, even then, a bit short of close relatives. On my mother's side there was only a cousin, Irene Gray, of about my own age. She was serving in the WAAF and we were in touch. My father's sister, Joyce Garlick, lived in Cape Town, so I would have to cable her. My grandfather, Henry Charles Allen, having died the previous year, meant that my aged grandmother was living on her own in Oxted, Surrey. She had to be told as soon as possible and I had to be the one to tell her.

I then made one of the worst decisions of my life – certainly, the most heartless. I rang up my grandmother and broke the news to her, over the telephone. I had entirely overlooked the fact that whereas Harry and I had become accustomed to death, sometimes on a daily basis, in effect accepting it as part of everyday life – those who were not subjected to that sort of experience still, and understandably, found death a great shock, particularly when it was that of a beloved son and daughter-in-law. I had also forgotten that my grandmother had lost her eldest son, in France in 1918, whilst serving in the Buffs. Lieutenant (Acting Captain) Geoffrey Charles Allen was an uncle whom I had never known . . .

I had it in my mind that my grandmother might hear of the deaths from some other source – perhaps a friend, the wireless or in the press – before I could drive down to Oxted and tell her myself. I could not get away from Ashford until I had made arrangements for the funeral. I felt I had to ring her without delay.

Of course, if I had only stopped to think, I should have realised that no information regarding damage and casualties caused by enemy action would be released to the media until it had been carefully censored by the Ministry of Information, to ensure that nothing was published which might be of any value to the enemy (e.g. the names of the victims and the location of the incident). In those days next-of-kin did not have to suffer at the hands of intrusive press reporters and there were no television cameras at Clarendon Road on Saturday 28 October 1944. I need not have worried.

I rang my grandmother's number and she answered – I was told, some time later, that when I had rung off, a few minutes later, and she had put the phone down, she collapsed, as a result of the shock which I had given her. She had doted on her youngest child, Brian, and was very fond of her daughter-in-law, Kathleen. Worse still, in view of my flawed decision to tell her the news over the phone, she was alone in the house. She lay unconscious on the floor.

Rodney's diary has already told us that he and I did drive over to Oxted on the following day and that Granny was very brave. She told us then, that she would be at the funeral, already arranged for Thursday at Woking, Surrey.

Our parents were cremated at Woking Crematorium on Thursday 2 November. Again Rodney bravely wrote the following entry into his diary:

CREMATION
THURSDAY, NOVEMBER 2, 1944
R.I.P.

'Mother and Father cremated at Woking 11.00hrs. Service not as trying as I had expected. Chapel full. Irene Gray turned up. Granny Allen very strong. Service conducted by Revd. Penny.

   Went to "The Green Man" after the Service. Drank beer and played darts to relieve strain.'

Rodney and I arranged for the service to be short, it was under 20 minutes, and we worked on the principle that when people have been hurt badly, they should not be hurt any more than is absolutely necessary. We arranged with Lock's, the undertakers, that the coffins of our father and mother should be in position, side by side, before the service started so that there should be no heart-rending procession into the chapel, with the bearers manoeuvring the coffins into position, watched with bated breath by all.

Rodney and I had asked that there should be no flowers, except for our one wreath. Those who wished to do so were invited to send a donation to the Royal Air Force Benevolent Fund, in their memory. I remember that over £150 was collected, which was quite a lot of money in those days and, with the constrictions of wartime, it was a significant tribute to them. It was also a source of satisfaction to Rodney and me.

I can't remember the hymns that Rodney and I chose, or any other of the details of the service, except the following passage from Ephesians, Chapter 6, Verses 10–13.

10. Finally, my brethren, be strong in the Lord, and in the power of his might.

11. Put on the whole armour of God, that ye may be able to stand against the wiles of the devil.

12. For we wrestle not against flesh and blood, but against the principalities, against powers, against the rulers of the darkness of this world, against spiritual wickedness in high places.

13. Wherefore take unto you the whole armour of God, that ye may be able to withstand in the evil day, and having done all, to stand.

It was the Reverend Penny who suggested these verses to us and they seemed appropriate, both then and now. We asked him, above all, to keep the service short, and he did so. I had seen a number of funerals in the preceding three years, and people – brave at the beginning of the service – reduced to a pulp, if it went on for too long. Rodney and I did not want that to happen, and it did not.

We did not hold a reception after the funeral was over. As Rodney said in his diary, the chapel was full and there were many of my parents' friends and business associates at Woking. But when Rodney and I led the congregation out into the autumn sunshine we said our goodbyes, thanked as many as possible for coming, and we all went our separate ways. In one of the popular catch phrases of the time 'There is a war on, you know!'

Apart from the fact that there was a war on I had made up my mind where Rodney and our close friends would be going, as soon as we could – with decency – remove ourselves from that woeful crematorium. We were both sure that what our parents would have liked us to do was to head for one of my father's favourite pubs, and unwind a bit.

Together with Harry, Teddy Sessions and one or two more we set off for the Green Man at Hatton Corner just off the old Great West Road and, today, right in the flight-path of Heathrow! There, my father's old friend 'Charlie' looked after our needs until late into the afternoon. As Rodney wrote in his diary, we '. . . Drank beer and played darts to relieve the strain.'

Our mother's and father's names are in the Roll of Honour for 'Civilian War Dead 1939–1945', which was compiled by the Imperial War Graves Commission and later placed in Westminster Abbey. I went to the Abbey with Pam, a few years ago, and one of the vergers kindly opened the Roll of Honour for me, at the page on which their names are entered.

'URBAN DISTRICT OF STAINES

ALLEN, Brian Seamer, age 45; A.T.C.; Home Guard; of Westwick, Clarendon Road, Ashford. Son of Mrs. E. Allen, of Fairfield, Westhill, Oxted, Surrey, and of the late H.C. Allen; husband of Kathleen Margaret Jessie Allen. 28 October 1944, at Westwick, Clarendon Road.

ALLEN, Kathleen Margaret Jessie, age 46; of Westwick, Clarendon Road, Ashford. Daughter of Mrs. Gray, of 13 Salisbury Street, Hull, Yorkshire; wife of Brian Seamer Allen. 28 October 1944, at Westwick, Clarendon Road.'

In all of this, I am ashamed to say that I have no recollection of my other grandmother, Mrs Gray, or of seeing her. She was a remote figure.

My father had been well known in British aviation throughout the thirties and the death of our parents did not go unnoticed. A week passed and then the following notice appeared in *Flight*. *Flight* and *The Aeroplane* were the two great weekly magazines which kept everyone in civilian aviation in touch with what was going on.

'DEATH OF BRIAN ALLEN

The British aviation community learnt with sincere regret of the death, through enemy action, of Brian Allen and his wife, Kathleen, in October last. Cremation was at Woking last Thursday, November 2nd, and at the request of the sons, F/Lt Michael Allen and F/O Rodney Allen, both serving in the R.A.F., remembrances took the form of donations to the R.A.F. Benevolent Fund.

Brian Seamer Allen was born in London on May 1st, 1899. After making a name in the motor world, he entered civil aviation as manager and pilot of the aviation department of Henly's, having previously served in the first world war. Later he formed his own company, Brian Allen Aviation Ltd and became a well-known figure at Croydon and Heston. In addition to taxi work, the firm acted as agents and distributors of various civil aircraft types, including the diminutive Tipsy models, one of which Brian Allen demonstrated very effectively at one of the Royal Aeronautical Society's garden parties at Fairey's airfield. [Now London's Heathrow airport!]

Private flying will be a great deal poorer after the war without Brian.'

In the aftermath of the death of our parents it may be asked, what happened to Rodney's posting as a potential glider pilot and where did he go when his embarkation leave expired on 28 October?

The answer is that four days after the funeral Rodney went off up to Harrogate to present himself to the Air Crew Selection Board, accompanied by the powerful figure of Flight Lieutenant Harry White! In short, supported by Harry, he got an extra week's leave and his posting onto gliders was cancelled. It was a very satisfactory outcome to their long journey and I was grateful to Harry. As I was to say, many years later, in an after-dinner speech at West Raynham, he always used to behave as if he was an air commodore – long before he reached that rank!

By 13 November – having done my best, with the aid of the family solicitor, to clear up my parents' affairs – I was back at Foulsham. On the 23rd Harry and I went on ops with a trip to the Ruhr, in support of a spoof raid by 100 Group. Once more, the Germans were not spoofed. There was no reaction from their GCI Controllers and we had no AI contacts throughout the trip. There is, however, an entry made in my log-book of particular significance for me, which reads: 'WE SAW 2 V-2s GOING UP'.

As we flew over Holland, on our way to 'Happy Valley', our attention was attracted by two fiery trails ascending vertically into the night sky and disappearing into the dark, many miles above us. We both had the same unspoken thought in our minds: within five or six minutes two V-2 rockets, similar to the one which had killed my parents and destroyed my home a few days earlier, would be crashing to earth somewhere in England and there was nothing anyone could do about it. We flew on . . .

We didn't operate again in November, but managed to get in some more practice on the Mk X AI before the end of the month.

I have mentioned that my father's sister, Mrs Joyce Garlick, was living in South Africa and that all I could do immediately after the rocket fell was to cable her with the news. There was no way of avoiding giving her the shock of opening the telegram and I could not, because of wartime restrictions, telephone her. It was unlikely that she would hear the news from the media or any other source, so one of my next tasks, once the funeral was over, was to write to her . . .

Thanks to my cousin Neil Garlick (who returned the letter I wrote to his parents, after his mother's death) I have my letter beside me, and believe it might be of interest to reproduce it in full, because it describes the situation immediately after our parents' death – as Rodney and I saw it.

The following is a fair copy of the letter I wrote to my uncle and aunt, Mr and Mrs Donald Garlick, at their home, 'Chilterns', Wynberg, Cape Town. The letter was written from our adopted home with Mrs Sessions. For some reason I forgot to date it, but it was most probably written in the second week of November 1944, before I returned to duty with BSDU at Foulsham. It reads:

'F/Lt M.S. Allen
77, Church Road
Ashford
Middlesex

My Dear Uncle Don and Auntie Joyce,
    You will by this time be aware of the rather cruel blow that fate has dealt us and I feel that I should try and tell you the story in as simple and straight forward manner as possible. I realise that the news that Daddy and Mummy had lost their lives owing to enemy action must have come as a tremendous shock, and I wish most earnestly to be able to spare you any further anxiety.
    Let me begin by telling you that the Hun threw his spanner into our lives early on Saturday morning the 28th October at about 5 o'clock when all the household was asleep. Daddy and Mummy were in the back room, Rodney (who was on leave at the time) in the front room, and there was also a friend Joan Wesson sleeping in another little room in the far side of the house. Since the bomb fell in the back garden about twenty yards away from the building Daddy and Mummy lost their lives owing to shock or blast from the explosion. I do want you to know that they had no knowledge of the incident and were taken as they slept.
    I rather feel that although it must be very painful for you to read, you would rather have these details than to be wondering and turning over all the time in your mind what has actually happened. You will feel so helpless and lost because of the distance which lies between us that every scrap of information must be better than awful uncertainty.
    I shall continue by telling you that neither of them suffered, or was mutilated and I think we may be grateful that they were spared the horrors of suffocation or those of being maimed or imprisoned.
    As you will probably realise the house partially collapsed and Rodney awoke to find his bed descending into the dining room with him still in it and when it finally came to rest he scrambled out into the garden through the hole in the side of the house. Apart from a few minor scratches and cuts which are now healed [I realise this conflicts with the account of Rodney being rescued by the ARP team.], he was completely unhurt and it is needless for me to say that his composure and grip of the situation throughout the last ten days has been

superb. Our friend Joan Wesson was also pulled out by the wardens unhurt and only a trifle shaken although of course it has been a wretched business for her since she was so fond of Mummy and Daddy and her husband who used to fly for us before the war was killed over three years ago in the Air Force. She has a small girl aged five who thank goodness was not in the house, and has virtually had the bottom knocked out of her life for the second time.

I think perhaps you will now be wondering where I was during this time so I must take you back to Norfolk to continue my story.

I awoke on the Saturday morning to receive a message from my batman to ring the telephone exchange as the police were trying to get in touch with me. On doing this I found a wire which said: "House damaged, Brother Rodney at Sessions." (Mrs Sessions is the person at whose house we are staying.) I also had another wire, this time from Rodney saying: "House destroyed, am at Sessions, return immediately." So I put two and two together and decided that I did not like the look of things one little bit. You see, it was more by what the wires did not say, than by what they said, that I felt the worst had happened.

I had already arranged to have a forty-eight hour leave over the weekend so I was already organised with ration cards and petrol coupons etc. since I am now running my car again. So I told my C.O. and Harry, my pilot, of the messages in case my fears proved to be correct and left the camp at 10.30 although my car is a small 1938 Ford 8 h.p. Saloon I can honestly say that nothing overtook me on the way down, and I arrived back in Ashford at 1.45 to find Rodney and Joan Wesson where my worst fears were confirmed.

I am continuing this letter a few days later back at camp, to be precise it is the 15th November today, and I am writing to you from my room which I share with Harry, the time is about 8.45 p.m. and in the background I have the strains of the Symphony Orchestra coming from my radio. I also have a lovely fire to keep out the chill as the frost sets in outside. But I am wandering a little from my story and must go on:-

Rodney returned to Harrogate on Sunday the 12th and I managed to get away a day later on the Monday.

Throughout the two weeks that we were in Ashford clearing up our affairs we stayed with the Sessions family and were most kindly looked after by this most friendly and big hearted household. Needless to say we had so many offers of temporary homes that we could have slept in a different bed every night if we had so desired.

Mrs Sessions has a family of six, boys and girls equally divided and she has brought them up alone since the death of her husband some fifteen years ago. All the three boys are in the R.A.F. and the youngest, Teddy aged 22 I knew when I was at prep school at The Mall, Twickenham. Of the three girls the eldest two are married but living at home owing to their husbands being in the forces and the youngest Betty aged 20, I have known for nearly four years. I think, I may add here that neither Rodney nor I are married, engaged, or have any immediate intention of getting "hitched"!

Although the house is a complete write off most of our personal possessions have been salvaged by the A.R.P. Wardens who have put up a splendid show in getting everything possible out of the wreckage. As you will probably realise most of the furniture is I am afraid completely wrecked but this is only to be expected as the house collapsed.

We have Captain Birkett of Tipsy Aircraft, whom you will possibly remember, acting as our executor and we also have our own solicitor, a Mr Roy Newberry, who knew both Daddy and Mummy personally and had previously done some business for the family. I should also like you to know that so far as the financial situation is concerned there is nothing to worry about and as soon as I can give you our figures when the situation has cleared I will do so.

I realise that you will be anxious to know these facts but I do want you to understand that everything that can be done is being done. If by any chance something too big for me to handle does break then I will not hesitate to wire you, but for goodness sake do not worry yourselves unduly because that will not help. I have found the antidote for pain and that is work, during the two weeks that I have been home sorting out our affairs I have hardly stopped. Once you stop, you start to think, and, to think back, which is ridiculous. My theory, which I have told so many people in the past few days, is to thank God for what you have had in the past and look to the future.

I know that your thoughts will be with Grannie since it is a bitter blow for her, but I can still find many people who are far worse off than Rodney and I and are far less in a position to tackle such a situation. We are not the sort of blokes who sit down and start feeling sorry for ourselves, we are going to hit back and I can promise you that somebody in Hunland is going to pay our debt.

You must not get the idea that the country is under any great menace. This was just the odd one out of the blue, it has done little damage, and it just happens that we were the unfortunate ones.

Please do not get the idea that I am being offhand or callous about Mummy and Daddy, believe me I am not. But the Hun is trying to kill our spirit and we must not let that happen. Neither am I being in any way heroic, but I believe that there is only one way to take a blow like we have suffered and Rodney and I are taking it on the chin.

I will write to you again in about a week's time but I feel I have said enough for the present. My address is:

F/Lt. M.S. Allen   or c/o Mrs Sessions
Officers Mess   77 Church Road
R.A.F.   Ashford
Foulsham   Middlesex
Dereham
Norfolk
All my Love I send you tonight and Always
Michael
There is so much to tell you that I could go on for pages but as I want this to go to post it must suffice for the present.
P.S. I have a Second Bar to my D.F.C.'

As Guy Gibson said, in the Foreword and Dedication to his book *Enemy Coast Ahead* (when wondering if he could retell the story of his four years of war), 'A memory is a short thing, and flak never does it much good'. I am well aware that some of the details in my letter to my aunt and uncle are at variance with the description of the death of my parents which preceded it. I make no apologies for that. My memory did not suffer the effects of so much flak as Guy Gibson's, but it had a bit.

Further, I know my letter suffers from almost a complete lack of punctuation! I have been tempted to put some in but, again, I have decided to leave my letter exactly as I wrote it over fifty years ago, as the style reflects the fashion and the phrases of the time. I have a letter written by my uncle, Lieutenant Geoffrey Allen, during the First World War – and the style and fashion is different again.

If, at times, and to use modern parlance, I went 'OTT' my readers must try to imagine the situation as it was in November 1944: the war was still on; I was writing to two people who lived in another world, 7,000 miles away and who perforce had no knowledge of life in wartime England. The 'proof of the pudding', if I may put it that way, 'lay in the eating'. My aunt kept my letter, amongst her treasures, for the rest of her life . . .

On 2 December 1944 we did an op to the Ruhr, still carrying out trials with Monica, and we had a Mosquito fitted with Mk X AI. Somewhere over the Ruhr – which was being attacked by a force of 400 bombers – we picked up an AI contact, completed the interception and Harry got a visual on a twin-engined aircraft, with twin tails. It could have been a Heinkel 219 (one of the new German night-fighters) or an American 'Black Widow' night-fighter (some of which, we had heard, were starting to operate over Europe).

Whether it was an E/A or a Black Widow it must have been equipped with an efficient rearward-looking AI and the AI operator in it must have picked us up as we came in behind them. Our target, still not identified, suddenly started to take violent evasive action and Harry followed him visually through two tight orbits, before he dived away into the cloud layer below us. Harry lost the visual and I lost the AI contact. We returned home to base after 4.20 hours in the air – both extremely disappointed.

Two nights later we went to Karlsruhe on the Mosquito XXX, our old friend, 797. My log refers to the bombers' target as being a 'Nice Prang' but there was very little reaction from the German night-fighters. We did get one AI contact and completed the interception. When Harry got a visual on our target, it turned out to be a lone Lancaster, heading north away from Karlsruhe, and appearing to be completely clueless.

On the 6th we operated again and went to Osnabrück, and again we took 797. In my log, at the top of the page, is written: ' "To be turned from one's course by misrepresentation shows a man unfit to hold an office." Plutarch.'

Further down the page – for the op on the 6th – one may read: 'Osnabrück. Lost contact on Hun three miles away, after he had dropped fighter flare.'

We landed back at Foulsham after 4.30 hrs in the air, both bitterly disappointed. I had (in Plutarch's words of centuries earlier) turned Harry from his course, and I was clearly a man unfit to hold office.

Six days later we took off on ops, again in 797 – at least, we tried to take off! We were half-way down the runway, when the port engine cut, virtually at the point of no return, and Harry chopped the starboard engine. We sped on down the runway. As our speed slowly dropped off, Harry gingerly started to apply the brakes. We eventually ran out of runway, trundled onto the grass and finally came to a stop with the nose of the Mosquito a few feet from the boundary fence.

Harry and I found ourselves looking at some rather surprised cows, busy chewing the cud, in the field beyond. Number 797 was towed ignominiously back to the BSDU Dispersal where the engine fitters could find nothing wrong with the port engine!

Harry and I were beginning to view 797 with some suspicion, and to wonder whether it had a jinx on it. When another BSDU crew experienced engine failure on 797, a few days later, people were overheard referring to it as 'the dreaded XXX'. My log-book entry reads: 'Tues 12th 18.30 Mosquito XXX F/Lt White OPS. Port engine cut on take-off. Pulled up. All OK JUST!' The space normally filled in with our flying time is noticeably blank!

At about this time BSDU moved, lock, stock and barrel from Foulsham across to Swanton Morley. The unit was out of action for two weeks and we did not operate again until after Christmas. Swanton Morley was only five miles south of Foulsham, we were still very much part of 100 Group, so little changed except that it was a grass airfield and there were no concrete runways. Swanton was still very much within range of Aylsham (where I was still seeing both Jill and Ursula) so there was no problem there. However, in view of what happened later, it was a pity that we didn't leave 797 behind, when we moved out of Foulsham!

Whilst we were settling in at Swanton Morley, I had to make a quick visit to Ashford. Today, when many instances of misbehaviour and vandalism are reported, in gory detail, by the media, the older generation tend to say, smugly, 'Tut, Tut, Tut! That wouldn't have happened in our time'. Don't you believe it! It could and did happen in our younger days and in wartime too, as we shall see!

I was rung up at Swanton by the Inspector of Staines Police Station, the same officer whom I had met at the time 60 Clarendon Road was destroyed by the V-2. He sounded uncomfortable, and asked me apologetically if I could get down to Ashford and come and see him (I started to wonder what I had done wrong!). I took two more days' leave and drove straight to Staines. There, the Inspector was waiting for me with a police car. We drove out to some school buildings on the Kingston road. On the way he explained the reason for his call.

A day or two after the missile had fallen the ARP teams went back to the site to salvage what they could of our belongings from the ruins of the house. They also went to adjoining houses, which had been badly damaged, and were no longer habitable. The rather pitiful bits and pieces had been removed, and taken for storage at a new school which was being built on the Staines to Kingston road. They would remain there until reclaimed by their owners. The Inspector proceeded to tell me that a gang of youths had broken into the building. They had ransacked the school and vandalised a number of the classrooms. They had applied the same treatment to our possessions which had been stored on the first floor.

The school, half built, with walls not yet plastered, and the upper windows open to the elements, was not a good security risk. Perhaps someone in authority did not consider that anyone would think of breaking into the building and vandalising what few possessions were left to the victims of the recent bombing. He should have thought again.

The Inspector, visibly embarrassed, showed me over the whole building, and the sight which I saw stays with me yet. Everywhere we looked was a scene of wanton destruction and obscenity. When I eventually went into the bare room to which our possessions had been taken by the ARP men and neatly stacked, I saw that everything had been disarranged, there was total chaos. I remember, in particular, four things – they still turn my stomach.

Our Trix Twin train set had been thrown out of the window. When I looked out, I could see the engine and carriages lying on the ground below, and a set of snooker balls had been treated likewise. Rodney's loose stamps (he had a formidable stamp collection) had been found in an attaché case. The lid of the leather case had been forced open – and the contents were scattered all over the room.

And then there was my mother's camera. In the unsophisticated days of the 1930s, the camera for the amateur family photographer was the five shilling Brownie box camera. It was a small and compact oblong black box. Inside, was a roll of Kodak film which was inserted into the back, and wound around two spools. I spotted it lying on the floor, in the midst of the debris, where it had been thrown carelessly down. However, it had not been discarded before the back of the camera had been ripped off and the film – which was inside – ripped out and left hanging forlornly, and quite ruined, from the back of it.

As we drove back to Staines, the Inspector apologised to me again and promised that, if they caught up with those responsible, retribution would follow swiftly and without mercy. In those days the police could sometimes take matters into their own hands, without the danger of being sued by some criminal for compensation.

I made an overnight stop at Dencliff House and returned to Swanton Morley the following day, thinking that I had now seen everything. As usual, I was wrong.

Shortly after the move to Swanton Morley we had a visitor. Harry and I were in the bar one night when the CO, Rupert Clerke, came across to us, and rather apologetically asked if we could help him out. He went on to explain that a Canon Marriott had arrived and would be staying in the mess for two or three days, as the guest of the Station Commander. The Canon, Rupert explained, was the representative of the Bishop of London and he was one of several clerics who had been deputed to visit units in all three Services. Their brief was to spend a day or two with a regiment, on board one of the Navy's ships or at an RAF station. Their task was to ascertain the feelings of those serving in the Armed Forces in respect of religion and religious matters, then to report back to the bishop with their findings.

Rupert wanted Harry and I to look after the Canon during his short stay at Swanton Morley. To say the least, we were not enthralled by the prospect. Religious considerations had not figured prominently in our partnership! Of course there had been that disturbing few weeks at Tangmere when Harry, shortly after being commissioned, had fallen under the spell of Squadron Leader the Reverend Howard Guinness!

I remember it well, because, for a short spell, he gave me stick for drinking too much, swearing too much, and staying out too late at night! He was impossible to live with but, I am pleased to record, he soon snapped out of it and equilibrium was restored to the White/Allen relationship. To say that we were concerned by the CO's request to host the worthy Canon was putting it mildly.

In the event, we need not have worried. Canon Marriott was a delightful and charming man. He was, additionally, a most interesting and open-minded person. We enjoyed looking after him and Harry and I never forgot him. I have also not forgotten his opening remarks, when we first met. He was elderly in appearance, white haired, distinguished and he had a genuine sense of humour. When Rupert had introduced him to us we bought him a beer, and the three of us settled down comfortably in a corner of the bar. He opened on the following lines:

'When we visit the Navy and spend a few days on board ship, we find amongst members of the crew, and at "Divisions", that there is some feeling for religion and some positive reaction. It is the same when we visit units of the Army – particularly when they are serving abroad – and attendance at their "Drum Head" Services are a rewarding experience. But, Harry and Michael, when it comes to visiting you chaps – we have to confess that we have no idea whatsoever, what makes the RAF tick!'

I am not at all sure that we were able to say anything to enlighten him. We did our best to be helpful and constructive and, at a guess, may have tried to put forward some of the following points, all of which I am sure he must have heard before, but was too polite to say so!

In the Navy, the chaplains can go to sea in the larger vessels and they form part of the ship's company. When the ship engages the enemy, they have their 'Action Stations' like every other member of the crew, they can share the experience of war. It is the same in the Army. The regimental chaplains are part and parcel of the unit and, when battle is joined, they go into action with it. They again are able to share the experience of war with their 'congregation' and they rightly merit the respect and admiration of their men for having done so. In both cases it is reasonable to assume that something of the chaplain's calling rubs off on the sailors and soldiers after the battle is over.

The Royal Air Force chaplains are not so lucky. They cannot share the experience of war with those who fly, any more than the ground crews and administrative personnel on an RAF station. The crew of a Spitfire is one, the crew of a Mosquito is two, the crew of a Lancaster is seven. There is no more room for a chaplain than there is for the Engineer Officer or the Station Adjutant.

In the Air Force, a whole squadron did not go into action together, only the aircrew took off on ops. Their ground crews, representing 70–75 per cent of the squadron strength, remained on the ground. There was no such being as a Squadron Chaplain, only two or three Station Chaplains representing the various denominations, and they too had to remain on the ground. In short, they could not share the feelings and emotions of men going into action, in the way their opposite numbers in the Navy and the Army could. Therefore, they knew nothing of the world in which the aircrew lived – and frequently died.

We felt sorry for the Station Chaplains, we were tolerant towards them, but we did not want to see them around too much. Especially, we did not want them hanging about the crew room or near our aircraft just before we took off on ops. Unlike some wartime films, which depict padres going round to American crews – due to take off on a mission – to administer the sacraments and give a blessing. If we had seen any of the Station Chaplains at dispersal, in the 'twitchy' few moments before having to climb into our machines, many of us would have regarded it as an ill omen for the trip!

There were some notable exceptions like Branse Burbridge and Bill Skelton and of course, John Brachi. But, in the main, we were a fairly carefree lot where religious matters were concerned. We were not, of course, oblivious to the intangible – far from it – but we tended to put our faith in luck, fate, chance or call it what you will. More likely than not, just before climbing into our aircraft, we would be checking up to make sure that we had not forgotten our own special lucky charm or talisman, which we hoped would ward off the perils of the night. Mine was my old House Colour scarf, from Hurstpierpoint College days. We would also be going through a well-established routine, without which we would feel unsettled when we were in the aircraft. For many, this routine included the act of relieving themselves against the tail-wheel!

From being unsettled (as we all are when we've forgotten something) it is a short step to being worried and finally, to our minds not being on our job. From that, for a member of aircrew on operations, it is a quick step to disaster. Not just for him, but probably his whole crew. There is an example of this in the film, *The Way to the Stars*, when the CO mislays his cigarette lighter, just before taking off on an op. He does not return.

Some of the RAF chaplains – I am sure – were able to do a splendid job amongst the administrative personnel on a station, but many of our squadron ground crew (who were much closer to us) thought as we did and would have been likely to give the padre fairly short shrift! I have heard that there were one or two of the American chaplains who flew on the odd operation with Fortress or Liberator crews. These aircraft carried a crew of ten and a keen chaplain could get himself a ride as a waist gunner if he felt so inclined! I am sure he never regretted it and that he would enjoy the esteem and comradeship of his 'congregation' for ever after. There may have been some RAF padres who went on an op but I have never heard of one. For most of them I am afraid that the barrier, between their lives and ours, proved impenetrable and we stuck to our lucky charms.

All this, and a lot more, we thrashed out with Canon Marriott, and his time at Swanton Morley passed quickly. We enjoyed having him with us and were sorry to see him go.

A few days later it was Christmas, and the Church's fears about what made the Air Force tick were seen in stark reality at Swanton Morley. It was Christmas Day, bitterly cold and there was a blanket of snow covering the whole airfield. At the station Chapel for the Christmas Day service was the Chaplain; Wing Commander Rupert Clerke (who as acting Station Commander felt he ought to be there); the station administrative officer; Harry and I (because Rupert had asked us to support him); and Rupert's WAAF driver (who came in because it was too cold for her to sit in the car outside!).

Admittedly, there were not a large number of personnel at Swanton at the time, but if those were all who could be mustered in church for Christmas Day (and five out of those attended as a result of some form of persuasion!), it is little wonder that the Bishop of London wanted to know what made the RAF tick.

My three previous Christmases (two at Tangmere, and one at West Raynham) had been spent in uninhibited celebrations, starting with serving the airmen with their Christmas dinner in traditional style, moving back to the sergeants' mess in 1941 and latterly, once we were commissioned, moving eventually to the officers' mess, for our own meal. By then, I would not like to say we were drunk but we were 'very nicely thank you'. I have no recollection of how I spent the rest of Christmas Day 1944.

Three days later, when the snow had been swept off the wings of our Mosquitoes and thawed from the airfield, we ended the year by doing an op to Bonn and München Gladbach. Once again we had no joy, and saw only one bomber shot down (and that, by flak). We were busy testing out one of the 'George boxes' but there were no 'George' noises from enemy aircraft to be heard that night.

So ended 1944, one way and another, it had been quite a year: more was still to come. The New Year dawned with us making a hurried return flight to West Raynham in the Anson to pick up some equipment and then doing a very rushed NFT of only 20 minutes, in the dreaded XXX 797, prior to setting off on a task, loosely defined in our Combat Report as 'Patrol Bremen to Ruhr'.

Somewhere, 30 miles east of Dortmund at a height of 15,000 feet, we picked up two AI contacts at a range of about seven miles. We selected the contact on our port side and completed the interception on a target which was weaving violently. Harry got a fleeting visual at 3,000 ft, and again at 2,000 ft – where he was able to hold it, as we continued to close in. At 200 ft in front of us Harry identified the target – still weaving – as a Junkers 88. I then picked up the night glasses, saw the distinctive tail unit of a Ju 88 with the swastika on it, and confirmed the identification of the E/A to Harry.

We then dropped back to 250 ft behind the Junkers, and from slightly below it, opened fire with a one-second burst. We saw several strikes, followed by an explosion, and some small pieces were seen to come away. The flash of the explosion caused Harry to lose his visual, then the Ju 88 broke away in a hard diving turn to starboard. I tried to follow him on the AI, but failed in my attempt to do so, and lost the contact. Harry fired another short burst at the estimated position of the E/A.

Nothing further was seen of him, so all we could claim was one Ju 88 damaged. The real culprit for our failure to destroy the Junkers – which would have given us so much satisfaction was, once again, poor old 797! When we had opened fire both port cannon had failed! We learned later, after we had landed, that we had fired 125 rounds from the two starboard cannon, but there were stoppages in both the port inner and outer guns.

It is tempting to say that the failure of 50 per cent of our armament made the difference between us being able to destroy the enemy aircraft and only being able to claim it as damaged. But life is never quite as simple as that. If, with the benefit of hindsight, you are tempted to alter one aspect of your story in your favour, who can tell whether another aspect of the story might not have varied, which could have been distinctly against your best interests, i.e. the Ju 88 might have got a shot at us!

What is certain is that our failure to destroy the 88 had tangible repercussions on the following day, which were distinctly unpleasant for all concerned and nearly resulted in someone else having to write this story.

My log-book entry for Tuesday 2 January 1945 is as follows:

'Tues 2nd 17.15 Mosquito MM797 F/Lt White OPS 797

Pranged shortly after take off in the dreaded XXX owing to a glycol leak in the Port Engine and we were unable to feather. Harry jettisoned our droptanks and put up a terrific show in crash landing the kite in a field in the half light and very poor vis. although both unhurt, we were unable to get out of the wrecked and burning remains owing to my left leg being trapped. After several minutes three farmer types arrived and at the risk of their own lives succeeded in pulling us out with the kite now very well alight and ammunition exploding right, left, and centre. This; my first prang could not have been cut any finer! And we both owe our lives to those three men.

    Time in the air: 5 minutes.'

Some weeks later I pasted the following extract from *The Eastern Daily Press* into my log-book beside the above entry. It was dated 9 May 1945 and read:

'AIRMEN RESCUED BY NORFOLK MEN. B.E.M. AWARDS

Awards of the B.E.M. have been made to three Norfolk men for splendid service in extricating R.A.F. Officers from a plane which crashed, and burst into flames at Scarning in January.

The recipients are Mr. Walter William Ward, farm labourer employed by Mr. Samuel Steward of Laurence House Farm Scarning, and living at 17 Washbridge, Dereham; Mr. Herbert George Farrow, farmer of Broadway Farm, Scarning; and Mr. James Andrews of 2 Council Houses Scarning, a labourer employed by Mr. Farrow.

At about 5.20 p.m. in the gathering dusk, their attention was drawn to a low-flying aircraft which skimmed hedges and then crashed in a ploughed field, bursting into flames. The men raced to the scene and saw one of the airmen in the cockpit. He was unable to get out because his left leg was trapped.

Farrow and Andrews worked strenuously to extricate him but were unable to do so until Ward managed to get this Airman's boot off. Having freed him they rolled him into a ditch nearby. It was then seen that the pilot had been lying underneath the first airman, and the three men lifted him bodily out of the blazing aircraft.

Then, in compliance with one airman's shout to "run before it goes up," they sought the safety of the ditch. During the whole of this time there were explosions of ammunition and the flames grew in intensity. A second or two after all the men had flattened themselves in the ditch the petrol tank exploded. The airmen were F/Lt. Allen navigator, and F/Lt. White pilot, and both were removed to Broadway Farm for attention before being taken away by ambulance.'

To go back to the morning of 2 January, Harry and I found, when we had slept late after the previous night's trip, that ops were on again. Still feeling disappointed after only damaging the Junkers 88, we found – when we went down to Dispersal – that another pilot and navigator (Dennis Welfare and 'Sticky' Clay, an exceptional crew), were on the programme and were down to take 797.

On the spur of the moment, Harry said to Dennis, 'Mike and I would like to have another go, there's only one aircraft available, I'll toss you for it, to see who does the trip!' Rupert Clerke had no objections, so we tossed a coin and Harry won. It was all a big joke, because I don't think any of us had ever spun a coin before, to decide such an issue. Dennis and Sticky took themselves off happily enough and Harry and I went to look at 797.

We then learned that the Mosquito was still being serviced after the previous night's op and was unlikely to be ready until the late afternoon. We went to Briefing and 797 still hadn't come up. It was an early time when we were due to be over the target and we were scheduled to take off at 5.15 p.m. When the aircraft was still not ready at 4.00 p.m. we said we would take it on the op without bothering to carry out an NFT. We had never – in three and a half years of night-fighter operations – taken an aircraft on ops without an NFT – let alone the dreaded XXX!

At 5.10 p.m. we picked up our things and walked out to 797. Five minutes later Harry opened the throttles and we took off, heading east to west, from Swanton

Morley before planning to turn port and climb onto our course for the Ruhr. But we had no sooner cleared the hedge and climbed to 600 feet than the port engine failed. Harry could feel the immediate loss of power and when I looked back, over my left shoulder, I could see a long stream of glycol trailing from the port engine.

Writing to Rodney, several days later, Harry – in his usual succinct style – said:

'. . . about an accident some little time ago, there really is so little to say. As Mike has no doubt told you the port engine failed soon after take off but the position, although "dicie" never appeared critical till it suddenly became drastic. You probably know the whole story, Mike could never miss such an opportunity to tell all that happened. [Note: "Ahem!" Au.]'

The Bomber Support Development Unit, Swanton Morley: on 2 January 1945 we crashed shortly after taking off on an operation to the Ruhr. Harry and I were trapped in the burning wreckage until we were rescued by the selfless courage of three Norfolk farmers. Harry returned the following morning and took these two photographs. One is of the wreckage of the cockpit, the engines and wings and the other is of the tail unit, which broke off as we bumped across the field in a 'wheels-up' landing.

A glycol leak, 716 gals. of petrol and an engine which would not feather. The touch down, which soon became inevitable in the half light was very heavy; much heavier than it should have been with the possible excuse that a glide approach with such a load at 140 m.p.h. could not be otherwise. Although the machine was a complete and utter wreck before it came to rest, it was not that which caused all the trouble. If it had not been for a dreaded and unavoidable ditch we should both have found no difficulty in extricating ourselves from the resulting shambles.'

When the port engine failed – and Harry could not feather it, to reduce the drag – we knew that we would not be able to maintain our altitude, let alone climb to a safer height. It was before the days of ejection seats and we were too low to bale out. Our only chance was to try and find a field and put the Mosquito down with a wheels-up landing – and hope that the aircraft would not sustain too much damage when we slid across the field on our belly.

Harry jettisoned the two 100 gallon drop-tanks, reducing our fuel to 516 gallons, and I released the top hatch above our heads in hope that we would be able to scramble quickly out of the cockpit and drop onto the ground. With a wheels-up landing we would not have far to drop(!) once the Mosquito had come to rest . . .

From Swanton Morley, on our westerly heading, we must have passed just to the North of East Dereham and we were gradually turning to port all the time. We must have been down to about 300 feet when we crossed the East Dereham/Swaffham Road and by then we were heading south as we passed over the village of Scarning. A few seconds later Harry spotted a field which might just be large enough, if he could get the Mosquito down onto the ground as soon as we had cleared the lane and the hedge.

He did it and we were down and bumping across the field; although how he managed it in the dusk and half-light, with no other choice, I will never know. It was his supreme moment as a pilot. The ground was hard, because there had been some frost and there was a light covering of snow so we slid across the field in fine style without 797 sustaining too much damage. As Harry says, it was only when we had nearly come to rest, that we went over a hidden ditch (which we could not have avoided anyway) that caused the tail unit to break off. Worse still, the wooden fuselage was broken and crumpled in several places, the cockpit layout had suffered certain modifications, and the aircraft was on fire.

Harry and I, although mercifully unscratched, and sitting now in the wreckage of the cockpit, found that we both had a problem. Having been around for some time, we knew we had not got long in which to solve these problems!

Harry's problem was that his seat – on the port side – had shifted and come off its mountings. He had been thrown forward into the bottom right-hand corner of the cockpit. He found himself trapped in his seat, surrounded by the wreckage of my Mk X AI radar, and jammed tightly down in front of me. He could not get out until I got out.

My problem was that, when I tried to stand up and pull myself out of the now open canopy above us, I found my left leg was sticking out through a narrow slit of the broken fuselage. The slit was small and there was pressure on it which prevented me from forcing it open any wider. I was wearing the standard black leather flying boots of the time, the bottom part being the tightly laced 'shoes' which could be cut off from the top half (if one was trying to evade capture, in enemy-occupied territory), with its wide flange and sheepskin lining. The complete boot with its wide floppy top and its laced-up shoe was on the outside of the fuselage, with my leg firmly encased in it.

The rest of me was on the inside and, try as I may, I could not pull my leg back through the slit. The harder I pulled, holding on to the edge of the canopy, and with (I was told years later by Herbert Farrow) perspiration pouring down my face, the harder the wide rim of my boot was forced against the outside of the fuselage. I too was trapped. So we both were.

Herbert Farrow and James Andrews, at Broadway Farm, were just finishing work as darkness fell and they had seen us come down. 'Old Walter' Ward had been cycling home along the lane which lay past the field which Harry had chosen for our crash-landing. Later he was to tell us '. . . you come over so bliddy low, you bliddy near cut me 'ead orf!'

After several futile attempts to pull myself out of the cockpit, I shouted for help. I shouted 'HELP! HELP!' several times, at the pitch of my lungs.

In retrospect, the chances of anyone hearing me must seem remote, to say the least! We had crashed somewhere in the Norfolk countryside about four miles south-west of Swanton Morley. It was almost dark, bitterly cold and the nearest village was a mile away. In wartime England, with the blackout and no lights anywhere, no one stayed out at night if it could possibly be avoided.

Even if, by any chance, someone heard my cries for help, it was unlikely that they would be prepared to approach the burning wreck in the field, which was likely to blow up at any moment.

Incredible though it was, three men *had* seen us come down and they *had* heard my cries for help. Furthermore, they were three men who were brave enough to run right up to the burning Mosquito. Above all, the three had the courage to stay at the scene until they had got us out.

Still struggling to pull myself out, but weakening from my efforts, I was still calling out for help when I suddenly saw two faces above me, peering down through the open canopy into the cockpit. Herbert Farrow and James Andrews had clambered up onto the wings and, leaning over the top of the Perspex canopy, they tried to pull me out of the aircraft.

Even with their joint strength, the wide rim of the flying-boot on my left leg bearing hard against the outside of the fuselage could still not be forced back through the narrow slit in the broken woodwork, so I remained trapped. So did Harry. I slumped back, exhausted, into my seat and I heard one of them say: 'I think she's going up now!'. We weren't the first aircraft they had seen come down and they knew what was likely to happen at any moment, just as well as we did. I remember thinking that they would not stay any longer. I also remember thinking that I would not blame them, if they did go.

As I have said earlier, we were both unhurt when the broken and battered Mosquito came to a stop and it might well be asked, what was Harry White doing whilst I was struggling to get clear and calling for help? Harry was a forceful character. He was also struggling and trying to get out of his seat from somewhere underneath my smashed AI set, whilst urging me on in my endeavours with characteristically forceful language!

When I slumped back in my seat, exhausted, and thought the men outside were going to leave us, I virtually gave up the struggle. I didn't think it was of use bothering any more. I didn't know how long we had been on the ground – and on fire – but I thought it must be two or three minutes and this is a long time under such circumstances. I only knew that things could not go on like this for very much longer – and as we have seen, my log-book entry (made a day or two afterwards) refers to 'THE KITE BEING NOW VERY WELL ALIGHT AND AMMUNITION EXPLODING'.

I sat back and started to contemplate what death would be like. I found myself looking forward to it with a warm sense of anticipation. I thought it would be good. I also made a mental note that I would probably find out what had happened to my parents killed two months earlier by the V-2 rocket. I didn't think I would see them again, but I did think I would find out what had happened to them. I felt a warm glow as I sat there, making no further efforts to get out, and was looking forward to dying within the next few seconds.

Harry White, however, had other ideas. He was more concerned about the warm glow under us – and he most certainly had not given up! I was dragged back to reality by the sound of his voice shouting 'GET THE AXE OUT!' All aircraft carried an axe (like a fireman's axe) so that aircrew could supposedly chop their way out if they found themselves in a predicament – such as ours in fact! I should have looked for it earlier, when I had first found that my leg was trapped.

His language urged me on, although I never did find the axe. I have always thought since, that if Harry had been able to get his hands on the axe, he would have had my leg off in a trice!

Instead, I suddenly thought if one of those people outside (if they were still there?) could pull my left boot right off my foot – then my leg, minus the cumbersome boot, might pass back through the slit in the starboard side of the fuselage, when the others tried again from the top of the canopy to pull me out of the wreckage.

I shouted out to them (they were still there), to pull my boot off, and Old Walter it was who got his hands round the boot – still sticking out of the side of the fuselage – and started pulling. By this time, I was fully back in the land of the living and was yelling 'HEAVE! HEAVE!' to Old Walter.

Eventually, I have no idea how long it took him, the flying boot (complete with its tightly laced shoe) came off in his hands. Herbert Farrow and Jimmy Andrews leaned over the canopy once more, and pulled me straight out – my stockinged left leg coming through the narrow slit without any further trouble. As the local paper said, they bundled me unceremoniously into a ditch and ran back for Harry.

They were able to shift his seat (with me now out of the way) and get him out very quickly. It was he who shouted to them 'RUN BEFORE IT GOES UP!', which they did – falling into the ditch in a heap beside me. A few seconds later 797, the dreaded XXX, blew up . . .

The BSDU Operational Report for 2/3 January 1945 reads as follows:

'Mosquito XXX F/Lt H. White D.F.C.& F/Lt M. Allen D.F.C.– High level Intruder

M.M. 797 Take off 17.25 hrs. ABORTIVE

Port engine cut out soon after take off and airscrew would not feather. Pilot unable to maintain height although he jettisoned wing tanks and A/C force-landed near Dereham (Cat E) Crew unhurt apart from shock to Navigator.'

Harry and I were taken back to Broadway Farm by our rescuers, where he phoned up Swanton Morley, got through to BSDU and told them what had happened. They sent out an ambulance to pick us up.

By the time the ambulance arrived, my left leg had stiffened up after the treatment it had received, and I could hardly walk. When we arrived back at Swanton Morley I was carted off to station sick quarters, where I spent a couple of days, whilst my left leg thawed out after the tug-of-war with the boot. I had no idea that I was suffering from shock, until I read the above Operational Report many years later!

I remember being completely spoilt by the nursing staff in sick quarters; and then, when I came out, I spent the next few days limping round the camp with a stick, shooting the most awful line. In the meantime, Harry had been back to Broadway Farm and taken two photographs of the wreckage of 797 (see page 265). One was of the tail unit, which it will be recalled had broken off as we careered across the frozen field, and the other shows all that was left of the front part of the Mosquito after the petrol tanks had exploded. We also decided that we must go back to see our rescuers and thank them. I used the time whilst I was off flying to go to London, where I ordered three silver tankards from Goldsmiths & Silversmiths and had them suitably engraved.

When the tankards were delivered, early in February, we went to Broadway Farm – this time by car! We took a crate of beer, as well as the tankards, and we had a party! Some of those on BSDU came along, together with one or two of our old friends from 141, including, I remember, Roger Osborn. Apart from Herbert Farrow, Jimmy Andrews and Old Walter Ward, there were a number of their friends, from the village of Scarning, who had come along to help them celebrate with 'they boys from the Air Force' – and to drink up the free beer!

It was a riotous evening; and after the tankards had been duly presented, an awful lot of beer disappeared down RAF and Norfolk throats! I well remember Old Walter telling me that someone (presumably either Herbert or Jimmy) had told him, after the rescue was over, that there had been ammunition going off, but that he had never heard it!

Harry and I were both also convinced that all three of them should be put up for one of the bravery awards, to give public recognition of their courage in risking their own lives to save ours. Harry wrote out a full report of the crash and the rescue, and with Rupert Clerke's support, it was steered towards the right Government Department for the handling of recommendations of honours and awards to civilians. *The Eastern Daily Press* announced the award of the BEM (the British Empire Medal, now sadly discontinued) to Herbert Farrow, James Andrews and Walter Ward, when it printed the story of the rescue on 9 May, just as the war in Europe came to an end. There was a postscript to these awards, given for conspicuous gallantry.

Years later, when Pam and I visited Herbert Farrow, I asked him to show me his BEM. He pointed to the sideboard, in his tiny sitting room, and said: 'It's in there, Michael.' I opened one of the drawers and found a small cardboard box, held together by a rubber-band. I said, in astonishment, 'Is this it?' and Herbert nodded, adding: 'And that's how it come.' He had been sent his BEM through the post.

As already mentioned elsewhere, there was a long queue of recipients of awards waiting to be summoned to Buckingham Palace but I have never been able to understand why the services of the county Lord Lieutenants and High

Sheriffs were not called upon to perform the presentations (in the King's name), as being far more acceptable than sending medals, awarded for bravery, through the post.

Later, I heard of one or two other people who had received their DFCs through the post. What a let-down and disappointment that must have been. So far as Herbert Farrow was concerned, I always got the impression that he was more pleased with the silver tankard, that Harry and I had given him, than he was with his BEM!

It was, in fact, thirty-three years before Pam and I went to see Herbert Farrow and learned how he had received his BEM. In the post-war years I had always ducked going back, and then in 1966 I had emigrated to South Africa. Now, on home leave in 1978, Pam would hear of no more stalling on my part. She said: 'You owe it to them to go back.' So we found ourselves walking up the path to Herbert's small cottage, just outside East Dereham, meeting his wife, Doris, and seeing him for the first time since the night at Broadway Farm, when Harry and I gave the three of them their tankards.

Later we drove out to find the field where Harry and I had crashed, all those years before. As we stood there together, I asked Herbert if he could remember where our Mosquito had come down because all Pam and I could see was a dark green crop of sugar beet. He pointed immediately to a circular patch of beet, in the middle of the field, about 40 yards in diameter, which was *of a different colour*, and said 'That's where it were, my Booty!' Then we saw – the patch which marked the spot where our Mosquito finally came to rest – was light green.

We squelched through the thick Norfolk mud and sure enough, among the tell-tale light green leaves of the ripening beet, we looked down and saw some fragments of 797 lying there at our feet.

Sadly, both Jimmy Andrews and Old Walter had died before Pam and I went back to East Dereham but we kept in touch with Herbert until his death in 1992. I was invited to give the address at his funeral and was thus able to pay a public tribute to Herbert Farrow BEM, and to the other two, who had saved our lives on 2 January 1945. (The official citation for their awards is in Appendix 2.)

The story of the crash was first told in 1970 in the Johannesburg Newspaper, *The Star*, and later, after Pam and I had returned to England in 1982, it was included in *Out Of The Blue*. Harry's account of our sortie on the night of the Peenemünde raid also features in that book. When, out of courtesy, I sent Harry a copy of my masterly account of the crash, he was extremely rude! He wrote back to me and said: 'Dear Mike, I still can't think how you made so many mistakes that night. Yours ever, Harry.'

Amongst the incredible stories in *Out Of The Blue* is an account by Squadron Leader T. Bennett. Ben Bennett, as a Navigator Leader of 617 Squadron, was to have a distinguished career in Bomber Command. He spoke of his Lancaster plunging earthwards and 'the absolute terror of it', with the certainty of an immediate and frightening death. 'Then, a buoyant calm seemed to come and soothe away all my hysteria, all my unspeakable fear . . .' It will be remembered that Paddy Engelbach's Sonnet also appears in *Out of the Blue*, including the words '. . . a strange, warm comfort calms you with its kiss.'

When I had slumped back into my seat, after failing to get clear of our wrecked and burning Mosquito and knowing that the petrol tanks were liable to blow up at any second, it was the same calm that I found – when I knew, beyond doubt, that I was going to die within a matter of seconds.

It will come as no surprise to my readers to be told that I have never forgotten those few moments and often recall them. For many years I had nightmares, as the story was played out, night after night, in my dreams.

Fifty-four years on and now turned 76, I venture to suggest that in such terminal moments, one's early religious upbringing returns and brings with it this wonderful calm which helps you to die peacefully.

It does not matter that one has spent adult years denying most of the Christian tenets to which one was introduced as a child. When that moment comes, and you know you are going to die, the faith in which you were brought up as a child reasserts itself. I feel sure that this must hold good for the whole range of religious beliefs, as well as it does for the Christian faith. I only know that there is no price that one can put on one's early religious training and no price which I can put on the fifty-four bonus years of life which I have been fortunate enough to enjoy since 2 January 1945.

As already mentioned, Harry wrote to Rodney and outlined what had happened when 797 played her last trick on us. I also wrote to him, and in his diary for 11 January he made the following entry:

> 'Got a long letter from Michael telling me of his dicey do on Jan 2nd when the port engine of their Mosquito caught fire just after take off, forcing Harry to crash land 8 minutes later, in a field with both Mick and Harry caught in cockpit. A/C on fire. Lusty shouts brought farmers who got them out – Thank God – that I still have a brother.'

What of Mosquito MM797, the dreaded XXX? Is there such a thing as a rogue aircraft (or a rogue car, for that matter?) Was there really a jinx on it?

What should you do when your aircraft (or your car) continually gives fault, and nobody seems to be able to find the trouble? Or was it all par for the course, the average happening that one must expect on any operational unit, in wartime conditions? In other words, was it all a part of the intangible elements of luck, fate, chance – or call it what you will?

Some people call 'IT' God. I further venture to think, that if they do, they have in mind *WHATEVER, WHEREVER and WHOEVER* their own particular God may be . . .

8 Our Return to 141 Squadron – and the Napalm Attacks

– and how the German night-fighter force remained to the end – undefeated

Harry and I were operational again by 11 January and on 12 January we did an NFT on a Mosquito XIX, No. 638, and a late trip was cancelled due to bad weather. We tried again the following day with the same aircraft; but were only up for 20 minutes on our NFT. The Remarks column in my log-book reads: 'Weather awful. Cloud almost on the deck. We scrubbed ops. at 15.00 hrs – and were justified.'

The next day we tried once more and on the NFT found the the starboard hydraulic jack was u/s! This was repaired and at 18.50 hours we took off for Merseburg, only to be forced to turn back soon after crossing the enemy coast. The Mk X AI, the Monica equipment and the Gee set all went u/s, for different reasons. We had hoped that, with the demise of 797, our problems caused by the recurrent unserviceability of aircraft and equipment on BSDU might be coming to an end. No such luck. The remainder of the month was spent carrying out daylight trials on Perfectos 11 and the backward-looking Mk X AI, and we reached the end of January without further incident.

On the first day of the month, February 1945, which was to see our departure from BSDU, we operated in support of a raid on Mannheim and were given a patrol line Karlsruhe–Frankfurt. About 30 miles south-east of Frankfurt we intercepted a Ju 88, but Harry could not get a shot at it because the German pilot was taking such violent evasive action. Because this encounter was typical of the changes which had come about in the High-Level Bomber Support operations in recent months it may be worthwhile to include our report for 1/2 February, made out when we landed back at Swanton Morley, after 4.35 hours in the air. (We took a Mosquito XIX, No. 684, equipped with Mk X AI and Serrate IV, taking off at 17.10 hours.)

> 'Patrol was uneventful till 19.10 hrs. at 49.40'N, 09.15'E when an A.I. contact was obtained 5 miles away on the port side. Mosquito was heading South. This contact was chased and found to be weaving and range was closed to 500ft., where a visual was obtained. Mosquito closed further on violently jinking aircraft to 150ft. and identified a Ju 88. E/A was followed visually for 7–10 mins. at speeds varying between 140 and 210mph., weaving violently in azimuth and elevation.
>
> Several times Mosquito had to throttle right back causing exhausts to back-fire. Ju 88 eventually evaded by a climbing turn to stbd. followed by a peel-off to port. Visual was lost but A.I. contact maintained. Range increased to 12,000ft. and contact became mixed up with Window and two other A.I. contacts.

One of these contacts was chased (believed at the time to be the same contact), at full throttle for 15 mins. course varying between East, South and West. Range could not be decreased so since contact was above Mosquito chase was abandoned in a position approximately 49.00'N, 07.30'E, time being 19.45 hrs. It is believed Ju 88 peeled off after seeing Mosquito's exhausts back-fire and that the second contact chased was not the original contact, but possibly a P.F.F. Mosquito.

Patrol was continued uneventfully till 20.30 hrs. when course was set for base. Height was lost to 6,000 ft. as the Dutch coast was approached and a dozen searchlights were seen to be active in the Schelde Estuary, some attempt being made to cone Mosquito, despite I.F.F. being shown. Colours of the Day were fired (later found to be the wrong colours) and considerable light A.A. activity was experienced. Mosquito evaded in cloud and landed at base without further incident.'

By the beginning of February, the Allied armies held most of Belgium and were preparing for the Rhine Crossings, so we could afford to lose height, on approaching the coast, at a much earlier point than a few months earlier when the Germans held all of Holland and Belgium (or so we thought!). The ack-ack batteries which fired at us that night were our own! And, to add insult to injury, we heard later that they were 'manned' by the ATS! It was a good thing for Harry and I that the women on those guns did not match up to the German flak gunners!

The entry in my log is somewhat shorter than our report, but shows our disappointment at not being able to destroy the Junkers: 'Mannheim & Mainz. Visual on Ju 88. Unable to attack owing to Hun behaving like a bastard.'

One of the achievements of the fighter squadrons in No. 100 Group was that ranging all over Germany – high level and low level – the defending German night-fighters never knew when they might find a Mosquito behind them. In 1995, at Duxford, I met Heinz Rökker, who had flown Ju 88s with great distinction (whilst with I/NJG 2.), and for the past years we have enjoyed a close correspondence and a warm friendship. In one of his letters he wrote: 'I always had a great respect about the excellent performance of the English intruders. You must have a lot of courage to fly a so long time over enemy country, never knowing what happens the next minute. However I had this feeling flying over England.'

The German night-fighters were forced, whilst searching for the British bombers, to take continuous evasive action, just as day-fighters had been forced to do since the days of World War 1. They had by this time developed their own backward-looking AI, so my opposite numbers in the Ju 88s and Me 110s could warn their pilots, like Heinz Rökker, when there was another aircraft closing in on them from astern, and many of our friends on 141 and the other squadrons suffered the same experience we did on 1/2 February, when closing in on their prey.

Additionally, the German twin-engined fighters carried an air-gunner who, facing aft, might get his own visual on the pursuing British fighter. It is highly probable, as we said in our report, that when Harry had to suddenly throttle back the engines, the gunner in the Junkers 88 saw the flames from our exhausts – as our engines backfired. This could easily account for the 'steep climbing turn to starboard', and then the 'peel off' to port.

Once again, disappointed, we did another op the following night and patrolled in the Weisbaden/Karlsruhe area. We chased one AI contact and got a visual on a clueless Mosquito but saw little else.

On 3 February we had some fun. We flew a Mosquito to East Wretham – only a few miles south of Swanton Morley – which was a USAAF base and from which the Americans were flying Mustangs on long-range fighter escort for the Fortresses and Liberators. Harry and I had been invited to give a talk on High-Level Bomber Support operations and we found ourselves standing up on the platform, in an enormous Nissen hut, facing a crowd of Mustang pilots, who had only shortly landed back at East Wretham, after escorting a group of Flying Fortresses to 'the Big City' – Berlin. In addition to the Mustang pilots, there were a number of Signals GIs, so we had a fairly mixed, and boisterous, audience!

The scene – with all the 'Yanks' lounging in front of us, in their brown leather jackets and chewing gum – was just like those out of one of the many films, made after the war, depicting the Americans flying on operations from their English bases!

Harry spoke first, and I followed, rather as we had done at Cranfield, the previous year. I think things went reasonably well, but all I have been able to remember of the proceedings was the introduction by the Colonel! This was memorable and some of his words passed into family history. He said when he eventually succeeded in quietening the audience down: 'I would now like to inter-dooce you to Flight Lootenant White and Flight Lootenant Allen of the 141st Night Persoot Squadron . . .'!

We did one more NFT on BSDU, for an op to Leipzig, but there were thunderstorms over the continent and yet another trip was scrubbed. There was a final air test on the 7th, but we were only airborne for five minutes so something must have gone wrong to bring us back so quickly.

On this low note, our leave-taking of BSDU seemed to typify the frustrating seven months which we had spent on the unit, since leaving 141 Squadron the previous June.

On the same day Squadron Leader Peter Bates DFC, the 'A' Flight Commander of 141 Squadron, with his Nav/Rad, Flying Officer Bill Cadman DFC, took off on a patrol to Ladbergen (between Münster and Osnabrück) Germany. They did not return.

In Don Aris's History, a few days later, on 13 February 1945, there is the following entry:

> 'The "A" Flight Commander of 141 Squadron, S/L P.A.Bates had been killed on operations on the 7th February 1945. The vacancy has been filled by F/L H.E.White DFC** who was posted to 141 Squadron together with his Nav/Rad F/L M.S.Allen DFC** from the Bomber Support Development Unit at Swanton Morley, Norfolk. F/L White was promoted to S/L to take up this Command.
>
> They had previously been long serving members of 141 Squadron and when their tour expired they were posted to B.S.D.U. on the 14.6.1944. Their time with B.S.D.U. was certainly not a rest from operations as while they were with this unit they carried out 20 operations together and F/L White carried out a further one with another Nav/Rad. These operations were to try out, under operational conditions, new or modified radar equipment being developed by B.S.D.U. for all the 100 (BS) Group Mosquitoes.'

So we went back to West Raynham and rejoined 141 Squadron. We even found ourselves in our old room (No. 13) in the mess, which had been occupied, until the previous week, by Peter Bates and Bill Cadman. They had been a very successful crew and apart from destroying an Me 110 in September they had carried out a number of low-level operations, both being awarded the DFC in the previous November. We never heard what had happened to them, but Don Aris found out when researching his History of the Squadron, that they were both buried in the Hanover War Cemetery, Germany; from which he concluded that they must have been brought down over Germany. They were a loss to the squadron.

Our first flight was in an Avro Anson, so that Mark Webster could demonstrate for me the ASH Mk XV AI centimetric radar with which 141's Mosquito Mk VIIs had been equipped in December. ASH, he told me, was an improvement on the old Mk IV AI, but not a patch on the Mk X sets, which we had been using on BSDU and which were being used to such good effect by 85 and 157 Squadrons at Swannington. Mark Webster and I had been on the same course at No. 54 OTU, at Church Fenton in August 1941.

We had lost touch with each other in the intervening years and he was now Navigator Leader of 141. I wrote in my log-book for the first time, (under 'Pilot') Squadron Leader White (and added GOOD SHOW!). Harry's promotion to the rank of Acting Squadron Leader came through on 8 March, although, of course, he took up his new duties as Flight Commander of 'A' Flight when we rejoined the squadron on 13 February.

We did three practice trips in daylight on the ASH AI, then on 21 February an NFT in a Mosquito VI No. 180 and at 17.10 took off on a low-level Intruder to an airfield at Kassel.

We picked up one AI contact over Kassel airfield at a range of 3,500 ft on the port side, but we were only at 5,000 ft ourselves and I lost the contact when we started to turn after the target. Perhaps if we had had Mk X AI we might have been able to complete the interception, who can tell? The rest of the trip was uneventful and we returned to West Raynham after five hours in the air, and at least we were operational again.

Bomber Command attacked a variety of strategic and tactical targets, and the changes which had taken place as the Allied armies had driven across northern France, Belgium and into Holland may be seen by the fact that they put up 1,110 sorties and only lost 34 aircraft.

Earlier in the month, on the night 13/14 February 1945, just as we were rejoining 141, the great raid on Dresden had been carried out. Twelve Mosquitoes of 141 had flown in support of the attack and that night Bomber Command flew 1,406 sorties on this (and other) operations, and only lost nine aircraft. Although we were not personally involved in this raid, I shall deal with it at length to rebut the adverse criticism that has arisen. Don Aris, in his Squadron History, comments on the raid which was to cause so much controversy in the post-war years and about which so many books and articles have been written:

'It has been blamed for the subsequent "playing down" of the magnificent role, together with the enormous loss of aircrew lives, that Bomber Command played in winning World War 2 and for the fact that Air Chief Marshal Sir Arthur Harris GCB, OBE, AFC was not given the honours and public acclaim bestowed on the other Service Chiefs. It has also been blamed for the fact that Bomber Command air and ground crews were not awarded a special medal even though more Bomber Command aircrew were lost on one raid on Nuremberg, on the night of 30/31st March 1944, than in the whole of the Battle of Britain. In so far as the ground crews were concerned, Harris, in a letter to Portal (Chief of Air Staff), on the 1st June 1945 putting forward the case for a medal for ground crews, said "I have lost more armourers etc. than the Army lost men crossing the Rhine".'

Certainly our ground crews in Bomber Command deserved similar recognition to that received by every butcher and baker who served with and behind the Allied armies, i.e. the Africa Star or the France and Germany Star. No finer tribute to the RAF ground crews has ever appeared than that written by John Terraine in his book *The Right of the Line*, published by Hodder and Stoughton. It reads:

'The overwhelming majority of the R.A.F.'s million (men) were to be found in the ground crew – that assembly of skilled, educated, individualistic, irreverent, dependable men without whose untiring labours the aircraft would not have flown, the operations would not have happened, and the victory could never have been won. The off-hand diffidence of their generation still causes many of them to brush aside their war service with comic or sardonic anecdotes, an attitude reflected in their scurrilous joyful songs, and summed up in what may almost be called the anthem of the "erks"

"Bless (or otherwise) 'Em All":

Bless all the Sergeants and WOs,

Bless all the Corporals, etc., etc."

From the beginning to end "Binding" every inch of the way, they made victory possible. They were splendid.'

Don Aris continues:

'The town of Dresden was a vital communication and supply centre for the Eastern Front which had now crossed the borders of Germany and also was a route through which reinforcements of the German Army could be moved from West to East. The attack was carried out by 796 Lancasters and 9 Mosquitoes in two separate attacks and 1,478 tons of high explosive and 1,182 tons of incendiary bombs were dropped, creating a firestorm similar to the one experienced by Hamburg in July 1943. The result was that large areas of the city were destroyed and the number of people killed was never accurately discovered, but it was in excess of 50,000. Contributing to the damage and loss of life was an attack the next day by 311 B-17 Flying Fortresses of the American 8th USAAF.'

The facts concerning the Dresden raid (for anyone who is interested enough to think beyond the emotive headlines and inaccurate articles served up by the mass-media) may be found in *Bomber Harris*, the authorised biography by Group Captain Dudley Saward OBE. Suffice to say here that the decision to bomb Dresden, along with Berlin, Chemnitz and Leipzig, was conveyed to the C-in-C of Bomber Command in a letter from Air Vice-Marshal Norman

Bottomley, the Deputy Chief of Air Staff, dated 27 January 1945. The Chief of Air Staff, Sir Charles Portal, had commented:

'We should use available effort in one big attack on Berlin and attacks on Dresden, Leipzig, Chemnitz, or any other cities where a severe blitz will not only cause confusion in the evacuation from the East but will also hamper the movements of troops from the West.'

The day before, the Prime Minister was clearly not satisfied with the urgency being given to the matter of support for the Russians by bombing eastern German towns lying in the path of Russian advances. Churchill wrote to the Air Minister, Sir Archibald Sinclair, on 26 January, as follows:

'I did not ask you last night about plans for harrying the German retreat from Breslau. On the contrary, I asked whether Berlin, and no doubt other large cities in East Germany, should not now be considered especially attractive targets. I am glad that this is under examination. Pray report to me tomorrow what is being done.'

On the following day Sir Arthur received his instructions. It is clear, beyond any possible doubt, from the mass of evidence set out in Group Captain Saward's book, that the decision to bomb Dresden (and the other three named cities) was *not* taken by the C-in-C of Bomber Command and anyone, with the slightest understanding of the line of authority from the British Government to its Military Chiefs, would be aware that Sir Arthur Harris could never have taken such a decision on his own.

Some six weeks after the bombing of Dresden, the climate changed. Churchill himself wrote to the Chiefs of Staff Committee and started to raise doubts about the continuation of the Allied bombing policy and he specifically queried the destruction of Dresden. It was already clear, even though the war in Europe had not yet been won, and the war in the Far East was still very much on, that the two main political parties in Great Britain were taking up the cudgels again, and preparing for an early General Election. Perhaps that had something to do with Churchill's volte-face so soon after he had pressed for attacks on eastern Germany prior to his meeting with Stalin in Yalta on 4 February.

Whatever reason it was, Churchill's Minute of 28 March sparked off a memorandum from the hapless Deputy Chief of Air Staff (of the same date) to C-in-C Bomber Command querying '. . . whether the time has not come when the question of bombing of German cities simply for the sake of increasing the terror, though under other pretexts, should not be reviewed . . .', etc., etc.

Although the letter had been sent on the instructions of the Chief of the Air Staff, Sir Arthur Harris had no hesitation in administering a suitable flea in the ear to Norman Bottomley! Sir Arthur's skill with the pen matched that of his with the sword! He was rightly infuriated by the insidious allegations contained in Air Vice-Marshal Bottomley's letter. His reply, sent off the following day, was a masterpiece. His complete and devastating answer of 29 March deserves to be read in full. Sadly, there is only space here to reproduce two of its paragraphs; they are as follows:

'. . . To suggest that we have bombed German cities simply for the sake of increasing the terror though under other pretexts and to speak of our offensive as including mere acts of terror and wanton destruction is an insult both to the bombing policy of the Air Ministry and to the manner in which that policy has been executed by Bomber Command. This sort of thing if it deserves an answer will certainly receive none from me, after three years of implementing official policy.

As regards the specific points raised in your letter, namely the adverse economic effects on ourselves by increasing yet further the material havoc in Germany and the destruction of Dresden in particular the answer is surely very simple. (The feeling, such as there is, over Dresden could be easily explained by any psychiatrist. It is connected with German bands and Dresden shepherdesses. Actually Dresden was a mass of munition works, an intact government centre, and a key transportation point to the East. It is now none of those things.) It is already demonstrated in the liberated countries that what really makes any sort of recovery almost impossible is less the destruction of buildings than the complete dislocation of transportation . . .'

In the light of the controversy that has raged since the end of the war about our bombing offensive, I have always nurtured a slight feeling of regret that Harry and I were not on the Dresden raid. Although Bomber Command, the work that we did and the intrepid Sir Arthur Harris have been widely denigrated since the end of World War II, we had the support of virtually the whole population of this country behind us during the war years, when Great Britain was the target for widespread and varied attack for five years, and it will do no harm to give a firsthand example.

When the bombing of London started in September 1940 many of its citizens sought shelter in the London Underground. Deep down, on the platforms – sometimes on the stationary escalators themselves – people felt safe and could get a good night's sleep before making their way to work the following morning. As the months went by, wooden and steel bunks were assembled on the platforms and some people took up an almost permanent residence in the Underground. The trains continued to run and often there was only a narrow gap, on the platform, between the sliding doors of the coaches and the bunks where the occupants were sleeping. I remember well trying to clamber over people, sitting wrapped, in blankets – and having no bunk to go to – as I passed through Piccadilly, Charing Cross or Leicester Square, on my way home on leave, or returning late at night to a bomber station in East Anglia and rushing to catch the last train out of King's Cross. Some of those, crouching on the ground and clutching a few precious possessions, would look up when they heard someone coming.

If they saw that you were in Air Force uniform, they would peer again through the gloom and discomfort of their surroundings, to see if you were wearing a flying badge. If you were, their faces would light up, and they would quite often say (as you went past): 'Drop one for us, Guv!'

Arthur Harris, like other commanders in the Second World War, had been a junior officer in 1914–18. The slaughter witnessed in France was in the back of their minds. These men, Montgomery, Brooke, Alexander, Portal and Harris, now commanded large forces themselves and were determined that, as long as it was humanly possible, every step would be taken to avoid a repetition of these horrific casualties, particularly in the Allied armies. The prosecution of the war was their first priority, carrying out the policies of the war cabinet.

Harris, using an expression from an even earlier time of battle, said:

'No German City, is worth the bones of one British Grenadier.'

On the night 23/24 February 1945, we did a trip to Pforzheim, between Karlsruhe and Stuttgart. It was uneventful except that the weather closed in as we and the other 11 Mosquitoes operating from West Raynham were returning across the North Sea, and we were all diverted to other airfields. Harry and I landed at Little Snoring (It seems an unbelievable name now!). The mist was rolling in across Norfolk and blotting out everything in its path as we finished our landing run, and turned to port, off the main runway onto the perimeter track. I looked over my left shoulder and saw the mist covering the airfield behind us! The next aircraft in the circuit could not get down and was directed to go further west to one of the airfields which was still open.

Sadly, one of the 239 Squadron aircraft, diverted to our old base at Foulsham, crashed on landing, injuring the navigator and killing the pilot. As it was, at Little Snoring the mist was so thick, the Airfield Controller had to send out a tractor to guide us round the perimeter track to a spot near the Watch office where we could park our Mosquito VI for the night. There was a party on, back at West Raynham, so we quickly got ourselves debriefed and organised some transport.

Back in the mess we changed out of our battle-dress and joined the party at about 11 p.m. In the morning, not too early, and feeling slightly groggy, we were driven back to Little Snoring, where we retrieved our aircraft and flew back to Raynham. Before we left I made enquiries for Dick Sessions (older brother of Teddy) who was stationed at Snoring as a PT instructor, having had the frustrating experience of being failed on his pilot's course in Canada, earlier in the war. Dick was a very decent and hard-working chap, who did well in the post-war years as a leather chemist and subsequently emigrated to South Africa. We met up at the gymnasium and enjoyed a few minutes' chat before I had to fly back to West Raynham, and after the war we became good friends.

We went air-to-air firing before the end of the month and Squadron Leader White distinguished himself by missing the drogue altogether! The 'Remarks' column in my log-book was rather scathing! It read: '"SCREWBALL WHITE" (after the famous day-fighter ace, "Screwball Beurling") "THEY FIRED ALL THEIR 'BALLS', AND HAD NO HITS AT ALL".'

And before February was out we went to Wilhelmshaven in support of a raid by the 'Yanks'. We got visuals on a Liberator, a Mosquito and a Stirling but saw nothing of our opposite numbers! Our ASH radar equipment went u/s when we were on our way back across the North Sea.

Starting out on one of these trips, and shortly after we had returned to 141 Squadron, I got a visual – and in broad daylight! It was one that nearly spelt the end of us. We had just taken off from West Raynham and were climbing up on our way across out over the English coast at Happisburgh.

All around we could see other aircraft, also climbing and heading east towards Germany. I glanced out to our starboard side and was shocked to see a Halifax, probably from Foulsham, 3–400 yards away also climbing, but on a converging course with our own! I took a second terrified look, realised that he had not seen us and saw that we were, in fact, on a collision course! I shouted one word, over the intercom, to Harry: '*DOWN!*'

By that time, in all our years together, we had worked out various simple emergency procedures, which we both obeyed immediately and without question. Harry pushed the stick hard forward with all his strength – and, as our Mosquito lurched downward, we heard the sound of the Halifax's four engines as he passed over the top of us. We began to regain our lost height and went on our way, badly shaken before we had even crossed out over the English coast.

During February, 141 had operated on 20 nights and carried out 149 sorties. Nearly all these were listed as high-level ASH patrols but although the Group claims for the month were 11 (10?) for the month, none of these successes came the way of our squadron. What was happening was that increasingly, as crews found no 'trade' at 15,000–23,000 feet, they were dropping down to look for targets on the ground. Airfields, trains and road transport were attacked as we went low level. The news had also come through that we were to be re-equipped with the Mosquito XXX with Mk X AI. Both aircraft and radar would be a better proposition than the Mk VIs with ASH.

Our rivals at West Raynham, 239 Squadron, already had these aircraft and equipment and had now destroyed 47 E/A in the air, compared to our 31 (this figure does not take into account our score on Serrate operations prior to coming into 100 Group). On the other hand, our claims of damage done on low-level strafing runs were showing a handsome return.

At the beginning of March a Wellington aircraft, from the Bomber Support Training Unit at Great Massingham, arrived for the training of the 141 Nav/Rads in Mk X AI. The Wellington was flown by a Flying Officer Smith, and on 2 March 'Scotty', Charles Winn's navigator, and about five more of us went up with him for a couple of hours' training on the Mk X AI using a Hurricane as a target. We were up for 2.40 hours and my log records the following succinct comment: 'This is the worst pilot with whom I have ever flown. Scotty agrees!'

That was the first and last time I flew with F/O Smith and I considered myself fortunate that I had already had quite a bit of experience with the Mk X AI,

No. 141 Squadron, West Raynham: group photo taken in March 1945. The Commanding Officer, Wing Commander C.V. Winn DFC is in the centre and Squadron Leader H.E. White DFC**, the 'A' Flight Commander, is on his right. I am sitting, second in from the right, in the front row.

whilst at BSDU. I would manage the rest of my training with Harry, when our new Mosquitoes were delivered. When on the same day Bomber Command attacked Cologne with 858 aircraft and lost only nine of them, it was again a sign of the times, and a welcome one at that. It was to be the last raid of the war on that much bombed city.

On 3/4 March what some of us had been fearing would happen happened! A large number of German night-fighters followed the bomber stream back to England and made a killing. Bomber Command had put up a total of 785 aircraft on targets in and near the Ruhr, and they lost only eight bombers over Germany. At long last, the Germans mounted an intruder operation – code-named it 'GISELLA' – and sent about 200 of their night-fighters across the North Sea in the wake of the returning bomber force.

As the Lancasters and Halifaxes started to lose height, on approaching the English coast, sometimes switching on their navigation lights (to avoid the risk of collision, when nearing their home airfields), the Ju 88s and a mixed bag of other twin-engined fighters (operating freelance, as we did when over Germany) fell on them.

Some of the four-engined bombers of 100 Group (which had been engaged on radar countermeasure duties) were attacked as they were in the circuit and whilst on their approach to land, with wheels and flaps down. Twenty of the returning bombers were shot down over England, five crashing in Norfolk (including a Lancaster which fell a mile to the north of West Raynham).

It was a bad night for Bomber Command, but many of us had talked about the possibility of the Germans infiltrating the returning bomber stream, by using some of their Home Defence night-fighters as intruders – in the same way that we had done (notably by 1, 23 and 605 Squadrons) since the early days of the war. It was not entirely a new venture for the Germans, because it will be recalled that in 1941, when Harry and I were at Church Fenton, their intruders were quite active for a period.

However, once Bomber Command's attacks started to increase in intensity in 1942, the defence of the Third Reich became top priority and the German night-fighter groups were ordered to restrict their operations to the skies above the Fatherland. There is no doubt that Bomber Command were extremely lucky that the *Nachtjagdgeschwader* were not released to intrude on us much earlier in the proceedings. With crews starting to relax – as we did, coming back over the North Sea, once we had left the enemy coast behind – navigation lights and airfield lighting making for good targets, all the way up the East Coast, the pickings would have been rich.

Of course, lights were soon turned out once it was realised by the Airfield Controllers and the crews that there were 'BANDITS! BANDITS!' in the circuit. But the disruption to a large force (700/800 aircraft) trying to get down, with some carrying wounded, some short of fuel and others damaged as a result of enemy action, would have been considerable and could have had a significant effect on the whole bomber offensive.

On 5 March we did our longest trip yet, 6.40 hours. We went to Chemnitz, one of the four targets specially selected for our attention (along with Berlin, Leipzig and Dresden). We went together with over 800 other crews, of which 31 aircraft were lost over Germany and 10 more crashed in England on their return, some perhaps due to bad weather.

My log entry showed how, once more, Harry and I were disappointed not to have done better: '. . . 800 Heavies on Chemnitz & Bohlen. ASH results very disappointing, Huns about but heavy cloud en route seem to have affected the wretched ASHCAN. W/C Gibb of 239 got 2 making us both mad. Longest trip yet. No intruders on return, as on 3rd.'

Two nights later, when the Command attacked Dessau in eastern Germany and other targets, we lost a total of 41 aircraft (out of 1,276 sorties), showing that the German night-fighters were far from being a spent force. Indeed, our opposite numbers were never defeated. They were simply overtaken by the course of events, as the Third Reich collapsed around them . . .

Harry and I didn't operate again before going on leave on 15 March, my 22nd birthday. I had made arrangements to spend the first part of my leave with Mr and Mrs Lock, at Church Farm, East Lavant (just to the north of Chichester). I had tried to do this during the intervening years, both to keep in touch with Ken's movements and because I genuinely enjoyed staying in the old farm house, walking with Ernest Lock over his fields and soaking up the peace and beauty of the Sussex countryside. Mr Lock regarded me, quite rightly, as a townie who knew nothing about farming and he used to chuckle away to himself when I couldn't tell the difference between a field of potatoes and another of mangels. I had a great regard for him and everything that he stood for. Whenever I hear the term 'yeoman farmer' I think of Ernest Lock and all that was best in the England of those days.

Life was looking good, with nine days' leave coming up, plenty of petrol coupons for my car, Harry off to spend his leave with Joan – his wife of eight months – and myself to see Betty Sessions after spending the first two days at Church Farm with Ernest and Dorothy Lock.

Then Group Captain Cheshire's views on life ('Just as you think all is well, things start to go wrong') were proved in the most cruel way. Because the telegram arrived. It was from Mrs Lock and it read: 'KENNETH KILLED WHILST ON ACTIVE SERVICE. STILL COME FOR THE WEEKEND, IF YOU WANT TO.' It was exactly four years – to the day – since we had gone together to the Recruiting Office at Euston. Who was it who said, two thousand years earlier, 'Beware the Ides of March'?

In the years which had passed since March 1941, all of us had grown up a bit, not least Harry and I, and we had grown used to losing friends on a weekly – and sometimes on a daily – basis. So it was easier for us than for those who had not been so involved. I wired back to Mrs Lock to the effect that I was still coming and a few hours later said, 'Cheerio, Boy!' to Harry and got into my car to drive south.

I don't remember much about that weekend with poor Ernest and Dorothy Lock, except that they were both incredibly brave and that, when I was out walking with Ernest over his land, sloping away off Goodwood towards Tangmere and the Channel beyond, he said quietly: 'I can see him walking the farm with me when I go out, Michael.' He didn't say much more than that, the whole of the morning . . .

The coincidence that I should learn of Ken's death exactly four years to the day after we had so joyfully signed on at the Recruiting Office at Euston in March 1941 struck me forcibly and has stayed with me in the years which have passed since my 22nd birthday. By March 1945 Ken had become an experienced pilot and, like myself, was also a flight lieutenant. He would have had a wonderful life ahead of him, farming in West Sussex on the slopes of Goodwood if he had survived the war. His name is on the Roll of Honour in the O.J. Chapel at Hurstpierpoint College. I always make for the chapel when I go back to the school, and it gives me an odd sensation to stand there looking up at the gold embossed letters of the 67 Old Johnians who were not so lucky and seeing 'K. LOCK'. I miss him yet.

When I got back to the mess at West Raynham I found a small parcel, with a Scottish postmark on it, in my letter-rack. Inside, was a set of gold cuff-links and a letter from Harry (he and Joan had spent their leave in Scotland, to be near her mother). The letter was couched in unusually polite tones (for my esteemed pilot) and I still have it!

> 'Hospital Lodge
> Forres
> Morayshire
> 21/3/45

Dear Michael,

As a token of my appreciation and of our affection I hope you will accept what we have been able to get for your birthday. And in wishing yourself the very best for the future I express the hope that it may exceed the past in achievement and lasting happiness.

More could be said but such time as we have spent together makes the interplay of words superfluous.

Give our regards to the Sessions family and to Rodney if he is at home. Enjoy the little that remains of your leave and let us hope that there is still something remaining to be done when we return!

Sincerely yours,

Harry'

On one side of the gold links was engraved the badge of 141 Squadron and on the other the initials, in Harry's own hand, 'HEW'.

We need not have worried about missing any ops, whilst away on this leave, because the re-equipment of the squadron with Mosquito XXXs was now going on apace and 141 did not carry out any operations between 15 March and 3 April. However, the month did not end entirely without incident!

We had got back, at the end of our leave, on 26 March, did some daylight Mk X AI practice the following day; and then did not fly on the three succeeding days. On the 30th, having not flown all day and there being no ops, we had an impromptu party in the mess and retired to bed sometime after midnight, a trifle the worse for wear (but not in too bad a state!). It seemed as if my head had only just touched the pillow, when I was being shaken, and awoke to see Harry scrambling out of bed. I don't know who it was in our room – perhaps the Duty Officer – but he was pouring out a story to the effect that there was a Catalina flying boat of the American USAAF down in the North Sea, and two Mosquitoes from 141 were wanted to fly an Air-Sea Rescue sortie and help in the search for the missing crew members. By 01.15 hrs on 31 March we were in the air and heading for the Frisian Islands, north of the Dutch coast, which was the area in which the Catalina was supposed to have come down.

We were in the air for five and a quarter hours and, sadly, found no trace of the missing flying boat. There is the following forthright entry in my log (with yet another disappointment!):

'Fri. 30th 01.15 Mosquito V1 Sqd/Ldr White AIR SEA RESCUE 578

PATROL OFF FRISIAN ISLANDS LOOKING FOR CATALINA DOWN
ON WATER WITH U.S.CREW – NO JOY – ASH CONTACT ON THREE
SMALL NAVAL BOATS HEADING FOR HELIGOLAND ATTACKED
THE GRAND FLEET BUT GUNS FROZEN UP! SOME LIGHT FLAK,
THEN ON HOMEWARD JOURNEY FOUND A LIGHT ON THE
WATER 53.30N/04.10E POSSIBLY SOME TYPE IN THE DRINK. POOR
OLD HARRY TIRED AS HELL, JUST TIRED. HAIL THE DAWN!
   BAH THE EVILS OF ALC! 05.15 hours.'

Flying at 3–4,000 feet above sea-level, looking for any sign of the Catalina, I picked up the three ships as they were heading east, and to the north of the Frisians, and we thought we would come down and have a go at them. We headed north for a few minutes, then turned back in order to make our attack from the dark part of the sky. The blips of the ships were showing up well on the ASH, and we got right down 'on the deck' to attack the port side of the leading ship. We could see them quite clearly and when we were within range Harry pressed the gun-button. We braced ourselves for the thudding of the four cannons . . . absolutely nothing happened – except that as Harry pulled the stick back to climb over the height of the masts, they opened fire on us with several bursts of light flak!

We felt a bit foolish, as we pulled away to get out of their range, and tried to figure out why our cannons had failed us at the crucial moment. The answer was this: taking off on an Air-Sea Rescue sortie (and at night) we had not expected to encounter any enemy aircraft and I had, foolishly, not switched on the gun-heater when we were airborne, which was my usual practice. When we decided to attack the ships, I forgot that the gun-heater had not been switched on! Perhaps the fact that we had been roused out of bed in the early hours also had something to do with it, but the guns were simply frozen up! Perhaps we really had been operating for too long and were simply tired.

We were certainly tired that night, and again I remember we tried singing (over the intercom!) to keep each other awake as we flew back across the North Sea, with the dawn coming up behind us. We landed safely at West Raynham at 6.30 a.m. and took ourselves wearily back to bed.

The month of March had seen the Crossing of the Rhine and the Allied armies sweeping into Germany. Bomber Command had, for some time, been attacking by day (with massive fighter escort) a variety of tactical targets, some-times softening up the territory in front of the troops and saving them untold casualties.

There were still some targets in Germany which were strategic, rather than tactical, as the first few days of April started to unfold but the land forces were moving so fast, in some areas of the advance, that the targets given to us in the morning were often scrubbed by the afternoon! To further illustrate how much things had changed for the better since the horrific winter of 1943/44, on 25 March Bomber Command had attacked Hanover, Münster and Osnabrück, all important reinforcement routes to the Rhine battle area, during the day, and lost only four aircraft out of 606 sorties.

On 2 April ops to Kiel were scrubbed and I wrote in my log, 'Has Montgomery got there too?!'

He hadn't, as it happened! But the next day, when targets at Nordhausen and

Erfurt were cancelled, I was correct when I wrote: 'I think the Army has beaten us to it!'

On the 4th it was a case of third time lucky and we went to Merseburg. We now had our new Mosquito XXXs and Mk X AI (which the squadron would have given its eye teeth to have had eight months earlier). Harry and I intercepted two hopeful-looking AI contacts, only to get visuals on, first, a Flying Fortress, and then, a Halifax. We were now using several advanced bases on the continent, and we landed back at Brussels/Melsbroek airfield, refuelled very quickly and returned to Raynham via Dungeness and Gravesend.

On 10 and 14 April we carried out our last high-level operations in support of the bombers, going to Leipzig and Potsdam respectively. There were a lot of searchlights over Leipzig, but only six bombers were lost. My entry for the raid on Potsdam reflects the mood prevailing on the bomber stations at that time. Everyone knew now that the war in Europe was rapidly coming to an end and there was a general feeling of 'let's hit Germany as hard as we can whilst we have still got the opportunity to do so!'

Losses from enemy action were now minimal and the old crews all wanted to go on and, as it were, be in at the death. The new crews – still being posted in to the squadron – were desperate (after all their years of training) to get a few ops in before the whole show packed up. From my log-book:

'Sat.14th 20.45 Mosquito XXX S/Ldr White OPS

Potsdam – 450 Heavies – 2 lost – a military objective? Who cares! The more Huns killed whilst we still have the opportunity, the better. Dennis Raby got the only 100 Group claim, a Ju 88 illuminated beautifully in its own S/Ls. 4.50 hours.'

Potsdam had never been a target for us before, and we had no idea whether it was a military target or not but, as I wrote at the time, we didn't care! Perhaps by then, as the Allied armies overran the German concentration camps, reports of the unspeakable horrors of Buchenwald, Sachsenhausen, Auschwitz and the others were starting to filter through as the unbelievable actions of the Third Reich – so long a secret from most of us – were uncovered by the advancing British, American and Russian troops.

Perhaps it was the memories of the indiscriminate bombing of civilian targets, launched first – beyond any doubt – by the Germans, which led to that intangible feeling in the last days of the war of 'no mercy for them'. Perhaps it was simply – as in childish squabbles – a case of 'Well, he started it!' Whatever the reason, as the war in Europe drew to a close in April 1945, everyone wanted to be in on the act.

To keep the record straight, Harry and I did have one more attempt at a high-level support operation – to Munich – but our radar and all our electrics packed up and we struggled home. As logged: 'Both very tired & brassed off.'

It is only when coming to write this account that I have fully realised the extent of the unserviceability experienced by the crews of the bomber support fighter squadrons.

In the meantime our irrepressible CO, Charles Winn (he was universally and affectionately known as 'Winnie'), was determined that 141 Squadron should go out with a bang, not a whimper! Don's History for 6.4.1945 contains the following, and somewhat surprising, entry:

'At 15.00 hours, at West Raynham, W/C C.V.Winn DFC carried out the first of three trials of types of Napalmgel by dropping it on the airfield. He flew parallel to the main No.1 runway, flying low from NE to SW and dropped 100-gallon drop-tanks filled with Napalmgel on the grass of the airfield. He carried out further trials and demonstrations on the 12th and 13th April and, according to ex F/Lt Roy Marriott speaking to the writer in 1991, this was to test out three types of Napalmgel, each with different consistencies, thick, medium and thin and apparently the thick failed to ignite. These trials caused enormous interest on the Station and aircrew crowded onto the flying control tower while the ground crews climbed on to the roofs of the hangars in order to get a good view.'

Napalmgel, or napalm as we came to call it, was a highly inflammable liquid made up of naphthaline, palm oil and white phosphorus. We carried it in the 100-gallon drop-tanks, affixed to the port and starboard wings, which were normally filled with petrol. It will be recalled that Harry and I had been carrying these tanks, and promptly jettisoned them, the night we had to make a crash-landing in Mosquito 797!

The tanks – when containing napalm – were released by the same switches and mechanism that were used when they had been emptied of fuel and the pilot wished to reduce the extra drag for the journey home. Don reports that his friend Johnny Claxton, ex-LAC Armourer (and a long-serving member of 141 Squadron) remembers that a 1 lb 'all way' phosphorus fuse was fitted in each tank to ignite the napalm on impact.

The fuse was called 'all way' because, no matter how the tank fell, it would ignite! As we were to find out for ourselves, the napalm-filled tanks burst into flames upon hitting the ground or landing on a building, and set fire to everything in close proximity to the spot where it had fallen. We believed that we were the first squadron in the RAF to use napalm against the enemy.

A few days before Charles Winn burned up two long swathes of grass in front of the control tower at West Raynham, he had returned from leave. When he came into the bar, in the mess, he was bubbling over with a new plan for our low-level sorties, which were becoming more and more the order of the day, now that there were hardly any German night-fighters operating at high-level.

Charles was a big man, and full of fun. When he got enthusiastic about anything, which he frequently did, his whole body used to quiver with laughter and he always reminded me of those wonderful advertisements for the 'Michelin Man', ensconced in his mass of rubber tyres!

The story that he was soon pouring out, once he had got a glass of beer in his hand, was that in the train coming up from King's Cross he had got into conversation with an American Air Force colonel. Winnie soon learned that the USAAF had got a supply of Napalmgel, which they intended using on the enemy in Europe, and it was not long before he had asked the colonel (in his most persuasive way!) if he could 'borrow' some of the inflammable liquid, having quickly worked out in his mind how the stuff could be dropped from 141's Mosquitoes! The colonel told Charles that they had a good stock at the airfield, which was somewhere in East Anglia, and not far from Raynham, and the deal was done.

The next thing which happened was that we looked out of the mess windows, a day or two later, and saw a convoy of massive grey petrol tankers (each with a large white star on the side) moving slowly in through the main gates, and past the guard room! The Americans were doing things in style, as usual, and the colonel had come up trumps! Winnie had already obtained permission from Group to use napalm, providing he could secure his own supply of the stuff. For a man like Winnie that was no problem!

Don tells us that the 100 (BS) Group's Report for April speaks of 141 Squadron practising Napalmgel-dropping on various corners of West Raynham airfield, but, as Roy Marriott has said, that was not the case. By that time most of the pilots had carried out some attacks at low level with cannon and bombs (or like us, over the Frisians, with no cannon!), so when the time came, off we went! If we had all started with practice drops over West Raynham there wouldn't have been a blade of grass left on the airfield anyway!

The first napalm attacks were carried out on 14/15 April, when five 141 Mosquitoes went to Neuruppin and Juterborg airfields, and the last on 2 May, when 12 aircraft attacked the aerodromes at Flensburg and Hohn. In the space of about three weeks the squadron carried out nearly 60 sorties and dropped 11,050 gallons of Napalmgel on ten different airfields in Germany.

Although quite a lot of light flak was encountered when we went in, one after the other, to make our strafing run at low level and drop our napalm tanks, the

No. 141 Squadron, West Raynham: Harry and myself in front of our Mosquito XXX F 507, with which we carried out a number of sorties – including the napalm attacks – between March and May 1945. With us are Flt/Sgt 'Chiefy' Stanley, the Senior NCO in charge of our ground crews, and Sgt Hale.

only casualties we suffered were on 18 April, when we lost our New Zealand crew (W/O Dawson and F/O Childs) during the attack on Munich/Neubiberg airfield. There was a master bomber, F/Lt J.S. Rivaz, with F/Sgt Spender, from 23 Squadron, directing the proceedings and he gave instructions for Dawson in 141/R to come in and bomb, but to mind the flak.

Several of the other crews saw some moderate but accurate light flak come up as Dawson went in to make his attack, then they saw an explosion in mid-air and flaming wreckage falling to the ground and another explosion about 2–3 miles north-west of the airfield. 'WINBALL 7', which was Dawson's call-sign, was not heard to report 'CLEAR OF TARGET'. Ronnie Dawson and Charlie Childs were both killed outright and lie in adjoining graves in Durnbach War Cemetery, south of Munich, in the foothills of the Alps, a long way from their homes in New Zealand. It was their 10th operation with the squadron.

The code word used for the napalm operations was, appropriately, 'FIRE-BASH' and on 22 April I wrote in my log: '141st Night Pursuit Squadron go fire bashing to Westerland A/F on Sylt. Three or four good fires burning fiercely. A few searchlights and some inaccurate light flak. Had a good 10-second burst into camp area on way in.'

As I said, Harry got in a long burst of cannon fire (at some of the airfield build-ings) on our run in, and we came right down to 100 feet to drop our two 100-gallon drop-tanks on the incendiaries, which were burning on the east side of Westerland airfield. Four fires were to be seen afterwards in that area. On our way out over the seaplane base at Sylt, we were accurately coned by five search-lights (we were then at 2,000 feet), but we managed to slip out of the beams before the flak opened up. We landed safely back at West Raynham after only three hours in the air.

We had now got our own Mosquito NT507F, and on 24 April six aircraft from the squadron went back to the airfield at Munich/Neubiberg, with Harry, as 'A' Flight Commander, leading the attack in F 507. Earlier in the evening we had flown across to an advanced base in northern France where we had refuelled and picked up the latest met. report. The airfield where we landed was Juvincourt, and many months before, in the summer of 1943, we had had our first successes in the skies above that part of France, when we returned to Wittering claiming an Me 110 as destroyed. It gave us quite a thrill to land there.

I remember that we had to fly from Juvincourt down to two lakes south of Munich and then set course for the airfield where the master bomber, S/Ldr Penny from 515 Squadron, was marking the target and controlling the attack. Circling over the two lakes, we had an awe-inspiring view of the Alps, before starting to lose height and going in to make our attack. We approached in a dive from 3,000 feet east to west and Harry opened fire with a 12-second burst at 1,000 feet. We saw several strikes on the airfield buildings and one sizeable explosion in the light of which we saw that we had hit a single-engined enemy aircraft. Part of the wing blew off and there were several other small explosions.

We dropped our tanks from a height of 100 feet onto the hangars, which were clearly silhouetted in the light of the incendiaries dropped by the master bomber. I think, in the back of our minds, we remembered that Dawson and Childs had been shot down over Munich/Neubiberg four nights earlier, and Harry got down as low as possible as we raced across the airfield.

The master bomber's marking and control were first rate and the whole attack was over in six minutes. There was some slight – but inaccurate – flak from four points round the airfield, but there were no searchlights. At 01.20 hours, when we left, there were several fires burning amongst the hangars and aerodrome buildings. We landed at Brussels/Melsbroek and once again flew home across the North Sea as dawn was breaking. After we had landed at Raynham we finally got to bed at 08.30 hours. I slept all day.

It was on one of these ops that we took off, with a full war load, banked round and came back across the airfield at about 100 ft, aiming directly at the Watch office! Just before we pulled up and over the top of them, we saw the startled faces of the Flying Control officers. Then we flew between the two hangars directly behind the Watch office, right over the centre of the camp, before turning east to head for Germany.

Throughout April there was a rising air of excitement on the station. Resettlement Officers (so named) were coming and going. Meetings were being held for the airmen and airwomen to inform them about demobilisation plans and the return to civilian life, and by 23 April the British Second Army had arrived opposite Hamburg. The following day its advanced units were on the west bank of the Elbe poised ready for their last thrust to Lübeck and Kiel.

On the 25th, when we were asleep all day after the attack on Munich/ Neubiberg, Bomber Command attacked the Frisian island of Wangerooge with 482 aircraft, losing only two Lancasters. The raid was to knock out the coastal batteries controlling the approaches to Bremen and Wilhelmshaven. They also attacked Hitler's retreat, 'the Eagle's Nest' at Berchtesgaden in the Bavarian Alps. Some 370 aircraft went on what must have been a satisfying trip, and only two were lost. For many of those taking part this was to be their last operation of the war.

There were many signs that the war in Europe was coming to an end. The American 69th Division and the Russian 59th Guards Division made the first meeting of East and West battle fronts, on the banks of the Elbe, and the Russians finally encircled Berlin.

Bomber Command then came in for two new and different kinds of operations. Both of them must have been extremely satisfying, and both of them brought tears to the eyes of men who, for the years spent on bombing operations, had become adjusted to suppressing their feelings and emotions.

On 26 April some Lancasters from Bomber Command, carrying no bombs, landed at Brussels, initially, and then other airfields on the continent to start Operation 'Exodus'. Their objective was no longer to bomb targets in Germany, but to fly released British prisoners-of-war home to England!

A day or two later Bomber Command started on its second new task when they commenced Operation 'Manna'. A large pocket in western Holland was still in German hands and the Dutch population was approaching starvation. A truce had been arranged with the German commander to allow our Lancasters to fly over the area and drop food and medical supplies. At West Raynham we wished that our Mosquitoes had been large enough for us to join in these deeply moving and humanitarian operations.

After the war, a number of Dutch children were brought to England for three or four weeks at a time, where they were lodged with kindly families – and fed! Many came to homes in East Anglia and some of these children were accommodated in Aylsham, where I was still friendly with the Jenners and the Holmans. They were painfully thin when they first arrived, but the good people of Norfolk soon had them eating properly again and putting on weight!

Mrs Jenner (it will be remembered that she was the local District Nurse) had two of the children. We called them 'Big Johnny' and 'Little Johnny', and I got to know them quite well. They were about 12 and 10 years of age, and both of them begged me to let them have an RAF button. They were pathetically grateful for what the Air Force had done to help bring about the liberation of their country.

Back on the squadron, as each day passed, we kept on thinking that Germany would surrender and that we had flown our last op or, at least, our last op over Europe! Although many people were now thinking of peace and of returning to civilian life, Harry and I, and others who were still flying, could not forget that the war in the Far East, against the Japanese, was very far from being over.

There was a squadron party on the 27th, but I have no recollection of it. The weather was still unbelievably bad for the springtime, at Raynham we had sleet and snow showers. We only did one NFT during the last four days of April; and that, too, helped to lull us into a false sense of security!

April had been an exciting month and we all felt that we were seeing history in the making and that perhaps, to a small extent were helping to make it. The squadron had operated on 15 nights and carried out 86 operational sorties. Harry and I had been on seven of them and after the attack on Munich/Neubiberg had claimed one unidentified single-engined aircraft destroyed on the ground. This type of claim was nothing like so satisfying as destroying an enemy aircraft in the air.

As April closed news came through that both Adolf Hitler and Benito Mussolini were dead and we all thought that the European war must be over. I had even had time to go into the Link Trainer – normally used by the pilots to keep their instrument flying up to the mark – and spent a happy hour in its mock cockpit 'flying' a series of set courses, and regretting once more that I had not been a pilot!

When I had finished and looked at the replica of the courses which I had been steering, as traced out by the 'crab', I found a handsome sketch of 'the Irremovable Finger' (so long the trademark of the immortal Pilot Officer Prune!). Still, the unexpected accuracy of my 'flying' brought a grunt of approval from Harry.

May Day dawned and much to our dismay we learned, when we went down to Dispersal, that ops were on! We could hardly believe it but we got on with an NFT and were up for 35 minutes in F 507 even though I had a slight cold. But later in the day I was to enter: 'Ops Scrubbed we all think it is The End.'

On the following day my log entry was quite different:

'Wed 2nd 21.10 Mosquito XXX S/Ldr White   OPS   507

We were fooled again. Target Flensburg A/F. A memorable take off in pouring rain, rushing around taking out the locks etc. Pretty dark and Harry could not manage his usual long burst. One of our napalm tanks hung up, then dropped on far side of the drome. Flak average, so we strafed some of it to fix the b******s. Several fires and all in and out OK.

   Two Window Halifaxes lost. A bloody poor show at this stage of the War. 03.25 hours.'

Thirteen crews from 141 took part in what was to be the very last operation of the war for Bomber Command. The CO led six of the aircraft to Hohn airfield,

35–40 km west of Kiel, and Harry led the remainder to Flensburg A/F, close to the German/Danish Border. In both areas, we were told, there was a pocket of Germans holding out.

On top of our surprise (and horror!) to hear that ops were on, the weather was still frightful! As we went out to our aircraft, just before nine o'clock, the rain was pouring down and I had to dash round to the rear of the Mosquito (as I always did) to check that the locks had been removed from the elevators and the ailerons by our ground crew. By the time that I had done so and clawed my way up the ladder, to join Harry in the cockpit, I was soaked to the skin! I was muttering something to the effect that we must all be mad to be going off in such appalling weather at this stage of the war, until Harry told me to shut up and get on with my cockpit checks!

The squadron records show that we '. . . took off at 21.10 hrs on a low level fire bomb attack on Flensburg airfield . . .' and as it proved to be the last operational trip that Harry and I ever did, and the last night of the ops over Europe, it may be of some small historical interest to include the rest of the report in full:

> 'They crossed in over the German island of Pellworm at 22.35 hrs and arrived at Flensburg at 22.48 hrs and dropped 2 x 100 gallon drop tanks of Napalmgel at 22.53 hrs from 100 ft., on incendiaries; their approach was SE/NW. One tank caused a fire in buildings South of the perimeter and the other hung up before falling to the ground West of the airfield. They saw other fires concentrated on buildings South of the perimeter. They strafed with cannon fire buildings and gun positions to the South of the airfield. The gun positions were one four-barrel pom-pom half a mile to the East of the airfield, three light flak guns to the South and one light flak gun SW of the airfield. They crossed out and landed at West Raynham at 00.35 hrs.'

A copy of the Night Battle Order, on which I wrote 'NOT ONE OF OUR AIRCRAFT WAS MISSING', and listing the names of the crews who took part in the operation, may be found in Appendix 3. Only twelve crews are listed but thirteen crews operated. The crew missing from the list was F/L J.A.H. Edwards and his Nav/Rad, F/Sgt A.C. Pynn.

As it happened only twelve crews actually carried out bombing with Napalmgel, as one crew, F/O W.P. Rimer with his Nav/Rad, F/O H.B. Farnfield, obtained an AI contact on an enemy aircraft on the way to the target and became engaged in an AI dogfight with the contact, as a result of which they had to abort the bomb attack.

Three other crews from 100 Group were not so lucky. As recorded in my log at the time, two Window Halifaxes from 199 Squadron at North Creake were lost, engaged on RCM operations. All eight men in each aircraft were killed. The Halifaxes suffered a mid-air collision over Kiel.

That was not all; F/O R. Catterall DFC and his navigator, F/Sgt D.J. Beadle, from 169 Squadron at Great Massingham, were killed whilst carrying out a Napalmgel attack on Jagel/Schleswig airfield, when their Mosquito was shot down by flak.

We can only imagine the agony suffered by the next-of-kin of these 18 men, when they received the news of their deaths and realised it was truly a case of 'so near . . . but yet so far'. On the same page of my log-book on which I had entered my notes on our last op, I wrote:

'UNCONDITIONAL SURRENDER OF GERMANY TO THE ALLIES
TUESDAY MAY 8TH 1945.'

The Squadron History talks about a Service of Thanksgiving on the parade
ground at West Raynham and various other activities on 8 May (the instrument
of total surrender having been signed by General Jodl for Germany on the
previous day), but I remember very little of what came to be known as 'VE-Day'.

Six days after our attack on Flensburg airfield, it was all over, although Harry
and I did get into the air again twice before peace fell over a scarred and devas-
tated Europe on 8 May 1945.

Rodney had, at long last, almost completed his training and was flying
Spitfires at an aerodrome in Shropshire, called Montford Bridge. We took a
Mosquito VI and (after I had carefully checked on the length of the runways)
flew over to have lunch with Rodney. We found him in great form and flying
Spit. VIs. We also had a bit of a lunch-time session with some of the 'day boys'
who were instructing there, whilst on rest. In the event, Rodney finally got his
posting to an operational squadron, No. 1, just a week after the war was over.

On the day before VE-Day, there is the following entry, and it is one that I
never thought I would be able to write:

'Mon 7th 11.45 Mosquito VI S/Ldr White RUHR COOK'S TOUR

With memories of Düsseldorf – Essen – Bochum – Duisberg – Hamm – the
Möhne Dam – Cologne (which is really everything) – Aachen. Harry and I
never thought we should fly over the Ruhr in daylight at 1,500 ft. 04.00 hrs.'

All across Bomber Command, crews were taking off to fly over Germany in
daylight to have a look at what they had done, flying in safety, with the terrors
of the once vivid night skies above the Third Reich only a memory.

The heavy bombers could take their faithful ground crews with them, so that
they could also see where they had gone once they had waved their precious
charges out of the dispersal bays and into the night. With our two-seater
Mosquitoes, we could not, sadly, take our ground crews on the 'Cook's Tours'.

We flew low over the great cities of the Ruhr (still half expecting a burst of
flak) and saw the devastation caused by our bombing, but we saw it without
emotion. Then we headed south down the Rhine Valley to look for the scene of
our former Flight Commander's successful raid on the Dams, whilst leading No.
617 Squadron. We found the Möhne Dam, where Guy Gibson became part of
the Air Force legend, the breach in the dam wall still showing up clearly. We
marvelled that the crews had been able to get down to 60 ft, in the dark, to cross
the lake and drop their special bombs so accurately.

Then we turned west and flew back up the Rhine Valley at a height of
2–3,000 ft – passing over Koblenz and Bonn – on our way to have a look at
Cologne. Flying low over the beautiful countryside of southern Germany, and
looking all around us with great interest, we did get an odd feeling, and spon-
taneously we both voiced the same thoughts to each other, over the intercom: I
remember what we said, as clearly as if it was yesterday . . . 'Why on earth did it
have to happen?'

We lost height again as we approached Cologne, with the twin spires of its
great cathedral pointing up 660 feet into the sky and the building underneath
them virtually unscathed. Like St Paul's in London, Cologne's cathedral had

been spared the ravages of the bombing, for no tangible reason. As we circled the city at 1,500 ft we could see the outline of where the three main streets had been, radiating out from the vicinity of the cathedral, and that was all, for about a quarter of a mile in each direction. The Hohenzollern Bridge was down, across the Rhine, and staring down at the ruined city we both agreed that it presented the worst scene of devastation that either of us had ever seen. We set course for home and landed back at West Raynham after a flight of four hours.

As we climbed out of 507, knowing that it was the end to a chapter in our lives, we were both slightly chastened by what we had seen over the other side, but by no means did we regret what had been done to Germany, and our small part in its execution.

I have already observed that I could remember very little of the happenings on VE-Day at West Raynham. To be more accurate, I could remember *absolutely nothing* of the proceedings between 10.30 a.m. and about 6 p.m., when I awoke in Roger and Joan Osborn's house, a mile or two away from the station!

The Station Commander, George Heycock, threw the officers' mess bar open immediately after breakfast was over (although I cannot find any mention of this in the Squadron History!). Within moments the bar was crammed with most of the pilots and navigators from the two squadrons operating from Raynham, together with nearly all the officers from SHQ who could leave their desks! The noise and clamour was such that you could hardly hear yourself speak, as everybody seemed to be talking at once!

Before I passed out there was one remark which I managed to hear above the uproar, as more and more beer was consumed, and during the 'Cold War' with our former allies, the Russians, it often came to mind . . .

One must remember that in May 1945 the combined strength of Bomber Command and the US 8th Air Force was a formidable bombing weapon. It was capable of round-the-clock bombing, with us operating at night and the Americans bombing by day; although with air superiority over Europe since the spring of '44, Bomber Command had been able to operate successfully by day, as well as by night.

The remark I heard, above the noise that was going on was this: 'Why don't we and the Americans go on now, and push the Russians back to their own border?' One man, at least, in that crowd, was already concerned about the onward movement of the Russian Army to the West – and the consequences of the Allies allowing them to occupy the Eastern half of Berlin. One man could see the menace that was going to face the Western World in the post-war years – the menace of Communism. This menace, sadly, is still there, notwithstanding the fall of the Iron Curtain and the changes that have taken place in Russia over the past decade, to say nothing of the 'sleeping giant' further to the East.

I have no idea if any one else took up the cry for a combined British and American air assault on 'Uncle Joe' (as Joseph Stalin, the Russian dictator, was referred to during the war). If they did, it was swallowed up in the general uproar that was going on in the bar, and I never heard it. But that unknown prophet helped to open my eyes to what was going on when the Iron Curtain fell across East Germany in 1946, and the pathetic stream of refugees (that has come to typify the 20th Century more than anything else) started to make their way across to the West, frequently at the risk of their lives.

In any case, it must be said that we were all conscious that the war in the Far East was still going on – and with no knowledge of the development of the

Atomic Bomb by the Americans, and the cataclysmic outcome over Hiroshima in August, we felt that we were going to have our hands full, for some time to come. Rumours of the formation of a force of 1,000 heavy bombers from Bomber Command, to be called 'Tiger Force', to go out to the Pacific and carry on the war against the Japanese were already circulating.

Harry and I saw VE-Day as only a temporary respite and that as soon as the celebrations were over (and we had recovered from our hangovers), we would be swotting up on our Japanese aircraft recognition – doing a few long-range navigation exercises – and then we would be on our way. In two/three weeks we would be recommencing operations and assisting the Americans, island hopping to the Japanese mainland, and it would be a case of '*Tokyo, Here we come*'.

Anyway, shortly after hearing that epic remark (but not its answer!) I must have passed out! because I remember no more of VE-Day until about 6 o'clock that evening, when I awoke to hear (through rather a mist!) Joan Osborn saying, 'I think he's coming to now!' Much to my surprise I found myself lying on the settee in their sitting-room and VE-Day was nearly over!

There was another reason – apart from the Japanese War looming in the offing – why I always remember viewing VE-Day with mixed feelings . . . possibly it was also the explanation of why I drank so much, and so quickly, when the bar opened in the morning?

The destruction of our home in Ashford, six months earlier, and the death of our parents, had left Rodney and I without any permanent home. To that extent it had left us both with a strangely unsettled feeling, even though the 'cracks had been papered over' and we knew that we could stay for as long as we liked with the Sessions family. Both the present and the future looked rather uncertain. I missed not being able to phone my parents up and to plan my next leave at 60 Clarendon Road. I was glad when VE-Day was over.

Don Aris has found, amongst the records of 239 Squadron, a description of the happenings at West Raynham on VE-Day, and although I took no part in them, it seems a pity that readers of this narrative should not hear the following account, which reflects, so well, the emotions of many living in England at the time. Don reports that all that the 141 Squadron records say about this momentous day is: 'VE-Day. Thanksgiving Service on the Parade Ground. Bonfire, fireworks and dance at night.'

The records of the other Mosquito Squadron at West Raynham, No. 239, are not only more detailed but give a bit of the atmosphere of the day:

> 'This was VE-Day and although all the "erks" did not have breakfast in bed as anticipated, they were able to relax a little and had an hour or two extra in bed. Our celebrations started with a short but impressive Service of Thanksgiving on the parade ground at 11.00 hrs., most people then adjourned to their Messes or NAAFI to have a quiet drink or two and then after listening to the Prime Minister's talk at 15.00 hrs., the afternoon was spent in gathering material for a gigantic bonfire behind the Airmen's Mess.
>
> In the evening there was an All Ranks Dance in the Airmen's Mess with plenty of "eats" and 22 barrels of beer. At about 22.30 hrs., the bonfire was lit and with "SANDRA" lights playing and the Beacon flashing "V" (in Morse) instead of "WR", and everyone on the Station gathering round. It was a most impressive show. There was lots of quiet fun but no excesses of any kind.'

Don continues with the Station Records for May:

'VE-Day and VE + 1 were the highlights of this month's recreation. A Dance was held on both days and a very impressive bonfire, complete with three dummies (Hitler, Mussolini and Tojo) hanging from the gallows, was lit on VE-Day. The dances were extremely well run and all personnel on the Station had an exceedingly good time.'

There was a ban on all flying from VE-Day to 10 May (incl.), but in point of fact, Harry and I didn't fly again for two weeks after our sightseeing tour of Germany. On 24 May we carried out a X-country exercise. I navigated F 507 across to Newquay, in Cornwall, and back to West Raynham and we started to get ready to go to Japan.

After the celebrations marking the end of the war in Europe were over, before Harry and I got down to our Japanese aircraft recognition (and trying to improve my navigational skills!), I made a brief summary of our efforts during the three and three-quarter years that we had been flying together. It amounted to some 111 operations, of which 56 were Bomber Support operations. Twelve enemy aircraft were claimed to have been destroyed and four more damaged; one of the latter was subsequently upgraded to destroyed, as a result of post-war research. It did not seem much to show for nearly 1,200 hours in the air.

When I had completed this summary, I inserted a quotation from Joshua, Chapter VIII, Verse 28, which seemed to me to be appropriate: 'And Joshua burnt AI, and made it a heap for ever, even a desolation unto this day.' And I think that is how some AI operators, who had spent so many hours peering into our AI sets, felt in the days following the cessation of hostilities in Europe and as the atmosphere of anticlimax started to set in.

But there is another summary which must be made if the story of our activities, from July 1943 onwards, is to be seen in its proper perspective: namely, the bomber support operations carried out, firstly in Fighter Command and latterly in Bomber Command. The facts are that, between December 1943 and May 1945, the Mosquito squadrons of 100 (BS) Group showed the following successes:

Location	Quantity	Category
In the air	236	Destroyed
	12	Probably Destroyed
	64	Damaged
On the ground	21	Destroyed
	1	Probably Destroyed
	62	Damaged

To these figures must be added the claims of 141 Squadron when they were pioneering the Serrate operations with their Beaufighters between June and September 1943.

In the air	16	Destroyed
	1	Probably Destroyed
	6	Damaged

As Don Aris has said, on top of these successes were the attacks made at low level against a variety of ground targets and including the destruction of trains, lorries, airfield buildings and defences.

Additionally, the very presence of the 100 Group fighters over Germany and Occupied Europe, on the hunt for the defending German fighters, had a detri-

Former Hauptmann Heinz Rökker: in April 1995 I received a letter from a distinguished German night fighter pilot, who wrote to me from his home in Oldenburg, Germany. He was research-ing the losses amongst German night-fighter crews and had been given my name. I promptly replied and we have been in close and regular correspondence ever since. We met at Duxford Aero-drome in July 1995 and my wife and I have a standing invitation to visit him and his wife at Oldenburg. He is holder of the Knight's Cross with Oak Leaves and flew a Ju 88 with I/NJG 2 for more than three years. His claims amount to 65 British aircraft destroyed, putting him in the very top rank of the German night-fighter

aces. Here is a photo of Heinz (second in from the right) standing with his crew by the nose of his Ju 88 in 1945, and another of us meeting at Duxford in 1995 fifty years on.

mental effect on the German Ground Controllers, and even more so on their colleagues in the air. The value just of our presence over the Third Reich cannot be calculated, but a number of former German pilots have written about their constant worry of being intercepted by a long-range British night-fighter, all the time that they were in the air trying to find and destroy the British bombers.

Heinz Rökker was a leading German night-fighter ace who, by the end of the war, held the rank of *Hauptmann* and had been awarded the Knight's Cross with

Oak Leaves. He had 65 victories, nearly all our four-engined bombers, and in one of his letters to me has written '. . . I always had great respect about the excellent performance of the English intruders.'

Here it is worthy of note that our friendship bears no trace of that word, much loved of politicians and churchmen, 'reconciliation'. My friendship with Heinz is founded on a mutual interest in what we were doing and the mutual respect for what the other did. I am sure it is the same for him and that we would not have it any other way. Government and Church leaders may find it desirable (and politically expedient) to pontificate on reconciliation. Those of us, on both sides, who were fortunate to be nearer the action, find no such need.

In March 1993 – fifty years after the commencement of the attempt to protect our heavy bomber force over enemy territory – I wrote some notes on the different phases of the High-Level Bomber Support operations prior to attending a meeting arranged by the Royal Air Force Historical Society at the RAF Staff College at Bracknell. I concluded by saying:

> 'The Bomber Support operations were created to cause as much destruction and confusion to the air and ground defences of Germany as possible. The records of over 250 enemy aircraft destroyed in the air – and many more damaged – speak for themselves. And for the Beaufighter and Mosquito crews it was the most satisfying job in the night-fighter business.'

As they say today, that was the good news, but what about the other side of the coin? What about the bad news?

As the story of bomber support has unfolded – since the idea of putting British night-fighters over Germany at high level was first conceived in the autumn of 1942 – I have criticised, in fairly forthright style, a number of aspects of these operations, starting with the fact that only one squadron was allocated to pioneer the Serrate operation.

We, on 141, were only equipped with Beaufighters, which were short on speed and short on range. When, within a few weeks, German night-fighters were being shot down and the operation proved to be a success – there was no follow-up. It must be pointed out that Wing Commander Braham destroyed a Messerschmitt 110 on 14 June 1943, on the very first Serrate sortie, yet no other squadrons were formed to take advantage of 141's initial successes.

From October onwards there were delays in 141 being re-equipped with the speedier and longer-range Mosquito, and then, as related in full earlier in the narrative, we were given old and clapped-out Mosquito IIs, with disastrous results. When eventually two additional Serrate squadrons were formed (169 and 239) in December, they too were allocated worn-out Mosquito IIs. They were not able to claim their first successes until the end of January 1944. A start was made on replacing 141's Beaufighters with Mosquitoes in October 1943, only to be met with unserviceability of both the aircraft and the radar equipment.

The net result was that the squadron was virtually non-operational for October, November, December '43 and January 1944. One of the ironies of the situation was that there were new Mosquito VIs on the Home Defence squadrons which were being under-employed due to the lack of incoming German bombers. Since the last heavy Blitz of May 1941 there had been spasmodic light raids by 20 to 30 bombers, but seldom anything more.

In the meantime, as we sat by, the heavy bomber crews (like those Harry and

I had met on No. 35 (PFF) Squadron at Graveley) were being harvested by the brilliant, courageous and efficient German night-fighter arm. Nos. 141, 169 and 239 Squadrons were left to struggle on with their old Mosquito IIs until after D-Day, and they left the bones of a number of their crews scattered in the North Sea and on German soil as a direct consequence.

When, eventually, 85 and 157 Squadrons were transferred from Fighter Command into 100 Group, with their newer aircraft and radar equipment, they quickly made their mark. But, as I have observed earlier on, by then 'the ball was over'. Is it being too fanciful, too wise after the event, to ask why 85 and 157 (and maybe others) were not transferred at a much earlier date? Say, at the time 100 Group was being formed in October 1943?

If 141 and the two new squadrons being formed, 169 and 239, had, at the same time, been re-equipped with new Mosquitoes and newer radar, there could have been five Mosquito squadrons supporting the bomber force from November 1943 onwards, as the Battle for Berlin was joined, and when the strategic bomber offensive was at its peak. As things were, for four long and bloody months, the 'bomber boys' had no fighter support at all!

In my notes, written in 1993, I had said that 'for the Beaufighter and Mosquito crews [engaged on bomber support] it was the most satisfying job in the night-fighter business.' I have no reason to alter my opinion in that regard. The feeling that by shooting down a Junkers 88 you might have helped to save the lives of one, or more, heavy-bomber crews was marvellous. But I added the last rather sad paragraph to my notes:

> '. . . for the handful of 141 pilots and navigators who were on the Squadron between October 1943 and January 1944 – and are still alive today – there must always be the nagging feeling that we let "the Bomber Boys" down when they needed us most.'

With the benefits of hindsight, of course, anything is possible, but this is not hindsight. *We knew it then.* If any of my readers are still moved to think that I am being wise after the event I have, in the last few months, been sent a most interesting and revealing document, namely the minutes of a meeting chaired by Sir Robert Renwick at the Air Ministry on Friday 16 July 1943 to discuss Serrate and Mausoleum.

At the time of this meeting, 141 had already been operating for a month and had destroyed six German night-fighters in fact, Harry and I had got our first Me 110 the night before! It is surely of interest that, at the highest level, the powers that be were already committed to providing '. . . the best possible protection for our Bombers over enemy territory' and were already thinking in terms of three Serrate squadrons.

No lesser person than David Jackson (who had flown successfully as an AI operator on Home Defence, and is mentioned earlier in the narrative) was, even then, thinking of three squadrons of Mosquitoes! If one squadron of Beaufighters could – in the pioneering stage of the new operation – claim 16 E/A destroyed, how many could three squadrons of Mosquitoes (with their longer range and higher top speed) have intercepted and shot down as autumn 1943 gave way to winter?

And if their successes were comparable, or better, than those of 141 surely when all three squadrons were transferred into Bomber Command (on the formation of No. 100 Group) 85 and 157 and maybe others would have been relieved from kicking their heels in Fighter Command to go where the real battle was unfolding over the Third Reich?

If there had been five, or even six, squadrons of Mosquitoes operating on bomber support from October 1943 onwards (and from reading the minutes of the meeting held on 16 July, that is not inconceivable) then it is reasonable to presume that a real blow could have been struck at the German night-fighter arm; that the 'Battle of Berlin' would not have taken such a terrible toll; that we would not have lost 78 bombers over Leipzig in February 1944; and that the name Nuremberg would not have carried for ever such dreadful memories for all who served in Bomber Command. The minutes of Sir Robert Renwick's meeting were paved with good intentions . . . I wonder what happened to them?

It was to be six months after Sir Robert's meeting before three squadrons of Mosquitoes would be operational on the business of bomber support, and another two before their claims of German night-fighters started to mount. They were ineffective in support of the Nuremberg raid at the end of March 1944, and this ill-fated raid virtually signalled the end of the strategic bombing offensive for the winter of 1943/44. Much has been written about Allied air superiority, even supremacy, in the latter part of the war, but air superiority over Germany and Occupied Europe – during the hours of darkness – still lay firmly in the hands of the German night-fighter arm.

It was the 'bomber boys' who paid the price.

9 The Anti-climax and the Parting of the Ways

– 'Farewell – Othello's occupation's gone'

Don Aris continued his incomparable History of the Squadron, right up to 7 September 1945, when it was disbanded shortly after the second Atomic Bomb was dropped, and the Japanese surrendered. At the end of May, by which time many of our ground crews had been taken on one of the 'Cook's Tours' over Germany provided by the Halifaxes of 100 Group's heavy-bomber squadrons, 171 and 199, he wrote:

> 'The Squadron had flown a reduced programme of cross-country and formation flying which some today believe were for Far East training. Much to the dislike of all, a peacetime routine started to come back to West Raynham with Colour Hoisting and Church Parades and the tightening up of discipline. The Station Medical Officer makes the comment in his end of month report that there had been a 100% increase in the numbers on Sick Parade since the resumption of peacetime routine and early morning working parades!'

Throughout the war operational stations, squadrons and both aircrew and their ground crews had been remarkably free from what was known in the Air Force as 'bull'. Everybody had a job to do and when you were off duty you were largely left to your own devices. None of us took too kindly to 'square bashing' and enforced Church Parades but it was not long before I got involved in one! I was rung up one day and told by the Station Administrative Officer that I would be taking the Church Parade the following Sunday! I was horrified and asked him politely what I was supposed to do? He said:

> 'Well Mike, all you have to do is to accept the parade from the Station Warrant Officer, when he's got them all lined up then, as soon as you see the Station Commander walking onto the Parade Ground, you call the parade 'to attention' and give the order to the Corporal in charge of the Colour Party to raise the RAF Standard to the top of the flag-pole. After that you accompany the Station Commander, whilst he inspects the parade. It's a piece of cake, you can't go wrong!'

The great day came and everything went according to plan. It was just like being back at Hurstpierpoint College on one of the OTC parades. Everything went according to plan – that is – until the moment before the great man was due to arrive! I was walking up and down in front of my 'troops', feeling rather like the Noble Duke of York, when the corporal in charge of the colour party sidled up to me and saluted. Then, in sepulchral tones, he said 'Sorry, Sir, but the rope 'as gorn . . .' Then, as I tried desperately to collect my thoughts, 'What are we going to do Sir?'

I glanced up at the flag-pole and, where the halyard should have been gaily flapping in the breeze, saw that the wretched corporal was indeed speaking the truth. The rope had gorn! I took another quick turn, up and back, with the corporal more or less hanging on to my coat-tails and then said, out of the side of my mouth, 'Tie the standard to the rope that goes out to the yardarm, he'll have to make do with that for today!' He saluted thankfully and the day was saved, but not before the 'penny had dropped'.

I realised that, during the week, it had got around that 'Mike's taking the Church Parade on Sunday' and that some of my 'friends' had improved the shining hour on Saturday evening by making a sortie to the parade ground and quietly removed the rope from the flag-pole. It was some time before I was asked to take another Church Parade.

There seemed to be plenty of leave and not very much serious flying but I can't remember where I went, maybe to Ashford, but things were understandably no longer the same there . . . maybe to Aylsham to see Jill Holman who, mad keen on horses, was teaching me to ride.

During the whole of June, Harry and I did only 6.05 hrs flying, one night-flying test and two X-countries, and July was even worse, with only 3.30 hrs in the air. It began to look as if our chances of going out to the Far East, as part of Tiger Force were receding rapidly.

Then, during July, there was a squadron posting and we were all uprooted from our comfortable mess and quarters to go to a hutted camp, NE of Raynham, with the unlikely name of Little Snoring.

Little Snoring. The very name conjures up the countryside of England, so beloved by John Betjeman and so evocatively expressed in his poems. 'Snoring', as it inevitably became, lay only three miles to the north-east of Fakenham, so we were even closer to our old haunt at the Crown. We also found ourselves close to Great Walsingham, where the ancient Catholic Shrine attracted – and still does attract – pilgrims from all over the world. The local pub in Great Walsingham had an odd name; it was called (if I remember rightly) the Oxford Stores and was located quite close to the Shrine.

It was not too long before we found ourselves making our pilgrimage there – to the pub, not the Shrine – for 'a Gin and Holy Water'. We also found that the landlord of the Oxford Stores had a supply of petrol, quite illegally, and after closing time we could drive our cars round to his pump at the back of the pub and fill up our tanks. Petrol, at that time, was still strictly rationed.

Whilst on this subject I recall that, back in Ashford, there was a chap in the Feltham Road who had built an illicit still from which he was able to produce a strange-looking fluid called 'Chrysanthemum Juice'! He sold it at an exorbitant price, with a bit of a discount if you were in the Air Force and local!

We also found ourselves nearer to the coast and often at a loose end. We would gather ourselves together in a fleet of three or four cars and head for Holkham, Overy Staithe, to finish up at the Lestrange Arms at Hunstanton. Frequently these outings started in the morning with a swim in the sea, off Holkham, and ended with a hectic lunch-time session, in Hunstanton. From one of these, I remember driving most of the way back to Snoring with Harry balanced precariously on the bonnet of my Ford.

On other occasions, during some very hot days in July and August, we helped the farmers out with the harvest. Some of the big farmers in Norfolk had always been very good in entertaining us, so we were only too willing to help them out at harvest time. I remember sweating all day in the fields, stacking the corn, and then eating a gargantuan dinner in the evening, which bore no relationship to the ordinary civilian ration cards!

I also remember being introduced to Norfolk's own special tipple, gin and cider! A substantial tot of gin, emptied into a pint glass of raw cider! After a full day in the harvest fields I knocked the first one back and it hardly seemed to touch the sides. The second went down scarcely less quickly and I thought how innocuous was their much vaunted Norfolk brew! The only trouble was that, shortly after I had started to down my third pint glass of this same innocuous brew, I remembered no more of the proceedings until two hours later!

Although I have mentioned that I had a drink from time to time, during those days, I never smoked. Our parents had always given Rodney and I permission to smoke from the time that we were about 13 years old. They both smoked, my father 50 to 60 a day, but neither of us ever took up the habit, which was in those days very much in fashion. Every film star had a cigarette dangling nonchalantly from his, or her, finger tips and it was twenty years before the disclosures of the early sixties, revealing the correlation between the incidence of cancer and cigarette smoking.

For me, the deciding factor had been the sound of my father coughing his heart out, as he got up in the mornings, when he was still a young man in his mid-thirties. Whenever I was offered a cigarette, I always had my stock answer ready to hand, to the effect that I had never smoked, and 'Thank you, but NO', spelt out politely, but quite firmly! All this worked quite well for a long time, although sometime I used to dream that I was smoking and wake up in a mock sweat thinking 'My God, I've started!'

Then one morning – back in the mess at Raynham – with breakfast over, the cigarettes were handed round and, when offered one, I launched forth with my usual spiel. I was doing fine until someone cut in on my protestations that I did not smoke, had never smoked, etc., etc. with 'Don't be such a "BF" Mike, you were smoking at the party last night!'

But in that summer of anticlimax the parties which we had did not feel the same. We were no longer celebrating a victory or a survival. The exhilaration of 'playing in the 1st XV', i.e. of being on an operational squadron and going hunting for the enemy over the other side was gone from our lives, and for the vast majority of us, gone for ever. On the other hand, the drug of operational flying lingered on – with many of us – for a long time.

Bomber Command's Tiger Force, to go to the Pacific was – we heard – being reduced from 1,000 aircraft to 900, and then to 800. As our chances of going out to the Far East diminished in June and July, Harry and I often used to say to each other, 'I wish we could do just one more trip.' Like other 'artists' the drug of going 'on stage', night after night, had eaten deep into our souls. Just how deep, I did not know at the time . . .

100 (Bomber Support) Group was already starting to disintegrate: West Raynham had been handed over to Fighter Command, earmarked for a new unit being formed, called grandiosely 'The Central Fighter Establishment'. Squadrons 169 and 239 were both disbanded at the beginning of July '45. Our old unit, BSDU and the Training Unit at Massingham soon went, and almost every day, on 141, personnel were being posted away.

Surprisingly, we had some new crews posted in to us from the disbanded BSTU at Great Massingham! It must have been an anticlimax for them, as it was for

Rodney, now on Spitfires, to be posted onto an operational squadron, with the war over and no chance of putting all their years of training to the test by actually flying on ops.

We were even losing our aircraft! Early in July all of the Mosquito XXXs of 141 were grounded and eventually – after being stripped of their armament and some of their instruments – flown away ignominiously to various RAF Maintenance Units for storage. We had to take over 515 Squadron's old Mosquito Mk VIs! Still, it was not to be for long, 'our number' would soon be coming up!

During July (when as mentioned, I only put in 3.30 hours flying) and in August, I flew with several of the other pilots on the squadron, including the New Zealander, F/Lt McClymont, Rocky Brady and surprisingly, Paddy Engelbach! It will be remembered that 'Angels' (which was his more customary nickname!) had been shot down in June 1944 and been taken prisoner. Ron Mallett DFC, his navigator, had sadly been killed.

Shortly after Angels, along with thousands of other prisoners-of-war, had been released and repatriated in May/June, he turned up again at his old squadron! He was still as large as life, and the harrowing experience of being shot down and his subsequent incarceration for 12 months had done nothing to lessen his bouncy, endearing and entertaining personality. It may also be recalled that Angels had enjoyed rather a chequered career as a pilot on 141, and at one time only Bob Braham's influence enabled us to continue with the undoubted pleasure of his company! I see from my log-book that I did actually go up with him in a Mosquito VI for 15 minutes of local flying in the vicinity of Little Snoring, but I did not venture any further with him!

I remember him coming into the mess wearing a German uniform that he had brought back with him. He was very keen to take a Mosquito and fly back over Germany to look for the site of *Stalag Luft 3*, the camp in East Germany to which he had been taken after being interrogated at *Dulag Luft*, near Frankfurt. He asked me if I would go with him and navigate for him! I had a mental picture of dear old Angels 'beating up' his old camp in joyous fashion and at low level looking out at the remains of *Stalag Luft 3* rather than where he was going – I declined the offer! I remember saying 'Angels, I love you dearly and I am delighted to see you back. But I'm not going to risk my neck by flying over Germany with you, on that sort of trip!'

Needless to say, he was not at all offended, and we continued to enjoy a close friendship until his tragic loss in a post-war flying accident. He stayed on in the Air Force, was a brilliant linguist – amongst his other talents – and was sent to France to learn Russian. He was 'a natural' for a post as one of the Military Attachés on the British Embassy staff in Moscow in the 'fifties as the Cold War developed, following the fall of the 'Iron Curtain' and the blockade of Berlin in 1948.

Angels would have enjoyed trying to outwit 'Uncle Joe' and he would have been very good at it. However, like Rodney and many others who have been bitten by the flying bug, he only wanted to fly and nobody could persuade him any differently.

Apart from the many memories I have of him, I still have copies of the exceptional poems he wrote when he was a POW. Some moving, some light-hearted, one long one about life and death on a squadron, one about his feelings when he was shot down, and one supremely unselfish one to Helena, his fiancée, abjuring her from waiting for him. She too was a wonderfully staunch person – she waited for him. Angels, I will always remember, was short of stature but long on courage.

Early in July, 1945 I received a letter from the Central Chancery of the Orders of Knighthood which opened: 'The King will hold an Investiture . . .' Harry had been up to the Palace in June (it will be remembered that his award of the DFC had come through several weeks before mine). The date of the investiture at Buckingham Palace '. . . at which your attendance is requested' was to be 20 July. The letter further advised me that I could be accompanied by two relations or friends to witness the investiture.

So I promptly got in touch with Rodney and my grandmother. We were told to be at the Palace not later than 10.15 a.m., but the doors would be open at 9.45. Harry had already briefed me that it was advisable to be there an hour early, if one wanted to ensure good seats for one's relatives. So, with Rodney and Granny Allen, at 8.45 we were outside the gates of the Palace, where the queue was already forming. When the doors opened the queue soon started moving and we walked across the outer courtyard, through the centre arch, and on into the inner courtyard.

Once inside the Palace, Rodney and Granny were guided away to be shown their seats in the Audience Chamber, and I was ushered through to one of the large rooms overlooking the garden. There I found a crowd of other RAF officers, and there we waited, milling around and chatting to old friends. Later, a Palace official came round and affixed a small clip to the top of the left-hand breast pocket of our uniform and told us that we would not need to wear our caps when we went up to receive our decorations from the King.

In the meantime, Rodney and Granny were already watching the King investing the first recipients with their honours and awards. These were the various Orders and the Knights Bachelor which were, of course, ranked before the Service Crosses. There was, however, one decoration which took precedence even over the Garter, the most noble Order in the Land, and there was a recipient of that decoration at the Palace on 20 July, who was the first man to stand before His Majesty the King that day.

A Gurkha soldier had won the Victoria Cross in Italy at the crossing of the Sangro River. He was there, accompanied by one of his officers, to receive his VC. What ensued turned out to be almost the most entertaining part of the day but, waiting patiently in our room overlooking the gardens, we missed it all. Rodney told me what happened when we met again after the investiture was over, and the story went like this.

The only award for which the citation was read out (prior to the recipient step-ping forward to have the medal pinned on) was the Victoria Cross. So, Rodney said, there was the Gurkha standing rigidly at attention at the foot of the ramp, which led up to the dais where the King stood, whilst the story of his almost incredible bravery was read out by one of the Palace officials.

But for this courageous little man the thought of having to stand in the presence of his King, the King Emperor as he was in those days, was worse than having to fight his way across the Sangro River! For him it must have been like having to meet God! Rodney said that, when the citation had been read out, his officer gave him a nudge and he set off up the ramp. But apparently he was in such a state that when he reached the dais he walked right on past the King, who was dressed in naval uniform, and headed for one of the officials, resplendent in blue and gold lace! He must have thought that the official, in his more impressive and imposing uniform, was the King! Anyway, his officer soon hauled him back to the dais where he could turn left, face the Monarch, who was now smiling kindly at him, and receive his Victoria Cross.

In due course they got to the DSCs and then to the MCs. Then it was our turn to form ourselves into a queue and move towards the Throne Room. I found myself heading the line of Air Force officers who were to receive the DFC, then, as I reached the foot of the ramp, I heard my name being called out and I started to walk towards the King.

When I had been working as an apprentice at Fairey's, five long years before, the King and Queen visited the factory (following the success of the Fairey Swordfish over Taranto) and walked through the main assembly bay. I have recorded how, right up to a few minutes before their arrival, nobody (including myself) took the slightest notice, or was moved in any way . . . and how, once we found ourselves in their presence, things changed and one felt differently. Of course, at Fairey's, I was only an apprentice and nowhere near them. I was just one of hundreds, standing on the benches, cheering them as they walked past.

But at the Palace, waiting to receive our medals, it was just the same. In the garden room, chatting away to each other, we had been blasé, and almost uninterested in the whole performance. Once Peter Townsend formed us up into the queue things were different and, like the Gurkha VC, our throats became dry and our heart-strings started to tighten. We were in the presence of our King – and nobody felt blasé any more.

As I walked up the ramp I could hear the soft background music of the Guards' Band and I thought to myself 'I shall always remember this piece of music because of where I am standing now.' . . . I have never remembered a single note! I walked onto the dais, turned to my left and bowed. The King reached behind him for the medal and – transferring it to his right hand – slipped it over the small hook above my pocket, which had been placed there earlier. I had determined that, when I went to get my decorations, I would try to tell him that – since its award – my parents had been killed as a result of enemy action. I did tell the King but, as with the music, I have no recollection of what I said, or of his reply. I know that he was immensely kind and considerate before he put his arm forward, for me to shake his hand.

I then took one pace backwards, turned to my right and stepped off down the ramp beyond the dais. I had barely reached level ground – and had no time to get used to the medal hanging from my chest – before an official leapt forward and whipped the Cross from its hook! He slapped it cheerfully into its little box, removed the hook, and handed the box back to me. I walked on out into the inner courtyard, where I was soon joined by Rodney and Granny.

Outside the Palace, where we were joined by my cousin, Irene Gray, still in the WAAF, we had an awful photograph taken (of which I have always been ashamed), then we all bundled into a taxi and drove off to have lunch at Bellometti's in Leicester Square, which had been one of my parents' favourite restaurants. There Bellometti himself 'rolled out the red carpet' and later we saw our grandmother back to Victoria and safely onto the train for Oxted.

I missed not being able to attend the Palace with Harry and to receive our decorations together. Also, needless to say, 20 July 1945 was the day on which I missed my Mother and Father more than at any other time . . .

At the beginning of August Harry and I did some more X-country flights, more map reading, and I put in more than 20 hours in the Link Trainer; plotting courses, taking bearings, and working out problems on 'the Triangle of Velocities' and of 'DR'. But as the uncertainty of a posting to the Far East grew daily and as talk about something called 'demobilisation' started to creep into the conversation, one started to think, 'What am I going to do? Should I try to stay in the Air Force, or should I head for civvy street?'

Forms for applying for a permanent commission in the Royal Air Force were in circulation, and like many others, I filled one in and sent it off, without thinking seriously whether I wanted to stay in if I were to be granted one. In any case, there seemed to be nothing to lose. About this time I think that Joan, Harry's wife, got her discharge from the Wrens and they found some accommodation in Fakenham, so four years of sharing a room with him, in all sorts of funny places, came to an end.

In the meantime, when we refer (almost for the last time) to the Squadron History, we find on 6 August:

'. . . that the war in the Far East [*Note: which even to this day is so often overlooked by people in England*] against the Japanese had been continuing with heavy losses. Burma had been reconquered by the British and the Japanese mainland had been under aerial bombardment since October 1944 with American B-29 bombers from Saipan and Guam in the Marianas. Okinawa in the Ryuku Islands and Iwo Jima in the Bonin Islands, both close to Japan, had been taken and air attacks from these as well as from Saipan and Guam and from carrier-borne aircraft meant that raids of a 1,000 aircraft could be made on Japan. Tokyo had suffered the terrible fire storm raid by B-29s on the 9th/10th March 1945 when some 80,000 to 90,000 casualties were caused.

An ultimatum had been sent to the Japanese Government on the 26 July jointly by the American, British and Chinese Governments calling for unconditional surrender, this was rejected. Leaflets had been dropped on all major Japanese cities warning that unless they surrendered they would be subjected to intensive aerial attacks.

On the 6 August 1945 therefore, the American B-29 bomber *ENOLA GAY* dropped an Atomic Bomb on Hiroshima with the awesome results now so well documented. The dead were estimated by the Americans as 78,000 but the Japanese give figures as high as 240,000, half the population of the city.'

The 6th of August 1945 changed everybody's life. The dropping of the Atomic Bomb transcended anything – and any weapon – that had featured in six years of war. Every man, woman and child, whether in the Armed Forces or not, in this country and in countries around the world, woke up on 7 August to find that they were living in a new dimension. That they were living with the greatest force, for both evil and good, ever known to man: a force that was to dominate the world political scene, from that moment onwards.

Three days later a second Atomic Bomb was dropped on Nagasaki in Japan, with estimated casualties of 35,000. Five days after that Japan agreed to surrender unconditionally . . . and it was all over.

In my log-book, I wrote: 'THAT'S THAT'. The Second World War was over.

Neither Tiger Force nor Harry and I would now be going to the Far East. We would all, except those who had been on regular engagements when the war broke out, have to re-think our future . . .

There had been VE-Day when the war in Europe had come to an end, now the

15 August was 'Victory over Japan', and declared as VJ-Day. A national holiday was pronounced for both the 15th and 16th, although the celebrations were, understandably, on a lesser scale to those in May. Don reports that: 'Emperor Hirohito went on the radio – for the first time ever – and ordered all Japanese troops to lay down their arms.'

Although some units of the Japanese forces continued to fight for a while in China, Manchuria until the Russians came in, and on remote islands in the Pacific, officially World War Two was now over, subject to the signing of various surrender documents. On 2 September the formal instrument of surrender was signed by the Japanese on the American battleship USS *Missouri* in Tokyo Bay.

At Little Snoring there was no flying of any kind for 141 and 23 Squadrons from 15 to 19 August, inclusive.

Although the sudden ending of the war in the Far East, and the method by which it was achieved, came as a shock, it was probably just as well that things happened as they did. Up to 6 August few people, outside those directly concerned with the policy design, manufacture and delivery of the Atomic Bomb, had any knowledge of it or of its awesome potential; it was a very well kept secret.

So the general impression, back in England, was that – with the fanatical spirit of the Japanese troops and the *Kamikaze* attacks launched by the Japanese Air Force – the Americans and their Allies were faced with island hopping all the way up to the Japanese mainland. Furthermore, it was estimated that this strategy would take another 18 months and a million casualties amongst the Allied forces, before victory could be achieved.

Controversy concerning the dropping of two Atomic Bombs on Japan has raged on moral and other grounds since the end of World War Two. But the fact that they saved the lives of countless American and British soldiers, sailors and airmen is beyond dispute. Harry and I may have been initially disappointed that we could not do just one more trip (and maybe a few more on top of that!), but if we were honest with ourselves the use of the bombs may well have saved our lives as well!

One has, of course, no means of telling, it is all in the realms of fantasy, but I have often thought, as the post-war years have unfolded, that if Tiger Force had gone out – and us with it – and we had begun in effect a fourth tour of operations, we would not have been much good for anything else when we got back – if we had got back.

I, for one, have always been deeply grateful for the courage of President Truman and his other fellow Americans who took the most difficult decision of the 20th century, when they authorised the dropping of the Atomic Bomb on Hiroshima, Japan.

But now, much closer to home, other decisions had to be made. These were the personal ones which could be summed up quite simply into 'What am I going to do? Am I going to try to stay in the Air Force or am I going to go out into "Civvy Street"?' As so often in life, it was simpler to ask the question than to answer it!

Restricting our thoughts to the aircrew, the pilots and navigators, the former were somewhat better placed than their companions. The Air Force had taught them to fly and in the post-war world, with the inevitable expansion of civil aviation, those of them for whom the RAF in peace-time had no appeal could pursue their calling as an airline captain. It might be thought, by some, to be a trifle mundane after the excitement of flying on ops, but it could – and subsequently did – provide a marvellous career for many wartime pilots.

But who wanted an Observer (Radio) – to revert to our old job title? Let alone an AI Operator – and let alone those of us who had been rushed through our training in 1941, without doing a navigation course!

Admittedly, many of the airlines still carried 'Navigators' and '2nd Pilots'; and there would be a few permanent commissions granted to 'Observers' in the Air Force. But for the majority of us, particularly for those who had flown for a long time with one pilot, the prospect of crewing up again, or of having to fly with just any pilot, was not an attractive one.

I had already put in my application for a permanent commission, so there was nothing more to do in that direction, except to wait and see. But I felt I must start to put some other irons in the fire regarding my future, now that the war was finally over. I made some enquiries, should the Air Force decide that they could manage without my services, and, through a friend of mine, who had been a navigator on 239 Squadron, I got an introduction to Lever Bros & Unilever Limited, the multi-national industrial group.

He advised me to write off to Lever's, and apply for an opening as a management trainee. This I did and, again, I had to sit back and await results. I had also ascertained that if I left the Royal Air Force, my likely date for demobilisation would be June 1946. This meant that I had about nine more months in which to sort out my future.

I was glad that by the time the VJ-Day celebrations were over and we started flying again, albeit in somewhat desultory fashion, I had taken some steps to sort out a future career, although I was still pretty uncertain of what I really wanted to do. Our first peacetime flight, made on 21 August, was an air firing exercise carried out off the North Norfolk coast. Earlier in the month some of us had indulged in some 'gannet bashing' in the Bristol Channel with some low-level

Harry White and myself at the first 141 Squadron Reunion held at Oddenino's Restaurant, in London, in 1946. 'Jacko' Flight Lieutenant Jacobs DFC*, AFC is next but one on my left.

mock strafing attacks on Lundy Island. In those days, Lundy was uninhabited – except for the gannets – and the animal rights people (even then) had been quick to take exception to our activities!

Nearly every day now, someone or other was posted off the squadron: John Sheldon DFC, a navigator, had gone on 4 August; Norman Barber, on the 7th; 'Scotty' DFC and Bar, Charles Winn's navigator, had already gone; and on the 24th, the CO himself, Charles, who had recently added the DSO to his DFC in well-earned recognition of his leadership of 141 Squadron during the last years of the war, was posted to take command of RAF Bathurst in Gambia, West Africa. Like others of the pre-war regulars who had survived, Charles Winn could now resume, and look forward to, a normal peacetime Service career.

These were unsettling days for everyone on the squadron – aircrew and ground crew alike – and with the rapid disintegration of 100 Group it was becoming obvious that, like 169 and 239 Squadrons, 141 Squadron would also soon be disbanded. Harry and I began to wonder what was in store for us. We were not to be left long in doubt!

Number 141 Squadron was disbanded on 7 September 1945, and three days later Harry and I got our posting. There were a series of farewell parties at Little Snoring, but I can't remember any of them. Which is, perhaps, just as well. Happily, the post-war Air Force found that it could not get along without the '141st Night Pursuit Squadron', and the squadron was later re-formed in June, 1946.

By 12 September Harry and I were flying again, in a Mosquito XIX No. 682, from, of all places, Tangmere! Tangmere, where we had spent so many fruitless months in 1941/42 flying the airborne searchlight and so many valuable months learning our trade. We found ourselves back there again! We had joined the Fighter Interception Development Squadron, which was one of many similar units making up the newly formed Central Fighter Establishment: the same CFE which was destined for West Raynham as soon as it had been finally evacuated by 100 Group. In other words we soon learned that within a matter of days we would find ourselves back in Norfolk, and stationed for the third time at West Raynham.

Before we left Tangmere we did one trip which must be recorded. The 15th of September 1945 marked the first of many succeeding anniversaries held to commemorate the Battle of Britain. For, on that day in 1940, the claims for the number of German aircraft shot down reached its peak. Now, with the coming of peace, the RAF could for the first time celebrate it in style.

A massive formation of Hurricanes and Spitfires was assembled from all over Fighter Command and, led by some of the survivors of the battle, including Douglas Bader (recently returned from Colditz), flew right across London and plumb over Trafalgar Square where, I am sure, that Lord Nelson was looking approvingly up at them from his column!

Amongst that formation, flying a Spitfire from No. 1 Squadron, was Rodney, my brother, now a Flying Officer. Our part in the great day was, by comparison, very insignificant. Royal Air Force stations all over England were thrown open to the public. Local air displays were laid on and aircraft were lined up on the edges of the airfields for the public to crawl into the cockpits, and clamber about, to their heart's content!

Some stations, particularly the Training Units, were a bit short on operational aircraft, so there were lots of Station Commanders who had rung up to say, 'Can you send me a Spitfire?' or 'Can you let me have a Mosquito?' So it came about that Harry and I took off from Tangmere early on Saturday the 15th in a Mosquito Mk VI No. 470, and flew to a small station located at Aberporth on the Welsh coast, some miles to the south of Aberystwyth where I had started my ITW course, but never finished it, in June/July 1941.

The OC RAF Aberporth, a wing commander, welcomed us with open arms and we duly lined our Mosquito up with the other visiting aircraft and spent the rest of the day showing the 'Wooden Wonder' to the good people of Wales. Harry and I took it in turns to stand at the bottom of the steps and push them up through the narrow door and to sit in the pilot's seat, answering numerous questions, which came from young and old alike.

The atmosphere was marvellous throughout the day and, if truth be told, we thoroughly enjoyed ourselves. When the time came for us to stop 'shooting a line', and return to Tangmere, the CO said to us, 'Give them a bit of a show, when you leave, will you?' That was enough for Harold White! We taxied out, took off, climbed to 2,000 ft, banked round, put the nose down, and came back across the airfield at Aberporth at a height of 50 ft – flat out! I caught a glimpse of the crowd and their white faces, staring at us – and then we were gone. Harry had indeed given them 'a bit of a show'.

On our return journey, from Aberporth to Tangmere, we dropped in at Silverstone to see Jack, the eldest of the three Sessions brothers. Jack, married with two children, had just completed a successful tour on Halifaxes as a navigator on 158 Squadron, for which he was awarded a DFC. Later he emigrated to South Africa. When I, too, moved there in the mid-60s, he and I became great friends.

Younger readers might wonder how we dropped in at Silverstone? Had we perhaps used the main straight of the racing track? It was the reverse – the runway was to become the race track! After the war, a number of airfields provided the ideal foundation for motor-racing; RAF Silverstone was one such. On that first Battle of Britain Day, we found Jack in great form and, after a happy hour, we went on our way back to Tangmere.

I was thrilled when I heard, a day or two later, that Rodney had been in the great formation that had flown over London and that having been together at Clarendon Road on the day that war broke out we both took part in the celebrations which ended it.

Talking of the Sessions family reminds me that, during the last winter of the war, when Bomber Command were still operating, I gave Teddy Sessions a lift back to his airfield (a pilot, he was on his second tour flying PFF Mosquitoes). We had found ourselves on leave in Ashford at the same time and I realised that I could drop him off at his station, just outside Cambridge, as we were due to finish our leave at the same time. Mrs Sessions packed us up some sandwiches and off we went, leaving Ashford after lunch.

All round Cambridge lay the wartime airfields of the Pathfinder Force, No. 8 Group, Bomber Command, and just to the north of the city we pulled off the road to eat our picnic. There, on the other side of the hedge, we saw the Lancasters and an airfield beyond. There were signs of activity, engines were being started up, buses full of aircrew were on the move – and we realised immediately that ops were on.

As we watched, fascinated, one of the buses pulled up near to a Lancaster, which was parked in a dispersal bay not far from where we were sitting. The seven crew climbed out of the bus and walked towards their aircraft. I even spotted the navigator, with his green bag containing all his charts and maps for the coming op. They stood around for a few minutes; those last few pregnant minutes that both Teddy and I knew so well, some of them smoking, and the difference between their situation and ours hit us both like a thunderbolt! Them just setting out to face the flak, the night-fighters and the hell of the target area – and us sitting there eating our sandwiches and enjoying the English countryside, knowing that we would sleep safely in our beds that night. The contrast was too much for us. We hastily bolted the remainder of our picnic, gave them a tentative wave through the gap in the hedge, got back in the car and drove on.

By the beginning of October the Central Fighter Establishment, with its various offshoots had completed its move from Tangmere, and settled down at West Raynham, now a station within the aegis of Fighter Command. Harry and I, who found ourselves there for the third time, did not really settle. The future for both of us still appeared to be uncertain and the job, on the Fighter Interception Development Squadron, was all a bit of a sham. We went through the motions and did a number of flight trials during the month, but it all seemed rather futile, and our hearts were not in it.

Central Fighter Establishment was a conglomeration of all the day-fighter and night-fighter activities that one could possibly think of! It was jammed pack-full of the most experienced and distinguished fighter pilots in the Royal Air Force (there were also a few AI operators there!). I think the idea was to capitalise on the experience gained during the war years, review and examine every aspect of fighter tactics, aircraft, equipment, crewing, etc. and by flight trials, plan and develop the policy and strategy for Fighter Command in the post-war years which lay ahead. I am making no attempt to knock this objective. I am quite sure that, at the time, it was perfectly laudable and the only logical course that could be taken by the Air Ministry.

So in Fighter Interception Development Squadron (or FIDS as our unit was known, for short) we were made up of night-fighter pilots and AI operators, and we had a variety of Mosquitoes, and even one Beaufighter, to fly. Our main task (not unlike that on the BSDU) was to carry out flight trials on new instruments and equipment for the night-fighter squadrons still being retained in the Air Force. The difference was that we could not now take them on ops and try them out for real! Also, the boffins had disappeared back to their universities and their laboratories, and the designers of any new equipment were from the companies supplying the Defence Industry.

We tested a new type of cathode-ray tube for the Mk X AI called 'the Birmingham University Tube'. I remember that there was one version with a yellow screen and another with a green screen. When we landed I wrote in my report that the latter was easier to read at night (we had actually flown at night to make sure that the trials were authentic), and jokingly said that the Air Force should order 5,000 of 'the green sort'!

When we took off one day in a Mosquito equipped with a new Mk IX AI to carry out a practice interception – it was all practice now – it was on one of our old adversaries, a Messerschmitt 110. Unfortunately the E/A went u/s shortly after becoming airborne, but not before we had got in behind it and had a good look at it – in the daylight! Then we were given a magnificent new instrument in Mosquito VI No. 470; it was called the 'Non-Topple Artificial Horizon'.

The ordinary artificial horizon on the blind flying panel was liable to 'topple' during any extreme manoeuvre, so that by the time that the pilot had righted the aircraft the instrument would no longer be giving an accurate reading. At night, or in cloud, this could be uncomfortable, to say the least!

So our task for this trial was to take No. 470 up to a safe altitude, and throw it about all over the sky to see if we could topple the intriguing 'Non-Topple Artificial Horizon' on our instrument panel. Almost for the last time we can refer to my flying log-books to see what happened: 'After an hour's gyrations the N.T.A.H. still remained untoppled – not so our stomachs!'

The trial was obviously successful!

At the end of October Harry received a telegram, a copy of which I pasted into my log-book. It read, as follows:

'FROM AIR MINISTRY

TO C.F.E.

POST 119508 F/LT.H.E.WHITE. PILOT FROM C.F.E. TO A.M.U. W.E.F. 12.11.45. SUPERNUMERARY P.P. TO S/LDR. POST DGM/M10 VICE S/LDR. RAFFAELLI. TO REPORT A.M.U., 77, HALLAM STREET, LONDON BEFORE REPORTING FOR DUTY.'

As I pasted the copy of the telegram into my log I wrote across it one word and underlined it:

FINIS!

Harry's permanent commission had come through. He had got a posting to an administrative job in London and he and Joan were off in a matter of days to begin the search for accommodation, which at that time in London was at a premium.

A few weeks later I received the following letter:

'111, Church Road,
Richmond,
Surrey,
18.11.45.

My Dear Mike,

First, an explanation. Four years odd is a long time and one would think that there might have been a little more appreciation shown even by such as myself when we came to the temporary parting of the ways. Let me say now that I do appreciate all you have done for me during that time. Not only have I learned to fly an aeroplane better under your helpful, critical eye but have grown up a better and more wise man than I should have done without your companionship – something I shall always prize greatly. My sincere thanks Mike. The explanation for such a belated appreciation is simple if not obvious.

It would have been easy to succumb to emotional regret at no longer being able to take the air at leisure, being no longer part of 'the many'; being no longer able to enjoy the pleasant line-shooting company of those more akin to men than any I have yet met – and many more regrets too. I say it would have been easy but it would have been slightly foreign and what was more important and upmost in my mind during those last couple of days was the unenviable prospect of finding somewhere to live in London. That is temporarily settled, re above address, unsatisfactory as it is, it will serve till we can find somewhere better. Though during our search and several enquiries I was most unfavourably impressed by the continued rudeness of the inhabitants of this district – though there is one very amusing story, well illustrating the point, which I'll tell when we have the pleasure of seeing you next.

Armed only with the thought that a flying record would impress no one, and possibly be a hindrance, and with that alone I attended Air Ministry on Monday. As expected, I was not to replace the P.A. to the D.G. but some other bod who was expecting to be discharged in January/February. Quite reasonably he wanted someone with more experience than I had had. I won't go into details – you wouldn't have any more clues than I had. It revolves around the question of applying the policy of demob to all special cases which arise. You may think that straight forward, it is of itself, but when so many others are concerned (departments) it has to be appreciated that one has to know the Air Ministry fairly well to get along. I am in the process of learning, and find it extremely interesting. If anyone had told me, three weeks ago, that I should be quite happy in Air M. I should have told them they were talking through their hat. But that, strange as it may sound, is perfectly true. Here, there most certainly is a job to be done; and of such a kind that one has to think and concentrate hard. It is really the first mental exercise I have had since I left S.F.T.S. If you have any queries just phone Holborn 3434 Ex.227 – we have the answers! My title is 'M' 10 – Manning Dept.

The fellow from whom I will be taking over, in good time, is an ex-nav from 4 Group who, before coming here, did the Staff College Course. To my reckoning he has been off flying for at least 18 months – and from his conversation it is clear to see that he was little asset to any crew – though it is equally clear to see that he does know his present job. Unfortunately he adopts a school master's attitude to a naughty boy when Joe makes a boob and that doesn't go down well. I like straight talking. The other types in my office are both penguins but again know what they are engaged upon. The first thing to realise, something I did before I set foot inside the building, is that flying just doesn't mean a thing. It is a pity but perfectly true.

Till I take over from S/L Raffaelli I am acting unpaid without even the A.M. allowance of £90 per year which doesn't go down at all well in London. Before I have even bought a drink I reckon it will cost me £8 a week to live and you reckon that out on F/Lts pay you will see how far money goes in London – but then you know already.

I have chased up my medical (C.M.B.) and expect it next week. Once my P.C. has actually been gazetted I shall feel more settled. Upon making enquiries from Pat I learned that two lists of short service Coms. have already been issued; the first in Sept on a typed sheet of bumph, not yet published in A.M.O.s, which, she says, contained your name. If you haven't heard officially I suggest you make enquiries because several types up here seem to know all about it. I have seen the most recent list of P.C.s and saw Togg's name down (9.11.45), Mellersh was the name but I am not certain about the initials. If this is correct I hope you will pass on my congrats. I don't know what to think about this Short Service stunt, and hope really that it isn't as true as it sounds, thus leaving the way open for your P.C. Incidentally I should mention that the hours at A.M. are 9.30 to 6.30 with only penguin leave every 3 months so if anyone else is thinking of coming ask them to think again.

I stayed with Roger [Roger Osborn from 141] my first weekend in Town and found him hale and hearty as expected, Joan [Roger's wife] too, is well and full of life. Roger, the dodger, was pleased to find someone who could tell him more of the eclipse of 100 Group and the "empire building" of others. You must drop in to see them if ever you have the chance. A 19, 22 or 137 bus from Sloane Sq. will take you to Prince of Wales Drive in five minutes. It's South of the River bordering on Battersea Park.

I ran into Tillney (think the name is correct – the Station Adj at Swanton) the other day. He too is polishing a chair! Bill Williams is the only other type I have seen who brings back memories! Saw him in Kingsway and had a brief word with him. Just back from India – wearing the appropriate medals! and looking fit only for the grave. I've never seen a man so yellow, he was on his way to a Medical Board. I honestly reckon a one-way ticket to St. Peter will be his lot before long.

Usually I find London unpleasant, hate-making and temper-fraying but have so far been able to accept it without too much trouble. If I have the money I shall at last be able to see some of the things worth seeing, but that I reckon will have to wait for the paid scraper-ring. Everyone here is in the same boat. It is a damned nuisance.

For your enjoyment I can add that there is an A.M. flight at Hendon for those that want to keep their hands in at flying . . . Proctors! Just give me a little more time and I shall be back at Raynham to sample the "air" the "mess" and the other things which make up the real Air Force. I reckon I should manage a few days now and again.

This is all for now chum. When you happen to be down this way next just give me a tinkle if you feel inclined and we'll have that night out we promised ourselves.

Cheerio Mike, and watch those pilots. From us to you,
and regards to Rodney
Yours, as ever
HARRY'

Thus our partnership of four and a quarter years became a friendship that lasted for the ensuing forty-five years, broken only by his death on 25 March, 1990.

It will also have been noted from his letter that the Air Force had decided that it could struggle along without my services on a permanent basis. Additionally I found out – when I followed up on Harry's letter – that the four-year extended service commission, which had been offered to me, only carried the substantive rank of Flying Officer. When, over the next few weeks, I was struggling with my disappointment and with the problem as to whether I should accept a short service commission I often thought about my father's guidance on this subject.

When I was still at school and trying to decide on my future career we had discussed the possibility of my applying for a short service commission, and he had always spoken against it. Perhaps he had considered one himself and then drawn back because, as he told me, 'you will come out into civvy street and all the good jobs will have gone'. This observation of his must be related to the nineteen-twenties when, although he himself was selling motor-cycles and running the Allen Bennett Motor Company, he saw plenty of his friends from the Royal Flying Corps who were struggling to get a job. He also observed wisely that, in the Services, one tended to become used to a way of life that could be difficult to sustain in civvy street, unless one had a source of private income.

I had three other fundamental problems.

Firstly, as already mentioned, I was not keen to fly with any pilot who came along. After having the good fortune to fly with one pilot for four and a quarter years, I was spoilt, and getting fussy in my old age! (Even in his letter Harry had said, at the end: '. . . Cheerio Mike, and watch those pilots . . .') I *was* watching!

Secondly, the idea of staying in the RAF as a penguin, i.e. with a ground job in the Administrative & Secretarial Branch, did not appeal to me as aircrew were all commissioned into the General Duties Branch. There was some pride in that, and as one can see – by referring again to Harry's letter – we were prejudiced against the 'penguins', as we so rudely referred to all officers who did not wear a flying badge.

Thirdly, I was always conscious that I was only an AI operator, as a result of being hauled off the observer's course so precipitously in July 1941 to go into the night-fighting business. I had never been to a Navigation School.

Additionally, I was probably tired and due to come off flying for a spell anyway, and I certainly had a bit of a twitch! After all, although our first operations on Home Defence were not very hazardous in 1941 and 1942, we had had a fairly long spell on the bomber support operations from July 1943 to May 1945. I realised, some years after the war, that one does not really know at the time what effects any prolonged activity are having on one's mental and physical state of health.

It will be recalled that I could not return to the Fairey Aviation Company. One of the conditions for my release in March 1941 to join the Air Force (from a Reserved Occupation) was that I should 'never darken their doorways again'. It began to look as if I must try hard to get the job as a management trainee at Lever Bros and to prepare myself for leaving the RAF in the June of the following year.

In November, the month following Harry's departure, I flew with some of the other pilots as the Fighter Interception Development Squadron continued to carry out its flight trials on a variety of weird and wonderful pieces of equipment, notably with Joe Singleton, who had had a distinguished career in the night-fighter business (his former AI operator had been a very nice – and competent – chap called Geoff Haslam). He took a Wellington up one day and I found myself looking at a mass of large cathode-ray tubes and other 'black boxes'. In fact they represented the early attempts at taking the GCI stations from the ground and turning them into Airborne Early Warning Stations. Thus, for example, by putting the aircraft out over the North Sea, it was possible to greatly extend the range at which incoming enemy aircraft could be picked up and intercepted.

Fifty years on all this has become commonplace except that, today's early warning (AWACS) aircraft are modern jets and their targets are not only aircraft, but missiles too! Joe was an exceptional pilot and he thought he'd have a go at toppling the previously mentioned instrument, the 'Non-Topple Artificial Horizon'! We went up in Mosquito No. 470 for 50 minutes on 15 November and once again I was thrown about all over the sky! In the end we looped the loop but I have no record of whether Joe succeeded in toppling this obstinate instrument and I have no idea what the loop did to the structure of our poor old Mosquito!

Then there was something called 'BEECHNUT' but, for the life of me, I cannot recall anything about the equipment or its purpose! However, we did have a film explaining its mysteries which opened memorably with: 'THIS FILM IS MADE SILENT FOR REASONS OF SECURITY'!

Early in December the Adjutant of FIDS was demobilised and I applied for his job. I did one more flight trial with Joe on some equipment code-named 'NAXOS', which I think Harry and I had been playing with at BSDU at Swanton Morley. Fifty minutes, appropriately in a Beaufighter, and that was it, my flying career in the Air Force was over . . .

I had a grand flying total of 1,216 hours, 474 of which had been at night. For my remaining six months in the RAF I became a penguin.

*   *   *

Christmas 1945 was memorable in several ways. It was the first peacetime Christmas for six years and Rodney and I drove down together to Oxted to spend it with Granny Allen. Her daughter, Joyce Garlick, had somehow managed to secure a berth on a cargo-boat, out of Cape Town, to come to England to look after her mother, following the death of our parents the previous year. Only Aunt Joyce could have talked Union-Castle into giving her a passage to the UK at that time, but she was that sort of person!

On Christmas Eve we all went to the Midnight Service in the tiny village church, Rodney and I still of course in uniform. It was the 'old fashioned' service, with the 'old fashioned' Prayer Book. The church was packed, the service was traditional and there were none of the recent changes which now tend to make so many of the older generation feel uncomfortable when they attend church. Above all, there were no vestments, no 'bells and smells', no 'popery' and no 'passing the Peace'. We were all genuinely at peace that night in Oxted and I have treasured the memory of that Christmas Eve Service all my life.

Back from leave at West Raynham, I quickly settled into the Adjutant's chair at FIDS and like Harry – down at the Air Ministry in London – found that I thoroughly enjoyed the variety of administrative and clerical duties that came across my desk. As the prospect of civvy street started to loom even nearer I thought that I was probably gaining some useful experience anyway. There is no doubt that I was enjoying being off flying!

I was still driving over to Aylsham whenever the opportunity presented itself – to see either Jill Holman or Ursula – and my love for the Norfolk countryside grew, as petrol became easier and we could explore its villages and coastline. Jill continued my riding lessons, mostly in Blickling Park, and before I left Aylsham for the last time, just before I was demobilised, I had learned enough (including mucking out) not to make too much of a fool of myself.

In return, I let her drive my car and attempted to give her one or two driving lessons! Her parents, Dr and Mrs Holman, were a delightful couple and he was the much respected local GP. They had lost their only son, a navigator in the Air Force, flying on coastal Beaus in the Middle East. This had been a terrible blow for them but they bravely carried on and hid their grief. Their son had been awarded a DFC not long before he was reported missing, and it lay, in its case, on the mantelpiece in their drawing-room. I was very conscious that, being a navigator myself and the same rank, my presence in their home may have made things even more painful for them.

I also saw quite a lot of Ursula Jenner and her parents. Everybody knew everybody in the village and most of the boy/girl friendships were so innocent in those days – at least mine were! When later in the year the time came for me to go to

London, for my interview with Lever Bros, it was Ursula's father who stepped into the breach. I had thought quite a lot about the interview, after receiving the letter giving me the date and time on which to present myself at Unilever House, the imposing UK home of the vast Unilever empire, not forgetting, of course, Port Sunlight!

I was quite convinced that it would not be the right thing to wear uniform. If I was coming out into civilian life, then the sooner I got used to wearing civilian dress the better! Also I did not want them to give me the job out of sympathy for the fact that I was an ex-serviceman. Ursula's father was not as broadly built as I was but, with a bit of a struggle, I managed to squeeze myself into his best suit. In my wardrobe, all I had was an old sports jacket which I did not think would be appropriate for the VIPs I was scheduled to see! Off I went and spent the whole day going from one interview to another at Blackfriars House and went to the Royal Aero Club in the evening, where I thankfully let myself out of Mr Jenner's suit and got back into uniform.

The Royal Aero Club of the United Kingdom had premises at 119 Piccadilly, not far from the Royal Air Force Club at 128. Sadly the former is no longer there but the latter is thriving, and continues to go from strength to strength. My father had put me up for membership of the Royal Aero Club as my 21st birthday present, hoping it would stand me in good stead after the war if I continued to follow a career in aviation, whether I remained in the Service or, like him, took up civil flying.

At that time, the Club was the focus of civil aviation in the UK and its activities could be likened to those of the MCC in the world of cricket. My father had been a member for years and was well known and liked there, I counted it a privilege to follow him. By the time Rodney's 21st had come up on the 4 June 1945, our parents had been killed and it fell to me to put Rodney's name forward for membership and for him to keep up the family tradition.

As I have said, I was taken to see a number of people during my day at Lever's HQ and most of them seemed to be Departmental Heads, sitting in large and imposing offices. I have only one vivid memory, I think it was in the office of the Head Buyer. What followed was no fault of his, he was only trying to put me at my ease, and to be affable to the raw youngster who stood in front of him, in the sadly ill-fitting suit.

He opened cheerfully with, 'I've never met a man with three DFCs before!' and then followed it with, 'What was it like?' Of course he could not be expected to ask me anything about buying because I had no experience whatever in that direction, but I had been trying so hard to keep away from my flying record and life in the Air Force. I wanted so badly to do well at the various interviews and to try and show that I was fit for something else *other than flying*!

I remember choking and stumbling to find a reply and the tempo of our conversation sagged miserably into a strained silence. Eventually I managed to blurt out: 'I'm very sorry Sir, but I can't tell you what it was like . . .', and a few minutes later I was shuffling awkwardly out of the room.

There was no way on earth whereby I could have told him 'what it was like' and if I had had any sense I would have walked out of Unilever House – there and then – and thought of something else. In the event, I received a letter, a few days later, offering me a job as a management trainee at a starting salary of £300 a year, with instructions to join one of their subsidiary companies, the British Oil & Cake Mills, in Hull, Yorkshire, as soon as I was demobilised from the RAF.

On my next visit to Aylsham, I duly returned Mr Jenner's suit, which did not fit him as well as before!

I now had somewhere to go if I decided finally to pass up the idea of taking the four-year extended service commission and I settled back into my adjutant's job at FIDS that much easier in my mind.

Sometime in the period March/April 1946 I was talking to Bill Skelton and he issued me with a rather strange invitation, which also included Harry. Bill, together with his pilot, Branse Burbridge, had been the AI operating half of the most successful crew in 100 Group. Together they had destroyed 20 enemy aircraft in the period 1944/45, whilst flying with 85 Squadron. Both had received the DSO and Bar, and DFC and Bar for their exceptional achievements, both were exceptional men in every regard. Bill had also turned up at CFE and we became good friends. Bill Skelton and Branse Burbridge also had another interesting side to their personalities: they were amongst the relatively few members of aircrew who were active in Church matters.

It was not unheard of, in the winter of 1944/45, to learn that they had been operating over Germany on the Saturday night and busy 'putting round holes into square heads'. Then on the Sunday morning they would be found in the village church near Swannington, with one reading the Lesson and the other giving the Sermon (as a Lay Preacher). I remember admiring them and thinking it was the best example of the Church Militant which I had ever seen. They were a remarkable and charming couple.

The invitation was for us to join them at a meeting to be held at the Albert Hall in London on a Friday night, and then to drive on down to a large country house somewhere in Kent, where we, with a group of others, would spend the remainder of the weekend! It did not sound quite like our cup of tea, but I rang Harry up at his office in London to sound him out.

As well as having a high regard for both Bill and Branse we liked them and enjoyed their company so, after some hesitation, Harry agreed to come and it was all fixed up. In any case, we thought, it is an opportunity for us to see each other again and perhaps we can treat ourselves to that night out in London that we had promised ourselves 'when peace came . . .' Still I did begin to wonder what I could have said to Bill that produced such an invitation and what it might lead to. I started to ask a few more questions!

As may be guessed now, the meeting at the Albert Hall was an Evangelical Meeting and the weekend at the country house in Kent was to sound out various selected people to see if they were interested in entering the Church. At the meeting, which was a forerunner of the type held by the great American Evangelist Billy Graham, there were a number of speakers, and quite a lot of incidental music. The climax came when those in the audience who had 'seen the light' were invited to declare their faith in God and to step forward, walk up onto the stage and be welcomed into the church.

Harry and I started to feel uncomfortable long before the meeting was called to a close, and for two pins we would have quietly slipped off there and then and stayed in London. However, being more polite than was our wont, and out of respect for our hosts, we stayed on and duly took our place in the convoy of vehicles which set off for Kent. Our time at the glorious country mansion, in the heart of Kent, was spent in attending meetings and a service and in talking. No pressure was put on us, but the suggestion was never far away that if we had evinced the slightest interest in entering the Church our mentors would have been delighted, and we would soon have been involved in some serious discussions.

Again, as the day wore on, both Harry and I began to feel more and more uncomfortable and out of place. We managed to sneak away from our 'escorts' shortly after lunch, had a quick conference of our own behind a thick hedge in the beautiful gardens and made our decision. We picked up our kit from our room and, without saying our farewells to anyone, drove quietly out of the main gates and away.

I am glad to say that I retained my friendship with Bill (who did enter the Church) for many years afterwards. He had the ability to go far and I always hoped that he would be appointed one day as a bishop. He had a charisma as well as his faith. When he entered a room full of people, you knew that somebody had entered that room.

*   *   *

While I was settling into my chair at West Raynham, Rodney was well settled in with No. 1 Squadron, and flying Spitfire F 21s had achieved his ambition of becoming a fighter pilot. Even though along with many others, he had had to experience the anticlimax and disappointment of just missing the chance to become operational. I think, in the spring of 1946, he must already have been thinking about staying in the RAF and applying for a permanent commission. But he was also following the latest developments in the new jet aircraft, built at Glosters, and using the engines designed and pioneered by Group Captain Frank (later Air Commodore Sir Frank) Whittle.

He heard that Power Jets Ltd, the small company formed by G/C Whittle, with others like Dr Roxbee Cox, to further develop his invention for commercial purposes, was looking for staff. This was just the sort of project for which, with his exceptional natural talent for figures, he was well suited, although he would have had to return to Cambridge first, to complete his degree. I remember accompanying him to the offices of Power Jets Ltd in Lower Park Lane when he attended for his interview with Dr Cox. He got an offer from them, but after much consideration decided to turn it down and try to stay on in the Air Force.

By then, the RAF was becoming a home to him and like myself, he was probably influenced, albeit unconsciously, by the lack of a family home and the loss of our parents. As things happened, the Service recognised his exceptional talents and he was successful in gaining a permanent commission. He stayed on until his death, in a flying accident, in 1952. Needless to say, in the years that followed, I often regretted that I had not tried harder to persuade him to go back to Cambridge and resume his studies. Power Jets was soon swallowed up by 'the big boys'.

In the Adjutant's office in No. 1 Hangar, West Raynham, looking out over the runways, from which Harry and I had taken off so often, I was getting some of the administrative experience that set me on the road to taking up a career in Personnel Management.

I think there were about 130 officers and men in FIDS, and I found myself dealing with anything from leave applications to organising a cricket team, from postings to personal problems. We had one or two marvellous cricket matches against the local village teams with plenty of beer in the evenings, to round off the day! We played at Raynham Park and Houghton Park on pitches barely recovered after the depredations of war, and the balls were bouncing over our heads, or skating along under our bats, but nobody minded. I think many of us were struck by the thought that village cricket followed by an evening at the pub, was one of the things that the country had been fighting for. I was sorry when I had to leave the team in the middle of the season.

The war being over, the Air Force was, understandably, returning to peace-time procedures and discipline (the latter being commonly referred to as 'bull'). Consequently there were aspects of our life which we found difficult to accept, particularly those of us who were coming out of the Service – and I had practically made up my mind to refuse the extended service commission and take up the offer from Lever Bros. Then, on 26 April I received my copy of the following telegram from the Air Ministry in London to CFE at West Raynham:

> 'P.926 PIIL. 1946 UNCLASSIFIED REQUEST YOU INFORM THE UNDER-MENTIONED PILOTS THAT THEY ARE TO REPORT TO ROOM 350. ADASTRAL HOUSE. KINGSWAY AT 10.30 HOURS ON THE 29/4/46 FOR INTERVIEW. F/LT. ALLEN M.S. (120723) F/LT. BENT B. (52078) F/LT. CARPENTER (113426) ACKNOWLEDGE.
>
> BT 1640
>
> E. WILKINSON'

The telegram was marked 'Pass to Adjutant, FIDS', which was, of course, me! I read: 'THE UNDERMENTIONED PILOTS . . .' and scrawled across it: 'A PILOT'S AIR FORCE TO THE LAST!'

Just as I had made up my mind to go out and face the rigours of civilian life, I was, at the eleventh hour, to be presented with another option. Anyway, this summons to attend at the Air Ministry led to the last entry in my flying log-book, from which I have quoted so many times since I began this story. Without my two log-books there would have been no story, and the entry which covers the thirty-minute flight to Boxted, Essex, is strangely prophetic (Joe Singleton flew me down in an Oxford):

> 'Sat 27th. 11.10 Airspeed S/L Singleton TO BOXTED Oxford
>
> ON A WEEKEND FOR AN INTERVIEW AT THE AIR MINISTRY WITH TOMMY CARPENTER, WE TOOK HARRY OUT TO LUNCH AND POURED HIM BACK INTO HIS OFFICE AT 4 O'CLOCK AFTER MAKING A SUCCESSFUL SORTIE ON BUSTER – MAYBE OUR LAST FLING? 00.30 hrs.'

I knew Tommy Carpenter well. He had been Paul Evans's navigator when Paul had command of 239 Squadron at Raynham but I had not met the third navigator summoned to Adastral House on Monday 29 April. Buster, to whom I referred in my log entry, was of course our former 141 Squadron Intelligence Officer, the inimitable Buster Reynolds, now once again a sedate and upright London solicitor. His firm's offices were quite close to Kingsway, so we were soon able to upset his day!

After my interview I had found where Harry was working and was introduced to everybody in his office. He had already made a name for himself in the Manning Department by sorting out his secretary's knitting! I am not joking, there was nothing that Harry could not do if he set his mind to it.

To return to the purpose of our interviews at the Air Ministry. They were looking for Ground Controllers for a new 'blind landing' system which was just being developed and was called the 'Instrument Landing System', or ILS, for short.

All three of us were experienced AI operators, who had spent three or four years peering into cathode-ray tubes and interpreting the signals, so we should have encountered no difficulty in operating the new ILS equipment. Although it will be appreciated that, in 1946, such instrument landing systems were still in their infancy, a cloud base of under 500 ft was a matter to be reckoned with.

Apart from the fact that my mind was virtually made up already to take the job at Levers', I found myself strangely worried about the idea of becoming a Ground Controller, with the task of guiding aircraft in to land in bad weather, thick fog or with aircraft/engine failure.

Fifty years on the computers have taken over and thousands of ordinary airline passengers have sat comfortably, sipping the last of their gin and tonics, as their aircraft descended through 'the clag', turned onto the approach, broke cloud at under 300 ft in line with the runway, and landed safely. Up in front on the flight-deck the pilot is no longer peering out, desperately looking for a hole in the clouds, with the sweat pouring off his brow; more often than not, he is sitting there with his hands in his lap, watching the computer do the work!

There had been frequent occasions when Harry and I had had to rely on the early AI sets to get us back to base, and even onto the line of the approach. It may be recalled that when we had flown down from Scotland to Wittering (in a Beaufighter in June 1943), we had been engulfed in solid cloud all the way back to base, only seeing the ground when we broke cloud, at under 500 ft, two miles to the east of Wittering.

But, to sit safely on the ground in the Controller's hut, giving instructions over the VHF to some poor pilot, perhaps carrying a full load of passengers, struggling to make an emergency landing in appalling weather conditions, had no attractions for me. I felt strongly that if anyone should be recruited for these Controllers' jobs they should be pilots and not navigators. Perhaps the telegram asking for 'THE UNDERMENTIONED PILOTS TO REPORT TO ROOM 350' had been right after all? Above all, I had the thought of making a mistake, giving the wrong instructions to the pilot and being responsible for a horrendous accident and consequent loss of life. It was too much for me and I politely asked the interviewing officer to withdraw my name from the list of candidates.

As with many of the decisions I made in the years immediately following the war I was of course quite wrong! Many men who had hardly flown at all – far less as pilots or navigators – became Flying Control Officers, and were extremely good at their job. But 'MAYBE OUR LAST FLING?' proved to be the last line I ever wrote in my flying log-books.

I mentioned earlier that some of us found the transition to peacetime procedures difficult to accept. The following account illustrates what I had in mind. The Commandant of the Central Fighter Establishment was now an Air Commodore, and I'm afraid to say that I crossed swords badly with him on more than one occasion as he, like Charles Winn and others, resumed their peacetime careers after the interruptions of war. But A/Cdre Harvey was not like Charles Winn, who was to go right up to Air Vice-Marshal. He was not like Winnie at all! Our worst clash came about in the following manner.

Before the war the senior NCOs – the Regulars – who had wives and families had married quarters on the station on which they were serving, a normal peace-time procedure. During the war all this ceased, since every bit of accommodation on the station was needed to house the airmen and airwomen supporting the operational squadrons and Training Units. In the early part of 1946, as the married quarters on the various Stations were restored and refurbished, a certain flight sergeant, a Fitter 1 (the cream of all our ground crew NCOs) with some 20 or more years of service behind him, was allocated new quarters on a station somewhere in the south of England.

After seven years of separation from his family, he joyfully moved in with his wife and children. They had barely settled in before he found that he had been posted to West Raynham – with no married quarters, because ours had not yet been restored!

Worse still (for me) he had been posted to FIDS. One morning in the period April/May he walked in to my office, with his posting in his hand. When he had told me his story I rang up the Station Adjutant and made an appointment to see the Commandant of CFE with a view to getting the posting cancelled on com-passionate grounds. I thought I had a good case because, apart from the wretched situation in which the F/Sgt found himself, I thought about the demoralising effect that such a thoughtless posting would have on his colleagues, i.e. if the peacetime Air Force could treat people like that, then what future was there in it for them?

There was another angle to it as well. A lot of the ground crew had, like the aircrew, joined up for 'hostilities only'. Many of the corporals and leading aircraftmen, some already being demobilised, were fitters and electricians who had served full apprenticeships before coming into the Air Force. They were skilled men. The authorities were trying to attract some of them into signing on as they could see the day coming when they might fill the gaps as the long-serving Regulars became due for retirement. What sort of encouragement would such treatment be to men like these, who were already returning to civvy street in droves?

I went across to Station Headquarters to see the Commandant full of hope that he would agree with my views on the situation and cancel the posting imme-diately, so that the flight sergeant could be restored to his family, and that others considering remaining in the Air Force would be encouraged to do so when 'the buzz' went round that they could expect fair and humane treatment from their senior officers.

I could not have been more wrong! I walked out of SHQ some twenty minutes later after getting a flat refusal from the Air Commodore to alter the posting. Furthermore, when I had told him in somewhat forcible language what I thought of his decision (and the effect it would have on other personnel), he did not like it! Any chance that still remained of me being granted a permanent commission must have vanished in those few moments of an awful 'set to' before he said: 'That's enough, Allen.' Perhaps this incident had something to do with the fact that shortly afterwards I made my own decision to accept the job at Lever's and leave the Air Force when my 'Demob Number' (No. 40) came up in June.

I was left with the dismal task of informing the flight sergeant that I had failed and that there was nothing I could do for him.

There were still a few parties – often as people were being demobilised – and the period must have been as unsettling for those who were staying in, as it was for those of us who would shortly be taking 'the King's shilling' for the last time.

Twice I ran into trouble and the second time was serious. One night, coming back from a pub somewhere on the north coast with a car full, I missed a sharp right hand bend in one of the lanes and drove straight on into a field. I was twenty yards on, before I got the car round to the right. My companions cheerfully piled out, pushed me back onto the road and we went happily on our way.

Worse was to come! One night in May, only a few weeks before I was due to be released, I was driving back to West Raynham from Fakenham with Bill Bailey (a pilot on FIDS and a very nice chap) after an evening spent in the Crown. Just to the east of Helhoughton, and about one and a half miles out of Raynham, there is a steepish hill, at least steep for Norfolk! At the bottom there is a 90 degree turn to the left, with a bridge on an angle in the middle of the bend. When I had finished up in the field, a few days earlier, the only mishap which had occurred was the loss of a Sikh officer's turban (when he was bounced around in the back of the Ford). This time, I was to write off my car completely.

I got down the hill all right, and through the bridge, but I did not make it through the remainder of the left-hand bend. We went off the road and finished up deep in a ditch on the far side with my beloved Ford lying on its right-hand side. The engine was still going and, after I had switched it off, I said to Bill: 'OK Bill, out you get, after you, old boy!' Amazingly, and undeservedly as far as I was concerned, we were both in one piece and, somehow, unharmed. We helped each other out and completed our journey back to West Raynham on foot. The following morning the CO, Wing Commander Gonsalves, drove us back to the scene so that I could start to make arrangements for the recovery of the vehicle.

We were shocked to find that the Ford was so far below the level of the road that we could not see it until we were level with the spot where it had come to rest in the ditch. In short, having managed to survive nearly four years of wartime flying, I came near to killing myself, and another man, through drinking too much – and then getting into the driving-seat of a motor car. My last few months in the Air Force were distinguished more by my stupidity than anything else.

When my father and I had bought the 1938 Ford 8 in May 1940 for £50 second-hand we thought we'd got a good deal, and I had it for six years before I foolishly crashed it in a Norfolk lane. I still have the letter from my insurance company paying me out £135 on the basis of my claim that the car was a total loss. A handsome sum, in those days, and almost three times what we had paid for the car in 1940. Clearly, I did not deserve such good fortune.

It was the second paragraph of Thos. Stephens & Sons Ltd's letter that has caused me to keep it all these years. It read as follows:

> '. . . We hope to be favoured with your future instructions when you obtain another car and would also like to remind you that we are at your service in respect of any other insurances you may wish to effect.
>
> Yours truly
> THOS. STEPHENS & SONS, LTD.
> (Signed) M.S.Vickers'

I just could not believe that they – or any other firm of insurers – would ever take on the risk of having me on their books, after what had happened! I could never make out whether they were just being kind to me because I was in the Air Force. I still don't know! I didn't buy another car for several years, but Rodney had an Austin 7 which he trustingly lent me, and I managed not to get it caught up in any sharp left-hand bends.

Time was now starting to run out. May passed quickly, and on the last day of the month a 'Demobilisation Dinner' was held for five of us, from FIDS, who were going out. They were:

W/Cdr Gonsalves DSO, DFC.
S/Ldr Singleton DSO, DFC.
S/Ldr Head DFC.
F/Lt Haslam DFC.
F/Lt Allen DFC.

The menu, emblazoned significantly with a bowler hat, contained such items as 'Creme Rue Bourgeoisie' to herald the soup, and 'Carrelet Bowler Hat' for the fish. But I did not enjoy the evening. I found myself continually looking at the quotation and the cartoon that had been cleverly used to introduce the menu!

The quote was, needless to say, from Shakespeare, and had been aptly chosen. It was: 'Farewell – Othello's Occupation's Gone.'

The cartoon depicted an airfield. Five old airmen with long beards, wearing flying helmets and goggles, leaning on their walking sticks, staggering past the hangars towards a signpost which had on it the single word 'OUT'. It was all too true!

At the beginning of June I started to hand over my duties to my successor. I was due 'OUT' in the middle of the month. However, I had to brace myself for one more party. I was tipped off that my presence was desired at 7.00 p.m. on the 5th at a certain pub in Castle Acre, to the south-west of Raynham. I think it was called the Castle. There, I found that all the airmen and airwomen from FIDS had gathered, and at the end of a riotous evening they presented me with a tankard on which they had had engraved the following:

Presented to
"MIKE" S ALLEN
by
The Ground Crews of
F.I.D.S.
June 5th 1946

That same much treasured tankard is standing on the sideboard as I write, and close to hand!

I have another item beside me which brings back less pleasant memories. It is 'RAF FORM 2520C, for Officers', the blue Royal Air Force Service and Release Book. When I left West Raynham for the last time I had, in common with everyone else being demobilised, to report to a 'Demob Centre', where we would be finally released from the Service and given an issue of civilian clothing. There have been many ex-Servicemen who have described their feelings on going through these 'Demob Centres'. I will make mine brief.

I am quite sure that everything, arranged by the Government of the day, for the demobilisation of thousands of Service men and women, was well and efficiently done. It could not have been done better. However, for me, passing from one queue to another in the Demobilisation Centre (in a large warehouse located at Wembley) it was one of the most miserable and unreal days in the whole of my life.

By the time that I had signed all the necessary release documents and walked past a long line of cardboard boxes, picking out so many shirts and pants and socks, and finally choosing a brown 'Demob' suit, I only wanted to run from the building – and never stop running.

Late on 26 June I drove back to Ashford and joined the Sessions family. So in June 1946 I left the Air Force. It was almost exactly five years since I had been seen off in the train, by my parents at Paddington Station, *en route* for the Receiving Wing at Stratford-upon-Avon in the June of 1941. I went out, with fear and trepidation, into civilian life and five weeks later I started work at the British Oil & Cake Mills Ltd in Hull and moved into digs.

By Christmas I had been transferred to Port Sunlight, the great soap factory, with its adjacent village, created by William Lever at the turn of the century. It was there that I received a Christmas present from Harry.

When I unwrapped the paper I found that he had sent me a copy of *Enemy Coast Ahead*. In this book Guy Gibson had set down the story of his wartime life in both Bomber Command and Fighter Command, culminating in the authentic account of the Dams Raid on 16/17 May 1943. It was completed shortly before he met his own death in September 1944.

It will be remembered that I started this narrative by describing how he had been our Flight Commander in September 1941, when we had been posted – with little training and completely clueless – to No. 29 Squadron at West Malling.

When I opened the book I found that Harry had written the following words in the flyleaf:

'Mike

For neither of us will the "vector" ever again be zero nine zero – the night is over now and the sun has risen in that quarter. Until the sun sets elsewhere, when we again may be "driven to the slaughter", let us be thankful that we did our duty when we reached the "Enemy Coast Ahead".

Harry.'

FINIS

Epilogue

Death By The Roadside in Hampshire

In the August of 1952 (when I was living and working in Manchester) my brother Rodney, by then a Flight Lieutenant with a Permanent Commission, died in a flying accident together with a pupil pilot. Based at RAF Stradishall, he was giving dual instruction on a Gloster Meteor when the aircraft crashed close to the airfield, and both he and his pupil were killed instantaneously. He was 28, single, had been awarded a 'Mention in Dispatches' the previous year and was making a name for himself in the post-war Air Force. He was a great loss to us, his family – and to the Service. Nearly forty years later I received the news that Harry White too – was dead. It happened like this . . .

It was on Monday 26 March 1990 – when I had been retired for nearly two years – and Pam and I were living at Mothecombe in South Devon, that the telephone rang in the middle of the afternoon. It was Michael Tagg, phoning from the Royal Air Force Museum, where he held the post of Public Relations Officer. I had met Michael on several occasions and he knew that I had been Harry White's wartime navigator. What followed proved to be one of the worst telephone calls it has ever been my misfortune to receive . . .

Michael apologised for calling me but he wanted to know if I had heard of the death of Air Commodore White, in a road accident the previous day? I was trying to take this in, when I heard him ask a second question. He had the Press on the phone, and would it be all right for him to give them my address and telephone number?

I gathered my wits together and told him, firstly, that I had not heard of Harry's death and that, secondly, he was under no circumstances to release my address and telephone number to the Press. I tried to find out a few more details, and it appeared that Harry had stopped his car in a lay-by on the A303, just south of Basingstoke. After getting out of his Mercedes, he had stepped into the path of an oncoming lorry – and been killed instantaneously. I had last seen Harry in April of the previous year, when we had attended a dinner in the officers' mess at RAF West Raynham. To say that I was shattered would have been putting it mildly.

I would normally be reluctant to speak to anyone from the media over the telephone: under the above circumstances, nothing would have induced me to do so.

When I had thanked Michael for putting me in the picture I put the phone down, then I picked it up again and rang Harry's home number at Hartlip, in Kent. His younger son (by his second marriage) answered the telephone and confirmed that his father had been killed the previous day, in a road accident. Ten days later Pam and I attended Harry's funeral, which was followed by a cremation.

Harry's obituary appeared in *The Daily Telegraph* on 2 March and in *The Times* three days later. The latter carried the heading 'AIR COMMODORE HAROLD WHITE – Wartime Ace in crack night-fighter Squadron'. On 30 July Pam and I drove to Winchester to attend the inquest into Harry's death, and for two hours we sat and listened to the awful details of what had happened, and the evidence of those who had been involved. At the end, the Coroner, Mr Tim Milligan, said that he would record an Open Verdict.

It will be remembered that Harry and Joan married in June of 1944, and as he rose up in the Service they enjoyed fifteen happy years, and set about rearing their three children, Michael (my namesake), Roger and Rosemary. It was Christmas 1959, when their card arrived from Singapore signed 'Joan and Harry'. Except that there was a note inside the card, from someone signing themselves 'Joan Ingle'. The note read:

> 'Since this card was written I regret to say Harry and Joan were involved in a car accident. Joan was killed and Harry is in B.M.H. Singapore with a broken pelvis. He will be there for at least ten weeks, meanwhile the children are being looked after by other neighbours.
> Joan Ingle'

I wrote back as follows:

> 'Dear Joan Ingle,
> Thank you for your note telling me about the motor accident in which Harry and Joan were involved. I have sent Harry a cable and he will know how I feel.
> Will you please let me know if there is anything I can do at this end? Will you also keep me in touch with what is going on until Harry is well enough to write to me.
> Yours,
> Michael Allen.'

When he had recovered a bit, he did write:

> 'Far East Defence Secretariat,
> Phoenix Park,
> Singapore, 10.
> 5th March, 1960
>
> Dear Mike,
> Having passed through the various stages of lying down for six weeks, sitting up for two, a wheelchair for a fortnight, a walking frame and then crutches, I was eventually "allowed out" on the 17th February – still grasping my crutches. Several days later I was able to discard these in favour of a stout stick and though I have to take my time, just as well in this heat, I look more normal and feel more normal. In six months time I should be able to play tennis again. That should be the end of the affair. I was told I could play up to two holes of golf in two months time but since I have only been round twice in my life, for 146 and 147 I thought I might be pardoned for evading that part of my physio-therapy. It wouldn't be fair on my navigator!'

And again on the 13th June:

> '. . . Still writing letters at the rate of about 50 per month I can afford to miss you out some of the time but not quite all of the time. If I don't tap the keys in

your direction this evening you won't be hearing from me for about a month – Captain Cook will have nothing on me by the time I have finished my next trip. But first, your letter . . .'

He made a trip back to the UK as soon as he was fit to fly. He went up to Scotland to see Joan's mother and her relations, sorted out the children's schooling and visited his own mother – before returning to Singapore to complete his tour in the Far East.

He just carried on as if nothing had happened, without a shred of self-pity, and a year or so later he was back in England to attend the Joint Services Defence Course at Latimer and promoted to the rank of Group Captain. I learned that he was the youngest group captain in the Service at the time. Many years later he was to tell me, wryly, that he was now the oldest group captain!

He invited me to a 'Dining-In Night' whilst he was at Latimer, and I drove down from Cambridge. He was in tremendous form, laughing and joking with all the admirals and generals and recognised by all on the course as a bit of a character, and someone to be reckoned with. Later, when we got back from the mess to his quarters in the early hours of the morning, we opened a bottle of brandy and sat through the rest of the night, talking. It was then that he told me of the accident in Singapore, and of Joan's death. He gave me the story in the most minute detail, never sparing himself in any degree. In the weeks

In 1967 Harry White, now Group Captain H.E. White DFC**, AFC commanded the RAF Radar Station at Buchan in Scotland.

following Joan's tragic death he never, for one instance, allowed himself a shred of self-pity.

As in the war years, my admiration and regard for him knew no bounds. As the dawn rose I crawled into my car to drive back to Cambridge and went straight to my office at Pye Telecommunications. I don't think I was much use for work that day.

Later, whilst Harry was still at the Joint Services Staff College, I took Miles (his godson) down to Latimer to spend the day with him. We had drinks before lunch, then he disappeared into the kitchen. A few minutes later we found ourselves sitting down to a three-course meal, with all the trimmings. Group Captain White had prepared, cooked and now served the lunch, himself.

The next thing we heard was that he was to re-marry. On 8 June 1963, at the Central Church of the Royal Air Force, St Clement Danes, he was married to Pilot Officer Diana K. Pottinger, WRAF, many years his junior in age. It was a big Service wedding, but I found it difficult to get our epic trip to Scarborough and Aberdeen, and his marriage to Joan in 1944, out of my mind. His best man was one of his friends, still serving. They were all in full uniform. I felt strangely out of place.

Before Harry and Joan went out to Singapore in the late fifties he had, as a wing commander, been Chief Flying Instructor at RAF Leeming, in Yorkshire. In 1956 he received command of No. 46 Squadron, at RAF Odiham, in which position he was responsible for introducing the Gloster Javelin all-weather fighter to operational service. His name is still held in awe by those who served under him on 46 Squadron.

He also added an Air Force Cross and a Mention in Dispatches to his wartime decorations. As a young group captain with two Staff College courses behind him, he was – in the middle sixties – obviously marked out for higher things, and ultimately for appointment to Air Rank.

When he had been at the Central Flying School at RAF Little Rissington we had gone down from Wilmslow to stay with him and Joan and to attend a Summer Ball. All the officers were in mess kit, and I think it was the last time that I wore white tie and tails. It was a marvellous evening, almost the end of an era. When he had command of 46 Squadron I went to spend a few nights with him at Odiham.

Harry had taken over when their previous CO had been killed, and the future of the Javelin as the RAF's all-weather fighter was still in doubt. He led them through several weeks of intensive flight trials; the situation was saved; and his name became known throughout the Service. I went down to dispersal to watch him and some of his other crews take off on night-flying practice sorties. It was a strange feeling to see him walk out to his aircraft, with his peacetime navigator beside him, and then taxi out as we had first done at Church Fenton, all those years before.

When I emigrated to South Africa in 1966 – and remained out there until 1982 – the close contact, which we had been able to maintain since I had left the Air Force in 1946, faded somewhat and only a few desultory letters were exchanged until 1974. Harry was, by then, an air commodore and the Air Officer i/c Administration for the RAF in Germany, and stationed at Rheindahlen.

I was visiting England and the Continent, partly on business and partly on holiday. Travelling through France, Belgium and Holland into Germany, I was met off the train by Air Commodore White and, with his driver at the wheel of his staff car, we settled ourselves in state, in the back, and drove off to his married quarters on the camp at Rheindahlen.

There I met Diana again and was introduced to his 'second family'. Their two boys, Andrew and Julian, were growing up fast. My own marriage had come to an end, a few months before when, after 25 years, my first wife and I decided to go our separate ways. The last thing Harry said to me, at the end of a first-rate weekend and just as I was leaving, was, 'Look after yourself, Boy, and get yourself re-married.' Fifteen months later I met Pam, took his advice, and with it, a second chance in life.

By the time Pam and I returned to England in 1982, Harry and Diana were living at Hartlip, near Sittingbourne, in Kent. He had retired from the Air Force and embarked on a second career as Chief Executive of the Swale District Council where, by all accounts, he was doing an outstanding job.

In 1980, when Pam and I had been back in England on leave, we had had our marriage blessed in the crypt of St Clement Danes, Harry and Diana had come

Out of the Blue, edited by 'Laddie' Lucas, was published in 1985. Harry and I both contributed to Laddie's collection of stories, all highlighting the element of 'luck' in air operations. Harry gave an account of our trip on the night of The Peenemünde Raid in August 1943, and I sent in the account of our crash in January 1945 and our rescue by the three Norfolk farmers. By the time the book was published there was sadly only one survivor, Herbert Farrow BEM. I got Laddie to sign a copy of Out of the Blue specially for Herbert, and Harry and I went to his home in East Dereham to present it to him. This is the photograph taken at the time, with Herbert on the left of the picture, Harry in the centre, and myself on the right.

up from Kent, to be our two witnesses. On our first Sunday back in London, in March 1982, we went to Morning Service there and who was waiting for us in the entrance of the church but Harry and Diana! It was a well-kept secret, carefully pre-planned by Pam and a marvellous moment for me. We went back to the RAF Club for lunch and Harry and I drank the old Scottish toast together, 'Here's to us – there aren't many like us – and those that are – are dead!!!'

In the ensuing years, whilst we were living in London and I was working at the Officer's Association in Pall Mall, we used to meet up from time to time either to go to the theatre, or for us to drive out to Hartlip for the day, at a weekend.

The previous year 'Laddie' Lucas had edited a book entitled *Out of the Blue – The Role of Luck in Aerial Warfare 1917–1966*. Under the title of 'Norfolk Courage' Laddie had published my account of the crash and the rescue by Herbert Farrow, Jimmy Andrews and Old Walter Ward. I thought it would be right for Harry and I to present Herbert (the only surviving member of the trio) with a copy of the book in which his story was contained. I duly asked Laddie if he would sign a copy of *Out of the Blue* for Herbert, and a date was arranged.

Pam's treasured memory of that day is of us passing each other – in our cars, in the centre of East Dereham – on our way to Herbert's cottage on the Scarning Road, both going in opposite directions! The old man was greatly touched by the gift. It was in fact the first time he had seen Harry since the night of the crash 41 years earlier. It was to be the only time he saw us together.

In the mid-eighties, when Harry was again making a name for himself, as the Chief Executive of Swale District Council, someone asked him why his name did not appear in *Who's Who*. He replied, in typical dusty fashion, to the effect that 'Why should he care whether it was in *Who's Who*, when it was in *The Guinness Book of Records*? Sure enough, in the 1986 Edition, Norris McWhirter had published a list of the names of those who had won the DFC three times. There are 58 names, going back to the days of the Royal Flying Corps, and ours are the 33rd and 34th on the list.

There should be 59, but for some unaccountable mischance, Mickey Martin's name is left off: the late Air Marshal Sir Harold Martin KCB, DSO*, DFC**, AFC, the former Australian bomber ace who flew on the Dams raid in May 1943.

On 14 April 1989, a Dining-in Night was held in the officers' mess at RAF West Raynham to mark the 50th Anniversary of the opening of the airfield, in 1939. Group Captain Graeme Smith OBE, AFC, the Station Commander, kindly invited Harry and I to attend as joint Guests of Honour. It was a memorable evening, in more ways than one, with the officers in mess kit and civilians, like myself, in dinner jackets and wearing miniatures, if they possessed them.

It was the first time I had seen Harry in Mess Kit since the Summer Ball at the Central Flying School in 1952. Now he was wearing the uniform of an air commodore, with the CBE preceding his many medals and decorations. We met in his room (we both had VIP quarters), looked each other over and then, with a couple of approving grunts, headed out into the corridor, which we had so often trodden forty-six years earlier. Then, as like as not, we were wearing battledress, and on our way to briefing an hour or two before taking off on operations and heading for Germany. On 14 April 1989 we headed on along the corridor to the ante-room and to meet our hosts.

Towards the end of the dinner, Group Captain Smith gave a short speech outlining the history of RAF West Raynham, to which Harry was invited to

The Family Service at the RAF Memorial at Runnymede: I was involved for five years with what I chose to call 'The Family Service' at Runnymede, which emerged from an idea I had seen at the Memorial to The South African Air Force, at Swartkop just South of Pretoria. This photograph features Don Aris, a former member of 141 Squadron, and the devoted Squadron Historian. (The Family Service originated in England in the City of London Branch of The Aircrew Association.)

respond. He duly did so. His words and pithy down-to-earth style of delivery were received with acclamation by his audience. Graeme Smith then turned to me and, amidst considerable barracking led by the air commodore on his right, he said, 'I wonder if Mike would like to say a few words?' With Harry still muttering to the effect that 'if Mike gets up and starts speaking, we'll be here all night', I got up on my feet.

I thought, 'Right, Harry, now I'm going to fix you!' I opened thus:

> 'It is always nice if you can say of someone, who has worked his way up in the world: "he hasn't changed a bit". This is true whether the chap has worked his way up from being an office boy to Managing Director, or again if he has risen from Sergeant Pilot to Air Commodore. And it gives me much pleasure to be able to say this about Air Commodore White!
>
> I can truthfully tell you that, since the days when he was a Sergeant Pilot in 1941, "he hasn't changed a bit"! When he was a Sergeant Pilot he always behaved exactly as if he was an Air Commodore!'

The rows of expectant faces, already cheered by quite a few 'wee drams' which were looking up at me, seemed to like that! I don't think they'd heard anyone pull the leg of an Air Officer in public before and from then on the evening 'went'!

I don't know what the time was when we tottered off to bed, or how many 'wee drams' later it was, but as I have said, it was a memorable evening in more ways than one because, apart from the thrill of being back at Raynham together, I never saw Harry again.

Harry lived three times as long as many of his friends, he enjoyed over forty 'bonus' years of life; what more can any of us ask?

I am still in close touch with Harry's younger brother, Captain Gerald White (who had a distinguished career in the Merchant Navy), and his caring wife Pat. Also with courageous Rosemary, Harry's daughter, with his grandson Zac. And every now and again, I receive a letter which opens 'Dear Namesake' and is always signed off as from 'Your Namesake'. A thrill goes through me because it will be from Harry's eldest son (now just turned 52!), Michael Alan White.

In the Introduction which he wrote for Guy Gibson's book *Enemy Coast Ahead*, Air Chief Marshal Sir Arthur Harris (as he then was) describes how he 'quite wrongly' allowed Wing Commander Gibson to return to air operations. After three and a half years of operational flying culminating in the epic Dams raid, Guy did return, but was killed in September 1944. The opening chapter of my story tells how Harry and I served under him in the far-off days of 1941.

The C-in-C Bomber Command concluded his Introduction with the following unsurpassed tribute to him:

> 'If there is a Valhalla, Guy Gibson and his band of brothers will be found there at all the parties, seated far above the salt.'

Never again will I watch whilst Harry pushes the throttles open and hear him say, as we gather speed down the runway, 'OK Boy, off like a bomb!' But if there is a Valhalla, Harry White will be found there at all the parties and he too will be seated far above the salt.

The main runway at RAF West Raynham – from which Harry and I used to take off so often on operations against the enemy – lies empty and deserted after the station was closed down in 1997.

Appendix 1A
AI Mk IV

AI Mk IV was the first mass-produced AI set and was relatively unsophisticated. The operating frequency was 190 to 195 MHz with a wave length of 1.5 m. The system comprised a receiver, transmitter, control panel, modulator, indicator unit and associated aerial system, consisting of a transmitter mounted in the nose, azimuth aerials mounted above and below each wing about two feet in from the tip and elevation aerials above and below the starboard wing outboard of the engine nacelle. (see diagram 1).

The indicator unit consisted of two CRTs displaying elevation and azimuth respectively (see diagram 2). The three items shown on the diagram are the transmitter pulse (the root of the Christmas tree), the target blip somewhere on the time trace (trunk of the tree) and the ground return (the branches of the tree). It is evident from the diagram that a target could not be detected at any range beyond the ground returns. The detection range was limited to the altitude of the aircraft. Thus at 20,000 ft the range would be just under 4 miles, which was about the limiting range of the set. A good height to fly. The minimum range (at which the AI operator could see the target blip on the time trace) was about 400 ft – below which the target merged with the transmission pulse.

It should be noted that the two small CRTs of the Mk IV AI were completely blank – there were no scales on them, and no calibration marks, to assist the AI Operator in guiding his pilot towards their target. His directions (and running commentary of what was happening in the night sky) were based on his estimate of where the target was in relation to his own aircraft – in a constantly changing situation. It was guesswork, based on experience, as to how many degrees the

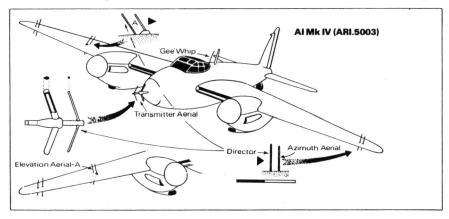

Diagram 1

Diagram 2: the Mk IV AI set

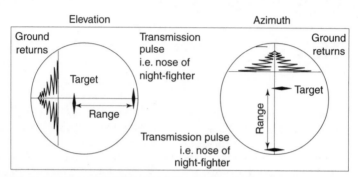

1. Night-fighter flying at height of 20,000 ft. Target blip ahead at range of 18,000 ft, 20 degrees to starboard and 20 degrees below. (The 'minimum range' diamond at the root of the 'Christmas tree' may be taken to represent the nose of the night-fighter).

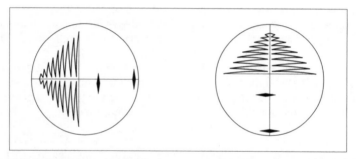

2. The night-fighter has now lost height down to 13,000 ft. The target is still ahead, but the range has decreased to 8,000 ft. The target is now 20 degrees on the port side, and 10 degrees below.

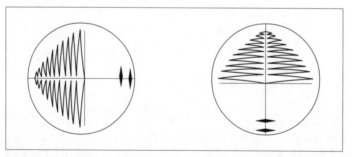

3. The night-fighter has now come down to a height of 11,000 ft – the target's range is 1,000 ft, dead ahead and 15 degrees above the night-fighter . . . closing slowly, the pilot should soon obtain 'a visual' as the blip disappears into the 'minimum range' diamond at the 'root' of the 'Christmas tree'.

target was to port/starboard in the azimuth plane . . . how many feet the target was above/below the pursuing night-fighter in the vertical plane . . . and how far it was in front of them – guesswork, pure and simple!

In the air defence role the night-fighter crew would depend on the GCI to get them within range of the target. In the Bomber Support role, with the night-fighter operating beyond GCI cover, the AI Operator, using Serrate, assumed this additional responsibility.

The diagrams of a typical interception, and the use of 'MOTHER' for homing to base, do not precisely represent what the AI operator would see. In reality, the picture would be confused by spurious echoes and 'noise', presenting a shimmering, pulsating mass of green lines and signals from which he would have to identify the one that mattered. The AI Operator would spend up to four hours peering at this display. If he took a break, he might miss the one and only contact of the sortie. That is a measure of what it took to be a successful AI operator (Ed.).

Diagram 3: Mk IV AI set – homing beacon (code-name 'MOTHER')

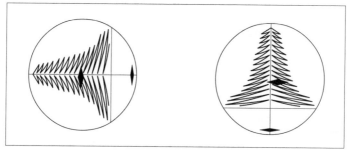

1. The blip of the Homing Beacon – code-named 'MOTHER' shows up through truncated ground returns. There was one sited at each night-fighter airfield – flashing the Morse-code letters of the base, for identification. In this diagram the night-fighter's airfield is about 30 miles away and 15 degrees to his starboard.

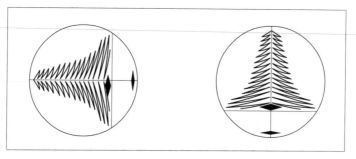

2. In this diagram the blip received from 'MOTHER' is dead ahead and right on the bottom of the ground returns, indicating that the night-fighter is over base.

Appendix 1B
AI Mk IV and the Serrate Homer

The following diagrams represent an interception, on a Bomber Support operation.

The following diagrams represent an interception, on a Bomber Support operation.

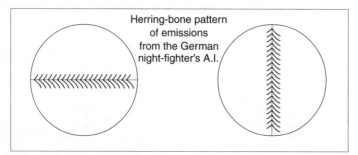

1. Serrate signals (herring-bone pattern on the time-trace, and no ground returns) emitted from the AI set in a German night-fighter – target over to starboard, and below the British night-fighter. There is no precise indication of range, but it could be 30/40 miles away – or even more.

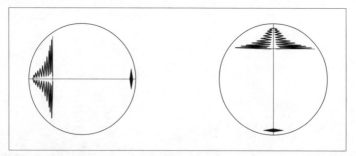

2. The AI operator in the Serrate fighter, switching back to his Mk IV set, sees no sign of a blip, which might correspond with his Serrate signals, anywhere on his time-trace. He and his pilot are flying at a height of 20,000 ft, which gives him a maximum range of 4 miles ahead, in his search. The target must therefore be more than 4 miles away, and they must carry on homing onto the Serrate signals – hoping to reduce the range to enable them to pick up a contact on the Mk IV AI, and complete the interception

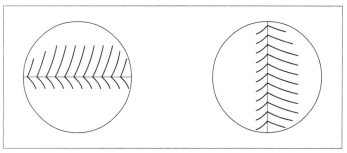

3. The Serrate fighter turns to starboard, and begins to lose height. The AI operator, switching back to the Serrate frequency, finds that the herring-bone pattern is getting stronger and increasing in size. The signals start to swamp the starboard side of the azimuth tube, and the volume control on his set has to be turned down. The target is now above the British fighter.

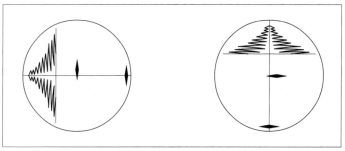

4. Switching once more back to his Mk IV AI, the AI operator sees a blip at about 10,000 ft away (they are now down at 16,000 ft) it is on his starboard side and above. The crew now set out to complete the interception on the Mk IV AI, with the operator constantly checking back on the Serrate frequency to ensure that the two signals match one another. Hopefully, the 'visual' can now be attained, identification confirmed and the German night-fighter shot down …

Appendix 2

Citation for Awards to James Andrews, Herbert George Farrow and Walter William Ward

CENTRAL CHANCERY OF THE ORDERS OF KNIGHTHOOD
S͞T JAMES'S PALACE, SW1A 1BG
TELEPHONE - 01-834 2837 & 2838

CENTRAL CHANCERY OF THE ORDERS OF KNIGHTHOOD,

St. James's Palace, S.W.1.
8th May, 1945.

The KING has been graciously pleased to give orders for the undermentioned appointments to the Most Excellent Order of the British Empire, for the following awards of the British Empire Medal, and for the publication in the London Gazette of the names of the persons specially shown below as having received an expression of Commendation for their brave conduct.

Awarded the British Empire Medal
(Civil Division):—

James ANDREWS, Farm Labourer, Dereham, Norfolk.

Herbert George FARROW, Farmer, Dereham, Norfolk.

Walter William WARD, Farm Labourer, East Dereham, Norfolk.

An aircraft crashed and immediately burst into flames. Ward, Farrow and Andrews, acting independently, at once ran to the scene of the crash and found two men trapped in the burning aircraft. The fire had taken firm hold of the port wing and bomb bay, ammunition was exploding, and the petrol tank was liable to explode at any moment. Despite the known risks and the possibility of the presence of a bomb load, the three men persisted in their efforts and succeeded, with difficulty, in freeing the navigator. They carried him to safety and and then, notwithstanding that the flames had by this time reached the cockpit, they renewed their efforts and rescued the pilot. The three men, by their courage and disregard of danger, saved two lives.

Appendix 3
141 Squadron Order of Battle for 2 May 1945

NO.141 (BS) SQUADRON			NIGHT BATTLE ORDER		
Aircraft & Letter	Petrol	Pilot	Navigator	Call Sign	Remarks
Mos. 578 W.	516	W/C WINN	F/L SCOTT	50	
" 554 R.	516	S/L THATCHER	F/O WARD	30	
" 551 S.	516	F/L BREARLEY	F/O SHELDON	33	
" 486 V.	516	F/O HARRIOTT	F/O BARBER	35	
" 485 N.	516	F/O RIDER	F/O FARNFIELD	36	
" 483 L.	516	F/S EVEREST	P/O PEARSON	42	
" 507 F.	516	S/L WHITE	F/L ALLEN	10	
" 502 C.	516	F/L YOUNG	F/O SANDERSON	12	
" 472 H.	516	F/L McCLYMONT	W/O COULTER	14	
" 500 K.	516	F/O BARTON	SGT BERLIN	15	
" 504 G.	516	W/O FLEMING	F/S CAMPBELL	20	
" 371 D.	516	W/O WATERFIELD	SGT SAMPSON	21	

Officer i/c Night Flying:- To be detailed by 239 Squadron.
Relief:- P/O Fisher.
(u/t F/O Anderson)
Duty N.C.O, Sgt. McConnell.

2nd. May, 1945.

for Wing Commander, Commanding,
No.141 (BS) Squadron

The last op. of 141 in the European War. Twelve aircraft napalm dropping and strafing Hohn & Flensburg airfields. Not one of our aircraft were missing.

Bibliography

Bowman, Martin (1996) *Confounding the Reich*.

Bowyer, Chaz (1983) *Bomber Barons*.

Braham, Wing Commander R.J.D. (1961) *Scramble*.

Chisholm, Roderick (1953) *Cover of Darkness*.

Gibson, Guy (1946) *Enemy Coast Ahead*.

Gunston, Bill (1976) *Night Fighters*. Patrick Stephens.

Hillary, Richard (1942) *The Last Enemy*.

Lucas, 'Laddie' (1989) *Thanks for the Memory – Unforgettable characters in air warfare 1939–45*.

Lucas *ed.* (1985) *Out of the Blue*, Sonnet by Engelbach, P.S. Hutchinson.

Middlebrook, Martin (1982) *The Peenemünde Raid*. Allen Lane.

Middlebrook, Martin (1973) *The Nuremberg Raid*. Allen Lane.

Moran, The Lord (1966) *The Anatomy of Courage*.

Saward, Dudley (1984) *Bomber Harris*. Cassell Buchan & Enright.

Streetly, Martin (1978) *Confound and Destroy – 100 Group and the Bomber Support Campaign*. Macdonald and Jane.

Streetly, Martin (1984) *The Aircraft of 100 Group*. Robert Hale Ltd.

Terraine, John (1985) *The Right of the Line*. Hodder and Stoughton.

Index

Addison, AVM EB   150, 154, 183, 216, 244
Aindow, F/Sgt C   68
Alexander, FM Sir H   278
Allen, Pam   vii, 54, 123, 184, 253, 269, 270, 326, 330–1
Allen, Simon   viii
Allen, Donna   viii
Allen, F/L Rodney   3, 15, 18, 19, 20, 27, 53, 66, 132, 140, 179,199, 227–8, 237–8, 242, 248–9, 250, 251–6, 260, 265, 271, 283, 292, 294, 302, 304, 309, 316, 317, 319, 326
Allen, BS   3, 13, 15–16, 17, 18, 20, 21, 22, 26, 27, 28, 29–30, 32, 36, 53, 66, 76, 133, 140, 142, 145, 179, 249–58, 305, 314, 317, 323
Allen, Mrs K MJ   13, 15, 20, 32, 36, 46, 53, 132–3, 243, 249–58, 305
Allen, Lt GC   13, 15, 18, 252
Allen, Henry Charles   251
Allen, Mrs E (Granny)   251–3, 304, 346
Allen family   13–15, 18, 243, 251
Andrews, J   xi, 264, 267–70, 337
Appleton, G/C CH   65, 78
Aris, Don   92, 93, 94, 100, 105, 106–7, 111–12, 114, 124, 125, 128, 129, 133, 134, 150, 152, 153, 154, 156, 159, 160–1, 166, 172, 174, 177, 193, 198, 201, 210, 225, 241, 276, 285–6, 287, 294–5, 300–1, 322
Ashworth, S/L HJV   66–7
Austin, F/Sgt S   56

Bader, G/C DRS   309
Bailey, F/O R   197, 212–13
Bailey, George   221, 229, 234
Bailey, F/L Bill   323

Baldwin, F/O K   151
Barber, F/Sgt C   68
Barber, F/O N   309
Bardwell, Sgt   75
Barrie, JM   132
Bates, S/L PA   274–5
Beadle, F/Sgt DJ   291
Beaverbrook, Lord   24
Becker, Oblt M   188
Beechey, P   30
Bennett, AVM D   xi, 189
Bennett, S/L T
Benson, W/C JG   55, 239
Bent, F/L B   320
Berry, S/L J   235
Betjeman, John   153, 301
Bigoray, F/S W   95
Birkett, Capt G   257
Black, TC   16
Bliss, F/L G   165
Booth, S/L J   192
Bottomley, AVM N   276, 277–8
Bowman, Martin   ix, 102
Bowyer, RC 'Chaz'   ix, 157–8
Brachi, F/L J   165–6, 177, 261
Brady, F/O 'Rocky'   303
Braham, G/C JRD   viii, xi, 80, 91–2, 93, 97, 101, 104, 105, 107–8, 110–11, 112–13, 115, 116, 123, 125, 126, 127, 130, 131–2, 136, 137, 138, 140, 142–3, 145, 152, 166, 176, 178, 193, 204, 206, 207–8, 219, 222, 223–4, 225, 297, 303
Braham, Mrs Joan   viii, ix
Brandon, S/L L   55, 239
Brooke, Rupert   121
Brooke, FM Sir A   278
Buchanan, Jack   185

Budd, S/L GO   51, 58, 65, 66–7, 68, 75, 184
Bulling, F/L J   248
Bundschuh, Uffz T   124
Burbridge, W/C BA   223, 247, 261

Cadman, F/O WG   274–5
Calvert, F/O   241
Carpenter, F/L T   320
Carter, F/L GHF   156, 157, 158, 159
Catterall, F/O R   291
Chadwick, Roy   172
Chamberlain, Neville   20, 24
Cheshire, G/C L   xi, 31, 101, 103, 168, 185, 282
Childs, F/O C   288
Chisholm, A/C R   xi, 149, 183–4, 188, 222
Churchill, Winston   24, 277
Clark, F/Sgt T   63, 68
Claxton, LAC J   286
Clay, F/L 'Sticky'   264
Cleall, F/Sgt J   68, 73–4
Clerke, W/C RFH   221, 222, 244, 249, 251, 256, 260, 262, 264, 269, 290
Cochrane, AVM Sir R   218
Connolly, S/L R   37, 55, 84–5, 140, 166
Cooper, S/L J   84, 85, 140, 166
Cox, Dr R   319
Cunningham, G/C J   11, 47, 142, 145, 184, 224

D'Houtecourt, F/L   217
Davies, Sgt   75
Davis, W/C FP   97, 107, 113, 130, 131, 136, 145, 160, 161, 174, 176, 177, 193, 199, 201, 204, 215, 216–7
Dawson, W/O R   288
Dear, F/O K   159, 162, 192
Dittman, Ltn G   124
Dobson, Sir Roy   16
Donaldson, G/C   76, 250–1
Dormann, Hptm W   124, 126
Dougall, F/L J   133–4

Earhart, Amelia   16
Edwards, F/L JAH   291
Eeles, J   19, 20, 27, 64
Ellis, F/O   45, 46

Engelbach, Helena   ix, 303–4
Engelbach, S/L PS   ix, 89–90, 160, 194, 211, 224, 225–6, 270, 303
Evans, F/S G   58, 66–7, 68, 75
Evans, W/C PMJ   169, 320

Farnfield, F/O HB   291
Farrow, HG   xi, 264, 267–70, 330, 331
Ferguson, F/L RW   128, 138–9
Folley, P/O FS   131, 148, 161, 167, 169–70, 180, 182, 185, 187, 198, 199
Forbes, Sgt   68
Forshaw, S/L JCN   131, 148, 161, 167, 168, 169–70, 180, 182, 183, 185, 187, 198, 199, 201, 205
Franks, Norman LR   ix
Franks, Hugh   ix
Frost, F/Sgt   111, 130
Fuller, WF   250

Gallacher, F/L   215
Garlick, Neil   ix, 54, 140, 255
Garlick, Joyce   53–4, 251, 255, 258, 316
Garlick, Donald   53, 255
Geiger, Hptm A   142
George VI, HRH King   2, 4, 5, 24–5, 55, 95, 192, 243, 304–5
Gibb, W/C WF   282
Gibson, W/C GP   xi, 1, 4, 7–8, 55, 56, 80, 101, 234, 257–8, 292, 325, 334
Gillam, F/Sgt DJ   68, 114, 130
Gonsalves, W/C FS   323, 324
Gracie, W/C EJ   173
Graham, Billy   318
Gray, F/Sgt   215
Gray, Mrs   254
Greatrex, Mr   76
Gregory, S/L WJ   5, 56, 80, 91–2, 107, 110, 112, 130, 141, 145, 193, 208–9, 224
Gregory, F/Sgt D   68, 73
Gregory, P/O I D   176, 230
Guinness, S/L Rev H   260
Gunnill, F/O J   160

Hair, P/O   99
Hale, Sgt   287
Hall, Sgt   6

Hamer, W/O RC   137
Hampshire, F/L HR   237
Hanson, F/Sgt H   160
Harris, Lt H   17
Harris, ACM Sir A   94, 152, 180, 192,
    275–6, 277, 278
Harvey, A/Cdr   321–2
Harwood, S/L MJ   vii, xi–xii
Haslam, F/L WG   315, 324
Head, S/L NS   324
Helmore, G/C E   56
Heycock, A/Cdr G   293
Hill, AVM Sir R   141, 145
Hitler, Adolf   20, 24, 62, 289, 290, 295
Hobbis, S/L D   63
Holman, Jill & family   301, 316
Holman, F/O CP   316
Horrocks, E   37, 38
Hough, Frank   16
Howard, AB   149
Hurley, F/O AR   165

Ingle, Joan   327
Irvin, Leslie   16, 17

Jackson, W/C DA   236–7, 298
Jacobs, F/L H   110, 115, 116, 123, 124,
    127, 129, 130, 138, 141, 145
Jardine, F/Sgt   73
Jenner, Ursula & family   234, 289–90,
    316–17
Jodl, Gen A   292
Johnson, Amy   16
Johnson, AVM JE   92
Joll, F/L IKS   46, 47, 49–50, 58
Jones, F/O G   194
Jordan, P/O H   95
Joy, S/L   80
Joyce, F/O   146, 163

Kelsey, W/C HC   115, 130, 160, 162,
    168–9, 172, 184, 185, 193, 216
Kendrick, J   229
Kent, HRH Duke of   75
Kinchin, S/L   195
Kingsford-Smith, Sir C   16
Kocher, P/O   217
Kraft, Fw G   125

Lamb, F/L R   158

Lambert, W/C EFF   159, 162
Lampkin, W/O   241
Latimer, S/L J   58, 65
Lawrence, TE   15
Lawrence, Sgt   3
Leader, P/O   73
Le Boutte, Lt-Gen LJG   111, 131,
    206–7, 210–11, 216, 224
Lee, A/Cdr AGS   101
Legg, G/C RG   109, 133
Lilley, W/O RC   199
Lindley, P/O   73
Lock, F/L K   19, 26, 27, 28,30, 31, 32,
    33–4, 64, 282–3
Lovell, F/L VC   199, 201
Lucas, W/C PB   ix, 112, 118, 121, 123,
    226, 330

MacAndrew, S/L R   198
MacLeod, F/O AP   165–6, 177
Mallett, F/O RS   111, 194, 206, 210,
    211, 224–5, 287, 303
Maltby, F/L D   135
Mamoutoff, F/O G   185, 210
Marriott, F/L R   218, 286
Marriott, Canon   260–2
Marsh, P/O P   249
Martin, AM Sir HB   168, 331
Matthews, S/L K   68
Matthews, S/L JO   239
McCairns, F/O JA   77, 78
McClymont, F/L   303
McGovern, Maj DR   129
McLean, W/O   215
McWhirter, Norris   331
Melrose, W/O AAW   237
Middlebrook, Martin   ix, 100, 121,
    123, 124, 134, 188, 189
Miles, F/O   6
Milligan, Tim   327
Moll, JJ   16
Mollison, J A   16
Montgomery, FM Sir B   278, 284
Moran, Lord   132
Munro, F/O N   165
Murray, S/L W   165, 185
Mussolini, Benito   290, 295

Nelson, G/C ETT   159, 160, 217
Newberry, Roy   257

Norfolk, HRH Duke of   79

O'Leary, P/O M   193, 212, 215
Okell, P/O   52
Osborn, F/L R W   128, 137–9, 269,
    293, 313–14

Pamment, F/L KJ   161
Pantry, F/S T   209
Park, AVM Sir KR   8
Parmentier, KD   16
Penny, Rev.   253
Penny, S/L   288
Penrose, W/O A   239
Phillipson A/Cdr JR   11
Pickard, G/C P   77
Pollard, F/O   147, 155, 161–2, 167
Portal, ACM Sir P   276, 277, 278
Potter, W/O   215
Poulton, P/O E   95
Prchyl, F/L   86
Pugsley, W/O   156, 158
Pynn, F/Sgt AC   291

Raby, S/L D   285
Raffaelli, S/L   313
Rauh, Maj H   102–3
Rawnsley, F/L CF   47
Reeves, W/C N   193, 212, 215, 240
Renaldi, Sgt   151, 154
Renson, F/O LF   151
Renwick, Sir R   298, 299
Reynolds, F/L CHF   97, 99, 103, 113,
    116, 126, 128, 129, 131, 133–4, 137,
    142–3, 161, 204, 320
Rice, S/L GJ   166, 176, 194, 201, 206,
    224
Richthofen, Baron M von   163, 205
Riddoch, F/L PA   218
Rimer, F/O WP   291
Ripley, F/O W   148, 184
Rivaz, F/L JS   288
Roberts, W/C KC   145–6, 163, 169,
    174–5, 176, 215
Robertson, F/Sgt MM   114, 130
Robertson, LAC   149
Rogerson, F/L JG   166, 176, 194, 201,
    206, 224
Rökker, Hptm H   247, 273, 296–7
Ronayne, F/O CS   218

Sale, S/L DJ   156, 157–8, 159, 189
Saunders, F/L   44
Saward, G/C D   276, 277
Sawyer, F/O DC   135
Schmalscheidt, Ofw F   124
Schnaufer, Ltn H-W   125
Scott, CWA   16
Scott, F/L RAW   80, 114, 229, 230,
    280, 309
Scott, F/L   229–30
Selassie, Haile   18
Sellers, F/L   195
Sessions, Betty   132, 199, 242, 251,
    256, 282
Sessions, Harriet   199, 249, 250, 251,
    256, 310
Sessions, Teddy   253, 256, 279, 310–11
Sessions, Dick   279
Sessions, F/O JWG   310
Sessions family   199–200, 256, 283,
    310, 325
Sheldon, F/O J   309
Sherman, P/O P   248
Sikorski, Gen W   87
Sinclair, Sir A   6, 95, 145, 277
Singleton, S/LJ   315, 320, 324
Skelton, S/L FS   247, 262, 318, 319
Slee, G/C LC   218, 243, 244
Smith, Sgt A   135
Smith, Mr EJ   155
Smith, F/L EM   115, 130, 160, 162,
    168–9, 172, 185, 193, 216
Smith, F/L   280
Smith, G/C G   331, 333
Snape, P/O D   162, 176
Sparrowe, F/L   81, 92, 93, 126, 152,
    204
Spender, F/Sgt   288
Stalin, Joseph   293
Stanley, F/Sgt   99, 167, 229, 287
Stephens, F/L DH   230
Stevens, F/L RP   9
Steward, S   264
Streetly, Martin   181

Tagg, Michael   326
Terraine, John   276
Thatcher, S/L JV   241
Thornton, F/O CB   111, 149
Tillney, F/L   314

Tojo, Gen H   295
Tolkien, J   81–2
Towler, Sgt   111, 130
Townsend, Lord   190
Townsend, G/C PW   305
Trenchard, Lord H   75–6
Truman, Pres. H   307

Van den Plassche, F/O FE   185, 210
Verity, G/C HB   3, 77
Vink, Fw H   125–6

Walch, F/L DC   223–4
Wallis, Barnes   221
Wallnutt, F/Sgt   241
Walsh, F/O E   137
Ward, WW   xi, 264, 267–70, 331
Watkins, F/O J   209
Webb, Sgt   6
Webster, F/L M   275
Welfare, F/L D   264
Welsh, F/O D   148, 184
Wesson, T & J   35–6, 242–3, 250, 256
Wheldon, F/O J   113, 130, 162, 176
White, AB   149
White, F/O J   197, 212–13
White, Mrs Joan   200–1, 223–3, 242, 306, 312, 327

White, Mrs DK   329, 330
White, A/Cdr HE   vii, viii, ix, xi, 1–8, 33, 46–53, 55, 57–65, 68–72, 76–81, 83–92, 95–110, 112, 114–23, 126–7, 130–2, 134–7, 140–1, 143–5, 147, 148, 150–61, 163–6, 169–71, 173, 175–7, 179–84, 186–8, 190–2, 192–5, 197, 199–201, 203–18, 221–3, 228, 229–30, 232, 233, 236, 238–48, 251, 254, 256, 258–75, 278–92, 294, 297, 301–2, 304–6, 308–10, 312–16, 318–21, 325–7, 330–1, 333–4
White family   200–1, 203, 327–8, 330, 334
Whittle, A/Cdr Sir F   319
Wilk, F/O L   198
Wilkinson, E   320
Williams, F/O AH   314
Wilton-Todd   173
Winn, AVM CV   viii, 80, 114, 123, 124, 137, 191, 217, 229–30, 242, 243, 280, 285–6, 309, 321
Winn, Mrs S   123
Winter, F/O M   73
Wittgenstein, Maj H z Sayn   163
Wright, F/L   193

Airlife Classics

is an exciting new collection of classic aviation titles now reproduced in affordable paperback editions. This superbly produced series brings back into print the best and most popular writing from Airlife's archive library.

THEY GAVE ME A SEAFIRE *Commander R. 'Mike' Crosley*

'Mike' Crosley started training with the Fleet Air Arm on the very day of the battle of Taranto and went on to serve aboard HMS *Eagle* on the notorious Malta convoy run, shooting down his first enemy aircraft in two days. Surviving *Eagle*'s sinking in August 1942, the author graduated to Seafires – and flew this beautiful but often troublesome aircraft in Combat Air Patrols and 'ramrod' strikes until the end of the war. From hilarious episodes during training and working up in the West Country and Scotland, through the Allied landings in north Africa, the author describes in vivid detail the experiences, the excitement and the terror of this type of flying.

222 x 147mm, 296 pages, 20 pages photographs, 1 84037 247 1

VCs OF THE AIR *John Frayn Turner*

There were thirty-two VCs of the air during the Second World War, yet how many of their names are known today? We have all heard of the exploits of Guy Gibson and Leonard Cheshire, but every one of the VCs of the air is associated with deeds equally daring and courageous. *VCs of the Air* reflects the whole war in the air more graphically than any impersonal history could do. The story starts in the days before Dunkirk, and finishes a few days before the atom bombs were dropped on Japan.

216 x 235mm, 176 pages, 8 pages photographs, 1 84037 234 6

DOUGLAS BADER *John Frayn Turner*

Based on extensive interviews which the author had with Douglas Bader during the last thirteen years of Bader's life, this biography tells the full story from his childhood to his work with the disabled in later life. The story of his war-time activities, both in the air and as a POW, is told in some detail and makes fascinating reading. John Frayn Turner's account of a remarkable life is a fitting tribute to one of this country's most heroic figures.

234 x 156mm, 272 pages, b/w photographs, 1 84037 244 3

HURRICANES OVER MURMANSK *John Golley*

On 21 June 1941, Adolf Hitler gave the momentous order for Operation 'Barbarossa' to be put into action. Within 24 hours the invasion of Russia was under way. As the Red Army fell back in full-scale retreat, Stalin's pleas for British help fell on sympathetic ears in Downing Street. On 27 July, Churchill agreed to a plan to send two squadrons of RAF Hurricanes to protect the vital ice-free port of Murmansk. This is the incredible, hitherto untold, story of those two squadrons, Nos 81 and 134, suddenly plucked from Britain to the defence of Russia, and their spirited resistance to the Nazi onslaught.

216 x 135mm, 224 pages, b/w photographs, 1 84037 298 2

THE REMORSELESS ROAD *James McEwan*

This is the compelling and at times harrowing account of the author's experiences whilst serving in the RAF during the Second World War. His autobiography recounts his posting to the Far East, where he served alongside those resolute airmen who fought the Japanese against all odds and to the bitter end, the survivors eventually laying down their arms. Then follows his account of the ordeal and humiliation of imprisonment for the last three-and-a-half years of the war, with only the atomic bombs putting an end to their plight.

234 x 156mm, 320 pages, photographs, 1 84037 301 6

AIRLIFE CLASSICS

DESERT EAGLES *Humphrey Wynn*

Desert Eagles tells the story of two American pilots who served in P-40 Kittyhawk fighter/bomber squadrons in the desert air force in 1942 before, during and after the Battle of El Alamein. Both pilots kept diaries of their Middle East experiences and it is on these first-hand accounts that the book is based. Humphrey Wynn has used his own knowledge of the period to provide a background to the diary material and has produced a fascinating account of these two men's war.

> *210 x 135mm, 164 pages, photographs, 1 84037 293 1*

THE LAST PATROL *Harry Holmes*

The Last Patrol is an operational history of the fifty-two United States submarines lost during the Second World War. The Submarine Service of the US Navy suffered the highest percentage of losses of any branch of the American armed forces with almost one in five vessels failing to return. However, the achievements of United States submarines are legend as their crews, while representing only two per cent of Navy personnel, accounted for over fifty-five per cent of Japanese shipping losses. This is the story of those submarines.

> *216 x 150mm, 216 pages, photographs, 1 84037 270 2*

SKY FEVER *Sir Geoffrey de Havilland*

Geoffrey de Havilland was one of the world's true pioneers of powered flight. Without experience, plans or instructions, he built his own first flying machine and the engine to power it in 1910, and by painstaking trial and error taught himself to fly. His autobiography contrives to tell the story of British aviation through the people and the events with which he was associated, while revealing his own unusually powerful, compassionate and diversified personality.

> *216 x 135mm, 256 pages, 1 84037 148 X*

MARCH OR DIE *Philip Chinnery*

This is the story of the deadly struggle between fanatical Japanese Imperial troops and the British Army that was fought in the dense tropical jungle of Burma in 1943 and 1944. Major-General Orde Wingate employed fighting tactics gleaned from his previous experiences of guerilla warfare learned in Palestine and Abyssinia. He played the Japanese at their own game, taking his troops deep behind enemy lines and using hit-and-run tactics to break communications, disrupt supply lines and shatter the morale of the Japanese Emperor's disciples. The men of this force became known as Chindits.

> *234 x 156mm, 288 pages, b/w photographs, 1 84037 289 3*

THE OTHER BATTLE *Peter Hinchliffe*

This book traces the parallel development of night bombing within the RAF and that of the *Luftwaffe*'s Night Fighter Force, culminating in the strategic bombing offensive and the German aerial defence against that offensive. It encompasses the historical, strategic, tactical and technical aspects of the subject, and contains a large amount of material based on personal experience.

> *234 x 156mm, 368 pages, b/w photographs, 1 84037 303 2*

LUCK AND A LANCASTER
Harry Yates, DFC

This book takes you, raid by raid, through the author's tour of operational duty over the last five months of 1944. It is a bomber pilot's story, but it is also about the grinding operational pressure, the brotherhood of the crew and their fears of injury and death. It is about a squadron of Bomber Command that bore a barely-equalled burden in operational effort and losses.

234 x 156mm, 272 pages, 16 pages b/w photographs, 1 84037 291 5

THE AIR BATTLE FOR MALTA
Lord James Douglas-Hamilton

For both the Axis and the Allied Powers, Malta was a vital key to victory – not only in the Mediterranean, but in north Africa and the Middle East as well. *The Air Battle For Malta*, provides one of the most intriguing and realistic accounts of the struggle for possession of the island, a fight to the death which lasted two-and-a-half years, during which time 14,000 tons of bombs were dropped on a defiant population.

240 x 172mm, 160 pages, b/w photographs, 1 84037 145 5

ONE NIGHT IN JUNE *Kevin Shannon and Stephen Wright*

This is an account of the Glider Pilot Regiment's role in Operation 'Tonga', the first stage of the Airborne assault in the Normandy landings in June 1944. The story is told through the eyes of those who were there – glider pilots, paratroops, pathfinders, tug crews and passengers and covers the Operation from training through to evacuations after D-Day. The account includes stories of crew who evaded capture by the Germans and pays tribute to the help they received from local Resistance fighters.

234 x 156mm, 224 pages, b/w photographs, 1 84037 183 8

AIR BATTLE OF THE RUHR *Alan Cooper*

Bomber Command's first real assault on Germany industry in the Ruhr took place in March 1942 but the results were disappointing. It was not until the following year that the RAF was to have more success and Alan Cooper describes in detail individual raids, their targets, the aircraft used and the German defences. Throughout, the author has used personal accounts and anecdotes and he gives vivid descriptions of the fearful effect of German searchlight skills and the strain of flying on raids of up to five to six hours' duration, three hours of which were over enemy territory.

234 x 156mm, 256 pages, b/w photographs, 1 84037 213 3

THE DAY OF THE TYPHOON *John Golley*

Reading more like fiction than fact, and a fast-moving action-packed novel of war at that, this account of rocket Typhoon operations over Normandy in the weeks immediately following the D-Day invasion of Europe is all the more enthralling for its authenticity. Written by a former ground attack pilot who flew 73 missions with 245 Squadron over Northern France in 1944–5, the book has all the immediacy of a first-hand account of the action, excitement, terror and the camaraderie experienced by a close ground support squadron 'moving up the line'.

216 x 138mm, 216 pages, b/w photographs, 1 84037 181 1

BARRACUDA PILOT *Dunstan Hadley*

Dunstan Hadley served as a pilot in the Fleet Air Arm during World War II. *Barracuda Pilot* is his account of those times and is written in a light-hearted and often humorous style. He writes about his experiences as a trainee pilot, an operational pilot and as a flight deck officer. The author was in action against the Japanese in Sumatra and the raid on Sigli is vividly recounted.

220 x 150mm, 224 pages, b/w photographs, 1 84037 225 7

THE BADER WING *John Frayn Turner*

This book reveals the fascinating story of the charismatic Wing Commander and the five squadrons which he led. The story is set against the broader canvas and controversy of the Big Wing. The tactics and strategy favouring the Wing are forcibly argued by the author, who comes down heavily on the side of Bader the man, whose outspoken views and forceful personality made the Wing possible.

216 x 135mm, 176 pages, 1 84037 126 9

AIRYMOUSE *Harald Penrose*

Harald Penrose made his first flight in 1919 in an Avro 504K. There followed a long and distinguished career in aviation mainly as a test pilot. During this period he flew many unusual types such as the tail-less Pterodactyl, the Whirlwind and the Wyvern. This book describes flights in 'Airymouse' – 'A diminutive single seater aeroplane of insignificant horse power' – which he bought in his retirement. He sets out to recapture earlier times in his life when he first experienced the pure enjoyment of flight.

216 x 135mm, 160 pages, 1 84037 144 7

AN ANCIENT AIR *Harald Penrose*

An Ancient Air portrays the hitherto only briefly recorded life of John Stringfellow of Chard (1799–1883), the first man in the world to demonstrate that engine-powered winged flight was practicable. Whereas earlier general aviation histories tend to discount Stringfellow's work, *An Ancient Air* reveals that his absorption with aviation was lifelong, starting with the construction of balloons, recorded here for the first time.

234 x 156mm, 192 pages, b/w photographs, 1 84037 184 6

CLOUD CUCKOOLAND

Harald Penrose

Cloud Cuckooland is a volume of delightful reminiscences. This book highlights Harald Penrose's love of light aviation by conjuring up graphic images of a golden age of private flying in the UK. The book comprises a series of charming and often funny stories involving a variety of types.

216 x 135mm, 160 pages, 1 84037 127 7